Sunset

BEST HOME PLANS

500 Best Vacation Home Plans

SUNSET BOOKS INC.
Director, Sales & Marketing:
Richard A. Smeby
Editorial Director:
Bob Doyle
Production Director:
Lory Day
Group Marketing Manager:
Becky Ellis
Art Director:
Vasken Guiragossian
Consulting Editor:
Don Vandervort

Cover: Pictured is plan H-930-1 on
page 250. Cover design by Vasken
Guiragossian. Photography by Bob
Halline...

For more information on Sunset's 500 *Best
Vacation Home Plans* or any other Sunset
book, call (800) 526-5111.

 Printed on recycled paper

What the Plans Include

Complete construction blueprints are available for every house shown in this book. Clear and concise, these detailed blueprints are designed by licensed architects or members of the American Institute of Building Design (AIBD). Each plan is designed to meet standards set down by nationally recognized building codes (the Uniform Building Code, Standard Building Code, or Basic Building Code) at the time and for the area where they were drawn.

Remember, however, that every state, county, and municipality has its own codes, zoning requirements, ordinances, and building regulations. Modifications may be necessary to comply with such local requirements as snow loads, energy codes, seismic zones, and flood areas.

Although blueprint sets vary depending on the size and complexity of the house and on the individual designer's style, each set may include the elements described below and shown at right.

■ **Exterior elevations** show the front, rear, and sides of the house, including exterior materials, details, and measurements.

■ **Foundation plans** include drawings for a full, partial, or daylight basement, crawlspace, pole, pier, or slab foundation. All necessary notations and dimensions are included. (Foundation options will vary for each plan. If the plan you choose doesn't have the type of foundation you desire, a generic conversion diagram is available.)

■ **Detailed floor plans** show the placement of interior walls and the dimensions of rooms, doors, windows, stairways, and similar elements for each level of the house.

■ **Cross sections** show details of the house as though it were cut in slices from the roof to the foundation. The cross sections give the home's construction, insulation, flooring, and roofing details.

■ **Interior elevations** show the specific details of cabinets (kitchen, bathroom, and utility room), fireplaces, built-in units, and other special interior features.

■ **Roof details** give the layout of rafters, dormers, gables, and other roof elements, including clerestory windows and skylights. These details may be shown on the elevation sheet or on a separate diagram.

■ **Schematic electrical layouts** show the suggested locations for switches, fixtures, and outlets. These details may be shown on the floor plan or on a separate diagram.

■ **General specifications** provide instructions and information regarding excavation and grading, masonry and concrete work, carpentry and woodwork, thermal and moisture protection, drywall, tile, flooring, glazing, and caulking and sealants.

Other Helpful Building Aids

In addition to the construction information on every set of plans, you can buy the following guides.

■ **Reproducible sets** are helpful if you'll be making changes to the stock plan you've chosen. These blueprints are line drawings produced on erasable, reproducible paper for the purpose of modification. When alterations are complete, working copies can be made.

■ **Itemized materials list** details the quantity, type, and size of materials needed to build your home. (This list is extremely helpful in obtaining an accurate construction bid. It's not intended for use to order materials.)

■ **Mirror-reverse sets** are useful if you want to build your home in the reverse of the plan that's shown. Because the lettering and dimensions read backwards, be sure to buy at least one regular-reading set of blueprints.

■ **Description of materials** gives the type and quality of materials suggested for the home. This form may be required for obtaining FHA or VA financing.

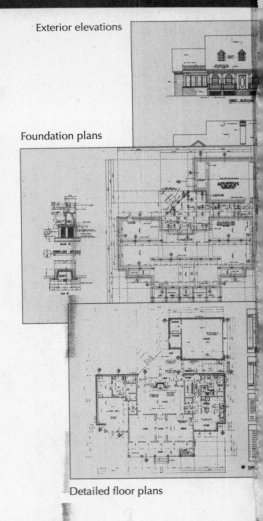

Exterior elevations

Foundation plans

Detailed floor plans

■ **How-to diagrams** for plumbing, wiring, solar heating, framing and foundation conversions show how to plumb, wire, install a solar heating system, convert plans with 2 by 4 exterior walls to 2 by 6 construction (or vice versa), and adapt a plan for a basement, crawlspace, or slab foundation. These diagrams are not specific to any one plan.

NOTE: Due to regional variations, local availability of materials, local codes, methods of installation, and individual preferences, detailed heating, plumbing, and electrical specifications are not included on plans. The duct work, venting, and other details will vary, depending on the heating and cooling system you use and the type of energy that operates it. These details and specifications are easily obtained from your builder or local supplier.

Having a Grand Time

- This attractive home is planned around a central Grand Room, which boasts a vaulted ceiling, an adjoining dining area, a serving bar and sliding glass doors to a lovely screened porch.
- The U-shaped kitchen boasts a handy pass-through to an attached dining deck. Volume ceilings enhance all of the rooms on the main floor.
- The owner (master) suite offers a walk-in closet, a private bath and access to a secluded deck.
- A second bedroom makes a great guest room, with a full bath nearby.
- The daylight basement provides two more bedrooms , which could be used for guests or for recreation. Also included are a full bath, a covered patio, a tuck-under garage and a large storage area.

Plan EOF-45

Bedrooms: 3+	Baths: 3
Living Area:	
Main floor	1448 sq. ft.
Daylight basement	673 sq. ft.
Total Living Area:	**2121 sq. ft.**
Tuck-under garage	550 sq. ft.
Storage	150 sq. ft.
Exterior Wall Framing:	2x4

Foundation Options:

Daylight basement

(All plans can be built with your choice of foundation and framing. A generic conversion diagram is available. See order form.)

BLUEPRINT PRICE CODE:	C

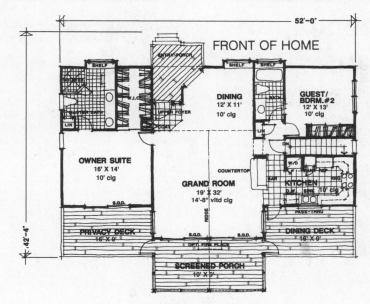

MAIN FLOOR

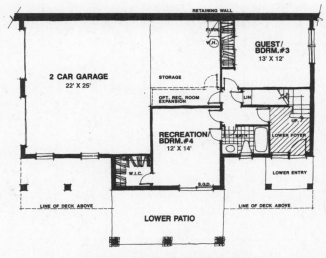

DAYLIGHT BASEMENT

Contemporary Elegance

- This striking contemporary design combines vertical siding with elegant traditional overtones.
- Inside, an expansive activity area is created with the joining of the vaulted living room, the family/dining room and the kitchen. The openness of the rooms creates a spacious, dramatic feeling, which extends to an exciting two-story sun space and a patio beyond.

- A convenient utility/service area near the garage includes a clothes-sorting counter, a deep sink and ironing space.
- Two bedrooms share a bright bath to round out the main floor.
- Upstairs, the master suite includes a sumptuous skylighted bath with two entrances. The tub is positioned on an angled wall, while the shower and toilet are secluded behind a pocket door. An optional overlook provides views down into the sun space, which is accessed by a spiral staircase.
- A versatile loft area and a large bonus room complete this design.

Plan LRD-1971

Bedrooms: 3+	Baths: 2
Living Area:	
Upper floor	723 sq. ft.
Main floor	1,248 sq. ft.
Sun space	116 sq. ft.
Bonus room	225 sq. ft.
Total Living Area:	**2,312 sq. ft.**
Standard basement	1,248 sq. ft.
Garage	483 sq. ft.
Exterior Wall Framing:	2x6

Foundation Options:

Standard basement
Crawlspace
(All plans can be built with your choice of foundation and framing. A generic conversion diagram is available. See order form.)

BLUEPRINT PRICE CODE:	C

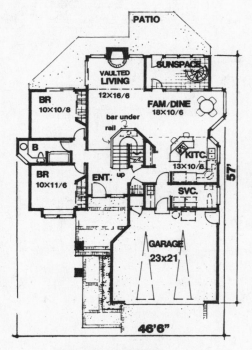

MAIN FLOOR

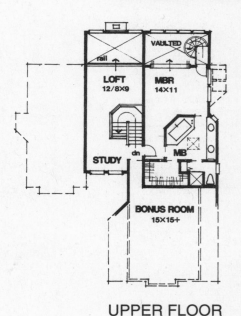

UPPER FLOOR

ORDER BLUEPRINTS ANYTIME!
CALL TOLL-FREE 1-800-820-1283

Plan LRD-1971

PRICES AND DETAILS
ON PAGES 2-5

495

Photo by Kevin Robinson

Striking Hillside Home Design

- This striking home is designed for a sloping site. The two-car garage and sideyard deck are nestled into the hillside, while cedar siding and a shake roof blend in nicely with the terrain.
- Clerestory windows brighten the entry and the living room, which unfold from the covered front porch. The huge living/dining area instantly catches the eye, with its corner fireplace, 17-ft. sloped ceiling and exciting window treatments. The living room also offers an inviting window seat, while the dining room has sliding glass doors to the large deck.
- The adjoining nook and kitchen also have access to the deck, along with lots of storage and work space.
- The isolated bedroom wing includes a master suite with his-and-hers closets and a private bath. The two smaller bedrooms share a hall bath.
- The daylight basement hosts a laundry room, a recreation room with a fireplace and a bedroom with two closets, plus a large general-use area.

Plan H-2045-5

Bedrooms: 4	Baths: 3
Living Area:	
Main floor	1,602 sq. ft.
Daylight basement	1,133 sq. ft.
Total Living Area:	**2,735 sq. ft.**
Tuck-under garage	508 sq. ft.
Exterior Wall Framing:	2x4

Foundation Options:

Daylight basement

(All plans can be built with your choice of foundation and framing. A generic conversion diagram is available. See order form.)

BLUEPRINT PRICE CODE:	D

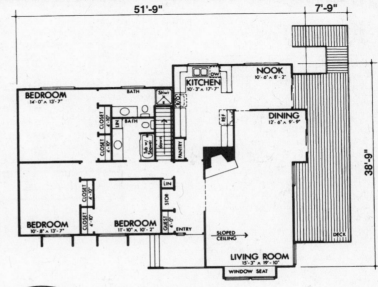

**NOTE: The above photographed home may have been modified by the homeowner. Please refer to floor plan and/or drawn elevation shown for actual blueprint details.

MAIN FLOOR

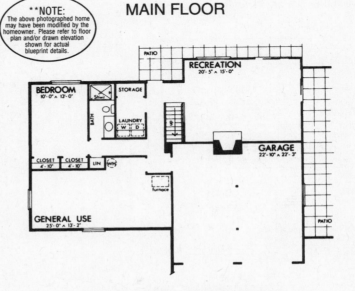

DAYLIGHT BASEMENT

Plan H-2045-5

PRICES AND DETAILS ON PAGES 2-5

Bright and Spacious

- Vaulted ceilings, plenty of windows and two rear decks make this home bright, spacious and perfect for entertaining.
- From the vaulted foyer, take guests to the vaulted, sunken living room, which features a charming fireplace. The adjacent dining room boasts French doors to a huge, partially covered wraparound deck.
- The informal family room, nook and kitchen are open and sunny, and boast a second fireplace, an island cooktop and access to the deck.
- A cozy corner den can serve as a spare bedroom, if needed.
- On the upper floor, a central balcony overlooks the foyer and the living room.
- A secluded bath, a private deck and a walk-in closet give the master suite a strong appeal.

Plan LRD-9186

Bedrooms: 3+	Baths: 2½
Living Area:	
Upper floor	1,025 sq. ft.
Main floor	1,460 sq. ft.
Total Living Area:	**2,485 sq. ft.**
Standard basement	1,460 sq. ft.
Garage	680 sq. ft.
Storage	133 sq. ft.
Exterior Wall Framing:	2x6

Foundation Options:

Standard basement

Crawlspace

(All plans can be built with your choice of foundation and framing. A generic conversion diagram is available. See order form.)

BLUEPRINT PRICE CODE:	C

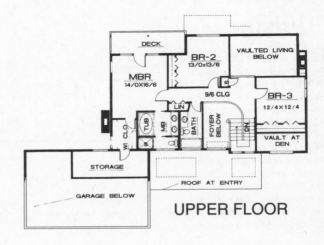

UPPER FLOOR

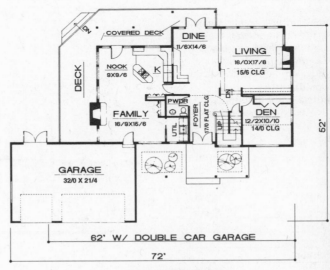

MAIN FLOOR

ORDER BLUEPRINTS ANYTIME!
CALL TOLL-FREE 1-800-820-1283

Plan LRD-9186

PRICES AND DETAILS
ON PAGES 2-5
493

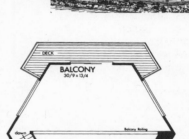

REAR VIEW

Quadruple the Fun!

- There is nothing ordinary about this innovative design. A cluster of hexagons brings together the living areas, a carport and an entry deck, creating an incredibly fun place to live.
- Cedar siding that follows the many angles of the home enhances its appeal.
- Ahead from the entry hall, the humongous living room unfolds in splendor. Brilliant windows allow sunlight to fill the space, and the railed deck can be accessed through a sliding glass door.
- A stroll up the sweeping staircase reveals the cozy balcony loft, featuring a private viewing deck.
- To the right of the entry lies the casual living areas. A majestic fireplace warms the family room, which shares a snack bar with the U-shaped, walk-through kitchen. The laundry room and a full bath are also nearby.
- Across the home, three uniquely angled bedrooms, one with a private bath, round out the floor plan.

Plan H-899-1A

Bedrooms: 3+	Baths: 3
Living Area:	
Upper floor	333 sq. ft.
Main floor	1,995 sq. ft.
Total Living Area:	**2,328 sq. ft.**
Carport	280 sq. ft.
Exterior Wall Framing:	2x4

Foundation Options:

Crawlspace

(All plans can be built with your choice of foundation and framing. A generic conversion diagram is available. See order form.)

BLUEPRINT PRICE CODE:	C

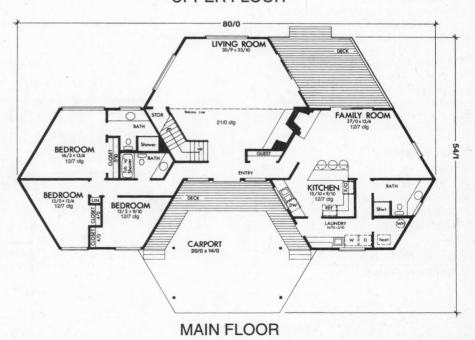

UPPER FLOOR

MAIN FLOOR

Plan H-899-1A
PRICES AND DETAILS
ON PAGES 2-5

Multi-Level with Dynamic Flair

- Bold geometrics lend a dynamic flair to this multi-level design. Wide roof overhangs and protected balconies offer privacy and shelter from the sun.
- Up a stairway from the split entry, the living room unfolds beneath a vaulted ceiling. This space is warmed by a fireplace, and sliding glass doors open to a front-facing deck.
- The dining room expands into the living room for extra space during holidays or large-scale entertaining. The dining room also features sliding doors to a backyard deck.
- The good-sized kitchen features a large nook for casual dining.
- Down the hall, the master suite boasts a private bath.
- In the daylight basement, a recreation room with a fireplace hosts laid-back family times. An extra bedroom and a full bath are just around the corner.
- Roomy laundry facilities take the hassle out of daily chores.

Plan H-2090-1

Bedrooms: 4	Baths: 3
Living Area:	
Main floor	1,520 sq. ft.
Daylight basement	735 sq. ft.
Total Living Area:	**2,255 sq. ft.**
Tuck-under garage	653 sq. ft.
Exterior Wall Framing:	2x4

Foundation Options:

Daylight basement

(All plans can be built with your choice of foundation and framing. A generic conversion diagram is available. See order form.)

BLUEPRINT PRICE CODE:	C

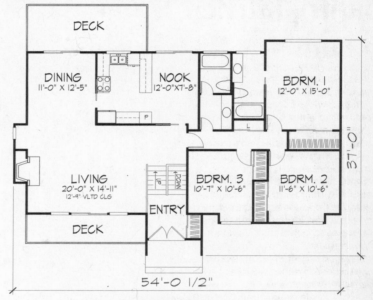

MAIN FLOOR

DECK

DINING
11'-0" X 12'-5"

NOOK
12'-0" X 7'-8"

BDRM. 1
12'-0" X 15'-0"

LIVING
20'-0" X 14'-11"
12'-4" VLTD CLG

BDRM. 3
10'-7" X 10'-6"

BDRM. 2
11'-6" X 10'-6"

ENTRY

DECK

37'-0"

54'-0 1/2"

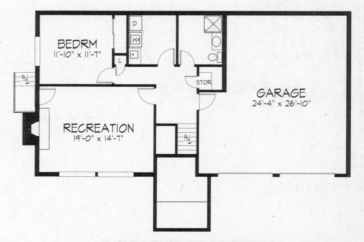

DAYLIGHT BASEMENT

BEDRM
11'-10" X 11'-7"

RECREATION
19'-0" X 14'-7"

STOR

GARAGE
24'-4" X 26'-10"

ORDER BLUEPRINTS ANYTIME!
CALL TOLL-FREE 1-800-820-1283

Plan H-2090-1

PRICES AND DETAILS
ON PAGES 2-5

491

Country Kitchen

- A lovely front porch, dormers and shutters give this home a country-style exterior and complement its comfortable and informal interior.
- The roomy country kitchen connects with the sunny breakfast nook and the formal dining room.
- The central portion of the home consists of a large family room with a handsome fireplace and easy access to a backyard deck.
- The main-floor master suite, particularly impressive for a home of this size, features a majestic master bath with a corner garden tub, two walk-in closets and a dual-sink vanity with knee space.
- Upstairs, you will find two more good-sized bedrooms, a double bath and a large storage area.

Plan C-8645

Bedrooms: 3	Baths: 2½
Living Area:	
Upper floor	704 sq. ft.
Main floor	1,477 sq. ft.
Total Living Area:	**2,181 sq. ft.**
Daylight basement	1,400 sq. ft.
Garage and storage	561 sq. ft.
Exterior Wall Framing:	2x4

Foundation Options:

Daylight basement
Crawlspace
Slab
(All plans can be built with your choice of foundation and framing. A generic conversion diagram is available. See order form.)

BLUEPRINT PRICE CODE: C

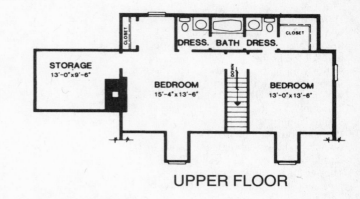

UPPER FLOOR

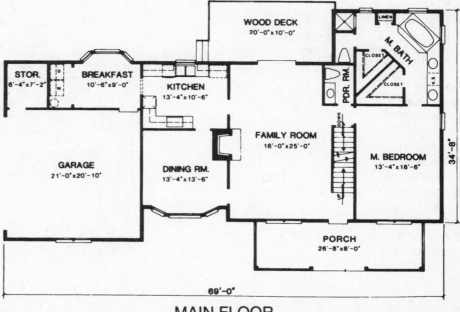

MAIN FLOOR

Plan C-8645

PRICES AND DETAILS
ON PAGES 2-5

Home with Sparkle

- This dynamite design simply sparkles, with the main living areas geared toward a gorgeous greenhouse at the back of the home.
- At the front of the home, a sunken foyer introduces the formal dining room, which is framed by a curved half-wall. The sunken living room boasts a 17-ft. vaulted ceiling and a nice fireplace.
- The spacious kitchen features a bright, two-story skywell above the island. The family room's ceiling rises to 17 feet. These rooms culminate at a solar greenhouse with an indulgent hot tub and a 12-ft. vaulted ceiling. The neighboring bath has a raised spa tub.
- Upstairs, the impressive master suite includes its own deck and a stairway to the greenhouse. A vaulted library with a woodstove augments the suite. Ceilings soar to 16 ft. in both areas.

Plan S-8217

Bedrooms: 3+	Baths: 2
Living Area:	
Upper floor	789 sq. ft.
Main floor	1,709 sq. ft.
Bonus room	336 sq. ft.
Total Living Area:	**2,834 sq. ft.**
Partial basement	1,242 sq. ft.
Garage	441 sq. ft.
Exterior Wall Framing:	2x6

Foundation Options:
Partial basement
Crawlspace
Slab
(All plans can be built with your choice of foundation and framing. A generic conversion diagram is available. See order form.)

BLUEPRINT PRICE CODE: D

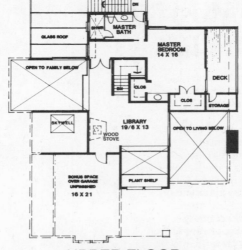

UPPER FLOOR

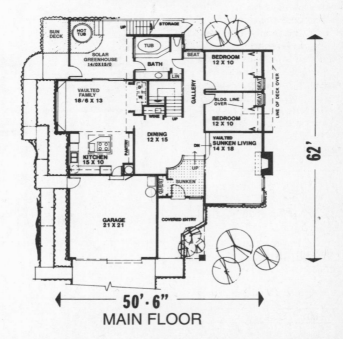

50'·6"
MAIN FLOOR

62'

ORDER BLUEPRINTS ANYTIME!
CALL TOLL-FREE 1-800-820-1283

Plan S-8217

PRICES AND DETAILS
ON PAGES 2-5

489

Make the Most of a Hillside Lot

- This striking design is just right for a hillside lot. It takes advantage of all usable space, creating a home you'll enjoy for years to come.
- Decorative stonework along the front of the home adds curbside appeal.
- Inside, the airy entry opens to the spacious living room. Its windows offer grand views, while the fireplace provides comfort on crisp autumn days.
- Stylish half-walls define the formal dining room; when weather permits, step out to the shaded deck to enjoy the fresh air. The kitchen is perfectly placed to easily service both this room and the cozy breakfast nook.
- With its own fireplace and access to a sun deck in back, the family room will be a favorite spot to unwind.
- An open-railed staircase leads down to the sleeping quarters. The master bedroom features a private patio and a separate dressing area and bath. Two additional bedrooms are identically sized, and share another full bath.

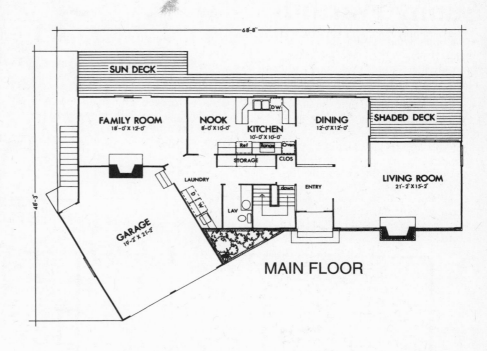

MAIN FLOOR

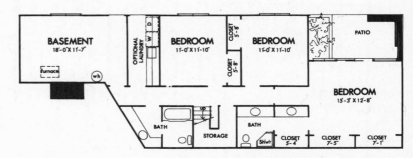

DAYLIGHT BASEMENT

Plan H-2072-1

Bedrooms: 3	Baths: 2½
Living Area:	
Main floor	1,205 sq. ft.
Daylight basement	1,205 sq. ft.
Total Living Area:	**2,410 sq. ft.**
Garage	405 sq. ft.
Exterior Wall Framing:	2x4

Foundation Options:

Daylight basement

(All plans can be built with your choice of foundation and framing. A generic conversion diagram is available. See order form.)

BLUEPRINT PRICE CODE:	C

488

ORDER BLUEPRINTS ANYTIME!
CALL TOLL-FREE 1-800-820-1283

Plan H-2072-1

PRICES AND DETAILS
ON PAGES 2-5

Rays of Sunny Warmth

- Big bright windows throughout and a glass roof over the breakfast nook ensure that the sun's warm rays will add sparkling cheer to this fascinating multi-level home.
- A glass roof over the entry creates a dramatic effect for arriving guests. From there, walk up to the spacious formal living areas.

- The nice-sized living room offers a charming fireplace and access to a huge back deck.
- Sensationally sunny, the breakfast nook's window wall and glass ceiling bring an unequalled beauty to the whole area.
- Three additional bedrooms—including the master suite, which boasts a walk-in closet, its own bath and private deck access—round out the main floor.
- The daylight basement provides a fourth bedroom, a third full bath and an enormous recreation room.

Plan H-2106-1	
Bedrooms: 4	**Baths:** 3
Living Area:	
Main floor	1,408 sq. ft.
Daylight basement	855 sq. ft.
Total Living Area:	**2,263 sq. ft.**
Tuck-under garage	515 sq. ft.
Exterior Wall Framing:	2x6
Foundation Options:	
Daylight basement	

(All plans can be built with your choice of foundation and framing. A generic conversion diagram is available. See order form.)

BLUEPRINT PRICE CODE:	**C**

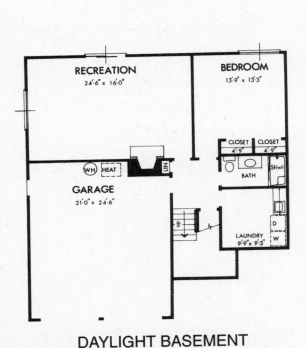

DAYLIGHT BASEMENT

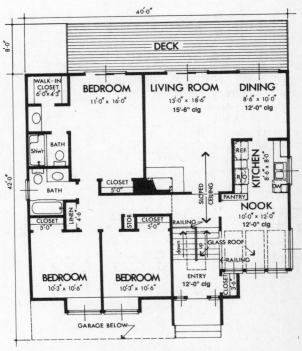

MAIN FLOOR

ORDER BLUEPRINTS ANYTIME!
CALL TOLL-FREE 1-800-820-1283

Plan H-2106-1

PRICES AND DETAILS
ON PAGES 2-5

487

REAR VIEW

Tucked Away in the Woods

- Tucked away in the woods, or in the heart of the city, this exciting contemporary home is sure to stand out beautifully in any neighborhood.
- From the entry, head straight to the huge living room. The perfect place to hold family get-togethers, its cozy corner fireplace gives the room a charming ambience, while access to the incredible back deck lets the party spill outdoors on hot summer nights.

- A breakfast bar between the kitchen and dining room creates a casual spot for bagels and cream cheese. You can get two tasks done at once with the kitchen's close proximity to the laundry room. Extra storage space and a convenient half-bath are nearby.
- Four bedrooms provide room enough for a growing family or overnight guests. Two of the upper-floor bedrooms offer private decks.
- The spacious upper-floor recreation room is just right for weekend billiards or canasta tournaments. A railed balcony lets you keep an eye on the fireplace below.

Plans H-914-1 & -1A	
Bedrooms: 4	**Baths:** 2½
Living Area:	
Upper floor	958 sq. ft.
Main floor	1,216 sq. ft.
Total Living Area:	**2,174 sq. ft.**
Daylight basement	1,216 sq. ft.
Garage	441 sq. ft.
Exterior Wall Framing:	2x6
Foundation Options:	**Plan #**
Daylight basement	H-914-1
Crawlspace	H-914-1A
(All plans can be built with your choice of foundation and framing. A generic conversion diagram is available. See order form.)	
BLUEPRINT PRICE CODE:	**C**

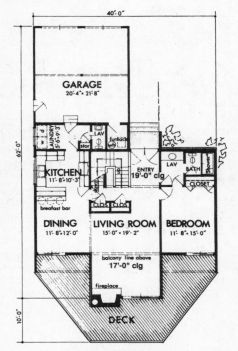

MAIN FLOOR

UPPER FLOOR

Dramatic Rear Views

- Columned front and rear porches offer country styling to this elegant two-story.
- The formal dining room and living room flank the two-story-high foyer.
- A dramatic array of windows stretches along the informal, rear-oriented living areas, where the central family room features a 17-ft.-high vaulted ceiling and a striking fireplace.
- The modern kitchen features an angled snack counter, a walk-in pantry and a work island, in addition to the bayed morning room.
- The exciting and secluded master suite has a sunny bayed sitting area with its own fireplace. Large walk-in closets lead to a luxurious private bath with angled dual vanities, a garden spa tub and a separate shower.
- The centrally located stairway leads to three extra bedrooms and two full baths on the upper floor.

Plan DD-2912

Bedrooms: 4	Baths: 3½
Living Area:	
Upper floor	916 sq. ft.
Main floor	2,046 sq. ft.
Total Living Area:	**2,962 sq. ft.**
Standard basement	1,811 sq. ft.
Garage	513 sq. ft.
Exterior Wall Framing:	2x4

Foundation Options:

Standard basement
Crawlspace
Slab
(All plans can be built with your choice of foundation and framing. A generic conversion diagram is available. See order form.)

BLUEPRINT PRICE CODE: D

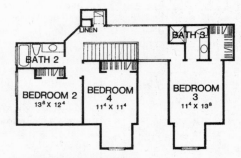

UPPER FLOOR

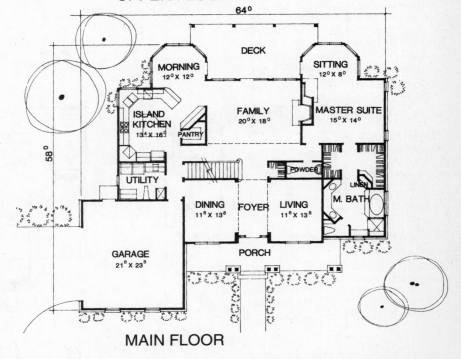

MAIN FLOOR

Plan DD-2912

Unparalleled Contemporary

- Incredible architectural skill turns clever ideas into reality in this brilliantly livable contemporary home!
- The exterior boasts a unique rooftop deck and a wonderful main-floor deck that wraps around half the home.
- The huge sunken living room is a natural gathering spot during holiday parties. Its handsome fireplace and trio of skylights create a warm, cozy feel.
- Gourmet meals have a home in the formal dining room; the galley-style kitchen is just steps away.
- Three bedrooms add room enough for fine family living. Each offers ample closet space and is near a full-size bath.
- Imagine nights on the incredible rooftop deck, searching for stars and planets with a telescope.

Plans H-935-1 & -1A

Bedrooms: 3	Baths: 2
Living Area:	
Upper floor	844 sq. ft.
Main floor	1,323 sq. ft.
Total Living Area:	**2,167 sq. ft.**
Standard basement	1,323 sq. ft.
Carport	516 sq. ft.
Exterior Wall Framing:	2x6

Foundation Options:

Standard basement

Crawlspace

(All plans can be built with your choice of foundation and framing. A generic conversion diagram is available. See order form.)

BLUEPRINT PRICE CODE:	C

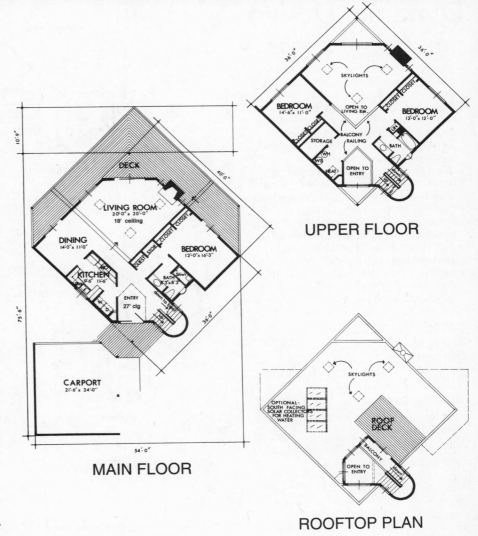

UPPER FLOOR

MAIN FLOOR

ROOFTOP PLAN

Plans H-935-1 & -1A

PRICES AND DETAILS
ON PAGES 2-5

Dynamic Design

- Angled walls, vaulted ceilings and lots of glass set the tempo for this dynamic home.
- The covered front entry opens to a raised foyer and a beautiful staircase with a bayed landing.
- One step down, a spectacular see-through fireplace with a raised hearth and built-in wood storage is visible from both the bayed dining room and the stunning Great Room.
- The Great Room also showcases an 18-ft.-high vaulted ceiling, wraparound windows and access to a deck or patio.
- The adjoining nook has a door to the deck and is served by the kitchen's snack bar. The kitchen is enhanced by a 9-ft. ceiling, corner windows and a pass-through to the dining room.
- Upstairs, the master suite offers a 10-ft.-high coved ceiling, a splendid bath, a large walk-in closet and a private deck.

Plan S-41587

Bedrooms: 3+	Baths: 3
Living Area:	
Upper floor	1,001 sq. ft.
Main floor	1,550 sq. ft.
Total Living Area:	**2,551 sq. ft.**
Basement	1,550 sq. ft.
Garage (three-car)	773 sq. ft.
Exterior Wall Framing:	2x6

Foundation Options:
Daylight basement
Standard basement
Crawlspace
Slab
(All plans can be built with your choice of foundation and framing. A generic conversion diagram is available. See order form.)

BLUEPRINT PRICE CODE: D

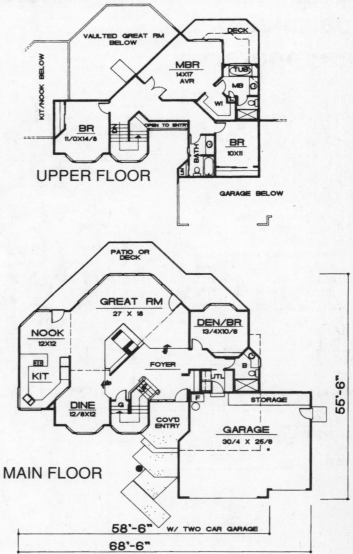

UPPER FLOOR

MAIN FLOOR

ORDER BLUEPRINTS ANYTIME!
CALL TOLL-FREE 1-800-820-1283

Plan S-41587

PRICES AND DETAILS
ON PAGES 2-5

483

REAR VIEW

Glass Galore

- The rear view of this home reveals window walls and a ceiling of glass that allow the sun to pour into this stunning contemporary design.
- The sheltered front porch opens to an entry hall with access to each of the home's living areas.
- Straight ahead, the wall and ceiling windows that surround you in the living room make you feel at one with the outdoors. A beckoning fireplace serves as a cozy focal point.
- The U-shaped kitchen conveniently envelops the family chef with thoughtful

amenities like a pantry closet and a built-in china cabinet.
- The dining area and the family room flow into one another to create a large entertainment zone that's perfect for casual get-togethers.
- The main-floor sleeping wing features a bedroom with dual closets and a private bath for overnight guests. Two more bedrooms share a full bath.
- Upstairs, the master retreat consists of a bedroom lit by a transom-topped wall of windows, as well as a private bath and a dressing area with a walk-in closet. At the end of a balcony hallway, a den overlooks the living room.

Plans H-3721-1 & -1A	
Bedrooms: 4	**Baths:** 3½
Living Area:	
Upper floor	757 sq. ft.
Main floor	1,888 sq. ft.
Total Living Area:	**2,645 sq. ft.**
Standard basement	1,888 sq. ft.
Garage	459 sq. ft.
Exterior Wall Framing:	2x6
Foundation Options:	**Plan #**
Standard basement	H-3721-1
Crawlspace	H-3721-1A

(All plans can be built with your choice of foundation and framing. A generic conversion diagram is available. See order form.)

BLUEPRINT PRICE CODE:	D

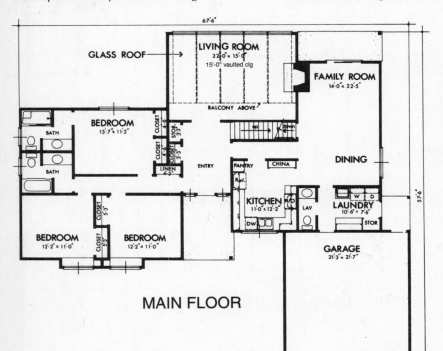

MAIN FLOOR

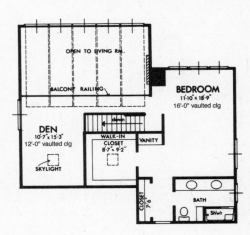

UPPER FLOOR

Plans H-3721-1 & -1A
PRICES AND DETAILS ON PAGES 2-5

Sun-Filled Excitement

- The spacious interior of this exciting contemporary design is awash in warmth and sunlight.
- Centered at the rear of the home, the brilliant sun room is the prime source of natural light. Surrounded by greenhouse windows and ventable skylights, it helps heat the home in winter and beat the heat in summer.

- Spend some quality time with your loved ones in the comfortable family room. Among its highlights are a cozy fireplace and sliding glass doors leading out to a back patio.
- Open to the family room, the well designed kitchen easily accesses both the formal dining room and the casual eating nook.
- Upstairs, a pair of skylights brightens the hallway connecting the three bedrooms. Double doors introduce the master bedroom, which boasts a large walk-in closet and a tidy private bath.

Plans H-3713-1 & -1A	
Bedrooms: 3	**Baths:** 2½
Living Area:	
Upper floor	816 sq. ft.
Main floor	1,357 sq. ft.
Sun room	123 sq. ft.
Daylight basement	954 sq. ft.
Total Living Area:	**2,296/3,250 sq. ft.**
Garage	460 sq. ft.
Exterior Wall Framing:	**2x6**
Foundation Options:	**Plan #**
Daylight basement	H-3713-1
Crawlspace	H-3713-1A

(All plans can be built with your choice of foundation and framing. A generic conversion diagram is available. See order form.)

BLUEPRINT PRICE CODE:	**C/E**

DAYLIGHT BASEMENT

BASEMENT STAIRWAY LOCATION

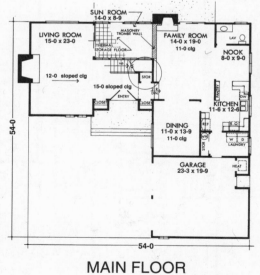

MAIN FLOOR

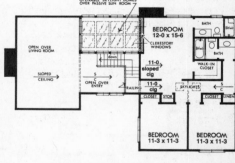

UPPER FLOOR

Geometric Gem

- This striking contemporary flaunts a unique exterior of vertical siding, shed roofs and glass. With the tuck-under garage, the home would be ideal for a sloping lot. Without the garage, it may be built on a level lot.
- A semi-circular silo houses the stairway to the private master suite on the upper floor, which features a skylighted bath and a private balcony.
- The skylighted foyer opens to a huge Great Room, also with skylights. A cathedral ceiling, a large fireplace and lots of glass are other highlights. Sliders at the rear access the expansive backyard deck.
- The centrally located kitchen is open to the Great Room and includes a functional snack counter, a work desk, a pantry and its own deck access.
- A full bath, a discreet laundry closet and three bedrooms are located in the sleeping wing.

Plan AX-98489

Bedrooms: 4	Baths: 2
Living Area:	
Upper floor	485 sq. ft.
Main floor	1,560 sq. ft.
Total Living Area:	**2,045 sq. ft.**
Standard basement	1,218 sq. ft.
Tuck-under garage	342 sq. ft.
Exterior Wall Framing:	2x4

Foundation Options:

Standard basement

(All plans can be built with your choice of foundation and framing. A generic conversion diagram is available. See order form.)

BLUEPRINT PRICE CODE: C

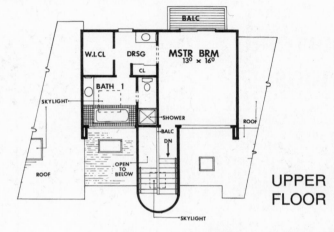

UPPER FLOOR

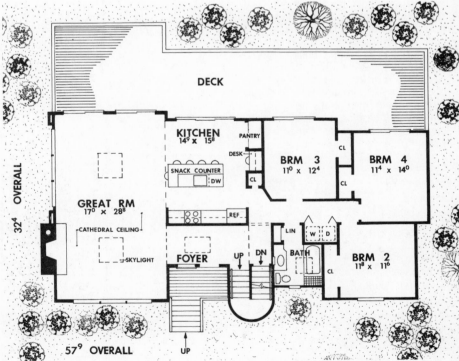

MAIN FLOOR

Plan AX-98489

PRICES AND DETAILS
ON PAGES 2-5

Charming Details

- A peaceful covered porch accented by three graceful arches is just one of this home's many charming details.
- Inside, the Great Room is an inviting spot for casual and formal gatherings. A warm fireplace adds a cozy glow.
- The dining area nearby extends to the efficient U-shaped kitchen. Beautiful French doors open to a relaxing deck.
- Across the home, an attractive bay window highlights the master bedroom. A luxurious whirlpool tub is the focal point of the suite's private bath.
- Laundry facilities and a convenient powder room complete the main floor.
- A centrally located staircase leads up to two more bedrooms, which share a hall bath. A bonus room across the hall can be adapted to meet family needs.
- The daylight basement includes a two-car garage that is located beneath the Great Room and the kitchen.

Plan C-9435

Bedrooms: 3+	Baths: 2½
Living Area:	
Upper floor	606 sq. ft.
Main floor	1,224 sq. ft.
Bonus room	306 sq. ft.
Total Living Area:	**2,136 sq. ft.**
Daylight basement/garage	1,204 sq. ft.
Exterior Wall Framing:	2x4

Foundation Options:

Daylight basement

Crawlspace

(All plans can be built with your choice of foundation and framing. A generic conversion diagram is available. See order form.)

BLUEPRINT PRICE CODE: C

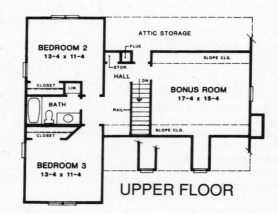

UPPER FLOOR

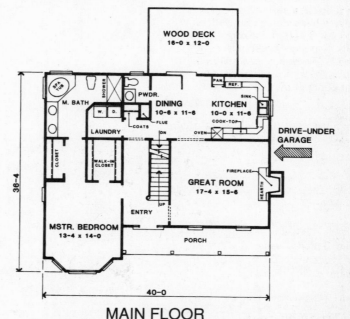

MAIN FLOOR

ORDER BLUEPRINTS ANYTIME!
CALL TOLL-FREE 1-800-820-1283

Plan C-9435

PRICES AND DETAILS
ON PAGES 2-5

479

Spectacular Front Porch

- A roomy covered front porch, perfect for outdoor entertaining, provides an inviting entrance to this classic home.
- Just past the entry, the spacious living room showcases 6-ft.-high arched windows and a warming fireplace.
- Convenient to the living room is the modern U-shaped kitchen, which boasts a bay-windowed sink and access to a covered rear porch. A bright 6x6 window brings sunlight into the adjoining dining area.
- The master suite offers a luxurious private bath, complete with a step-up garden tub, a separate shower, dual vanities and a walk-in closet.
- An additional main-floor bedroom, ideal for use as a den or home office, has private bathroom access. All main-floor rooms have 9-ft. ceilings.
- Upstairs, two more bedrooms share a third bath. The bonus area makes a great playroom or reading loft. All upper-floor ceilings slope to 8 feet.

Plan J-91024

Bedrooms: 4	Baths: 3
Living Area:	
Upper floor	863 sq. ft.
Main floor	1,463 sq. ft.
Total Living Area:	**2,326 sq. ft.**
Standard basement	1,463 sq. ft.
Garage	529 sq. ft.
Exterior Wall Framing:	2x6

Foundation Options:

Standard basement

Crawlspace

Slab

(All plans can be built with your choice of foundation and framing. A generic conversion diagram is available. See order form.)

BLUEPRINT PRICE CODE: C

UPPER FLOOR

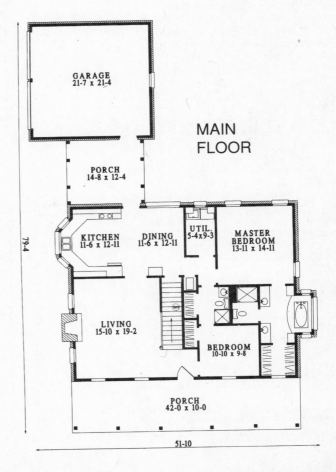

MAIN FLOOR

PRICES AND DETAILS ON PAGES 2-5

Heartwarmer

- Unique window treatments and a stone and cedar exterior highlight the design of this rustic retreat.
- An abundance of natural light pours into the Great Room through a stunning rear window wall. Skylights heighten the impressive two-story effect of a railed balcony open to the recreation room below.
- A dramatic central fireplace further warms your heart. A wet bar and a built-in entertainment center add to the generous appeal of this truly "great" room. A 14-ft. ceiling tops both this room and the foyer.
- Conveniently serving the dining room and the breakfast nook, the kitchen boasts a 9-ft. tray ceiling.
- Enjoy special occasions under the dining room's elegant 10-ft. tray ceiling.
- Across the home, the master bedroom features a high, arched transom window and a 15-ft. vaulted ceiling. The private bath includes a garden tub, a separate shower and twin walk-in closets.
- Use the adjoining study for a home office or a convenient nursery.

Plan GA-9605

Bedrooms: 3	Baths: 3
Living Area:	
Main floor	1,818 sq. ft.
Daylight basement (finished)	1,248 sq. ft.
Total Living Area:	**3,066 sq. ft.**
Daylight basement (unfinished)	634 sq. ft.
Garage	684 sq. ft.
Exterior Wall Framing:	2x6

Foundation Options:

Daylight basement

(All plans can be built with your choice of foundation and framing. A generic conversion diagram is available. See order form.)

BLUEPRINT PRICE CODE:	E

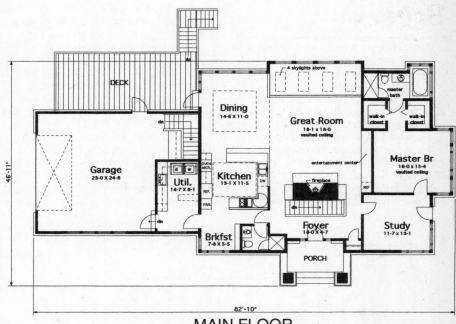

MAIN FLOOR

DAYLIGHT BASEMENT

ORDER BLUEPRINTS ANYTIME!
CALL TOLL-FREE 1-800-820-1283

Plan GA-9605

PRICES AND DETAILS
ON PAGES 2-5

477

Bright and Breezy

- With a breezy porch and multiple sunny decks, this pretty home will be a delightful refuge all year long.
- Inside, the two-story foyer serves as a bridge between the living room and the dining room, two important spaces when you entertain. Off the living room, a covered deck lets guests step outside for conversation after dinner.
- Because the majority of your time is spent on casual, day-to-day activities, the layout of the family room is large and welcoming. During kids' birthday parties, plenty of room is available for boisterous games of Twister.
- Nearby, the kitchen and the adjacent morning room function efficiently and comfortably. At the center, a space-saving island workstation lets helping hands join in meal preparation.
- Upstairs, the angled balcony opens to another charming deck.
- The deluxe master suite also offers a private deck. What a great place for morning coffee! If the air turns chilly, try the quiet sitting area inside.
- Two of the remaining bedrooms share a semi-private bath, while the third one boasts its own full bath.
- Unless otherwise mentioned, all rooms include 10-ft. ceilings.

Plan DD-2757	
Bedrooms: 4	**Baths: 3½**
Living Area:	
Upper floor	1,345 sq. ft.
Main floor	1,407 sq. ft.
Total Living Area:	**2,752 sq. ft.**
Standard basement	1,407 sq. ft.
Detached garage	498 sq. ft.
Exterior Wall Framing:	2x4
Foundation Options:	
Standard basement	
Crawlspace	
Slab	

(All plans can be built with your choice of foundation and framing. A generic conversion diagram is available. See order form.)

BLUEPRINT PRICE CODE:	**D**

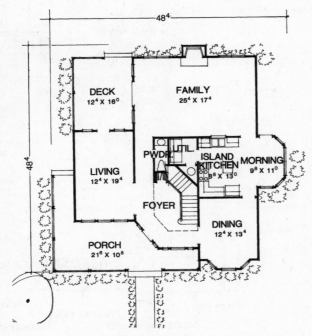

MAIN FLOOR

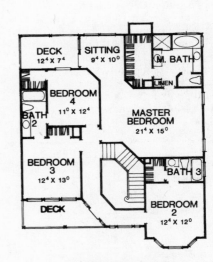

UPPER FLOOR

Dreams Do Come True

- The first time you return home to this delightful two-story, you'll realize all your dreams have come true.
- Out front, a charming porch hails back to the days when neighbors enjoyed Sunday afternoons together, rocking and visiting.
- Inside, the living and dining rooms provide an integrated area for gatherings. Whether you plan to hang out by the fireplace in a pair of sweats, or mingle with colleagues at the wet bar, this spot will fit your needs. Both rooms overlook a charming porch.

- For everyday meals, the eating nook offers a comfortable setting. Round up the troops for a big bowl of chili or some extra special lasagna.
- The open design of the nearby kitchen makes serving dinner simple. A handy desk is perfect for planning meals, while sunny windows allow a great view of a unique atrium.
- Off the master suite, a private porch is perfect for a romantic night of stargazing. Make a date with your significant other and enjoy. The master bath offers private access to the atrium.
- Upstairs, a fun balcony would serve well as a bedroom or a study. When the kids need to work on the computer, they can still be within earshot of parents downstairs.

Plan E-2504	
Bedrooms: 3+	**Baths: 3½**
Living Area:	
Upper floor	984 sq. ft.
Main floor	1,568 sq. ft.
Total Living Area:	**2,552 sq. ft.**
Standard basement	1,568 sq. ft.
Garage and storage	532 sq. ft.
Exterior Wall Framing:	2x6
Foundation Options:	

Standard basement
Crawlspace
Slab
(All plans can be built with your choice of foundation and framing. A generic conversion diagram is available. See order form.)

BLUEPRINT PRICE CODE: D

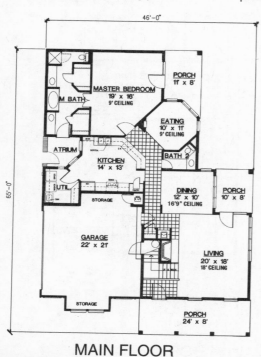

MAIN FLOOR

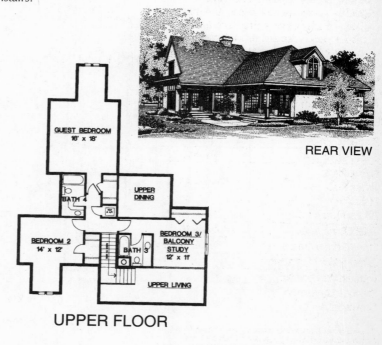

REAR VIEW

UPPER FLOOR

Indulge Yourself

- You'll find all manner of indulgence in this nostalgic country-style home, beginning with its fabulous wraparound porch that promises relaxation.
- Flanking the foyer are the formal dining room and living room or study. With shelves lining two walls, the living room could easily become a library.
- Ahead of the foyer, the Great Room rests, a welcome retreat and gathering place for your loved ones.
- Your morning fruit cup can be enjoyed either in the nook or on the porch. If you crave hot cereal, fix some oatmeal on the kitchen's island cooktop.
- Double doors swing open to the master suite, which boasts a fireplace and private porch access. Its bath delivers a garden tub and a separate shower under a dramatic greenhouse window.
- Upstairs, a big bonus room with a boxed-out window would make a fantastic game room. There's plenty of room for a slumber party, too!

Plan DW-2420

Bedrooms: 3+	Baths: 2½
Living Area:	
Upper floor	488 sq. ft.
Main floor	1,932 sq. ft.
Bonus room	240 sq. ft.
Total Living Area:	**2,660 sq. ft.**
Standard basement	1,932 sq. ft.
Exterior Wall Framing:	**2x4**

Foundation Options:

Standard basement

Crawlspace

Slab

(All plans can be built with your choice of foundation and framing. A generic conversion diagram is available. See order form.)

BLUEPRINT PRICE CODE:	**D**

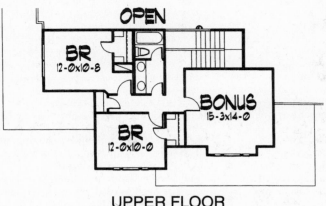

UPPER FLOOR

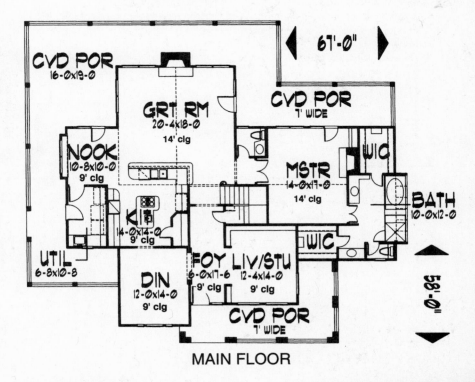

MAIN FLOOR

Plan DW-2420

PRICES AND DETAILS
ON PAGES 2-5

Abundant Amenities

- Charming window seats, beautiful built-in bookshelves and elegant French doors grace the interior of this lovely country home.
- A columned covered porch leads to a sidelighted 18-ft.-high foyer. The foyer is open to the formal dining and living rooms, which have 9-ft. ceilings.
- Adjacent to the living room, the master bedroom and bath boast 10-ft. ceilings. A separate tub and shower, a walk-in closet and a private toilet highlight the master bath.
- Handsome French doors topped with transom windows separate the study

from the living room and the central hall. A window seat, built-in bookshelves and a 9-ft. ceiling make this room a perfect retreat.
- A 17-ft. cathedral ceiling crowns the family room, where a French door leads to a covered deck. With its cozy fireplace, windowed walls and built-in bookshelves and cabinets, this room has a decidedly affectionate air.
- The gourmet kitchen features an island cooktop, a serving bar and a 9-ft. ceiling. This high ceiling extends to the adjoining morning room, which offers a cheery, open view of the deck.
- Stylish window seats adorn two upstairs bedrooms. Each bedroom has private access to a shared, compartmentalized bath; each access flaunts a walk-in closet, a window seat and a vanity.

Plan DD-2390

Bedrooms: 3+	Baths: 2½
Living Area:	
Upper floor	677 sq. ft.
Main floor	1,791 sq. ft.
Total Living Area:	**2,468 sq. ft.**
Partial basement	912 sq. ft.
Garage	500 sq. ft.
Exterior Wall Framing:	2x4

Foundation Options:

Partial basement
Crawlspace
Slab

(All plans can be built with your choice of foundation and framing. A generic conversion diagram is available. See order form.)

BLUEPRINT PRICE CODE:	C

VIEW INTO FAMILY ROOM

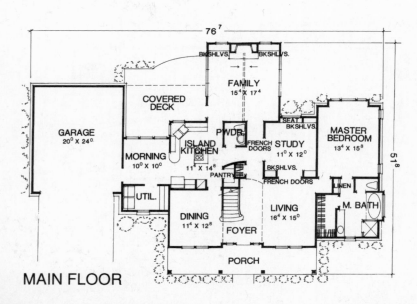

MAIN FLOOR

UPPER FLOOR

ORDER BLUEPRINTS ANYTIME!
CALL TOLL-FREE 1-800-820-1283

Plan DD-2390

PRICES AND DETAILS
ON PAGES 2-5

473

Terrific Tiered Contemporary

- This contemporary design features a tiered floor plan that allows for dramatic multi-level living.
- The side entry is sheltered from the elements by the roof of the carport.
- Inside, a stairway leads up to the prowed living room, which is on the home's highest level. A 15½-ft. cathedral ceiling crowns this space, and oversized transom windows flood the room with sunshine. Two sets of sliding glass doors lead out to a big deck; a massive fireplace casts a warm glow.
- Two stairways diverge at the corner of the living room. One leads down to a dining room that's visible over a railing. Sliding glass doors access a nice deck.
- The kitchen, a half-bath and a utility room are conveniently close together.
- The second stairway leads from the living room to the sleeping quarters, where every bedroom boasts a sunny window seat. The master suite includes a private bath and a walk-in closet.
- The partial basement features a glass-prowed recreation room with its own fireplace.

Plan H-888-1	
Bedrooms: 3	**Baths:** 2½
Living Area:	
Main floor	1,640 sq. ft.
Partial basement	510 sq. ft.
Total Living Area:	**2,150 sq. ft.**
Carport	556 sq. ft.
Exterior Wall Framing:	2x4
Foundation Options:	

Partial basement
(All plans can be built with your choice of foundation and framing. A generic conversion diagram is available. See order form.)

BLUEPRINT PRICE CODE: **C**

BASEMENT

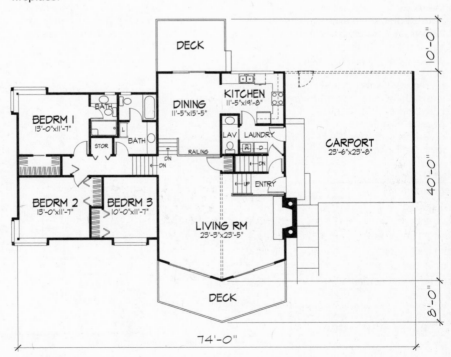

MAIN FLOOR

Plan H-888-1

PRICES AND DETAILS
ON PAGES 2-5

Sloping Split-Level

- Generously sized rooms and little hallway space make this split-level roomy, while its design allows it to take advantage of a laterally sloping lot.
- A nook and expandable dining alcove flank the kitchen, and both overlook the elevated deck at the rear of the home.
- The L-shaped living and dining room area takes advantage of a log-sized fireplace that also borders the entry.
- Three bedrooms share the other half of the main floor; the master bedroom corners plenty of space with its dual closets and private bathroom.
- The finished daylight basement includes a commodious recreation room for entertaining in style! Buffered from the recreation room by its configuration of walls, the house's fourth bedroom is complete with its own bath.
- Also downstairs, the utility room connects smartly with the rear garden for added convenience.

Plan H-2045-7

Bedrooms: 4	Baths: 3
Living Area:	
Main floor	1,502 sq. ft.
Daylight basement	964 sq. ft.
Total Living Area:	**2,466 sq. ft.**
Tuck-under garage	472 sq. ft.
Exterior Wall Framing:	2x6
Daylight basement	

(All plans can be built with your choice of foundation and framing. A generic conversion diagram is available. See order form.)

BLUEPRINT PRICE CODE:	C

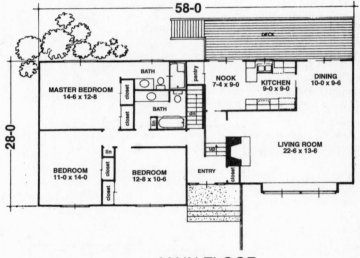

MAIN FLOOR

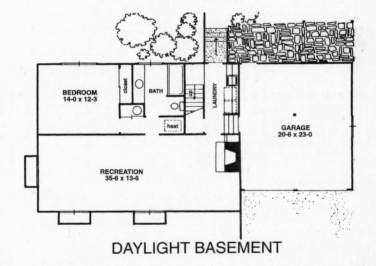

DAYLIGHT BASEMENT

ORDER BLUEPRINTS ANYTIME!
CALL TOLL-FREE 1-800-820-1283

Plan H-2045-7

PRICES AND DETAILS
ON PAGES 2-5

471

Garden Party

- Who doesn't love a garden party? This sunny home showcases a porch, partially covered by an arbor, that lends itself perfectly to those summer events.
- Inside, the dining room sits just to the right of the foyer, inviting guests in for a tasty meal. French doors open to the porch, making hors d'oeuvres in the fresh air a pleasing possibility.
- Across the foyer, the living room hosts gatherings of any sort, from the most casual to those when appearances

count. A pass-through to the kitchen saves trips back and forth.
- For everyday meals, a built-in table and seat off the kitchen keep things simple.
- Nearby, a skylighted hobby room could also serve as an office or guest room.
- When the day comes to an end, the master suite upstairs promises an inviting retreat. The bath's Jacuzzi tub is a well-deserved treat after a long jog.
- Down the hall, a skylight brings cheer to the secondary bathroom.
- Unless otherwise noted, all rooms include 9-ft. ceilings.

Plan L-75-CSB	
Bedrooms: 3+	**Baths:** 2½
Living Area:	
Upper floor	953 sq. ft.
Main floor	1,124 sq. ft.
Total Living Area:	**2,077 sq. ft.**
Garage	433 sq. ft.
Exterior Wall Framing:	2x4

Foundation Options:

Slab
(All plans can be built with your choice of foundation and framing. A generic conversion diagram is available. See order form.)

BLUEPRINT PRICE CODE: C

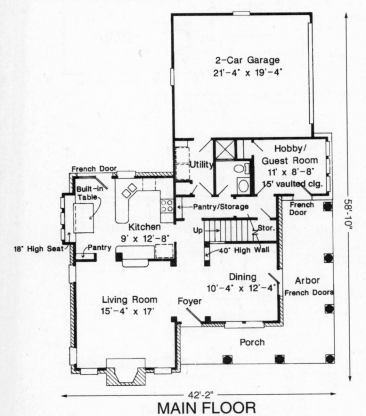

MAIN FLOOR

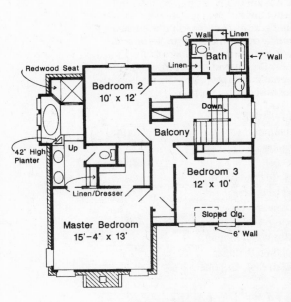

UPPER FLOOR

Plan L-75-CSB

PRICES AND DETAILS
ON PAGES 2-5

High-Style Hillside Home

- This beautiful hillside home is loaded with stylish features.
- The foyer leads into the Great Room, which is crowned by a 13-ft. vaulted ceiling. A fireplace warms this inviting space, and a door leads out to a wide sun deck that hugs the back of the home, offering sweeping views.
- The U-shaped kitchen includes a walk-in pantry, a greenhouse window, an eating bar and an adjoining nook.
- A vaulted ceiling in the master bedroom flattens out at 9 ft. for a spacious feel. A door offers private access to a relaxing hot tub on the deck. The private bath boasts a whirlpool tub and a separate shower with a seat.
- The versatile den could be used as a media room or as an extra bedroom.
- Two bedrooms downstairs share a full bath. The central bedroom would make a great guest room, with its walk-in closet and private patio.

Plan S-41892

Bedrooms: 3+	Baths: 3
Living Area:	
Main floor	1,485 sq. ft.
Partial daylight basement	590 sq. ft.
Total Living Area:	**2,075 sq. ft.**
Mechanical room	30 sq. ft.
Garage	429 sq. ft.
Exterior Wall Framing:	2x6

Foundation Options:
Partial daylight basement
(All plans can be built with your choice of foundation and framing. A generic conversion diagram is available. See order form.)

BLUEPRINT PRICE CODE:	C

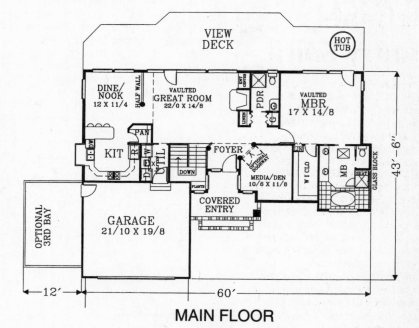

MAIN FLOOR

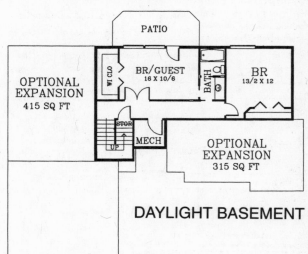

DAYLIGHT BASEMENT

ORDER BLUEPRINTS ANYTIME!
CALL TOLL-FREE 1-800-820-1283

Plan S-41892

PRICES AND DETAILS
ON PAGES 2-5

469

Catch the Country Spirit

- A railed porch and a matched trio of dormers fill this two-story with a heartwarming country spirit!
- The pretty porch is a great place to greet guests as they arrive for holiday gatherings. Hang some flower baskets to add a pleasant touch of extra color.
- Inside, the huge sunken family room is at the heart of the main floor. Its grand fireplace lights up the whole area.
- Big and efficient, the island kitchen is just a few short steps from the dining room, where access to the back porch lets you step out and enjoy the weather after enjoying a fine meal.
- Secluded at the opposite end of the home is the spacious master suite, complete with a large walk-in closet and a private bath with a garden tub.
- Two additional bedrooms are on the upper floor. Each has ample closet space and a built-in desk.
- A cozy study can easily be used as a fourth bedroom.

Plan J-86171

Bedrooms: 3+	Baths: 2½
Living Area:	
Upper floor	792 sq. ft.
Main floor	1,573 sq. ft.
Total Living Area:	**2,365 sq. ft.**
Garage and storage	569 sq. ft.
Exterior Wall Framing:	2x4

Foundation Options:

Crawlspace

Slab

(All plans can be built with your choice of foundation and framing. A generic conversion diagram is available. See order form.)

BLUEPRINT PRICE CODE: C

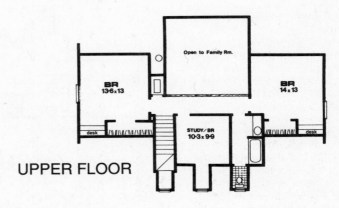

UPPER FLOOR

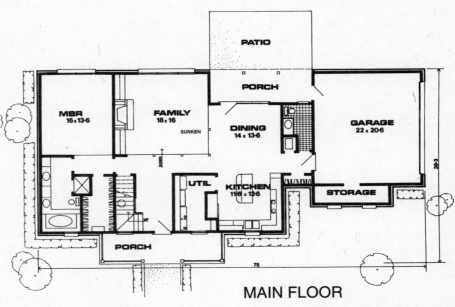

MAIN FLOOR

Plan J-86171

PRICES AND DETAILS
ON PAGES 2-5

Phenomenal French Flair!

- This classically designed home has a French Provincial flair and a stylish stucco facade that gives it a phenomenal appeal to prospective home owners.
- An attractive hip roof, elegant quoins and oval windows give the exterior an exquisite beauty.
- Located on the main floor for convenience, the master suite adds a touch of welcome luxury. It features a big walk-in closet, a private bath and gorgeous French doors leading out to the enormous back deck.
- Adjacent to the master suite is the huge library, where you'll find a cozy corner fireplace and deck access.
- A second fireplace, as well as French doors to the deck, are featured in the living room.
- Two more bedrooms—each with walk-in closets—are on the upper floor.
- The daylight basement includes a side-entry, two-car garage.

Plan AX-8619

Bedrooms: 3	Baths: 2½
Living Area:	
Upper floor	1,068 sq. ft.
Main floor	2,592 sq. ft.
Total Living Area:	**3,660 sq. ft.**
Daylight basement	2,168 sq. ft.
Tuck-under garage	424 sq. ft.
Exterior Wall Framing:	2x4

Foundation Options:

Daylight basement

(All plans can be built with your choice of foundation and framing. A generic conversion diagram is available. See order form.)

BLUEPRINT PRICE CODE:	F

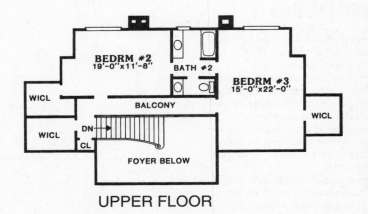

UPPER FLOOR

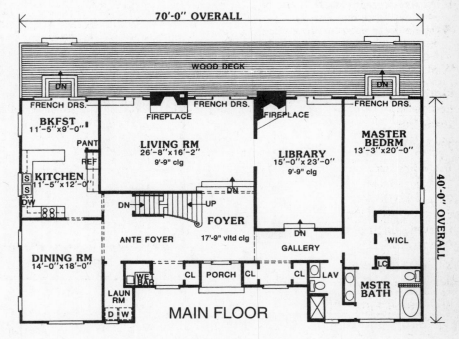

MAIN FLOOR

ORDER BLUEPRINTS ANYTIME!
CALL TOLL-FREE 1-800-820-1283

Plan AX-8619

PRICES AND DETAILS
ON PAGES 2-5
467

Comfortable Livability

- This comfortable cottage combines a highly livable floor plan with a charming Cape Cod exterior.
- The covered front porch ushers guests into the spacious central living room, which features a striking fireplace and direct access to a backyard deck.
- The roomy island kitchen easily serves the bright dining room and the bay-windowed breakfast nook. A laundry closet is nearby.
- The master suite boasts a walk-in closet and a compartmentalized bath that connects to a powder room.
- The second bedroom could also be used as a nursery or a den.
- On the upper floor, two good-sized bedrooms share a second full bath.
- A convenient storage area is provided off the side-entry, two-car garage.

Plan C-8030

Bedrooms: 4	Baths: 2½
Living Area:	
Upper floor	728 sq. ft.
Main floor	1,499 sq. ft.
Total Living Area:	**2,227 sq. ft.**
Daylight basement	1,381 sq. ft.
Garage and storage	441 sq. ft.
Exterior Wall Framing:	2x4

Foundation Options:

Daylight basement
Crawlspace
Slab

(All plans can be built with your choice of foundation and framing. A generic conversion diagram is available. See order form.)

BLUEPRINT PRICE CODE: C

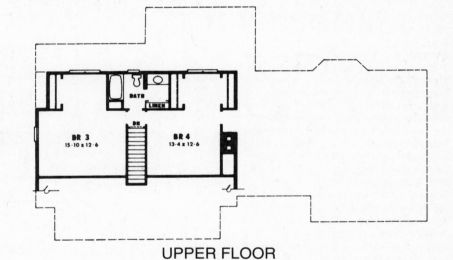

UPPER FLOOR

MAIN FLOOR

Plan C-8030

Especially Attractive!

- Wood posts, attractive shutters and decorative dentils give this beautiful home a classic look.
- The half-round transoms along the front porch allow extra light to flow into the formal living spaces. The warmth and drama of the living room's inviting fireplace can be felt from the foyer.
- The foyer also offers a view into the spacious Great Room and the expansive backyard deck beyond. French doors alongside another handsome fireplace open to the deck.
- The Great Room unfolds to the open kitchen, which includes a sunny bayed dinette with deck access.
- A convenient half-bath and a nice-sized laundry room are located between the kitchen and the garage entrance. All main-floor rooms boast 9-ft. ceilings.
- Four bedrooms and two full baths occupy the upper floor. The master suite boasts a unique ceiling that slopes to 12 feet. the master bath offers a whirlpool tub and a separate shower.

Plan AHP-9410

Bedrooms: 4	Baths: 2½
Living Area:	
Upper floor	1,116 sq. ft.
Main floor	1,222 sq. ft.
Total Living Area:	**2,338 sq. ft.**
Standard basement	1,222 sq. ft.
Garage and storage	497 sq. ft.
Exterior Wall Framing:	2x4 or 2x6

Foundation Options:

Standard basement

Crawlspace

Slab

(All plans can be built with your choice of foundation and framing. A generic conversion diagram is available. See order form.)

BLUEPRINT PRICE CODE:	C

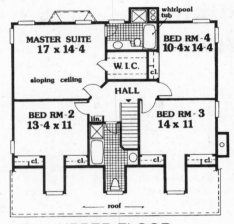

UPPER FLOOR

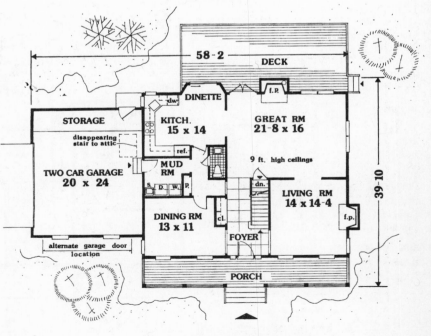

MAIN FLOOR

ORDER BLUEPRINTS ANYTIME!
CALL TOLL-FREE 1-800-820-1283

Plan AHP-9410

PRICES AND DETAILS
ON PAGES 2-5
465

Enfolding Spanish Arms

- A masonry half-wall surrounds a pleasant courtyard and garden walkway leading to this luxurious home. The wall rises to follow the slope of the tiered roofline, where clay tiles complement the stucco exterior.
- Double doors flanked by sidelight windows open to the tiled entry. Step down into the living room, which features a fireplace, picture windows overlooking the courtyard, and glass doors opening to a covered patio at the rear of the home.
- The open central staircase also adds to the living room's spaciousness.
- A pocket door separates the dining room from the kitchen, helping to keep food prep noise to a minimum.
- The family room is highlighted by false beams in the ceiling, another fireplace, and patio doors leading to the backyard.
- The garage provides direct access to a mudroom area in the laundry room.
- Upstairs bedrooms are large, but there's still room for three full baths and plenty of closet and linen storage.

Plan H-3717-M1A	
Bedrooms: 4	**Baths:** 3½
Living Area:	
Upper floor	1,308 sq. ft.
Main floor	1,363 sq. ft.
Total Living Area:	**2,671 sq. ft.**
Garage	550 sq. ft.
Exterior Wall Framing:	2x6
Foundation Options:	

Slab
(All plans can be built with your choice of foundation and framing. A generic conversion diagram is available. See order form.)

BLUEPRINT PRICE CODE:	D

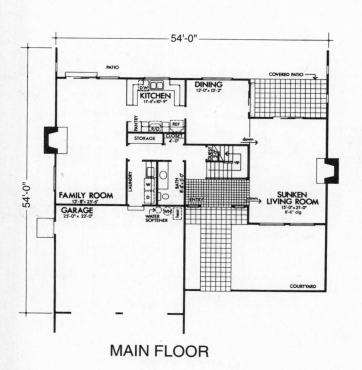

MAIN FLOOR

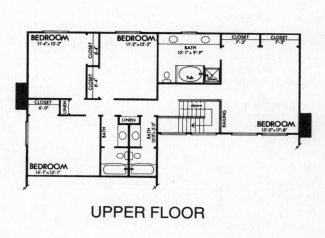

UPPER FLOOR

A Hint of Victorian Charm

- Half-timbering, patterned wood shingles and decorative trim give this country home a hint of Victorian-style charm.
- A covered front porch, triple dormers and a pretty bay window complete the attractive exterior.
- Inside, the sizable living room's handsome fireplace sets a cozy mood for intimate evenings.
- A second gathering space is the family room. It's the perfect place to gather on movie night. Its proximity to the kitchen means snacks are just a few steps away.
- The kitchen also serves the beautiful formal dining room, whose bay window adds a dramatic touch at dinnertime.
- A private bath and a walk-in closet are highlights in the master suite.
- Upstairs, two bedrooms and a full bath create room for your growing family. A loft over the garage offers expansion possibilities.

Plan AX-8272-A

Bedrooms: 3+	Baths: 2½
Living Area:	
Upper floor	674 sq. ft.
Main floor	1,296 sq. ft.
Bonus room	245 sq. ft.
Total Living Area:	**2,215 sq. ft.**
Standard basement	1,296 sq. ft.
Optional garage and storage	440 sq. ft.
Exterior Wall Framing:	2x4

Foundation Options:

Standard basement

Slab

(All plans can be built with your choice of foundation and framing. A generic conversion diagram is available. See order form.)

BLUEPRINT PRICE CODE:	C

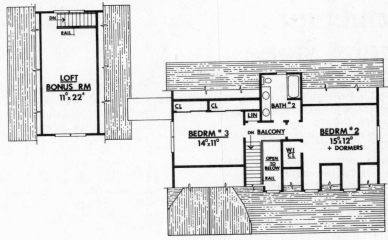

UPPER FLOOR

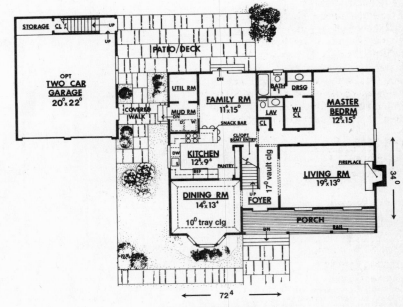

MAIN FLOOR

ORDER BLUEPRINTS ANYTIME!
CALL TOLL-FREE 1-800-820-1283

Plan AX-8272-A

PRICES AND DETAILS
ON PAGES 2-5

463

Perfect for a Lateral Slope

- Side-to-side sloping lots are often difficult to cope with, but this clever design accepts the challenge and comes out a clear winner!
- The dramatic exterior's rustic feel is highlighted by a wall of windows that looks out over a cantilevered deck and an interesting tuck-under carport.
- Once inside, you'll be impressed by the open spaciousness of the floor plan. The huge living room/dining room area is perfect for large gatherings of friends and family. Listen to the crackling flame in the fireplace and watch the sun fade into the horizon out the beautiful, panoramic windows.
- Three nice-sized bedrooms assure you that there will be room enough if your family expands or you have surprise overnight guests. The master suite features a private bath.
- Downstairs, the daylight basement offers a wonderful recreation room with its own cheery fireplace. The "general area" is a great spot for a workroom.

Plan H-2015-1

Bedrooms: 3	Baths: 2
Living Area:	
Main floor	1,192 sq. ft.
Daylight basement	810 sq. ft.
Total Living Area:	**2,002 sq. ft.**
Tuck-under carport	392 sq. ft.
Exterior Wall Framing:	2x6

Foundation Options:

Daylight basement

(All plans can be built with your choice of foundation and framing. A generic conversion diagram is available. See order form.)

BLUEPRINT PRICE CODE:	C

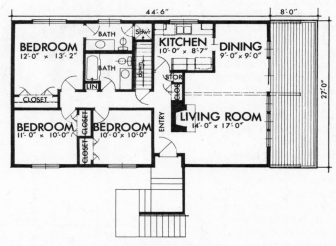

MAIN FLOOR

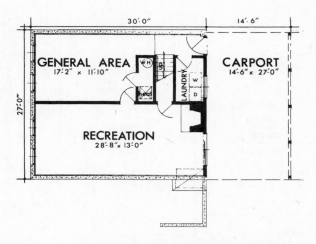

DAYLIGHT BASEMENT

ORDER BLUEPRINTS ANYTIME!
CALL TOLL-FREE 1-800-820-1283

Plan H-2015-1

PRICES AND DETAILS
ON PAGES 2-5

A Custom Contemporary

- Clean lines and custom design touches are found in this contemporary home.
- The recessed entry unveils an open foyer with a convenient coat closet and a good-sized storage area. A powder room with a shower is located nearby.
- Straight ahead, a 16½-ft. vaulted ceiling soars over the Great Room. Bright windows frame the space, which features a fireplace and a built-in entertainment center. Beautiful French doors lead to the backyard.
- The dining area merges with the skylighted kitchen, where a desk and an island cooktop with a snack bar for four make the most of the space.
- Across the home, a 10-ft. coved ceiling tops the master suite, which boasts built-in cabinets. Two closets and a dresser lead to the skylighted bath, which includes a whirlpool tub.
- Upstairs, two bedrooms share another skylighted bath. A third room that overlooks the Great Room could serve as a quiet den or a guest room.

Plan LRD-51391

Bedrooms: 3+	Baths: 3
Living Area:	
Upper floor	545 sq. ft.
Main floor	1,645 sq. ft.
Total Living Area:	**2,190 sq. ft.**
Standard basement	1,645 sq. ft.
Garage	552 sq. ft.
Exterior Wall Framing:	2x6

Foundation Options:

Standard basement

Crawlspace

(All plans can be built with your choice of foundation and framing. A generic conversion diagram is available. See order form.)

BLUEPRINT PRICE CODE:	C

VIEW INTO GREAT ROOM

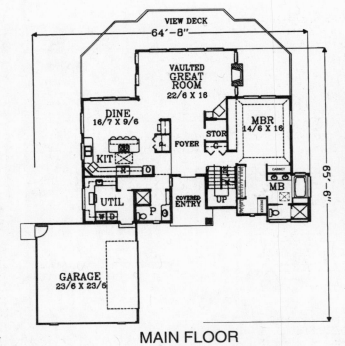

MAIN FLOOR

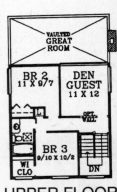

UPPER FLOOR

Open Arches

- This home welcomes you with open arches. Its covered entry and lovely window treatments create a graceful exterior. Inside, plenty of open spaces embrace family members and friends.
- To the left of the double door entry, the formal living and dining rooms flow together under a 15-ft., 10-in. vaulted ceiling.
- The efficient, walk-through kitchen shares a snack bar with the bayed breakfast nook.
- Spend some quality time relaxing with the kids in the vaulted family room. Under an 18-ft., 4-in. ceiling, a glowing fireplace adds just the right touch of warmth and coziness.
- Whether as an extra bedroom or as a den, the room at the front of the home is sure to meet your needs. It offers a 10-ft, 8-in. vaulted ceiling.
- Double doors open to the master suite, where an 11-ft. vaulted ceiling graces the sleeping area. The 12-ft. vaulted bath promises a spa tub, a separate shower and a dual-sink vanity.
- Off the balcony hall, two secondary bedrooms share another bath.

Plan LS-95825-BJ

Bedrooms: 3+	Baths: 2½
Living Area:	
Upper floor	1,001 sq. ft.
Main floor	1,530 sq. ft.
Total Living Area:	**2,531 sq. ft.**
Garage and storage	638 sq. ft.
Exterior Wall Framing:	2x6

Foundation Options:

Slab

(All plans can be built with your choice of foundation and framing. A generic conversion diagram is available. See order form.)

BLUEPRINT PRICE CODE:	**D**

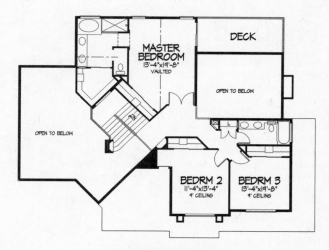

UPPER FLOOR

MAIN FLOOR

 Plan LS-95825-BJ

Shades of New England

- This home shows a traditional New England look to the world, while the interior is very modern and open. Formal in exterior appearance, it is definitely a home that is designed for informal living throughout the interior.
- A large two-story vaulted foyer greets guests upon arrival. Upon entering the Great Room, passing by either side of the fieldstone fireplace, they are then treated to a room flooded with light from the multiple window treatments. The large kitchen with central island range contains a secondary bar sink with room for four bar stools.
- An open picketed staircase leads one to the "supersuite" complete with a gas-log fireplace, private deck and luxurious master bath that includes a raised garden tub.
- The study may be used as a bedroom or left as a study/library as shown. The utility area is part of the second floor design for easier access from the bedrooms.

Plan LRD-33090

Bedrooms: 3+	Baths: 3
Living Area:	
Upper floor	1,361 sq. ft.
Main floor	1,693 sq. ft.
Total Living Area:	**3,054 sq. ft.**
Standard basement	1,693 sq. ft.
Garage	463 sq. ft.
Exterior Wall Framing:	2x6

Foundation Options:

Standard basement

Crawlspace

(All plans can be built with your choice of foundation and framing. A generic conversion diagram is available. See order form.)

BLUEPRINT PRICE CODE:	**E**

MAIN FLOOR

UPPER FLOOR

ORDER BLUEPRINTS ANYTIME!
CALL TOLL-FREE 1-800-820-1283

Plan LRD-33090

PRICES AND DETAILS
ON PAGES 2-5

459

A Spanish Flair

- A stucco exterior crowned by a zesty Spanish-tile roof gives this home flair. The covered entry is striking, with its gorgeous transom and sidelights.
- Inside, a dramatic view of a 17-ft. vaulted ceiling over the living room greets visitors in the entry. Natural sunlight pours into the room through beautiful transom windows.
- An oversized bay window and a 10-ft. ceiling in the dining room provide a cheerful spot for breakfast, lunch and dinner. A handy island workstation in

the kitchen allows ample room to gather in the home's busiest spot.
- A den is close enough to the living areas to be within earshot of children, but secluded enough for you to work on quiet chores. This room could also accommodate overnight guests.
- The master suite's gem is a private bath, where a dual-sink vanity and a separate tub and shower allow spouses to get ready for the day together.
- Upstairs, a loft is a great place for a computer desk for the kids, and a versatile bonus room can be adapted to meet your family's needs.

Plan B-94032	
Bedrooms: 3+	**Baths:** 2½
Living Area:	
Upper floor	549 sq. ft.
Main floor	1,395 sq. ft.
Bonus room	268 sq. ft.
Total Living Area:	**2,212 sq. ft.**
Standard basement	1,395 sq. ft.
Garage	478 sq. ft.
Exterior Wall Framing:	2x6
Foundation Options:	

Standard basement
(All plans can be built with your choice of foundation and framing. A generic conversion diagram is available. See order form.)

BLUEPRINT PRICE CODE: C

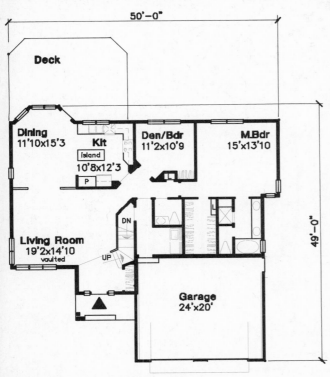

MAIN FLOOR

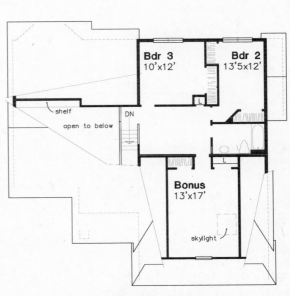

UPPER FLOOR

Plan B-94032

PRICES AND DETAILS
ON PAGES 2-5

Sunny Spaces

- Graced by skylights and clerestory windows, this bright and airy home is filled with sunny spaces.
- The skylighted foyer showcases a sunstreaked open-railed stairway under a 12-ft., 3-in. sloped ceiling.
- Off the foyer, the intimate sunken living room is augmented by a 16-ft. cathedral ceiling and tall corner windows.
- Defined by columns and railings, the formal dining room is enhanced by an arched window arrangement.
- The skylighted island kitchen includes a bright breakfast space, which is separated from the family room by a half-wall. Expanded by a skylighted 16-ft. cathedral ceiling, the family room offers a handsome fireplace and access to a sunken rear sun room.
- The deluxe master suite features a stepped ceiling, a bayed sitting room and a private bath. Sliding glass doors open to the sun room, which boasts an 11-ft., 7-in. vaulted ceiling.
- Two more bedrooms, a study alcove and a full bath are found upstairs.

Plan AX-91314

Bedrooms: 3+	Baths: 3
Living Area:	
Upper floor	544 sq. ft.
Main floor	1,959 sq. ft.
Sun room	202 sq. ft.
Total Living Area:	**2,705 sq. ft.**
Standard basement	1,833 sq. ft.
Garage	482 sq. ft.
Exterior Wall Framing:	2x4

Foundation Options:

Standard basement

Crawlspace

Slab

(All plans can be built with your choice of foundation and framing. A generic conversion diagram is available. See order form.)

BLUEPRINT PRICE CODE: D

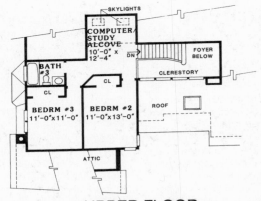

UPPER FLOOR

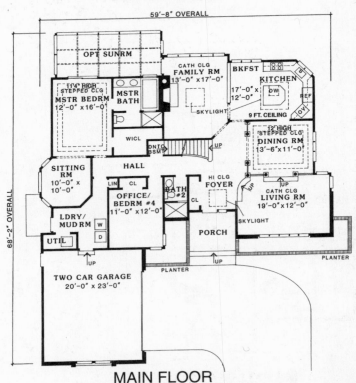

MAIN FLOOR

Touch of Drama

- Usually the little things make a home something special. But in this contemporary design's case, it's the prominent features that add the extra touch of drama.
- Rustic stonework on the facade and a breathtaking picture window accent the sharp angles of the roofline.
- Just off the entry, the sunken living room beckons visitors to rest for a spell. Open

to the elegant formal dining room, it also has access to a covered patio.
- The large, efficient island kitchen adjoins the sprawling family room and the casual dining area, allowing the family chef to participate in conversations while preparing dinner.
- An appealing wood deck stretches the entire right side of the home.
- A breathtaking, open-railed staircase leads upstairs, introducing three good-sized bedrooms and a compartmentalized bath. The master bedroom boasts a charming window seat and a large walk-in closet.

Plans H-3697-6 & -6A	
Bedrooms: 3	**Baths:** 2½
Living Area:	
Upper floor	921 sq. ft.
Main floor	1,410 sq. ft.
Total Living Area:	**2,331 sq. ft.**
Standard basement	1,410 sq. ft.
Garage	452 sq. ft.
Exterior Wall Framing:	2x4
Foundation Options:	**Plan #**
Standard basement	H-3697-6
Crawlspace	H-3697-6A
(All plans can be built with your choice of foundation and framing. A generic conversion diagram is available. See order form.)	
BLUEPRINT PRICE CODE:	**C**

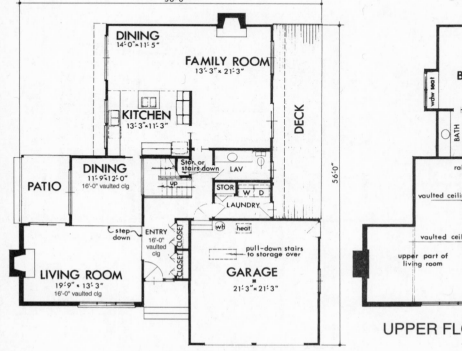

MAIN FLOOR

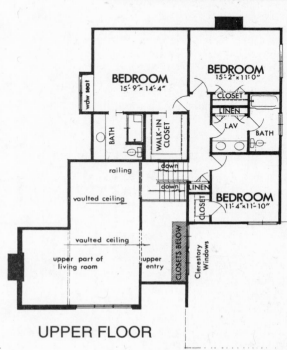

UPPER FLOOR

Plans H-3697-6 & -6A

PRICES AND DETAILS
ON PAGES 2-5

Breakfast by a Woodstove

- Skylights and clerestory windows shine from all angles of this floor plan and, with the help of vaulted ceilings scattered throughout, bathe the rooms in natural light.
- Enjoy breakfast by the woodstove while you look out to the pretty covered patio.
- An island with a cooktop and a snack bar complement the gourmet kitchen.

- The sunken living room includes a fireplace for cozy family gatherings.
- A traditional curved staircase to the upper level features a curved, open-railed balcony that looks out over the entry foyer and the living room.
- The master bedroom has a walk-in closet, a private bath, and access to a wood deck overlooking the backyard.
- The secondary bedrooms share a full-size bath.
- The garage has a work area that looks out on the home's front entry, and offers plenty of storage space above.

Plan LRD-52883

Bedrooms: 3+	**Baths:** 2½

Living Area:	
Upper floor	890 sq. ft.
Main floor	1,330 sq. ft.
Total Living Area:	**2,220 sq. ft.**
Basement	1,330 sq. ft.
Garage	420 sq. ft.
Exterior Wall Framing:	2x6

Foundation Options:

Daylight basement
Standard basement
Crawlspace
(All plans can be built with your choice of foundation and framing. A generic conversion diagram is available. See order form.)

BLUEPRINT PRICE CODE: C

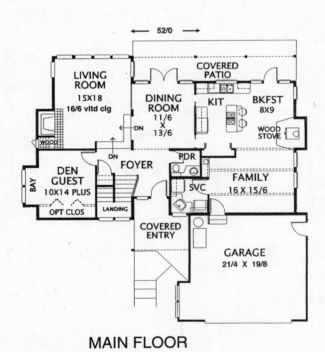

MAIN FLOOR

UPPER FLOOR

Bold, Exciting Design

- Vertical siding, a bold roofline, two decks and lots of glass are the hallmarks of this exciting design.
- An open room arrangement dominates the main level.
- The vaulted entry leads to the informal living areas straight ahead or to the formal living and dining rooms on the right. A half-bath is centrally located.
- The combination family room, breakfast area and kitchen is sure to be the hot spot of the house. Lots of windows, a fireplace and an adjoining deck make this spacious area warm and inviting.
- The upper level is highlighted by the vaulted master bedroom with windows that overlook a private deck. A large bathroom and a walk-in closet complete the master suite.
- A sitting area is just off the balcony hallway, as are two more bedrooms and another full bath.

Plan B-7833

Bedrooms: 3	Baths: 2½
Living Area:	
Upper floor	1,260 sq. ft.
Main floor	1,400 sq. ft.
Total Living Area:	**2,660 sq. ft.**
Daylight basement	1,400 sq. ft.
Garage	550 sq. ft.
Exterior Wall Framing:	2x4

Foundation Options:

Daylight basement

(All plans can be built with your choice of foundation and framing. A generic conversion diagram is available. See order form.)

BLUEPRINT PRICE CODE:	D

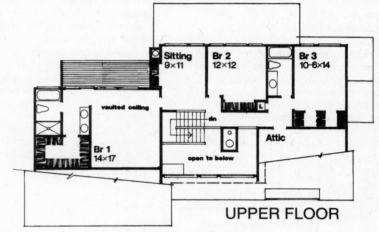

UPPER FLOOR

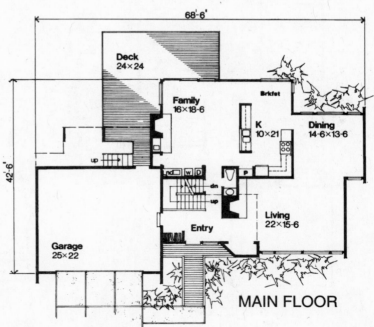

MAIN FLOOR

Room for a Growing Family

- Suitable for a narrow lot, this stylish home may have two, three or four bedrooms, depending on the needs of your family.
- The living room boasts a 13-ft.-high vaulted ceiling and a large bay window. Striking columns set off the adjoining formal dining room.
- The spacious family room features a handsome fireplace and a ceiling that vaults to 17 feet. Sliding glass doors provide access to an inviting deck.
- The efficiently designed kitchen offers an angled serving counter, a handy pantry and a sunny breakfast nook.
- A 10-ft. tray ceiling and private deck access highlight the master suite, which also includes his-and-hers closets and an opulent spa bath.
- A second bedroom is found upstairs, along with a nice loft that overlooks the family room and could serve as a third bedroom. The unfinished bonus room may be completed later as a fourth bedroom, a playroom or a home office.

Plan B-92001	
Bedrooms: 2+	**Baths:** 2½
Living Area:	
Upper floor	522 sq. ft.
Main floor	1,750 sq. ft.
Total Living Area:	**2,272 sq. ft.**
Bonus room (unfinished)	207 sq. ft.
Standard basement	1,750 sq. ft.
Garage	406 sq. ft.
Exterior Wall Framing:	**2x6**

Foundation Options:

Standard basement
(All plans can be built with your choice of foundation and framing. A generic conversion diagram is available. See order form.)

BLUEPRINT PRICE CODE: C

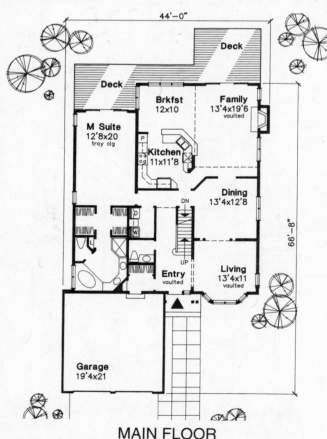

MAIN FLOOR

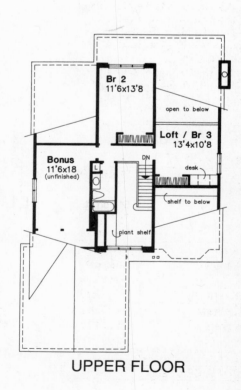

UPPER FLOOR

ORDER BLUEPRINTS ANYTIME!
CALL TOLL-FREE 1-800-820-1283

Plan B-92001

PRICES AND DETAILS
ON PAGES 2-5

451

Clever Contemporary

- A wide, sweeping facade introduces this striking contemporary design.
- Inside, the good impression continues, with the sight of a huge Great Room with a large masonry fireplace.
- The passive sun room can serve as a breakfast room, family room or arboretum, while at the same time collecting and redistributing the sun's heat throughout the house.
- Adjoining the sun room is the nice-sized master suite that features a luxurious private bath and a big walk-in closet. A pretty window seat lets you keep an eye on outdoor activities.
- Upstairs, you'll find an enormous and versatile bonus room that can serve as a kids' playroom, a home office or an exercise area. A full bath and an impressive wardrobe/storage area add to the area's usefulness.

Plans H-958-1A & -1B

Bedrooms: 2+	Baths: 3
Living Area:	
Upper floor	511 sq. ft.
Main floor	1,568 sq. ft.
Sun room	194 sq. ft.
Total Living Area:	**2,273 sq. ft.**
Daylight basement	1,568 sq. ft.
Garage	484 sq. ft.
Exterior Wall Framing:	2x6
Foundation Options:	**Plan #**
Daylight basement	H-958-1B
Crawlspace	H-958-1A

(All plans can be built with your choice of foundation and framing. A generic conversion diagram is available. See order form.)

BLUEPRINT PRICE CODE:	C

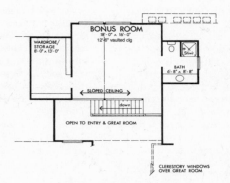

UPPER FLOOR

MAIN FLOOR

BASEMENT STAIRWAY LOCATION

Narrow Escape

- This plan makes the most of even a narrow, urban lot. At 36 ft. wide, its deluxe living space is further maximized by an open floor plan.
- The front door, sheltered by a roof overhang, opens to a tiled entry. The entry leads to virtually every room in the house, with the living areas straight ahead and the stairway to the second-floor bedrooms on the right.
- The living space is open, yet each room is given its own definition. The kitchen features an island counter that includes a cooktop and plenty of room for casual dining. The adjoining nook is encased in glass, providing a pleasant view to the backyard deck.
- The dining room flows into the Great Room, creating one huge area for relaxing and entertaining. Imagine the grand parties you'll throw here!
- The second floor hosts a cozy loft or den, three bedrooms and two baths. The master bedroom features a vaulted ceiling, a walk-in closet with a clothes chute and a private dressing area. The inviting master bath includes a platform tub, another vanity plus a shower.

Plan S-9288	
Bedrooms: 3+	**Baths:** 2½
Living Area:	
Upper floor	1,094 sq. ft.
Main floor	1,140 sq. ft.
Total Living Area:	**2,234 sq. ft.**
Standard basement	1,140 sq. ft.
Garage	502 sq. ft.
Exterior Wall Framing:	2x6

Foundation Options:

Standard basement
Crawlspace
Slab
(All plans can be built with your choice of foundation and framing. A generic conversion diagram is available. See order form.)

BLUEPRINT PRICE CODE:	C

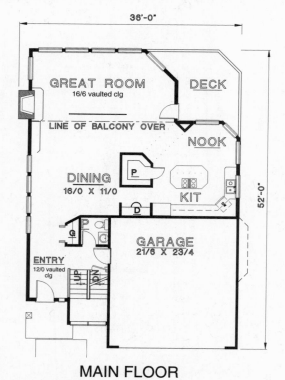

MAIN FLOOR

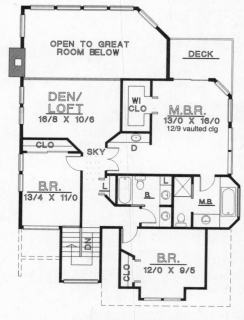

UPPER FLOOR

ORDER BLUEPRINTS ANYTIME!
CALL TOLL-FREE 1-800-820-1283

Plan S-9288

PRICES AND DETAILS
ON PAGES 2-5

449

Resplendent Contemporary

- A dramatic roofline and a combination of vertical and horizontal siding give a resplendent look to this two-story home. They serve as appropriate introductions to the home's 14-ft.-high foyer.
- The enormous, sunken living room is at the heart of the home. It boasts a grand fireplace, a remarkable 22-ft. vaulted ceiling, a pair of skylights and access to an amazing back deck via sliding glass doors on three sides!
- Perfect for sun-worshipping or festive summer barbecues, the back deck is a natural spot for fair-weather fun.
- Another incredible spot is the master suite, which offers a luxurious bath with skylights set into its breathtaking, 15-ft. vaulted ceiling.
- Spacious and efficient, the L-shaped kitchen has a huge pantry for all your canned goods.
- Three comfortable bedrooms and a full-sized bath comprise the upper floor.

Plan AX-98712

Bedrooms: 4	Baths: 2½
Living Area:	
Upper floor	815 sq. ft.
Main floor	1,343 sq. ft.
Total Living Area:	**2,158 sq. ft.**
Standard basement	1,298 sq. ft.
Garage	400 sq. ft.
Exterior Wall Framing:	2x4

Foundation Options:

Standard basement
Slab
(All plans can be built with your choice of foundation and framing. A generic conversion diagram is available. See order form.)

BLUEPRINT PRICE CODE: C

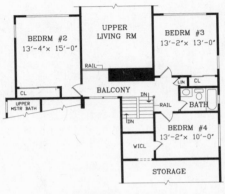

UPPER FLOOR

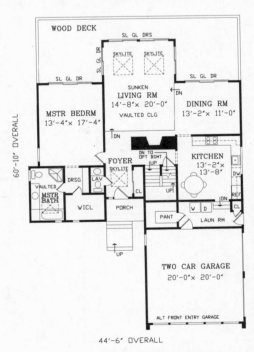

MAIN FLOOR

Whispering Windsong

- Merging its interior rooms with the beautiful outdoors all around it, this two-story lets the windsong flow freely through its fresh, open design.
- Fascinating details are everywhere! On the exterior, a privacy fence hides a bubbly hot tub.
- Inside, you'll marvel at the vaulted Great Room on the upper floor; this enormous open space that features a cozy corner fireplace, a built-in wine storage area, two double doors to the sparkling sun room and access to the incredible view deck in the rear.
- A walk-in closet, a private entrance to a full bath and scenic views out the home's front and side give the master suite a luxurious feel.
- The U-shaped kitchen offers a handy eating bar and a unique dumbwaiter to serve the main floor below.
- Perfect for intimate nights for just the two of you, the main-floor den boasts its own corner fireplace plus a built-in bookshelf. If an extra bedroom is needed, this is just the spot!
- A shop/exercise room, a full bath and two bedrooms complete the floor plan. The bath opens to the hot tub area.

Plan LRD-60983

Bedrooms: 3+	Baths: 2
Living Area:	
Upper floor	1,600 sq. ft.
Main floor	1,197 sq. ft.
Shop/exercise	250 sq. ft.
Sun room	200 sq. ft.
Total Living Area:	**3,247 sq. ft.**
Tuck-under garage and storage	638 sq. ft.
Exterior Wall Framing:	**2x6**

Foundation Options:

Crawlspace
(All plans can be built with your choice of foundation and framing. A generic conversion diagram is available. See order form.)

BLUEPRINT PRICE CODE: E

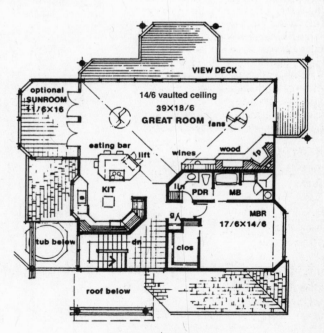

MAIN FLOOR

UPPER FLOOR

ORDER BLUEPRINTS ANYTIME!
CALL TOLL-FREE 1-800-820-1283

Plan LRD-60983

PRICES AND DETAILS
ON PAGES 2-5

447

Cheerful Aspect

- A cozy gambrel roof, a turret-like bay window and a detailed, covered front porch enhance the cheerful appeal of this unusual home. Shingles on the exterior walls as well as the roof add a touch of 19th-century charm.
- The entry creates a stunning first impression of the interior, with a vaulted ceiling accented by an overhead window and plant shelf.
- French doors enclose the bayed library, which overlooks the front yard.
- On the other side of the entry, the living room and dining room flow together. An angled fireplace and built-in shelves highlight the area, and the dining room includes a door to a covered side porch.
- The island kitchen enjoys a sunny eating nook with access to a backyard deck. The laundry area houses a pantry.
- The secluded master suite boasts a large bedroom and a lush spa bath.
- Upstairs, two secondary bedrooms share a compartmentalized bath. The family room overlooks the entry below.

Plans H-3747-1 & -1A

Bedrooms: 3	Baths: 2½
Living Area:	
Upper floor	1,002 sq. ft.
Main floor	2,232 sq. ft.
Total Living Area:	**3,234 sq. ft.**
Standard basement	2,232 sq. ft.
Garage	774 sq. ft.
Exterior Wall Framing:	2x6
Foundation Options:	**Plan #**
Standard basement	H-3747-1
Crawlspace	H-3747-1A

(All plans can be built with your choice of foundation and framing. A generic conversion diagram is available. See order form.)

BLUEPRINT PRICE CODE: E

MAIN FLOOR

GARAGE 24'-0" X 27'-0"

DECK

NOOK 9'-0" X 11'-4"

KITCHEN 15'-4" X 12'-0"

PANTRY

LAUNDRY

BATH

SHWR LIN

WALK-IN CLOSET

HOT TUB

BEDROOM 19'-0" X 16'-6"

STORAGE

DINING 12'-0" X 16'-0"

Guest Shelves

LIVING ROOM 16'-0" X 20'-0" 12'-0" vltd clg

LIBRARY 13'-0" X 15'-0"

ENTRY 17'-0" vltd clg

PORCH

87'-6"

59'-6"

UPPER FLOOR

BEDROOM 15'-0" X 12'-6"

BEDROOM 10'-0" X 14'-10"

FAMILY ROOM 15'-6" X 25'-0"

OPEN TO ENTRY

42" high wall

SHELF

BASEMENT STAIRWAY LOCATION

down

Hillside Charmer

- This charming multi-level design is a masterful blend of contemporary and classic details and is designed to fit a hillside lot.
- A sidelighted entry opens into the living room, where a fireplace takes the chill off long winter nights. The angles of the vaulted ceiling frame a round window that lets in extra sunlight.
- Up a short flight of stairs, the dining and family room combination is brightened by a unique window wall. In the kitchen, a handy work island is topped by extra cabinet space.
- In the vaulted master suite you'll find a private bath with a large soaking tub, a separate shower, dual sinks and a big walk-in closet.
- An adjoining den makes a nice guest room when necessary and has sliding glass doors to a big backyard deck.
- The daylight basement includes two bedrooms that share a full bath, plus a utility area and a recreation room.

Plan B-89037

Bedrooms: 3+	Baths: 3
Living Area:	
Upper floor	1,160 sq. ft.
Main floor	255 sq. ft.
Partial daylight basement	913 sq. ft.
Total Living Area:	**2,328 sq. ft.**
Garage	468 sq. ft.
Exterior Wall Framing:	2x6

Foundation Options:

Partial daylight basement

(All plans can be built with your choice of foundation and framing. A generic conversion diagram is available. See order form.)

BLUEPRINT PRICE CODE: **C**

UPPER FLOOR

MAIN FLOOR/DAYLIGHT BASEMENT

H-944-1A REAR VIEW

Whatever the Weather

- You'll be smiling when the bills come, with this energy-efficient home that puts heat-retaining masonry walls, earth-shelter berms that can insulate as well as cool, a Plenwood heating system (described in the plans), and solar skylights to work for you.
- The living room is spectacular. Its masonry wall is a beautiful backdrop for the woodstove, collecting and redistributing warmth throughout the home.

- The master suite is sweet indeed. Bigger than the average living room, it also has its own private bath and huge walk-in closet.
- If you've never had a kitchen pantry before, you'll love it! Also enjoy other time-saving utility features like the spacious laundry, plentiful storage and wraparound kitchen configuration.
- Landscape the rear of the home for maximum patio enjoyment.
- French doors separate the living room from the family room.
- Order this home with either an all-weather wood or concrete foundation, as specified.

Plans H-944-1A & -1B	
Bedrooms: 3	**Baths:** 2½
Living Area:	
Main floor	484 sq. ft.
Daylight basement	1,640 sq. ft.
Total Living Area:	**2,124 sq. ft.**
Garage	471 sq. ft.
Exterior Wall Framing:	2x6
Foundation Options:	**Plan #**
Daylight basement (wood)	H-944-1A
Daylight basement (concrete)	H-944-1B

(All plans can be built with your choice of foundation and framing. A generic conversion diagram is available. See order form.)

BLUEPRINT PRICE CODE:	**C**

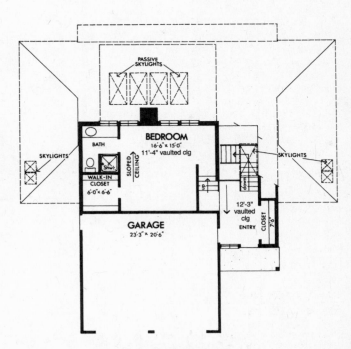

DAYLIGHT BASEMENT

MAIN FLOOR

Narrow-Lot Luxury

- At only 40 ft. wide, this 1½-story home is ideal for a narrow lot.
- Vaulted ceilings in the entry, living room, family room and master suite contribute to the overall spaciousness of the home's open design.
- Special touches – like a plant shelf above the vaulted entry, decorative columns between the dining room and the living room and a loft with two overlooks – make an exciting interior statement.
- The main-floor master suite opens to a private deck and features his-and-hers closets. The personal bath boasts a vaulted ceiling, double sinks, an oval tub and a separate shower.
- The family gathering area includes an open kitchen, a sunny breakfast room and a vaulted family room with a fireplace and an adjoining deck.
- A second bedroom and another bath share the upper floor, along with a loft area that could serve as an extra bedroom, a TV room or a home office.

Plan B-90002	
Bedrooms: 2+	**Baths:** 2½
Living Area:	
Upper floor	527 sq. ft.
Main floor	1,730 sq. ft.
Total Living Area:	**2,257 sq. ft.**
Standard basement	1,730 sq. ft.
Garage	406 sq. ft.
Exterior Wall Framing:	2x6
Foundation Options:	

Standard basement
(All plans can be built with your choice of foundation and framing. A generic conversion diagram is available. See order form.)

BLUEPRINT PRICE CODE:	**C**

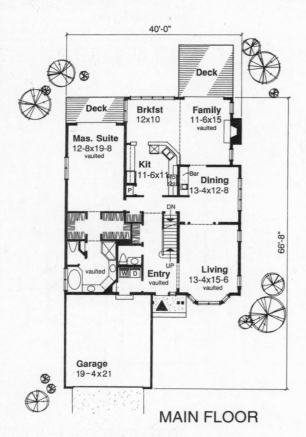

MAIN FLOOR

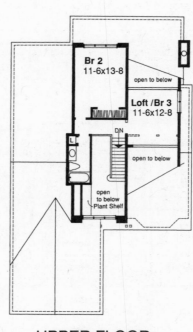

UPPER FLOOR

Rustic Year-Round Home

- This rustic home allows the year-round enjoyment of a scenic site. Visitors will be impressed by the home's attractive wood exterior, enormous railed deck and striking chimney.
- The front stairs lead past a storage closet to the deck and the main entrance.
- Inside, the open foyer introduces the magnificent Great Room, which is warmed by a cozy fireplace and enhanced by a 15½-ft. cathedral ceiling. Four sets of sliding glass doors extend the entertaining area to the wraparound deck. Note the handy serving shelf with a pass-through from the kitchen.
- The welcoming country kitchen is sure to be the center of casual family activities. Features here include a handy

pantry closet, a large snack bar and a second fireplace.
- The spacious master bedroom offers private access to the main-floor bath, which shows off a relaxing whirlpool tub and a linen closet.
- Convenient laundry and coat closets complete the main floor.
- A railed, skylighted stairway leads to two bedrooms, a second bath and another linen closet on the upper floor. The railed hallway provides views to the Great Room below.
- Perfect for a sloping lot, this home's daylight basement includes a fabulous recreation room with a third fireplace and sliding glass doors to a nice patio. A third bath and an unfinished area are other extras.
- Also on the lower level is a unique tuck-under garage, which may be entered from two directions and is suitable for boat storage.

Plan AX-7944-A	
Bedrooms: 3	**Baths:** 3
Living Area:	
Upper floor	457 sq. ft.
Main floor	1,191 sq. ft.
Daylight basement (finished)	545 sq. ft.
Total Living Area:	**2,193 sq. ft.**
Daylight basement (unfinished)	246 sq. ft.
Tuck-under garage	382 sq. ft.
Exterior Wall Framing:	2x4

Foundation Options:

Daylight basement
(All plans can be built with your choice of foundation and framing. A generic conversion diagram is available. See order form.)

BLUEPRINT PRICE CODE: C

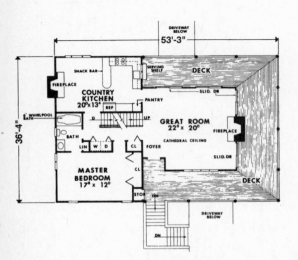

MAIN FLOOR

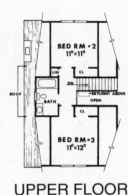

UPPER FLOOR

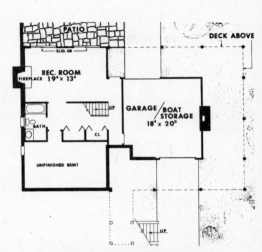

DAYLIGHT BASEMENT

Plan AX-7944-A

PRICES AND DETAILS
ON PAGES 2-5

Worth a Second Look!

- If you're looking for a home that commands a second look, this design is for you! Its striking columns, concrete tile roof and curved glass-block wall create an enduring impression.
- The entry's high transom window radiates light into the foyer and the adjacent formal living areas. The living room's French doors open to a covered patio with a cool summer kitchen.
- With a gourmet island, a large pantry and lots of storage and work space, the indoor kitchen is well equipped.
- The breakfast nook and family room enjoy the warmth of a gas fireplace and the sights and sounds of your favorite entertainment media. Both areas have outdoor views and expand to the patio.
- The amenities don't end here. Wrapped by glass block, the master bath's grand soaking tub is fit for a king! The quarter-round glass-block shower and dual vanities add to the royal treatment.
- Two main-floor bedrooms and one upstairs bedroom suite accommodate the rest of the family; the den offers a fifth bedroom option.

Plan HDS-99-216

Bedrooms: 4+	Baths: 4
Living Area:	
Upper floor	441 sq. ft.
Main floor	2,898 sq. ft.
Total Living Area:	**3,339 sq. ft.**
Garage	673 sq. ft.
Exterior Wall Framing:	2x4

Foundation Options:
Slab
(All plans can be built with your choice of foundation and framing. A generic conversion diagram is available. See order form.)

BLUEPRINT PRICE CODE: **E**

UPPER FLOOR

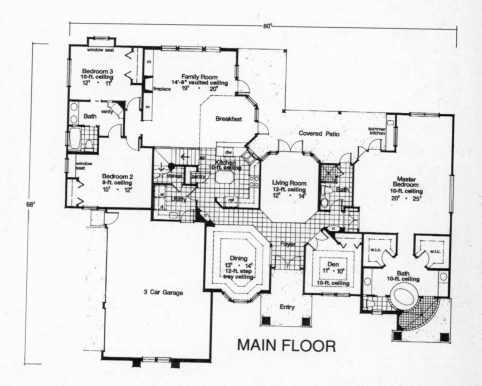

MAIN FLOOR

Plan HDS-99-216

PRICES AND DETAILS
ON PAGES 2-5

A Natural Setting

- The large front porch of this traditionally styled home offers a warm accent to its durable stone exterior.
- The spacious living and dining rooms feature a fireplace, sloped ceilings and outdoor views. An inviting deck is accessed through double doors in the bright window wall. Transom windows, including an attractive half-round window above the double doors, bring in even more sunshine.
- The island kitchen and the morning room are separated by a snack bar.
- Privacy and relaxation are found in the master suite, which offers 10-ft. ceilings. The sitting area has a romantic fireplace and a corner window with transoms; the master bath offers a whirlpool tub, a separate shower and a dual-sink vanity.
- A third bedroom and an optional bonus room are found on the upper level, at either end of a railed gallery. The gallery overlooks the living, dining and morning rooms, and features two window seats and built-in bookshelves.

Plan DD-3467

Bedrooms: 3+	**Baths:** 3½
Living Area:	
Upper floor	822 sq. ft.
Main floor	2,645 sq. ft.
Bonus room	215 sq. ft.
Total Living Area:	**3,682 sq. ft.**
Standard basement	2,645 sq. ft.
Garage	491 sq. ft.
Exterior Wall Framing:	2x4

Foundation Options:

Standard basement

Crawlspace

Slab

(All plans can be built with your choice of foundation and framing. A generic conversion diagram is available. See order form.)

BLUEPRINT PRICE CODE: F

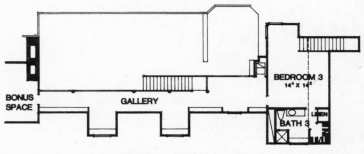

UPPER FLOOR

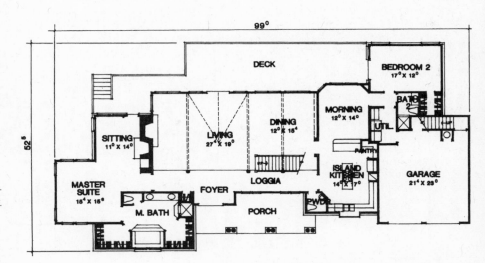

MAIN FLOOR

Old European Tradition

- Old European tradition blends with contemporary spatial and functional design concepts in this luxurious two-story home.
- You'll love relaxing on the spacious deck, which winds conveniently from the dining room to the family room.
- The living room is highlighted by a stunning fireplace and a beautiful vaulted ceiling. Nearby, the dining room features a handy wet bar.
- The informal areas offer a spacious family room with a second fireplace, an island kitchen and a breakfast room overlooking the rear yard.
- Sleeping areas upstairs feature a master suite with its own deck and a pair of big walk-in closets.
- Three additional bedrooms provide plenty of space for growing families or overnight guests. The rear-most bedroom offers the use of a lovely, full-sized private bath.

Plan B-87166	
Bedrooms: 4	**Baths: 3½**
Living Area:	
Upper floor	1,318 sq. ft.
Main floor	1,598 sq. ft.
Total Living Area:	**2,916 sq. ft.**
Standard basement	1,598 sq. ft.
Garage	638 sq. ft.
Exterior Wall Framing:	2x4
Foundation Options:	

Standard basement
(All plans can be built with your choice of foundation and framing. A generic conversion diagram is available. See order form.)

BLUEPRINT PRICE CODE: D

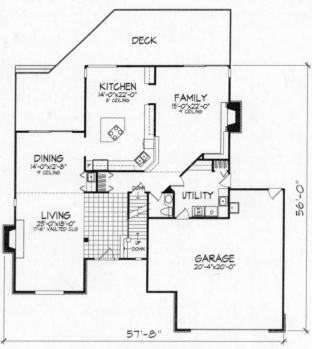

MAIN FLOOR

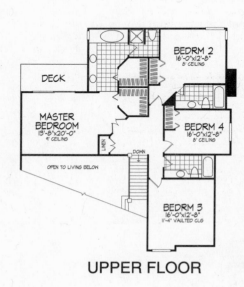

UPPER FLOOR

Better All the Time!

- Designed to cope with an uphill site, this efficient design features an appealing layout that will just seem to get better all the time.
- Two well-thought-out floor plans are available to accommodate your needs and preferences.
- Plan H-2029-4 offers a charming formal dining room—a wonderfully romantic location for candlelit evenings. Invite friends over after you've mastered your new recipes.
- Plan H-2029-5 replaces the dining room with a nice-sized family room, where the kids can work on their homework or you can all meet about next winter's vacation plans.

- Each design boasts a big living room that's spacious enough for large gatherings; a cozy fireplace makes it a great spot for intimate nights, as well.
- A wraparound deck is ideal for sunbathing or barbecuing on pleasant summer days. At night, turn it into an outdoor classroom and teach the kids how to find constellations.
- The master suite features extra closet space and a private bath.
- Two additional bedrooms provide room for expanding families or overnight guests. A full-sized bath is just down the hall.
- Extra living space is found in the basement, which is highlighted by a pleasant recreation room. It's just the right size to turn into a surround-sound movie room when the next giant, scary dinosaur flick comes out. A fireplace adds to the fun.

Plans H-2029-4 & -5	
Bedrooms: 3	**Baths:** 3
Living Area:	
Main floor	1,664 sq. ft.
Daylight basement	1,090 sq. ft.
Total Living Area:	**2,754 sq. ft.**
Tuck-under garage	573 sq. ft.
Exterior Wall Framing:	2x6
Foundation Options:	
Daylight basement	
(All plans can be built with your choice of foundation and framing. A generic conversion diagram is available. See order form.)	
BLUEPRINT PRICE CODE:	D

MAIN FLOOR
Plan H-2029-4

MAIN FLOOR
Plan H-2029-5

DAYLIGHT BASEMENT

Impressive Impression

- This stunning two-story's exterior makes a strong first impression on visitors and passersby; its interior will bring it even more praise!
- A bow window and a half-circle window over the entry add touches of pleasant elegance to the front facade.
- Inside, you'll be impressed with the main-floor's two large gathering areas, the family room and the living room.
- The sunken living room's fireplace and bow window make it the perfect place for formal or casual entertaining.
- A second fireplace and a trio of sunny skylights are found in the family room. A serving bar shared with the kitchen means snacks are just a step away.
- Enormous and luxurious, the master suite boasts a walk-in closet and a private bath.
- Two bedrooms, a bath and a computer room highlight the upper floor. The front-most bedroom has its own deck.

Plans H-2124-1 & -1A

Bedrooms: 3	Baths: 2½
Living Area:	
Upper floor	772 sq. ft.
Main floor	1,736 sq. ft.
Total Living Area:	**2,508 sq. ft.**
Standard basement	1,736 sq. ft.
Garage	462 sq. ft.
Exterior Wall Framing:	**2x6**
Foundation Options:	**Plan #**
Standard basement	H-2124-1
Crawlspace	H-2124-1A

(All plans can be built with your choice of foundation and framing. A generic conversion diagram is available. See order form.)

BLUEPRINT PRICE CODE:	**D**

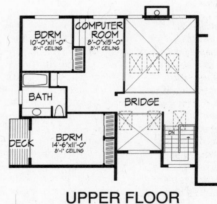

UPPER FLOOR

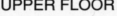

MAIN FLOOR

ORDER BLUEPRINTS ANYTIME!
CALL TOLL-FREE 1-800-820-1283

Plans H-2124-1 & -1A

PRICES AND DETAILS
ON PAGES 2-5

437

Two-Story with Curb Appeal

- This two-story home is thoughtfully designed to dress up any street and offer you the latest in convenient amenities.
- A covered porch gives way to a soaring entry hall that leads directly into the central Great Room. Here, a tray ceiling creates an elegant atmosphere that's warmed by a fireplace. A wet bar is available for festive occasions, and a door opens to a backyard deck.
- The adjacent den is entered through double doors and features a bayed window seat. The room's easy access to a full bath allows it to be used as a guest room, when needed.
- The island kitchen and the breakfast area adjoin a formal dining room, where a door leads out to a patio.
- The vaulted master suite is brightened by a boxed-out window and boasts a private bath and a walk-in closet.
- Two upper-floor bedrooms share a full bath. A large storage space is useful.

Plan B-89060

Bedrooms: 3+	Baths: 3
Living Area:	
Upper floor	502 sq. ft.
Main floor	1,698 sq. ft.
Total Living Area:	**2,200 sq. ft.**
Standard basement	1,698 sq. ft.
Garage	462 sq. ft.
Exterior Wall Framing:	2x4

Foundation Options:

Standard basement

(All plans can be built with your choice of foundation and framing. A generic conversion diagram is available. See order form.)

BLUEPRINT PRICE CODE:	C

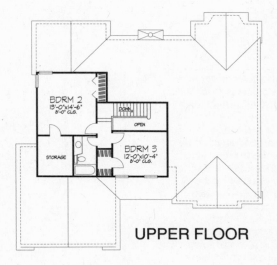

UPPER FLOOR

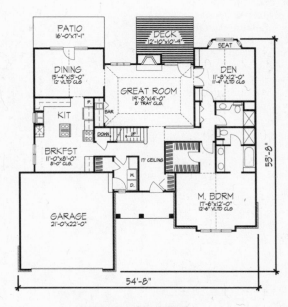

MAIN FLOOR

Plan B-89060

European Appeal

- A colonnaded, covered front porch, fieldstone and lap siding, Prairie-style windows and a standing-seam metal roof create European appeal.
- The floor plan is symmetrically organized, with a central formal living/dining area flanked by two-story wings to the right and left. A main- and upper-floor gallery, accessed by an interesting stair tower, overlook the formal living/dining rooms with a covered rear patio beyond.
- The right wing houses the family room with a fireplace, plus a bay-windowed breakfast room and an island kitchen.
- The left wing includes a guest bedroom and bath, as well as the master suite. The master bedroom features a stairway leading up to a studio. There is also a master bath and two walk-in closets.

Plan DD-3623

Bedrooms: 5	Baths: 4
Living Area:	
Upper floor	1,273 sq. ft.
Main floor	2,393 sq. ft.
Total Living Area:	**3,666 sq. ft.**
Standard basement	1,420 sq. ft.
Garage	473 sq. ft.
Exterior Wall Framing:	2x4

Foundation Options:

Standard basement
Crawlspace
Slab

(All plans can be built with your choice of foundation and framing. A generic conversion diagram is available. See order form.)

BLUEPRINT PRICE CODE: F

UPPER FLOOR

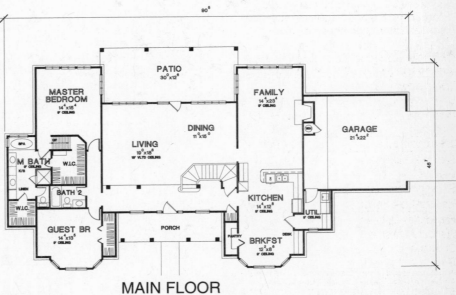

MAIN FLOOR

ORDER BLUEPRINTS ANYTIME!
CALL TOLL-FREE 1-800-820-1283

Plan DD-3623

PRICES AND DETAILS
ON PAGES 2-5

435

FRONT VIEW

Geometric Sunshine

- Clean geometric lines join forces with wonderful windows and high ceilings to make this contemporary home bright and airy.
- The vaulted living room is warmed by a fireplace, while the dining room offers double doors to a sheltered patio.
- The spacious family room boasts an exposed-beam ceiling, an inviting woodstove and a bright window wall facing a delightful sun space.
- A hot tub or spa can be added to the sun space, which offers a spiral staircase to the upper-floor master suite.
- The kitchen is a gourmet cook's dream, with an angled cooktop/snack bar, a built-in pantry and a boxed-out window over the sink.
- The secluded den can perform double duty as a guest room or fourth bedroom when needed.
- The upper floor hosts three roomy bedrooms, including a luxurious master suite with a deluxe bath that includes a corner spa tub and a soothing sauna. A storage room is another nice extra.

REAR VIEW

UPPER FLOOR

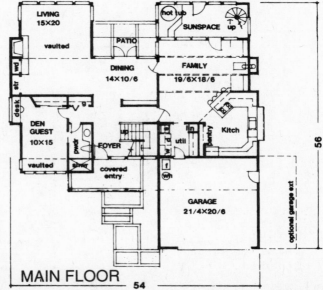

MAIN FLOOR

Plan S-6777

Bedrooms: 3+	Baths: 2½
Living Area:	
Upper floor	1,342 sq. ft.
Main floor	1,514 sq. ft.
Sun space	160 sq. ft.
Total Living Area:	**3,016 sq. ft.**
Standard basement	1,500 sq. ft.
Garage	437 sq. ft.
Storage above den	146 sq. ft.
Exterior Wall Framing:	2x6

Foundation Options:
Standard basement
Crawlspace
Slab
(All plans can be built with your choice of foundation and framing. A generic conversion diagram is available. See order form.)

BLUEPRINT PRICE CODE: E

Upbeat Design

- Roof gables featuring fantail wood detailing and an arched window provide strong focal points for this upbeat design.
- The important-looking entry opens to a vaulted foyer. The sunken living room, just to the right, features a vaulted ceiling, a boxed-out window and a two-way fireplace with a wide raised hearth.
- Straight ahead lie the fabulous family room, nook and kitchen, which are embraced by lots of windows overlooking a wraparound deck.
- The adjoining dining room is highlighted by a vaulted ceiling and a spectacular arched window.
- Upstairs, double doors open to an especially nice master suite. In addition to a luxurious bath, the suite offers a private deck with a spiral staircase to the lower deck.
- Two additional bedrooms, a second full bath and a multipurpose bonus room round out this ingenious design.

Plan S-62586

Bedrooms: 3+	Baths: 2½
Living Area:	
Upper floor	1,056 sq. ft.
Main floor	1,416 sq. ft.
Bonus room	144 sq. ft.
Total Living Area:	**2,616 sq. ft.**
Standard basement	1,416 sq. ft.
Two-car garage	476 sq. ft.
Three-car garage	676 sq. ft.
Exterior Wall Framing:	2x6

Foundation Options:

Standard basement
Crawlspace
Slab

(All plans can be built with your choice of foundation and framing. A generic conversion diagram is available. See order form.)

BLUEPRINT PRICE CODE: D

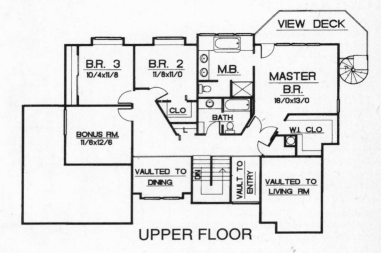

UPPER FLOOR

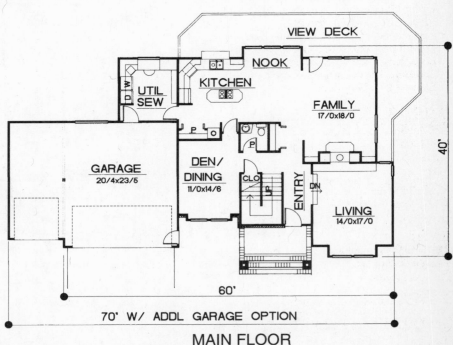

MAIN FLOOR

ORDER BLUEPRINTS ANYTIME!
CALL TOLL-FREE 1-800-820-1283

Plan S-62586

PRICES AND DETAILS
ON PAGES 2-5

433

Rustic Relaxation

- A covered front porch, a pair of dormers and a combination of wood and brick create a rustic exterior for this traditional home. An expansive screen porch doubles as a breezeway connecting the home with the garage.

- The front porch opens directly into the large Great Room, with its handsome fireplace. With a nearby snack bar and French-door access to the screen porch, a dining area would fit nicely between the Great Room and the kitchen.

- Also adjoining the kitchen is an oversized utility room with space for a washer, a dryer and an extra freezer.

- The deluxe master suite offers a private bath with a separate tub and shower and a dual-sink vanity with knee space for a makeup table. Generous closet space for two is also provided.

- The second main-floor bedroom uses the full bath across the hall. Two more bedrooms, each with a window seat and storage space access, share a full bath on the upper floor.

Plan C-7746

Bedrooms: 4	Baths: 3
Living Area:	
Upper floor	773 sq. ft.
Main floor	1,694 sq. ft.
Total Living Area:	**2,467 sq. ft.**
Daylight basement	1,694 sq. ft.
Screen porch	353 sq. ft.
Garage	552 sq. ft.
Exterior Wall Framing:	2x4

Foundation Options:

Daylight basement

Crawlspace

(All plans can be built with your choice of foundation and framing. A generic conversion diagram is available. See order form.)

BLUEPRINT PRICE CODE: C

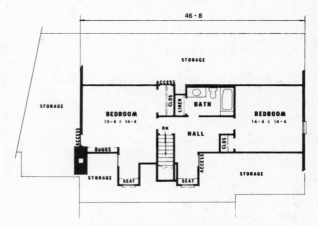

UPPER FLOOR

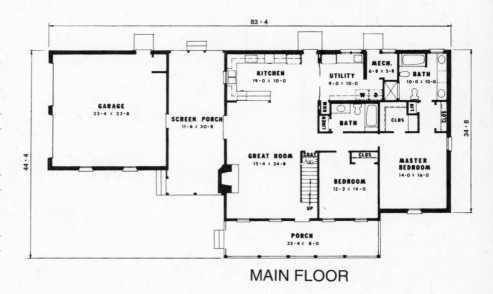

MAIN FLOOR

Joyful Reawakening!

- Multiple decks, a sun roof, lots of family areas and a secluded, luxurious master suite turn this contemporary home into a welcome retreat that's sure to reawaken the fun in your life!
- From the entry, guests are just steps from the huge living room—the ideal spot for big celebrations. Charmed by its 17-ft. vaulted ceiling, a woodstove

and a passive sun roof, guests will delight in the festive ambience.
- The upper floor is completely devoted to the amazing master suite. A spacious walk-in closet, a balcony overlooking the living room, a private deck and a bath with a spa tub top the long list of amenities.
- Two additional bedrooms, a full bath and an oversized family room occupy the daylight basement. The family room offers a handsome fireplace and access to a patio. An extra storage room is sure to come in handy.

Plan H-2110-1B

Bedrooms: 3	**Baths:** 2½

Living Area:	
Upper floor	649 sq. ft.
Main floor	1,044 sq. ft.
Daylight basement	1,044 sq. ft.
Total Living Area:	**2,737 sq. ft.**
Garage	462 sq. ft.
Exterior Wall Framing:	2x6

Foundation Options:

Daylight basement
(All plans can be built with your choice of foundation and framing. A generic conversion diagram is available. See order form.)

BLUEPRINT PRICE CODE:	**D**

DAYLIGHT BASEMENT

PATIO

FAMILY ROOM
13'-6"x22'-0"

BEDROOM
10'-0"x13'-4"

BEDROOM
10'-8"x11'-8"

CLOSET

LIN.

CLOSET

BATH
15'-6"x5'-8"

FURNACE

STORAGE

STOR.

UP

MAIN FLOOR

36'-0"

55'-0"

DECK

KITCHEN
10'-3"x9'-5"

DINING
10'-9"x14'-0"

LIVING RM.
13'-6"x22'-0"

WOOD STOVE

NOOK
10'-3"x8'-0"

LARDER

REF

LAUNDRY
9'-6"x6'-0"

BATH

CLOSET

ENTRY

UP

GARAGE
21'-4"x21'-8"

UPPER FLOOR

DECK

PASSIVE SUN ROOF

MASTER BEDROOM
21'-0"x13'-4"

SLOPED CEILING

BALCONY RAILING

OPEN TO LIVING ROOM

BRIDGE

BATH
12'-4"x10'-0"

LIN.

OPEN TO ENTRY

STORAGE
12'-4"x5'-0"

WALK-IN CLOSET
7'-9"x11'-6"

DN

REAR VIEW

ORDER BLUEPRINTS ANYTIME!
CALL TOLL-FREE 1-800-820-1283

Plan H-2110-1B

PRICES AND DETAILS
ON PAGES 2-5

431

Convenient Contemporary

- In this plan, a thoroughly contemporary exterior wraps a design with so many convenient features, you'll wonder how you ever lived without them.
- The vaulted foyer leads into the vaulted Great Room, which features a warm woodstove and a built-in entertainment center. The two spaces are separated by a balcony bridge on the upper floor that creates a spacious, modern look with an immediate impression.

- The large, open kitchen includes plenty of working space. An island cooktop features a snack bar for casual meals. The adjoining dining room has sliding doors to a wraparound deck.
- Two secondary bedrooms each have an alcove designed to hold a study desk.
- Secluded upstairs, the master suite boasts a walk-in closet and a dressing area that leads to a skylighted bath, which is also accessible from the den.
- As an option, the vaulted area over the Great Room may be enclosed to create a fourth bedroom or a rec room.
- A long closet at the end of the hall provides the extra storage you need.

Plan S-72485

Bedrooms: 3+	Baths: 2
Living Area:	
Upper floor	650 sq. ft.
Main floor	1,450 sq. ft.
Total Living Area:	**2,100 sq. ft.**
Standard basement	1,450 sq. ft.
Garage	502 sq. ft.
Exterior Wall Framing:	2x6

Foundation Options:

Standard basement
Crawlspace
(All plans can be built with your choice of foundation and framing. A generic conversion diagram is available. See order form.)

BLUEPRINT PRICE CODE:	C

MAIN FLOOR

UPPER FLOOR

Plan S-72485

Alluring
Two-Story

- This dramatic contemporary is adorned with staggered rooflines that overlap and outline large expanses of glass.
- Flanking the two-story-high foyer are the formal dining room and the sunken living room, which is expanded by an airy 16-ft. cathedral ceiling.
- The adjoining sunken family room boasts a fireplace and sliding glass doors to a backyard patio.
- A step up, the bright breakfast area enjoys an eating bar that extends from the efficient U-shaped kitchen. A half-bath and laundry facilities are convenient.
- The second level features a spacious master bedroom with a 12-ft. sloped ceiling, dual closets and a private bath. Two secondary bedrooms, another full bath and an optional expansion room above the garage are also included.

Plan AX-8596-A

Bedrooms: 3+	Baths: 2½
Living Area:	
Upper floor	738 sq. ft.
Main floor	1,160 sq. ft.
Bonus room	226 sq. ft.
Total Living Area:	**2,124 sq. ft.**
Standard basement	1,160 sq. ft.
Garage	465 sq. ft.
Exterior Wall Framing:	2x4

Foundation Options:

Standard basement
(All plans can be built with your choice of foundation and framing. A generic conversion diagram is available. See order form.)

BLUEPRINT PRICE CODE: **C**

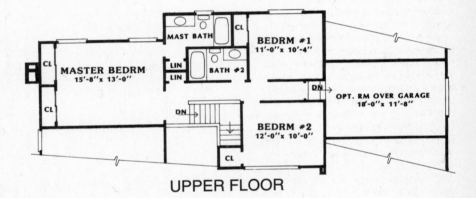

UPPER FLOOR

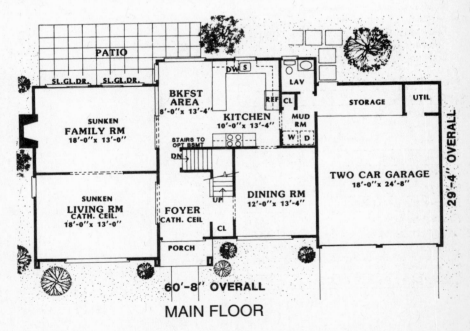

MAIN FLOOR

CALL TOLL-FREE 1-800-820-1283

Plan AX-8596-A

PRICES AND DETAILS ON PAGES 2-5

429

Dramatic Contemporary

- Dramatic rooflines and appealing outdoor spaces combine with a functional floor plan to create this comfortable contemporary home.
- Skylights shed light on the soaring entry, which offers views of the living room and the distinctive staircase.
- A striking fireplace accents the sunken living room. Together with the dining room, this space is ideal for entertaining large or small gatherings.
- The sprawling family room features its own fireplace, and shares a snack bar with the U-shaped kitchen.
- With its own deck and a sumptuous private bath, the master bedroom is sure to please.
- Upstairs, three identically sized bedrooms share a spacious full bath. A balcony area accesses a covered deck, and overlooks the living room.

Plans H-3708-1 & -1A

Bedrooms: 4	Baths: 2½
Living Area:	
Upper floor	893 sq. ft.
Main floor	2,006 sq. ft.
Total Living Area:	**2,899 sq. ft.**
Daylight basement	2,006 sq. ft.
Garage	512 sq. ft.
Exterior Wall Framing:	2x6
Foundation Options:	**Plan #**
Daylight basement	H-3708-1
Crawlspace	H-3708-1A
(All plans can be built with your choice of foundation and framing. A generic conversion diagram is available. See order form.)	
BLUEPRINT PRICE CODE:	**D**

REAR VIEW

UPPER FLOOR

MAIN FLOOR

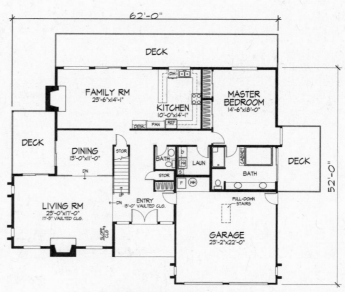

Plans H-3708-1 & -1A

An Octagon with Options

- Four floor plans are available for this striking octagonal vacation home. Each includes a wraparound deck that offers panoramic views and glorious outdoor living options.
- The main floor is essentially the same in each version. A large combination living and dining room is topped by a 12-ft., 8-in. vaulted ceiling, creating an air of spaciousness. A fireplace is a cozy focal point. Sliding glass doors open to the deck.
- Except for the central bath, which rises to a height of 8 ft., 8 in., the main-floor rooms are topped by 12-ft., 8-in. vaulted ceilings.
- The U-shaped kitchen puts everything within reach of the family chef. The laundry facilities are nearby.
- Plan H-861-2B includes a recreation room in the daylight basement and a master suite with a private bath.
- Plan H-861-2C features a garage and an optional bath in the daylight basement, as well as a private bath in the master suite.
- Plan H-861-3B omits the private bath in the master suite, allowing a larger sleeping area, and has a rec room in the daylight basement.
- Plan H-861-3C omits the master bath and includes a garage and optional bath in the daylight basement.

Plans H-861-2B, -2C, -3B & -3C	
Bedrooms: 3+	**Baths:** 2-3
Living Area:	
Main floor	1,236 sq. ft.
Daylight bsmt.	905 sq. ft.
Daylight bsmt. (rec room version)	1,236 sq. ft.
Total Living Area:	**2,141/2,472 sq. ft.**
Tuck-under garage	331 sq. ft.
Exterior Wall Framing:	2x6
Foundation Options:	
Daylight basement	

(All plans can be built with your choice of foundation and framing. A generic conversion diagram is available. See order form.)

BLUEPRINT PRICE CODE:	**C**

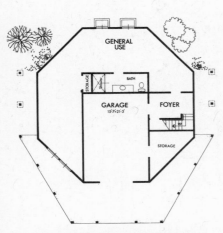

DAYLIGHT BASEMENT WITH GARAGE

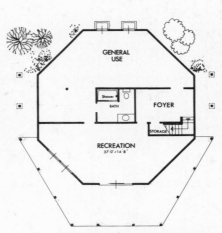

DAYLIGHT BASEMENT WITH REC ROOM

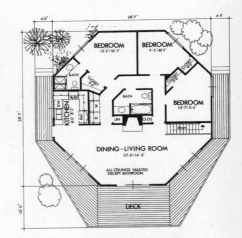

MAIN FLOOR

Plans H-861-2B, -2C, -3B & -3C

Innovative Use of Space

- This fascinating design is recognized for its innovative use of space.
- You can't help feeling the draw of its inviting exterior layout.
- The central formal spaces separate the master suite and the den or study from the informal spaces. The rear window wall in the living room allows a view of the outdoors from the oversized foyer.

- The unique arrangement of the master suite lets traffic flow easily from the bedroom to the dressing areas, to the garden tub and to a walk-in closet that you could get lost in.
- The spacious two-story family room, kitchen and breakfast room open to one another, forming a large family activity area with corner fireplace, snack counter and surrounding windows.
- A second main-floor bedroom, two upper-floor bedrooms and three extra baths complete the floor plan.

Plan HDS-99-166

Bedrooms: 4+	Baths: 4
Living Area:	
Upper floor	540 sq. ft.
Main floor	2,624 sq. ft.
Total Living Area:	**3,164 sq. ft.**
Garage	770 sq. ft.
Exterior Wall Framing:	2x4

Foundation Options:

Slab

(All plans can be built with your choice of foundation and framing. A generic conversion diagram is available. See order form.)

BLUEPRINT PRICE CODE: E

MAIN FLOOR

UPPER FLOOR

Plan HDS-99-166

Luxurious Country Home

- This country cottage hosts many luxuries, such as an expansive Great Room, good-sized sleeping areas and a large, screened back porch.
- The rustic front porch opens to the inviting Great Room, which is warmed by a handsome fireplace. Entertaining may be expanded to the rear porch when the weather is suitable.
- The bright kitchen features a huge work island and a windowed sink, and flows into both the formal dining room and the cozy breakfast bay.
- The two-car, side-entry garage is located nearby to facilitate the unloading of groceries. A handy storage room is perfect for the lawn mower and sports equipment.
- The removed master suite boasts a private bath with a spa tub, a separate shower, a dual-sink vanity and two walk-in closets.
- Upstairs are two oversized bedrooms, each with a dressing room that adjoins a shared bathing area.

Plan C-8535

Bedrooms: 3	**Baths:** 2½
Living Area:	
Upper floor	765 sq. ft.
Main floor	1,535 sq. ft.
Total Living Area:	**2,300 sq. ft.**
Partial daylight basement	1,091 sq. ft.
Garage	424 sq. ft.
Exterior Wall Framing:	2x4

Foundation Options:

Partial daylight basement
(All plans can be built with your choice of foundation and framing. A generic conversion diagram is available. See order form.)

BLUEPRINT PRICE CODE: C

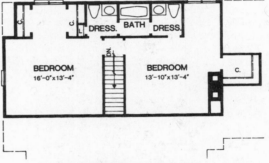

UPPER FLOOR

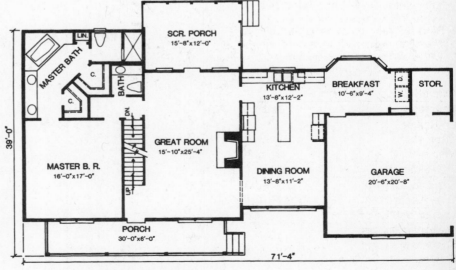

MAIN FLOOR

ORDER BLUEPRINTS ANYTIME!
CALL TOLL-FREE 1-800-820-1283

Plan C-8535

PRICES AND DETAILS
ON PAGES 2-5

425

Home at Last!

- Whether you're returning from a business trip or a personal vacation, you'll never get tired of coming home to this spectacular stucco delight.
- Breezy outdoor spaces parade around the home, starting with a nostalgic front porch and ending at a relaxing spa tub on a sprawling backyard deck.
- The spacious interior is bright and open. Past the entry, a gallery with French doors leads to the superb kitchen.
- The family can discuss the day's news over breakfast at the big snack bar or in the sunny bayed morning room.
- For activities of a larger scale, the living room offers an engaging fireplace, exciting views and enough space to house your entertainment equipment.
- A two-sided fireplace adds a romantic glow to the master bedroom and private sitting area. The elegant, skylighted master bath promises luxury for two!
- All main-floor rooms have 9-ft. ceilings.
- The upper-floor bedrooms are furnished with a shared bath and their own walk-in closets and sunny sitting spaces.

Plan DD-2617

Bedrooms: 4	Baths: 3
Living Area:	
Upper floor	609 sq. ft.
Main floor	2,034 sq. ft.
Total Living Area:	**2,643 sq. ft.**
Standard basement	2,034 sq. ft.
Garage and storage	544 sq. ft.
Exterior Wall Framing:	2x4

Foundation Options:

Standard basement
Crawlspace
Slab
(All plans can be built with your choice of foundation and framing. A generic conversion diagram is available. See order form.)

BLUEPRINT PRICE CODE:	D

UPPER FLOOR

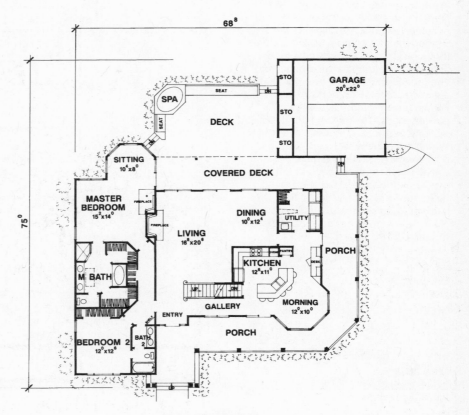

MAIN FLOOR

Plan DD-2617

PRICES AND DETAILS
ON PAGES 2-5

Comfortable Contemporary

- This home's contemporary facade and roofline give way to an impressive Great Room for ultimate comfort.
- The sidelighted two-story foyer unfolds directly to the spectacular sunken Great Room, which is highlighted by a 10-ft., open-beam ceiling. A wood-burning stove, a pair of ceiling fans and two French doors that open to a rear wraparound deck are also showcased.
- Sharing the Great Room's 10-ft. ceiling, the open kitchen boasts an eating bar and a pass-through to the dining area.
- The secluded master bedroom features a TV wall with his-and-hers dressers. A French door provides access to a covered deck. The master bath flaunts a relaxing whirlpool tub and two vanities.
- Where not otherwise noted, the main-floor rooms have 9-ft. ceilings.
- A long balcony on the second level overlooks the foyer. Two good-sized bedrooms offer nice views of the backyard and share a full bath.

Plan LRD-22994

Bedrooms: 3	Baths: 2½
Living Area:	
Upper floor	692 sq. ft.
Main floor	1,777 sq. ft.
Total Living Area:	**2,469 sq. ft.**
Standard basement	1,655 sq. ft.
Garage	550 sq. ft.
Exterior Wall Framing:	2x6

Foundation Options:

Standard basement

Crawlspace

Slab

(All plans can be built with your choice of foundation and framing. A generic conversion diagram is available. See order form.)

BLUEPRINT PRICE CODE: **C**

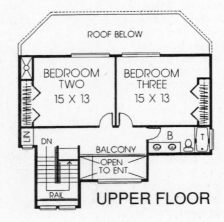

UPPER FLOOR

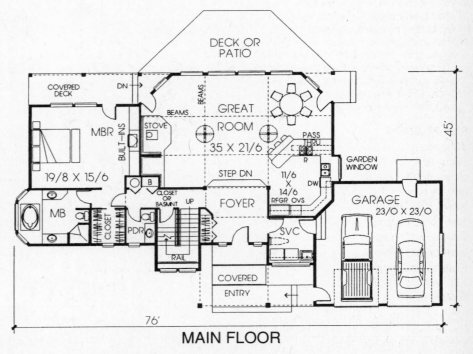

MAIN FLOOR

ORDER BLUEPRINTS ANYTIME!
CALL TOLL-FREE 1-800-820-1283

Plan LRD-22994

PRICES AND DETAILS
ON PAGES 2-5

423

Balcony Bonus

- This home's stone facade and unique metal roof add appeal, while balconies at the front and rear are extra bonuses.
- Inside, the entry flows past a bookcase to the living room. A 20-ft. sloped ceiling soars over both rooms.
- In the living room, a warm fireplace and a neat media center topped by an attractive arch serve as fun diversions.
- The breakfast nook, which opens to a patio through a French door, shares a snack bar with the island kitchen. A pass-through between the kitchen and the dining room simplifies meals.
- Across the home, a bayed sitting area and an entertainment center make the master bedroom an exciting retreat. The master bath leads to a double walk-in closet, where shoe shelves and a bench make the most of the space.
- Unless otherwise mentioned, every main-floor room includes a 9-ft. ceiling.
- Upstairs, two bedrooms and a study, all with sloped 10-ft. ceilings, share a hall bath. The study has a private balcony, and the rear bedroom has its own deck.

Plan DD-2703-1

Bedrooms: 3+	Baths: 2½
Living Area:	
Upper floor	727 sq. ft.
Main floor	1,921 sq. ft.
Total Living Area:	**2,648 sq. ft.**
Standard basement	1,921 sq. ft.
Garage and storage	600 sq. ft.
Exterior Wall Framing:	2x4

Foundation Options:

Standard basement
Crawlspace
Slab

(All plans can be built with your choice of foundation and framing. A generic conversion diagram is available. See order form.)

BLUEPRINT PRICE CODE: D

UPPER FLOOR

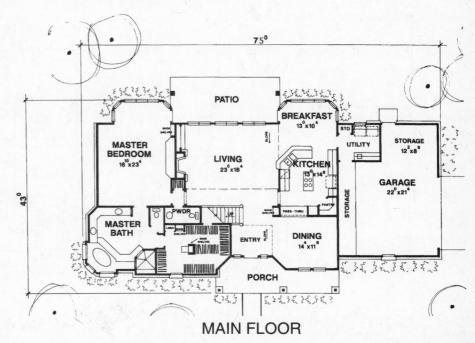

MAIN FLOOR

Gentle Breezes

- With or without palm trees, this design invokes a breezy sense of tropical relaxation. A unique front porch and upper- and lower-level rear verandas embrace the open outdoors.
- From the foyer, an arched opening sweeps guests into the expansive Grand Room, which boasts a fireplace, a 14-ft. tray ceiling and an optional aquarium.
- The breakfast nook flows into the kitchen, which shares an eating bar with the Grand Room. A large pantry and easy access to the formal dining room add to its practicality.
- A versatile study, to the left of the foyer, provides the perfect haven for you and your favorite books. It can also be converted to an extra bedroom.
- The master suite encompasses the entire left wing of the home. Its fantastic features treat you as though you are at a spa resort!
- When you wake, throw open the French doors to the veranda for a breath of fresh air. Large walk-in closets connect the bedroom to its opulent private bath. Here, a garden tub, a separate shower, a dual-sink vanity and a compartmentalized toilet keep you feeling sane.
- Two additional bedrooms across the home share another full bath.
- Unless otherwise specified, all main-floor rooms feature 9-ft., 4-in. ceilings.

Plan SG-6622

Bedrooms: 3+	Baths: 2
Living Area:	
Main floor	2,190 sq. ft.
Lower floor	1,383 sq. ft.
Total Living Area:	**3,573 sq. ft.**
Tuck-under garage	583 sq. ft.
Exterior Wall Framing:	2x6

Foundation Options:

Slab

(All plans can be built with your choice of foundation and framing. A generic conversion diagram is available. See order form.)

BLUEPRINT PRICE CODE:	**F**

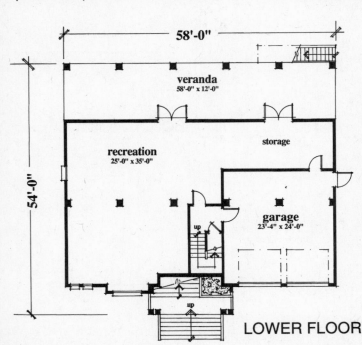

LOWER FLOOR

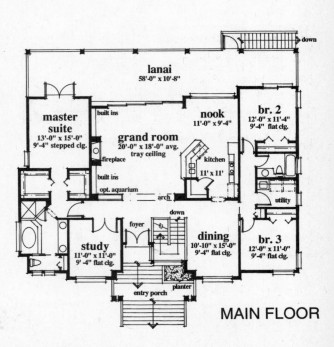

MAIN FLOOR

A Deck for Each Room

- Exciting outdoor living is made possible by the many decks of this three-level contemporary design.
- The front entrance and garage are located at the daylight basement level, along with a dressing room, a full bath and laundry facilities.
- A lofty 16½-ft. vaulted ceiling tops the living room, highlighting the main floor. This expansive room includes a massive stone wall with a heat-circulating

fireplace; two sets of sliding glass doors step out to a sprawling front deck, the perfect spot for watching colorful summer sunsets.
- Designed to make efficient use of space, the U-shaped kitchen will please the chef in your family. When warmer weather permits, use the outdoor barbecue to add a little zest to your favorite meats.
- Upstairs, the exquisite master bedroom boasts a 13½-ft. vaulted ceiling, its own fireplace and a private viewing deck.
- The other upper-floor bedroom sports a 9½-ft. vaulted ceiling. Both secondary bedrooms access private decks.

Plan HFL-2176

Bedrooms: 3	Baths: 3½
Living Area:	
Upper floor	712 sq. ft.
Main floor	1,001 sq. ft.
Daylight basement	463 sq. ft.
Total Living Area:	**2,176 sq. ft.**
Tuck-under garage/storage	448 sq. ft.
Exterior Wall Framing:	2x6

Foundation Options:

Daylight basement

(All plans can be built with your choice of foundation and framing. A generic conversion diagram is available. See order form.)

BLUEPRINT PRICE CODE:	C

DAYLIGHT BASEMENT

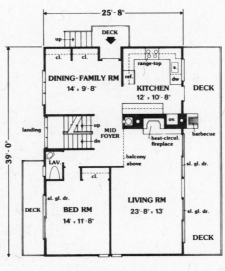

MAIN FLOOR

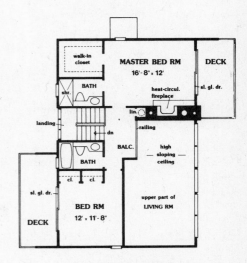

UPPER FLOOR

Plan HFL-2176

PRICES AND DETAILS
ON PAGES 2-5

Design Leaves Out Nothing

- This design has it all, from the elegant detailing of the exterior to the exciting, luxurious spaces of the interior.
- High ceilings, large, open rooms and lots of glass are found throughout the home. Nearly all of the main living areas, as well as the master suite, overlook the veranda.
- Unusual features include an ale bar in the formal dining room, an art niche in the Grand Room and a TV niche in the Gathering Room. The Gathering Room also features a fireplace framed by window seats, a wall of windows facing the backyard and a half-wall open to the sunny morning room.
- The centrally located cooktop-island kitchen is conveniently accessible from all of the living areas.
- The delicious master suite includes a raised lounge, a three-sided fireplace and French doors that open to the veranda. The spiral stairs nearby lead to the "evening deck" above. The master bath boasts two walk-in closets, a sunken shower and a Roman tub.
- The upper floor hosts two complete suites and a loft, plus a vaulted bonus room reached via a separate stairway.

Plan EOF-61

Bedrooms: 3+	Baths: 4½
Living Area:	
Upper floor	877 sq. ft.
Main floor	3,094 sq. ft.
Bonus room	280 sq. ft.
Total Living Area:	**4,251 sq. ft.**
Garage	774 sq. ft.
Exterior Wall Framing:	2x6

Foundation Options:

Slab

(All plans can be built with your choice of foundation and framing. A generic conversion diagram is available. See order form.)

BLUEPRINT PRICE CODE: G

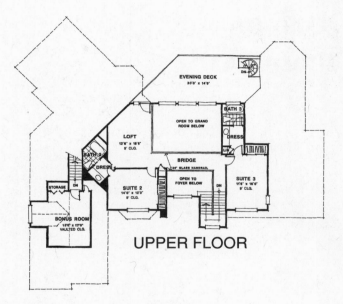

UPPER FLOOR

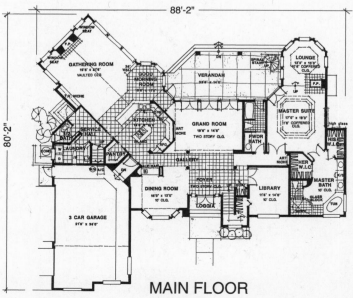

MAIN FLOOR

Pure Luxury

- This executive-style home exudes a feeling of pure luxury.
- A sidelighted entry opens into the living room, which is topped by a vaulted ceiling crowned by clerestory windows. A cozy fireplace adds a warm glow.
- The casual family room has its own fireplace and sliding glass doors that open to a big backyard patio. The patio is also accessible via sliding glass doors from the dining room.
- The main-floor master suite boasts a walk-in closet and a skylighted private bath with a time-saving dual-sink vanity, an oval soaking tub and a

separate shower. Two sets of sliding glass doors access an outdoor spa surrounded by a 6-ft. privacy fence.
- Across from the master suite, a study looks out to the front yard. The room's easy access to a full hall bath makes it a nice guest room, if needed.
- On the upper floor, a balcony hallway connects three bedrooms that share a skylighted full bath. The balcony looks down on the living room.
- The basement versions of this plan include a rec room with a fireplace, as well as lots of work and storage space.
- The facade of plan H-3714-M2A has stucco walls, arched windows and a tile roof that give it a Spanish look.

Plans H-3714-1, -1A, -1B & -M2A	
Bedrooms: 4+	**Baths:** 3
Living Area:	
Upper floor	740 sq. ft.
Main floor	2,190 sq. ft.
Total Living Area:	**2,930 sq. ft.**
Basement	1,842 sq. ft.
Garage	576 sq. ft.
Exterior Wall Framing:	2x6
Foundation Options:	**Plan #**
Daylight basement	H-3714-1B
Standard basement	H-3714-1
Crawlspace	H-3714-1A
Slab	H-3714-M2A
(All plans can be built with your choice of foundation and framing. A generic conversion diagram is available. See order form.)	

BLUEPRINT PRICE CODE: D

MAIN FLOOR

UPPER FLOOR

Plans H-3714-1, -1A, -1B & -M2A

**PRICES AND DETAILS
ON PAGES 2-5**

Visible Wonders

- A lattice-trimmed front porch, a sturdy stone and siding facade and dramatic transom windows are visible exterior evidence of the wonderful treasures you'll find within this two-story home.
- The pretty porch opens to the incredible Grand Room, which is highlighted by a heartwarming fireplace and two sets of doors leading to a remarkable view deck in back. Two covered decks on either side of the room further enhance its special rapport with the outdoors.
- The back deck is large enough to host a giant neighborhood barbecue; dazzle your friends with your selection of spicy sauces. A variety of benches gives guests a place to sit down.
- A unique covered dining deck flanks the island kitchen; let the open air add flavor to each meal. When the weather's a bit chilly, dine inside in the pleasant morning room or the formal dining room.
- Luxury lives in the fantastic master suite, which boasts a large walk-in closet, deck access and an unparalleled private bath with a corner spa tub.
- The daylight basement offers just as much contact with the outdoors as the upper floor, with a giant patio that extends the width of the home. A huge Gathering Room with a woodstove, plus two bedrooms and a home office complete the design. The office easily converts to a fourth bedroom.

Plan EOF-14	
Bedrooms: 3+	**Baths:** 2
Living Area:	
Main floor	1,431 sq. ft.
Daylight basement	1,054 sq. ft.
Total Living Area:	**2,485 sq. ft.**
Tuck-under garage	480 sq. ft.
Exterior Wall Framing:	2x4
Foundation Options:	

Daylight basement
(All plans can be built with your choice of foundation and framing. A generic conversion diagram is available. See order form.)

BLUEPRINT PRICE CODE:	C

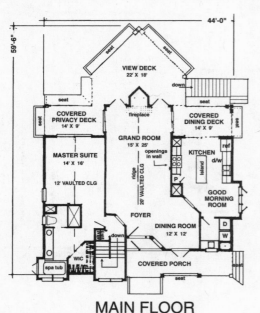

MAIN FLOOR

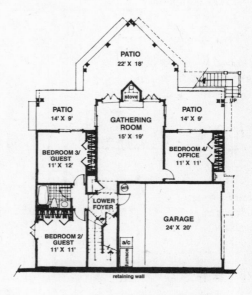

DAYLIGHT BASEMENT

ORDER BLUEPRINTS ANYTIME!
CALL TOLL-FREE 1-800-820-1283

Plan EOF-14

PRICES AND DETAILS
ON PAGES 2-5

415

Hot Tub, Deck Highlighted

- Designed for indoor/outdoor living, this home features a skylighted spa room with a hot tub and a backyard deck that spans the width of the home.
- A central hall leads to the sunny kitchen and nook, which offer corner windows, a snack bar and a pantry.
- Straight ahead, the open dining and living rooms form one huge space, further pronounced by expansive windows. The 16-ft. vaulted living room also features a fireplace and sliding glass doors to the deck.
- The master suite includes a cozy window seat, a large walk-in closet, a private bath and access to the tiled spa room. The spa may also be entered from the deck and an inner hall.
- Upstairs, two more bedrooms share a full bath and a balcony that overlooks the living room below.
- The optional daylight basement offers a deluxe sauna, a fourth bedroom, a laundry room and a wide recreation room with a fireplace. A large game room and storage are also included.

Plans H-2114-1A & -1B

Bedrooms: 3+	Baths: 2½-3½
Living Area:	
Upper floor	732 sq. ft.
Main floor	1,682 sq. ft.
Spa room	147 sq. ft.
Daylight basement	1,386 sq. ft.
Total Living Area:	**2,561/3,947 sq. ft.**
Garage	547 sq. ft.
Exterior Wall Framing:	2x6
Foundation Options:	**Plan #**
Daylight basement	H-2114-1B
Crawlspace	H-2114-1A

(All plans can be built with your choice of foundation and framing. A generic conversion diagram is available. See order form.)

BLUEPRINT PRICE CODE: **D/F**

REAR VIEW

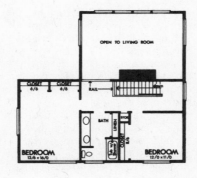

UPPER FLOOR

DAYLIGHT BASEMENT

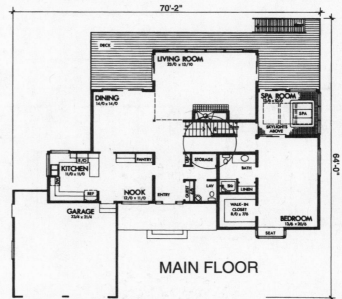

MAIN FLOOR

STAIRWAY AREA IN CRAWLSPACE VERSION

Plans H-2114-1A & -1B

PRICES AND DETAILS ON PAGES 2-5

REAR VIEW

Hillside Haven

- Designed for a sloping lot, this three-level home boasts an exterior that blends smoothly with the contours of its surroundings. The front facade greets guests with a gracious entrance deck.
- Doors at the front deck and in the garage open to the upper-floor entry, which welcomes guests with skylights, a sloped ceiling and a railing overlooking the living room below.
- A loft, with a sloped ceiling and a railing overlooking the dining room below, lies adjacent to the entry.
- A central staircase leads down to a main-floor entry area that can also be reached from the outside, via a walkway and stairs from the upper front deck.
- The open living room lies straight ahead. Its rustic woodstove is flanked by sliding glass doors to the angled backyard deck.
- Formal and casual meals are equally at home in the dining room. The nearby kitchen receives natural light through a window over the sink.
- Across the home, the primary bedroom features a private, dual-sink bath. A half-bath is available for use by the rest of the main floor.
- The daylight basement houses a huge rec room, two bedrooms and a bath.

Plan H-966-1B	
Bedrooms: 3+	**Baths:** 2½
Living Area:	
Upper floor	378 sq. ft.
Main floor	1,256 sq. ft.
Daylight basement	1,256 sq. ft.
Total Living Area:	**2,890 sq. ft.**
Garage	528 sq. ft.
Exterior Wall Framing:	2x6
Foundation Options:	
Daylight basement	

(All plans can be built with your choice of foundation and framing. A generic conversion diagram is available. See order form.)

BLUEPRINT PRICE CODE: D

DAYLIGHT BASEMENT

MAIN FLOOR

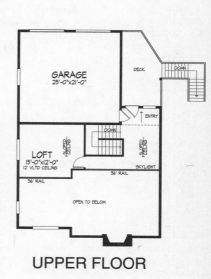

UPPER FLOOR

ORDER BLUEPRINTS ANYTIME!
CALL TOLL-FREE 1-800-820-1283

Plan H-966-1B

PRICES AND DETAILS
ON PAGES 2-5

413

One-of-a-Kind Contemporary

- A unique exterior design and distinctive use of space confirm this five-level contemporary home as truly one-of-a-kind.
- Inside, the entry level opens to the winding staircase. Also included on this level are the comfortable family room and the U-shaped kitchen.
- Up a set of stairs, the expansive living room is a secluded space to entertain family and friends. It features a cozy fireplace and a pair of sliding glass doors to a wide viewing deck.
- The next level up contains the huge, skylighted master bedroom. It is highlighted by a small deck, a walk-in closet, a private bath and a separate dressing area.
- One more flight of stairs reveals two good-sized secondary bedrooms and a full bath.

Plans H-932-1 & -1A

Bedrooms: 3	Baths: 2½
Living Area:	
Upper floor	1,028 sq. ft.
Main floor	983 sq. ft.
Lower floor (entry)	122 sq. ft.
Total Living Area:	**2,133 sq. ft.**
Standard basement	550 sq. ft.
Carport	403 sq. ft.
Exterior Wall Framing:	2x6
Foundation Options:	**Plan #**
Standard basement	H-932-1
Crawlspace	H-932-1A

(All plans can be built with your choice of foundation and framing. A generic conversion diagram is available. See order form.)

BLUEPRINT PRICE CODE:	C

UPPER FLOOR

MAIN FLOOR

LOWER FLOOR

Plans H-932-1 & -1A

PRICES AND DETAILS ON PAGES 2-5

Sweeping, Sunny Spaces

- A sweeping roofline, punctuated with a cutout in the covered front porch and a clerestory window, attracts attention to this stylish contemporary home.
- The vaulted entry is brightened by the clerestory window above.
- Sunlight invades the main floor by way of a window wall in the vaulted living room and an optional sun space off the patio or deck.
- The open family room shares a wood-stove with the kitchen and nook. A wet bar and an island cooktop/snack bar make casual entertaining a breeze.
- A formal dining room features French doors opening to the sun space.
- Upstairs, the large master suite offers a private deck, a walk-in closet and a personal bath with a corner spa tub, a separate shower and dual sinks.
- The skylighted balcony hall overlooks the vaulted spaces below.

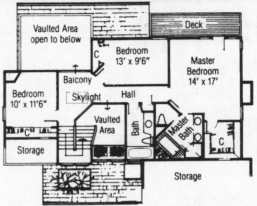

UPPER FLOOR

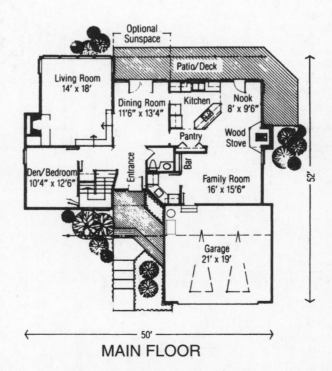

MAIN FLOOR

Plan S-2001

Bedrooms: 3+	Baths: 2½
Living Area:	
Upper floor	890 sq. ft.
Main floor	1,249 sq. ft.
Total Living Area:	**2,139 sq. ft.**
Basement	1,249 sq. ft.
Garage	399 sq. ft.
Exterior Wall Framing:	2x6

Foundation Options:
Daylight basement
Standard basement
Crawlspace
Slab
(All plans can be built with your choice of foundation and framing. A generic conversion diagram is available. See order form.)

BLUEPRINT PRICE CODE: C

ORDER BLUEPRINTS ANYTIME!
CALL TOLL-FREE 1-800-820-1283

Plan S-2001

PRICES AND DETAILS
ON PAGES 2-5

411

More than Meets the Eye

- Striking angles of unique rooflines characterize the exterior of this contemporary design. But there's more to this home than meets the eye.
- A step in from the front deck reveals a roomy entry and a beautiful open-railed staircase.
- Two distinct areas combine to form the gracious living room. The formal area is distinguished by several columns, while the intimate, sunken conversation area is nestled around a rustic fireplace.

- Well placed to easily access the living areas, the U-shaped kitchen and the dining area present a wonderful spot to prepare and serve special meals. The dining room includes a sliding glass door out to a covered deck.
- The main-floor bedroom boasts a large walk-in closet, a dual-sink private bath and its own covered deck.
- Clerestory windows illuminate the upper floor, where a balcony hall connects the two identically sized bedrooms with a den and a full bath.
- The daylight basement includes a full bath and a fun-filled recreation room.
- In the crawlspace version, the garage is attached just off the entry.

Plans H-928-1 & -1A	
Bedrooms: 3+	**Baths:** 2½-3½
Living Area:	
Upper floor	656 sq. ft.
Main floor	1,605 sq. ft.
Daylight basement	642 sq. ft.
Total Living Area:	**2,261/2,903 sq. ft.**
Garage (crawlspace)	812 sq. ft.
Garage (daylight basement)	425 sq. ft.
Exterior Wall Framing:	**2x6**
Foundation Options:	**Plan #**
Daylight basement	H-928-1
Crawlspace	H-928-1A

(All plans can be built with your choice of foundation and framing. A generic conversion diagram is available. See order form.)

BLUEPRINT PRICE CODE:	**C/D**

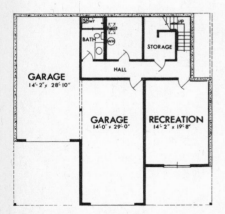

DAYLIGHT BASEMENT

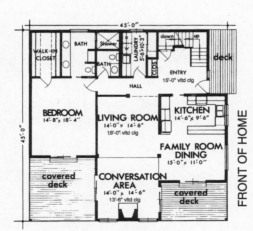

MAIN FLOOR

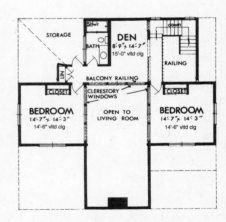

UPPER FLOOR

Plans H-928-1 & -1A
PRICES AND DETAILS
ON PAGES 2-5

Move-up Comfort

- Luxurious and vastly open, this contemporary home is ideal for the established family and for couples who enjoy entertaining.
- At the airy foyer, step down to the expansive living spaces that circulate around a woodstove and stone fireplace focal point. Spectacular views along the perimeter, and a vaulted ceiling above the Great Room, add visual drama.
- A uniquely shaped formal dining room is well-suited for gourmet meals.
- The island kitchen boasts a garden window at the sink, a built-in menu desk and a walk-in pantry.
- Upstairs, find two more bedrooms, a fantastic home library and a superb master suite with a sitting bay that overlooks a private deck!

Plan LRD-52382

Bedrooms: 3+	Baths: 2½
Living Area:	
Upper floor	1,409 sq. ft.
Main floor	2,030 sq. ft.
Total Living Area:	**3,439 sq. ft.**
Daylight basement	2,000 sq. ft.
Garage	830 sq. ft.
Exterior Wall Framing:	2x6

Foundation Options:

Daylight basement

Crawlspace

(All plans can be built with your choice of foundation and framing. A generic conversion diagram is available. See order form.)

BLUEPRINT PRICE CODE:	E

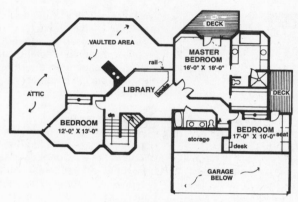

UPPER FLOOR

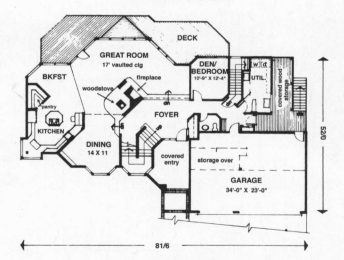

MAIN FLOOR

ORDER BLUEPRINTS ANYTIME!
CALL TOLL-FREE 1-800-820-1283

Plan LRD-52382

*PRICES AND DETAILS
ON PAGES 2-5*

409

REAR VIEW

Something Special

- From its spacious, semi-enclosed entrance deck and unique expanses of windows to its stunning interior, this home is something special.
- Sidelighted double doors open to a wide entry, the highlight of which is a gracious staircase to the upper floor.
- Straight ahead, the sunken living room showcases a wall of windows to the backyard. A massive fireplace with a raised hearth stands across from the

view. A pitched, beamed ceiling tops the room, and sliding glass doors on either side access twin covered decks.
- A level above, the dining room features windows on two sides and a breakfast bar shared with the kitchen.
- A short hallway, flanked by a half-bath and the laundry room, leads to the garage entrance.
- Across the home, two secondary bedrooms share a hall bath. Each room has an eye-catching vaulted ceiling.
- Upstairs, a railed balcony overlooks the living room and catches its marvelous view. The adjoining master suite enjoys a private bath and two walk-in closets.

Plans H-865-2 & -2A	
Bedrooms: 3	**Baths:** 2½
Living Area:	
Upper floor	576 sq. ft.
Main floor	1,490 sq. ft.
Total Living Area:	**2,066 sq. ft.**
Standard basement	1,490 sq. ft.
Garage	414 sq. ft.
Exterior Wall Framing:	2x4
Foundation Options:	**Plan #**
Standard basement	H-865-2
Crawlspace	H-865-2A

(All plans can be built with your choice of foundation and framing. A generic conversion diagram is available. See order form.)

BLUEPRINT PRICE CODE:	C

MAIN FLOOR

UPPER FLOOR

Plans H-865-2 & -2A

PRICES AND DETAILS
ON PAGES 2-5

Magical Vistas

- This smart contemporary home features a living room where a window wall and a glass ceiling combine to provide an unparalleled view of the great outdoors.
- The U-shaped kitchen offers plenty of counter space for the family chef. A pantry closet and a built-in china cabinet, which stands at the entrance to the dining area, are thoughtful touches.
- One of the three main-floor bedrooms has its own bath and double closets, making it a perfect in-law or guest suite. Two more bedrooms share a full bath.
- Upstairs, the exquisite master suite boasts windows that reach nearly the full height of an extended wall, framing the spectacular scenery beyond. A private bath and a skylighted walk-in closet ease you into each day.
- Down a balcony hallway, a skylighted den overlooks the living room, taking advantage of the view. You may choose to use this space as a studio or an office.

Plans H-3721-M1 & -M1A

Bedrooms: 4	Baths: 3½
Living Area:	
Upper floor	757 sq. ft.
Main floor	1,888 sq. ft.
Total Living Area:	**2,645 sq. ft.**
Partial basement	1,234 sq. ft.
Garage	458 sq. ft.
Exterior Wall Framing:	2x6
Foundation Options:	**Plan #**
Partial basement	H-3721-M1
Crawlspace	H-3721-M1A

(All plans can be built with your choice of foundation and framing. A generic conversion diagram is available. See order form.)

BLUEPRINT PRICE CODE:	**D**

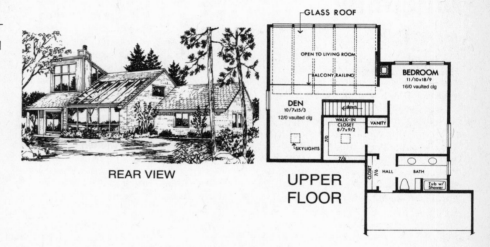

REAR VIEW

UPPER FLOOR

STAIRWAY AREA IN CRAWLSPACE VERSION

MAIN FLOOR

ORDER BLUEPRINTS ANYTIME!
CALL TOLL-FREE 1-800-820-1283

Plans H-3721-M1 & M1A

PRICES AND DETAILS
ON PAGES 2-5

407

Dynamic Multi-Level

- Suitable for a sloping lot with attractive views, this dynamic multi-level contemporary home design offers its owners sheer delight.
- The wide entry looks dramatically into the formal dining room and the vaulted living room a flight of stairs below.
- Skylighted and warmed by a fireplace, the living room expands to a rear deck through sliding glass doors.
- Behind stairways to the basement and the upper floor, the U-shaped kitchen sits snugly at the center of the home.
- A sloped ceiling, a radiant skylight and a raised hearth spark interest for the sprawling family room. Sliding glass doors access a backyard covered patio.
- Upstairs are three roomy bedrooms and two full baths. Clerestory windows shower the master bedroom with light.

Plan H-2103-1

Bedrooms: 3	Baths: 2½
Living Area:	
Upper floor	770 sq. ft.
Main floor	1,409 sq. ft.
Total Living Area:	**2,179 sq. ft.**
Daylight basement	620 sq. ft.
Garage	448 sq. ft.
Exterior Wall Framing:	2x6

Foundation Options:

Daylight basement

(All plans can be built with your choice of foundation and framing. A generic conversion diagram is available. See order form.)

BLUEPRINT PRICE CODE:	C

UPPER FLOOR

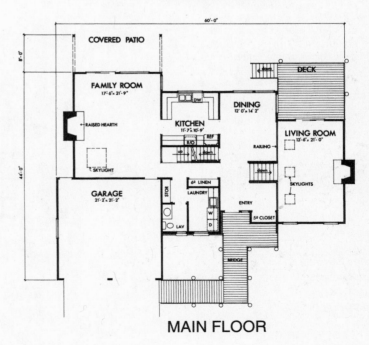

MAIN FLOOR

Plan H-2103-1

PRICES AND DETAILS
ON PAGES 2-5

State-of-the-Art Floor Plan

- This design's state-of-the-art floor plan begins with a two-story-high foyer that introduces a stunning open staircase and a bright Great Room.
- The Great Room is expanded by a 17-ft. vaulted ceiling and a window wall with French doors that open to a rear deck.
- Short sections of half-walls separate the Great Room from the open kitchen and dining room. Natural light streams in through a greenhouse window above the sink and lots of glass facing the deck.
- The main-floor master suite has a 9-ft. coved ceiling and private access to an inviting hot tub on the deck. Walk-in closets frame the entrance to the luxurious bath, highlighted by a 10-ft. vaulted ceiling and an arched window above a raised spa tub.
- Upstairs, a balcony hall leads to two bedrooms and a continental bath, plus a den and a storage room.

Plan S-2100

Bedrooms: 3+	Baths: 2½
Living Area:	
Upper floor	660 sq. ft.
Main floor	1,440 sq. ft.
Total Living Area:	**2,100 sq. ft.**
Standard basement	1,440 sq. ft.
Garage	552 sq. ft.
Exterior Wall Framing:	2x6

Foundation Options:

Standard basement

Crawlspace

Slab

(All plans can be built with your choice of foundation and framing. A generic conversion diagram is available. See order form.)

BLUEPRINT PRICE CODE: C

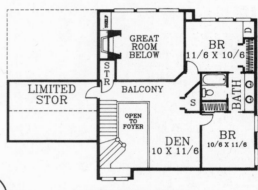

NOTE: The above photographed home may have been modified by the homeowner. Please refer to floor plan and/or drawn elevation shown for actual blueprint details.

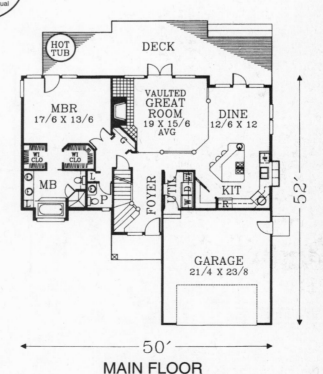

UPPER FLOOR

MAIN FLOOR

Casa Grande

- The street-side view of this charming Spanish villa arouses a desire for further inspection behind the adobe-style garden walls. The shake-style tile roof lends Old World authenticity to the many amenities found inside.
- Greet family and friends in the outdoor entry court before ushering them through the dramatic double doors.
- Stroll into the sunken living room to enjoy an evening of good conversation. The room includes a fireplace and sliding-glass-door access to a covered patio, and is distinguished from the dining room by a wrought-iron railing.
- Sunlight pours into the expansive family room through a sparkling wall of windows. The room shares a snack bar with the tidy, U-shaped kitchen.
- Secluded on the main floor for privacy, the master bedroom boasts a pair of closets and a lavish bath with a spa tub, dual sinks and access to a private patio.
- Upstairs, three identically sized bedrooms share a full bath. A balcony loft allows you to step out to a covered viewing deck.

Plan H-3708-M3A

Bedrooms: 4+	Baths: 2½
Living Area:	
Upper floor	893 sq. ft.
Main floor	2,006 sq. ft.
Total Living Area:	**2,899 sq. ft.**
Garage	513 sq. ft.
Storage	280 sq. ft.
Exterior Wall Framing:	2x6

Foundation Options:

Slab
(All plans can be built with your choice of foundation and framing. A generic conversion diagram is available. See order form.)

BLUEPRINT PRICE CODE:	**D**

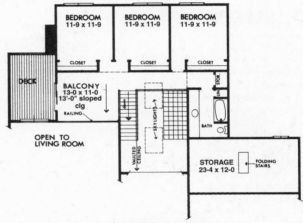

UPPER FLOOR

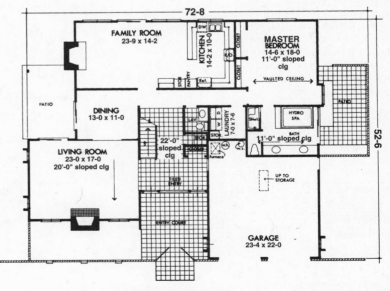

MAIN FLOOR

The Joy of Daily Pleasures

- The easy charm of a big, sun-blessed porch and the joy of a well-designed interior will bring everyday pleasure to the owners of this two-story home.
- Perfect for rocking chairs and swinging hammocks, the porch is also a natural spot to pour glasses of punch during summertime family reunions.
- Step inside via the entry or by one of two doors to the living room, which is highlighted by a handsome fireplace and a 16-ft. ceiling. Exposed beams in the ceiling add to the cozy ambience.
- The kitchen is at the heart of the home.
- For casual eating the sunny nook is the choice. On pleasant days, you can step out to a peaceful enclosed garden.
- The large master suite boasts a walk-in closet and a private bath, and is just a step from a back door to the porch.
- Two bedrooms and a sizable game room comprise the upper floor.
- Plans include a detached two-car garage with storage space.

Plan E-2103

Bedrooms: 3+	Baths: 2½
Living Area:	
Upper floor	736 sq. ft.
Main floor	1,431 sq. ft.
Total Living Area:	**2,167 sq. ft.**
Detached garage and storage	540 sq. ft.
Exterior Wall Framing:	2x6

Foundation Options:

Crawlspace

Slab

(All plans can be built with your choice of foundation and framing. A generic conversion diagram is available. See order form.)

BLUEPRINT PRICE CODE: C

UPPER FLOOR

MAIN FLOOR

ORDER BLUEPRINTS ANYTIME!
CALL TOLL-FREE 1-800-820-1283

Plan E-2103

PRICES AND DETAILS
ON PAGES 2-5

403

Luxurious Interior

- This luxurious home is introduced by an exciting tiled entry with a 17½-ft. vaulted ceiling and a skylight.
- The highlight of the home is the expansive Great Room and dining area, with its fireplace, planter, 17½-ft. vaulted ceiling and bay windows. The fabulous wraparound deck with a step-up hot tub is the perfect complement to this large entertainment space.
- The kitchen features lots of counter space, a large pantry and an adjoining bay-windowed breakfast nook.
- The exquisite master suite flaunts a sunken garden tub, a separate shower, a dual-sink vanity, a walk-in closet and private access to the deck area.
- The game room downstairs is perfect for casual entertaining, with its warm woodstove, oversized wet bar and patio access. Two bedrooms, a full bath and a large utility area are also included.

Plan P-6595-3D

Bedrooms: 3	Baths: 2½
Living Area:	
Main floor	1,530 sq. ft.
Daylight basement	1,145 sq. ft.
Total Living Area:	**2,675 sq. ft.**
Garage	462 sq. ft.
Exterior Wall Framing:	2x6

Foundation Options:
Daylight basement
(All plans can be built with your choice of foundation and framing. A generic conversion diagram is available. See order form.)

BLUEPRINT PRICE CODE:	**D**

MAIN FLOOR

DAYLIGHT BASEMENT

Contemporary Solar Chalet

- Designed to house even the largest family, this expansive solar chalet easily serves as either a primary residence or a recreational retreat.
- The conveniently arranged main floor is tailor-made for family living, allowing for a smooth flow of traffic.
- Refreshing outdoor areas enhance the design; the spacious deck acts as a great spot for summer entertaining, and the sun room brings light and warmth.
- Three good-sized bedrooms and two full baths lie upstairs. Plenty of windows in the master suite provide lots of sunshine and cheer. The private bath is accessed through a walk-in closet.
- A one-car tuck-under garage comes with the daylight basement version, while a two-car garage comes with the crawlspace plan

Plans H-962-1A & -1B

Bedrooms: 4+	Baths: 3-4
Living Area:	
Upper floor	970 sq. ft.
Main floor	1,248/1,266 sq. ft.
Sun room	135 sq. ft.
Daylight basement	884 sq. ft.
Total Living Area:	**3,237/2,371 sq. ft.**
Two-car garage	572 sq. ft.
One-car/tuck-under garage	338 sq. ft.
Exterior Wall Framing:	2x6
Foundation Options:	**Plan #**
Daylight basement	H-962-1B
Crawlspace	H-962-1A

(All plans can be built with your choice of foundation and framing. A generic conversion diagram is available. See order form.)

BLUEPRINT PRICE CODE: C

UPPER FLOOR

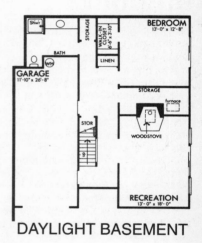

DAYLIGHT BASEMENT

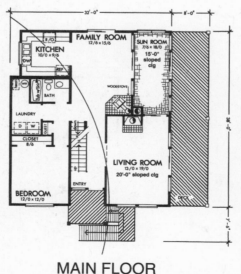

MAIN FLOOR

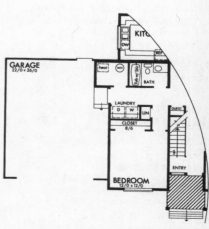

ALTERNATE MAIN FLOOR WITH CRAWLSPACE VERSION

ORDER BLUEPRINTS ANYTIME!
CALL TOLL-FREE 1-800-820-1283

Plans H-962-1A & -1B

PRICES AND DETAILS
ON PAGES 2-5

401

Unique Farmhouse

- Tapered columns, half-round windowed dormers and a cupola above the garage lend a unique flavor to this farmhouse-style home.
- Nestled between the living room and the trayed dining room, the foyer leads to the centrally located family room.
- Expanded by a two-story ceiling, the skylighted family room boasts a cozy fireplace and French doors leading to a covered backyard patio.
- The tiled kitchen area includes a handy island worktop, a roomy pantry and a sunny breakfast nook with patio access. The nearby laundry room opens to a two-car garage.
- The secluded main-floor master bedroom opens to the patio and features a huge walk-in closet and a private bath with an angled spa tub, an oversized shower stall and a dual-sink vanity.
- Unless otherwise specified, all main-floor rooms have 10-ft. ceilings.
- Upstairs, a lovely view into the family room can be enjoyed from the hallway. Three more bedrooms, each with private bath access, complete this floor.

Plan HDS-99-188

Bedrooms: 4	Baths: 3½
Living Area:	
Upper floor	879 sq. ft.
Main floor	1,747 sq. ft.
Total Living Area:	**2,626 sq. ft.**
Garage	538 sq. ft.
Exterior Wall Framing:	2x4

Foundation Options:

Slab
(All plans can be built with your choice of foundation and framing. A generic conversion diagram is available. See order form.)

BLUEPRINT PRICE CODE:	D

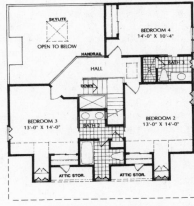

UPPER FLOOR

MAIN FLOOR

Plan HDS-99-188

PRICES AND DETAILS ON PAGES 2-5

Bring It Outside!

- This stylish country classic welcomes you outside, with its front porch, covered patio and backyard deck with a summer kitchen and a spa tub!
- In from the front porch, the formal dining room merges with the living room. This space is enhanced by a fireplace flanked by built-in shelves.
- Around the corner, the kitchen offers easy service to the morning room, the family room and the dining room. Nearby are a half-bath and a large utility room, plus easy access to the garage, storage space and patio.

- A lovely Palladian window, a soaring brick fireplace and a 12-ft. ceiling augment the family room, which shares a long snack counter with the kitchen.
- The master bedroom features a bayed sitting area with a fireplace, a 10-ft. coffered ceiling and direct patio access. The plush private bath boasts a spa tub set into a bay window.
- The study/bedroom would make a perfect guest room, with a second full bath a few steps away.
- All main-floor rooms have 9-ft. ceilings unless otherwise specified.
- Upstairs, two good-sized bedrooms share a third full bath.

Plan DD-3052

Bedrooms: 3+	Baths: 3½
Living Area:	
Upper floor	840 sq. ft.
Main floor	2,348 sq. ft.
Total Living Area:	**3,188 sq. ft.**
Standard basement	2,293 sq. ft.
Garage and storage	500 sq. ft.
Exterior Wall Framing:	2x4

Foundation Options:

Standard basement
Crawlspace
Slab
(All plans can be built with your choice of foundation and framing. A generic conversion diagram is available. See order form.)

BLUEPRINT PRICE CODE: E

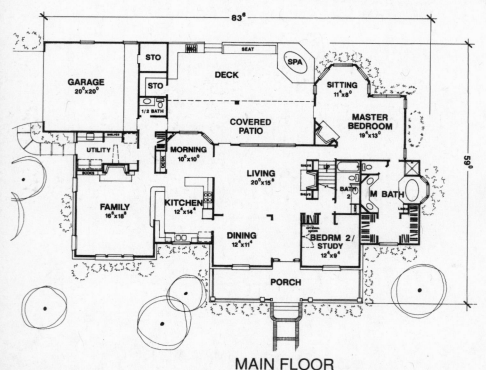

MAIN FLOOR

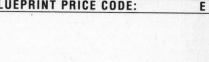

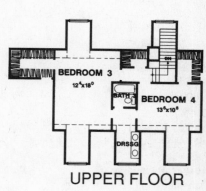

UPPER FLOOR

ORDER BLUEPRINTS ANYTIME!
CALL TOLL-FREE 1-800-820-1283

Plan DD-3052

PRICES AND DETAILS
ON PAGES 2-5

399

At Home
on the Farm

- With its magnificent wraparound covered porch, this classic country-style design would look at home nestled into green, rolling farmland.
- The airy foyer introduces the Great Room to the right, where a gorgeous fireplace resides.
- A central breakfast nook basks in the glow from a wide window arrangement. Porch access is immediate and laundry facilities are out of sight.
- Amenities in the kitchen include a tidy pantry and an oversized island for meal preparation. A door to the formal dining room muffles kitchen noise.
- Upstairs, the master bedroom flaunts a walk-in closet and a stunning bath that includes a spa tub, a separate shower and his-and-hers vanities.
- Along the hallway, two large secondary bedrooms share another full bath.
- A breathtaking Palladian window lights up a window seat in a restful sitting area off the balcony, making it a wonderful place to finish that novel or cross-stitch pattern.

Plan C-9430

Bedrooms: 3	Baths: 2½
Living Area:	
Upper floor	1,138 sq. ft.
Main floor	1,125 sq. ft.
Total Living Area:	**2,263 sq. ft.**
Daylight basement	1,125 sq. ft.
Exterior Wall Framing:	2x4

Foundation Options:

Daylight basement
Crawlspace
(All plans can be built with your choice of foundation and framing. A generic conversion diagram is available. See order form.)

BLUEPRINT PRICE CODE: C

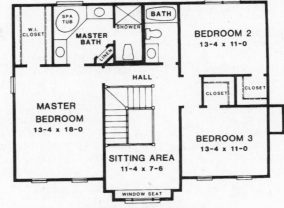

UPPER FLOOR

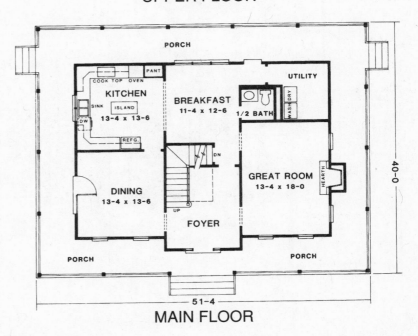

MAIN FLOOR

ORDER BLUEPRINTS ANYTIME!
CALL TOLL-FREE 1-800-820-1283

Plan C-9430

PRICES AND DETAILS
ON PAGES 2-5

Memorable Mediterranean

- A covered portico shades the entry to this lovely Mediterranean design, where memories are yours to make in the wonderful years to come.
- The foyer is brightened by an arched picture window set above the double entry doors. Ahead is a spacious two-story Great Room with a wet bar and sliding glass doors to the rear patio. Here you'll find a second wet bar that complements the summer kitchen.

- The interior kitchen and adjoining breakfast room are tiled. The kitchen features a large pantry closet and discreet access to the formal dining room off the foyer.
- A handy guest room on the main floor adjoins a full bath.
- The upper floor contains the family sleeping quarters. The master suite boasts its own deck, which is accessed via French doors. The private master bath includes his-and-hers vanities, a garden tub and an oversized shower with a seat.
- One of two secondary bedrooms has a roomy study area and its own deck.

Plan HDS-99-132	
Bedrooms: 4	**Baths:** 3
Living Area:	
Upper floor	1,000 sq. ft.
Main floor	1,352 sq. ft.
Total Living Area:	**2,352 sq. ft.**
Garage	384 sq. ft.
Exterior Wall Framing:	2x4 and
	8-in. concrete block

Foundation Options:
Slab
(All plans can be built with your choice of foundation and framing. A generic conversion diagram is available. See order form.)

BLUEPRINT PRICE CODE: C

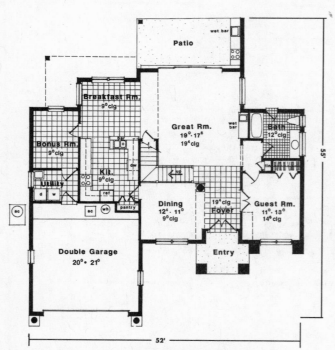

MAIN FLOOR

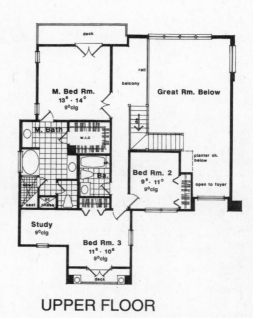

UPPER FLOOR

ORDER BLUEPRINTS ANYTIME!
CALL TOLL-FREE 1-800-820-1283

Plan HDS-99-132

PRICES AND DETAILS
ON PAGES 2-5

397

Quiet Quarters

- Quiet living spaces are located in and above this home's detached garage. The two areas may function as guest quarters or as a studio or home office.
- A lovely columned porch leads from the garage to the welcoming foyer. Enviable wood floors attract attention in the foyer and the living and dining rooms.
- A columned half-wall defines the living room, where a fine fireplace is the focus of attention. A built-in media center facilitates relaxation, while the sitting room is nice for reading.
- Columned half-walls with bookshelves introduce the formal dining room.

- The wide-open island kitchen flows into a sunny breakfast room, where a French door accesses a covered porch. A sizable laundry room is nearby.
- All main-floor rooms have 9-ft. ceilings.
- On the upper floor, a railed balcony overlooks the foyer below.
- The luxurious master suite features two large walk-in closets. The bedroom's 9-ft. ceiling steps up to 11 ft. to accommodate the interesting window arrangement.
- The master bath shows off a columned bathing bay with a garden tub and a separate shower.
- Two secondary bedrooms share a nice hall bath.

Plan L-222-VSB

Bedrooms: 3+	**Baths:** 3½

Living Area:

Upper floor	932 sq. ft.
Main floor	1,213 sq. ft.
Guest quarters/studio	434 sq. ft.
Bonus room/home office	304 sq. ft.
Total Living Area:	**2,883 sq. ft.**
Garage	517 sq. ft.
Exterior Wall Framing:	2x4

Foundation Options:

Slab
(All plans can be built with your choice of foundation and framing. A generic conversion diagram is available. See order form.)

BLUEPRINT PRICE CODE: D

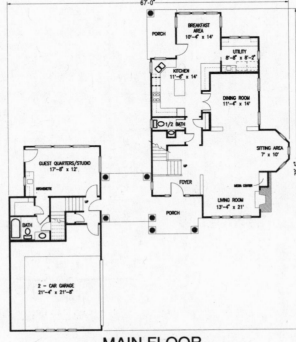

MAIN FLOOR

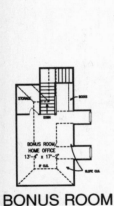

BONUS ROOM

UPPER FLOOR

Plan L-222-VSB

Natural State

- This home's nostalgic facade seems to blend with its natural surroundings, making it a prime choice for those who wish communion with the environment.
- There's plenty of room for interaction with nature. At the rear of the home, a covered patio flows into a fabulous deck, where a barbecue, a fun spa tub and built-in bench seats are arranged for the ultimate in excitement!
- The master bedroom cashes in on its location with a bayed window to view the festivities on the deck, and a private entrance in case the temptation to join in the frolicking becomes irresistible.
- A bay window also brightens the morning room, where your whole family may gather for waffles on those sleep-in Saturdays. In the fall months, you'll appreciate the kitchen's oversized island, which is big enough for four prize pumpkins!
- Your social obligations have not been overlooked, either. The large dining room practically guarantees successful formal dinners.

Plan DD-1914

Bedrooms: 3+	Baths: 2½
Living Area:	
Upper floor (bonus space)	1,216 sq. ft.
Main floor	1,917 sq. ft.
Total Living Area:	**3,133 sq. ft.**
Standard basement	1,820 sq. ft.
Garage and storage	467 sq. ft.
Exterior Wall Framing:	2x4

Foundation Options:

Standard basement

Crawlspace

Slab

(All plans can be built with your choice of foundation and framing. A generic conversion diagram is available. See order form.)

BLUEPRINT PRICE CODE: E

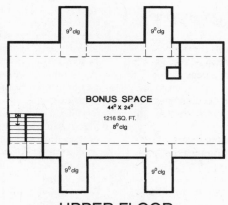

UPPER FLOOR

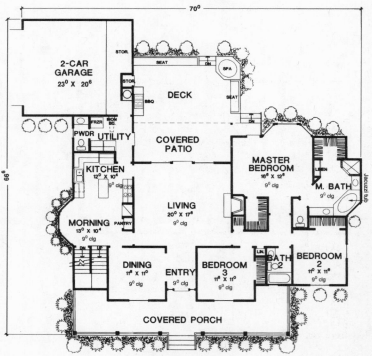

MAIN FLOOR

ORDER BLUEPRINTS ANYTIME!
CALL TOLL-FREE 1-800-820-1283

Plan DD-1914

PRICES AND DETAILS
ON PAGES 2-5

395

REAR VIEW

Victorian Vacation Home

- Victorian design accents, horizontal wood siding and decorative windows create an exciting exterior for this versatile home.
- A stairway to the back porch presents accesses to the living room, dining room and master suite.
- The spacious master suite offers a large sleeping area, built-in bookshelves, a walk-in closet, a dressing area and a corner tub. The toilet and a second vanity are set off to serve as a half-bath for rest of the main floor.
- The tiled kitchen offers a U-shaped counter, ample storage space and nearby laundry facilities.
- Three secondary bedrooms share the upper floor with two baths.
- Plenty of storage space is available in the attic.
- The open space underneath the house makes an excellent carport or storage area for boats or other equipment.

Plan E-2006	
Bedrooms: 4	**Baths:** 3
Living Area:	
Upper floor	838 sq. ft.
Main floor	1,182 sq. ft.
Total Living Area:	**2,020 sq. ft.**
Carport/storage	1,450 sq. ft.
Exterior Wall Framing:	2x6

Foundation Options:

Pole
(All plans can be built with your choice of foundation and framing. A generic conversion diagram is available. See order form.)

BLUEPRINT PRICE CODE:	C

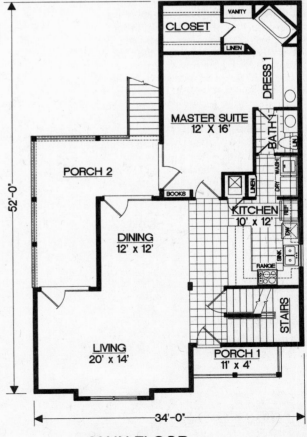

UPPER FLOOR

MAIN FLOOR

Plan E-2006

**PRICES AND DETAILS
ON PAGES 2-5**

Rise Above It All

- This plan offers "reverse living," with the main rooms located on the upper floor to take advantage of the view. The design's shingle siding is reminiscent of a New England oceanside cottage.
- The vaulted Great Room is the heart of the home. This generous space features bright windows and a fireplace with an attached wood storage box.
- The open kitchen is defined by a dropped ceiling. Its amenities include an island cooktop fronted by a snack bar, as well as a handy pantry closet and a built-in desk for jotting down grocery lists and menus.
- The vaulted master suite, which boasts a luxury private bath, opens to a rear deck. The deck may also be accessed via the utility area. A second deck overlooks the front of the home.
- The main floor contains two bedrooms that share a dual-sink bath. There's also a large rec room. Sliding glass doors in the hall open to the ground-level patio.

Plan LRD-9492

Bedrooms: 3	Baths: 2½
Living Area:	
Upper floor	1,373 sq. ft.
Main floor	1,057 sq. ft.
Total Living Area:	**2,430 sq. ft.**
Standard basement	1,057 sq. ft.
Garage	468 sq. ft.
Exterior Wall Framing:	2x6

Foundation Options:
Standard basement
Crawlspace
Slab
(All plans can be built with your choice of foundation and framing. A generic conversion diagram is available. See order form.)

BLUEPRINT PRICE CODE:	C

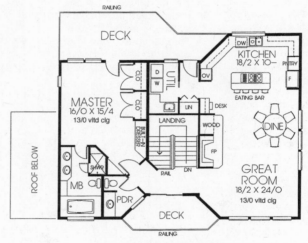

UPPER FLOOR

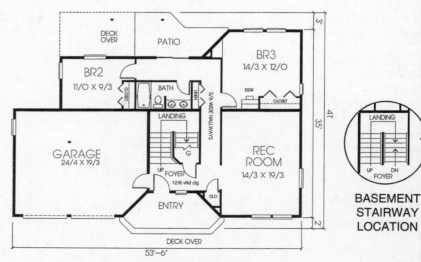

MAIN FLOOR

BASEMENT STAIRWAY LOCATION

Fall in Love!

- Easy, smart and stylish, this two-story design will lure you with its many charms. Its interesting expansion possibilities and the graceful flow between the indoor and outdoor areas will no doubt have you falling in love.
- A trio of dormers, a sprinkling of keystones and a columned front porch create a pleasant exterior. Big enough for the kids to use for games, the porch is also a great spot to gather friends.
- When the night turns chilly, come inside to the extra large Great Room and warm up by the inviting fire.
- The spacious master bedroom features a 14½-ft.-high vaulted ceiling and private access to the back patio. The master bath has an 11-ft., 9-in. vaulted ceiling.
- Off the island kitchen is an office/bonus room with a 15-ft. vaulted ceiling.
- Unless otherwise mentioned, all main floor rooms have 9-ft. ceilings.
- Three bedrooms and a versatile playroom comprise the upper floor.

Plan J-9409

Bedrooms: 3+	Baths: 2½
Living Area:	
Upper floor	707 sq. ft.
Main floor	1,768 sq. ft.
Total Living Area:	**2,475 sq. ft.**
Standard basement	1,768 sq. ft.
Garage	490 sq. ft.
Exterior Wall Framing:	2x4
Foundation Options:	
Standard basement	
Crawlspace	
Slab	

(All plans can be built with your choice of foundation and framing. A generic conversion diagram is available. See order form.)

BLUEPRINT PRICE CODE:	C

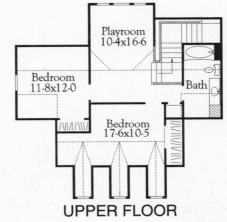

UPPER FLOOR

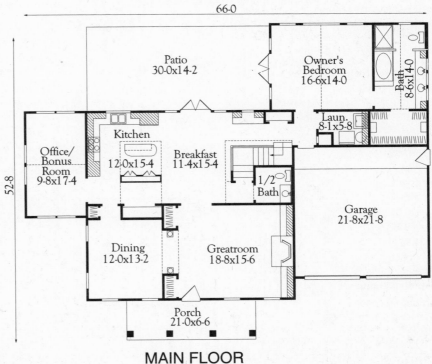

MAIN FLOOR

Vibrant Victorian

- The vibrant style and refined grace of the Victorian era is alive and well in this beautiful two-story home.
- Beyond the wraparound porch, the foyer is flanked by the formal areas.
- The quiet parlor features handsome built-in bookshelves and a decorative fireplace. The formal dining room shows off a lovely window seat.
- A glass-flanked fireplace is the focal point of the family room, where French doors open to a nice deck.
- The good-sized kitchen offers an eating bar and unfolds to a sunny bayed breakfast area. A laundry room is tucked away nearby.
- Upstairs, the spacious master bedroom boasts his-and-hers walk-in closets and a private bath with a whirlpool tub.
- Three additional bedrooms share a second full bath.
- The bonus area above the garage is great for use as a secluded home office or an extra bedroom.

Plan C-9330

Bedrooms: 4+	Baths: 2½
Living Area:	
Upper floor	1,178 sq. ft.
Main floor	1,240 sq. ft.
Bonus/office	288 sq. ft.
Total Living Area:	**2,706 sq. ft.**
Daylight basement	1,184 sq. ft.
Garage	528 sq. ft.
Exterior Wall Framing:	2x4

Foundation Options:

Daylight basement
Crawlspace

(All plans can be built with your choice of foundation and framing. A generic conversion diagram is available. See order form.)

BLUEPRINT PRICE CODE:	D

UPPER FLOOR

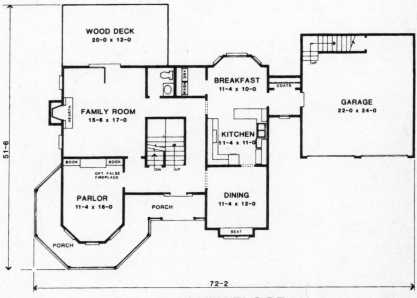

MAIN FLOOR

ORDER BLUEPRINTS ANYTIME!
CALL TOLL-FREE 1-800-820-1283

Plan C-9330

PRICES AND DETAILS
ON PAGES 2-5

391

European Calm

- Relaxation reigns in this European home, with its front covered porch, backyard deck and calming interior spaces. The facade recalls an Old World charm.
- The two-story foyer looks into the Great Room, which offers a fireplace and a window wall over the wraparound deck. Plant shelves and an 18-ft. ceiling command attention from above.
- A breakfast area and a built-in desk enhance the island kitchen. Sliding French doors open to the deck.
- Beautiful columns set off the elegant formal dining room.
- The master bedroom offers a bath with a garden tub and a separate shower. Sliding French doors access the deck.
- A secluded den has private access to a bath and can swing from function to function as family needs change.
- All main-floor rooms feature 9-ft. ceilings unless otherwise noted.
- Upstairs, two more spacious bedrooms share a full bath with a dual-sink vanity.
- An optional bonus room provides further expansion possibilities.

Plan B-94017

Bedrooms: 3+	Baths: 3
Living Area:	
Upper floor	666 sq. ft.
Main floor	1,725 sq. ft.
Total Living Area:	**2,391 sq. ft.**
Optional bonus room	216 sq. ft.
Basement	1,725 sq. ft.
Garage	470 sq. ft.
Exterior Wall Framing:	2x6

Foundation Options:

Daylight basement

Standard basement

(All plans can be built with your choice of foundation and framing. A generic conversion diagram is available. See order form.)

BLUEPRINT PRICE CODE: C

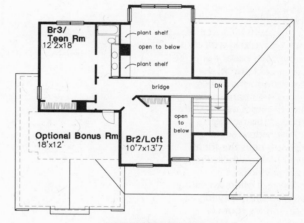

UPPER FLOOR

MAIN FLOOR

Plan B-94017

PRICES AND DETAILS
ON PAGES 2-5

Tomorrow's Memories

- Today's activities turn into tomorrow's memories, and this traditional home ensures that both will be sweet.
- Out front, a wraparound porch hosts summer afternoons with grace. The conversation and the iced tea will flow freely when friends gather here.
- Inside, French doors introduce a pretty parlor and a quiet den alongside the foyer. Both rooms include beautiful bay windows, and the den boasts an attractive bookcase.
- With its soothing fireplace and large, easygoing layout, the kitchen earns its title as a "country kitchen." At the center, folks will cluster around the island cooktop and snack bar to recount the events of the day.
- Upstairs, a balcony and a fireplace give the home owners a private, romantic place all their own in the master suite.
- A large storage area off the garage holds lawn equipment, bicycles and other outdoor gear, keeping the yard neat.

Plan GA-9602

Bedrooms: 4+	Baths: 2½
Living Area:	
Upper floor	1,036 sq. ft.
Main floor	1,113 sq. ft.
Total Living Area:	**2,149 sq. ft.**
Standard basement	1,020 sq. ft.
Garage	484 sq. ft.
Storage	213 sq. ft.
Exterior Wall Framing:	2x6

Foundation Options:

Standard basement
(All plans can be built with your choice of foundation and framing. A generic conversion diagram is available. See order form.)

BLUEPRINT PRICE CODE: C

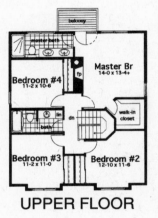

UPPER FLOOR

MAIN FLOOR

ORDER BLUEPRINTS ANYTIME!
CALL TOLL-FREE 1-800-820-1283

Plan GA-9602

PRICES AND DETAILS
ON PAGES 2-5

389

Cozy Comfort

- An efficient floor plan packed with amenities, and the savings you'll realize from energy-efficient construction make this new home an affordable alternative to an older one. The facade reflects the timeless design you've always wanted.
- The entry provides an open view of the main living areas. The dining room, the kitchen and the living room have no full walls between them, allowing shared family time together.
- The living room is anchored by a fireplace that invites you to draw close on frosty winter evenings. A snack bar that fronts the kitchen serves up delicious treats. A door opens to a big backyard deck for summertime fun.
- The main floor also includes two large bedrooms. The master bedroom boasts its own access to the backyard, a nice dressing area, a walk-in closet and private access to a full bath.
- A pair of upper-floor bedrooms and a full bath with a dual-sink vanity may be finished now or later.

Plan E-1310

Bedrooms: 2+	Baths: 1-2
Living Area:	
Upper floor	656 sq. ft.
Main floor	1,364 sq. ft.
Total Living Area:	**2,020 sq. ft.**
Standard basement	1,364 sq. ft.
Exterior Wall Framing:	2x6

Foundation Options:

Standard basement

Crawlspace

Slab

(All plans can be built with your choice of foundation and framing. A generic conversion diagram is available. See order form.)

BLUEPRINT PRICE CODE: C

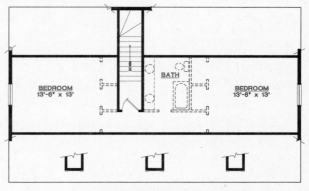

UPPER FLOOR

MAIN FLOOR

Plan E-1310

Old-World Appeal

- Stone and lap siding, repeated front-protecting gables, divided-light windows, and heavy wood trim all exude an Old-World character and appeal.
- From the raised entry, guests are greeted with interesting views of the formal living and dining rooms to the right and left, and the informal family room under the balcony straight ahead.
- The well-planned island kitchen overlooks the breakfast eating area with rear deck access and the sunken family room with a fireplace and a dramatic vaulted ceiling.
- The four upstairs bedrooms are highlighted by a 12-ft.-high vaulted master suite with an open-feeling master bath and a walk-in closet.

Plan B-88010

Bedrooms: 4	Baths: 2½
Living Area:	
Upper floor	1,468 sq. ft.
Main floor	1,639 sq. ft.
Total Living Area:	**3,107 sq. ft.**
Standard basement	1,639 sq. ft.
Garage	864 sq. ft.
Exterior Wall Framing:	2x4

Foundation Options:

Standard basement

(All plans can be built with your choice of foundation and framing. A generic conversion diagram is available. See order form.)

BLUEPRINT PRICE CODE: E

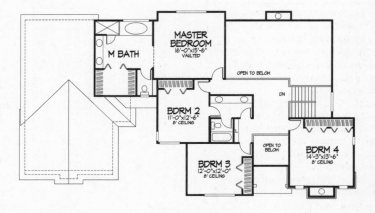

UPPER FLOOR

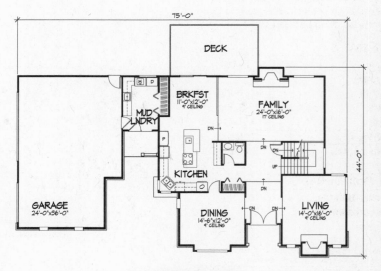

MAIN FLOOR

ORDER BLUEPRINTS ANYTIME!
CALL TOLL-FREE 1-800-820-1283

Plan B-88010

PRICES AND DETAILS
ON PAGES 2-5

387

Energy-Wise, Style-Conscious

- This passive-solar home flaunts lots of stylish details that guarantee its appeal to a wide variety of buyers!
- Energy-efficient techniques include berming, a south-facing sun porch with a masonry floor and heat-storing wall and two woodstoves.
- In from the 10-ft., 4-in.-high foyer, the huge living room is at the heart of the floor plan. Spacious enough to hold large family gatherings or office parties, you'll quickly fall in love with its intimate ambience.
- Another incredible room is the master suite, where you'll find lots of closet space, a 11-ft.-high vaulted bath and access to the sun porch.
- Two additional bedrooms, a full bath and a loft comprise the upper floor. The loft easily converts to an extra bedroom for surprise overnight guests.

Plan AX-8047-A

Bedrooms: 3+	Baths: 2½
Living Area:	
Upper floor	793 sq. ft.
Main floor	1,375 sq. ft.
Sun porch	258 sq. ft.
Total Living Area:	**2,426 sq. ft.**
Standard basement	1,375 sq. ft.
Garage	451 sq. ft.
Exterior Wall Framing:	2x6

Foundation Options:

Standard basement
Crawlspace
Slab

(All plans can be built with your choice of foundation and framing. A generic conversion diagram is available. See order form.)

BLUEPRINT PRICE CODE:	C

UPPER FLOOR

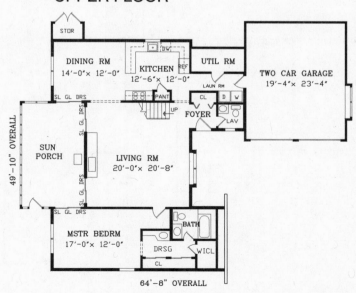

MAIN FLOOR

Plan AX-8047-A

PRICES AND DETAILS
ON PAGES 2-5

REAR VIEW

Three Levels of Fun!

- Step into this home, and step up to the three levels of fun that make this contemporary design a true winner!
- A soaring vaulted ceiling tops the sidelighted entry, introducing family and friends to the other surprises that await inside.
- The focal point of the sunken living room is the mood-setting fireplace. Two pairs of windows look out over the deck and let you soak in the views.

- A 6-ft.-high wall defines the cozy family room, creating a comfortable spot to relax before dinner is served.
- Tucked into the corner, the walk-through kitchen features a windowed sink and a handy serving bar.
- Upstairs, the master bedroom invites respite. The sleeping chamber is lighted by two windows to the backyard, while the private bath boasts a large walk-in closet and a pair of skylights.
- Two secondary bedrooms connect with another full bath by a balcony hall.
- The daylight basement includes a recreation room with its own fireplace and a huge all-purpose room.

Plans H-2100-1 & -1A

Bedrooms: 3	Baths: 2½
Living Area:	
Upper floor	1,031 sq. ft.
Main floor	1,036 sq. ft.
Daylight basement	770 sq. ft.
Total Living Area:	**2,067/2,837 sq. ft.**
Garage	502 sq. ft.
Exterior Wall Framing:	2x6
Foundation Options:	**Plan #**
Daylight basement	H-2100-1
Crawlspace	H-2100-1A

(All plans can be built with your choice of foundation and framing. A generic conversion diagram is available. See order form.)

BLUEPRINT PRICE CODE:	**C/D**

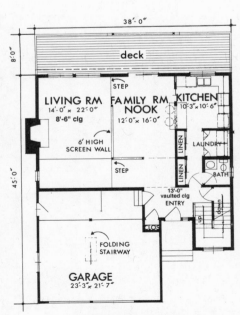

DAYLIGHT BASEMENT

MAIN FLOOR

UPPER FLOOR

ORDER BLUEPRINTS ANYTIME!
CALL TOLL-FREE 1-800-820-1283

Plans H-2100-1 & -1A

PRICES AND DETAILS
ON PAGES 2-5

385

Graceful Entry

- A stone and stucco exterior, combined with a graceful arched entry and transoms, creates this home's charm.
- The entry opens directly into the living room, which is highlighted by a 17-ft. vaulted ceiling and a fireplace.
- Stately columns and half-walls support a high plant shelf that defines the dining room. A 10-ft. ceiling and a bay window add style, while a beautiful French door opens to a huge deck.
- The kitchen also features a 10-ft. ceiling, along with a convenient island worktop, a pantry closet and a double sink topped by a bright window.
- A quiet den could serve as a home office or a guest room. Built-in shelves and sliding glass doors to the deck add to the room's appeal.
- In the main-floor master suite, a second set of sliding glass doors opens to the deck. The suite also includes a walk-in closet and a private bath with a lush garden tub, a sit-down shower and a dual-sink vanity.
- Upstairs, two more bedrooms share a hall bath. A skylighted bonus room offers space for further expansion.

Plan B-94023

Bedrooms: 3+	**Baths:** 3

Living Area:	
Upper floor	549 sq. ft.
Main floor	1,337 sq. ft.
Bonus room	323 sq. ft.
Total Living Area:	**2,209 sq. ft.**
Standard basement	1,337 sq. ft.
Garage	467 sq. ft.
Exterior Wall Framing:	2x6

Foundation Options:

Standard basement

(All plans can be built with your choice of foundation and framing. A generic conversion diagram is available. See order form.)

BLUEPRINT PRICE CODE:	C

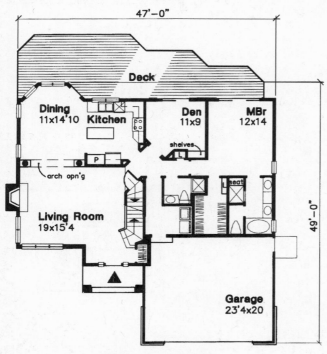

MAIN FLOOR

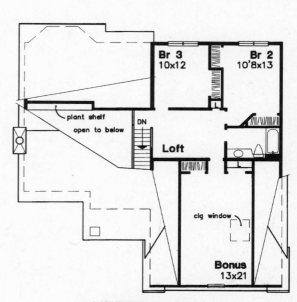

UPPER FLOOR

Plan B-94023

PRICES AND DETAILS
ON PAGES 2-5

Patience Pays!

- If you've waited to make your home-buying decision, your patience is about to pay off with this country-style home.
- A columned front porch spices up the facade and provides a fine introduction to the sidelighted foyer. The formal living and dining rooms reside to the left and right of the foyer.
- Ahead, the fabulous family room offers a fireplace, brilliant backyard views and access to a deck that is big enough to handle the largest extended family!
- The kitchen and its adjoining bayed breakfast nook combine to deliver a radiantly inviting morning retreat.
- Upstairs, double doors swing wide to reveal the master suite. A second set of double doors leads to its private bath, which boasts a dual-sink vanity, a large walk-in closet and a raised garden tub tucked into a boxed-out window.
- Three secondary bedrooms offer plenty of room for the kids to finish off that homework or pursue a favorite hobby.
- All rooms boast 9-ft. ceilings.

Plan DW-2127

Bedrooms: 4	Baths: 2½
Living Area:	
Upper floor	1,012 sq. ft.
Main floor	1,115 sq. ft.
Total Living Area:	**2,127 sq. ft.**
Standard basement	1,115 sq. ft.
Garage	464 sq. ft.
Exterior Wall Framing:	2x4

Foundation Options:

Standard basement

Crawlspace

Slab

(All plans can be built with your choice of foundation and framing. A generic conversion diagram is available. See order form.)

BLUEPRINT PRICE CODE:	C

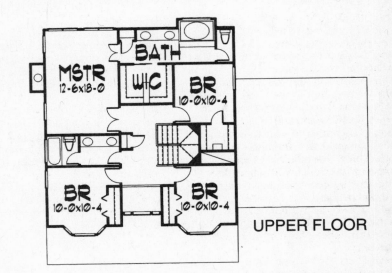

UPPER FLOOR

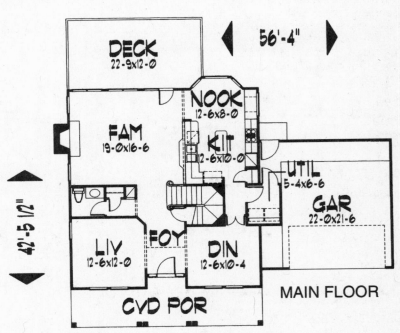

MAIN FLOOR

ORDER BLUEPRINTS ANYTIME!
CALL TOLL-FREE 1-800-820-1283

Plan DW-2127

PRICES AND DETAILS
ON PAGES 2-5

383

Country Home for Lake Lot

- The rear elevation of this country-style home is as exciting as the front, with a covered porch on each.
- A large central living room with a fireplace and built-in shelving overlooks the rear porch and offers three beautiful French doors to access it.
- An exciting sun room makes a great eating or sitting area and also extends to the porch. The adjoining kitchen features a functional work island, lots of counter space and access to the front porch.
- The oversized master bedroom has a private bath with a dual-sink vanity and a secluded toilet, plus a private door to the rear porch.
- The stairway to the upper level sits between the living room and the sun room, accessible from both rooms.
- Two bedrooms, a full bath and a versatile playroom occupy this level. The playroom and the balcony hall overlook the living room and sun room below.

REAR VIEW

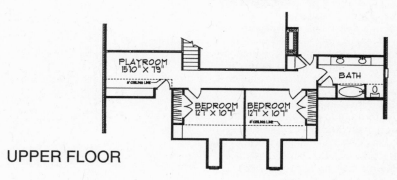

UPPER FLOOR

Plan J-91096

Bedrooms: 4	Baths: 3
Living Area:	
Upper floor	767 sq. ft.
Main floor	2,069 sq. ft.
Total Living Area:	**2,836 sq. ft.**
Standard basement	2,069 sq. ft.
Garage	550 sq. ft.
Exterior Wall Framing:	2x4

Foundation Options:

Standard basement
Crawlspace
Slab

(All plans can be built with your choice of foundation and framing. A generic conversion diagram is available. See order form.)

BLUEPRINT PRICE CODE:	D

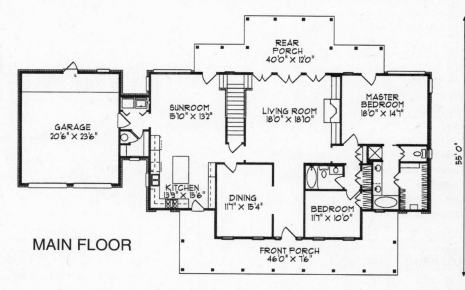

MAIN FLOOR

Rustic Luxury

- Cedar shingle siding and stone walls add a rustic flavor to this luxurious home.
- The glassed entry opens to a columned, two-story tiled foyer. To the left is the secluded living room, which is highlighted by a 15-ft.-high vaulted ceiling and plenty of tall windows.
- The centrally located family room shares the foyer's 17-ft. ceiling and boasts a handsome fireplace embraced by windows. Nestled between two columns, an entertainment center also serves as a pass-through to the kitchen.
- The spacious kitchen features an island cooktop, a corner pantry and a sunny breakfast nook with access to a backyard deck through sliding doors.
- Accented by a 15-ft. vaulted ceiling, the master bedroom shows off a private brick patio and a huge walk-in closet. The full bath includes dual pedestal sinks plus an incredible spa tub and shower encircled by a glass-block wall.
- A railed stairway leads to the upper floor where a lovely view into the family room can be enjoyed. This floor houses three more bedrooms and a full bath.

Plan B-93027

Bedrooms: 4	Baths: 2½
Living Area:	
Upper floor	591 sq. ft.
Main floor	1,750 sq. ft.
Total Living Area:	**2,341 sq. ft.**
Standard basement	1,750 sq. ft.
Garage	455 sq. ft.
Exterior Wall Framing:	2x4

Foundation Options:

Standard basement

(All plans can be built with your choice of foundation and framing. A generic conversion diagram is available. See order form.)

BLUEPRINT PRICE CODE:	C

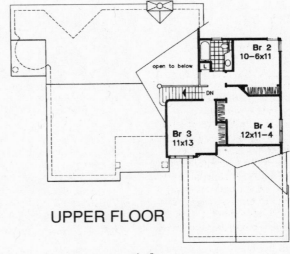

UPPER FLOOR

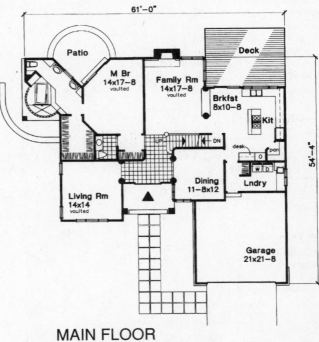

MAIN FLOOR

ORDER BLUEPRINTS ANYTIME!
CALL TOLL-FREE 1-800-820-1283

Plan B-93027

PRICES AND DETAILS
ON PAGES 2-5

381

Shaped for Scenic Sites

- An inviting conversation pit with a soaring fireplace and an 18-ft., 9-in. vaulted ceiling is the centerpiece of this unique octagonal home. It's topped by a window-ringed cupola that lets in plenty of sunlight.
- The kitchen opens directly into the large living- and dining-room combo. The kitchen's angled snack bar acts as a handy serving counter; sliding glass doors open to a covered deck. Lots of windows offer you a spectacular view.

- The master bedroom has its own bath, plenty of closet space and private access to the deck. Two secondary bedrooms share a full hall bath.
- All upper-floor rooms, unless noted otherwise, feature roomy 12-ft. vaulted ceilings for added spaciousness.
- The lower floor includes a roomy lounge or recreation room that's the perfect place to relax after a day of skiing or hiking. It could easily hold a pool table.
- A fourth bedroom with easy access to a full bath is opposite the lounge.
- The entry has two roomy closets for storing skis and jackets or other recreational equipment.

Plan AX-97833

Bedrooms: 4	**Baths:** 3

Living Area:

Upper floor	1,203 sq. ft.
Main floor	875 sq. ft.
Total Living Area:	**2,078 sq. ft.**
Carport	185 sq. ft.
Storage	25 sq. ft.
Exterior Wall Framing:	2x4

Foundation Options:

Slab

(All plans can be built with your choice of foundation and framing. A generic conversion diagram is available. See order form.)

BLUEPRINT PRICE CODE: C

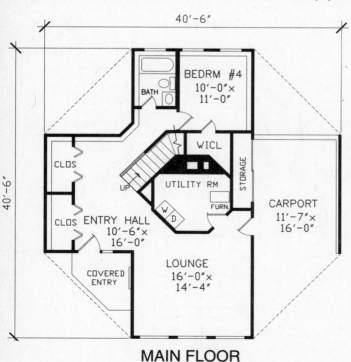

MAIN FLOOR

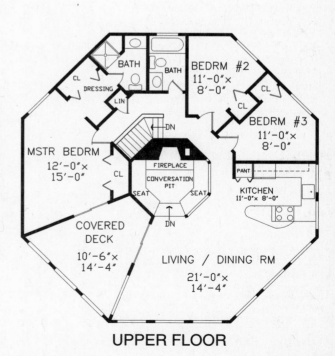

UPPER FLOOR

Plan AX-97833

PRICES AND DETAILS
ON PAGES 2-5

Five-Bedroom Farmhouse

- This five-bedroom farmhouse design offers the large or growing family five nice-sized bedrooms, including a private master suite on the main floor!
- The exterior of the home is embellished by shuttered windows and a winding, wraparound porch.
- The main entry opens directly into the living room, where a handsome fireplace is the focal point.
- The bright bayed dining room boasts a built-in china cabinet and sliding glass doors to the porch.
- The kitchen provides an island eating bar and a pantry closet as it unfolds to the breakfast nook and family room.
- The family room features a warm fireplace and sliding glass doors to a large backyard patio.
- The master suite showcases a private bath with a bayed spa tub and a separate shower. A French door in the bedroom opens to the porch.
- Four more bedrooms and two baths are housed on the upper floor. One bedroom features a private bath.

Plan U-93-210

Bedrooms: 5	Baths: 3½
Living Area:	
Upper floor	1,006 sq. ft.
Main floor	1,555 sq. ft.
Total Living Area:	**2,561 sq. ft.**
Standard basement	1,555 sq. ft.
Garage	514 sq. ft.
Exterior Wall Framing:	2x6

Foundation Options:

Standard basement

(All plans can be built with your choice of foundation and framing. A generic conversion diagram is available. See order form.)

BLUEPRINT PRICE CODE: D

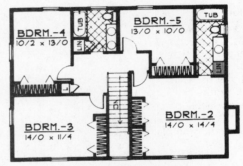

UPPER FLOOR

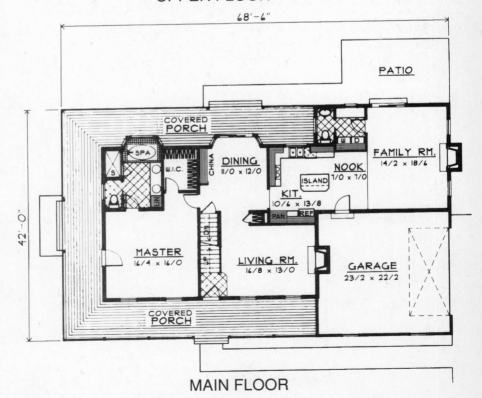

MAIN FLOOR

ORDER BLUEPRINTS ANYTIME!
CALL TOLL-FREE 1-800-820-1283

Plan U-93-210

PRICES AND DETAILS
ON PAGES 2-5

379

REAR VIEW

Double-Decker Does You Proud

- This exciting plan is for the family that wants a relationship with nature.
- The upper deck fans out over the lower deck, giving the home a beautifully layered multiple-use effectiveness.
- Corner glass walls accent the sunken, 14-ft.-high vaulted living room, inviting sunlight and breathtaking views to come inside with you!
- The U-shaped kitchen and bath are conveniently central to the main level.

The charming breakfast nook overlooks the dewy deck.
- A sewing/craft room makes space for the handcrafts and hobbies you always wanted to try.
- The dramatics continue as you climb stairs overlooking the living room.
- The master bedroom is a piece of work, with its private study, walk-in closet, dressing area, bath, and bay window. And the whole upper deck is all yours!
- Two more bedrooms share another bathroom at the front of the home.
- Finish this home with fieldstone accents, wood siding and cedar shakes for a one-of-a-kind gem in the rough.

Plan DD-2178	
Bedrooms: 3	**Baths:** 3
Living Area:	
Upper floor	994 sq. ft.
Main floor	1,174 sq. ft.
Total Living Area:	**2,168 sq. ft.**
Partial basement	815 sq. ft.
Carport	320 sq. ft.
Exterior Wall Framing:	2x4

Foundation Options:

Partial basement
Crawlspace
Slab

(All plans can be built with your choice of foundation and framing. A generic conversion diagram is available. See order form.)

BLUEPRINT PRICE CODE: **C**

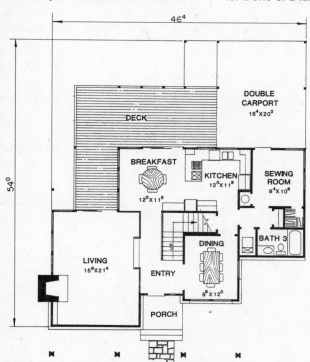

MAIN FLOOR

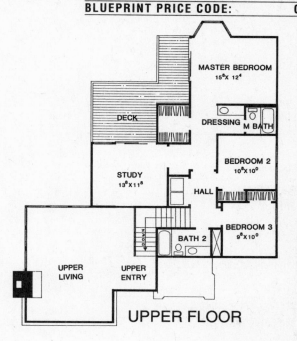

UPPER FLOOR

   ORDER BLUEPRINTS ANYTIME! CALL TOLL-FREE 1-800-820-1283   **Plan DD-2178**   *PRICES AND DETAILS ON PAGES 2-5*

Solarium Adds Sun and Fun!

- A large, south-facing solarium is beautifully incorporated into the sweeping roofline of this energy-efficient home.
- Adding sunny warmth in the winter months and lush, green foliage in the summer months, the luxurious solarium will instill a sparkling sense of fun into every season.
- The covered entry is protected from winds by an attractive wing wall.
- A two-story vestibule gives a dramatic greeting to guests, who'll get an immediate view into the sunken living room, with the dining room and solarium beyond.
- A large island workstation is at the center of the efficient kitchen. Nearby, the spacious family room boasts a handsome fireplace.
- Three bedrooms and a full bath are found on the upper floor, including the nicely equipped master suite.

Plan B-303

Bedrooms: 3	**Baths:** 2½
Living Area:	
Upper floor	837 sq. ft.
Main floor	1,055 sq. ft.
Solarium	280 sq. ft.
Total Living Area:	**2,172 sq. ft.**
Standard basement	1,055 sq. ft.
Garage	484 sq. ft.
Exterior Wall Framing:	2x4

Foundation Options:

Standard basement
(All plans can be built with your choice of foundation and framing. A generic conversion diagram is available. See order form.)

BLUEPRINT PRICE CODE: C

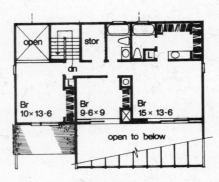

UPPER FLOOR

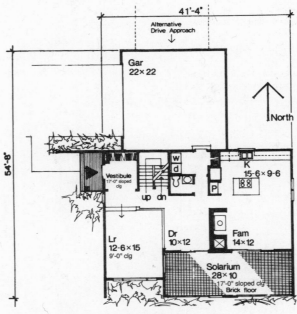

MAIN FLOOR

Clean Contemporary

- Sweeping rooflines with high, sparkling windows give the facade of this multi-level home a clean, contemporary look.
- Around back, plenty of glass and a neat sun space absorb the sun's energy and warmth on winter days.
- A protected entry opens to the dramatic living room, topped by a sloped ceiling and featuring a skylight, a rustic woodstove and a balcony overlooking the sun space below.
- Skylights brighten the U-shaped kitchen and the cheery breakfast nook, where sliding glass doors lead out to the expansive back deck.
- Secluded for privacy, the charming master suite includes a trio of closets, a private bath and sliding-glass-door access to the balcony.
- Downstairs, two good-sized bedrooms, the comfortable family room and the sun space share a full bath.

Plan AX-98266

Bedrooms: 3+	Baths: 2½
Living Area:	
Upper floor	261 sq. ft.
Main floor	1,192 sq. ft.
Daylight basement (finished)	665 sq. ft.
Sun space	132 sq. ft.
Total Living Area:	**2,250 sq. ft.**
Daylight basement (unfinished)	577 sq. ft.
Garage	451 sq. ft.
Exterior Wall Framing:	2x4

Foundation Options:

Daylight basement

(All plans can be built with your choice of foundation and framing. A generic conversion diagram is available. See order form.)

BLUEPRINT PRICE CODE:	C

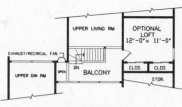

UPPER FLOOR

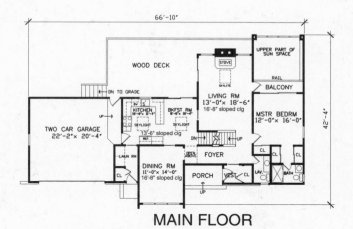

MAIN FLOOR

DAYLIGHT BASEMENT

REAR VIEW

Easy Living Every Day!

- You'll be able to feel the relaxed lifestyle each and every day in this easygoing two-story home.
- A deck at the entry is just one of four decks that help to merge the floor plan with the outdoors.
- Plenty of gathering space is available in the living room and the family room. Guests can cozy up to the living room's fireplace on cool nights; when the weather's warm, use the attached deck for a spicy summertime barbecue.
- The nearby kitchen is placed perfectly for serving hors d'oeuvres in the living areas or morning meals in the breakfast nook. A deck outside the nook is also accessible from the family room.
- Private and pleasant, the upper-floor master suite has its very own deck to add a special touch of romance. A skylighted walk-in closet and a secluded bath are other key features.
- Spacious walk-in closets are found in each of the two additional bedrooms.

Plan H-2099-1

Bedrooms: 3+	Baths: 2½
Living Area:	
Upper floor	1,210 sq. ft.
Main floor	1,180 sq. ft.
Daylight basement	1,087 sq. ft.
Total Living Area:	**3,477 sq. ft.**
Garage	460 sq. ft.
Exterior Wall Framing:	2x6

Foundation Options:

Daylight basement

(All plans can be built with your choice of foundation and framing. A generic conversion diagram is available. See order form.)

BLUEPRINT PRICE CODE: E

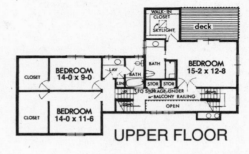

UPPER FLOOR

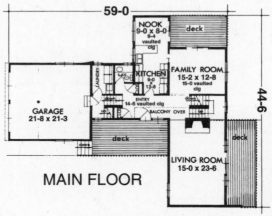

MAIN FLOOR

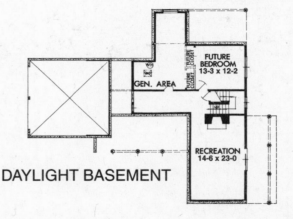

DAYLIGHT BASEMENT

ORDER BLUEPRINTS ANYTIME!
CALL TOLL-FREE 1-800-820-1283

Plan H-2099-1

PRICES AND DETAILS
ON PAGES 2-5

375

Instant Hit!

- Dignified country styling and an unusual, space-saving floor plan make this design an instant hit.
- A columned front porch leads to the cheerful entry, which is topped by an elegant, half-round window. The 18-ft. vaulted foyer presents a number of options for visiting family and friends.
- The living areas flow together smoothly, creating comfortable yet distinct spaces. French doors in the kitchen open to the covered rear porch.

- A bedroom or den also accesses the back porch. The main bath and the utility area are close to the living areas and to the garage entrance.
- Pure paradise exists in the dreamy master suite, offering a romantic fireplace, a luxurious private bath and a roomy walk-in closet.
- Unless otherwise specified, the main floor features 9-ft. ceilings.
- The upper floor includes a full bath, a loft and two good-sized bedrooms. Access your creative side to utilize the lengthy future space.

Plan J-91081

Bedrooms: 4+	Baths: 3
Living Area:	
Upper floor	872 sq. ft.
Main floor	1,645 sq. ft.
Future space	316 sq. ft.
Total Living Area:	**2,833 sq. ft.**
Standard basement	1,645 sq. ft.
Garage	491 sq. ft.
Exterior Wall Framing:	2x4

Foundation Options:

Standard basement
Crawlspace
Slab

(All plans can be built with your choice of foundation and framing. A generic conversion diagram is available. See order form.)

BLUEPRINT PRICE CODE: D

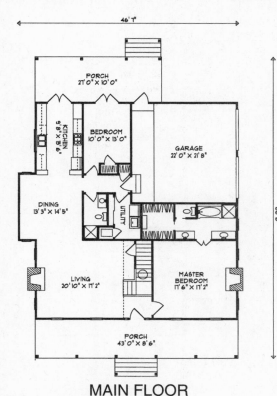

MAIN FLOOR

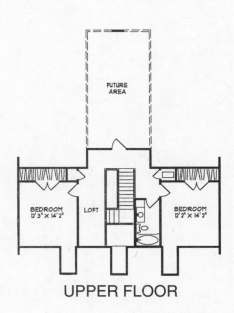

UPPER FLOOR

Plan J-91081

PRICES AND DETAILS
ON PAGES 2-5

Welcoming Country Style

- A columned and railed front porch highlights the facade of this home, creating an inviting country countenance.
- An overhead plant shelf adorns the two-story-high foyer. Flanking the foyer, the formal dining and living rooms are introduced by half-walls and columns.
- Straight ahead, a central fireplace anchors the family room, which is crowned by an 18-ft. vaulted ceiling. French doors flanking the fireplace open to a large backyard deck, which offers a nice spot for a refreshing backyard pool.

- A bow window provides great views from the breakfast nook adjoining the island kitchen. A handy pass-through nicely rounds out the area.
- Around the corner, a den flaunts a private bath, making it a good choice for an additional bedroom.
- The luxurious master bedroom boasts a half-circle sitting area and private deck access. The master bath enjoys a classy quarter-round tub, a separate shower and a walk-through closet.
- All main-floor rooms have 9-ft. ceilings unless otherwise noted.
- From the foyer, an elegant stairway leads up to two more bedrooms, each with a private bath and a built-in desk under a shuttered opening. A railed loft offers lovely views.

Plan B-94019

Bedrooms: 3+	Baths: 4½
Living Area:	
Upper floor	569 sq. ft.
Main floor	2,463 sq. ft.
Total Living Area:	**3,032 sq. ft.**
Basement	2,463 sq. ft.
Garage	717 sq. ft.
Exterior Wall Framing:	2x6

Foundation Options:

Daylight basement
Standard basement
(All plans can be built with your choice of foundation and framing. A generic conversion diagram is available. See order form.)

BLUEPRINT PRICE CODE:	E

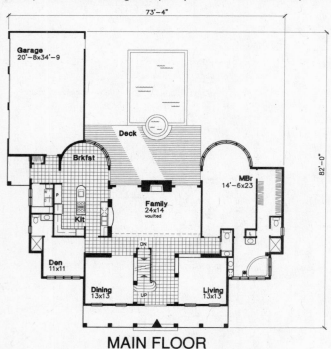

MAIN FLOOR

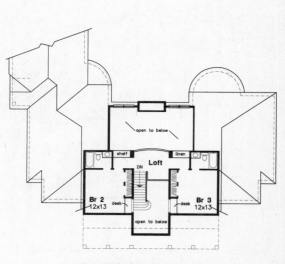

UPPER FLOOR

ORDER BLUEPRINTS ANYTIME!
CALL TOLL-FREE 1-800-820-1283

Plan B-94019

PRICES AND DETAILS
ON PAGES 2-5

373

Stairway to Paradise

- An open-railed stairway joins the heavenly interior spaces of this home. Abundant awe-inspiring views make this home the perfect choice for a wooded or mountainous setting.
- You'll breathe easier in the huge Great Room, which plays host to a gorgeous fireplace. The adjoining dining room offers French-door access to a sprawling wraparound deck that lets you get up close and personal with the wonders of the natural world. Fix a quick snack in the nearby kitchen.
- In the master suite you'll find sweet rest. Double doors introduce the sleeping chamber; the bath offers two sinks for comfort; for privacy, a pocket door shields the shower area.
- For the family's hobbyist or computer nut, a roomy loft provides a spot for weeknight relaxation.

Plan TS-9515	
Bedrooms: 3+	**Baths:** 2½
Living Area:	
Upper floor	664 sq. ft.
Main floor	1,418 sq. ft.
Total Living Area:	**2,082 sq. ft.**
Exterior Wall Framing:	2x6

Foundation Options:

Crawlspace
(All plans can be built with your choice of foundation and framing. A generic conversion diagram is available. See order form.)

BLUEPRINT PRICE CODE: C

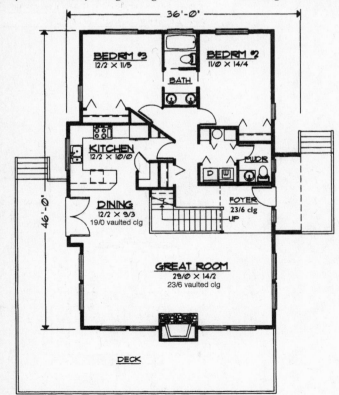

MAIN FLOOR

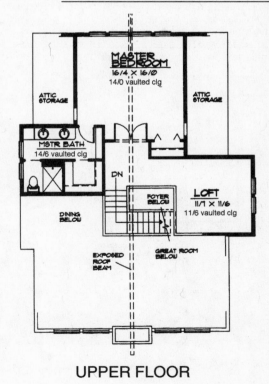

UPPER FLOOR

Plan TS-9515   *PRICES AND DETAILS*
ON PAGES 2-5

Surrounded by Shade

- Comfort reigns in this delightful domicile, which boasts a shaded veranda that nearly surrounds the home. There's enough room for a porch hammock! When it rains during the family reunion, the festivities can be moved to this glorious covered area.
- Inside, a fireplace-blessed living room joins seamlessly with the welcoming foyer. Opposite, the big dining room will hold the largest dinner parties.

- Your whole family can participate in meal preparation, since the kitchen and connecting breakfast room flow into each other. A French door gives veranda access.
- In the master bedroom, an atrium door offers private passage to the veranda. The private bath includes a bubbly tub, a separate shower and a planter for your lush greenery.
- Upstairs, two more bedrooms flank a peaceful sitting area. A large split bath features a dual-sink vanity.
- All rooms in the home are topped by airy 9-ft. ceilings, for added spaciousness.

Plan L-88-VB	
Bedrooms: 3	**Baths:** 2½
Living Area:	
Upper floor	751 sq. ft.
Main floor	1,308 sq. ft.
Total Living Area:	**2,059 sq. ft.**
Detached two-car garage	505 sq. ft.
Exterior Wall Framing:	2x4
Foundation Options:	

Slab
(All plans can be built with your choice of foundation and framing. A generic conversion diagram is available. See order form.)

BLUEPRINT PRICE CODE:	C

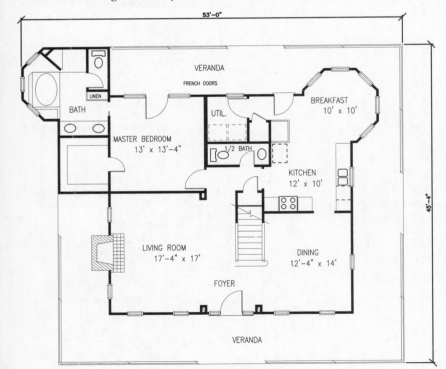

MAIN FLOOR

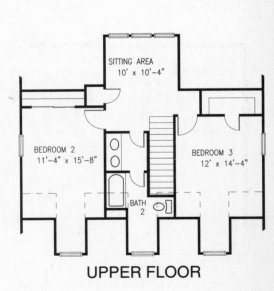

UPPER FLOOR

ORDER BLUEPRINTS ANYTIME!
CALL TOLL-FREE 1-800-820-1283

Plan L-88-VB

***PRICES AND DETAILS
ON PAGES 2-5***

371

Modern Multi-Level

- This contemporary multi-tiered design has living areas on three levels, making it perfect for a sloping lot.
- Just off the entry is the living room, which is brightened by a triple window arrangement that lets in lots of sun. The presence of a casual family room in the daylight basement allows you to reserve the living room for formal occasions.
- Up a short flight of stairs, the kitchen and dining area overlook the living room. A boxed-out window nook adds space to the kitchen; the dining room features sliding glass doors to a rear patio that's sure to be a favorite spot.
- The master suite has two closets and a private bath with a separate dressing area. The suite also boasts its own access to the patio.
- Two more bedrooms and another full bath round out the main floor.
- The daylight basement contains a family room with a fireplace to take the chill off winter nights. A nearby bonus room may be used as a bedroom.
- There's plenty of storage space on the lowest level of the home.

Plan B-7825	
Bedrooms: 3+	Baths: 3
Living Area:	
Main floor	1,440 sq. ft.
Daylight basement	723 sq. ft.
Total Living Area:	**2,163 sq. ft.**
Tuck-under garage	483 sq. ft.
Storage	295 sq. ft.
Exterior Wall Framing:	2x6
Foundation Options:	

Daylight basement
(All plans can be built with your choice of foundation and framing. A generic conversion diagram is available. See order form.)

BLUEPRINT PRICE CODE: C

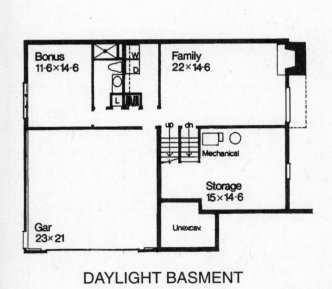

DAYLIGHT BASMENT

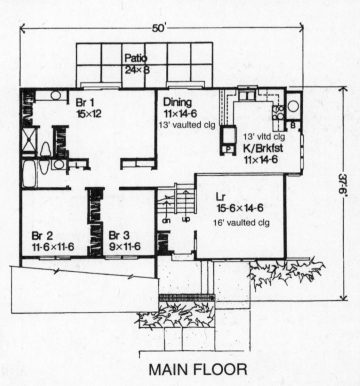

MAIN FLOOR

Plan B-7825

PRICES AND DETAILS
ON PAGES 2-5

True Grit

- Traditional Arts and Crafts styling gives this bungalow grit and durability. Its bold, low-maintenance exterior combines natural stone and cedar.
- Inside, skylights and transom windows produce plenty of natural light for the thoroughly modern floor plan.
- A lofty 20-ft.-high ceiling soars above the foyer and the Great Room, which are separated by a dramatic stone fireplace and a railed balcony.
- A decorative arch and wood-framed glass doors surround the Great Room's large-screen media center, while skylights overhead radiate sunshine.
- The functional island kitchen enjoys an ideal location near the busy living spaces and the laundry room. You won't miss your favorite TV show as you're washing the dinner dishes!
- A compartmentalized private bath with a delightful garden tub keeps the owners of this home pampered in style.
- Two more bedrooms share the upper floor with a versatile bonus room that can be tailored to your needs.

Plan GA-9601	
Bedrooms: 3+	**Baths:** 2½
Living Area:	
Upper floor	594 sq. ft.
Main floor	1,996 sq. ft.
Total Living Area:	**2,590 sq. ft.**
Unfinished bonus room	233 sq. ft.
Standard basement	1,996 sq. ft.
Garage	576 sq. ft.
Exterior Wall Framing:	2x6
Foundation Options:	

Standard basement
(All plans can be built with your choice of foundation and framing. A generic conversion diagram is available. See order form.)

BLUEPRINT PRICE CODE:	D

UPPER FLOOR

VIEW INTO GREAT ROOM

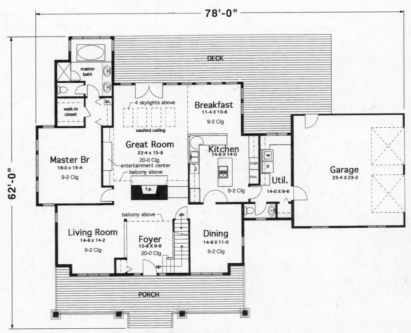

MAIN FLOOR

ORDER BLUEPRINTS ANYTIME!
CALL TOLL-FREE 1-800-820-1283

Plan GA-9601

PRICES AND DETAILS
ON PAGES 2-5

369

Plenty of Good Things

- The modest square footage of this ranch design offers maximum affordability, while plenty of exciting design features offer maximum livability.
- Covered main and secondary entries, a bay window and stone accents give exterior charm.
- The foyer opens to dramatic views into the living room and the dining room and rear yard straight ahead.
- The dining room has sliding-door access to the expansive rear deck, which wraps around the side to a front portico.
- The central kitchen serves the formal dining room and overlooks the sunny breakfast eating area, which also has sliding-door access to the deck.
- Three bedrooms and two full baths complete the main floor of the plan.
- The daylight basement floor plan includes a walkout family room with a fireplace, plus a fourth bedroom and third full bath.

Plan AX-7728-A

Bedrooms: 4	Baths: 3
Living Area:	
Main floor	1,653 sq. ft.
Daylight basement (finished)	641 sq. ft.
Total Living Area:	**2,294 sq. ft.**
Daylight basement (unfinished)	184 sq. ft.
Garage	500 sq. ft.
Exterior Wall Framing:	2x4

Foundation Options:

Daylight basement

(All plans can be built with your choice of foundation and framing. A generic conversion diagram is available. See order form.)

BLUEPRINT PRICE CODE: C

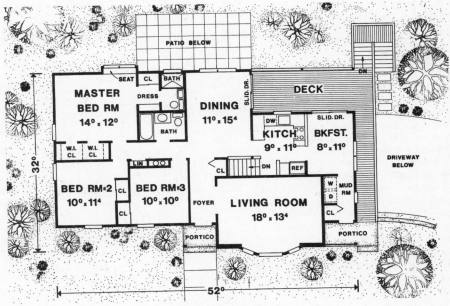

MAIN FLOOR

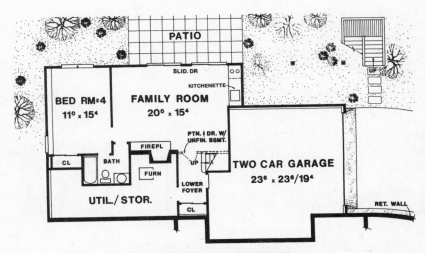

DAYLIGHT BASEMENT

ORDER BLUEPRINTS ANYTIME! **CALL TOLL-FREE 1-800-820-1283** Plan AX-7728-A **PRICES AND DETAILS ON PAGES 2-5**

Formal, Casual Entertainment

- This charming home has plenty of space for both formal and casual entertaining.
- On the main floor, the huge central living room will pamper your guests with an impressive fireplace, a wet bar and two sets of French doors that expand the room to a backyard porch.
- The large formal dining room hosts those special, sit-down dinners.
- There's still more space in the roomy island kitchen and breakfast nook to gather for snacks and conversation.
- For quiet evenings alone, the plush master suite offers pure relaxation! A romantic two-way fireplace between the bedroom and the bath serves as the focal point, yet the whirlpool garden tub is just as inviting.
- The main-floor rooms are enhanced by 10-ft. ceilings; the upper-floor rooms have 9-ft. ceilings.
- The kids' recreation time can be spent in the enormous game room on the upper floor. Private baths service each of the vaulted upper-floor bedrooms.

Plan L-105-VC

Bedrooms: 4+	Baths: 4
Living Area:	
Upper floor	1,077 sq. ft.
Main floor	1,995 sq. ft.
Total Living Area:	**3,072 sq. ft.**
Garage	529 sq. ft.
Storage	184 sq. ft.
Exterior Wall Framing:	2x4

Foundation Options:

Slab

(All plans can be built with your choice of foundation and framing. A generic conversion diagram is available. See order form.)

BLUEPRINT PRICE CODE: E

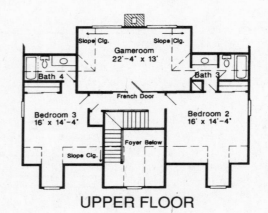

UPPER FLOOR

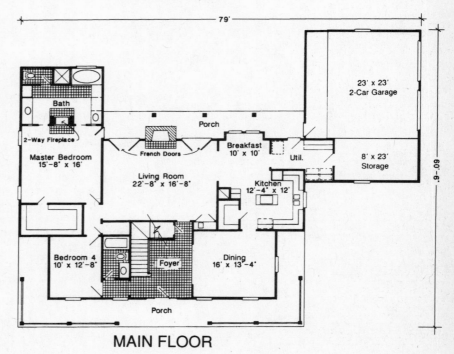

MAIN FLOOR

Hillside Plan, Room to Spare

- This modest-looking home contains a surprising amount of indoor and outdoor living space on two floors.
- From the covered porch, the foyer leads into a large living room with a fireplace. A cathedral ceiling that soars to a height of 16 ft. tops both spaces.
- The generous kitchen features a center work island and a walk-in pantry. The kitchen adjoins a handy breakfast area, which in turn opens onto a large deck or even an optional sun room.
- A mud room with a big closet is topped by a 9-ft., 3-in. ceiling for a spacious feeling uncommon in most utility areas.
- The master bedroom boasts a large walk-in closet and a private bath with a separate dressing area. Sliding glass doors open onto a secluded balcony.
- The lower level includes two bedrooms, a full bath, a big recreation room with a fireplace and plenty of space for you to finish as you see fit.

Plan AX-90308

Bedrooms: 5	Baths: 3
Living Area:	
Main floor	1,647 sq. ft.
Daylight basement (finished)	764 sq. ft.
Total Living Area:	**2,411 sq. ft.**
Daylight basement (unfinished)	883 sq. ft.
Garage	455 sq. ft.
Exterior Wall Framing:	2x4

Foundation Options:

Daylight basement

(All plans can be built with your choice of foundation and framing. A generic conversion diagram is available. See order form.)

BLUEPRINT PRICE CODE:	C

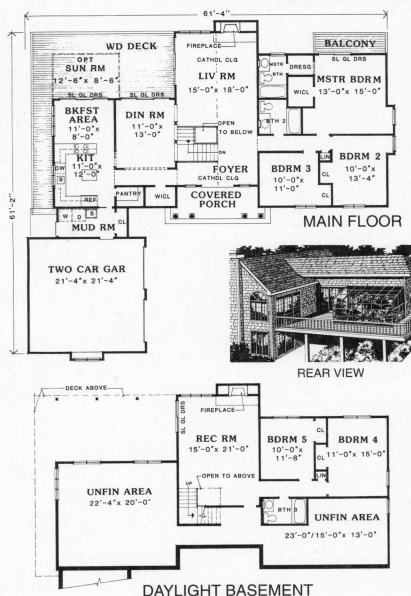

MAIN FLOOR

REAR VIEW

DAYLIGHT BASEMENT

Plan AX-90308

PRICES AND DETAILS
ON PAGES 2-5

Large Deck Wraps Home

- A full deck and an abundance of windows surround this exciting two-level contemporary.
- The brilliant living room boasts a huge fireplace and a 14-ft.-high cathedral ceiling, plus a stunning prow-shaped window wall.

- Skywalls brighten the island kitchen and the dining room. A pantry closet and laundry facilities are nearby.
- The master bedroom offers private access to the deck. The master bath includes a dual-sink vanity, a large tub and a separate shower. A roomy hall bath serves a second bedroom.
- A generous-sized family room, another full bath and two additional bedrooms share the lower level with a two-car garage and a shop area.

Plan NW-579

Bedrooms: 4	Baths: 3
Living Area:	
Main floor	1,707 sq. ft.
Daylight basement	901 sq. ft.
Total Living Area:	**2,608 sq. ft.**
Tuck-under garage	588 sq. ft.
Shop	162 sq. ft.
Exterior Wall Framing:	2x6

Foundation Options:

Daylight basement
(All plans can be built with your choice of foundation and framing. A generic conversion diagram is available. See order form.)

BLUEPRINT PRICE CODE:	D

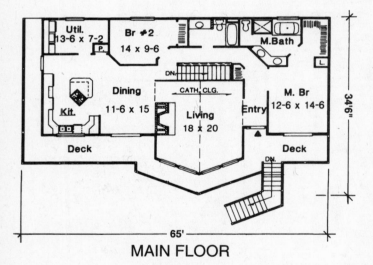

MAIN FLOOR

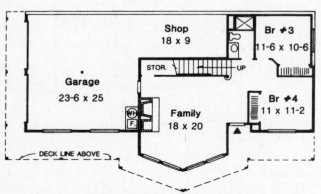

DAYLIGHT BASEMENT

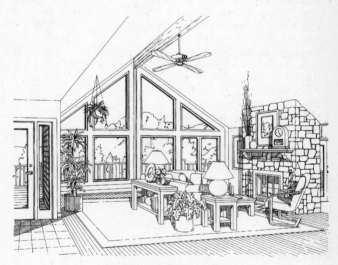

VIEW INTO LIVING ROOM

Practical Perfection

- This practical split-foyer home is perfect for a growing family, offering a huge lower area for a future recreation room.
- The vaulted foyer is brightened by transom and sidelight windows.
- A few steps up from the foyer, the living room boasts a cathedral ceiling and a fireplace flanked by angled window walls, one viewing to a large rear patio and the other to a wraparound deck.
- Sliding glass doors in the adjoining dining room open to the deck. The nearby eat-in kitchen also accesses the deck and has views of the front yard.
- The large master bedroom boasts a walk-in closet and a private bathroom with glass-block walls framing the designer shower. Two more main-floor bedrooms share a full bath.
- Downstairs, the future recreation room has space set aside for a wet bar and another fireplace. Laundry facilities and garage access are also convenient.

Plan AX-97511

Bedrooms: 3	Baths: 2
Living Area:	
Main floor	1,286 sq. ft.
Daylight basement (finished)	565 sq. ft.
Total Living Area:	**1,851 sq. ft.**
Utility room	140 sq. ft.
Tuck-under garage	400 sq. ft.
Exterior Wall Framing:	2x4

Foundation Options:

Daylight basement
(All plans can be built with your choice of foundation and framing. A generic conversion diagram is available. See order form.)

BLUEPRINT PRICE CODE:	**B**

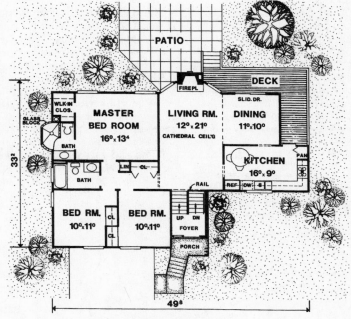

MAIN FLOOR

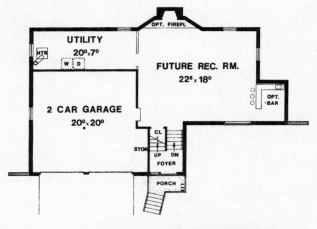

DAYLIGHT BASEMENT

ORDER BLUEPRINTS ANYTIME!
CALL TOLL-FREE 1-800-820-1283

Plan AX-97511

PRICES AND DETAILS
ON PAGES 2-5

Intimate Atmosphere

- Decorative wood detailing and an inviting covered front porch give this charming home its Victorian visage. In the front-facing living room, a bay window and a two-way fireplace create an intimate atmosphere.
- Sunlight floods the vast family room, which features an exciting media center wall and a French door that opens to a rear terrace.

- The kitchen provides lots of counter space and an eating bar for four that opens into the family room. Above the sink, a pair of windows drenches the scene with cheery natural light. The nearby laundry facilities let you perform multiple tasks at once.
- Upstairs, the master bedroom flaunts a cozy gas fireplace and two walk-in closets. A bayed area invites you to relax with a good book. The private bath includes a separate whirlpool tub and shower, plus a dual-sink vanity.
- Plans for a detached two-car garage are included with the blueprints.

Plan AHP-9560	
Bedrooms: 3	**Baths:** 2½
Living Area:	
Upper floor	778 sq. ft.
Main floor	780 sq. ft.
Total Living Area:	**1,558 sq. ft.**
Standard basement	780 sq. ft.
Garage (detached)	484 sq. ft.
Exterior Wall Framing:	2x4 or 2x6

Foundation Options:
Standard basement
Crawlspace
Slab
(All plans can be built with your choice of foundation and framing. A generic conversion diagram is available. See order form.)

BLUEPRINT PRICE CODE: B

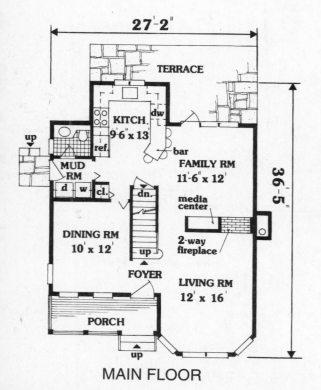

MAIN FLOOR

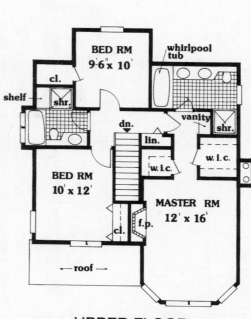

UPPER FLOOR

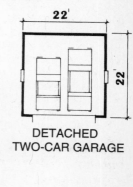

DETACHED
TWO-CAR GARAGE

Maximum Value

- This home was designed to provide maximum space at minimum cost, and it's loaded with the amenities you want: outdoor living spaces, separate formal and casual areas and much more!
- Note the feeling of spaciousness created by the 13-ft., 9-in. vaulted ceiling in the formal living room. Clerestory windows let in extra sunlight.
- The formal dining room resides in a quiet corner of the main floor. The nearby kitchen is positioned to easily serve the dining room without imposing on the elegant atmosphere you want to create here.
- One corner of the kitchen is reserved for a breakfast table. A half-wall offers a view into the adjoining family room.
- A fireplace is the focal point of the family room, where sliding glass doors access a backyard patio.
- Upstairs, the master suite enjoys its own full bath, a walk-in closet and a private deck accessed by sliding doors.
- Two more bedrooms share a full bath.
- The garage is large enough to hold a work bench for all your home projects.

Plan B-7609	
Bedrooms: 3	**Baths:** 2½
Living Area:	
Upper floor	854 sq. ft.
Main floor	1,017 sq. ft.
Total Living Area:	**1,871 sq. ft.**
Standard basement	1,017 sq. ft.
Garage	399 sq. ft.
Exterior Wall Framing:	2x4
Foundation Options:	

Standard basement

(All plans can be built with your choice of foundation and framing. A generic conversion diagram is available. See order form.)

| **BLUEPRINT PRICE CODE:** | B |

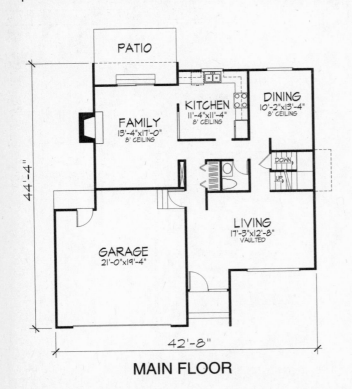

MAIN FLOOR

PATIO

KITCHEN 11'-4"x11'-4" 8' CEILING

DINING 10'-2"x13'-4" 8' CEILING

FAMILY 13'-4"x17'-0" 8' CEILING

DOWN UP

LIVING 17'-3"x12'-8" VAULTED

GARAGE 21'-0"x19'-4"

44'-4"

42'-8"

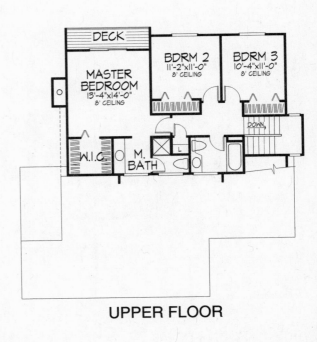

UPPER FLOOR

DECK

MASTER BEDROOM 13'-4"x14'-0" 8' CEILING

BDRM 2 11'-2"x11'-0" 8' CEILING

BDRM 3 10'-4"x11'-0" 8' CEILING

W.I.C.

M. BATH

DOWN

Plan B-7609

PRICES AND DETAILS ON PAGES 2-5

Meet Winter on Its Own Terms

- This earthy, low-profile design gives a grounded sense of domestic seclusion and solidity to your vacation dream.
- But come inside and feel the height inherent in the plan, from a sweeping spiral staircase to tall, sunny windows.
- Fireplaces in the living room and one of the upstairs bedrooms add to the home's rustic flavor.

- The main-floor bedroom has its own private bath and spacious closets.
- Bedrooms upstairs share easily accessible lavatories and plenty of closet space.
- You can store virtually anything under the home's steep eaves on both levels.
- The daylight basement has a full bath and a tuck-under garage.
- Plans suggest a solar heating option that puts a rear southern exposure to work for years of energy savings. Or install simple windows for passive-solar heat, plenty of natural light, and forest views.

Plans H-909-1 & -1A	
Bedrooms: 3	Baths: 2-3
Living Area:	
Upper floor	709 sq. ft.
Main floor	1,128 sq. ft.
Total Living Area:	**1,837 sq. ft.**
Daylight basement	1,016 sq. ft.
Garage (daylight basement only)	418 sq. ft.
Exterior Wall Framing:	2x4
Foundation Options:	**Plan #**
Daylight basement	H-909-1
Crawlspace	H-909-1A

(All plans can be built with your choice of foundation and framing. A generic conversion diagram is available. See order form.)

BLUEPRINT PRICE CODE: **B**

REAR VIEW

MAIN FLOOR

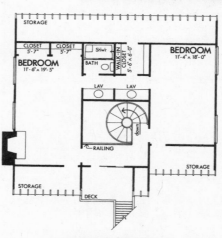

UPPER FLOOR

ORDER BLUEPRINTS ANYTIME!
CALL TOLL-FREE 1-800-820-1283

Plans H-909-1 & -1A

PRICES AND DETAILS
ON PAGES 2-5

361

REAR VIEW

A World Away

- This expanded A-frame getaway is the perfect place to separate yourself from the hustle and bustle of the workaday world any time you want.
- The design, which appears rather simple when viewed from the outside, contains a surprising amount of interior space.
- Double doors usher you into the entry, where a spiral staircase ascends to the upper floor. The back wall of the stone fireplace acts as a divider between the entry and the living room, giving the former space a separate, intimate feel.
- A window wall in the living room offers spectacular views. Sliding glass doors lead out to a large sun deck.
- An 11-ft snack and serving bar fronts the kitchen, which features a pantry closet.
- The main-floor master bedroom includes a walk-in closet and private access to a full bath.
- On the upper floor, a loft overlooks the living room and has a view through the window wall to the scenery beyond.
- Two roomy bedrooms flank the loft.

Plan DD-1026

Bedrooms: 3	Baths: 1½
Living Area:	
Upper floor	843 sq. ft.
Main floor	1,026 sq. ft.
Total Living Area:	**1,869 sq. ft.**
Standard basement	1,026 sq. ft.
Exterior Wall Framing:	2x4

Foundation Options:
Standard basement
Crawlspace
Slab
(All plans can be built with your choice of foundation and framing. A generic conversion diagram is available. See order form.)

BLUEPRINT PRICE CODE: B

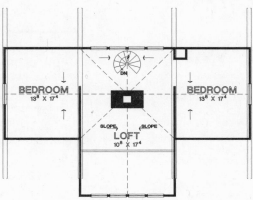

UPPER FLOOR

FRONT OF HOME

MAIN FLOOR

Exciting Fireplace Wall

- This exciting and versatile design would serve nicely as a starter, retirement or vacation home.
- Its rustic exterior shows off a dramatic roofline, an expansive sun deck and vertical pine siding.
- Off the portico is a handy storage area for tools and recreation or lawn equipment. The adjoining foyer area houses coat and laundry closets.
- The galley kitchen is well designed and includes a functional snack bar open to the Great Room.
- A soaring 17-ft.-high ceiling embraces the spacious Great Room, which overlooks the large side deck through two sets of sliding glass doors. The exciting fireplace wall is uniquely intersected by the upper-floor balcony.
- A nice-sized bedroom and a full bath complete the main floor, while two more bedrooms and another bath occupy the upper floor.

Plan AX-98271

Bedrooms: 3	Baths: 2
Living Area:	
Upper floor	452 sq. ft.
Main floor	967 sq. ft.
Total Living Area:	**1,419 sq. ft.**
Standard basement	967 sq. ft.
Exterior Wall Framing:	2x4

Foundation Options:

Standard basement
Crawlspace
Slab

(All plans can be built with your choice of foundation and framing. A generic conversion diagram is available. See order form.)

BLUEPRINT PRICE CODE: A

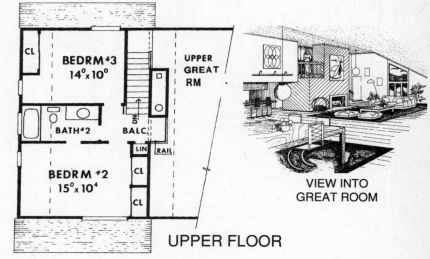

UPPER FLOOR

VIEW INTO GREAT ROOM

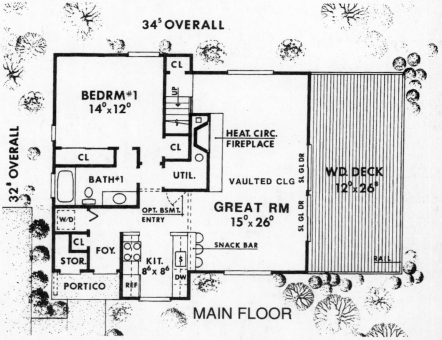

MAIN FLOOR

REAR VIEW

Nice Views from Above

- Don't let obstructions keep you from enjoying the view you love. This home puts the living space on the top floor, to maximize the beach or mountain view!
- A spacious deck not only capitalizes on the views, but also expands living and dining room space for entertaining.
- The kitchen is enhanced by a garden window for small potted flowers.

- A living-room fireplace warms the heart of the home, while three sliding glass doors light the area.
- A great private deck off the family room makes the perfect spot to relax and enjoy some peace and quiet over your coffee and the morning paper.
- The master bedroom enjoys its own private bath, ample closet space and sun-washed windows.
- Order this plan with a basement, and get another bedroom and bath, plus a recreation room that's easily converted to a hobby shop or workout room.

Plans H-933-1 & -1A

Bedrooms: 3+	Baths: 2½-3½
Living Area:	
Upper floor	863 sq. ft.
Main floor	784 sq. ft.
Standard basement	784 sq. ft.
Total Living Area:	**1,647/2,431 sq. ft.**
Garage	462 sq. ft.
Exterior Wall Framing:	2x6
Foundation Options:	**Plan #**
Standard basement	H-933-1
Crawlspace	H-933-1A

(All plans can be built with your choice of foundation and framing. A generic conversion diagram is available. See order form.)

BLUEPRINT PRICE CODE:	**B/C**

BASEMENT

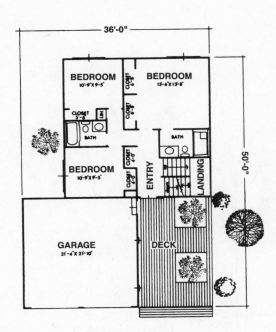

MAIN FLOOR

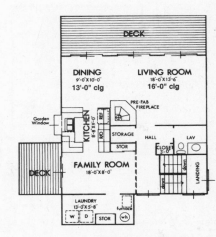

UPPER FLOOR

Plans H-933-1 & -1A

PRICES AND DETAILS
ON PAGES 2-5

A Fairy-Tale Life

- With its fancy-cut shingles and rustic stone exterior, this home is the perfect setting for a modern-day fairy tale.
- Inside, a 20-ft. vaulted ceiling crowns the living and dining rooms, where a shared fireplace sets an intimate tone for both dinner and conversation. Swing open the dining room's French doors to let soft, summer breezes drift in.
- Sunlight pours into the kitchen through a stunning wall of windows. Plenty of space is available to enjoy morning coffee, bagels and fresh fruit.

- The garage includes a handy shop with cabinets for the family do-it-yourselfer.
- Dramatic double doors under a plant shelf introduce the master bedroom, where a 17-ft. vaulted ceiling soars above, and sliding glass doors allow a private escape to the outdoors. A garden tub under skylights will pamper you after a long day away from home.
- Unless otherwise noted, every main-floor room includes a 9-ft. ceiling.
- Upstairs, two additional bedrooms share a unique split bath, which lets kids prepare for school at the same time, with privacy and without waiting.

Plan B-94027

Bedrooms: 3	**Baths:** 2½

Living Area:	
Upper floor	476 sq. ft.
Main floor	1,191 sq. ft.
Total Living Area:	**1,667 sq. ft.**
Standard basement	1,191 sq. ft.
Garage and shop	624 sq. ft.

Exterior Wall Framing:	2x4

Foundation Options:

Standard basement
(All plans can be built with your choice of foundation and framing. A generic conversion diagram is available. See order form.)

BLUEPRINT PRICE CODE:	**B**

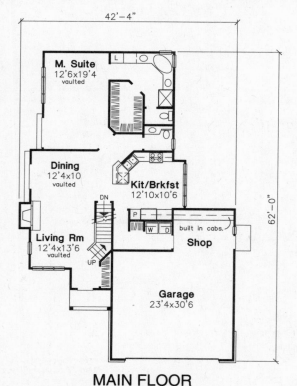

MAIN FLOOR

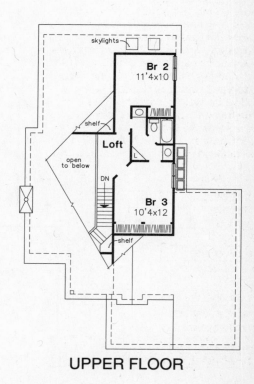

UPPER FLOOR

ORDER BLUEPRINTS ANYTIME!
CALL TOLL-FREE 1-800-820-1283

Plan B-94027

PRICES AND DETAILS
ON PAGES 2-5

357

Country Comfort

- From the covered front porch to the comfortable, open living spaces inside, this home offers an inviting warmth.
- The well-designed floor plan starts with a spacious formal living room that unfolds to a bright dining area, where sliding glass doors expand the area to the outdoors. A handy serving counter allows you to set up a buffet line when you're entertaining or hosting a big family get-together.
- An efficient, U-shaped kitchen adjoins the dining room and includes a convenient pantry closet.
- Everybody will enjoy the large family room and its appealing fireplace. A trio of windows allows a view of the backyard, so you can watch the snow fall while toasting marshmallows!
- The home's sleeping quarters are located on the upper floor. The master bedroom has a private bath; the two secondary bedrooms share a hall bath.

Plan GL-16792

Bedrooms: 3	Baths: 2½
Living Area:	
Upper floor	757 sq. ft.
Main floor	922 sq. ft.
Total Living Area:	**1,679 sq. ft.**
Standard basement	922 sq. ft.
Garage	462 sq. ft.
Exterior Wall Framing:	**2x6**

Foundation Options:

Standard basement

(All plans can be built with your choice of foundation and framing. A generic conversion diagram is available. See order form.)

BLUEPRINT PRICE CODE: **B**

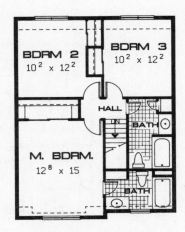

UPPER FLOOR

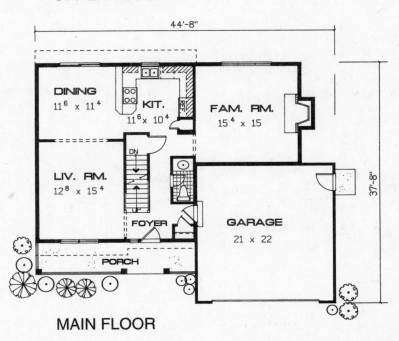

MAIN FLOOR

Growth Potential

- Ideal for the small or starter family, this two-story design stretches your dollar and your potential space.
- Vaulted ceilings at the entry and living room lend volume to the economical square footage.
- Behind the stairway to the upper floor, the open kitchen and dining area combination expands to a backyard patio. An island snack counter, a pantry and a laundry closet offer function.
- Separated from the other bedrooms, the main-floor master bedroom includes a walk-in closet and a skylighted bath that can also be accessed from the home's main entry.
- A dramatic view is offered from the upper-floor balcony, which connects two generous-sized secondary bedrooms and a skylighted central bath.
- Storage space is readily convertible to an extra bedroom, if desired.

Plan S-12883

Bedrooms: 3	Baths: 2
Living Area:	
Upper floor	578 sq. ft.
Main floor	1,021 sq. ft.
Total Living Area:	**1,599 sq. ft.**
Standard basement	1,021 sq. ft.
Garage and shop	462 sq. ft.
Exterior Wall Framing:	2x6

Foundation Options:

Standard basement

Crawlspace

Slab

(All plans can be built with your choice of foundation and framing. A generic conversion diagram is available. See order form.)

BLUEPRINT PRICE CODE: B

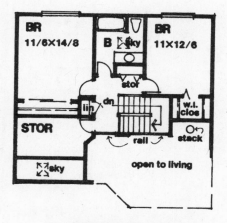

UPPER FLOOR

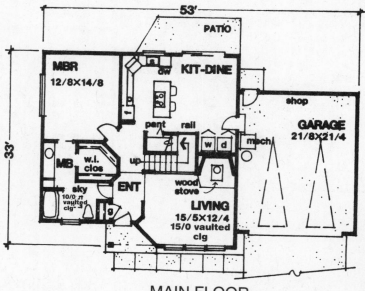

MAIN FLOOR

Striking Lines, Visual Appeal

- Numerous intersecting lines in this striking contemporary home create visual appeal both inside and out.
- In from the front porch, the bright entry is a veritable hub, offering an abundance of options for visiting guests.
- Rays of sunshine illuminate the long hallway that connects the entry with the living room, drawing friends and family to this cheery space. An attractive woodstove increases the appeal.

- The walk-through kitchen easily serves the all-purpose dining room. Access to the wraparound deck through sliding glass doors increases your options for entertainment.
- A short hallway connects two nicely sized bedrooms with a full bath.
- Upstairs, the master bedroom is private yet maintains an open feeling. Among its highlights are a huge walk-in closet, a separate bath and dressing area and a balcony overlooking the living room.
- The daylight basement plan includes a huge recreation and game area with a full wall of windows, a full bath and a general-use room.

Plan H-947-M1B	
Bedrooms: 3	**Baths:** 2-3
Living Area:	
Upper floor	516 sq. ft.
Main floor	1,162 sq. ft.
Daylight basement	966 sq. ft.
Total Living Area:	**2,644 sq. ft.**
Garage	280 sq. ft.
Exterior Wall Framing:	2x6
Foundation Options:	

Daylight basement
(All plans can be built with your choice of foundation and framing. A generic conversion diagram is available. See order form.)

BLUEPRINT PRICE CODE:	D

DAYLIGHT BASEMENT

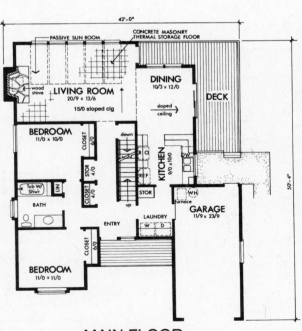

MAIN FLOOR

UPPER FLOOR

Plan H-947-M1B

PRICES AND DETAILS ON PAGES 2-5

Affordable Luxuries

- An attractive stucco exterior introduces a cozy home packed with luxuries.
- A bright French door in the covered entry opens into the dramatic foyer, which is highlighted by a soaring 17-ft. vaulted ceiling.
- An inviting archway, a half-wall and a 10-ft., 3-in. vaulted ceiling frame the sunken living/dining room.
- A large family room with a cozy fireplace highlights the casual living

areas at the rear of the home. A wall of windows brightens both the family room and the breakfast nook. A French door opens to a backyard patio.
- In the kitchen, a neat island with a cooktop and an eating bar for three makes casual and formal meals a snap.
- Upstairs, a sun-drenched loft with a skylight looks over the foyer below.
- A peaceful sitting area in the master suite serves as a welcome refuge after harried days. The compartmentalized master bath boasts a bright skylight and a dual-sink vanity.
- Two more good-sized bedrooms share a second full bath.

Plan S-70794	
Bedrooms: 3	**Baths:** 2½
Living Area:	
Upper floor	714 sq. ft.
Main floor	947 sq. ft.
Total Living Area:	**1,661 sq. ft.**
Partial basement	608 sq. ft.
Garage	451 sq. ft.
Exterior Wall Framing:	2x6

Foundation Options:
Partial basement
Crawlspace
Slab
(All plans can be built with your choice of foundation and framing. A generic conversion diagram is available. See order form.)

BLUEPRINT PRICE CODE:	B

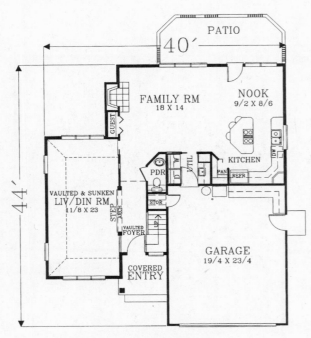

MAIN FLOOR

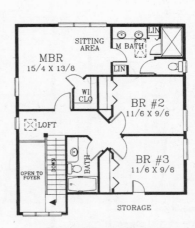

UPPER FLOOR

Charming and Space-Efficient

- Perfectly sized for a narrow lot, this charming modern cottage boasts space efficiency and affordability.
- The inviting raised foyer steps down into the two-story-high vaulted living room. Brightened by lovely front windows with high transoms, the living room also offers a handsome fireplace.
- The adjoining dining area is highlighted by overhead plant shelves and features sliding glass doors to a backyard deck.
- The cleverly designed, space-saving kitchen includes a stylish snack counter and a pantry shelf.
- Enhanced by a bright boxed-out bay with a window seat, the master bedroom also has a roomy walk-in closet and private bathroom access.
- Upstairs, a second bedroom and a loft or third bedroom share a convenient full bath with a linen closet.

Plan B-133-8510

Bedrooms: 2+	Baths: 2
Living Area:	
Upper floor	405 sq. ft.
Main floor	891 sq. ft.
Total Living Area:	**1,296 sq. ft.**
Standard basement	891 sq. ft.
Garage	402 sq. ft.
Exterior Wall Framing:	2x4

Foundation Options:

Standard basement

(All plans can be built with your choice of foundation and framing. A generic conversion diagram is available. See order form.)

BLUEPRINT PRICE CODE: A

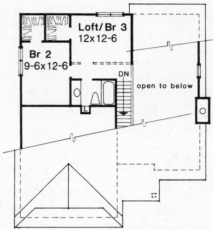

UPPER FLOOR

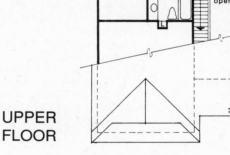

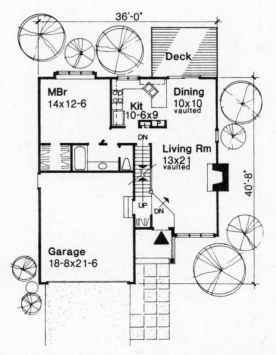

MAIN FLOOR

Sun-fully Appealing

- This appealing energy-efficient design uses a southern-exposure window wall to take advantage of the sun, and to give a dramatic look to the exterior.
- A trellis beam and built-in insulated shutters or drapes for summer shade, a concrete slab and trombe wall to store the sun's heat, full insulation and some earth berming all increase the home's energy and cost savings.

- Past the 11-ft., 3-in. vaulted entry, you'll find a living/dining room that's perfect for entertaining. It features a dramatic 13-ft. cathedral ceiling that adds a nice spaciousness to the area.
- With two closets and access to a full-sized bath, the master suite does a fine job of providing a nice dose of luxury for its occupants.
- A second bedroom and a den/studio make up the upper floor. If needed, the den can serve as a third bedroom. A full bath is just a few steps away.
- Included in the blueprints are plans for both a one- and a two-car garage.

Plan AX-98055	
Bedrooms: 2+	**Baths:** 2
Living Area:	
Upper floor	582 sq. ft.
Main floor	1,008 sq. ft.
Total Living Area:	**1,590 sq. ft.**
One-car garage	288 sq. ft.
Two-car garage	480 sq. ft.
Exterior Wall Framing:	2x6
Foundation Options:	
Slab	
(All plans can be built with your choice of foundation and framing. A generic conversion diagram is available. See order form.)	
BLUEPRINT PRICE CODE:	**B**

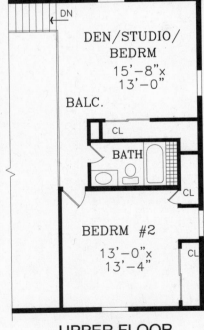

MAIN FLOOR

28'-0" OVERALL

36'-0" OVERALL

CL
UP
DN
MSTR BEDRM
12'-4"x 13'-6"
LIVING RM/ DINING RM
25'-0"x 13'-4"
CL
CL
BATH
D   W
PANT   REF
KITCHEN
12'-4"x 13'-4"
DW
CL
DN   DN

UPPER FLOOR

DN
DEN/STUDIO/ BEDRM
15'-8"x 13'-0"
BALC.
CL
BATH
CL
BEDRM #2
13'-0"x 13'-4"
CL

ORDER BLUEPRINTS ANYTIME!
CALL TOLL-FREE 1-800-820-1283

Plan AX-98055

PRICES AND DETAILS
ON PAGES 2-5

351

Stylish Family Living

- Stylish family living is the objective in this three-bedroom home.
- The vaulted entry opens to a vaulted living room with a fireplace and a corner window. Decorative columns define the adjoining formal dining room.
- A handy serving counter extends to the dining room from the kitchen and breakfast area. Patio dining is accessible from the kitchen.
- Elegant double doors open to the secluded master suite on the main floor.
- Two extra bedrooms and a second full bath share the upper floor with unfinished storage space.

Plan B-91004

Bedrooms: 3	Baths: 2½
Living Area:	
Upper floor	490 sq. ft.
Main floor	1,112 sq. ft.
Total Living Area:	**1,602 sq. ft.**
Standard basement	1,112 sq. ft.
Garage	374 sq. ft.
Exterior Wall Framing:	2x8

Foundation Options:

Standard basement

(All plans can be built with your choice of foundation and framing. A generic conversion diagram is available. See order form.)

BLUEPRINT PRICE CODE:	B

UPPER FLOOR

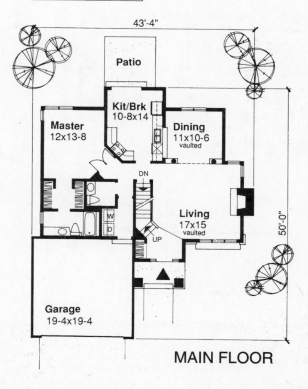

MAIN FLOOR

Plan B-91004

PRICES AND DETAILS
ON PAGES 2-5

Timeless Touches

- Classical touches like a rustic stone fireplace and paned windows give this home a quality look that never goes out of style.
- Past the rock kneewall and planters that border the covered front porch, the sidelighted entry steps down into the living room. This space is topped by an airy vaulted ceiling and is presided over by a fireplace that acts as a divider between the adjoining dining room.

- The kitchen extends a handy serving counter into a corner of the family room that may be used as a casual dining area. A convenient half-bath that serves the main floor is nearby.
- A big backyard deck accessible from the family room and the dining room becomes outdoor living space in warm weather. It's large enough to host a barbecue and invite the neighbors.
- The master suite is topped by a vaulted ceiling and includes a private bath with a walk-in closet.
- Two other bedrooms share a full bath. The connecting balcony hallway has a linen cabinet built into a half-wall.

Plan B-88004	
Bedrooms: 3	**Baths:** 2½
Living Area:	
Upper floor	777 sq. ft.
Main floor	888 sq. ft.
Total Living Area:	**1,665 sq. ft.**
Standard basement	888 sq. ft.
Garage	407 sq. ft.
Exterior Wall Framing:	2x4
Foundation Options:	

Standard basement
(All plans can be built with your choice of foundation and framing. A generic conversion diagram is available. See order form.)

BLUEPRINT PRICE CODE:	**B**

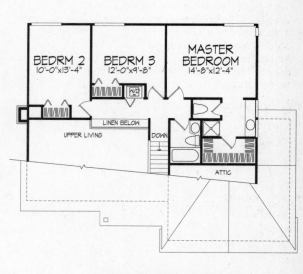

MAIN FLOOR

DECK

DINING
10'-0"x12'-0"

KIT
9'-4"x11'-4"

FAMILY
17'-8"x13'-8"

LIVING
19'-8"x13'-4"
17'-0" vaulted clg

GARAGE
20'-0"x20'-4"

DOWN

DOWN

UP

34'-8"

43'-4"

UPPER FLOOR

BEDRM 2
10'-0"x13'-4"

BEDRM 3
12'-0"x9'-8"

MASTER BEDROOM
14'-8"x12'-4"

LINEN BELOW

UPPER LIVING

DOWN

ATTIC

ORDER BLUEPRINTS ANYTIME!
CALL TOLL-FREE 1-800-820-1283

Plan B-88004

PRICES AND DETAILS
ON PAGES 2-5

349

Planned for Open Living

- A sweeping roofline, vertical wood siding and a covered entry porch give this design its curb appeal.
- A cutout in the roof of the entry porch lets in sunshine, while brick columns accentuate the sidelighted front door.
- The vaulted foyer leads to the center of the plan—a spacious Great Room that lends openness to the home. Brightened by four tall windows and warmed by a corner woodstove, the Great Room is wonderful for special occasions as well as for everyday living.
- A half-wall separates the Great Room from the dining room and the adjoining kitchen. The dining room has access to a backyard deck or patio; the kitchen boasts an island cooktop and snack bar.
- An open stairway leads to the upper floor, which offers three bedrooms, plus an optional bonus space.

Plan LRD-9292

Bedrooms: 3	Baths: 2½
Living Area:	
Upper floor	801 sq. ft.
Main floor	939 sq. ft.
Bonus room	214 sq. ft.
Total Living Area:	**1,954 sq. ft.**
Basement	869 sq. ft.
Garage	448 sq. ft.
Exterior Wall Framing:	2x6

Foundation Options:

Daylight basement

Standard basement

Crawlspace

(All plans can be built with your choice of foundation and framing. A generic conversion diagram is available. See order form.)

BLUEPRINT PRICE CODE: B

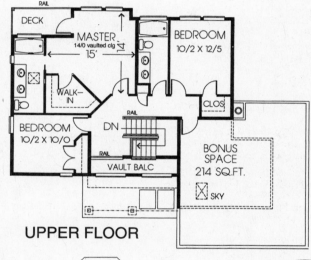

UPPER FLOOR

MAIN FLOOR

Plan LRD-9292

Wonderful Walk-Out

- A scenic or sloping lot can be accommodated nicely with this wonderful walk-out design. The optional daylight basement can be finished now if funds allow, or later as the family grows.
- The main floor includes a dramatic vaulted Great Room with windows on three sides and a two-story masonry woodstove on the other.
- The main-floor master suite features a vaulted ceiling, a window seat, a walk-in closet and a private skylighted bath.

Plans H-94003-A & -B

Bedrooms: 3+	Baths: 2½-3½
Living Area:	
Upper floor	560 sq. ft.
Main floor	1,340 sq. ft.
Daylight basement	1,340 sq. ft.
Total Living Area:	**1,900/3,240 sq. ft.**
Garage	496 sq. ft.
Exterior Wall Framing:	2x6
Foundation Options:	Plan #
Daylight basement	H-94003-B
Crawlspace	H-94003-A

(All plans can be built with your choice of foundation and framing. A generic conversion diagram is available. See order form.)

BLUEPRINT PRICE CODE: B/E

DAYLIGHT BASEMENT

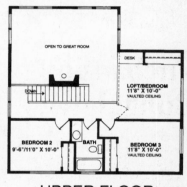

UPPER FLOOR

MAIN FLOOR

REAR VIEW

Enchanting Bungalow

- A charming stone and stucco exterior introduces this enchanting bungalow.
- Inside, a half-wall and a 17-ft. vaulted ceiling frame the living room, while sunlight pours in through a boxed-out window topped by an arched transom.
- A fireplace is shared with the dining room, where a cozy fire sets an intimate mood during dinner parties. The dining room also includes sliding glass doors

to a backyard deck, where you'll love to visit on summer evenings.
- The adjacent kitchen is roomy enough to place a breakfast table next to a bright bank of windows. An angled serving bar makes entertaining easy.
- The master bedroom is located on the main floor for added privacy. The room includes a walk-in closet and a convenient private bath.
- On the upper floor, two secondary bedrooms with walk-in closets share a centrally located hall bath. A railed media loft is ideal for TV watching, home computing and quiet reading.

Plan B-94026

Bedrooms: 3+	**Baths:** 2½
Living Area:	
Upper floor	645 sq. ft.
Main floor	1,055 sq. ft.
Total Living Area:	**1,700 sq. ft.**
Standard basement	1,055 sq. ft.
Garage	380 sq. ft.
Exterior Wall Framing:	2x4

Foundation Options:

Standard basement
(All plans can be built with your choice of foundation and framing. A generic conversion diagram is available. See order form.)

BLUEPRINT PRICE CODE:	B

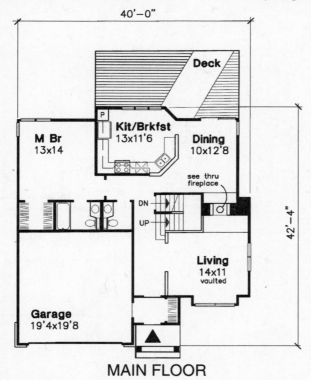

MAIN FLOOR

UPPER FLOOR

A Natural Complement

- Its rustic facade and woodsy appeal make this home a wonderful complement to nature's backdrop.
- A wide entry deck leads past a handy ski storage area to the 17-ft.-high foyer.
- To the right, the walk-through kitchen offers outdoor access.
- The adjoining dining room is brightened by a large window. A handsome fireplace warms the enormous living room, where two sets of sliding glass doors open to a sprawling deck in the backyard.
- Two large bedrooms down the hall share a full bath.
- On the upper floor, the luxurious master bedroom boasts sliding glass doors to a romantic balcony.
- Past a dressing area, the master bath is enhanced by a refreshing whirlpool tub and a separate shower. A balcony offers beautiful morning views.
- An unfinished attic space flaunts lots of natural light and could be used as a future bedroom, if desired.

Plan AX-8382

Bedrooms: 3+	**Baths:** 2

Living Area:

Upper floor	419 sq. ft.
Main floor	1,144 sq. ft.
Total Living Area:	**1,563 sq. ft.**
Unfinished attic (future bedroom)	235 sq. ft.
Standard basement	1,144 sq. ft.
Exterior Wall Framing:	2x4

Foundation Options:

Standard basement
Crawlspace
Slab

(All plans can be built with your choice of foundation and framing. A generic conversion diagram is available. See order form.)

BLUEPRINT PRICE CODE:	**B**

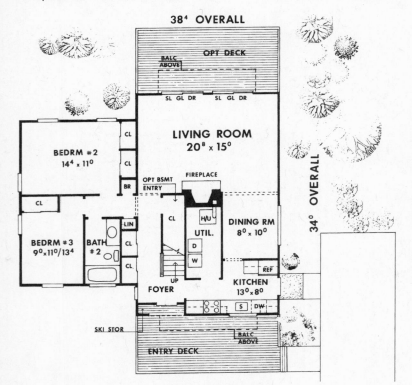

MAIN FLOOR

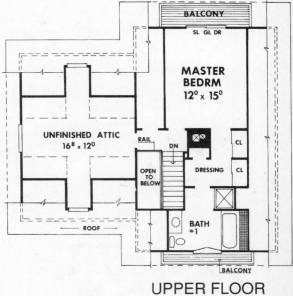

UPPER FLOOR

Contemporary Retreat

- Clean rooflines and a simple yet stylish facade distinguish this contemporary home, an ideal design for a mountain or woodsy retreat.
- Adjacent to the entry, the U-shaped kitchen is fully equipped to serve you and your family. A handy breakfast bar, a cheery windowed sink and ample cupboard and counter space are among its highlights.

- Experience the comfort and appeal of the spacious living room. A soaring fireplace flanked by bright windows warms the entire expanse. A sliding glass door provides access to the large rear deck. Relax in the shade of the covered section, or step out further to bask in the sun.
- Two good-sized bedrooms with built-in storage space are separated by a centrally located bath.
- Upstairs, the master bedroom is full of excitement. Open to the living room below, it includes a private bath and its own viewing deck.

Plan H-912-1S	
Bedrooms: 3	**Baths:** 2
Living Area:	
Upper floor	379 sq. ft.
Main floor	940 sq. ft.
Total Living Area:	**1,319 sq. ft.**
Garage	246 sq. ft.
Exterior Wall Framing:	2x4
Foundation Options:	
Crawlspace	

(All plans can be built with your choice of foundation and framing. A generic conversion diagram is available. See order form.)

BLUEPRINT PRICE CODE:	A

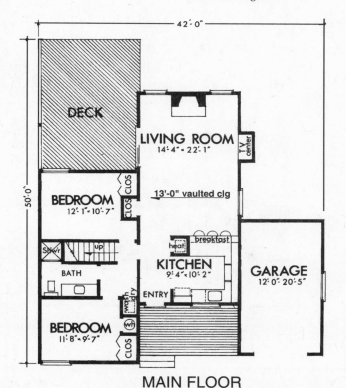

MAIN FLOOR

UPPER FLOOR

Plan H-912-1S

PRICES AND DETAILS
ON PAGES 2-5

Active Design

- The practical design of this plan allows room for your family's daytime activities while providing a secondary emphasis on sleeping accommodations.
- The flexible balcony room is the highlight of the upper floor. Not only does it provide dramatic views of the living room and dining room, but it provides an adaptable living space for family parties, children's sleepovers, and other overflow occasions.
- Warmed by a cozy fireplace, the living room is the main focus of the main floor. Its central location finds it flanked by a large bedroom and a fabulous formal dining room.
- A convenient kitchen arrangement makes dining room service easy, while a handy laundry closet off the kitchen helps consolidate the daily chores.
- A massive wraparound deck that provides abundant outdoor living space completes this well-rounded, comfortable dwelling that's sure to meet your family's needs.

Plans H-805-6 & -6A

Bedrooms: 2	Baths: 2
Living Area:	
Upper floor	504 sq. ft.
Main floor	1,063 sq. ft.
Total Living Area:	**1,567 sq. ft.**
Standard basement	1,063 sq. ft.
Carport	233 sq. ft.
Storage	20 sq. ft.
Exterior Wall Framing:	2x4

Foundation Options:

Standard basement

(All plans can be built with your choice of foundation and framing. A generic conversion diagram is available. See order form.)

BLUEPRINT PRICE CODE: B

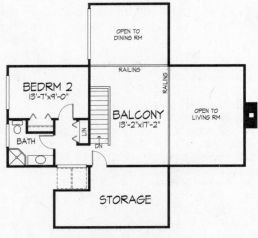

UPPER FLOOR

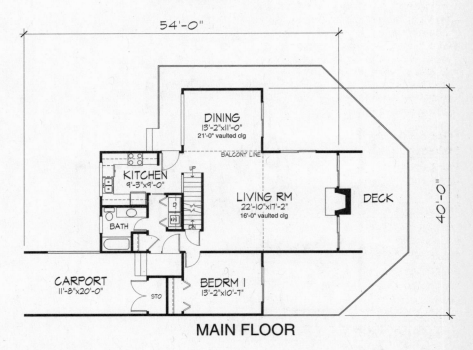

MAIN FLOOR

ORDER BLUEPRINTS ANYTIME!
CALL TOLL-FREE 1-800-820-1283

Plans H-805-6 & -6A

**PRICES AND DETAILS
ON PAGES 2-5**

343

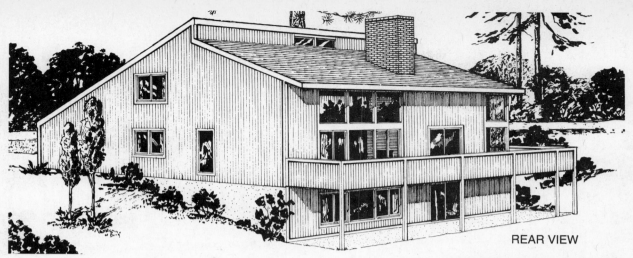

REAR VIEW

FRONT VIEW

Narrow-Lot Luxury

- This striking design takes into consideration your desire for luxury, as well as your need for a home to fit the lot of your choice—no matter its size.
- The comfortable entry hall leads straight ahead to the expansive living areas. Separated by a freestanding fireplace, the living room and dining room host any sort of gathering with ease.
- A wall of windows in the living room allows spectacular views to the outside, and nearby sliding glass doors to the wraparound deck invite you to catch a breath of fresh air.
- Adjacent to the dining room, the walk-through kitchen is conveniently near the laundry room.
- The main-floor bedroom provides a much-needed measure of privacy.
- Upstairs, two more bedrooms share another full bath. Wood railings in each room overlook the dining room and living room below.

Plans H-939-1 & -1A

Bedrooms: 3	Baths: 2
Living Area:	
Upper floor	627 sq. ft.
Main floor	1,168 sq. ft.
Total Living Area:	**1,795 sq. ft.**
Daylight basement	1,168 sq. ft.
Garage	460 sq. ft.
Exterior Wall Framing:	2x6
Foundation Options:	**Plan #**
Daylight basement	H-939-1
Crawlspace	H-939-1A
(All plans can be built with your choice of foundation and framing. A generic conversion diagram is available. See order form.)	
BLUEPRINT PRICE CODE:	**B**

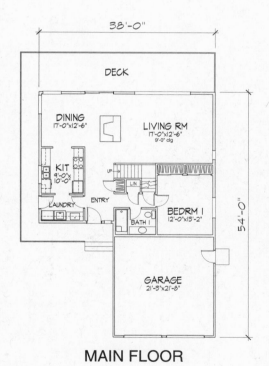

MAIN FLOOR

UPPER FLOOR

Plans H-939-1 & -1A

PRICES AND DETAILS ON PAGES 2-5

Quality Family Space

- This well-planned design makes the most of a small lot and still has space for four good-sized bedrooms.
- Off the raised entry, the living room is enhanced by a 17-ft.-high vaulted ceiling that is open to an upper-floor balcony. A handsome fireplace is flanked by built-in shelves, while a large boxed-out window allows in plenty of light.
- The formal dining room flows from the living room and expands to a rear deck.
- The kitchen is centrally located and open to the breakfast area and family room. A pass-through makes service to the dining room easy as well.
- A pantry, a coat closet and a powder room are conveniently located near the entrance from the two-car garage.
- All four bedrooms are housed on the upper floor and serviced by two full baths. The master bedroom boasts a partially vaulted ceiling, a private bath and a large walk-in closet.

Plan B-117-8506

Bedrooms: 4	Baths: 2½
Living Area:	
Upper floor	915 sq. ft.
Main floor	994 sq. ft.
Total Living Area:	**1,909 sq. ft.**
Standard basement	994 sq. ft.
Garage	505 sq. ft.
Exterior Wall Framing:	2x4

Foundation Options:

Standard basement
(All plans can be built with your choice of foundation and framing. A generic conversion diagram is available. See order form.)

BLUEPRINT PRICE CODE: B

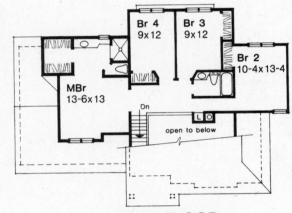

UPPER FLOOR

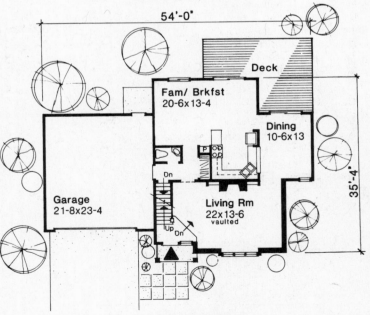

MAIN FLOOR

ORDER BLUEPRINTS ANYTIME!
CALL TOLL-FREE 1-800-820-1283

Plan B-117-8506

PRICES AND DETAILS
ON PAGES 2-5

341

Soaring Wings Accent Plan

- The soaring, wing-like roof of this plan is a striking eye-catcher, and the cross-shaped floor plan offers abundant windows and sensible traffic patterns.
- The central, sunken conversation pit is defined by a massive stone fireplace and is open to the dining area at the right and the living area, which opens to a huge wraparound deck.

- The rear arm of the cross is devoted to an efficient arrangement of kitchen, bath and laundry areas. A pair of windows lends cheer to the kitchen, where you'll find lots of elbow room.
- A bedroom with two closets and sliding glass doors that access the deck completes the main floor.
- The upper floor includes another bedroom and a second full bath, plus a balcony area that may be used as additional sleeping space. Other possible uses include a library or studio overlooking the living room below.

Plans H-805-4 & -4A	
Bedrooms: 2+	Baths: 2
Living Area:	
Upper floor	513 sq. ft.
Main floor	1,028 sq. ft.
Total Living Area:	**1,541 sq. ft.**
Standard basement	1,028 sq. ft.
Carport	231 sq. ft.
Storage	66 sq. ft.
Exterior Wall Framing:	2x4
Foundation Options:	**Plan #**
Standard basement	H-805-4
Crawlspace	H-805-4A

(All plans can be built with your choice of foundation and framing. A generic conversion diagram is available. See order form.)

BLUEPRINT PRICE CODE:	**B**

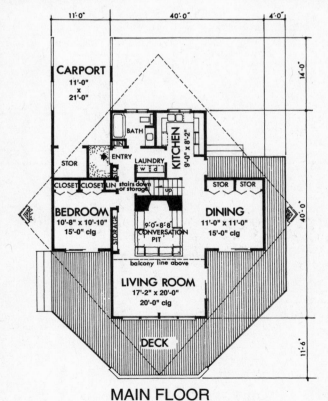

MAIN FLOOR

UPPER FLOOR

Plans H-805-4 & -4A

REAR VIEW

Log-Cabin Feel

- A simple, relaxing log-cabin feel is created in this design with wood siding over conventional wall construction.
- The large Great Room is anchored by a fireplace and topped by a 17-ft. vaulted ceiling. A window seat occupies one end of the room; on the other end, an open-railed stairway ascends to the upper floor.
- The kitchen includes enough space for a casual dining table, with a view over a half-wall into the main living area.
- The main-floor master bedroom boasts plenty of closet space and private access to a full bath.
- Upstairs, a balcony hallway that looks down on the Great Room leads to another full bath and a bedroom with a woodstove and its own deck. A nearby bedroom may be converted to a den.
- An optional screened porch provides a pleasant indoor/outdoor living area. The adjoining garage has plenty of storage.

Plan AX-8162-A

Bedrooms: 3	Baths: 2
Living Area:	
Upper floor	544 sq. ft.
Main floor	952 sq. ft.
Total Living Area:	**1,496 sq. ft.**
Standard basement	952 sq. ft.
Screened porch (optional)	271 sq. ft.
Garage	366 sq. ft.
Storage	84 sq. ft.
Exterior Wall Framing:	2x4

Foundation Options:

Standard basement
Slab

(All plans can be built with your choice of foundation and framing. A generic conversion diagram is available. See order form.)

BLUEPRINT PRICE CODE:	A

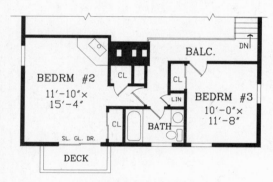

UPPER FLOOR

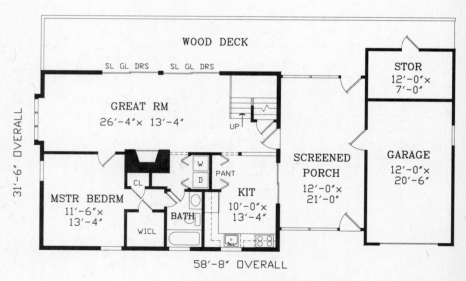

MAIN FLOOR

ORDER BLUEPRINTS ANYTIME!
CALL TOLL-FREE 1-800-820-1283

Plan AX-8162-A

PRICES AND DETAILS
ON PAGES 2-5

339

REAR VIEW

Indoor/Outdoor Advantage

- Great for a lake, weekend or permanent residence, this unique three-bedroom home utilizes every bit of living area to its advantage.
- An enormous living room spans the entire width of the floor plan and creates striking appeal and volume for the home. Sliding glass doors flank a handsome fireplace.

- A dining area and breakfast bar adjoin the living room and unfold to the kitchen. A doorway closes off a neat laundry room, utility room and mudroom combination, which accesses the two-car garage.
- One bedroom is located on the main floor; it has two closets and close proximity to the central bath.
- Another full bath serves the two upper-floor bedrooms, which are connected by a dramatic balcony overlook. High clerestory windows bring in sunlight from the outdoors.

Plans H-926-1 & -1A	
Bedrooms: 3	**Baths:** 2
Living Area:	
Upper floor	650 sq. ft.
Main floor	1,024 sq. ft.
Total Living Area:	**1,674 sq. ft.**
Daylight basement	1,024 sq. ft.
Garage	462 sq. ft.
Exterior Wall Framing:	2x6
Foundation Options:	**Plan #**
Daylight basement	H-926-1
Crawlspace	H-926-1A

(All plans can be built with your choice of foundation and framing. A generic conversion diagram is available. See order form.)

BLUEPRINT PRICE CODE:	**B**

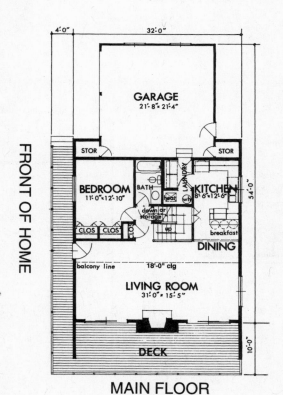

MAIN FLOOR

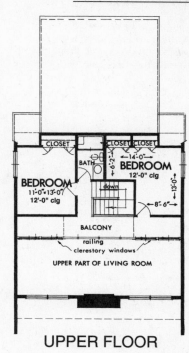

UPPER FLOOR

ORDER BLUEPRINTS ANYTIME! CALL TOLL-FREE 1-800-820-1283 **Plans H-926-1 & -1A** *PRICES AND DETAILS ON PAGES 2-5*

Openly Elegant

- Openness is the theme in this affordable story-and-a-half design, with its many windows, high ceilings and expansive entertaining area. A rugged stone exterior gives the home a country look with a touch of elegance.
- A lovely, free-standing staircase is immediately visible from the entryway. Beyond that is the spacious living room, with its massive fireplace. The adjoining bayed dining room features access to a rear patio. Both rooms enjoy a sloped ceiling and spectacular outdoor views.
- The U-shaped kitchen easily serves the dining area and is close to the garage for easy grocery transport.
- Two quiet bedrooms share a full bath in the sleeping wing of the main floor.
- The secluded master suite on the upper floor includes a large walk-in closet, a striking vaulted ceiling and a gorgeous Palladian window. The stairway landing offers a view of the living areas below.

Plan DD-1338	
Bedrooms: 3	**Baths:** 2
Living Area:	
Upper floor	358 sq. ft.
Main floor	1,022 sq. ft.
Total Living Area:	**1,380 sq. ft.**
Standard basement	1,022 sq. ft.
Garage	425 sq. ft.
Exterior Wall Framing:	2x4
Foundation Options:	
Standard basement	
Crawlspace	
Slab	

(All plans can be built with your choice of foundation and framing. A generic conversion diagram is available. See order form.)

BLUEPRINT PRICE CODE:	A

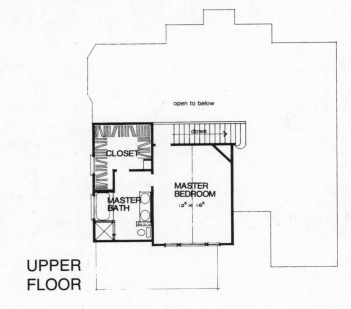

UPPER FLOOR

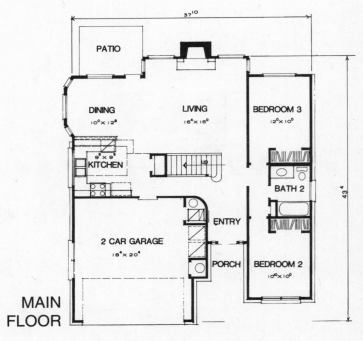

MAIN FLOOR

ORDER BLUEPRINTS ANYTIME!
CALL TOLL-FREE 1-800-820-1283

Plan DD-1338

PRICES AND DETAILS
ON PAGES 2-5

337

More than Meets the Eye

- With ample living space as well as a few hidden surprises, this one-story contemporary design is more than meets the eye.
- Spindled half-walls accentuate the entry, adding visual appeal to both the living and the dining rooms. Together these two rooms provide a wonderful space for entertaining guests.

- A peek through the kitchen door reveals the huge family room, the perfect spot for casual time at the end of the day. A sliding glass door allows you to step outside for a game of catch before dinner.
- Clerestory windows illuminate the balcony area that overlooks the family room. Use this space as a home office, hobby/game room or extra bedroom.
- The sleeping quarters are located across the home. The two front-facing bedrooms have charming window seats. A laundry closet stands nearby.

Plan H-3702-1A	
Bedrooms: 3+	**Baths:** 2
Living Area:	
Upper floor	250 sq. ft.
Main floor	1,633 sq. ft.
Total Living Area:	**1,883 sq. ft.**
Garage	405 sq. ft.
Exterior Wall Framing:	2x4

Foundation Options:

Crawlspace
(All plans can be built with your choice of foundation and framing. A generic conversion diagram is available. See order form.)

BLUEPRINT PRICE CODE:	**B**

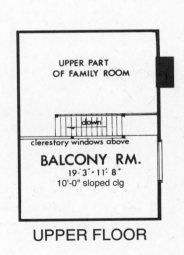

UPPER FLOOR

Upper part of family room — BALCONY RM. 19'-3" × 11'-8" 10'-0" sloped clg — clerestory windows above — down

MAIN FLOOR

- CLOSET
- BEDROOM 15'-0" × 12'-0"
- BATH
- BATH
- LAUNDRY
- LIN
- BEDROOM 12'-1" × 10'-2"
- CLOSET
- BEDROOM 10'-0" × 10'-2"
- CLOSET
- wdw. seat
- wdw. seat
- LIVING ROOM 14'-1" × 19'-5"
- KITCHEN 10'-2" × 12'-0"
- FAMILY ROOM 19'-3" × 12'-0" 14'-0" clg
- up
- STOR
- wh / heat
- ENTRY
- DINING 10'-2" × 14'-11"
- GARAGE 19'-3" × 21'-0"

60'-0"
37'-4"

Plan H-3702-1A

PRICES AND DETAILS ON PAGES 2-5

Bright, Indoor Sun Garden

- An indoor sun garden accessible from the back porch is the highlight of this Victorian-style farmhouse design. Grow exotic, hothouse plants all year round!
- Past the wraparound railed porch, the entry opens to a living room with a beamed volume ceiling and a fireplace that is the room's centerpiece.
- The dining room and the kitchen have views into the sun garden through multiple windows. The kitchen is fronted by a snack bar, and just around the corner is a utility room with enough space for a Deepfreeze™.
- The main-floor master suite boasts a boxed-out sitting area. Double doors access the private bath, which includes separate vanities and a walk-in closet. A door opens to a walled courtyard.
- Two good-sized secondary bedrooms are on the upper floor. Both feature plenty of closet space; the rooms share a full bath.
- The blueprints for this design include plans for a two-car detached garage.

Plan E-1814

Bedrooms: 3	Baths: 2
Living Area:	
Upper floor	576 sq. ft.
Main floor	1,251 sq. ft.
Sun garden	80 sq. ft.
Total Living Area:	**1,907 sq. ft.**
Detached garage and storage	540 sq. ft.
Exterior Wall Framing:	2x6

Foundation Options:

Crawlspace
Slab
(All plans can be built with your choice of foundation and framing. A generic conversion diagram is available. See order form.)

BLUEPRINT PRICE CODE: B

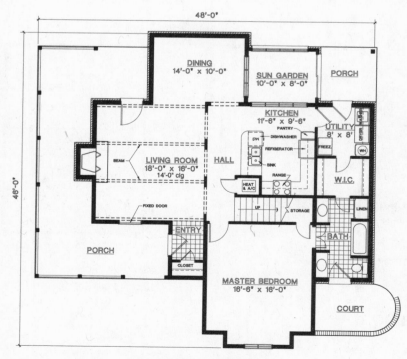

MAIN FLOOR

UPPER FLOOR

ORDER BLUEPRINTS ANYTIME!
CALL TOLL-FREE 1-800-820-1283

Plan E-1814

**PRICES AND DETAILS
ON PAGES 2-5**

335

Geometric Appeal

- With striking lines and fascinating angles, this home demonstrates the appealing aspects of geometry.
- In from the covered front porch, the entry accesses all parts of the home. Living and sleeping areas are zoned for privacy.
- The U-shaped kitchen boasts a windowed sink and a breakfast bar shared with the adjacent dining room.
- To the rear of the home, the living room is topped by a stunning 14½-ft. sloped ceiling. A large window and sliding glass doors to the rear deck enhance the feeling of bright spaciousness.
- The rear-facing bedroom also enjoys access to the deck, while the front bedroom features a charming boxed-out window seat. They share a full bath.
- Upstairs, a large bedroom loft overlooks the living room and could double as a recreation room.

Plans H-922-1 & -1A

Bedrooms: 3	Baths: 2
Living Area:	
Upper floor	461 sq. ft.
Main floor	1,001 sq. ft.
Total Living Area:	**1,462 sq. ft.**
Daylight basement	1,001 sq. ft.
Garage	313 sq. ft.
Exterior Wall Framing:	2x6

Foundation Options:

Daylight basement
Crawlspace

(All plans can be built with your choice of foundation and framing. A generic conversion diagram is available. See order form.)

BLUEPRINT PRICE CODE:	A

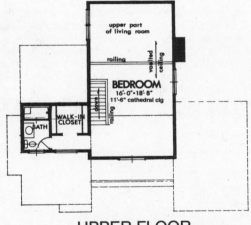

UPPER FLOOR

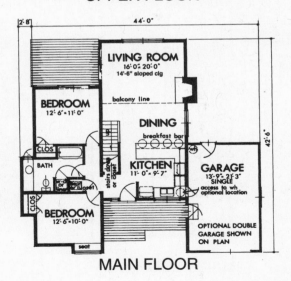

MAIN FLOOR

REAR VIEW

Bold Multi-Level

- This contemporary design features living spaces on five levels, vaulted ceilings and sharp exterior angles for a bold look in any setting.
- The entryway has a view up through the main staircase to the floor above. Nearby is a bedroom with two closets and easy access to a full bath.
- Short flights of stairs in two places access the main floor. Here, a vaulted ceiling soars above the living room and the dining area. A fireplace straddles the two rooms, providing warmth for the

entire space. The adjoining kitchen opens into a generous utility room.
- Sliding glass doors flank the fireplace, leading out to a large backyard deck that envelops the main-floor living area and offers panoramic views.
- Continuing upward, the main staircase ends in a balcony landing that connects two more bedrooms and a full bath.
- Up a short flight of stairs from the upper landing is an open loft suitable for use as a study or a fourth bedroom. It looks over the dining and living area below.
- A daylight basement with access to the backyard underlies the main floor.

Plan H-910-1

Bedrooms: 3+	Baths: 2
Living Area:	
Upper floor	674 sq. ft.
Main floor	1,117 sq. ft.
Total Living Area:	**1,791 sq. ft.**
Partial daylight basement	467 sq. ft.
Garage	392 sq. ft.
Storage	53 sq. ft.
Exterior Wall Framing:	2x4

Foundation Options:

Partial daylight basement
(All plans can be built with your choice of foundation and framing. A generic conversion diagram is available. See order form.)

BLUEPRINT PRICE CODE:	**B**

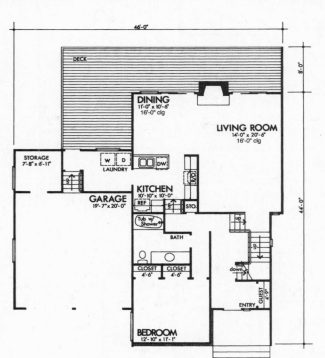

MAIN FLOOR

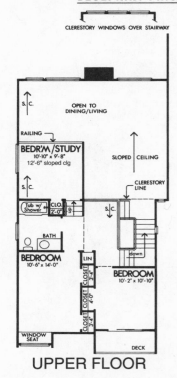

UPPER FLOOR

ORDER BLUEPRINTS ANYTIME!
CALL TOLL-FREE 1-800-820-1283

Plan H-910-1

PRICES AND DETAILS
ON PAGES 2-5

333

Decking the Day Away!

- An enormous wraparound deck serves as the heart of this recreational home.
- Rustic exterior styling presents the perfect image to the outside world, while the friendly interior will always offer a warm welcome.
- After a strenuous afternoon of water skiing, or an exhilarating day of fly fishing, you can spend the night resting your aching muscles on the amazing deck, counting stars and reliving the day's events.
- Once you head inside (if you must), you can continue your socializing around the living room's cozy fireplace.
- Before those early morning fishing excursions, you can flip pancakes and sip coffee in the efficient kitchen.
- Three bedrooms provide space for plenty of overnight guests.
- The daylight basement provides space for future expansion possibilities.

Plan H-806-M3

Bedrooms: 3	Baths: 1
Living Area:	
Main floor	952 sq. ft.
Daylight basement	676 sq. ft.
Total Living Area:	**1,628 sq. ft.**
Tuck-under garage	276 sq. ft.
Exterior Wall Framing:	**2x4**

Foundation Options:

Daylight basement

(All plans can be built with your choice of foundation and framing. A generic conversion diagram is available. See order form.)

BLUEPRINT PRICE CODE:	**B**

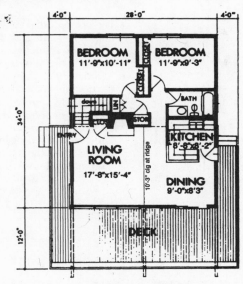

MAIN FLOOR

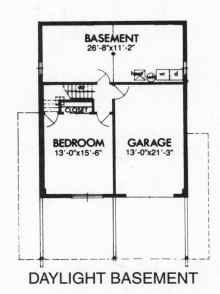

DAYLIGHT BASEMENT

Plan H-806-M3

PRICES AND DETAILS
ON PAGES 2-5

Panoramic Prow View

- This glass-filled prow gable design is almost as spectacular as the panoramic view from inside.
- French doors open from the front deck to the dining room. A stunning window wall illuminates the adjoining living room, which flaunts a 20-ft.-high cathedral ceiling.

- The open, corner kitchen is perfectly angled to service the dining room and the family room, while offering views of the front and rear decks.
- A handy utility/laundry room opens to the rear deck. Two bedrooms share a full bath, to complete the main floor.
- A dramatic, open-railed stairway leads up to the secluded master bedroom, which boasts a dressing room and a private bath with a dual-sink vanity and a separate tub and shower.

Plan NW-196	
Bedrooms: 3	**Baths:** 2
Living Area:	
Upper floor	394 sq. ft.
Main floor	1,317 sq. ft.
Total Living Area:	**1,711 sq. ft.**
Exterior Wall Framing:	2x6

Foundation Options:

Crawlspace
(All plans can be built with your choice of foundation and framing. A generic conversion diagram is available. See order form.)

BLUEPRINT PRICE CODE: B

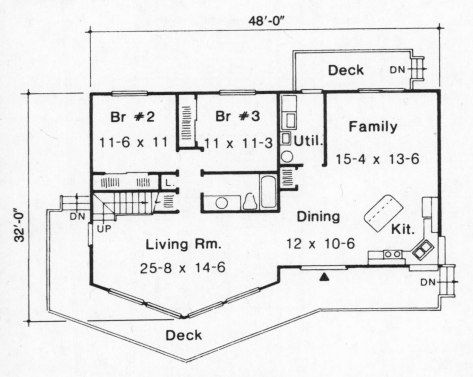

MAIN FLOOR

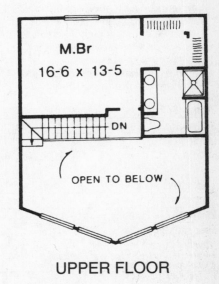

UPPER FLOOR

ORDER BLUEPRINTS ANYTIME!
CALL TOLL-FREE 1-800-820-1283

Plan NW-196

PRICES AND DETAILS
ON PAGES 2-5

331

REAR VIEW

Contemporary Split-Entry

- Striking contemporary rooflines and wood siding accent the exterior of this appealing split-entry design.
- A bright, cheery 13-ft.-high entry introduces the living areas upstairs and the sleeping quarters below.
- Open, free-flowing spaces define the light-filled main floor.
- With a ceiling that rises to 15½ feet, the living room stands poised to impress.

Among its features are a handy built-in wet bar, a majestic woodstove and access to both a small deck in front and a large octagonal-shaped deck in back.
- A dramatic sun roof brings warmth and light to the spacious dining room.
- A windowed sink eases the burden of daily chores in the cozy U-shaped kitchen. A nearby half-bath completes the main floor.
- Three generous bedrooms lie downstairs. The master bedroom has a pair of closets, a private bath and access to a covered patio; the two secondary bedrooms share a full bath.

Plan H-945-1A

Bedrooms: 3	Baths: 2½
Living Area:	
Main floor	886 sq. ft.
Lower floor	790 sq. ft.
Total Living Area:	**1,676 sq. ft.**
Garage	390 sq. ft.
Exterior Wall Framing:	2x6

Foundation Options:

Crawlspace
(All plans can be built with your choice of foundation and framing. A generic conversion diagram is available. See order form.)

BLUEPRINT PRICE CODE: **B**

LOWER FLOOR

PATIO

BEDROOM 12'0" x 17'0"

BEDROOM 10'0" x 11'6"

BEDROOM 9'0" x 11'6"

CLOSET 5'0"

CLOSET 5'0"

CLOSET 6'0"

CLOSET 6'0"

LINEN 4'3"

BATH

BATH

W D LAUNDRY

WH

furnace

ACCESS DOOR

MAIN FLOOR

40'-0"

DECK

PASSIVE SUN ROOF

LIVING ROOM 20'0" x 17'0"

DINING 10'0" x 18'0"

DW

KITCHEN 9'6" x 11'6"

R O

REF

SLOPED CEILING

WOOD STOVE

WET BAR

DECK

CLOSET 5'3"

CLERESTORY WDW. OVER

LAV

down

GARAGE 19'3" x 20'3"

ENTRY

47'-0"

FRONT VIEW

Full of Great Ideas

- This unique, rustic home features a sunken conversation pit, one of the many great design ideas located inside.
- Vertical siding, exposed timbers and a stone chimney enhance the home's exterior. The true gem, however, is the picturesque cathedral window, which is sure to offer incredible views of the natural landscape.
- Inside, the main floor revolves around the conversation pit. A sensational fireplace warms the entire living area.
- A soaring vaulted ceiling tops the living room, recipient of the splendor of the cathedral window. The living room, dining room and kitchen access the wraparound deck.
- Upstairs, a smaller bedroom and a large balcony bedroom share a full hall bath.

STAIRWAY AREA IN CRAWLSPACE VERSION STOR

Plans H-805-1 & -1A	
Bedrooms: 3	**Baths:** 2
Living Area:	
Upper floor	486 sq. ft.
Main floor	992 sq. ft.
Total Living Area:	**1,478 sq. ft.**
Standard basement	992 sq. ft.
Exterior Wall Framing:	2x4 and 2x6
Foundation Options:	**Plan #**
Standard basement	H-805-1
Crawlspace	H-805-1A
(All plans can be built with your choice of foundation and framing. A generic conversion diagram is available. See order form.)	
BLUEPRINT PRICE CODE:	**B**

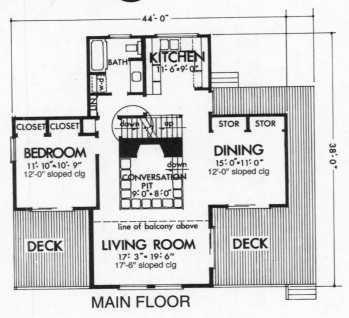

MAIN FLOOR

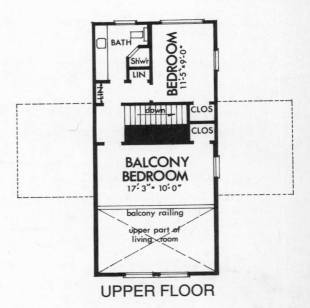

UPPER FLOOR

Skylighted Timber-Topper

- Illuminated by a pyramid-shaped skylight, this contemporary design has a sophisticated elegance about it. Getting the home off the ground gives you all kinds of sheltered space for protective storage, and also adds vast spaces to the available views.
- After a winter stroll through the woods, erase the chill beside a roaring fire in the spacious living room. Open to the other living spaces, this room is the heart of the home's charm.
- Serve up a wonderful meal of wild game in the all-purpose dining room. Afterwards, step out to the viewing deck to catch a glimpse of the setting sun.
- The efficient, U-shaped kitchen gives your frugal gourmet all the space necessary to create culinary delights.
- Three generously sized bedrooms, one with a cozy boxed-out window and another with its own full bath, complete the floor plan.
- A beautiful spiral staircase connects the main floor with the ground-level laundry room and entry.

Plan H-111-1

Bedrooms: 3	Baths: 2
Living Area:	
Main floor	1,248 sq. ft.
Lower floor	181 sq. ft.
Total Living Area:	**1,429 sq. ft.**
Exterior Wall Framing:	2x4

Foundation Options:

Slab

(All plans can be built with your choice of foundation and framing. A generic conversion diagram is available. See order form.)

BLUEPRINT PRICE CODE:	**A**

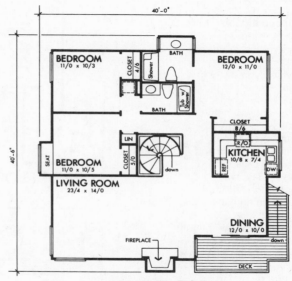

MAIN FLOOR

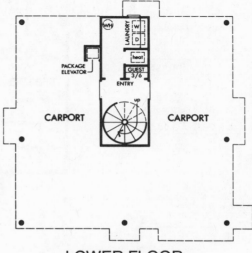

LOWER FLOOR

Swept Away

- With clever design and thoughtful use of space, this home's stunning exterior and spacious interior belie its modest square footage.

- Outdoor spaces sweep you away to a world of relaxation. A covered porch introduces the front of the home, and a large deck spans the entire length of the back. Another deck is nestled to the home's right, behind the garage.

- Inside, the kitchen, family room and living room form a vast area for entertaining and everyday living.

- Four windows brighten the modern kitchen, located conveniently near the laundry room and the garage.

- A nice wood railing separates the family room from the sunken living room, which boasts a handsome fireplace and sliding glass doors to the rear deck.

- Across the home, two secondary bedrooms—both with deck access—share a full bath.

- The upper floor houses the master suite, with a private bath and several closets.

Plan H-911-1A

Bedrooms: 3	Baths: 2
Living Area:	
Upper floor	429 sq. ft.
Main floor	1,342 sq. ft.
Total Living Area:	**1,771 sq. ft.**
Garage	452 sq. ft.
Exterior Wall Framing:	2x4

Foundation Options:

Crawlspace

(All plans can be built with your choice of foundation and framing. A generic conversion diagram is available. See order form.)

BLUEPRINT PRICE CODE:	**B**

UPPER FLOOR

BEDROOM
13'-0" x 16'-9"
14'-0" sloped clg
vaulted ceiling

BATH
11'-0"
sloped clg

CLOSET

WALK IN CLOSET

CLOS

down

MAIN FLOOR

58'-6"

8'-0"

50'-0"

DECK

BEDROOM
13'-0" x 12'-9"
10'-0" sloped clg

LIVING ROOM
20'-0" x 15'-3"
17'-6" sloped clg

CLOSET

railing

vaulted ceiling

DECK

BEDROOM
13'-3" x 11'-0"
8'-6" sloped clg

FAMILY ROOM
19'-4" x 12'-0"
16'-6" sloped clg

CLOSET

ENTRY
12'-0"
sloped clg

CLOS

KITCHEN
12'-0" x 11'-3"
14'-0" sloped clg

REF

D W

LAUNDRY
9'-3" x 6'-0"

HEAT

WH

GARAGE
21'-2" x 21'-4"

BATH
12'-0" sloped clg

DW

down

ORDER BLUEPRINTS ANYTIME!
CALL TOLL-FREE 1-800-820-1283

Plan H-911-1A

PRICES AND DETAILS
ON PAGES 2-5

327

Chalet with Options

- This attractive chalet offers three main-floor variations, with identical upper-floor and basement layouts.
- All versions feature a well-designed kitchen with dual sinks, a dishwasher and an adjacent dining area.
- A spacious, sun-filled living room boasting a wall of windows, deck access and a cozy fireplace can also be found in each main-floor plan.
- A full bath and a choice of one or two bedrooms are also offered.
- Upper-floor amenities include private decks off two more bedrooms, a full bath and plenty of storage space. Each bedroom has a 10-ft. vaulted ceiling.
- The optional daylight basement houses a one-stall garage, a large laundry room and additional storage space.

Plans H-720-10, -11 & -12A

Bedrooms: 3+	Baths: 2
Living Area:	
Upper floor	328 sq. ft.
Main floor	686 sq. ft.
Total Living Area:	**1,014 sq. ft.**
Daylight basement	408 sq. ft.
Tuck-under garage	278 sq. ft.
Exterior Wall Framing:	2x4
Foundation Options:	**Plan #**
Daylight basement	H-720-10 or -11
Crawlspace	H-720-12A

(All plans can be built with your choice of foundation and framing. A generic conversion diagram is available. See order form.)

BLUEPRINT PRICE CODE: **A**

UPPER FLOOR

DAYLIGHT BASEMENT

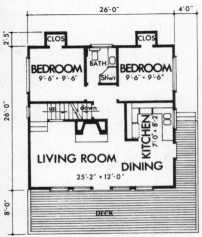

MAIN FLOOR
PLAN H-720-10

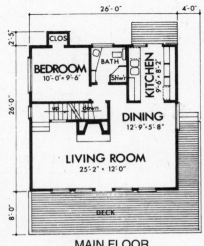

MAIN FLOOR
PLAN H-720-11

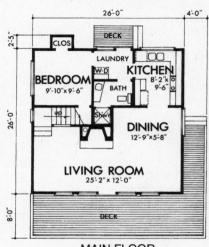

MAIN FLOOR
PLAN H-720-12A

Plans H-720-10, -11 & -12A

PRICES AND DETAILS
ON PAGES 2-5

REAR VIEW

Modern Rustic

- Expanses of deck beckon you to enjoy the outdoors, and two cozy fireplaces tempt you to hibernate inside this rustic—yet modern—home.
- Flanking the entry, a unique den houses your favorite books. It features a 14½-ft. sloped ceiling and sliding glass doors to a private deck. A 3-ft.-high wall separates it from the living room.
- Topped by a 17-ft. vaulted ceiling, the sunken living room lies steps below. Built-in bookshelves provide an ideal display area, while sliding glass doors to the rear deck visually expand the space.
- The free-flowing dining room shares a breakfast bar with the kitchen, which is close to the laundry room and the garage entrance.
- A nice-sized bedroom overlooks the front yard and easily accesses the nearby hall bath.
- Upstairs, the master suite has a deck, a private bath and an 11-ft., 9-in. ceiling.
- The daylight basement includes a rec room, a bedroom and another full bath.

UPPER FLOOR

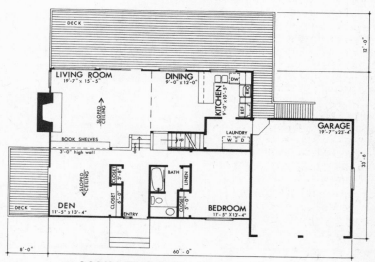

MAIN FLOOR

Plans H-877-2 & -2A

Bedrooms: 2+	Baths: 2-3
Living Area:	
Upper floor	320 sq. ft.
Main floor	1,200 sq. ft.
Daylight basement	1,200 sq. ft.
Total Living Area:	**1,520/2,720 sq. ft.**
Garage	457 sq. ft.
Exterior Wall Framing:	2x4
Foundation Options:	**Plan #**
Daylight basement	H-877-2
Crawlspace	H-877-2A

(All plans can be built with your choice of foundation and framing. A generic conversion diagram is available. See order form.)

BLUEPRINT PRICE CODE:	B/D

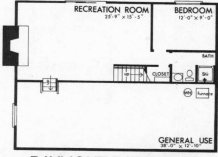

DAYLIGHT BASEMENT

ORDER BLUEPRINTS ANYTIME!
CALL TOLL-FREE 1-800-820-1283

Plans H-877-2 & -2A

**PRICES AND DETAILS
ON PAGES 2-5**

325

Lakefront Living

- This unique pentagonal plan is designed to take full advantage of your lakefront site, with a deck that wraps the entire main floor.
- A window wall interrupted only by a centerpiece fireplace offers exquisite views from the large living room and dining area. Sliding doors flanking the fireplace provide deck access.
- The kitchen is fronted by a breakfast bar that accommodates casual dining at any time of day. This allows you the option of setting up a formal dining suite in the adjoining dining area.
- A doorway in the kitchen leads to a utility room with a large storage closet and access to the attached garage.
- A full bath and a bedroom with two closets round out the main-floor plan.
- At the top of an open staircase, a balcony hallway connects two more bedrooms and another full bath. The balcony overlooks the living room and dining area, taking advantage of the view through the window wall.

Plans H-855-2 & -2A

Bedrooms: 3	Baths: 2
Living Area:	
Upper floor	660 sq. ft.
Main floor	1,174 sq. ft.
Total Living Area:	**1,834 sq. ft.**
Daylight basement	1,050 sq. ft.
Garage	326 sq. ft.
Exterior Wall Framing:	2x4
Foundation Options:	**Plan #**
Daylight basement	H-855-2
Crawlspace	H-855-2A

(All plans can be built with your choice of foundation and framing. A generic conversion diagram is available. See order form.)

BLUEPRINT PRICE CODE:	**B**

UPPER FLOOR

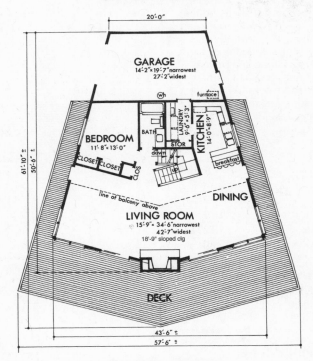

MAIN FLOOR

Plans H-855-2 & -2A

PRICES AND DETAILS
ON PAGES 2-5

Indoor/Outdoor Pleasure

- For a scenic lake or mountain lot, this spectacular design takes full advantage of the views.
- A three-sided wraparound deck makes indoor/outdoor living a pleasure.
- The sunken living room—with a 19-ft. cathedral ceiling, a skylight, a beautiful fireplace and glass galore—is the heart of the floor plan.
- Both the formal dining room and the kitchen overlook the living room and the surrounding deck beyond.
- The main-floor master bedroom has a 12-ft. cathedral ceiling and private access to the deck and hall bath.
- Upstairs, two more bedrooms share a skylighted bath and flank a dramatic balcony sitting area that views to the living room below.

Plan AX-98607

Bedrooms: 3	Baths: 2
Living Area:	
Upper floor	531 sq. ft.
Main floor	1,098 sq. ft.
Total Living Area:	**1,629 sq. ft.**
Standard basement	894 sq. ft.
Garage	327 sq. ft.
Exterior Wall Framing:	2x4

Foundation Options:
Standard basement
Slab
(All plans can be built with your choice of foundation and framing. A generic conversion diagram is available. See order form.)

BLUEPRINT PRICE CODE: B

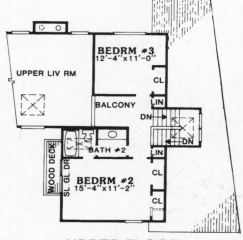

UPPER FLOOR

◀ 45'-0" ▶

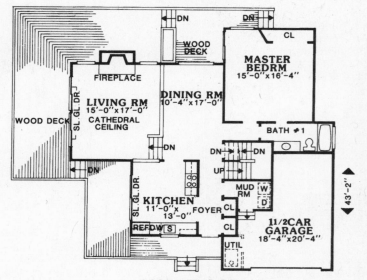

MAIN FLOOR

ORDER BLUEPRINTS ANYTIME!
CALL TOLL-FREE 1-800-820-1283

Plan AX-98607

PRICES AND DETAILS
ON PAGES 2-5

323

Pleasant and Affordable

- This affordable two-story offers a pleasant environment as a year-round home or as a great vacation retreat.
- Decks in front and back let you watch the sun rise and set, all while enjoying the beautiful outdoors.
- The spacious living room is sure to be a central gathering spot for family and friends. It offers a friendly fireplace and access to the big back deck.
- Three bedrooms provide room for growing families or weekend visitors. The main-floor bedroom is just a step away from the full-size bath.
- Each of the two upper-floor bedrooms has a door to the front deck. A balcony overlooking the living room gives you a grand view of the activities below.

Plan H-5

Bedrooms: 3	Baths: 1
Living Area:	
Upper floor	332 sq. ft.
Main floor	660 sq. ft.
Total Living Area:	**992 sq. ft.**
Exterior Wall Framing:	2x4

Foundation Options:

Crawlspace
(All plans can be built with your choice of foundation and framing. A generic conversion diagram is available. See order form.)

BLUEPRINT PRICE CODE:	**AA**

REAR VIEW

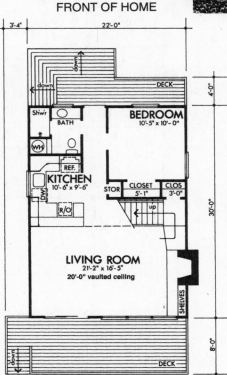

FRONT OF HOME

3'-4"   22'-0"

DECK

Sh'wr

BATH

BEDROOM
10'-5" x 10'-0"

WH

REF.

KITCHEN
10'-6" x 9'-6"

STOR

CLOSET
5'-1"

CLOS
3'-0"

DW

R/O

down   up

LIVING ROOM
21'-2" x 16'-5"
20'-0" vaulted ceiling

SHELVES

DECK

down

4'-0"

30'-0"

8'-0"

MAIN FLOOR

DECK

BEDR'M
7'-6" x 12'-5"
12'-4" vltd clg

CLOS
3'-0"

S.C.

BEDROOM
10'-5" x 12'-5"
12'-4" vltd clg

CLOSET
3'-0"

LIN

S.C.

BALCONY

down

RAILING

SLOPED CEILING

OPEN TO LIVING RM.

UPPER FLOOR

REAR VIEW

Flexible Design

- Designed for flexibility, this home can be built on a narrow or sloping lot, with either two bedrooms or three.
- The living room boasts a 16-ft.-high sloped ceiling and is warmed by a handsome woodstove. Sliding glass doors open to an inviting corner deck.
- The skylighted, passive-solar dining room is wrapped by windows and has a slate floor to capture and retain solar heat. A French door opens to the deck.
- The kitchen is open to the dining room but is separated from the living room by a 7½-ft.-high wall.
- The main-floor bedroom is located across the hall from a full bath with laundry facilities.
- In the plan's two-bedroom version, the upper-floor loft hosts a spacious master suite with a 12-ft. sloped ceiling, a huge walk-in closet and a private bath.
- In the plan's three-bedroom version, two bedrooms share the upper floor.

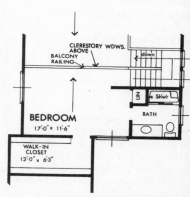

FRONT VIEW

Plans H-946-1A, -1B, -2A & -2B

Bedrooms: 2+	Baths: 1-2
Living Area:	
Upper floor (3-bedroom plan)	290 sq. ft.
Upper floor (2-bedroom plan)	381 sq. ft.
Main floor	814 sq. ft.
Total Living Area:	**1,104/1,195 sq. ft.**
Daylight basement	814 sq. ft.
Garage	315 sq. ft.
Exterior Wall Framing:	2x6
Foundation Options:	**Plan #**
Daylight basement (2 bedrooms)	H-946-1B
Daylight basement (3 bedrooms)	H-946-2B
Crawlspace (2 bedrooms)	H-946-1A
Crawlspace (3 bedrooms)	H-946-2A

(All plans can be built with your choice of foundation and framing. A generic conversion diagram is available. See order form.)

BLUEPRINT PRICE CODE:	**A**

MAIN FLOOR

**UPPER FLOOR
(TWO-BEDROOM PLAN)**

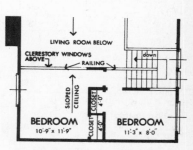

**UPPER FLOOR
(THREE-BEDROOM PLAN)**

Plans H-946-1A, -1B, -2A & -2B

**PRICES AND DETAILS
ON PAGES 2-5**

Pergola Perfection

- Here's a bungalow that understands the refreshment of tall windows in the traditional style, while providing outdoor living spaces that give it warmth and distinction.
- The pergola, wood-slatted and four-columned, redefines one corner of the home as a refined and shady place for reading the paper or sewing.
- Living and dining rooms rise up from the energy-saving airlock entry in a series of steps, adding spice to your decorative choices.
- A shapely rear deck off the kitchen adds to the outdoor luxury.
- The kitchen has a bay-windowed telephone desk, and a snack bar.
- The living room has built-in shelves, a fireplace and a stone hearth—all beneath a 9-ft. ceiling.
- Beautiful French doors separate the den from the living room.
- The master suite unfolds beneath an airy 9½-ft. vaulted ceiling. A built-in desk in the dormer puts a window over your work. The master bath complex maximizes your privacy and comfort.

Plans H-1459-1 & -1A	
Bedrooms: 2+	**Baths: 2**
Living Area:	
Upper floor	658 sq. ft.
Main floor	1,201 sq. ft.
Total Living Area:	**1,859 sq. ft.**
Partial basement	630 sq. ft.
Garage	280 sq. ft.
Exterior Wall Framing:	2x6
Foundation Options:	**Plan #**
Partial basement	H-1459-1
Crawlspace	H-1459-1A

(All plans can be built with your choice of foundation and framing. A generic conversion diagram is available. See order form.)

BLUEPRINT PRICE CODE:	**B**

MAIN FLOOR

UPPER FLOOR

Plans H-1459-1 & -1A

PRICES AND DETAILS
ON PAGES 2-5

REAR VIEW

Bold and Beautiful

- The bold form of this unusual design creates a feeling of spaciousness that's enhanced by the use of lots of large windows and huge decks.
- Compact and efficient, yet roomy enough to accommodate the average-sized family, its practicality will appeal to a wide variety of home owners.
- Sure to be a gathering spot for the whole family, the huge living room boasts a grand fireplace. When the weather's warm, you can take the festivities out to the enormous deck and enjoy the panoramic landscape spread out before you.
- The U-shaped kitchen stands ready to serve the charming dining room, perfect for formal or casual dining.
- Offering its own deck access is the main-floor bedroom. A full-sized bath is just a few steps away.
- A second bedroom and another full bath is found on the upper floor. An interesting balcony room looks down to the living room as well as the dining room. An extra large attic space provides plenty of room for storage.

Plans H-805-7 & -7A	
Bedrooms: 2	**Baths:** 2
Living Area:	
Upper floor	504 sq. ft.
Main floor	1,008 sq. ft.
Total Living Area:	**1,512 sq. ft.**
Attic storage	196 sq. ft.
Standard basement	1,008 sq. ft.
Garage	447 sq. ft.
Exterior Wall Framing:	2x4
Foundation Options:	**Plan #**
Standard basement	H-805-7
Crawlspace	H-805-7A

(All plans can be built with your choice of foundation and framing. A generic conversion diagram is available. See order form.)

BLUEPRINT PRICE CODE:	**B**

FRONT OF HOME — 49'-6"

GARAGE 20'-2" × 22'-2"

BATH
KITCHEN 9'-0" 9'-3"
CLOS
STORAGE
CLOSET
ENTRY W D
down to basement or furnace pit up
BEDROOM 10'-9" × 13'-2" 15'-8" sloped clg
DINING 11'-0" 13'-2"
LIVING ROOM 22'-10" × 17'-2" 16'-0" sloped clg
54'-0"
12'-0"
DECK

MAIN FLOOR

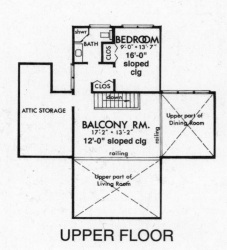

shwr
BATH
BEDROOM 9'-0" × 13'-7" 16'-0" sloped clg
CLOS
CLOS
down
ATTIC STORAGE
BALCONY RM. 17'-2" × 13'-2" 12'-0" sloped clg
railing
railing
Upper part of Dining Room
Upper part of Living Room

UPPER FLOOR

Elemental Two-Story

- Natural elements like stone and wood on the exterior of this two-story design make it the right choice for those who want a home that quietly reflects its surroundings.
- A sheltering front porch opens to a cozy entry hall that leads into the Great Room. Here, a fireplace invites you to gather around its comforting hearth; a bay window lets in plenty of sun.

- The kitchen extends a handy serving counter into the adjoining breakfast nook, where sliding glass doors access a big backyard deck.
- The 13-ft. vaulted ceiling that tops the family room gives the area a spacious feel. Wraparound corner windows are a bright touch.
- The home's sleeping quarters are on the upper floor. The master suite is entered through double doors. Inside you'll find his-and-hers closets on your way to a private bath.
- Two secondary bedrooms share a full hall bath.

Plan B-110-8504

Bedrooms: 3	**Baths:** 2½

Living Area:

Upper floor	712 sq. ft.
Main floor	900 sq. ft.
Total Living Area:	**1,612 sq. ft.**
Standard basement	900 sq. ft.
Garage	412 sq. ft.

Exterior Wall Framing: 2x4

Foundation Options:

Standard basement
(All plans can be built with your choice of foundation and framing. A generic conversion diagram is available. See order form.)

BLUEPRINT PRICE CODE: B

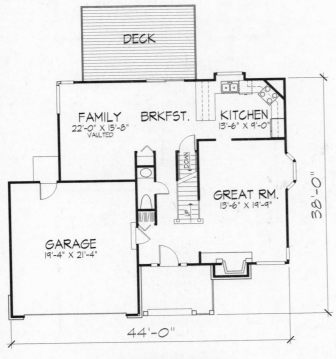

MAIN FLOOR

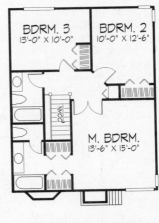

UPPER FLOOR

ORDER BLUEPRINTS ANYTIME!
CALL TOLL-FREE 1-800-820-1283
318

Plan B-110-8504

PRICES AND DETAILS
ON PAGES 2-5

Alpine Heritage

- Multiple open balconies and a steeply angled roof reflect the Alpine designs that inspired this vacation retreat.
- Past the covered porch, a two-story cathedral ceiling soars above a huge room where living, dining and kitchen activities flow into one another. This wonderful space is presided over by a corner fireplace. Oversized windows flood the area with bright sun.
- A doorway at the far end of this room leads out to a deck that spans the entire width of the home. The deck is ideal for daytime sunbathing or barbecuing and for stargazing at night.
- Two main-floor bedrooms, one of which features dual closets, share a full hall bath.
- Upstairs, a balcony hall overlooks the living area and takes advantage of the view through the uppermost windows.
- Two secondary bedrooms on the upper floor share a full bath. Each bedroom has its own access to a railed balcony on the side of the home. A front-facing balcony is accessible from the hall.

Plan C-7225

Bedrooms: 4	Baths: 2
Living Area:	
Upper floor	526 sq. ft.
Main floor	960 sq. ft.
Total Living Area:	**1,486 sq. ft.**
Daylight basement	960 sq. ft.
Exterior Wall Framing:	2x4

Foundation Options:

Daylight basement

Crawlspace

(All plans can be built with your choice of foundation and framing. A generic conversion diagram is available. See order form.)

BLUEPRINT PRICE CODE: A

UPPER FLOOR

MAIN FLOOR

ORDER BLUEPRINTS ANYTIME!
CALL TOLL-FREE 1-800-820-1283

Plan C-7225

PRICES AND DETAILS
ON PAGES 2-5

317

Home Split
Front to Back

- Here's a design for the person who wants things easy and efficient, with a sense of fun and character.
- First, you can have your choice of carport or indoor car storage.
- Enjoy the free-spirited simplicity of off-kitchen snack-bar dining.
- Customize the home further with your choice of living/dining room arrangements. Eat centrally near the kitchen, or take dinner to the fireside!
- There is only one bathroom to maintain on the lower level, and one upstairs, where your private master suite gives you seclusion and views.
- The spacious deck relaxes you twice: it's the perfect recreation area, and it adds virtually maintenance-free living space to your home.

Plan H-25-B

Bedrooms: 3	Baths: 2
Living Area:	
Upper floor	254 sq. ft.
Main floor	936 sq. ft.
Total Living Area:	**1,190 sq. ft.**
Partial basement	442 sq. ft.
Garage	276 sq. ft.
Carport	230 sq. ft.
Exterior Wall Framing:	2x4

Foundation Options:

Partial basement

(All plans can be built with your choice of foundation and framing. A generic conversion diagram is available. See order form.)

BLUEPRINT PRICE CODE:	A

UPPER FLOOR

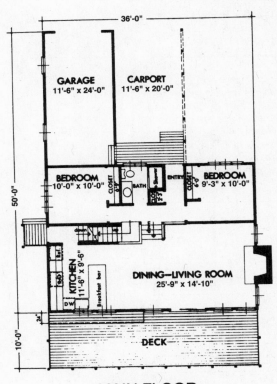

MAIN FLOOR

Plan H-25-B

PRICES AND DETAILS ON PAGES 2-5

Traditional Haven

- The young family in need of more space than their first home or condo will appreciate this well-planned three-bedroom design.
- A traditional exterior surrounds an efficient plan, offering affordable charm.

- The entry steps down into a dramatic living room with a fireplace, a 17-ft. vaulted ceiling, and open stairs.
- The kitchen serves the formal dining room, as well as an informal breakfast eating area with room enough for a couch and an entertainment center.
- There are three bedrooms upstairs, including a master suite with a walk-in closet and a dressing area with a sink and private access to the full bath.

Plan B-88032	
Bedrooms: 3	**Baths:** 1½
Living Area:	
Upper floor	691 sq. ft.
Main floor	713 sq. ft.
Total Living Area:	**1,404 sq. ft.**
Standard basement	713 sq. ft.
Garage	407 sq. ft.
Exterior Wall Framing:	2x4

Foundation Options:

Standard basement
(All plans can be built with your choice of foundation and framing. A generic conversion diagram is available. See order form.)

BLUEPRINT PRICE CODE: **A**

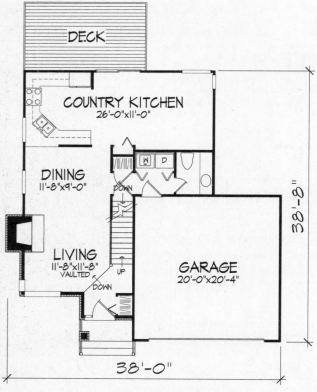

MAIN FLOOR

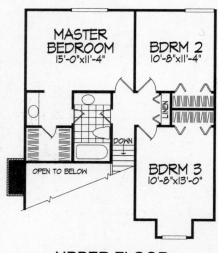

UPPER FLOOR

ORDER BLUEPRINTS ANYTIME!
CALL TOLL-FREE 1-800-820-1283

Plan B-88032

PRICES AND DETAILS
ON PAGES 2-5

315

1 Shoreview Dr.

- This two-story design is the perfect choice for an oceanfront or bay shore lot. Its wraparound sun deck offers uninterrupted views.
- A sidelighted entry gives way to a short hallway that leads you into the vaulted living room. Here, a sliding glass door opens to the deck and a fireplace takes the chill off late-summer evenings. Transom windows nestled against the ceiling let in extra sunlight.
- The dining area also features deck access. It is separated from the kitchen

by a handy serving bar. Windows over the kitchen sink afford you a view to the deck and beyond.
- One of two main-floor bedrooms boasts direct deck access. Both bedrooms share a full hall bath with a sunny window seat.
- A stairway leads to the upper floor where a bedroom with a private bath makes a wonderful master suite. A dressing area includes a lavatory and a walk-in closet. The bath features a window seat.
- The basement version of this plan gives you plenty of storage space.

Plans H-834-10 & -10A

Bedrooms: 3	Baths: 2
Living Area:	
Upper floor	387 sq. ft.
Main floor	1,144 sq. ft.
Total Living Area:	**1,531 sq. ft.**
Standard basement	1,144 sq. ft.
Garage	448 sq. ft.
Exterior Wall Framing:	**2x4**
Foundation Options:	**Plan #**
Standard basement	H-834-10
Crawlspace	H-834-10A

(All plans can be built with your choice of foundation and framing. A generic conversion diagram is available. See order form.)

BLUEPRINT PRICE CODE: **B**

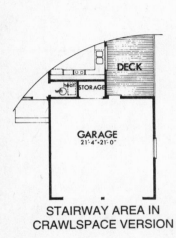

STAIRWAY AREA IN
CRAWLSPACE VERSION

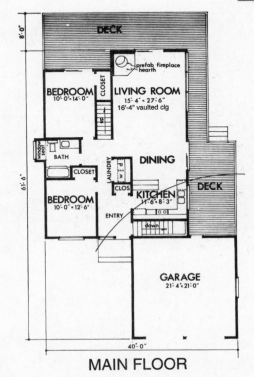

MAIN FLOOR

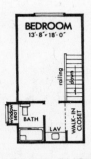

UPPER FLOOR

Plans H-834-10 & -10A

PRICES AND DETAILS
ON PAGES 2-5

Lake Home for Sloping Lot

- Large expanses of glass at the rear of this dynamic recreational home allow views to the outdoors through the dining room, the kitchen, the living room, the master bedroom and the upper loft!
- The living room features floor-to-ceiling windows that offer panoramic views; a fireplace takes the chill off late autumn evenings. A snack bar cozies up to the kitchen for casual meals at any time of day. Or use it as a serving buffet for hot appetizers when you entertain.
- The dining area offers easy deck access. Take your meals outside if you choose.
- The secluded master bedroom has its own romantic fireplace, as well as a personal bath and a private deck for stargazing or boat watching.
- A second bedroom on the main floor features easy access to a full bath.
- The upper-floor loft boasts another fireplace and overlooks the living room below. Use this area as a third bedroom, or turn it into a casual den, reserving the living room for more formal occasions.

Plan DD-1736	
Bedrooms: 2+	**Baths:** 2
Living Area:	
Upper floor	453 sq. ft.
Main floor	1,376 sq. ft.
Total Living Area:	**1,829 sq. ft.**
Standard basement	1,376 sq. ft.
Carport	360 sq. ft.
Exterior Wall Framing:	2x4
Foundation Options:	

Standard basement
Crawlspace
Slab
(All plans can be built with your choice of foundation and framing. A generic conversion diagram is available. See order form.)

BLUEPRINT PRICE CODE:	B

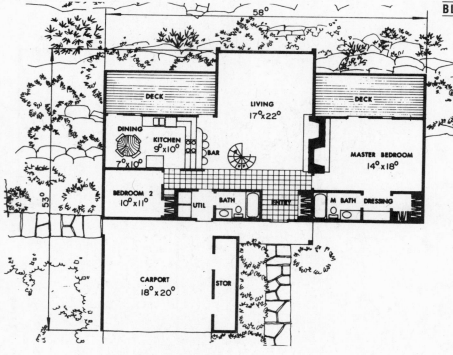

MAIN FLOOR

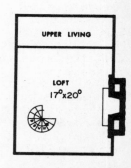

UPPER FLOOR

ORDER BLUEPRINTS ANYTIME!
CALL TOLL-FREE 1-800-820-1283

Plan DD-1736

PRICES AND DETAILS
ON PAGES 2-5

313

Cozy and Efficient

- This cozy and attractive vacation home is designed for efficiency.
- Functional benches flank the home's front porch, offering a perfect spot for relaxing conversation.
- Straight ahead, in the skylighted living areas, a 20-ft., 9-in. cathedral ceiling embraces a dramatic wall of glass. Double French doors open to a sizable backyard deck.
- The living room features an inviting inglenook: a nook that is warmed by a large, open fireplace.
- The bright dining area is large enough for any occasion.
- Columns set off both the L-shaped island kitchen and the convenient laundry area.
- The secluded main-floor bedroom is serviced by a spacious bath with a double-sink vanity.
- An 11-ft., 9-in. vaulted ceiling presides over the upstairs loft, which provides a stunning view of the living areas below and the outdoors beyond. The loft could serve as a playroom, a home office or additional sleeping quarters.

Plan U-93-201

Bedrooms: 1+	Baths: 1
Living Area:	
Upper floor	484 sq. ft.
Main floor	942 sq. ft.
Total Living Area:	**1,426 sq. ft.**
Exterior Wall Framing:	2x6

Foundation Options:

Crawlspace

(All plans can be built with your choice of foundation and framing. A generic conversion diagram is available. See order form.)

BLUEPRINT PRICE CODE: A

UPPER FLOOR

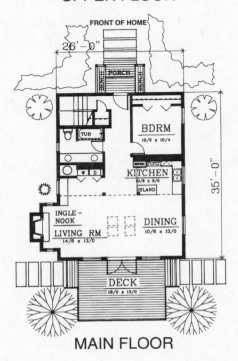

MAIN FLOOR

Plan U-93-201

FRONT VIEW

REAR VIEW

Dual-Purpose Dwelling

- This charming home is suitable as either a year-round residence or a weekend getaway home.
- From the covered front steps, the entry sweeps family and guests to any part of the home—without crossing another room. The massive living area is visible straight ahead.
- A freestanding fireplace is all that separates the living room and dining room. The living room benefits from

three windows overlooking the backyard deck, which spans the width of the home. Sliding glass doors in the dining room provide access to this sunny outdoor space.

- The kitchen has every convenience, including a separate outdoor entrance and a nearby laundry closet.
- A hall bath and a bedroom with double closets complete the main floor. Upstairs, two more bedrooms enjoy dual closets and share a full bath. One room includes a cozy alcove for hobbies, reading or daydreaming.
- The daylight basement version offers a rec room and another full bath.

Plans H-939-2 & -2A	
Bedrooms: 3	**Baths:** 2-3
Living Area:	
Upper floor	758 sq. ft.
Main floor	1,195 sq. ft.
Total Living Area:	**1,953 sq. ft.**
Daylight basement	1,012 sq. ft.
Garage	477 sq. ft.
Exterior Wall Framing:	2x6
Foundation Options:	**Plan #**
Daylight basement	H-939-2
Crawlspace	H-939-2A

(All plans can be built with your choice of foundation and framing. A generic conversion diagram is available. See order form.)

BLUEPRINT PRICE CODE:	**B**

DAYLIGHT BASEMENT

MAIN FLOOR

UPPER FLOOR

REAR VIEW

Contemporary Beach House

- A quick glance at this brilliant contemporary beach house and you can feel the sand between your toes.
- Compact enough to fit in a tidy-sized area, this clever design works well for even the smallest lot.
- The exterior offers plenty of outdoor spaces so you can take maximum advantage of every sunny day.

- Inside, the living room and dining room area boasts a nice openness suitable for entertaining. The nearby kitchen makes serving your guests quick and easy.
- Sunsets will never be more stunning or romantic than when viewed from the beautiful decks.
- The upper floor holds all four bedrooms, including the spacious master bedroom and its private bath.
- Extra storage space and a convenient pool shower adjoin the tuck-under carport below.

Plan BRF-1878

Bedrooms: 4	Baths: 3
Living Area:	
Upper floor	940 sq. ft.
Main floor	938 sq. ft.
Total Living Area:	**1,878 sq. ft.**
Tuck-under carport	533 sq. ft.
Storage	176 sq. ft.
Exterior Wall Framing:	2x4 or 2x8

Foundation Options:

Pole

(All plans can be built with your choice of foundation and framing. A generic conversion diagram is available. See order form.)

BLUEPRINT PRICE CODE:	**B**

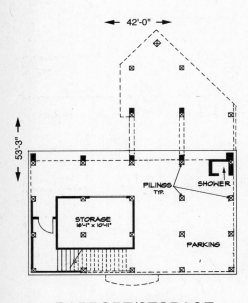

CARPORT/STORAGE

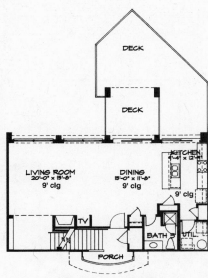

MAIN FLOOR

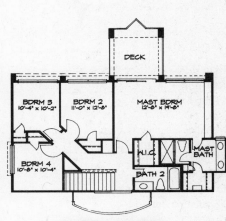

UPPER FLOOR

ORDER BLUEPRINTS ANYTIME!
CALL TOLL-FREE 1-800-820-1283

310

Plan BRF-1878

PRICES AND DETAILS
ON PAGES 2-5

Plenty of Space

- This four-bedroom home gives you plenty of living space, both indoors and out, while maintaining a cozy feel.
- The raised entry steps down into the Great Room, which is anchored by a handsome fireplace. A transom-topped, boxed-out window floods the room with light, and a 16-ft., 4-in. vaulted ceiling soars overhead.
- Quietly secluded to one side of the main floor, the dining room includes sliding glass doors that open to a big backyard deck.
- A casual area is created by the intimate arrangement of the kitchen and the family room. A serving counter fronts the kitchen, which also features a handy pantry closet. The family room has sliding glass doors to the deck.
- Upstairs, a balcony hallway connects the sleeping quarters and overlooks the Great Room. Double doors usher you into the master suite with its private bath and walk-in closet.
- The three secondary bedrooms share a full hall bath.

Plan B-905

Bedrooms: 4	Baths: 2½
Living Area:	
Upper floor	915 sq. ft.
Main floor	952 sq. ft.
Total Living Area:	**1,867 sq. ft.**
Standard basement	952 sq. ft.
Garage	505 sq. ft.
Exterior Wall Framing:	2x4
Foundation Options:	

Standard basement
(All plans can be built with your choice of foundation and framing. A generic conversion diagram is available. See order form.)

BLUEPRINT PRICE CODE:	**B**

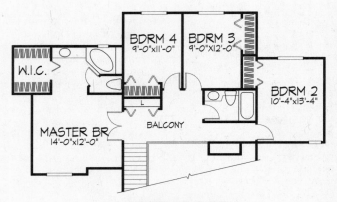

UPPER FLOOR

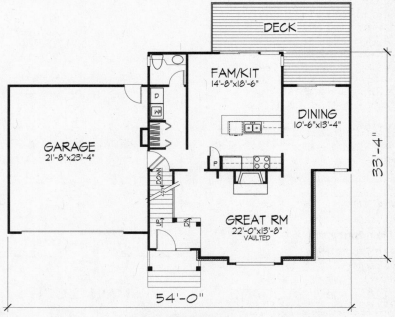

MAIN FLOOR

ORDER BLUEPRINTS ANYTIME!
CALL TOLL-FREE 1-800-820-1283

Plan B-905

PRICES AND DETAILS
ON PAGES 2-5

309

Charming
Symmetry

- Twin dormers and shuttered windows add stylish symmetry to the columned facade of this charming cottage.
- The covered entry opens to the large living room with its handsome tiled fireplace. Built-in cabinets on either side of the fireplace serve as an entertainment center or a storage area for books or personal treasures.
- A quaint dining area adjoins the kitchen at the rear of the home and opens to the backyard. The well-organized kitchen features a windowed sink and a neat laundry closet.
- The master bedroom unfolds to a full bath and a large walk-in closet.
- All main-floor rooms are expanded by 9-ft. ceilings.
- Upstairs are two more bedrooms and another full bath. Each bedroom has a unique dormer and generous closet space. The space between the bedrooms serves as a nice play area.

Plan DD-1392

Bedrooms: 3	Baths: 2
Living Area:	
Upper floor	552 sq. ft.
Main floor	840 sq. ft.
Total Living Area:	**1,392 sq. ft.**
Standard basement	840 sq. ft.
Exterior Wall Framing:	2x4

Foundation Options:
Standard basement
Crawlspace
Slab
(All plans can be built with your choice of foundation and framing. A generic conversion diagram is available. See order form.)

BLUEPRINT PRICE CODE: A

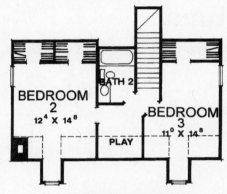

UPPER FLOOR

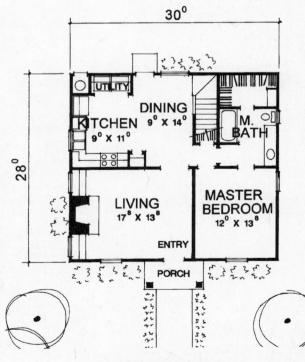

MAIN FLOOR

Plan DD-1392

Fresh as a Breeze, Trim as a Sail

- Its modest size making it easy to keep, this home offers plenty of space for the beginning family or for empty nesters who prefer a compact home.
- The living room provides ample space for gatherings of friends and family, and includes an impressive fireplace.
- The central area of the floor plan is devoted to a roomy kitchen/utility room and dining area.
- Both bedrooms feature large walk-in closets. The master bedroom includes a dressing room and a separate sink along its private entrance to the bath.
- The front porch, rear deck, and outside-access storage room are added features.
- The upper floor can be left open or finished later into two bedrooms and another bath. Added gables would nearly double the upstairs space and make this home irresistible.

Plan E-1215

Bedrooms: 2+	Baths: 1-2
Living Area:	
Upper floor	644 sq. ft.
Main floor	1,282 sq. ft.
Total Living Area:	**1,926 sq. ft.**
Standard basement	1,282 sq. ft.
Storage	54 sq. ft.
Exterior Wall Framing:	**2x6**

Foundation Options:

Standard basement

Crawlspace

Slab

(All plans can be built with your choice of foundation and framing. A generic conversion diagram is available. See order form.)

BLUEPRINT PRICE CODE: **B**

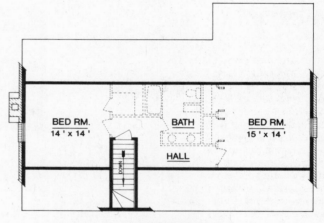

UPPER FLOOR

MAIN FLOOR

ORDER BLUEPRINTS ANYTIME!
CALL TOLL-FREE 1-800-820-1283

Plan E-1215

PRICES AND DETAILS
ON PAGES 2-5

307

REAR VIEW

Sunsational Two-story

- Sun worshipping was never classier than in this striking hideaway.
- Multiple skylights far above admit light from all directions, while a passive sun room collects rays that will help to heat the rest of the house.
- The walk-through kitchen delivers everything you need to create award-winning meals, while the nearby laundry facilities allow you to perform those Saturday chores with ease.
- A woodstove presides over the long living room, which offers sliding-glass-door access to a deck that stretches along the rear of the home.
- The second floor boasts two large bedrooms, including a lavish master suite with a walk-in closet, dressing space and its own private bath.
- The daylight basement version of this plan features room for a recreation room, an all-purpose room, an optional bath and storage space.

Plans H-956-1A & -1B

Bedrooms: 2	Baths: 2½
Living Area:	
Upper floor	572 sq. ft.
Main floor	703 sq. ft.
Passive sun room	120 sq. ft.
Total Living Area:	**1,395 sq. ft.**
Daylight basement	761 sq. ft.
Garage	337 sq. ft.
Exterior Wall Framing:	2x4

Foundation Options:

Daylight basement

(All plans can be built with your choice of foundation and framing. A generic conversion diagram is available. See order form.)

BLUEPRINT PRICE CODE:	**A**

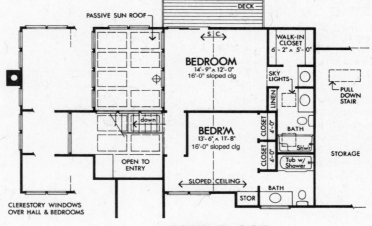

PASSIVE SUN ROOF

DECK

BEDROOM
14'-9" x 12'-0"
16'-0" sloped clg

WALK-IN CLOSET
6'-2" x 5'-0"

SKY LIGHTS

PULL DOWN STAIR

LINEN

BATH

BEDR'M
13'-6" x 11'-8"
16'-0" sloped clg

CLOSET 4'-0"

CLOSET 4'-0"

Shwr

STORAGE

Tub w/ Shower

OPEN TO ENTRY

SLOPED CEILING

STOR

BATH

CLERESTORY WINDOWS OVER HALL & BEDROOMS

UPPER FLOOR

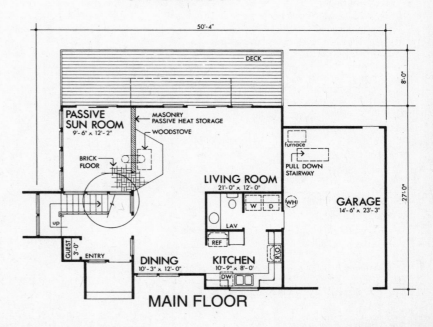

50'-4"

DECK

8'-0"

PASSIVE SUN ROOM
9'-6" x 12'-2"

MASONRY PASSIVE HEAT STORAGE

WOODSTOVE

furnace

BRICK FLOOR

PULL DOWN STAIRWAY

LIVING ROOM
21'-0" x 12'-0"

W   D

WH

GARAGE
14'-6" x 23'-3"

27'-0"

up

LAV

GUEST 3'-0"

ENTRY

REF

DINING
10'-3" x 12'-0"

KITCHEN
10'-9" x 8'-0"

R/O

DW

MAIN FLOOR

306

ORDER BLUEPRINTS ANYTIME!
CALL TOLL-FREE 1-800-820-1283

Plans H-956-1A & -1B

**PRICES AND DETAILS
ON PAGES 2-5**

Solution to Everyday Living

- This great getaway home works perfectly as a ski or hunting lodge, or as a quiet retreat for reviving your spirit after the pressures and demands of everyday living.
- Destined for big festive affairs, or intimate nights sipping hot buttered rum, the romantic Fireside Room features a grand fireplace that's perfect for a night of cozy cuddling. A unique built-in sofa provides extra comfort.

- Centrally located, the walk-through kitchen is able to quickly serve any room in the house, as well as the deck and patio.
- The dining room is formal enough for candlelight meals, but casual enough for morning waffles and juice. Access to both the deck and the patio bring the outdoors just a step away.
- Upstairs, you'll find a big sleeping room with a brilliant boxed-out window that bathes the area in sensational sunshine!
- A full bath and a sitting area that easily converts to a second bedroom complete the design.

Plan B-7635

Bedrooms: 1+	Baths: 2
Living Area:	
Upper floor	452 sq. ft.
Main floor	700 sq. ft.
Total Living Area:	**1,152 sq. ft.**
Exterior Wall Framing:	2x4

Foundation Options:

Crawlspace
(All plans can be built with your choice of foundation and framing. A generic conversion diagram is available. See order form.)

BLUEPRINT PRICE CODE:	**A**

MAIN FLOOR

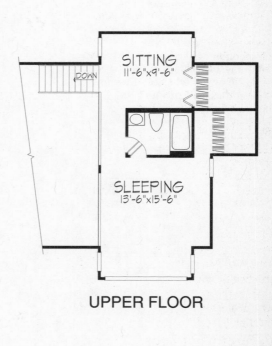

UPPER FLOOR

ORDER BLUEPRINTS ANYTIME!
CALL TOLL-FREE 1-800-820-1283
Plan B-7635
PRICES AND DETAILS
ON PAGES 2-5
305

Sweetness and Light

- Strategically placed windows in the front and a spectacular wall of windows in the back let natural light—and sweet outdoor views—into this dramatic multi-level home.
- The entry is flanked by two front-facing bedrooms and a hall bath, and leads to the living areas at the back of the home.
- The living room boasts a high, sloped ceiling, a rustic woodstove and access to the adjoining sun room, which is lit by a wall of windows and skylights. High clerestory windows at the front of the home also light the living room.
- With a view to the backyard deck and a snack bar shared with the kitchen, the dining room satisfies your good taste.
- Dominating the upper floor, the master suite features a private bath, a walk-in closet and a railing overlooking the living room below.

Plans H-877-M5A & -M5B

Bedrooms: 3+	Baths: 2-3
Living Area:	
Upper floor	382 sq. ft.
Main floor	1,200 sq. ft.
Sun room	162 sq. ft.
Daylight basement	1,200 sq. ft.
Total Living Area:	**1,744/2,944 sq. ft.**
Garage	457 sq. ft.
Exterior Wall Framing:	**2x6**
Foundation Options:	**Plan #**
Daylight basement	H-877-M5B
Crawlspace or slab	H-877-M5A

(All plans can be built with your choice of foundation and framing. A generic conversion diagram is available. See order form.)

BLUEPRINT PRICE CODE:	**B/D**

UPPER FLOOR

BASEMENT STAIRWAY LOCATION

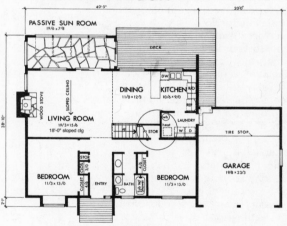

MAIN FLOOR

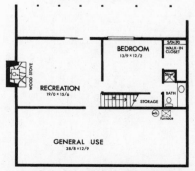

DAYLIGHT BASEMENT

Plans H-877-M5A & -M5B

PRICES AND DETAILS ON PAGES 2-5

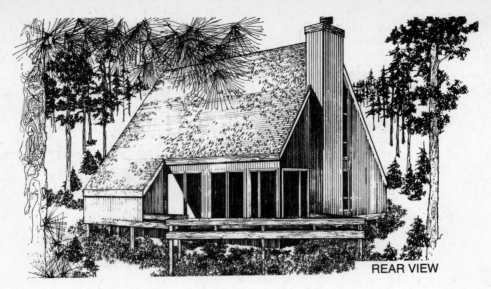

REAR VIEW

Chalet for the Soul

- Nestled in some peaceful forest at the edge of a clear lake or winding stream, this charming chalet is the perfect place to restore yourself after a long hard week at the office.
- Affordable and efficient, an open and spacious feel is still preserved by clever design and by merging the outdoors with the interior floor plan.
- A huge deck gives you a spot to quietly sit and observe all the wonderful nature around you. When guests are visiting, you can mix a pitcher of iced tea and socialize while enjoying the fresh air.
- Inside, the big living room/dining room area provides a place to entertain during inclement weather. Above the scene, a 19-ft. ceiling soars.
- The kitchen is just steps from the laundry area, which lets you get two tasks done at once. A full bath and a large bedroom complete the main floor.
- An upstairs bedroom and a loft give you extra sleeping space. Both boast hefty 10-ft. ceilings.

Plan B-7807

Bedrooms: 2+	Baths: 1½
Living Area:	
Upper floor	270 sq. ft.
Main floor	769 sq. ft.
Total Living Area:	**1,039 sq. ft.**
Storage	40 sq. ft.
Exterior Wall Framing:	2x4

Foundation Options:

Crawlspace
(All plans can be built with your choice of foundation and framing.
A generic conversion diagram is available. See order form.)

BLUEPRINT PRICE CODE: **A**

UPPER FLOOR

BR 2
10'-11"x9'-5"

LOFT
10'-11"x9'-7"

OPEN TO BELOW

DN

MAIN FLOOR

DECK

STOR

LIVING/DINING RM
26'-0"x11'-11"

UP

BR 1
10'-11"x11'-9"

KIT

30'-0"

33'-5"

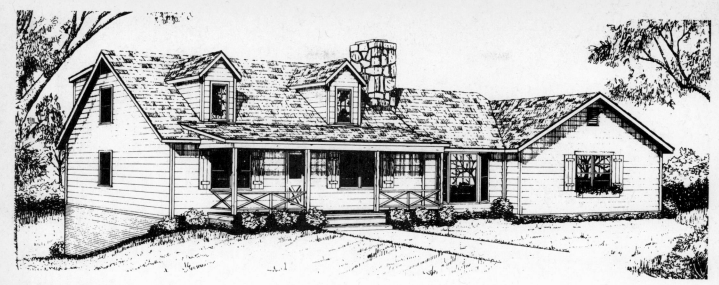

Country Comfort

- A welcoming front porch, window shutters and a bay window on the exterior of this country-style home are complemented by a comfortable, informal interior.
- A spacious country kitchen includes a bay-windowed breakfast area, a center work island and abundant counter and cabinet space.
- The large Great Room includes an impressive fireplace and a second eating area that features double doors opening to a nice-sized deck in back.
- Spacious and well-equipped, the master bedroom boasts a walk-in closet and a private bath.
- Two additional bedrooms, a full-size bath and a convenient storage room are found on the upper floor.

Plan C-8476

Bedrooms: 3	Baths: 2½
Living Area:	
Upper floor	720 sq. ft.
Main floor	1,277 sq. ft.
Total Living Area:	**1,997 sq. ft.**
Basement	1,200 sq. ft.
Garage and storage	461 sq. ft.
Exterior Wall Framing:	2x4

Foundation Options:

Daylight basement
Standard basement
Crawlspace
Slab

(All plans can be built with your choice of foundation and framing. A generic conversion diagram is available. See order form.)

BLUEPRINT PRICE CODE: B

UPPER FLOOR

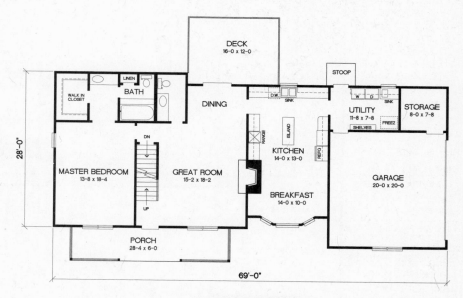

MAIN FLOOR

Plan C-8476

Narrow-Lot Contemporary

- Designed to accommodate a narrow lot, this economical, contemporary plan provides the amenities wanted by today's family.
- An efficient foyer distributes the traffic into several directions, including the formal dining room on the right, the living room on the left and the family room straight ahead.

- Cuddle up 'round the living room's cozy fireplace on chilly evenings. When the weather's nice, you can step out to the huge back deck.
- Another great entertaining space is the family room, which also accesses the deck and shares a handy serving bar with the breakfast nook.
- The kitchen is designed with practicality in mind, and features an angled snack counter and a sunny breakfast nook.
- Three secondary bedrooms and another full bath are also found upstairs.

Plan AX-98821	
Bedrooms: 4	**Baths:** 2½
Living Area:	
Upper floor	886 sq. ft.
Main floor	1,104 sq. ft.
Total Living Area:	**1,990 sq. ft.**
Standard basement	1,013 sq. ft.
Garage	383 sq. ft.
Exterior Wall Framing:	2x4

Foundation Options:
Standard basement
Crawlspace
Slab
(All plans can be built with your choice of foundation and framing. A generic conversion diagram is available. See order form.)

BLUEPRINT PRICE CODE:	B

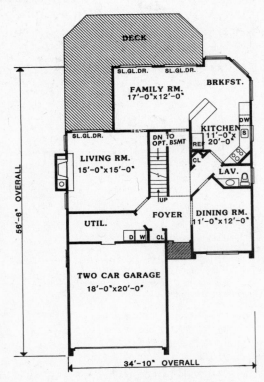

MAIN FLOOR

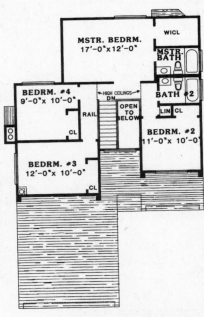

UPPER FLOOR

ORDER BLUEPRINTS ANYTIME!
CALL TOLL-FREE 1-800-820-1283

Plan AX-98821

PRICES AND DETAILS
ON PAGES 2-5

301

Level-Headed

- Designed to fit even the most narrow of lots, this home combines practicality with exciting good looks. The unique floor plan splits levels at the back of the home, allowing you to take advantage of a lot with a gradual slope to the rear.
- In from the covered front steps, the entry leads to all parts of the home. To the right, the U-shaped kitchen boasts a windowed sink and a serving bar shared with the adjacent dining room.
- The dining room overlooks the living room, and features sliding glass doors to a covered side deck. Savor summer meals outside, with the stars as the backdrop to after-dinner coffee.
- Down a short flight of stairs, the living room boasts a fireplace, a lofty high ceiling and sliding glass doors to the backyard deck.
- Two secondary bedrooms flank a hall bath on the left side of the home. The larger room lies down a set of stairs, and includes access to the rear deck.
- The master suite dominates the upper floor with a private bath and a dressing/sitting area overlooking the living room below.

Plan H-940-1A

Bedrooms: 3	Baths: 2
Living Area:	
Upper floor	591 sq. ft.
Main floor	1,170 sq. ft.
Total Living Area:	**1,761 sq. ft.**
Garage	448 sq. ft.
Exterior Wall Framing:	2x6

Foundation Options:

Crawlspace
(All plans can be built with your choice of foundation and framing. A generic conversion diagram is available. See order form.)

BLUEPRINT PRICE CODE: B

REAR VIEW

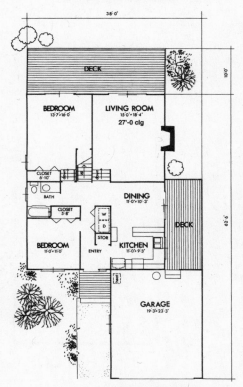

MAIN FLOOR

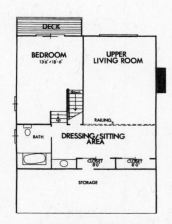

UPPER FLOOR

Plan H-940-1A

REAR VIEW

Lofty Living Room

- A beautiful two-story living room is at the heart of this fascinating design.
- Designed for fun, sunny living, two decks, a pair of skylights and an incredible number of windows bring the outdoors in and the indoors out!
- The living room's bold fireplace creates a cozy mood in an otherwise enormous space. This is the perfect spot to gather with friends and family to celebrate all of life's most important events. When

the weather cooperates, you can step out to the big back deck.
- Efficient and spacious, the U-shaped kitchen is ready for gourmet feasts or quick, casual snacks.
- Three bedrooms offer plenty of room when surprise overnight guests stop by. Each bedroom offers ample closet space, and each is just a step away from a full-sized bath.
- Above it all, the unique balcony room features incredible views of the surrounding landscapes and boasts a gorgeous private deck.
- The daylight basement has plenty of usable area.

FRONT OF HOME

Plans H-936-1 & -1A	
Bedrooms: 3+	**Baths:** 2
Living Area:	
Balcony room	150 sq. ft.
Upper floor	707 sq. ft.
Main floor	960 sq. ft.
Total Living Area	**1,817 sq. ft.**
Daylight basement	960 sq. ft.
Carport	624 sq. ft.
Exterior Wall Framing:	2x6
Foundation Options:	**Plan #**
Daylight basement	H-936-1
Crawlspace	H-936-1A
(All plans can be built with your choice of foundation and framing. A generic conversion diagram is available. See order form.)	
BLUEPRINT PRICE CODE:	**B**

MAIN FLOOR

30'- 0"

CARPORT
29'- 0" x 21'- 6"

BEDROOM
12'- 0" x 14'- 2"

BATH

ENTRY

CLOSET

54'- 0"

CLOSET   CLOSET   LIN

HALL

up

down

LAUNDRY

LIVING ROOM
20'- 0" x 14'- 0"

KITCHEN
9'- 0" x 8'- 6"

8'- 0"

deck

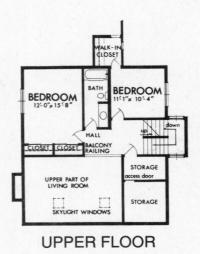

UPPER FLOOR

WALK-IN CLOSET

BATH

BEDROOM
12'- 0" x 15'- 8"

BEDROOM
11'- 1" x 10'- 4"

HALL

CLOSET   CLOSET

BALCONY RAILING

up   down

UPPER PART OF LIVING ROOM

STORAGE
access door

STORAGE

SKYLIGHT WINDOWS

BALCONY ROOM

BALCONY ROOM
12'- 1" x 10'- 5"

down

deck

ORDER BLUEPRINTS ANYTIME!
CALL TOLL-FREE 1-800-820-1283

Plans H-936-1 & -1A

PRICES AND DETAILS
ON PAGES 2-5

299

Yesterday Once More

- Shingle siding on portions of the exterior, and latticework on the front porch give this home a nostalgic look.
- A covered front porch gives way to a 17-ft. vaulted front entry that houses an open stairway to the upper floor.
- The living room and dining room boast 14-ft. vaulted ceilings. A fireplace warms the living room. The opening between the two spaces is bridged by a plant shelf.

- The kitchen is positioned to serve the dining room and the casual breakfast bay with equal ease.
- The cozy family room has its own fireplace. It's a great spot to kick back on a Friday evening and watch a video. Sliding glass doors lead out to a rear deck for summertime entertaining.
- On the upper floor, double doors open to the vaulted master suite, where an 11-ft. ceiling creates a spacious feel. The suite's private bath includes a walk-in closet and separate shower and tub facilities.
- Two secondary bedrooms share a full bath down the hall.

Plan B-88034	
Bedrooms: 3	**Baths:** 2½
Living Area:	
Upper floor	922 sq. ft.
Main floor	928 sq. ft.
Total Living Area:	**1,850 sq. ft.**
Standard basement	928 sq. ft.
Garage	459 sq. ft.
Exterior Wall Framing:	2x4
Foundation Options:	

Standard basement
(All plans can be built with your choice of foundation and framing. A generic conversion diagram is available. See order form.)

BLUEPRINT PRICE CODE: **B**

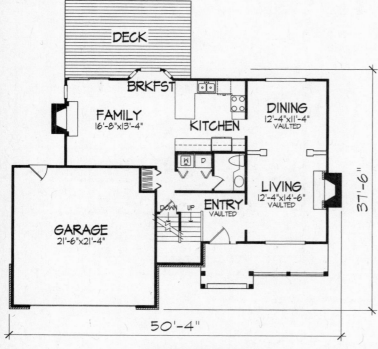

MAIN FLOOR

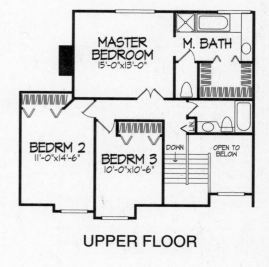

UPPER FLOOR

Plan B-88034

PRICES AND DETAILS
ON PAGES 2-5

REAR VIEW

Rustic Recreational

- Windows, sliding glass doors and an expansive covered rear deck provide a scenic view of your backyard and beyond in this two-level rustic home.
- The main level offers a vaulted living room, a dining area and an open kitchen, in addition to two bedrooms that share a full bath.
- The deck may be accessed from sliding glass doors in either the living room or the dining room.
- A fireplace at the front of the living room and clerestory windows to the rear add a dramatic effect.
- A space for a washer and dryer is tucked just outside the bathroom.
- A spiral staircase takes you to the vaulted loft and bath on the upper level.

Plan DD-1461

Bedrooms: 2+	Baths: 2
Living Area:	
Upper floor	294 sq. ft.
Main floor	1,116 sq. ft.
Total Living Area:	**1,410 sq. ft.**
Standard basement	1,116 sq. ft.
Carport	324 sq. ft.
Exterior Wall Framing:	2x4

Foundation Options:

Standard basement

Crawlspace

Slab

(All plans can be built with your choice of foundation and framing. A generic conversion diagram is available. See order form.)

BLUEPRINT PRICE CODE: **A**

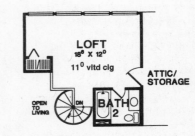

UPPER FLOOR

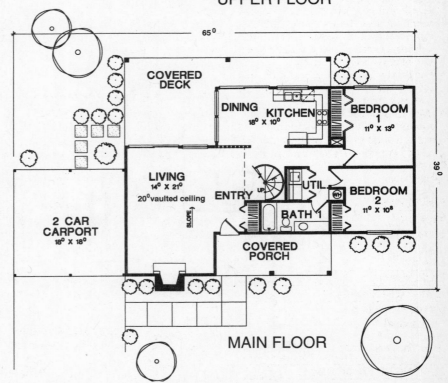

MAIN FLOOR

ORDER BLUEPRINTS ANYTIME!
CALL TOLL-FREE 1-800-820-1283

Plan DD-1461

PRICES AND DETAILS
ON PAGES 2-5

297

No Contest!

- You'll be hard-pressed to find another country-style home to rival this design!
- An incredible wraparound front porch is the perfect excuse to make those balmy summer evenings last a little longer. A porch swing would be right at home here, as would a lazy hammock with a tidy table for your soda.
- As fall approaches, you'll love the living room for its astounding 20-ft. cathedral ceiling, under which a glowing fireplace encourages romance!
- Entertaining is easy in the dining room. If your dinner party is large, you can invite your guests to the covered back porch for after-dinner drinks. Each morning, the kids can belly up to the kitchen's snack bar for a quick bowl of cereal and an English muffin.
- The master suite welcomes you with a private bath and bright windows overlooking the front porch.
- With its pleasant views to the living room below, the upper-floor loft would make a great game area! You may wish to add the optional bath and turn it into a nice spot for overnight guests to call their own.

Plan RD-1250

Bedrooms: 2+	Baths: 2-3
Living Area:	
Upper floor	341 sq. ft.
Main floor	1,250 sq. ft.
Total Living Area:	**1,591 sq. ft.**
Exterior Wall Framing:	2x4

Foundation Options:

Crawlspace

Slab

(All plans can be built with your choice of foundation and framing. A generic conversion diagram is available. See order form.)

BLUEPRINT PRICE CODE: B

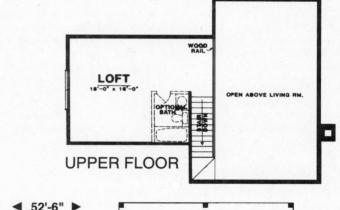

UPPER FLOOR

◄ 52'-6" ►

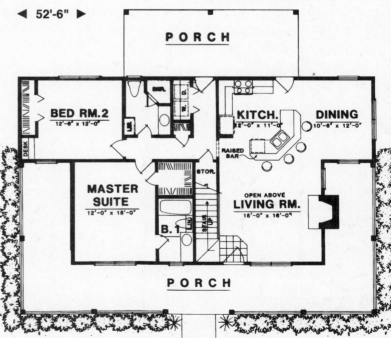

MAIN FLOOR

Plan RD-1250

PRICES AND DETAILS
ON PAGES 2-5

REAR VIEW

Gracious Chalet

- This appealing chalet-syle home offers a gracious welcome to family and friends. You'll appreciate the roomy sun deck and the romantic upper-floor balcony.
- The huge, sunken living area features a corner fireplace, sliding glass doors to the sun deck and plenty of room for entertaining. Up a set of stairs, the eating area shares a serving bar with the U-shaped kitchen.

- A windowed sink adds light to the kitchen, while a nice pantry closet contributes a place to stock extras. The kitchen is near a door to the outside.
- Nearby, a bedroom dwells close to the full bath.
- Upstairs, another bedroom enjoys storage space galore, as well as an intimate balcony outside.
- The sleeping area on the other side of the stairs also boasts a large storage capacity. Use this room as another bedroom, or let the kids claim it as their play area.

Plan C-6630	
Bedrooms: 3	**Baths:** 1
Living Area:	
Upper floor	540 sq. ft.
Main floor	864 sq. ft.
Total Living Area:	**1,404 sq. ft.**
Exterior Wall Framing:	2x4
Foundation Options:	
Crawlspace	
Slab	

(All plans can be built with your choice of foundation and framing. A generic conversion diagram is available. See order form.)

| **BLUEPRINT PRICE CODE:** | **A** |

FRONT OF HOME

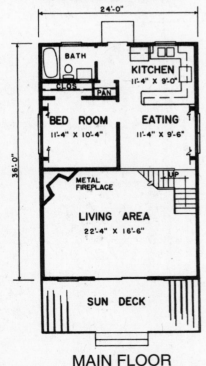

MAIN FLOOR

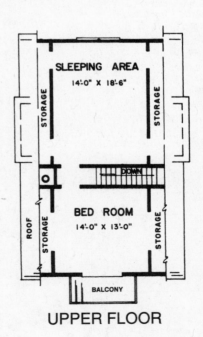

UPPER FLOOR

ORDER BLUEPRINTS ANYTIME!
CALL TOLL-FREE 1-800-820-1283

Plan C-6630

PRICES AND DETAILS
ON PAGES 2-5

295

Good Looks
Plus Smarts

- The charming stone facade of this intriguing design evokes the quaint feeling of an English cottage. The floor plan is just as smart, with an emphasis on using space wisely while infusing extra-special amenities.
- The sidelighted front door opens to the foyer, offering an impressive view of the living room and the dining room beyond. The living room is enhanced by a 17-ft. vaulted ceiling, a relaxing fireplace and elegant arched windows.
- Elegant columns frame the entrance to the dining room, which boasts a 10-ft. raised ceiling, a bay window and access to a full-width deck. The adjoining island kitchen features a pantry and views of the backyard.
- The main-floor master suite is hard to resist, with its see-through fireplace that is shared with the adjoining sitting room. The private master bath offers a garden tub and a separate shower.
- Upstairs, each bedroom has an oversized closet and easy access to a full bath. The loft features a built-in desk.

Plan B-91038

Bedrooms: 3	Baths: 2½
Living Area:	
Upper floor	550 sq. ft.
Main floor	1,256 sq. ft.
Total Living Area:	**1,806 sq. ft.**
Standard basement	1,256 sq. ft.
Garage	475 sq. ft.
Exterior Wall Framing:	2x6

Foundation Options:

Standard basement

(All plans can be built with your choice of foundation and framing. A generic conversion diagram is available. See order form.)

BLUEPRINT PRICE CODE:	B

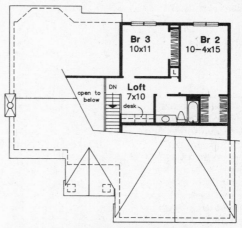

UPPER FLOOR

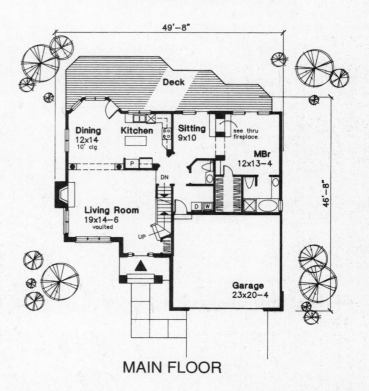

MAIN FLOOR

Plan B-91038

PRICES AND DETAILS
ON PAGES 2-5

Timeless Cape Cod

- The traditional Cape Cod is given an upbeat look in this design, featuring front dormers, interesting windows and window trim, plus a functional breezeway/patio between the house and the two-car garage.
- The front door opens into a 17-ft.-high vaulted foyer, further enhanced by a half-circle window above and an open stairway to the second floor.
- The foyer bridges the living and dining rooms, blending them together to create a harmonious atmosphere.
- The dining room flows easily into the kitchen, where a compact laundry area is concealed behind bifold doors.
- A bedroom and bath on the main level and two bedrooms with a shared bath upstairs offer plenty of room for family and friends.

Plans H-1446-1 & -1A

Bedrooms: 3	Baths: 2
Living Area:	
Upper floor	456 sq. ft.
Main floor	1,008 sq. ft.
Total Living Area:	**1,464 sq. ft.**
Standard basement	1,000 sq. ft.
Garage	484 sq. ft.
Exterior Wall Framing:	2x6
Foundation Options	**Plan #**
Standard basement	H-1446-1
Crawlspace	H-1446-1A
(All plans can be built with your choice of foundation and framing. A generic conversion diagram is available. See order form.)	
BLUEPRINT PRICE CODE:	**A**

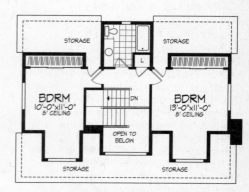

UPPER FLOOR

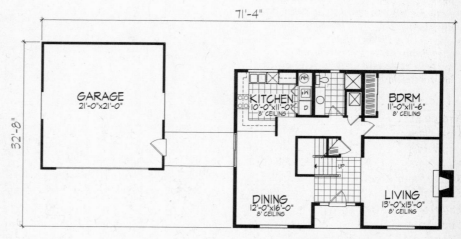

MAIN FLOOR

Saltbox with Open Interior

- This plan offers a classic traditional look on the outside but includes a thoroughly modern interior.
- The right side of the home is devoted to a large, open living and dining area, perfect for family gatherings or other events.
- The efficient kitchen is brightened by a skylight in the sloped ceiling and overlooks a large backyard deck. A compact laundry and an open bar are convenient to the major living areas.
- For economy and efficiency, the two main-floor bedrooms share a full bath. Note the large walk-in closet in the front bedroom.
- The second floor could be finished later if the space isn't needed right away. It offers room for two more bedrooms and another full bath.

Plan E-1003

Bedrooms: 2+4	Baths 1-2
Living Area:	
Upper floor	580 sq. ft.
Main floor	1,088 sq. ft.
Total Living Area	1,668 sq. ft.
Storage	32 sq. ft.
Exterior Wall Framing	2x6

Foundation Options:
Crawlspace
Slab
(All plans can be built with your choice of foundation and framing. A generic conversion diagram is available. See order form.)

BLUEPRINT PRICE CODE:	B

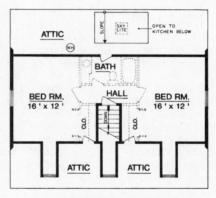

UPPER FLOOR

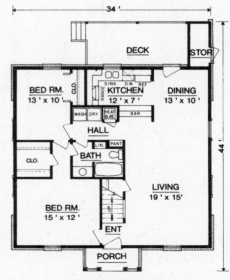

MAIN FLOOR

ORDER BLUEPRINTS ANYTIME!
CALL TOLL-FREE 1-800-820-1283

Plan E-1003

PRICES AND DETAILS
ON PAGES 2-5

Compact Chalet

- The three-sided wraparound deck makes outdoor living easy, and is accessible from the living room and the kitchen.
- The large living room offers a cozy fireplace and sliding doors to the deck.
- The fireplace is flanked by an open dining area that flows into the kitchen.

- The main-floor bedroom is adjacent to a bathroom with a shower.
- The upstairs includes two bedrooms and a half-bath.
- Large storage spaces straddle both sides of the bedrooms on the home's upper floor.
- One of the upstairs bedrooms opens onto a small private balcony, offering great views of the seaside, lake or mountains.
- The optional basement offers a garage, a recreation room and a laundry area.

Plans H-103-A & -B	
Bedrooms: 3	**Baths:** 1½
Living Area:	
Upper floor	378 sq. ft.
Main floor	624 sq. ft.
Daylight basement	312 sq. ft.
Total Living Area:	**1,002/1,314 sq. ft.**
Tuck-under garage (basement)	312 sq. ft.
Exterior Wall Framing:	2x4
Foundation Options	**Plan #**
Daylight basement	H-103-B
Crawlspace	H-103-A

(All plans can be built with your choice of foundation and framing. A generic conversion diagram is available. See order form.)

BLUEPRINT PRICE CODE: A

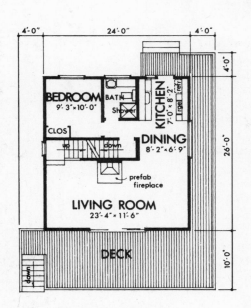

DAYLIGHT BASEMENT

MAIN FLOOR

UPPER FLOOR

ORDER BLUEPRINTS ANYTIME!
CALL TOLL-FREE 1-800-820-1283

Plans H-103-A & -B

PRICES AND DETAILS
ON PAGES 2-5

291

Adorable Country Loft

- Escape to the uncluttered simplicity of a country loft that's designed to elevate your spirits and calm your mind!
- The heart of this retreat is in the living room, where a soaring 17-ft.-high vaulted ceiling reflects the warm glow from the room's cozy fireplace.
- The country kitchen gives you just the space you need to keep preparations easy and cleanup simple. A pantry

closet ensures you'll always have something on hand.
- Outdoor dining is made possible by a pleasant patio off the kitchen in the back of the home.
- In the master suite, a private bath and a walk-in closet give you the comfort and space you need.
- The loft upstairs looks out over the living room in one direction and the great outdoors in the other—the perfect place for a studio or reading nook. Or use it to sleep extra guests.
- Another bedroom and a full-sized bath complete the upper floor.

Plan B-8305	
Bedrooms: 2+	**Baths:** 2
Living Area:	
Upper floor	488 sq. ft.
Main floor	801 sq. ft.
Total Living Area:	**1,289 sq. ft.**
Standard basement	801 sq. ft.
Garage	200 sq. ft.
Exterior Wall Framing:	2x4
Foundation Options:	

Standard basement
Slab
(All plans can be built with your choice of foundation and framing. A generic conversion diagram is available. See order form.)

BLUEPRINT PRICE CODE:	A

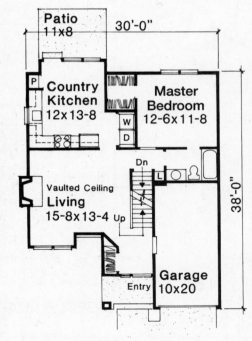

MAIN FLOOR

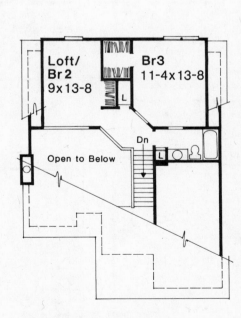

UPPER FLOOR

Shelter for Today

- Bold contemporary lines with wide sheltering overhangs, built-in planters and brick with wood siding combine to give this home a striking appearance.
- The foyer opens to a dramatic view of the cathedral-ceilinged living room with corner fireplace and railing overlook into the formal dining room, which has a 17-ft., 3-in. vaulted ceiling. Both the living room and foyer are topped by a gorgeous 14-ft., 9-in. vaulted ceiling.
- The kitchen is large enough for a breakfast table next to sliding doors leading to the patio.
- The family room, visible from the kitchen, features a second fireplace and a built-in wet bar.
- There are three bedrooms upstairs, including a master suite with double doors, a balcony, a walk-in closet and a private bath.

Plan AX-7625-A

Bedrooms: 3	Baths: 2½
Living Area:	
Upper floor	798 sq. ft.
Main floor	1,145 sq. ft.
Total Living Area:	**1,943 sq. ft.**
Partial basement	333 sq. ft.
Garage	420 sq. ft.
Exterior Wall Framing:	2x4

Foundation Options:

Partial basement
Slab

(All plans can be built with your choice of foundation and framing. A generic conversion diagram is available. See order form.)

BLUEPRINT PRICE CODE:	B

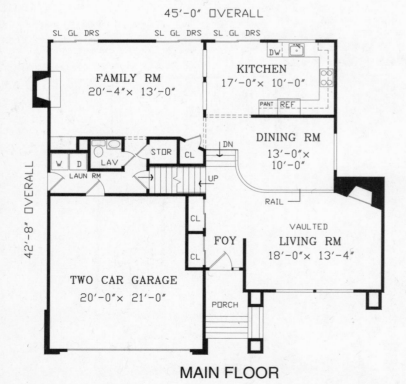

MAIN FLOOR

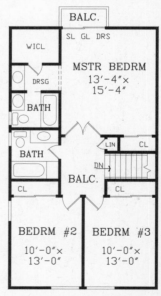

UPPER FLOOR

ORDER BLUEPRINTS ANYTIME!
CALL TOLL-FREE 1-800-820-1283

Plan AX-7625-A

PRICES AND DETAILS
ON PAGES 2-5

289

Nice Touches Add Charm

- A striking dormer window and a columned covered entry are just two of the many nice touches that make this appealing two-story home a truly charming dwelling.
- The entry opens directly into the living room, which boasts a 17-ft. vaulted ceiling and a high plant shelf.
- Easily accessed from the kitchen, the adjoining formal dining room provides a quiet area for special meals.

- Around the corner, the island kitchen offers deck access and a cheery breakfast nook.
- A low wall separates the kitchen from the family room, which is warmed by a handsome fireplace and brightened by corner windows. A handy powder room is just steps away.
- Upstairs, the master bedroom is highlighted by a 12-ft. ceiling and a walk-in closet. A cozy bay window is a nice spot to unwind.
- The private master bath flaunts a separate tub and shower.
- Another full bath services the two roomy secondary bedrooms.

Plan B-93018

Bedrooms: 3	Baths: 2½
Living Area:	
Upper floor	808 sq. ft.
Main floor	945 sq. ft.
Total Living Area:	**1,753 sq. ft.**
Standard basement	945 sq. ft.
Garage	410 sq. ft.
Exterior Wall Framing:	2x6

Foundation Options:

Standard basement
(All plans can be built with your choice of foundation and framing. A generic conversion diagram is available. See order form.)

BLUEPRINT PRICE CODE:	**B**

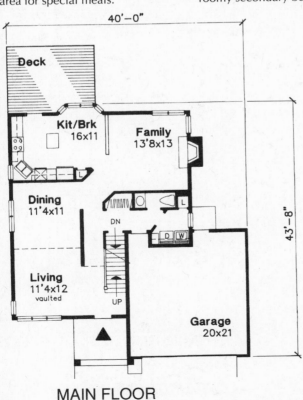

MAIN FLOOR

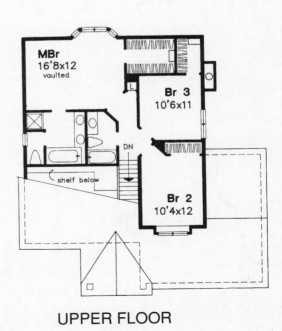

UPPER FLOOR

Plan B-93018

PRICES AND DETAILS
ON PAGES 2-5

Simple Pleasures

- It's evident in the clean, eye-catching exterior of this home that its interior pays attention to life's simple pleasures.
- Ascend to the unique covered front porch where a sidelighted door leads to the split entry inside. Upstairs, the main floor separates the sleeping quarters from the living areas for privacy.
- The living room overlooks the staircase with a nice wood railing, and views the front yard through two oversized windows. A cozy fireplace lies between this gathering area and the dining room, where there exist several dining options.
- Take advantage of the eating bar, shared with the kitchen, or enjoy summer meals outside on the backyard deck.
- The bright kitchen features a pantry for favorite foods and canned garden vegetables.
- Down the hall, the master bedroom includes its own bath. Two secondary bedrooms share a hall bath nearby.
- Downstairs, a large rec room makes space for the kids to play happily.

Plan LRD-45581

Bedrooms: 3	Baths: 2
Living Area:	
Main floor	1,073 sq. ft.
Lower floor	437 sq. ft.
Total Living Area:	**1,510 sq. ft.**
Tuck-under garage	456 sq. ft.
Exterior Wall Framing:	2x4

Foundation Options:

Slab

(All plans can be built with your choice of foundation and framing. A generic conversion diagram is available. See order form.)

BLUEPRINT PRICE CODE: B

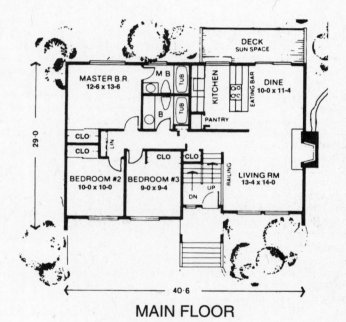

MAIN FLOOR

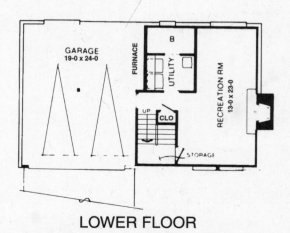

LOWER FLOOR

ORDER BLUEPRINTS ANYTIME!
CALL TOLL-FREE 1-800-820-1283

Plan LRD-45581

PRICES AND DETAILS
ON PAGES 2-5

287

Perfect Retreat

- This compact cabin-style home is the perfect vacation retreat.
- In the living room, a woodstove surrounded by a rustic brick hearth serves as a warm focal point.
- Upstairs, a good-sized loft with a 9-ft. vaulted ceiling overlooks the kitchen and dining area below.
- Skylights over the loft, kitchen and stairwell provide plenty of light to the living areas.
- The optional daylight basement plans feature either a second bedroom, bath and storage area, or a garage and storage area.

Plans H-967-1A, -1B & -1C

Bedrooms: 1	Baths: 1
Living Area:	
Upper floor	352 sq. ft.
Main floor	584 sq. ft.
Daylight basement	584 sq. ft.
Total Living Area:	**936/1,520 sq. ft.**
Tuck-under garage (basement)	584 sq. ft.
Exterior Wall Framing:	**2x6**
Foundation Options	**Plan #**
Daylight basement (with bedroom)	H-967-1B
Daylight basement (with garage)	H-967-1C
Crawlspace	H-967-1A

(All plans can be built with your choice of foundation and framing. A generic conversion diagram is available. See order form.)

BLUEPRINT PRICE CODE: **AA/B**

STORAGE

LOFT
14'-4"x26'-0"
VAULTED

OPEN TO BELOW

DN

UPPER FLOOR

34'-0"

20'-0"

LIVING
11'-10"x20'-0"
8' CEILING

DN

UP

REF

KITCHEN
14'-2"x14'-3"
8' CEILING

DECK

MAIN FLOOR

Full of Options

- This rustic A-frame offers an optional solar heating system, in addition to options for an attached screened porch and garage.
- Other exciting features of the design include a humongous deck that wraps around the house and an attached outdoor shower.
- The living/dining area has a vaulted ceiling and dramatic window walls. The room boasts a heat-circulating fireplace

with an opposite-facing barbecue, sliding glass doors on four sides and a snack bar off the kitchen.
- A whirlpool tub is located in the main-floor bath, shared by both the master and secondary bedroom.
- Two additional bedrooms on the upper floor have access to an outdoor balcony via sliding glass doors. A second bath is shared by the bedrooms on the upper floor.
- A second-floor balcony opens to the living/dining area below.
- Large closets and an outdoor-accessible utility area provide plenty of storage space for the home.

Plan AX-97729	
Bedrooms: 4	**Baths:** 2
Living Area:	
Upper floor	450 sq. ft.
Main floor	988 sq. ft.
Total Living Area:	**1,438 sq. ft.**
Screened porch	232 sq. ft.
Standard basement	905 sq. ft.
Garage	264 sq. ft.
Exterior Wall Framing:	2x4

Foundation Options:
Standard basement
Slab
(All plans can be built with your choice of foundation and framing. A generic conversion diagram is available. See order form.)

BLUEPRINT PRICE CODE:	**A**

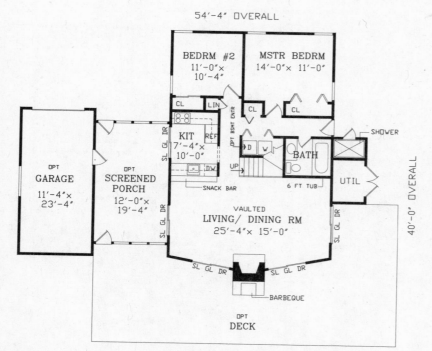

MAIN FLOOR

54'-4" OVERALL

- BEDRM #2 11'-0" x 10'-4"
- MSTR BEDRM 14'-0" x 11'-0"
- KIT 7'-4" x 10'-0"
- OPT GARAGE 11'-4" x 23'-4"
- OPT SCREENED PORCH 12'-0" x 19'-4"
- VAULTED LIVING/ DINING RM 25'-4" x 15'-0"
- BATH
- UTIL
- SNACK BAR
- 6 FT TUB
- SHOWER
- BARBEQUE
- OPT DECK
- 40'-0" OVERALL

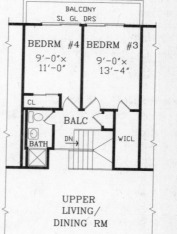

UPPER FLOOR

- BALCONY SL GL DRS
- BEDRM #4 9'-0" x 11'-0"
- BEDRM #3 9'-0" x 13'-4"
- BALC
- BATH
- WICL
- UPPER LIVING/ DINING RM

ORDER BLUEPRINTS ANYTIME!
CALL TOLL-FREE 1-800-820-1283

Plan AX-97729

PRICES AND DETAILS
ON PAGES 2-5

285

Simple Solution

- Within this dwelling's modest square footage lies the housing solution for many different people and situations. Its simple—and comfortable—design is ideal for young single persons, newly married couples or empty nesters.
- Its panoramic views and indulgent deck adapt it for satisfying vacations, as well.
- The main floor, accessible by a side staircase, provides a practical, well-arranged layout. The entry opens to a huge Great Room topped by a dramatic 14-ft., 2-in. vaulted ceiling. This living

and gathering area includes a dining area in the corner and a warm, rustic woodstove at the other end.
- Sliding glass doors flanked by windows and topped by high, angled windows brighten this area with views to the great outdoors.
- The U-shaped kitchen offers a convenient, well-lighted work space.
- The bedroom enjoys two closets and a nice window overlooking the backyard.
- Laundry facilities lie conveniently outside the full bath, as do a storage area and a linen closet.
- The two-car garage allows for storage.

Plan H-963-1A	
Bedrooms: 1	**Baths:** 1
Living Area:	
Main floor	728 sq. ft.
Total Living Area:	**728 sq. ft.**
Tuck-under garage	728 sq. ft.
Exterior Wall Framing:	2x4
Foundation Options:	
Slab	
(All plans can be built with your choice of foundation and framing. A generic conversion diagram is available. See order form.)	
BLUEPRINT PRICE CODE:	**AA**

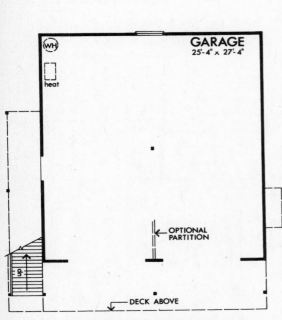

TUCK-UNDER GARAGE

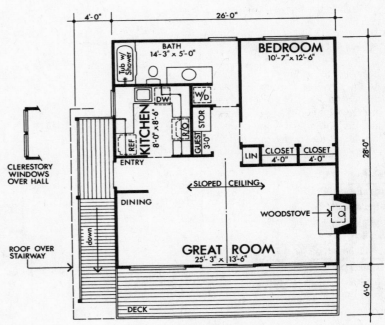

MAIN FLOOR

Plan H-963-1A

PRICES AND DETAILS
ON PAGES 2-5

Cute Cottage

- This home's rustic stone exterior gives it a charming, peaceful look, reminiscent of a cottage in a European village.
- Inside, a 17-ft. vaulted ceiling in the living room brings a bit of up-to-date comfort and style to the home. The greatest work of art can't hold a candle to the beauty of the picture window on the front wall. On winter nights, build a fire in the fireplace and enjoy the view from your own living room.
- Two handsome columns topped by a plant shelf usher guests into the adjacent dining room, where a 16-ft. vaulted ceiling soars above. During meals, the serving counter and pass-through to the kitchen save steps carrying dishes back and forth.
- The adjacent kitchen includes enough room for a casual breakfast table. Sliding glass doors open to a patio that is perfect for grilling outdoors.
- At day's end, sink into the serenity of the master suite. Here, a quiet sitting area gives you a place to read a novel and enjoy the peace and quiet.
- Upstairs, three bedrooms and a full bath complete the floor plan.

Plan B-92023

Bedrooms: 4	Baths: 2½
Living Area:	
Upper floor	564 sq. ft.
Main floor	1,134 sq. ft.
Total Living Area:	**1,698 sq. ft.**
Standard basement	1,134 sq. ft.
Garage	374 sq. ft.
Exterior Wall Framing:	2x6
Foundation Options:	

Standard basement
(All plans can be built with your choice of foundation and framing. A generic conversion diagram is available. See order form.)

BLUEPRINT PRICE CODE: **B**

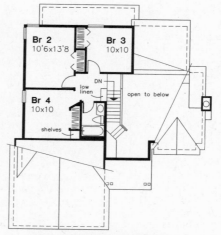

UPPER FLOOR

MAIN FLOOR

ORDER BLUEPRINTS ANYTIME!
CALL TOLL-FREE 1-800-820-1283

Plan B-92023

PRICES AND DETAILS
ON PAGES 2-5

283

Open Contemporary

- Nearly the entire main floor of this contemporary home is one Great Room, allowing everyone space to participate in family activities. Even the kitchen is completely open and accessible.
- Surrounded by glass and five large skylights overhead, the kitchen and dining area are connected to the outdoors. When weather permits, activity will gravitate to a huge deck just off the kitchen side of the Great Room.
- An oversized fireplace surrounded by native stone provides the focal point for the lounging and conversation area.
- A partially open staircase leads from the entry hall to a balcony study that could double as a bedroom.
- Sliding glass doors in the main bedroom provide access to a private sun deck.
- The second-floor full bath is divided into sections so that it can be used by two people at the same time.

Plans H-953-2A & -2B

Bedrooms: 1+	Baths: 1 full, 2 half
Living Area:	
Upper floor	689 sq. ft.
Main floor	623 sq. ft.
Total Living Area:	**1,312 sq. ft.**
Daylight basement	540 sq. ft.
Garage	319 sq. ft.
Exterior Wall Framing:	2x6
Foundation Options	**Plan #**
Daylight basement	H-953-2B
Crawlspace	H-953-2A

(All plans can be built with your choice of foundation and framing. A generic conversion diagram is available. See order form.)

BLUEPRINT PRICE CODE: A

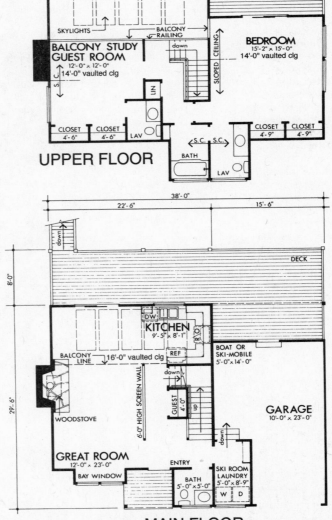

REAR VIEW

UPPER FLOOR

MAIN FLOOR

STAIRWAY AREA IN CRAWLSPACE VERSION

Fresh as a Cool Breeze

- A covered porch in front and a large patio in back help to keep you in touch with the fresh outdoor breezes.
- Set up a pair of lawn chairs, mix a pitcher of something cool and watch the neighborhood drift by from your front-porch observation post.
- The 18-ft. vaulted foyer makes a lasting first impression on arriving guests.
- Two sizable gathering rooms make entertaining a snap. At the front of the home, the sunken living room offers a 9-ft. ceiling, a big bay window and a handsome fireplace. You'll find a second fireplace in the spacious family room at the rear of the home, as well as access to the backyard patio.
- Centrally located, the island kitchen is well-equipped for gourmet nights; the formal dining room is ready for those special candlelit occasions.
- All three bedrooms are found on the upper floor, including the oversized master suite, which boasts a walk-in closet and a private dual-sink bath.
- Another full bath serves the remaining two bedrooms.

Plan S-21690

Bedrooms: 3	Baths: 2½
Living Area:	
Upper floor	900 sq. ft.
Main floor	1,080 sq. ft.
Total Living Area:	**1,980 sq. ft.**
Standard basement	900 sq. ft.
Garage	424 sq. ft.
Exterior Wall Framing:	**2x6**

Foundation Options:
Standard basement
Crawlspace
(All plans can be built with your choice of foundation and framing. A generic conversion diagram is available. See order form.)

BLUEPRINT PRICE CODE: **B**

MAIN FLOOR

UPPER FLOOR

ORDER BLUEPRINTS ANYTIME!
CALL TOLL-FREE 1-800-820-1283

Plan S-21690

PRICES AND DETAILS
ON PAGES 2-5

281

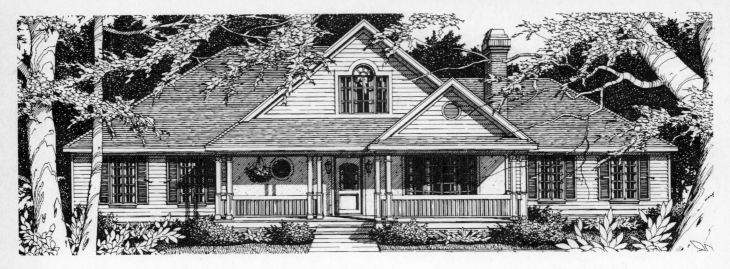

Nostalgic and Charming

- An inviting covered porch highlights the facade of this charming traditional design. Brick and stucco accents, nostalgic shutters and an elegant Palladian window arrangement add extra appeal.
- Inside, the spacious living room boasts a high 10-ft. ceiling and a fabulous fireplace with a striking mantel. Built-in shelves and cabinets are convenient features on either side.
- The gourmet kitchen offers a counter bar, a menu desk and nearby laundry

facilities. The dining room features a corner pantry plus a display shelf above the entrance from the living room.
- The two-car garage and a nice screened porch are just steps away.
- The secluded master bedroom is enhanced by a 10-ft.-high tray ceiling and lots of closet space. The private master bath includes a skylighted oval tub and a separate dressing area.
- The two front-facing bedrooms share the main bath across the hall.
- Upstairs, the skylighted loft and large closet may by used as a reading room, guest room or extra bedroom.
- An unfinished future expansion area is nicely brightened by the stunning Palladian window.

Plan J-9284

Bedrooms: 3+	Baths: 2
Living Area:	
Upper floor	255 sq. ft.
Main floor	1,611 sq. ft.
Total Living Area:	**1,866 sq. ft.**
Future space	231 sq. ft.
Screen porch	165 sq. ft.
Standard basement	1,611 sq. ft.
Garage	490 sq. ft.
Storage	123 sq. ft.
Exterior Wall Framing:	2x4

Foundation Options:

Standard basement
Crawlspace
Slab

(All plans can be built with your choice of foundation and framing. A generic conversion diagram is available. See order form.)

BLUEPRINT PRICE CODE:	B

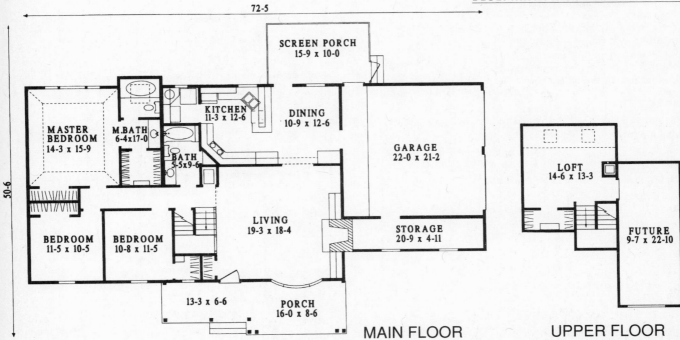

MAIN FLOOR UPPER FLOOR

Two-Story Treasure

- This plan features a charming wood and brick exterior, an ornate dormer and an very efficient interior floor plan.
- The vaulted entryway, open to the second floor, leads into a comfortable living room that is highlighted by a fireplace and tall windows.
- The dining area is open to the living room and offers sliding-door access to a backyard deck.
- The U-shaped kitchen adjoins a sunny breakfast area, designed with a built-in desk.
- The master bedroom features a large closet, a vaulted ceiling and a private bath with a built-in plant shelf.
- Two additional bedrooms share a full bath. The front bedroom boasts a beautiful half-round window set into a high-ceilinged area.
- A laundry closet is located near the bedrooms for convenience.

Plan B-87139

Bedrooms: 3	Baths: 2½
Living Area:	
Upper floor	928 sq. ft.
Main floor	788 sq. ft.
Total Living Area:	**1,716 sq. ft.**
Standard basement	788 sq. ft.
Garage	420 sq. ft.
Exterior Wall Framing:	2x4

Foundation Options:

Standard basement

(All plans can be built with your choice of foundation and framing. A generic conversion diagram is available. See order form.)

BLUEPRINT PRICE CODE: B

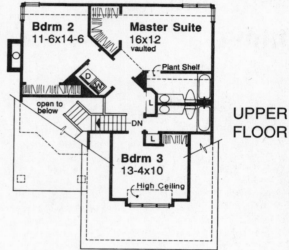

UPPER FLOOR

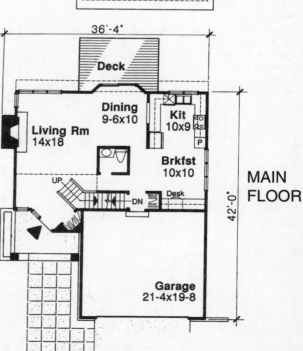

MAIN FLOOR

ORDER BLUEPRINTS ANYTIME!
CALL TOLL-FREE 1-800-820-1283

Plan B-87139

PRICES AND DETAILS
ON PAGES 2-5

279

Maximize Style and Space

- This unique transitional home is designed to maximize style, comfort and efficiency.
- The covered entry has an inviting traditional look, while the dramatic arched windows add an attractive contemporary flair.
- Inside is a functional floor plan enhanced with features such as the raised living room's 15-ft. vaulted ceiling and two-way woodstove.
- The woodstove is open to the family room on the other side and can be enjoyed from the adjoining dining area and kitchen. A rear French door opens to an outdoor patio.
- The kitchen features a snack bar, a pantry and a windowed sink.
- All three bedrooms are upstairs. The master bedroom has a private deck and bath. The bath features a dual-sink vanity, an isolated toilet and a separate tub and shower.

Plan LRD-31086

Bedrooms: 3	Baths: 2½
Living Area:	
Upper floor	860 sq. ft.
Main floor	924 sq. ft.
Total Living Area:	**1,784 sq. ft.**
Standard basement	924 sq. ft.
Garage	431 sq. ft.
Exterior Wall Framing:	2x6

Foundation Options:

Standard basement

Crawlspace

(All plans can be built with your choice of foundation and framing. A generic conversion diagram is available. See order form.)

BLUEPRINT PRICE CODE: B

UPPER FLOOR

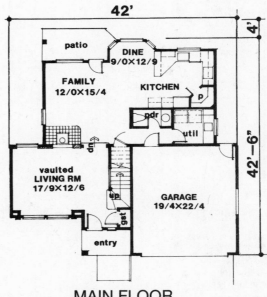

MAIN FLOOR

Plan LRD-31086

PRICES AND DETAILS
ON PAGES 2-5

Passive A-Frame

- Without breaking the lines, disturbing the A-frame shape or even interfering with the potential view, the passive sun room on this home performs its function of capturing, storing and gradually releasing the free heat from nature's furnace, the sun.
- The natural tendency of heat to rise will turn the loft over the back of the home into a warm and cozy retreat.

- The central location and comfortable rise of the stairway is a departure from the almost ladder-like access found in most A-frames.
- The triangular corner woodstove is situated so it doesn't spoil the view. At the same time, it allows furniture placement to take advantage of indoor warmth and outdoor view.
- The galley kitchen includes a pantry closet with plenty of room to stock food staples, and features access to a utility room with a washer and dryer.
- The optional daylight basement offers a garage and another bedroom and bath.

Plans H-959-1A & -1B

Bedrooms: 1+	Baths: 1-1½
Living Area:	
Upper floor	188 sq. ft.
Main floor	788 sq. ft.
Passive sun room	126 sq. ft.
Total Living Area:	**1,102 sq. ft.**
Daylight basement	461 sq. ft.
Garage (basement only)	450 sq. ft.
Exterior Wall Framing:	2x6
Foundation Options	**Plan #**
Daylight basement	H-959-1B
Slab	H-959-1A

(All plans can be built with your choice of foundation and framing. A generic conversion diagram is available. See order form.)

BLUEPRINT PRICE CODE: A

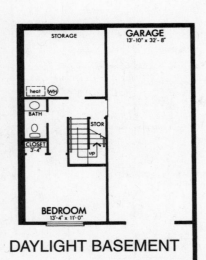

DAYLIGHT BASEMENT

STAIRWAY AREA IN CRAWLSPACE VERSION

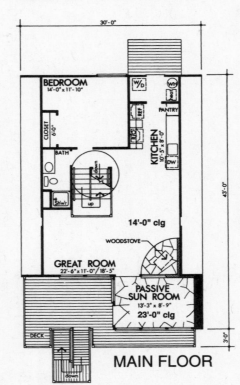

MAIN FLOOR

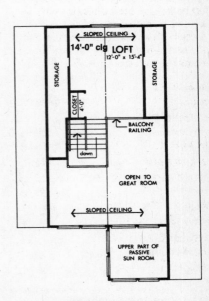

UPPER FLOOR

Family Farmhouse

- There's more to this house than its charming front porch, steeply pitched roof and dormer windows.
- A feeling of spaciousness is emphasized by the open floor plan, with the living room adjoining the kitchen and bayed breakfast area. A snack bar allows easy service to the living room.
- The back door leads from the carport to the utility room, which is convenient to the kitchen and half-bath.
- The secluded main-floor master bedroom offers a large walk-in closet and a private bathroom.
- Upstairs, two bedrooms share another full bath. One includes dormer windows and the other a window seat. A door at the top of the stairs provides access to attic space that could be turned into an extra bedroom.

Plan J-86133

Bedrooms: 3	Baths: 2½
Living Area:	
Upper floor	559 sq. ft.
Main floor	1,152 sq. ft.
Total Living Area:	**1,711 sq. ft.**
Standard basement	1,152 sq. ft.
Carport	387 sq. ft.
Storage	85 sq. ft.
Exterior Wall Framing:	2x4

Foundation Options:

Standard basement
Crawlspace
Slab
(All plans can be built with your choice of foundation and framing. A generic conversion diagram is available. See order form.)

BLUEPRINT PRICE CODE: B

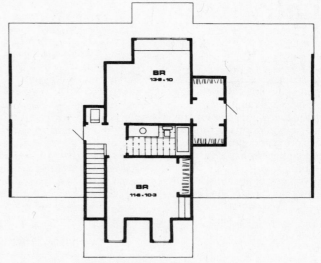

UPPER FLOOR

MAIN FLOOR

Plan J-86133

A Country Classic

- The exterior of this cozy country-style home boasts a charming combination of woodwork and stone.
- A graceful, arched entryway leads into the spacious living room with a 19-ft. vaulted ceiling, tall windows and a fireplace.
- The dining area has a lovely view of a patio and shares the living room's fireplace and vaulted ceiling.
- The impressive kitchen is brightened by a large window bank with skylights above, and offers ample counter space, a full pantry and easy access to the dining room.
- The master bedroom features a 14½-ft. vaulted ceiling, a walk-in closet, a linen closet, its own two-sink master bath and sliding-door access to the side patio.
- Two second-floor bedrooms share another full bath.

Plan B-87157

Bedrooms: 3	Baths: 2½
Living Area:	
Upper floor	452 sq. ft.
Main floor	1,099 sq. ft.
Total Living Area:	**1,551 sq. ft.**
Standard basement	1,099 sq. ft.
Garage	412 sq. ft.
Exterior Wall Framing:	2x4

Foundation Options:

Standard basement

(All plans can be built with your choice of foundation and framing. A generic conversion diagram is available. See order form.)

BLUEPRINT PRICE CODE: B

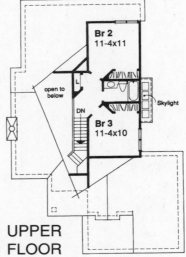

UPPER FLOOR

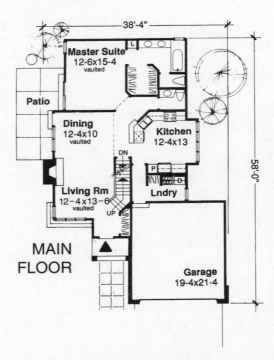

MAIN FLOOR

ORDER BLUEPRINTS ANYTIME!
CALL TOLL-FREE 1-800-820-1283

Plan B-87157

PRICES AND DETAILS
ON PAGES 2-5

275

Economical Construction

- This home offers simplicity and ease of construction, but still provides plenty of comfort and style.
- A fabulous 17-ft vaulted ceiling tops the airy entry.
- The living and dining rooms flow together to create a large space for entertaining. The area is anchored by a fireplace and includes a 16-ft. vaulted ceiling and a built-in wet bar off the dining room.
- The kitchen is designed for efficiency and adjoins a handy utility area. A serving area is easily accessible from the dining room.
- The main-floor master suite includes two large closets and a deluxe bath with dual vanities.
- Two upstairs bedrooms, each with lots of closet space, share a full bath.

Plan E-1507

Bedrooms: 3	Baths: 2
Living Area:	
Upper floor	495 sq. ft.
Main floor	1,091 sq. ft.
Total Living Area:	**1,586 sq. ft.**
Standard basement	1,091 sq. ft.
Garage	462 sq. ft.
Storage	88 sq. ft.
Exterior Wall Framing:	2x6

Foundation Options:

Standard basement

Crawlspace

Slab

(All plans can be built with your choice of foundation and framing. A generic conversion diagram is available. See order form.)

BLUEPRINT PRICE CODE: **B**

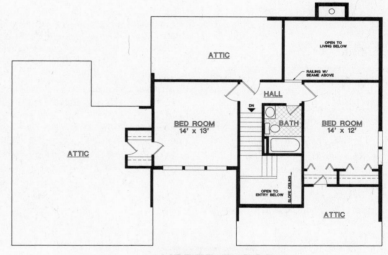

UPPER FLOOR

MAIN FLOOR

Weekend Hideaway

- Relaxed weekend and vacation lifestyles are reflected in this simple, yet dramatic plan which is easy to afford and easy to maintain.
- A contemporary exterior is created with a steeply pitched, skylighted roofline, vertical and diagonal wood siding and a wing wall for deck privacy.

- The interior centers on an open Great Room with a high sloped ceiling, a fireplace and dual sliders to the deck.
- The kitchen features an eating area next to an oversized window, plus a pantry and a view into the Great Room.
- A main-floor bedroom or den offers sleeping quarters without negotiating stairs.
- The upper floor houses two additional bedrooms, which are accessed from a dramatic open stair and a balcony overlooking the Great Room.

Plan AX-8470-A

Bedrooms: 2+	Baths: 2
Living Area:	
Upper floor	616 sq. ft.
Main floor	1,021 sq. ft.
Total Living Area:	**1,637 sq. ft.**
Standard basement	1,021 sq. ft.
Exterior Wall Framing:	2x4

Foundation Options:
Standard basement
Slab
(All plans can be built with your choice of foundation and framing. A generic conversion diagram is available. See order form.)

BLUEPRINT PRICE CODE:	**B**

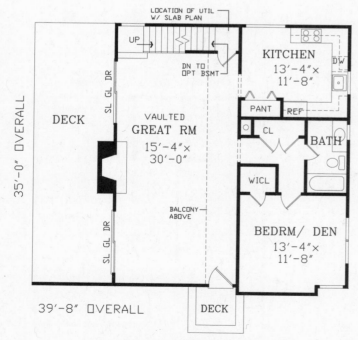

MAIN FLOOR

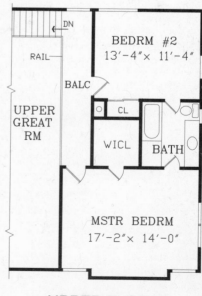

UPPER FLOOR

ORDER BLUEPRINTS ANYTIME!
CALL TOLL-FREE 1-800-820-1283

Plan AX-8470-A

PRICES AND DETAILS
ON PAGES 3-5

222

Smart Look, Smart Price

- Smart in looks, function and cost, this design is filled with flexible spaces and all the best in features.
- The exterior has a natural look, with its clean roofline, wood siding and stone veneer.
- The high-impact foyer has views of the winding stair tower brightened by a clerestory window.
- Straight ahead, the Great Room and the open kitchen serve as one huge, flexible living space. The Great Room features a cathedral ceiling, a built-in wet bar, a cozy fireplace and lots of glass overlooking the backyard deck. The kitchen is highlighted by a clever pass-through to the Great Room.
- The main-floor master suite offers all of today's amenities, including a window seat facing the backyard, a walk-in closet and a private bath.
- Another full bathroom, a roomy bedroom and a multipurpose loft are on the upper floor.

Plan B-711

Bedrooms: 2-3	Baths: 2½
Living Area:	
Upper floor	454 sq. ft.
Main floor	1,044 sq. ft.
Total Living Area:	**1,498 sq. ft.**
Standard basement	1,044 sq. ft.
Garage	380 sq. ft.
Exterior Wall Framing:	2x6

Foundation Options:

Standard basement

(All plans can be built with your choice of foundation and framing. A generic conversion diagram is available. See order form.)

BLUEPRINT PRICE CODE:	A

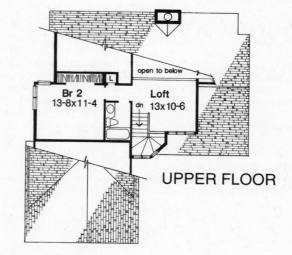

UPPER FLOOR

MAIN FLOOR

 Plan B-711 **PRICES AND DETAILS ON PAGES 2-5**

One-Bedroom Retreat

- This open one-bedroom retreat is the perfect solution for a private weekend getaway.
- Comforts you never had at home are featured in this unique A-frame design. A spacious, open, two-story living area with a vaulted ceiling, two-story fireplace, relaxing wet bar, walls of windows and a spiral staircase that draws you to the upperlevel master suite dominates the dramatic interior.
- A large island kitchen, dining area, full bath and expanisve outdoor deck complete the first level.
- Upstairs, the exciting master suite has a private sitting area with an attached deck, plus a walk-in closet and a dramatic balcony that overlooks the living room below.
- Skylights and soaring windows give the home an open, airy feeling.

Plan DD-2194

Bedrooms: 1	Baths: 2

Living Area:	
Upper floor	658 sq. ft.
Main floor	1,088 sq. ft.

Total Living Area:	**1,746 sq. ft.**
Exterior Wall Framing:	2x4

Foundation Options:

Crawlspace
Slab
(All plans can be built with your choice of foundation and framing. A generic conversion diagram is available. See order form.)

BLUEPRINT PRICE CODE: **B**

SIDE VIEW

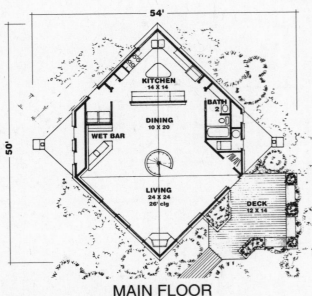

MAIN FLOOR

UPPER FLOOR

ORDER BLUEPRINTS ANYTIME!
CALL TOLL-FREE 1-800-820-1283

Plan DD-2194

PRICES AND DETAILS
ON PAGES 2-5

271

Warm Welcome

- A vaulted, covered porch adds warmth to the brick and cedar shingle facade of this cozy home.
- An inviting foyer opens into the living room, which boasts a 17-ft. vaulted ceiling and shares a see-through fireplace with the formal dining room. Sliding glass doors open to a spacious backyard deck.
- The gourmet kitchen wraps around a sunny breakfast nook. An angled serving counter facilitates entertaining.
- Just a few steps away, the master bedroom sports a walk-in closet and private bath access.
- Upstairs, a charming balcony leads to two secondary bedrooms, which are enhanced by roomy walk-in closets and share a full bath.
- An open loft area with built-ins may be used as an entertainment room or a third bedroom, if desired.

Plan B-93033

Bedrooms: 3+	Baths: 2
Living Area:	
Upper floor	645 sq. ft.
Main floor	1,042 sq. ft.
Total Living Area:	**1,687 sq. ft.**
Standard basement	1,042 sq. ft.
Garage	385 sq. ft.
Exterior Wall Framing:	2x4

Foundation Options:

Standard basement

(All plans can be built with your choice of foundation and framing. A generic conversion diagram is available. See order form.)

BLUEPRINT PRICE CODE: B

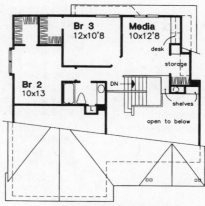

UPPER FLOOR

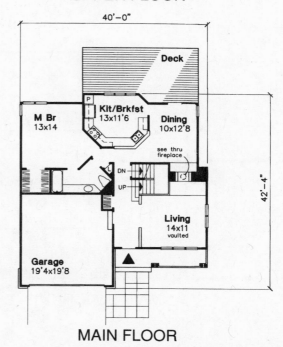

MAIN FLOOR

Plan B-93033

PRICES AND DETAILS ON PAGES 2-5

REAR VIEW

Crowd Shy, Mountain High

- Rising confidently into view, this solid, multi-tiered home will hold your attention for miles and miles.
- The home's floor plan shows how much it prefers nature views to the busy street. All the living areas, including two of the home's three bedrooms, are positioned to direct your eyes to your favorite views in two directions.
- The upstairs master bedroom suite is the home's most dramatic viewing point,

and the architectural crown of its design. It's a big room with a free sink and a walk-in closet.
- The kitchen wraps around the chef, and features a snack bar in the dining room.
- High sloped ceilings over the living and dining areas and an incredible fireplace keep the home's sense of height and energy alive inside.
- The laundry serves as an air-lock entry within the garage, convenient for snow-soaked children; it adjoins the kitchen, for easy grocery unloading.
- The optional basement has room for a big recreation room.

Plans H-937-1 & -1A	
Bedrooms: 3	**Baths:** 2
Living Area:	
Upper floor	462 sq. ft.
Main floor	1,446 sq. ft.
Total Living Area:	**1,908 sq. ft.**
Daylight basement	1,446 sq. ft.
Garage	644 sq. ft.
Exterior Wall Framing:	2x6
Foundation Options:	**Plan #**
Daylight basement	H-937-1
Crawlspace	H-937-1A

(All plans can be built with your choice of foundation and framing. A generic conversion diagram is available. See order form.)

BLUEPRINT PRICE CODE:	**B**

UPPER FLOOR

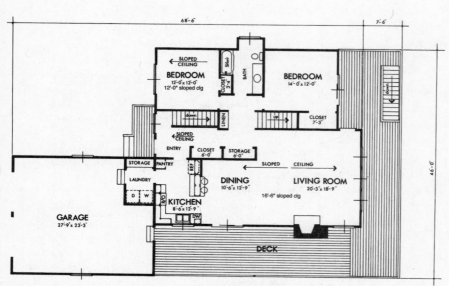

MAIN FLOOR

STAIRWAY AREA IN CRAWLSPACE VERSION

Cottage Suits Small Lot

- Designed to fit on a sloping or small lot, this compact country-style cottage has the amenities of a much larger home.
- The large front porch opens to the home's surprising two-story-high foyer, which views into the living room.
- The spacious living room is warmed by a handsome fireplace that is centered between built-in bookshelves.
- Enhanced by a sunny bay that opens to a backyard deck, the dining room offers a comfortable eating area that is easily served by the island kitchen.
- The secluded main-floor master bedroom includes a roomy walk-in closet. The spectacular master bath showcases a corner garden tub, a designer shower, a built-in bench and a dual-sink vanity.
- Upstairs, a railed balcony overlooks the foyer. Two secondary bedrooms with walk-in closets share a central bath.

Plan C-8870

Bedrooms: 3	Baths: 2
Living Area:	
Upper floor	664 sq. ft.
Main floor	1,100 sq. ft.
Total Living Area:	**1,764 sq. ft.**
Daylight basement/garage	1,100 sq. ft.
Exterior Wall Framing:	2x4

Foundation Options:

Daylight basement

(All plans can be built with your choice of foundation and framing. A generic conversion diagram is available. See order form.)

BLUEPRINT PRICE CODE: B

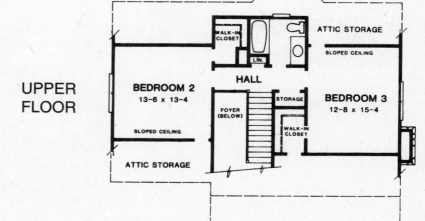

UPPER FLOOR

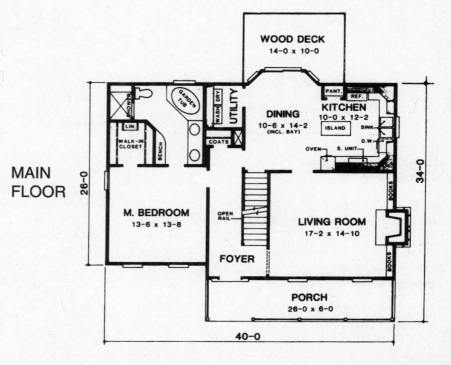

MAIN FLOOR

Plan C-8870

PRICES AND DETAILS ON PAGES 2-5

Stunning Home

- A stunning picture window arrangement highlights this split-foyer home, which is perfect for a sloping lot.
- Inside, a half-staircase leads up to the sunken living room. A 14-ft. cathedral ceiling soars over the room, which offers a spectacular view through a floor-to-ceiling wall of windows.
- A charming two-way stone fireplace is shared with the dining room, which features a 12-ft. cathedral ceiling. Sliding glass doors open to a backyard deck that beckons you for a summer afternoon barbecue.
- Nearby, a cheery bayed breakfast nook extends to the galley-style kitchen.
- In the master bedroom, sliding glass doors offer private deck access. The master bath boasts a garden tub and a dual-sink vanity.
- Across the hall, two good-sized bedrooms with large closets are serviced by a centrally located bath.
- Downstairs, a fun recreation room with handy built-in shelves is a great spot for boisterous family get togethers.

Plan AX-8486-A

Bedrooms: 3	Baths: 2
Living Area:	
Main floor	1,630 sq. ft.
Daylight basement (finished)	334 sq. ft.
Total Living Area:	**1,964 sq. ft.**
Daylight basement (unfinished)	754 sq. ft.
Tuck-under garage and storage	510 sq. ft.
Exterior Wall Framing:	2x4

Foundation Options:

Daylight basement
(All plans can be built with your choice of foundation and framing. A generic conversion diagram is available. See order form.)

BLUEPRINT PRICE CODE:	**B**

MAIN FLOOR

DAYLIGHT BASEMENT

ORDER BLUEPRINTS ANYTIME!
CALL TOLL-FREE 1-800-820-1283

Plan AX-8486-A

PRICES AND DETAILS
ON PAGES 2-5

267

FRONT VIEW

REAR VIEW

Sunny Hideaway

- A multitude of windows let in the sun, while a steeply pitched roofline and a private backyard deck lend this home an aura of intimacy.
- The living areas dominate the main floor. The massive living room features a sloped ceiling and a cozy fireplace.
- Two secondary bedrooms lie off to one corner. They share a hall bath with dual sinks, and each room enjoys a window with a built-in planter outside.
- Upstairs, the secluded master suite is a hideaway in itself. It includes a full bath, a walk-in closet and a bedroom window with a built-in planter outside.
- In the daylight basement version, a dramatic spiral staircase outside the living room leads downstairs, where the sun room—with open space above—is located. A rec room, another bedroom and a full bath complete the plan.

Plans H-975-1 & -1A

Bedrooms: 3+	Baths: 2-3
Living Area:	
Upper floor	370 sq. ft.
Main floor	1,231 sq. ft.
Sun room	163 sq. ft.
Daylight basement (finished)	782 sq. ft.
Total Living Area:	**1,764/2,546 sq. ft.**
Daylight basement (unfinished)	612 sq. ft.
Garage	448 sq. ft.
Exterior Wall Framing:	2x6
Foundation Options:	**Plan #**
Daylight basement	H-975-1
Crawlspace	H-975-1A

(All plans can be built with your choice of foundation and framing. A generic conversion diagram is available. See order form.)

BLUEPRINT PRICE CODE:	**B/D**

UPPER FLOOR

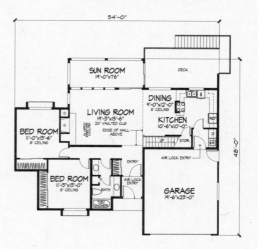

Your Choice

- This design provides a cozy, modern exterior and a number of choices for the interior. Mix and match foundations and upper-floor options as you please.
- For the plan with a crawlspace foundation and a bedroom/bath on the upper floor, order H-893-1A.
- For the plan with a crawlspace foundation and a dormitory on the upper floor, order H-893-2A.
- For the plan with a standard basement and a bedroom/bath on the upper floor, order H-893-1B.
- For the plan with a standard basement and a dormitory on the upper floor, order H-893-2B.
- For the plan with a daylight basement and a garage, plus a bedroom/bath on the upper floor, order H-893-1C.
- For the plan with a daylight basement and a garage, plus a dormitory on the upper floor, order H-893-2C.

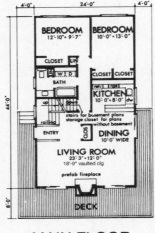

MAIN FLOOR

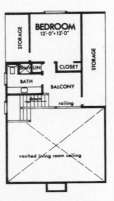

UPPER FLOOR

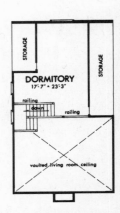

ALTERNATE UPPER FLOOR

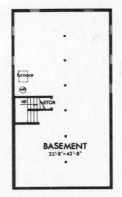

STANDARD BASEMENT

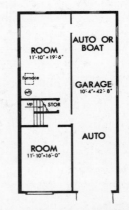

DAYLIGHT BASEMENT

Plans H-893-1A, -1B, -1C, -2A, -2B & -2C

Bedrooms: 2+	Baths: 1-2
Living Area:	
Upper floor	336 sq. ft.
Main floor	1,056 sq. ft.
Total Living Area:	**1,392 sq. ft.**
Daylight basement	615 sq. ft.
Standard basement	1,056 sq. ft.
Tuck-under garage	441 sq. ft.
Exterior Wall Framing:	2x4

Foundation Options:

Daylight basement
Standard basement
Crawlspace
(All plans can be built with your choice of foundation and framing. A generic conversion diagram is available. See order form.)

BLUEPRINT PRICE CODE:	**A**

Plans H-893-1A, -1B, -1C, -2A, -2B & -2C

New Yet Familiar

- You'll find style and value in this newly planned split-entry home.
- Ground-hugging front rooflines cover the vaulted Great Room, dining room, kitchen and master bedroom.
- The front-facing Great Room features a lovely fireplace flanked by windows

and entrance to a deck. The Great Room is presided over by a balcony dining room above.

- The breakfast room off the kitchen also offers an exciting adjoining deck, which may be entered through the master bedroom, as well.
- Two additional bedrooms are found on the upper level; a fourth bedroom and generous family room share the daylight basement with a bath and laundry room.

Plan B-903	
Bedrooms: 4	**Baths:** 2
Living Area:	
Main floor	1,197 sq. ft.
Lower floor	600 sq. ft.
Total Living Area:	**1,797 sq. ft.**
Partial basement	280 sq. ft.
Tuck-under garage	455 sq. ft.
Exterior Wall Framing:	2x4
Foundation Options:	

Partial basement
(All plans can be built with your choice of foundation and framing. A generic conversion diagram is available. See order form.)

BLUEPRINT PRICE CODE:	B

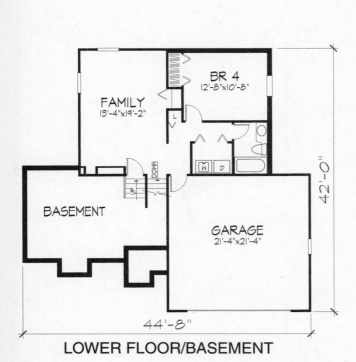

LOWER FLOOR/BASEMENT

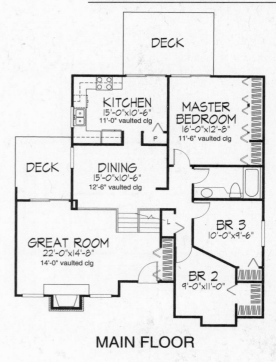

MAIN FLOOR

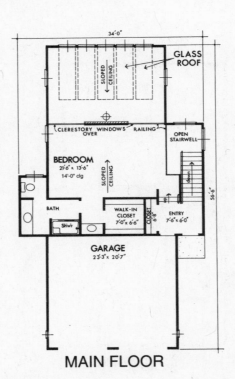

REAR VIEW

Drama in Many Levels

- High, stacked windows and glorious skylights sparkle in this modern, angular home. The dramatic flair of the exterior is echoed and embellished in the many levels of the interior.
- From the entry landing, step up to the spacious master suite. In the bedroom, a railing overlooks the open stairwell to the right, and two more railings flank a brick chimney and look down on the living room below.

- Clerestory windows above, in addition to skylights and a window wall in the living room, make for a dazzling view. A dual-sink bath and a walk-in closet add a practical—yet luxurious—touch.
- At the bottom of the stairway lies the lower floor. The bedroom is earth-sheltered for extra energy efficiency.
- The U-shaped kitchen includes a windowed sink, and is adjacent to the open dining room.
- A step down from the dining room, the living room is on center stage. Its glass expanses and free-standing fireplace attract admiration while it allows warm air to rise and heat the areas above.

Plan H-943-1A	
Bedrooms: 2	**Baths:** 2
Living Area:	
Main floor	575 sq. ft.
Lower floor	983 sq. ft.
Total Living Area:	**1,558 sq. ft.**
Garage	479 sq. ft.
Exterior Wall Framing:	2x6
Foundation Options:	
Crawlspace	
Slab	
(All plans can be built with your choice of foundation and framing. A generic conversion diagram is available. See order form.)	
BLUEPRINT PRICE CODE:	**B**

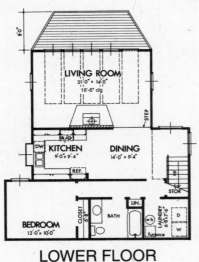

LOWER FLOOR

MAIN FLOOR

ORDER BLUEPRINTS ANYTIME!
CALL TOLL-FREE 1-800-820-1283

Plan H-943-1A

PRICES AND DETAILS
ON PAGES 2-5

263

Tradition Rekindled

- Stylish half-round windows and a quaint front porch rekindle family tradition in this warm country home.
- The porch opens to a spacious living and dining room combination that unfolds to the rest of the main floor. The open railing to the left provides a view of the stairway to the upper floor.
- Beyond the living room, an angled hallway flows past a convenient powder room and the luxurious master suite to the informal spaces.

- The comfortable family room features a 17-ft. vaulted ceiling and sliding glass doors that open to a covered patio.
- The kitchen's handy pass-through allows easy transporting of food and beverages into the family room. If desired, the opening could be closed off with bi-fold doors. A pantry and a sunny breakfast nook are also featured.
- The quiet master suite boasts a walk-in closet and a private bath with a spa tub.
- Off the upper-floor balcony are two nice-sized bedrooms, a full bath and a dramatic view into the family room.
- The optional bonus room above the garage could be finished and tailored to your needs.

Plan S-11993

Bedrooms: 3+	Baths: 2½
Living Area:	
Upper floor	489 sq. ft.
Main floor	1,128 sq. ft.
Total Living Area:	**1,617 sq. ft.**
Optional bonus room	256 sq. ft.
Standard basement	1,128 sq. ft.
Garage and shop	488 sq. ft.
Exterior Wall Framing:	2x6

Foundation Options:

Standard basement
Crawlspace
Slab

(All plans can be built with your choice of foundation and framing. A generic conversion diagram is available. See order form.)

BLUEPRINT PRICE CODE:	B

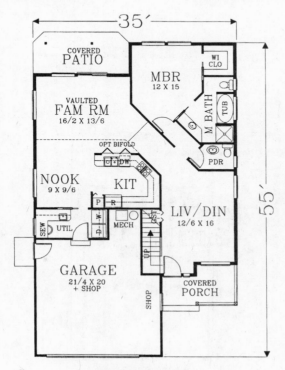

MAIN FLOOR

UPPER FLOOR

Plan S-11993

Excitement on a Narrow Lot!

- A stylish entry invites guests into this exciting, narrow-lot home.
- Exposed timbers, a Palladian window and decorative shingling create an attractive, rustic appeal.
- The enjoyment continues inside, beginning with a 17-ft. vaulted foyer that gives guests a great first impression.
- From the foyer, step into the spacious living room/dining room area, where a sparkling fireplace brightens the whole space with a sparkling charm.
- Sliding glass doors to a patio in back let you step out and enjoy the beautiful weather. If you want, enjoy your morning paper and breakfast alfresco!
- Upstairs, two walk-in closets and a private bath with a whirlpool tub highlight the master suite.
- Two additional bedrooms and a full bath provide room for growing families.

Plan AHP-9010

Bedrooms: 3	Baths: 2½
Living Area:	
Upper floor	826 sq. ft.
Main floor	794 sq. ft.
Total Living Area:	**1,620 sq. ft.**
Standard basement	794 sq. ft.
Garage	444 sq. ft.
Exterior Wall Framing:	2x6

Foundation Options:

Standard basement

Slab

(All plans can be built with your choice of foundation and framing. A generic conversion diagram is available. See order form.)

BLUEPRINT PRICE CODE:	B

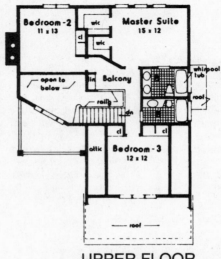

UPPER FLOOR

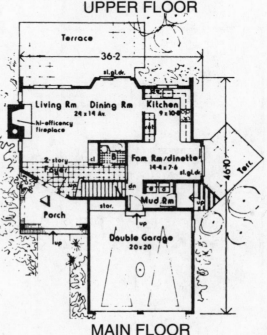

MAIN FLOOR

ORDER BLUEPRINTS ANYTIME!
CALL TOLL-FREE 1-800-820-1283

Plan AHP-9010

PRICES AND DETAILS
ON PAGES 2-5

261

Versatile A-Frame

- This traditional A-frame is designed for optimum comfort and minimum cost. The versatile interior can vary from plush to rustic, allowing the home to serve equally well as a weekend cabin, a summer retreat or a ski chalet.
- The highlight of the floor plan is the spacious living room, with its high 22-ft. vaulted ceiling and dramatic stone fireplace. The fireplace extends to the outdoors, where it doubles as a barbecue. A stunning window wall parallels the angles of the A-frame and includes sliding glass doors that access a huge deck. The adjoining U-shaped kitchen is open to the dining room.
- To the rear are two bedrooms and a full bath. Between the bedrooms is a hallway to a backyard deck.
- Upstairs is a third bedroom with a private deck and a half-bath. The balcony area that overlooks the living room can sleep overnight guests.

Plan H-6	
Bedrooms: 3+	**Baths:** 1½
Living Area:	
Upper floor	375 sq. ft.
Main floor	845 sq. ft.
Total Living Area:	**1,220 sq. ft.**
Exterior Wall Framing:	2x4

Foundation Options:

Crawlspace

(All plans can be built with your choice of foundation and framing. A generic conversion diagram is available. See order form.)

BLUEPRINT PRICE CODE: A

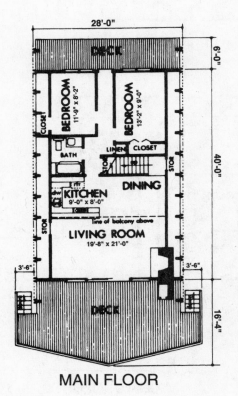

MAIN FLOOR

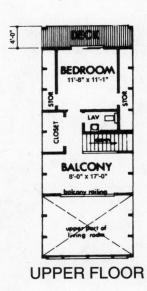

UPPER FLOOR

Stylish Blend

- A stylish blend of traditional and contemporary architecture distinguishes this striking compact home.
- A steeply pitched roofline, a covered front porch and decorative fishscale shingles lend drama to the front facade.
- Inside, a central hallway points ahead to the huge living room, which overlooks the backyard through a wall of windows. A woodstove lends warm charm to any gathering, and a side door invites you to take advantage of the wraparound side deck.
- A breathtaking sloped ceiling tops both the living room and the adjacent dining room. The eating area includes sliding glass doors to the deck.
- Natural light enters the kitchen through a window over the sink. Nearby, the laundry room provides an extra storage closet and access to the garage.
- The master suite occupies the entire upper floor. It features a sloped ceiling and a balcony overlooking the living room below. A full bath and a walk-in closet add final touches of luxury.

Plans H-947-2A & -2B

Bedrooms: 3	Baths: 2
Living Area:	
Upper floor	516 sq. ft.
Main floor	1,162 sq. ft.
Total Living Area:	**1,678 sq. ft.**
Daylight basement	1,162 sq. ft.
Garage	530 sq. ft.
Exterior Wall Framing:	2x6
Foundation Options:	**Plan #**
Daylight basement	H-947-2B
Crawlspace	H-947-2A

(All plans can be built with your choice of foundation and framing. A generic conversion diagram is available. See order form.)

BLUEPRINT PRICE CODE:	**B**

UPPER FLOOR

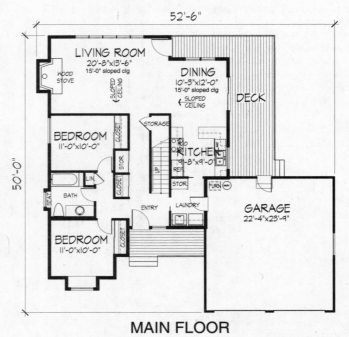

MAIN FLOOR

ORDER BLUEPRINTS ANYTIME!
CALL TOLL-FREE 1-800-820-1283

Plans H-947-2A & -2B

**PRICES AND DETAILS
ON PAGES 2-5**

259

Farmhouse for Today

- An inviting covered porch and decorative dormer windows lend traditional warmth and charm to this attractive design.
- The up-to-date interior includes ample space for entertaining as well as for daily family activities.
- The elegant foyer is flanked on one side by the formal, sunken living room and on the other by a sunken family room with a fireplace and an entertainment center. Each room features an 8½-ft. tray ceiling and views of the porch.
- The dining room flows from the living room to increase the entertaining space.
- The kitchen/nook/laundry area forms a large expanse for casual family living and domestic chores.
- Upstairs, the grand master suite includes a large closet and a private bath with a garden tub, a designer shower and a private deck.
- A second full bath serves the two secondary bedrooms.

Plan U-87-203

Bedrooms: 3	Baths: 2½
Living Area:	
Upper floor	857 sq. ft.
Main floor	1,064 sq. ft.
Total Living Area:	**1,921 sq. ft.**
Standard basement	1,064 sq. ft.
Garage	552 sq. ft.
Exterior Wall Framing:	2x4 or 2x6

Foundation Options:

Standard basement

Crawlspace

Slab

(All plans can be built with your choice of foundation and framing. A generic conversion diagram is available. See order form.)

BLUEPRINT PRICE CODE: B

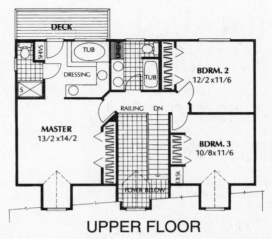

UPPER FLOOR

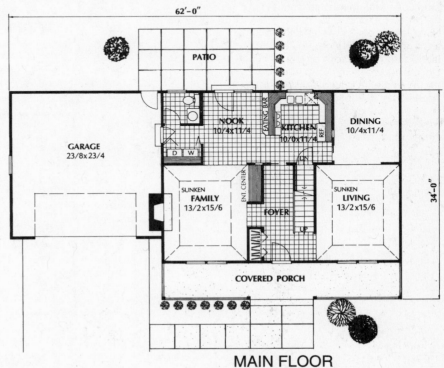

MAIN FLOOR

Cottage Basks in Brilliance

- The vaulted areas of this brilliant cottage bask in light that streams through its window walls and skylights.
- French doors are surrounded by dramatic glass to illuminate the 20-ft.-high entry as it flows into the formal areas.
- The soaring vaulted space of the living and dining rooms allows heat from the angled woodstove to spread into the loft area above.
- The U-shaped kitchen has a bright sink and abundant counter space. Laundry facilities are located by the back entry.
- Two corner bedrooms are separated by an oversized laundry room and are serviced by a full bath off the main hall.
- An outside stairway offers private access to the loft, which boasts a 10-ft.-high vaulted ceiling.

Plan NW-990-A

Bedrooms: 2+	Baths: 1
Living Area:	
Upper floor	330 sq. ft.
Main floor	1,008 sq. ft.
Total Living Area:	**1,338 sq. ft.**
Exterior Wall Framing:	**2x6**

Foundation Options:

Crawlspace

(All plans can be built with your choice of foundation and framing. A generic conversion diagram is available. See order form.)

BLUEPRINT PRICE CODE: **A**

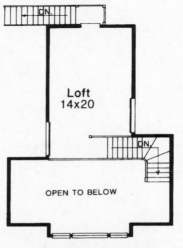

UPPER FLOOR

Loft 14x20

OPEN TO BELOW

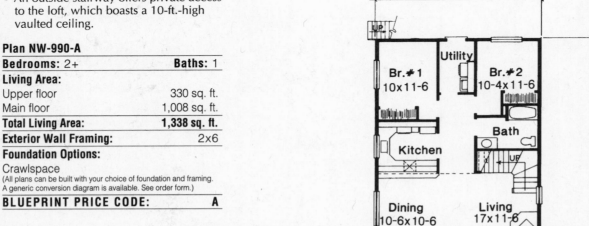

MAIN FLOOR

28'-0"

36'-0"

4'-0"

Br. #1 10x11-6

Utility

Br. #2 10-4x11-6

Bath

Kitchen

Dining 10-6x10-6

Living 17x11-6

ORDER BLUEPRINTS ANYTIME!
CALL TOLL-FREE 1-800-820-1283

Plan NW-990-A

PRICES AND DETAILS
ON PAGES 2-5

257

Seasonal Chalet

- This handsome chalet-style vacation home is so comfortable you may find yourself using it all year long.
- An entry hallway leads back to the main-floor living spaces. To the right is a generous living room that flows into a dining area. A fireplace separates the two rooms, warming them both and providing a sense of definition.
- The walk-through kitchen opens directly into the dining area.
- Sliding doors in the living room access a large side deck. You'll love using this area as additional outdoor living space in warm weather.
- The main-floor bedroom, with dual closets and easy access to a full bath, would make a nice master bedroom.
- Upstairs, two secondary bedrooms share a full bath. Each bedroom boasts a private deck.

Plans H-881-1 & -1A

Bedrooms: 3	Baths: 2
Living Area:	
Upper floor	462 sq. ft.
Main floor	1,008 sq. ft.
Total Living Area:	**1,470 sq. ft.**
Daylight basement	560 sq. ft.
Tuck-under garage	448 sq. ft.
Exterior Wall Framing:	2x4
Foundation Options:	**Plan #**
Daylight basement	H-881-1
Crawlspace	H-881-1A

(All plans can be built with your choice of foundation and framing. A generic conversion diagram is available. See order form.)

BLUEPRINT PRICE CODE:	**A**

UPPER FLOOR

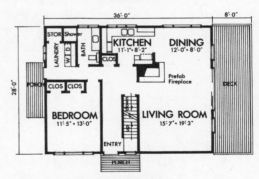

MAIN FLOOR

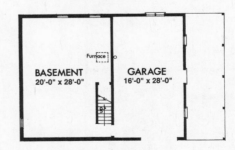

DAYLIGHT BASEMENT

Plans H-881-1 & -1A

PRICES AND DETAILS
ON PAGES 2-5

Quaint Retreat

- The main floor of this quaint retreat is accessed via stairs on either end of an inviting wraparound deck.
- The upper foyer introduces the Grand Room, with its large fireplace, TV niche and sliding glass doors to the deck.
- The kitchen boasts a handy island with a cooktop and a snack bar. Other features include a step-in pantry and a pass-through to the morning room.
- The morning room is brightened by incoming light through three walls of glass. Sliding glass doors give easy access to the deck and the street level.
- The master suite offers deck access, a dressing area and a walk-in closet. The unusual master bath has a stepped stone wall, a sunken shower and a dry-off area. Part of the bath is separate and functions as a powder room.
- The daylight basement houses two more bedroom suites, with a full bath between them. Each suite has outdoor access via sliding glass doors.
- The laundry room is large enough for a washer, a dryer and a laundry tub.

Plan EOF-15

Bedrooms: 3	Baths: 2
Living Area:	
Main floor	1,193 sq. ft.
Daylight basement	593 sq. ft.
Total Living Area:	**1,786 sq. ft.**
Tuck-under garage	360 sq. ft.
Exterior Wall Framing:	2x4

Foundation Options:

Daylight basement
(All plans can be built with your choice of foundation and framing. A generic conversion diagram is available. See order form.)

BLUEPRINT PRICE CODE: B

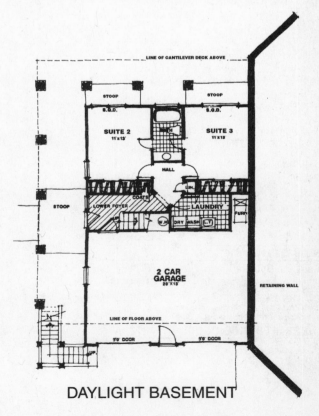

MAIN FLOOR

DAYLIGHT BASEMENT

ORDER BLUEPRINTS ANYTIME!
CALL TOLL-FREE 1-800-820-1283

Plan EOF-15

PRICES AND DETAILS
ON PAGES 2-5

255

The Sunshine of Your Life!

- A huge sun room and an abundance of windows in this fascinating home will bring the sunshine into your life!
- The huge living room's sparkling sun roof gathers solar heat, which is stored in the tile floor and the two-story-high masonry wall behind the woodstove. The cozy woodstove creates a glowing charm that's sure to light up all your family events.
- Efficiently designed, the galley-style kitchen makes meal preparation a breeze. Nearby access to a spacious deck lets you cool off after dining.
- Two nice-sized bedrooms and a full bath complete the main floor.
- Occupying the entire upper floor is the beautiful master suite, which features a big walk-in closet and a private bath. A balcony overlooking the living room lets you check in on the kids below.

Plans H-947-1A & -1B

Bedrooms: 3+	Baths: 2-3
Living Area:	
Upper floor	516 sq. ft.
Main floor	1,162 sq. ft.
Daylight basement	966 sq. ft.
Total Living Area:	**1,678/2,644 sq. ft.**
Garage	279 sq. ft.
Exterior Wall Framing:	2x6
Foundation Options:	**Plan #**
Daylight basement	H-947-1B
Crawlspace	H-947-1A

(All plans can be built with your choice of foundation and framing. A generic conversion diagram is available. See order form.)

BLUEPRINT PRICE CODE:	**B/D**

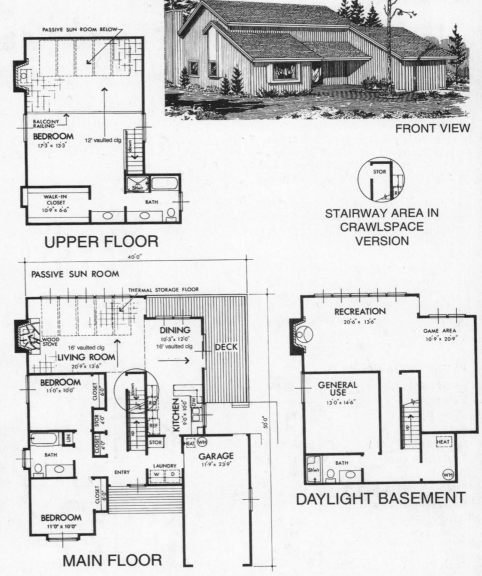

FRONT VIEW

STAIRWAY AREA IN CRAWLSPACE VERSION

UPPER FLOOR

MAIN FLOOR

DAYLIGHT BASEMENT

Plans H-947-1A & -1B

PRICES AND DETAILS ON PAGES 2-5

Octagonal Outlook

- Octagon homes are the ultimate design for providing stunning panoramic views. Besides an expansive wraparound deck, this unique plan features a huge living and dining area that is almost fully enclosed in glass!
- Solar heat is collected and stored by a dramatic masonry interior wall, while a central woodstove adds further warmth. The living area's high vaulted ceiling soars to over 15 ft., past the balcony railing of the master bedroom above.
- The efficient kitchen includes a pantry and a nice windowed sink.
- The oversized main-floor bedroom has a large walk-in closet and easy access to the nearby bath and laundry room.
- Luxurious vacation-style living is offered in the private master suite on the upper floor. An enormous bedroom with a cozy woodstove, a private bath and a gigantic separate dressing area make this retreat hard to beat!
- Space for a recreation room, a hobby room or extra bedrooms is available in the daylight basement.

Plans H-948-1A & -1B

Bedrooms: 2+	Baths: 2
Living Area:	
Upper floor	700 sq. ft.
Main floor	1,236 sq. ft.
Daylight basement	1,236 sq. ft.
Total Living Area:	**1,936/3,172 sq. ft.**
Garage	552 sq. ft.
Exterior Wall Framing:	**2x6**
Foundation Options:	**Plan #**
Daylight basement	H-948-1B
Crawlspace	H-948-1A

(All plans can be built with your choice of foundation and framing. A generic conversion diagram is available. See order form.)

BLUEPRINT PRICE CODE: **B/E**

REAR VIEW

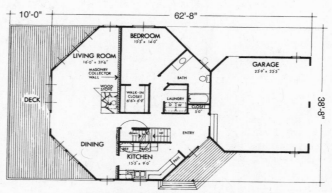

MAIN FLOOR

STAIRWAY AREA IN CRAWLSPACE VERSION

DAYLIGHT BASEMENT

UPPER FLOOR

SIDE VIEW

Get Away from it All!

- Load up the sport utility vehicle, change your voice-mail message to let people know you're out of town, and have the neighbors pick up the mail; summer's here and it's time to get away from it all in this classic A-frame!
- Affordable, yet gorgeous, this design stresses economics and an easy-going, open lifestyle.
- The incredible Great Room is clearly the heart of the home. A massive,

marvelous stone hearth surrounds its charming woodstove. Picturesque windows and access to the enormous deck bring you even closer to the wonderful outdoors.

- Energy savings are sure to result from the passive sun room, which collects, stores and redistributes the sun's heat. It also serves as a delightful breakfast nook or as a lovely arboretum.
- Surprisingly spacious, the master bedroom boasts its own walk-in closet and a private entry to a full-sized bath.
- Upstairs, you'll find two nice-sized bedrooms, a spacious full bath and extra storage space.

Plans H-957-1A & -1B	
Bedrooms: 3	**Baths: 2**
Living Area:	
Upper floor	590 sq. ft.
Main floor	1,074 sq. ft.
Passive sun room	136 sq. ft.
Total Living Area:	**1,800 sq. ft.**
Daylight basement	1,074 sq. ft.
Garage	595 sq. ft.
Exterior Wall Framing:	**2x6**
Foundation Options:	**Plan #**
Daylight basement	H-957-1B
Crawlspace	H-957-1A
(All plans can be built with your choice of foundation and framing. A generic conversion diagram is available. See order form.)	
BLUEPRINT PRICE CODE:	**B**

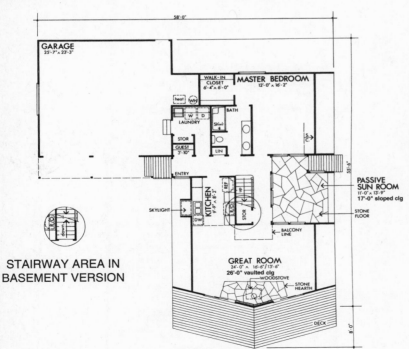

STAIRWAY AREA IN BASEMENT VERSION

MAIN FLOOR

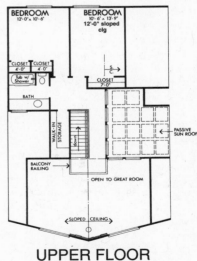

UPPER FLOOR

Plans H-957-1A & -1B

PRICES AND DETAILS ON PAGES 2-5

Lofty Cottage Retreat

- This generous cottage home offers wide-open living areas and a delightful balcony space.
- Off the recessed entry, the living room merges into the dining room for a spacious effect. A woodstove or fireplace adds an inviting ambience.
- The adjacent kitchen has a convenient raised service counter over the sink area and handy access to both the laundry closet and the back porch.
- The master suite offers a huge walk-in closet, a bayed sitting alcove and private access to the main bath, which features a soaking tub and a sit-down angled vanity.
- Upstairs, a large balcony bedroom overlooks the living areas below. This lofty space boasts a built-in desk and a bath with a shower.

Plan E-1002

Bedrooms: 1+	Baths: 2
Living Area:	
Upper floor	267 sq. ft.
Main floor	814 sq. ft.
Total Living Area:	**1,081 sq. ft.**
Standard basement	814 sq. ft.
Exterior Wall Framing:	2x4

Foundation Options:

Standard basement

Crawlspace

Slab

(All plans can be built with your choice of foundation and framing. A generic conversion diagram is available. See order form.)

BLUEPRINT PRICE CODE: A

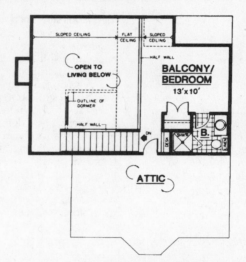

UPPER FLOOR

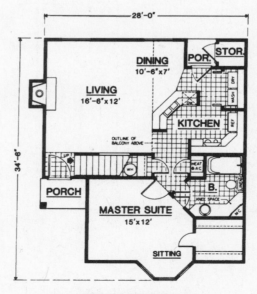

MAIN FLOOR

ORDER BLUEPRINTS ANYTIME!
CALL TOLL-FREE 1-800-820-1283

Plan E-1002

PRICES AND DETAILS
ON PAGES 2-5

251

Photo by Bob Hallinen

Soaring Design

- Dramatic windows soar to the peak of this prowed chalet, offering unlimited views of outdoor scenery.
- The spacious living room flaunts a fabulous fireplace, a soaring 26-ft. vaulted ceiling, a striking window wall and sliding glass doors to a wonderful wraparound deck.
- An oversized window brightens a dining area on the left side of the living room. The sunny, L-shaped kitchen is spacious and easily accessible.
- The secluded main-floor bedroom has convenient access to a full bath, a linen closet, a good-sized laundry room and the rear entrance.
- A central, open-railed staircase leads to the upper floor, which contains two more bedrooms and a full bath.
- A skylighted balcony is the high point of this design, offering a railed overlook into the living room below and sweeping outdoor vistas through the wall of windows.
- The optional daylight basement provides another fireplace in a versatile recreation room. The extra-long, tuck-under garage includes plenty of room for hobbies, while the service room offers additional storage space.

Plans H-930-1 & -1A	
Bedrooms: 3	**Baths:** 2
Living Area:	
Upper floor	710 sq. ft.
Main floor	1,210 sq. ft.
Daylight basement	605 sq. ft.
Total Living Area:	**1,920/2,525 sq. ft.**
Tuck-under garage/shop	605 sq. ft.
Exterior Wall Framing:	2x6
Foundation Options:	**Plan #**
Daylight basement	H-930-1
Crawlspace	H-930-1A
(All plans can be built with your choice of foundation and framing. A generic conversion diagram is available. See order form.)	
BLUEPRINT PRICE CODE:	**B/D**

DAYLIGHT BASEMENT

STAIRWAY AREA IN
CRAWLSPACE VERSION

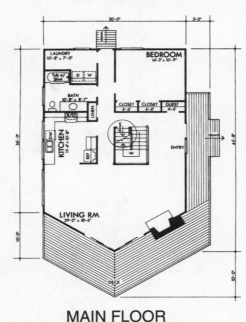

MAIN FLOOR

UPPER FLOOR

NOTE:
The above photographed home may have been modified by the homeowner. Please refer to floor plan and/or drawn elevation shown for actual blueprint details.

Every Room with a View!

- The unique octagonal design of this stunning home allows an outdoor view from each room.
- The entry opens into the spacious living room, which boasts a massive fireplace and a breathtaking, two-story-high skylighted atrium. Sliding glass doors in the adjoining dining area open to a huge angled deck.
- The efficient kitchen offers a windowed sink and access to another deck.

- A laundry room, a half-bath and storage space are conveniently nearby.
- An open-railed, angled staircase winds to the upper floor, where an octagonal balcony overlooks the living room.
- The master bedroom includes a private bath with a shower, dual vanities and a walk-in closet.
- Plans for both a three- and a four-bedroom version of this home are included with the blueprints. In the three-bedroom version, the fourth bedroom is replaced by an upper-floor deck. In each version, the bedrooms are enhanced by 11-ft. sloped ceilings and are serviced by two full baths.

Plan H-27

Bedrooms: 3+	**Baths:** 2½

Living Area:

Upper floor (3-bedroom version)   960 sq. ft.
Upper floor (4-bedroom version) 1,167 sq. ft.
Main floor   697 sq. ft.

Total Living Area:	**1,657/1,864 sq. ft.**
Exterior Wall Framing:	2x4

Foundation Options:

Crawlspace
(All plans can be built with your choice of foundation and framing. A generic conversion diagram is available. See order form.)

BLUEPRINT PRICE CODE:	**B**

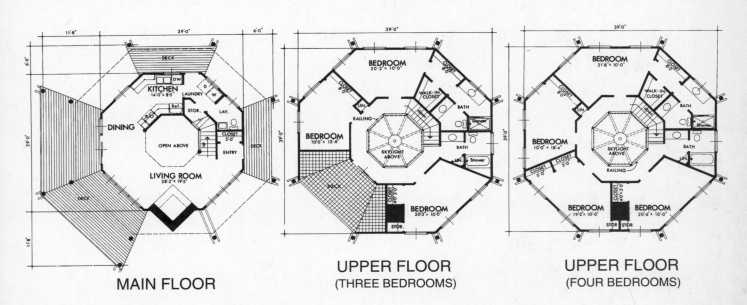

MAIN FLOOR

UPPER FLOOR
(THREE BEDROOMS)

UPPER FLOOR
(FOUR BEDROOMS)

ORDER BLUEPRINTS ANYTIME!
CALL TOLL-FREE 1-800-820-1283

Plan H-27

PRICES AND DETAILS
ON PAGES 2-5

249

Photo by Carren Strock

Solar Design that Shines

- A passive-solar sun room, an energy-efficient woodstove and a panorama of windows make this design really shine.
- The open living/dining room features a 16-ft.-high vaulted ceiling, glass-filled walls and access to the dramatic decking. A balcony above gives the huge living/dining area definition while offering spectacular views.
- The streamlined kitchen has a convenient serving bar that connects it to the living/dining area.
- The main-floor bedroom features dual closets and easy access to a full bath. The laundry room, located just off the garage, doubles as a mudroom and includes a handy coat closet.
- The balcony hallway upstairs is bathed in natural light. The two nice-sized bedrooms are separated by a second full bath.

Plans H-855-3A & -3B

Bedrooms: 3	Baths: 2-3
Living Area:	
Upper floor	586 sq. ft.
Main floor	1,192 sq. ft.
Sun room	132 sq. ft.
Daylight basement	1,192 sq. ft.
Total Living Area:	**1,910/3,102 sq. ft.**
Garage	520 sq. ft.
Exterior Wall Framing:	**2x6**
Foundation Options:	**Plan #**
Daylight basement	H-855-3B
Crawlspace	H-855-3A

(All plans can be built with your choice of foundation and framing. A generic conversion diagram is available. See order form.)

BLUEPRINT PRICE CODE:	**B/E**

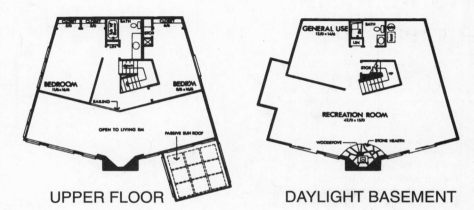

UPPER FLOOR

DAYLIGHT BASEMENT

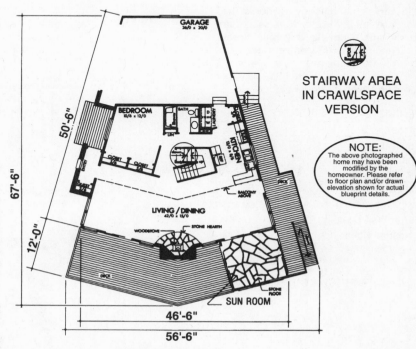

STAIRWAY AREA IN CRAWLSPACE VERSION

NOTE:
The above photographed home may have been modified by the homeowner. Please refer to floor plan and/or drawn elevation shown for actual blueprint details.

MAIN FLOOR

Plans H-855-3A & -3B
PRICES AND DETAILS ON PAGES 2-5

Warm, Rustic Appeal

- This quaint home has a warm, rustic appeal with a stone fireplace, paned windows and a covered front porch.
- Just off the two-story-high foyer, the living room hosts a raised-hearth fireplace and flows into the kitchen.
- The open L-shaped kitchen offers a pantry closet and a bright sink as it merges with the bayed dining room.
- The secluded master bedroom boasts a walk-in closet and a private bath with a dual-sink vanity. A laundry closet and access to a backyard deck are nearby.
- Upstairs, a hall balcony overlooks the foyer. A full bath serves two secondary bedrooms, each with a walk-in closet and access to extra storage space.
- Just off the dining room, a stairway descends to the daylight basement that contains the tuck-under garage.

Plan C-8339

Bedrooms: 3	Baths: 2
Living Area:	
Upper floor	660 sq. ft.
Main floor	1,100 sq. ft.
Total Living Area:	**1,760 sq. ft.**
Daylight basement/garage	1,100 sq. ft.
Exterior Wall Framing:	2x4

Foundation Options:

Daylight basement

(All plans can be built with your choice of foundation and framing. A generic conversion diagram is available. See order form.)

BLUEPRINT PRICE CODE:	**B**

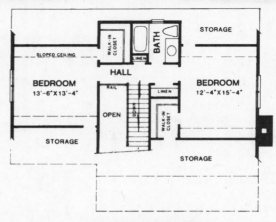

UPPER FLOOR

MAIN FLOOR

ORDER BLUEPRINTS ANYTIME!
CALL TOLL-FREE 1-800-820-1283

Plan C-8339

PRICES AND DETAILS
ON PAGES 2-5

247

Carefree Getaway

- Everything you need for a relaxing retreat can be found in this carefree getaway A-frame.
- A dramatic wall of glass allows sunshine to drench the expansive living room, which features a cozy woodstove and a soaring 24-ft.-high sloped ceiling.
- The U-shaped kitchen offers plenty of space for those essential appliances.

- The main-floor bedroom boasts a large rear-facing window and an ample closet with a handy storage area. Access to an expansive rear deck is nearby.
- Conveniently located right across the hall, the full bath includes a shower and easy access to a generous storage space.
- Upstairs, glorious views to both the front and rear can be enjoyed from the airy balcony room or extra bedroom. A dramatic 16-ft.-high ceiling slopes above.
- Sliding glass doors open to a romantic private deck—the perfect spot for an evening rendezvous.

Plan H-15-1

Bedrooms: 1+	Baths: 1
Living Area:	
Upper floor	254 sq. ft.
Main floor	654 sq. ft.
Total Living Area:	**908 sq. ft.**
Exterior Wall Framing:	**2x4**

Foundation Options:

Crawlspace
(All plans can be built with your choice of foundation and framing. A generic conversion diagram is available. See order form.)

BLUEPRINT PRICE CODE: AA

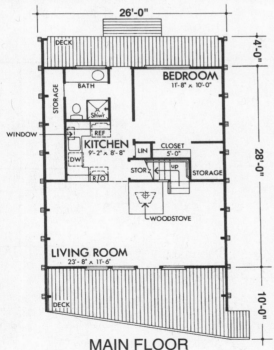

MAIN FLOOR

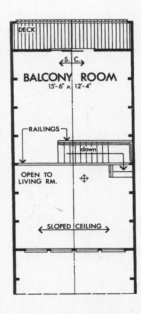

UPPER FLOOR

Eye-Catching Chalet

- Steep rooflines, dramatic windows and wide cornices give this chalet a distinctive alpine appearance.
- The large living and dining area offers a striking 20-ft.-high vaulted ceiling and a breathtaking view of the outdoors through a soaring wall of windows. Sliding glass doors access an inviting wood deck.

- The efficient U-shaped kitchen shares an eating bar with the dining area.
- Two main-floor bedrooms share a hall bath, and laundry facilities are nearby.
- The upper floor hosts a master bedroom with a 12-ft. vaulted ceiling, plenty of storage space and easy access to a full bath with a shower.
- The pièce de résistance is a balcony with a 12-ft. vaulted ceiling, offering sweeping outdoor views as well as an overlook into the living/dining area below. Additional storage areas flank the balcony.

Plans H-886-3 & -3A

Bedrooms: 3	Baths: 2
Living Area:	
Upper floor	486 sq. ft.
Main floor	994 sq. ft.
Total Living Area:	**1,480 sq. ft.**
Daylight basement	715 sq. ft.
Tuck-under garage	279 sq. ft.
Exterior Wall Framing:	2x6
Foundation Options:	**Plan #**
Daylight basement	H-886-3
Crawlspace	H-886-3A

(All plans can be built with your choice of foundation and framing. A generic conversion diagram is available. See order form.)

BLUEPRINT PRICE CODE:	A

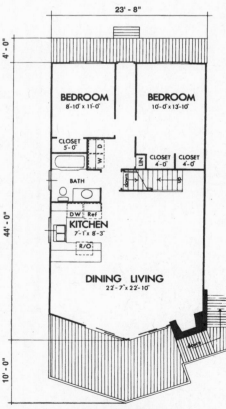

DAYLIGHT BASEMENT

GENERAL USE
22'-4" x 18'-8"

STOR

GARAGE
12'-6" x 22'-4"

FURNACE RM
9'-10" x 21'-3"

furnace

MAIN FLOOR

23' - 8"
4' - 0"
44' - 0"
10' - 0"

BEDROOM
8'-10" x 11'-0"

BEDROOM
10'-0" x 13'-10"

CLOSET
5'-0"

W D

LIN

CLOSET
4'-0"

CLOSET
4'-0"

BATH

down   up

DW   Ref

KITCHEN
7'-1" x 8'-3"

R/O

DINING   LIVING
22'-7" x 22'-10"

UPPER FLOOR

STORAGE

BEDROOM
12'-11" x 13'-10"

STORAGE

Shower

LIN

CLOSET
7'-9"

BATH

down

STORAGE

BALCONY
12'-10" x 9'-7"

STORAGE

Handrail

ORDER BLUEPRINTS ANYTIME!
CALL TOLL-FREE 1-800-820-1283

Plans H-886-3 & -3A

PRICES AND DETAILS
ON PAGES 2-5

245

Scenic Hideaway

- The perfect complement to any scenic hideaway spot, this A-frame is as affordable as it is adorable.
- A large deck embraces the front of the chalet, providing ample space for outdoor dining and recreation. Inside, vaulted ceilings and high windows lend a feeling of spaciousness.
- The living room is dramatically expanded by a 17-ft.-high vaulted ceiling and soaring windows facing the deck. This room also boasts a woodstove with a masonry hearth.
- The galley kitchen is well organized and includes a stacked washer/dryer unit and easy outdoor access. Nearby is a skylighted full bath.
- The romantic bedroom/loft overlooks the living room and features a 16-ft. ceiling. Windows at both ends of the room provide stunning views.
- On both floors, areas with limited headroom are utilized effectively for storage.

Plan H-968-1A

Bedrooms: 1	Baths: 1
Living Area:	
Upper floor	144 sq. ft.
Main floor	391 sq. ft.
Total Living Area:	**535 sq. ft.**
Exterior Wall Framing:	2x6

Foundation Options:

Crawlspace
(All plans can be built with your choice of foundation and framing. A generic conversion diagram is available. See order form.)

BLUEPRINT PRICE CODE:	**AA**

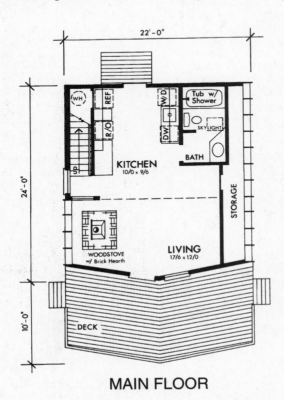

MAIN FLOOR

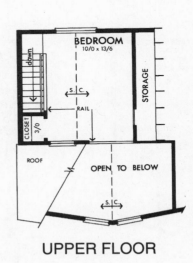

UPPER FLOOR

Plan H-968-1A

PRICES AND DETAILS
ON PAGES 2-5

A Chalet for Today

- With its wraparound deck and soaring windows, this chalet-style home is ideal for recreational living and scenic sites.
- The living and dining rooms are combined to take advantage of the dramatic 23-ft. cathedral ceiling, the rugged stone fireplace and the view through the spectacular windows.
- A quaint balcony above adds to the warm country feeling of the living area, which extends to the expansive deck.

- The open kitchen features a bright corner sink and a nifty breakfast bar that adjoins the living area.
- The handy main-floor laundry area is close to two bedrooms and a full bath.
- A 17-ft. sloped ceiling crowns the quiet study, which is a feature rarely found in a home of this size and style.
- The master suite and a storage area encompass the upper floor. A 13-ft., 8-in. cathedral ceiling, a whirlpool bath and sweeping views from the balcony give this space an elegant feel.
- The basement option includes a tuck-under garage, additional storage space and a separate utility area.

Plan AHP-9340

Bedrooms: 3+	Baths: 2
Living Area:	
Upper floor	332 sq. ft.
Main floor	974 sq. ft.
Total Living Area:	**1,306 sq. ft.**
Basement	624 sq. ft.
Tuck-under garage	350 sq. ft.
Exterior Wall Framing:	2x4 or 2x6

Foundation Options:
Standard basement
Daylight basement
Crawlspace
Slab
(All plans can be built with your choice of foundation and framing. A generic conversion diagram is available. See order form.)

BLUEPRINT PRICE CODE: A

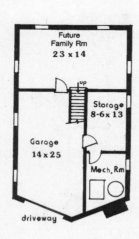

BASEMENT

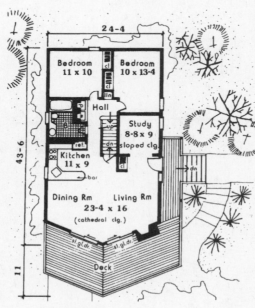

MAIN FLOOR

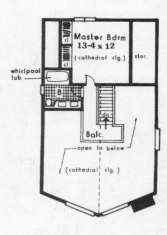

UPPER FLOOR

ORDER BLUEPRINTS ANYTIME!
CALL TOLL-FREE 1-800-820-1283

Plan AHP-9340

PRICES AND DETAILS
ON PAGES 2-5

243

Instant Impact

- Bold rooflines, interesting angles and unusual window treatments give this stylish home lots of impact.
- Inside, high ceilings and an open floor plan maximize the home's square footage. At only 28 ft. wide, the home also is ideal for a narrow lot.
- A covered deck leads to the main entry, which features a sidelighted door, angled glass walls and a view of the striking open staircase.
- The Great Room is stunning, with its 16-ft. vaulted ceiling, energy-efficient woodstove and access to a large deck.
- A flat ceiling distinguishes the dining area, which shares an angled snack bar/cooktop with the step-saving kitchen. A laundry/mudroom is nearby.
- Upstairs, the master suite offers a sloped 13-ft. ceiling and a clerestory window. A walk-through closet leads to the private bath, which is enhanced by a skylighted, sloped ceiling.
- Another full bath and plenty of storage serve the other bedrooms, one of which has a sloped ceiling and a dual closet.

Plans H-1427-3A & -3B

Bedrooms: 3	Baths: 2½
Living Area:	
Upper floor	880 sq. ft.
Main floor	810 sq. ft.
Total Living Area:	**1,690 sq. ft.**
Daylight basement	810 sq. ft.
Garage	409 sq. ft.
Exterior Wall Framing:	2x4
Foundation Options:	**Plan #**
Daylight basement	H-1427-3B
Crawlspace	H-1427-3A

(All plans can be built with your choice of foundation and framing. A generic conversion diagram is available. See order form.)

BLUEPRINT PRICE CODE:	**B**

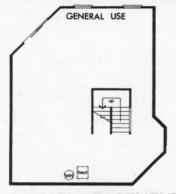

DAYLIGHT BASEMENT

UPPER FLOOR

BASEMENT STAIRWAY LOCATION

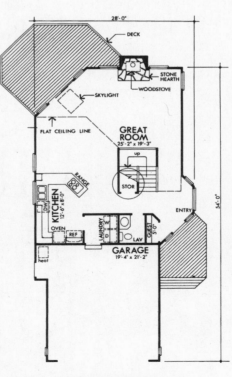

MAIN FLOOR

Plans H-1427-3A & -3B

PRICES AND DETAILS ON PAGES 2-5

Decked-Out Chalet

- This gorgeous chalet is partially surrounded by a large and roomy deck that is great for indoor/outdoor living.
- The living and dining area shows off a fireplace with a raised hearth, plus large windows to take in the outdoor views. The area is further expanded by a 17½-ft.-high vaulted ceiling in the dining room and sliding glass doors that lead to the deck.
- The kitchen offers a breakfast bar that separates it from the dining area. A convenient laundry room is nearby.
- The main-floor master bedroom is just steps away from a linen closet and a hall bath. Two upstairs bedrooms share a second full bath.
- The highlight of the upper floor is a balcony room with a 12½-ft.-high vaulted ceiling, exposed beams and tall windows. A decorative railing provides an overlook into the dining area below.

Plans H-919-1 & -1A

Bedrooms: 3	Baths: 2
Living Area:	
Upper floor	869 sq. ft.
Main floor	1,064 sq. ft.
Daylight basement	475 sq. ft.
Total Living Area:	**1,933/2,408 sq. ft.**
Tuck-under garage	501 sq. ft.
Exterior Wall Framing:	2x6
Foundation Options:	**Plan #**
Daylight basement	H-919-1
Crawlspace	H-919-1A
(All plans can be built with your choice of foundation and framing. A generic conversion diagram is available. See order form.)	
BLUEPRINT PRICE CODE:	B/C

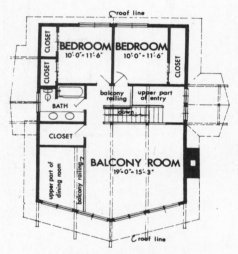

UPPER FLOOR

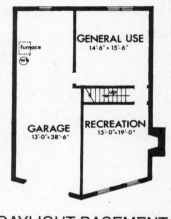

DAYLIGHT BASEMENT

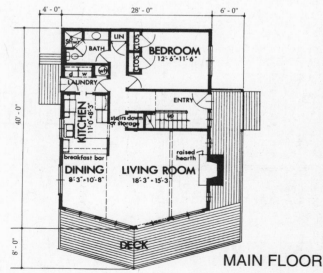

MAIN FLOOR

ORDER BLUEPRINTS ANYTIME!
CALL TOLL-FREE 1-800-820-1283

Plans H-919-1 & -1A

*PRICES AND DETAILS
ON PAGES 2-5*

241

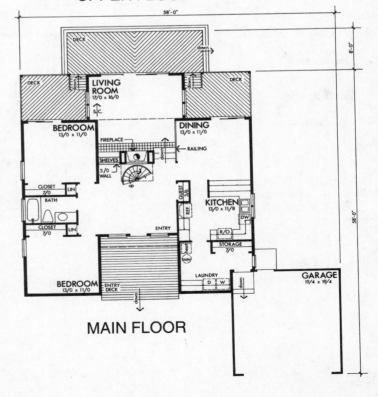

REAR VIEW

Intriguing Spaces

- Perfect as a rustic retreat or as a year-round mountain home, this refreshing design has a number of intriguing spaces, both inside and out.
- Extend a welcoming greeting to family and friends on the wide front deck.
- Cheery windows frame the entryway, adding a little class to the space. A picturesque spiral staircase stands in full view, just inside.
- Placing the living room a few steps below the main floor achieves a sense of comfort and warmth. This feeling is enhanced by the soaring fireplace, the clerestory windows that light the room and the breathtaking views out over the rear deck.
- Well equipped to satisfy the most finicky chef, the U-shaped kitchen is conveniently located near the garage to ease the burden of unloading groceries.
- Two identically sized bedrooms lie across the home and share a full bath.
- The trio of decks in back present a wonderful option for entertaining.

Plan H-971-1A

Bedrooms: 2+	Baths: 1
Living Area:	
Upper floor	230 sq. ft.
Main floor	1,385 sq. ft.
Total Living Area:	**1,615 sq. ft.**
Garage	373 sq. ft.
Exterior Wall Framing:	2x6

Foundation Options:

Crawlspace

(All plans can be built with your choice of foundation and framing. A generic conversion diagram is available. See order form.)

BLUEPRINT PRICE CODE: B

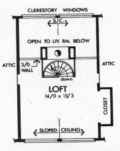

UPPER FLOOR

MAIN FLOOR

Plan H-971-1A

PRICES AND DETAILS ON PAGES 2-5

Chalet Charm

- A 17-ft. cathedral ceiling and a warm fireplace grace the Great Room of this rustic chalet. Two sets of sliding glass doors lead to a wide wraparound deck. Large windows above the doors provide a breathtaking panoramic view.
- The Great Room unfolds to the open kitchen, which features a six-person snack bar that is perfect for casual dining. Stacked laundry facilities are just steps away, as is a full bath that is shared by the two main-floor bedrooms.
- An open stairway leads to a balcony that overlooks the Great Room and the scenery beyond.
- The master bedroom is enhanced by a beautiful 14-ft. cathedral ceiling, a private bath and roomy closets. Attic storage space is also available.
- The optional basement plan offers a tuck-under garage, additional storage space and a large area for a future family room.

Plan AHP-9501

Bedrooms: 3	Baths: 2
Living Area:	
Upper floor	260 sq. ft.
Main floor	854 sq. ft.
Total Living Area:	**1,114 sq. ft.**
Daylight basement	344 sq. ft.
Tuck-under garage/storage	510 sq. ft.
Exterior Wall Framing:	2x4 or 2x6

Foundation Options:
Daylight basement
Crawlspace
Slab
(All plans can be built with your choice of foundation and framing. A generic conversion diagram is available. See order form.)

BLUEPRINT PRICE CODE: A

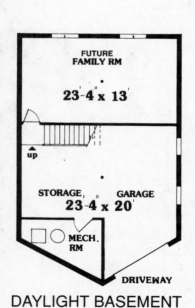

DAYLIGHT BASEMENT

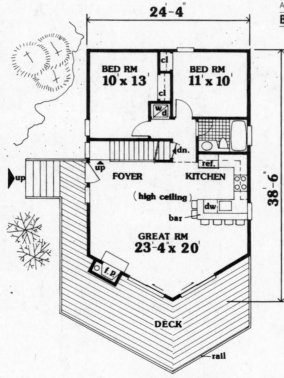

MAIN FLOOR

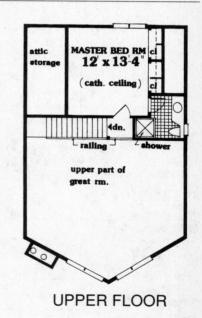

UPPER FLOOR

ORDER BLUEPRINTS ANYTIME!
CALL TOLL-FREE 1-800-820-1283

Plan AHP-9501

PRICES AND DETAILS
ON PAGES 2-5

239

Contemporary Creativity

- A dramatic row of clerestory windows surveys the sweeping roofscape of this creative contemporary design.
- This home contains the living spaces and amenities today's families demand at a price that's affordable.
- The entry opens to the 15-ft. vaulted living room brightened by a transom-topped window arrangement. A formal dining room is at the end of a short hall.

- The pass-through kitchen extends a handy serving bar to the dining room, and there's a bright corner suitable for a breakfast table.
- The adjoining family room is warmed by a fireplace. Sliding doors access a rear deck where you'll enjoy hosting summer barbecues.
- Upstairs, the master suite has its own bathroom, a walk-in closet and a private deck for soaking up the sun or some romantic moonlight.
- Two more bedrooms share a full bath.
- The master bath and the hall bath are brightened by the clerestory windows.

Plan B-812	
Bedrooms: 3	**Baths:** 2½
Living Area:	
Upper floor	785 sq. ft.
Main floor	920 sq. ft.
Total Living Area:	**1,705 sq. ft.**
Standard basement	920 sq. ft.
Garage	447 sq. ft.
Exterior Wall Framing:	2x4
Foundation Options:	

Standard basement
(All plans can be built with your choice of foundation and framing. A generic conversion diagram is available. See order form.)

BLUEPRINT PRICE CODE: **B**

MAIN FLOOR

- DECK
- DINING 10'-0"x13'-0"
- KITCHEN 9'-7"x11'-6"
- FAMILY 14'-0"x15'-8"
- DOWN / UP
- LIVING 14'-8"x13'-9" VAULTED
- GARAGE 22'-0"x20'-4"
- 41'-8"
- 39'-0"

UPPER FLOOR

- BEDRM 3 10'-0"x13'-0"
- BEDRM 2 9'-7"x13'-0"
- DECK
- MASTER BEDROOM 14'-0"x13'-2"
- DOWN
- LINEN
- CLERESTORY WINDOWS ABOVE

Captivating Cottage

- This modestly sized home delivers the impact of a much larger dwelling.
- Inside, the living areas unfold with the warmth of an old friend.
- The living room provides a quiet forum for conversation, enhanced by a charming fireplace and a 17-ft. vaulted ceiling above.
- An easy pace takes you to the family room, which offers plenty of space for the smallest family members, and boasts sliding glass doors to a backyard deck.
- In the kitchen you'll find the perfect setting for your culinary efforts.
- The dining area serves both casual and formal meals with ease. A second set of sliding glass doors to the deck allows for spontaneity on weekends. Anyone for a picnic?
- Upstairs, a sumptuous master bedroom awaits, complete with a private bath and a spacious walk-in closet.

Plan B-807	
Bedrooms: 3	**Baths: 2½**
Living Area:	
Upper floor	776 sq. ft.
Main floor	888 sq. ft.
Total Living Area:	**1,664 sq. ft.**
Standard basement	888 sq. ft.
Garage	406 sq. ft.
Exterior Wall Framing:	2x4
Foundation Options:	
Standard basement	
(All plans can be built with your choice of foundation and framing. A generic conversion diagram is available. See order form.)	
BLUEPRINT PRICE CODE:	**B**

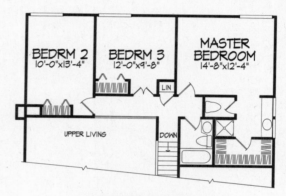

UPPER FLOOR

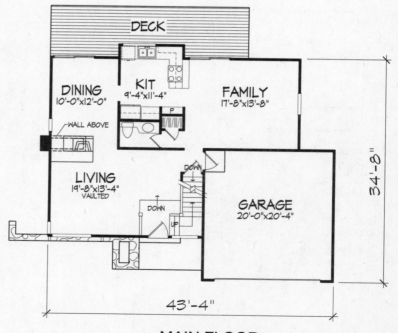

MAIN FLOOR

ORDER BLUEPRINTS ANYTIME!
CALL TOLL-FREE 1-800-820-1283

Plan B-807

PRICES AND DETAILS
ON PAGES 2-5

237

Breathtaking Great Room

- Stone veneer, log cabin siding, and a large covered porch are some of this rustic cabin's exterior attractions.
- Dramatic, contemporary and informal living is encompassed in the breathtaking Great Room with a massive stone fireplace flanked by sliding glass doors and a soaring 17-ft. cathedral ceiling that sweeps up to the second floor.
- A breakfast counter separates the Great Room from the adjoining U-shaped kitchen; a full bath and utility closet are convenient to both the kitchen and the master bedroom, which features twin closets and private access to the bath.
- Two additional bedrooms are located on the upper level, which is reached by an eye-catching circular stairway.

Plan AX-7836-A

Bedrooms: 3	**Baths:** 2

Living Area:	
Upper floor	375 sq. ft.
Main floor	970 sq. ft.
Total Living Area:	**1,345 sq. ft.**
Standard basement	970 sq. ft.
Exterior Wall Framing:	2x4

Foundation Options:
Standard basement
Slab
(All plans can be built with your choice of foundation and framing. A generic conversion diagram is available. See order form.)

BLUEPRINT PRICE CODE: **A**

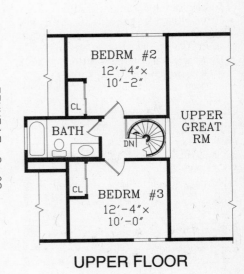

MSTR BEDRM 15'-2" x 12'-2"
CL
BATH
UTIL
D W
STOR CL
FOY
KIT 8'-6" x 8'-6"
REF
DW
PORCH
LOCATION OF OPT BSMT STAIR
VAULTED GREAT RM 15'-0" x 26'-0"
UP
SL GL DR
COVERED PORCH 12'-0" x 30'-8"
SL GL DR
30'-8" OVERALL
47'-6" OVERALL

MAIN FLOOR

BEDRM #2 12'-4" x 10'-2"
CL
BATH
DN
UPPER GREAT RM
CL
BEDRM #3 12'-4" x 10'-0"

UPPER FLOOR

Plan AX-7836-A

PRICES AND DETAILS ON PAGES 2-5

FRONT VIEW

REAR VIEW

See for Miles

- Plenty of dramatic windows, transoms and skylights let this sloping-lot design take full advantage of the breathtaking views around it.
- A covered front porch greets arriving guests and welcomes them into the spectacular Great Room. A woodstove, siding glass doors leading to the rear deck, and a bank of skylights above the vaulted rear of the home will let guests know they've arrived to a special place.
- The kitchen also overlooks the rear deck and views beyond.
- The single-car garage offers extra space for storing a boat, all-terrain vehicles or snowmobiles.
- There are two bedrooms upstairs, one with a special private deck to let you see for miles.

Plans H-953-1A & -1B

Bedrooms: 2	Baths: 1 full, 2 half
Living Area:	
Upper floor	689 sq. ft.
Main floor	623 sq. ft.
Total Living Area:	**1,312 sq. ft.**
Daylight basement	540 sq. ft.
Garage	319 sq. ft.
Exterior Wall Framing:	**2x6**
Foundation Options:	**Plan #**
Daylight basement	H-953-1B
Crawlspace	H-953-1A

(All plans can be built with your choice of foundation and framing. A generic conversion diagram is available. See order form.)

BLUEPRINT PRICE CODE:	**A**

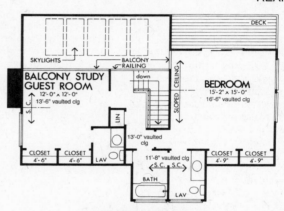

UPPER FLOOR

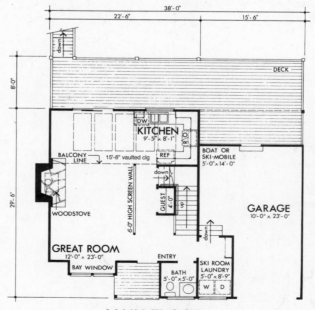

MAIN FLOOR

ORDER BLUEPRINTS ANYTIME!
CALL TOLL-FREE 1-800-820-1283

Plans H-953-1A & -1B

**PRICES AND DETAILS
ON PAGES 2-5**

235

Clean-Cut Two-Story

- A clean-cut roofline, a recessed entry and eye-catching window treatments give this design its good looks.
- Inside, the Great Room is graced with a vaulted ceiling, an inviting fireplace and corner windows. An open staircase and the adjoining dining room with a wet bar accentuate the Great Room's volume and add to its versatility.
- The kitchen and the breakfast nook are framed by bright corner windows. Casual gatherings will naturally spill over into the adjacent family room, where sliding doors open to a deck.
- Upstairs, the master suite boasts a sunken bath with a skylighted whirlpool tub, a separate shower, a toilet compartment and a walk-in closet.
- The upper floor also houses a second bedroom and an all-purpose loft.

Plan B-8329

Bedrooms: 2+	Baths: 2½
Living Area:	
Upper floor	797 sq. ft.
Main floor	904 sq. ft.
Total Living Area:	**1,701 sq. ft.**
Standard basement	904 sq. ft.
Garage	405 sq. ft.
Exterior Wall Framing:	**2x4**

Foundation Options:

Standard basement

(All plans can be built with your choice of foundation and framing. A generic conversion diagram is available. See order form.)

BLUEPRINT PRICE CODE: B

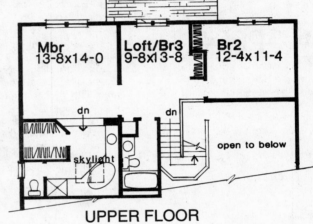

UPPER FLOOR

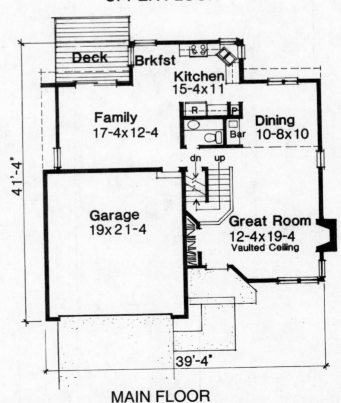

MAIN FLOOR

Equal Appeal

- This affordable home is equally appealing in the city or the country.
- The home is shown with an exterior of wood shingles, but lap siding is another equally attractive possibility.
- The open Great Room is the focal point of the floor plan. The raised-hearth fireplace extends the full height of the

26-ft. vaulted ceiling. It's the perfect place for warm family gatherings.
- A boxed-out dining room can be extended farther to increase the dining area. The kitchen offers a large island snack counter.
- The two bedrooms on the first floor share a hall bath.
- A dramatic overlook to the Great Room is possible from the master suite.

Plan LRD-4692

Bedrooms: 3	**Baths:** 2

Living Area:

Upper floor	380 sq. ft.
Main floor	1,082 sq. ft.
Total Living Area:	**1,462 sq. ft.**
Standard basement	1,082 sq. ft.
Garage	348 sq. ft.
Exterior Wall Framing:	**2x6**

Foundation Options:

Standard basement
Crawlspace
Slab

(All plans can be built with your choice of foundation and framing. A generic conversion diagram is available. See order form.)

BLUEPRINT PRICE CODE:	**A**

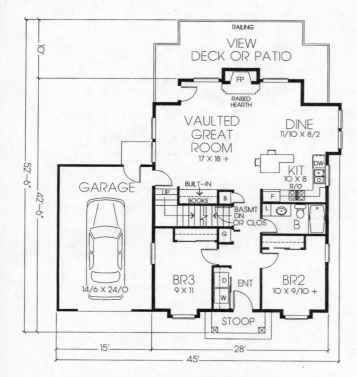

MAIN FLOOR

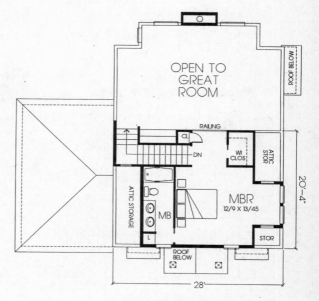

UPPER FLOOR

ORDER BLUEPRINTS ANYTIME!
CALL TOLL-FREE 1-800-820-1283

Plan LRD-4692

PRICES AND DETAILS
ON PAGES 2-5

233

Come Home to Comfort

- Due to its clever design, which includes a trio of decks, an abundance of windows and a free-flowing floor plan, this compact home allows you to come home to comfort.
- The courtyard-style entrance deck serves as a fitting introduction to what lies inside.
- Double doors open to reveal the spacious entry, a central hub which allows access to all the living areas.

- Flanked by charming sun decks, the sunken living room boasts a gleaming picture window and a wonderful raised-hearth fireplace.
- Feast on delectable morsels in the all-purpose dining room. The adjoining U-shaped kitchen features a windowed sink and ample cupboard and counter space. Laundry facilities and a half-bath are conveniently located nearby.
- Two good-sized bedrooms and a full hall bath occupy the opposite wing of the home.
- An open-railed staircase leads up to a cozy balcony loft, which would be perfect as a den or home office.

Plans H-865-1 & -1A	
Bedrooms: 2+	**Baths:** 1½
Living Area:	
Upper floor	352 sq. ft.
Main floor	1,520 sq. ft.
Total Living Area:	**1,872 sq. ft.**
Standard basement	1,096 sq. ft.
Exterior Wall Framing:	2x4
Foundation Options:	**Plan #**
Standard basement	H-865-1
Crawlspace	H-865-1A

(All plans can be built with your choice of foundation and framing. A generic conversion diagram is available. See order form.)

BLUEPRINT PRICE CODE:	**B**

MAIN FLOOR

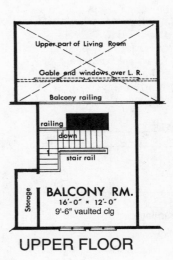

UPPER FLOOR

Plans H-865-1 & -1A

PRICES AND DETAILS ON PAGES 2-5

The Equalizer

- The unique pole foundation available with this design allows you to build on your rugged, scenic lot by varying the height of the supporting poles.
- This one-bedroom home is a fine choice for a site where you want to preserve the natural vegetation and terrain. In areas where the depth of snowfall is a factor, the elevated floor level and decks prove to be very functional.
- An open floor plan is the hallmark of this design, creating an interior of uncluttered spaciousness. A deck precedes the entry, which opens into a large combination living and dining room; a warm woodstove also radiates heat into the kitchen.
- Just around the corner are the home's full bath, utility closet with a stacked washer and dryer, and two storage spaces. A door leads to a rear deck.
- The bedroom is located on the upper floor to take full advantage of the view. It is generously sized and contains plenty of closet space.

Plans H-21-C & -D

Bedrooms: 1	Baths: 1
Living Area:	
Upper floor	256 sq. ft.
Main floor	648 sq. ft.
Total Living Area:	**904 sq. ft.**
Exterior Wall Framing:	2x6
Foundation Options:	**Plan #**
Crawlspace	H-21-D
Pole	H-21-C

(All plans can be built with your choice of foundation and framing. A generic conversion diagram is available. See order form.)

BLUEPRINT PRICE CODE:	**AA**

UPPER FLOOR

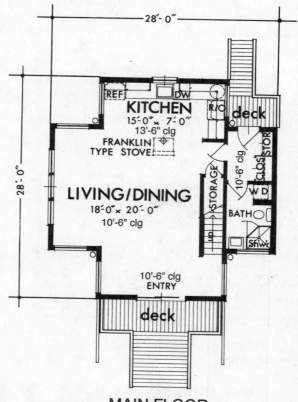

MAIN FLOOR

Into the Woods

- On the outside, this rustic tri-level home blends gently with its surroundings. The covered entry deck welcomes family and friends, and provides a nice place to enjoy nature's company.
- The entry opens directly to the living room, which includes a large boxed-out window, a woodstove and a dramatic vaulted ceiling that peaks at 13½ ft. over the woodstove's stone housing.
- The family room and dining area also benefit from the woodstove's warmth and cozy appearance. The dining room shares an eating bar with the kitchen,

and it offers sliding glass doors to the backyard patio—a perfect setting for summer meals outside.
- Storage space is plentiful in the U-shaped kitchen, which boasts a full-height pantry closet. The windowed sink lets in natural light, and allows parents doing chores to monitor the kids' play in the backyard.
- The sleeping wing lies a level above the living areas. Here, the master suite offers a private bath and a walk-in closet. Two secondary bedrooms share another full bath.
- Versatile by nature, the rec room in the basement can also work as a bedroom.

Plan S-50782	
Bedrooms: 3+	**Baths: 2½**
Living Area:	
Main floor	1,565 sq. ft.
Partial daylight basement	336 sq. ft.
Total Living Area:	**1,901 sq. ft.**
Tuck-under garage	440 sq. ft.
Exterior Wall Framing:	2x6
Foundation Options:	

Partial daylight basement
(All plans can be built with your choice of foundation and framing. A generic conversion diagram is available. See order form.)

BLUEPRINT PRICE CODE: B

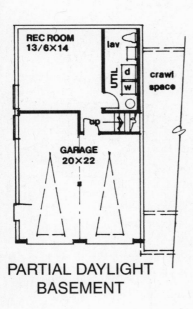

PARTIAL DAYLIGHT
BASEMENT

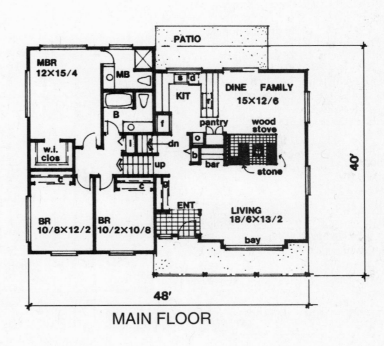

MAIN FLOOR

REAR VIEW

Easy-Living Country Lodge

- Contemporary styling is combined with the rustic atmosphere of a country lodge in this dynamic two-story home that virtually guarantees easy living!
- Decks abound! Three main-floor decks and another on the upper floor help merge the floor plan with the outdoors.
- Inside, the huge sunken living room is destined to host all your big family get-togethers. A warm fireplace brings a cheery ambience to the whole room.
- The U-shaped kitchen features a handy snack bar and a view of the front deck. The dining room is separated from the living room by a half-wall, and boasts sliding glass doors to the side deck.
- Upstairs you'll find the master suite, highlighted by a private deck and a oversized bath.

Plans H-834-5, -5A & -5B

Bedrooms: 3	Baths: 2-2½
Living Area:	
Upper floor	399 sq. ft.
Main floor	1,249 sq. ft.
Partial basement	640 sq. ft.
Daylight basement	1,249 sq. ft.
Total Living Area:	**1,648/2,288/2,897 sq. ft.**
Garage	398 sq. ft.
Exterior Wall Framing:	2x4
Foundation Options:	**Plan #**
Daylight basement	H-834-5B
Partial basement	H-834-5
Crawlspace	H-834-5A

(All plans can be built with your choice of foundation and framing. A generic conversion diagram is available. See order form.)

BLUEPRINT PRICE CODE:	**B/C/D**

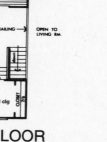

UPPER FLOOR

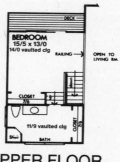

STAIRWAY AREA IN CRAWLSPACE VERSION

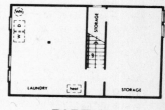

PARTIAL BASEMENT

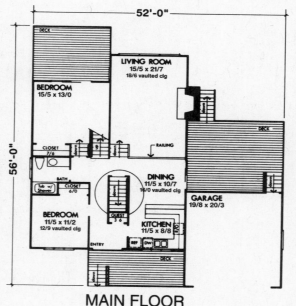

MAIN FLOOR

DAYLIGHT BASEMENT

ORDER BLUEPRINTS ANYTIME!
CALL TOLL-FREE 1-800-820-1283

Plans H-834-5, -5A & -5B

PRICES AND DETAILS
ON PAGES 2-5

229

Embracing Nature

- A plethora of decks and windows combine with a multi-level floor plan, allowing you to build a home that embraces the outdoors and all its natural beauty.
- Inside, the expansive living room is warmed by a majestic fireplace. Exposed rafters create a refreshing rustic feeling. Multiple windows view the natural landscape; step out to the expansive deck to experience the sights and sounds firsthand.
- Distinguishing the well-designed kitchen from the dining area is a wide snack counter. The tuck-under garage and storage area are accessed through the kitchen.
- Tucked away from the living areas, the secondary bedroom features a tidy wall closet. An elevated den with its own deck could easily double as a guest bedroom.
- Upstairs, the master bedroom boasts its own bath, a walk-in closet and a private viewing deck.

Plan H-863-2

Bedrooms: 2+	Baths: 2
Living Area:	
Upper floor	252 sq. ft.
Main floor	936 sq. ft.
Total Living Area:	**1,188 sq. ft.**
Daylight basement	558 sq. ft.
Tuck-under garage	378 sq. ft.
Exterior Wall Framing:	**2x4**

Foundation Options:

Daylight basement
(All plans can be built with your choice of foundation and framing. A generic conversion diagram is available. See order form.)

BLUEPRINT PRICE CODE:	**A**

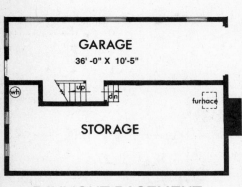

DAYLIGHT BASEMENT

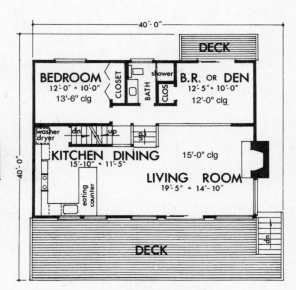

MAIN FLOOR

UPPER FLOOR

Plan H-863-2

PRICES AND DETAILS ON PAGES 2-5

REAR VIEW

Perfect for Year-Round Fun

- Whether it's used as a ski house, a cabin or a year-round residence, this delightful rustic home will be a pleasure to come home to.
- Steeply pitched rooflines, a unique blend of exterior materials and plenty of windows make the home delightfully picturesque from any angle.
- The main entrance stems from a porch with a covered entry and leads to a vaulted Great Room with a fireplace.
- The spacious eat-in kitchen, also with a dramatic high ceiling, offers a serving bar and a pantry.
- The vaulted sun porch at the back of the home has private access from the kitchen and the master bedroom, which also boasts a private bath and his-and-hers closets.
- Two extra bedrooms share the upper level's full bath.

Plan AX-91317

Bedrooms: 3	Baths: 2½
Living Area:	
Upper floor	411 sq. ft.
Main floor	1,008 sq. ft.
Sun porch	173 sq. ft.
Total Living Area:	**1,592 sq. ft.**
Standard basement	1,008 sq. ft.
Storage	42 sq. ft.
Exterior Wall Framing:	2x4

Foundation Options:

Standard basement
Slab

(All plans can be built with your choice of foundation and framing. A generic conversion diagram is available. See order form.)

BLUEPRINT PRICE CODE: B

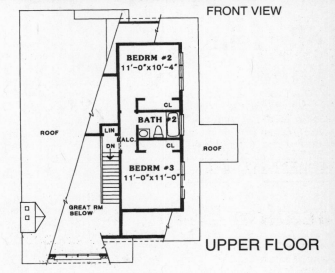

FRONT VIEW

UPPER FLOOR

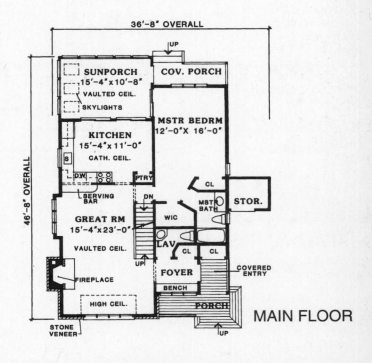

MAIN FLOOR

Economical Attraction

- This home is as economical as it is attractive. Two exteriors are available and included in the blueprints.
- The exciting space-saving floor plan has an open living area and a main-floor master suite.
- The vaulted living room is warmed by a fireplace. The kitchen features an angled sink set into a snack bar.
- Two nice-sized bedrooms and a full bath are found upstairs.

Plan B-8323

Bedrooms: 3	Baths: 2
Living Area:	
Upper floor	400 sq. ft.
Main floor	846 sq. ft.
Total Living Area:	**1,246 sq. ft.**
Standard basement	846 sq. ft.
Garage	400 sq. ft.
Exterior Wall Framing:	2x4
Foundation Options:	
Standard basement	
(All plans can be built with your choice of foundation and framing. A generic conversion diagram is available. See order form.)	
BLUEPRINT PRICE CODE:	**A**

CONTEMPORARY EXTERIOR

TRADITIONAL EXTERIOR

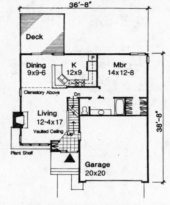

MAIN FLOOR

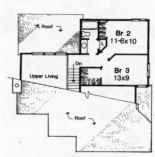

UPPER FLOOR

Plan B-8323

Vacation Living

- Double decks across the rear set the theme of casual outdoor living.
- For drama, the kitchen, the dining room and the vaulted living room are several steps down from the entry level.
- Upstairs, a hideaway bedroom includes a personal bath and a private deck.
- The optional daylight basement (not shown) features a large recreation room with a fireplace. Another bedroom and a third bath are also in the basement.

Plans H-877-1 & -1A

Bedrooms: 3+	Baths: 2-3
Living Area:	
Upper floor	320 sq. ft.
Main floor	1,200 sq. ft.
Daylight basement	1,200 sq. ft.
Total Living Area:	**1,520/2,720 sq. ft.**
Garage	155 sq. ft.
Exterior Wall Framing:	2x6
Foundation Options:	**Plan #**
Daylight basement	H-877-1
Crawlspace	H-877-1A
(All plans can be built with your choice of foundation and framing. A generic conversion diagram is available. See order form.)	
BLUEPRINT PRICE CODE:	**B/D**

REAR VIEW

BASEMENT STAIRWAY LOCATION

UPPER FLOOR

MAIN FLOOR

226

ORDER BLUEPRINTS ANYTIME!
CALL TOLL-FREE 1-800-820-1283

Plans H-877-1 & -1A

PRICES AND DETAILS
ON PAGES 2-5

Deluxe Cottage

- Plenty of luxuries are found in this cute cottage-style home.
- A 17-ft. vaulted ceiling, a massive fireplace, a corner window and a cozy library alcove highlight the living room.
- A window wall in the dining room provides views of the backyard and the deck, which are accessible through sliding glass doors in the bayed breakfast nook.
- The roomy country kitchen features a built-in desk, a pantry closet and a nearby powder room.
- Upstairs, the beautiful master suite offers such amenities as a 14-ft. vaulted ceiling, a corner window, a plant shelf and a private bath.
- Up one step are two more bedrooms, another full bath and a hall loft that overlooks the vaulted living room and the entryway.

Plan B-88002

Bedrooms: 3	**Baths:** 2½
Living Area:	
Upper floor	833 sq. ft.
Main floor	744 sq. ft.
Total Living Area:	**1,577 sq. ft.**
Standard basement	744 sq. ft.
Garage	528 sq. ft.
Exterior Wall Framing:	2x6

Foundation Options:

Standard basement

(All plans can be built with your choice of foundation and framing. A generic conversion diagram is available. See order form.)

BLUEPRINT PRICE CODE:　　　　**B**

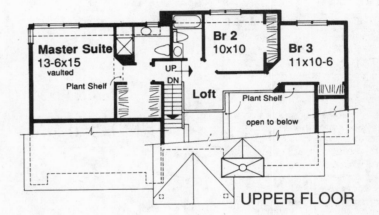

UPPER FLOOR

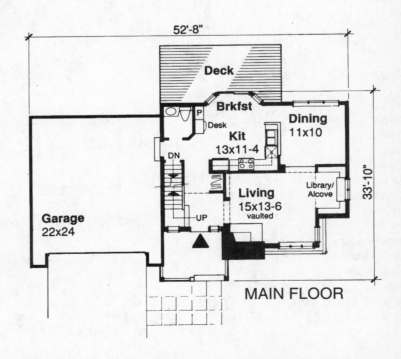

MAIN FLOOR

ORDER BLUEPRINTS ANYTIME!
CALL TOLL-FREE 1-800-820-1283

Plan B-88002

PRICES AND DETAILS
ON PAGES 2-5

225

Light-Filled Interior

- A stylish contemporary exterior and an open, light-filled interior define this two-level home.
- The covered entry leads to a central gallery. The huge living room and dining room combine to generate a spacious ambience that is enhanced by a 15½-ft. cathedral ceiling and a warm fireplace with tall flanking windows.
- Oriented to the rear and overlooking a terrace and backyard landscaping are the informal spaces. The family room, the sunny semi-circular dinette and the modern kitchen share a snack bar.
- The main-floor master suite boasts a 13-ft. sloped ceiling, a private terrace, a dressing area and a personal bath with a whirlpool tub.
- Two to three extra bedrooms with 11-ft. ceilings share a skylighted bath on the upper floor.

Plan K-683-D

Bedrooms: 3+	Baths: 2½+
Living Area:	
Upper floor	491 sq. ft.
Main floor	1,475 sq. ft.
Total Living Area:	**1,966 sq. ft.**
Standard basement	1,425 sq. ft.
Garage and storage	487 sq. ft.
Exterior Wall Framing:	2x4 or 2x6

Foundation Options:

Standard basement

Slab

(All plans can be built with your choice of foundation and framing. A generic conversion diagram is available. See order form.)

BLUEPRINT PRICE CODE:	**B**

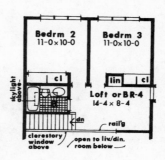

UPPER FLOOR

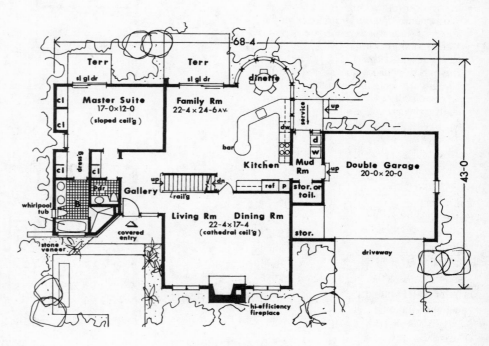

MAIN FLOOR

Relax in the Country

- This country home provides plenty of room to relax, with its covered porches and wide-open living spaces.
- Just off the front porch, the living room boasts a soothing fireplace with a raised brick hearth. The 18-ft. cathedral ceiling is shared with the adjoining dining room, which offers French-door access to the backyard porch.
- The walk-through kitchen features a handy pantry, plus a laundry closet that houses a stackable washer and dryer.
- A convenient pocket door leads to the secluded full bath.
- The master bedroom boasts two closets and private access to the bath.
- An open stairway with an oak handrail leads up to another bedroom, with a cozy seat under an arched window arrangement. Other features include a 9-ft. ceiling, a pair of closets and access to extra storage space.

Plan J-90016

Bedrooms: 2	Baths: 1
Living Area:	
Upper floor	203 sq. ft.
Main floor	720 sq. ft.
Total Living Area:	**923 sq. ft.**
Standard basement	720 sq. ft.
Exterior Wall Framing:	2x6

Foundation Options:

Standard basement
Crawlspace
Slab

(All plans can be built with your choice of foundation and framing. A generic conversion diagram is available. See order form.)

BLUEPRINT PRICE CODE: AA

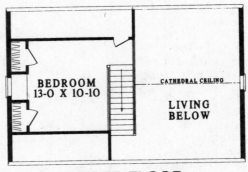

UPPER FLOOR

BEDROOM 13-0 X 10-10

CATHEDRAL CEILING

LIVING BELOW

32-0

38-6

PORCH 32-0 X 8-0

KITCHEN 11-6 X 7-4

DINING 14-2 X 8-0

MASTER BEDROOM 13-2 X 11-6

LIVING 14-2 X 13-6

PORCH 32-0 X 8-0

MAIN FLOOR

Easy Living

- The living is easy in this affordable home, which is perfect for a scenic lot.
- The main living areas look out over an inviting wraparound deck. The living room offers a 16-ft.-high sloped ceiling, a handsome fireplace and deck access.
- Two bedrooms near the main entrance feature 13-ft. sloped ceilings.
- The secluded upper-floor master suite boasts a 14-ft. vaulted ceiling, a walk-in closet, a full bath and a private deck.

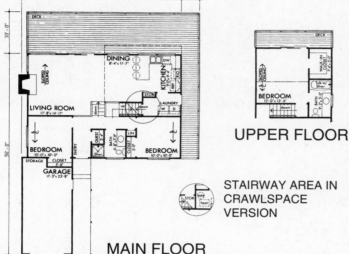

UPPER FLOOR

STAIRWAY AREA IN CRAWLSPACE VERSION

MAIN FLOOR

Plans H-925-1 & -1A

Plans H-925-1 & -1A	
Bedrooms: 3	**Baths: 2**
Living Area:	
Upper floor	288 sq. ft.
Main floor	951 sq. ft.
Total Living Area:	**1,239 sq. ft.**
Daylight basement	951 sq. ft.
Garage	266 sq. ft.
Exterior Wall Framing:	**2x4**
Foundation Options:	**Plan #**
Daylight basement	H-925-1
Crawlspace	H-925-1A

(All plans can be built with your choice of foundation and framing. A generic conversion diagram is available. See order form.)

BLUEPRINT PRICE CODE:	**A**

Comfortable, Rustic Styling

- A compact, space-efficient floor plan transforms this rustic-styled design into a comfortable place to call home.
- The living area spans the entire width of the home, and rises 14 ft. into the air.
- Several steps lead up to a pair of bedrooms with 11½-ft.-high ceilings and a full bath, all on the entry level.
- Upstairs, another large bedroom with a 10½-ft. ceiling includes a compact bath.

REAR VIEW

FRONT VIEW

UPPER FLOOR

MAIN FLOOR

Plan H-25-C	
Bedrooms: 3	**Baths: 2**
Living Area:	
Upper floor	222 sq. ft.
Main floor	936 sq. ft.
Total Living Area:	**1,158 sq. ft.**
Partial basement	365 sq. ft.
Garage	276 sq. ft.
Carport	230 sq. ft.
Exterior Wall Framing:	**2x4**
Foundation Options:	
Partial basement	

(All plans can be built with your choice of foundation and framing. A generic conversion diagram is available. See order form.)

BLUEPRINT PRICE CODE:	**A**

Plan H-25-C

PRICES AND DETAILS
ON PAGES 2-5

Economical and Convenient

REAR VIEW

- This home was designed to contain a relatively modest square footage without sacrificing the convenience afforded by an open, flowing floor plan.
- Down a short stairway from the entry, the main living area consists of a large living room with an airy vaulted ceiling and an inviting fireplace. The adjoining kitchen and dining area share a handy snack bar for quick meals.
- Sliding doors in the living room access the main-floor deck, which provides all the space you'll need to entertain in style during warm-weather months.
- Two secondary bedrooms and a full bath flank the entryway.
- Tucked away upstairs in complete privacy, the master suite is equipped with its own bath, a walk-in closet and a romantic private deck.
- The two decks make this home a perfect choice for a vacation retreat.

Plans H-925-2 & -2A

Bedrooms: 3	Baths: 2
Living Area:	
Upper floor	360 sq. ft.
Main floor	1,217 sq. ft.
Total Living Area:	**1,577 sq. ft.**
Daylight basement	1,217 sq. ft.
Garage and storage	309 sq. ft.
Exterior Wall Framing:	2x4
Foundation Options:	**Plan #**
Daylight basement	H-925-2
Crawlspace	H-925-2A

(All plans can be built with your choice of foundation and framing. A generic conversion diagram is available. See order form.)

BLUEPRINT PRICE CODE:	B

UPPER FLOOR

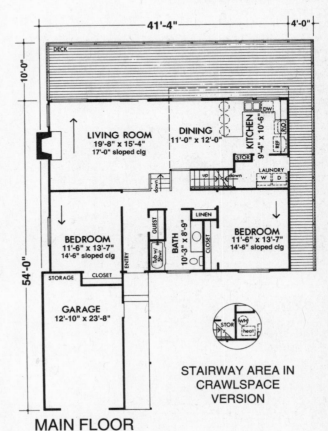

STAIRWAY AREA IN CRAWLSPACE VERSION

MAIN FLOOR

ORDER BLUEPRINTS ANYTIME!
CALL TOLL-FREE 1-800-820-1283

Plans H-925-2 & -2A

PRICES AND DETAILS
ON PAGES 2-5

221

Gorgeous Getaway!

- As you pull up at the start of a long weekend, the mere sight of this gorgeous getaway will cause the stress of the work week to fade right away.
- The huge living and dining room area provide a big place for family fun. Stoke the fireplace, pop some popcorn and spend the night assembling that 1,000-piece jigsaw puzzle while catching up on the week's activities.
- On warm summer days, take the action outdoors to the beautiful wood deck.
- Centrally located, the spacious kitchen can get nachos and cheese to any room in the house in a matter of minutes.
- Spacious and sunny, the master bedroom boasts a pair of closets, private access to a full bath and sliding glass doors to a pleasant patio.
- On the upper floor, two nice-sized bedrooms share a full bath. A charming balcony provides a dramatic view down into the living and dining rooms.

Plan C-7100

Bedrooms: 3	Baths: 2
Living Area:	
Upper floor	392 sq. ft.
Main floor	1,215 sq. ft.
Total Living Area:	**1,607 sq. ft.**
Carport	256 sq. ft.
Exterior Wall Framing:	2x4

Foundation Options:

Crawlspace
Slab

(All plans can be built with your choice of foundation and framing. A generic conversion diagram is available. See order form.)

BLUEPRINT PRICE CODE:	B

UPPER FLOOR

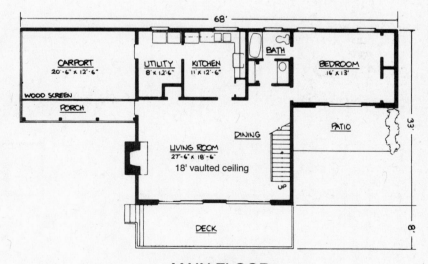

MAIN FLOOR

ORDER BLUEPRINTS ANYTIME!
CALL TOLL-FREE 1-800-820-1283

Plan C-7100

PRICES AND DETAILS
ON PAGES 2-5

Contemporary Retreat

- Designed for lots with spectacular views, this exciting contemporary home would make the perfect lake or mountain retreat.
- The side entryway opens to a relaxed and open atmosphere, which prevails throughout the home.
- A beamed ceiling and a charming balcony overlook the vast living area. Its highlights include a soaring 21½-ft.

vaulted ceiling, a majestic fireplace and sliding glass doors and windows that permit both visual and actual access to the splendid wraparound deck.
- Open to the living area, the dining room and U-shaped kitchen enhance the spacious feel.
- One large bedroom and a full bath complete the main floor.
- Upstairs, the master bedroom has a 12-ft., 10-in. vaulted ceiling and a private bath; a 10-ft. ceiling tops the other bedroom.
- The daylight basement has room for a huge recreation area, if you choose.

Plans H-929-1 & -1A	
Bedrooms: 3	**Baths:** 3
Living Area:	
Upper floor	685 sq. ft.
Main floor	960 sq. ft.
Total Living Area:	**1,645 sq. ft.**
Daylight basement	960 sq. ft.
Garage	460 sq. ft.
Exterior Wall Framing:	2x6
Foundation Options:	**Plan #**
Daylight basement	H-929-1
Crawlspace	H-929-1A
(All plans can be built with your choice of foundation and framing. A generic conversion diagram is available. See order form.)	
BLUEPRINT PRICE CODE:	B

MAIN FLOOR

UPPER FLOOR

ORDER BLUEPRINTS ANYTIME!
CALL TOLL-FREE 1-800-820-1283

Plans H-929-1 & -1A

PRICES AND DETAILS
ON PAGES 2-5

219

Cozy, Cost-Saving Retreat

- An 18½-ft. vaulted ceiling and expanses of glass add volume to this cozy cabin's living and dining area. Double doors access an inviting sun deck or patio that expands your outdoor living options.
- The U-shaped kitchen offers a bright sink and a convenient pass-through to the dining area.
- A quiet bedroom and a hall bath complete the main floor.
- The upper floor consists of a 9½-ft.-high vaulted loft that provides sweeping views of the living areas below and the scenery outside.

Plan I-880-A

Bedrooms: 1+	Baths: 1
Living Area:	
Upper floor	308 sq. ft.
Main floor	572 sq. ft.
Total Living Area:	**880 sq. ft.**
Exterior Wall Framing:	2x6
Foundation Options:	
Crawlspace	

(All plans can be built with your choice of foundation and framing. A generic conversion diagram is available. See order form.)

BLUEPRINT PRICE CODE:	**AA**

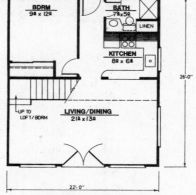

MAIN FLOOR

UPPER FLOOR

Plan I-880-A

Swiss Chalet

- Three decks, lots of views and Swiss styling make this three-bedroom chalet the perfect design for that special site.
- A stone-faced fireplace is the focal point of the central living area, which includes sliding glass doors to a deck.
- The main-floor bedroom is located conveniently close to a full bath.
- Upstairs, each of the two bedrooms has a sloped ceiling, accessible attic storage space and a private deck.
- The optional daylight basement provides opportunity for expansion.

Plans H-755-5E & -6E

Bedrooms: 3	Baths: 2
Living Area:	
Upper floor	454 sq. ft.
Main floor	896 sq. ft.
Daylight basement	896 sq. ft.
Total Living Area:	**1,350/2,246 sq. ft.**
Exterior Wall Framing:	2x4
Foundation Options:	**Plan #**
Daylight basement	H-755-6E
Crawlspace	H-755-5E

(All plans can be built with your choice of foundation and framing. A generic conversion diagram is available. See order form.)

BLUEPRINT PRICE CODE:	**A/C**

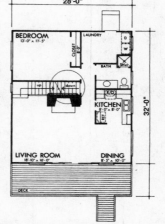

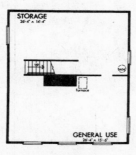

DAYLIGHT BASEMENT

MAIN FLOOR

UPPER FLOOR

Cottage with Open Interior

- The exterior of this contemporary cottage features a delightful covered porch and a pair of matching dormers.
- The entry has a dramatic 13-ft. ceiling and flows into an expansive Great Room. The Great Room is also highlighted by a vaulted ceiling that rises to a height of 17 feet. Tall windows brighten both corners, while a fireplace serves as a handsome centerpiece.
- Sliding doors between the Great Room and the breakfast nook open to an angled deck.
- The sunny 16½-ft.-high vaulted nook provides a cozy setting for family dining with a view of the backyard.
- Ample cabinets and counter space are offered in the efficient kitchen, which also features a handy snack counter that extends into the nook.
- The main-floor master bedroom has a walk-in closet and easy access to the full bath beyond.
- The upper floor offers another bedroom, plus a full bath with space for a laundry closet. The loft could serve as an extra sleeping space.

Plan JWB-9307	
Bedrooms: 2+	**Baths:** 2
Living Area:	
Upper floor	349 sq. ft.
Main floor	795 sq. ft.
Total Living Area:	**1,144 sq. ft.**
Standard basement	712 sq. ft.
Exterior Wall Framing:	2x4 or 2x6
Foundation Options:	

Standard basement
(All plans can be built with your choice of foundation and framing. A generic conversion diagram is available. See order form.)

BLUEPRINT PRICE CODE:	A

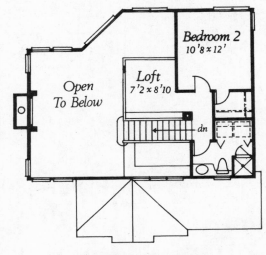

UPPER FLOOR

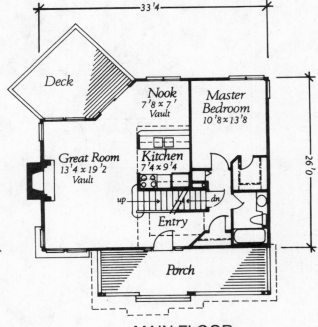

MAIN FLOOR

ORDER BLUEPRINTS ANYTIME!
CALL TOLL-FREE 1-800-820-1283

Plan JWB-9307

PRICES AND DETAILS
ON PAGES 2-5

217

Casual, Cozy Retreat

- This cozy home is perfect as a weekend retreat, a summer home or a casual permanent residence.
- The living room, the kitchen and the dining area flow together, creating a huge space for relaxing or entertaining guests. A 23-ft.-high cathedral ceiling soars above a striking wall of glass that overlooks a nice front deck. Sliding glass doors access the deck.
- Two bedrooms and a full bath round out the main floor.
- The upstairs loft could serve as a private master bedroom or as a quiet study, den or studio. An open railing provides gorgeous views of both the living area below and the scenery beyond.
- Two outside storage areas offer plenty of space for tools and equipment.

Plan CPS-1095

Bedrooms: 2+	Baths: 1
Living Area:	
Upper floor	320 sq. ft.
Main floor	784 sq. ft.
Total Living Area:	**1,104 sq. ft.**
Standard basement	784 sq. ft.
Exterior Wall Framing:	2x6

Foundation Options:

Standard basement

(All plans can be built with your choice of foundation and framing. A generic conversion diagram is available. See order form.)

BLUEPRINT PRICE CODE:	A

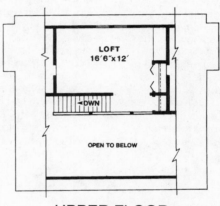

UPPER FLOOR

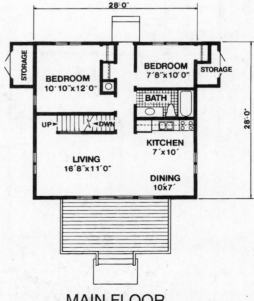

MAIN FLOOR

Plan CPS-1095

The Simple Life

- With a look that answers your call to get back to nature, this rustic home reminds you of a simpler life.
- Unfolding from the air-lock entry, the spacious living room is warmed by a beautiful woodstove and brightened by a pair of skylights. A 15-ft. vaulted ceiling soars overhead.
- The dining room is just steps away, and is easily serviced by the kitchen.
- French doors in the dining room offer access to the cheery sun room, a

wonderful spot to relax and enjoy the warm rays of the sun.
- A tidy pantry closet, a windowed sink and a central work island highlight the U-shaped kitchen.
- A versatile room near the entry could serve as a study or another bedroom.
- Step outside to the expansive deck for a summer barbecue with friends.
- An open staircase leads to the upper floor, where two bedrooms share a skylighted bath. The master bedroom features a trio of closets and a handy built-in desk.

Plans H-970-1 & -1A	
Bedrooms: 2+	**Baths:** 1½
Living Area:	
Upper floor	563 sq. ft.
Main floor	817 sq. ft.
Sun space	192 sq. ft.
Total Living Area:	**1,572 sq. ft.**
Standard basement	768 sq. ft.
Garage	288 sq. ft.
Exterior Wall Framing:	**2x6**
Foundation Options:	**Plan #**
Standard basement	H-970-1
Crawlspace	H-970-1A

(All plans can be built with your choice of foundation and framing. A generic conversion diagram is available. See order form.)

BLUEPRINT PRICE CODE:	**B**

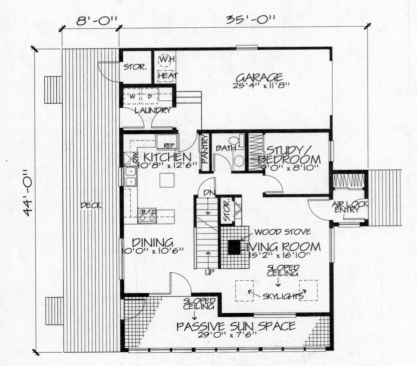

MAIN FLOOR

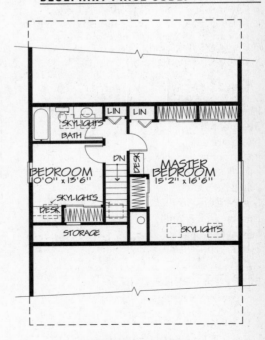

UPPER FLOOR

ORDER BLUEPRINTS ANYTIME!
CALL TOLL-FREE 1-800-820-1283

Plans H-970-1 & -1A

PRICES AND DETAILS
ON PAGES 2-5

215

BASEMENT
STAIRWAY

Super Chalet

- The charming Alpine detailing and the open, flexible interior make this one of our most popular plans.
- The living room wraps around a central fireplace or woodstove, providing a warm and expansive living space.
- The adjoining dining room is easily serviced from the galley-style kitchen.
- The larger upper-floor bedroom offers sliding glass doors to a lofty deck.
- In addition to a large general-use area and a shop, the optional daylight basement has space for a car or a boat.

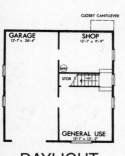

CLOSET CANTILEVER

GARAGE
12'-1" x 26'-4"

SHOP
12'-1" x 9'-9"

STOR

GENERAL USE
12'-1" x 13'-2"

DAYLIGHT BASEMENT

26'-0"

KITCHEN
7'-2" x 8'-9"

DW REF

BATH

BEDROOM
10'-0" x 10'-0"

DINING
6'-0" x 8'-9"

down

up

MASONRY BACKED
PRE-FAB FIREPLACE

LIVING ROOM
25'-2" x 13'-5"

DECK

MAIN FLOOR

CLOSET

SLOPED CEILING

BEDROOM
13'-7" x 10'-0"

STORAGE

STORAGE

Tub w/
Shower

BATH

down

CLOSET

STORAGE

BEDROOM
13'-7" x 11'-5"

CLOSET

STORAGE

DECK

UPPER FLOOR

Plans H-26-1 & -1A

Plans H-26-1 & -1A

Bedrooms: 3	Baths: 2
Living Area:	
Upper floor	476 sq. ft.
Main floor	728 sq. ft.
Daylight basement	410 sq. ft.
Total Living Area:	**1,204/1,614 sq. ft.**
Tuck-under garage	318 sq. ft.
Exterior Wall Framing:	2x4
Foundation Options:	**Plan #**
Daylight basement	H-26-1
Crawlspace	H-26-1A

(All plans can be built with your choice of foundation and framing. A generic conversion diagram is available. See order form.)

BLUEPRINT PRICE CODE:	**A/B**

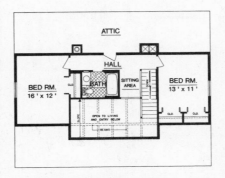

Compact, Cozy, Inviting

- Full-width porches at the front and rear of this home add plenty of space for outdoor living and entertaining.
- The living room features a corner fireplace, a 16-ft. sloped, open-beam ceiling and access to the back porch.
- The main-floor master suite offers a private bath with dual vanities and a large walk-in closet.
- A separate two-car garage is included with the blueprints.

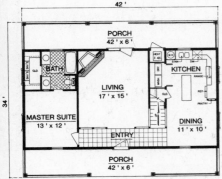

42'

PORCH
42' x 6'

BATH

HEAT
& AC

KITCHEN

RANGE

LIVING
17' x 15'

REF

PANTRY

34'

MASTER SUITE
13' x 12'

OPEN TO LIVING
AND ENTRY BELOW

DINING
11' x 10'

ENTRY

PORCH
42' x 6'

MAIN FLOOR

ATTIC

HALL

BED RM.
16' x 12'

BATH

SITTING
AREA

OPEN TO LIVING
AND ENTRY BELOW

BEAMS

BED RM.
13' x 11'

UPPER FLOOR

Plan E-1421

Bedrooms: 3	Baths: 2
Living Area:	
Upper floor	561 sq. ft.
Main floor	924 sq. ft.
Total Living Area:	**1,485 sq. ft.**
Standard basement	924 sq. ft.
Exterior Wall Framing:	2x6
Foundation Options:	
Standard basement	
Crawlspace	
Slab	

(All plans can be built with your choice of foundation and framing. A generic conversion diagram is available. See order form.)

BLUEPRINT PRICE CODE:	**A**

Space-Saving Tri-Level

- This clever tri-level design offers an open, airy interior while taking up a minimum of land space.
- The Great Room features a spectacular 15-ft. vaulted and skylighted ceiling, an inviting woodstove and sliding glass doors to a full-width deck.
- The Great Room also incorporates a dining area, which is easily serviced from the efficient, space-saving kitchen.
- The main-floor bedroom boasts two closets. A compact laundry closet, a guest closet and a storage area line the hallway to the spacious main bath.
- The large loft offers infinite possibilities, such as extra sleeping quarters, a home office, an art studio or a recreation room. Clerestory windows and a sloped ceiling enhance the bright, airy feeling.
- The tuck-under garage saves on building costs and lets you make the most of your lot.

Plan H-963-2A

Bedrooms: 1+	Baths: 1
Living Area:	
Upper floor	432 sq. ft.
Main floor	728 sq. ft.
Total Living Area:	**1,160 sq. ft.**
Tuck-under garage	728 sq. ft.
Exterior Wall Framing:	2x4

Foundation Options:

Slab

(All plans can be built with your choice of foundation and framing. A generic conversion diagram is available. See order form.)

BLUEPRINT PRICE CODE: **A**

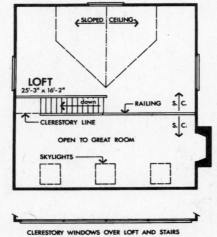

UPPER FLOOR

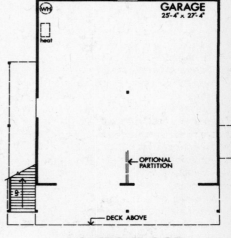

LOWER FLOOR

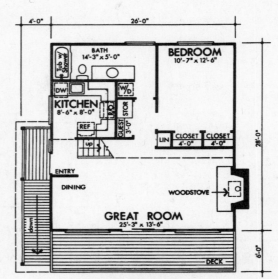

MAIN FLOOR

ORDER BLUEPRINTS ANYTIME!
CALL TOLL-FREE 1-800-820-1283

Plan H-963-2A

PRICES AND DETAILS
ON PAGES 2-5

213

FRONT VIEW

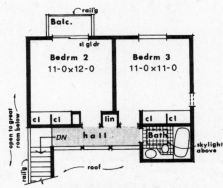

REAR VIEW

More for Less

- Big in function but small in square footage, this passive-solar plan can be built as a single-family home or as part of a multiple-unit complex.
- The floor plan flows visually from its open foyer to its high-ceilinged Great Room, where a high-efficiency fireplace is flanked by glass. Sliding glass doors open to a brilliant south-facing sun room that overlooks a backyard terrace.
- The eat-in kitchen has a pass-through to a bright dining area that opens to a nice side terrace.
- The master bedroom boasts a pair of tall windows, a deluxe private bath and three roomy closets.
- A handy laundry closet and a half-bath are located at the center of the floor plan, near the garage.
- Upstairs, a skylighted bath serves two more bedrooms, one with a private, rear-facing balcony.

Plan K-507-S

Bedrooms: 3	Baths: 2½
Living Area:	
Upper floor	397 sq. ft.
Main floor	915 sq. ft.
Sun room	162 sq. ft.
Total Living Area:	**1,474 sq. ft.**
Standard basement	915 sq. ft.
Garage	400 sq. ft.
Exterior Wall Framing:	2x4 or 2x6

Foundation Options:

Standard basement

Slab

(All plans can be built with your choice of foundation and framing. A generic conversion diagram is available. See order form.)

BLUEPRINT PRICE CODE: **A**

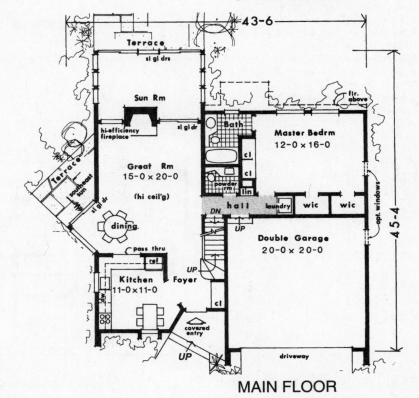

UPPER FLOOR

MAIN FLOOR

Plan K-507-S

PRICES AND DETAILS
ON PAGES 2-5

Hillside Design Fits Contours

- The daylight-basement version of this popular plan is perfect for a scenic, sloping lot.
- A large, wraparound deck embraces the rear-oriented living areas, accessed through sliding glass doors.
- The spectacular living room boasts a corner fireplace and a 19-ft. vaulted ceiling with three clerestory windows.
- The secluded master suite upstairs offers a walk-in closet, a private bath and sliding doors to a sun deck.
- The daylight basement (not shown) includes a fourth bedroom with a private bath and a walk-in closet, as well as a recreation room with a fireplace and access to a rear patio.
- The standard basement (not shown) includes a recreation room with a fireplace and a room for hobbies or child's play.
- Both basements also have a large unfinished area below the main-floor bedrooms.

Plans H-877-4, -4A & -4B

Bedrooms: 3+	Baths: 2-3
Living Area:	
Upper floor	333 sq. ft.
Main floor	1,200 sq. ft.
Basement (finished area)	591 sq. ft.
Total Living Area:	**1,533/2,124 sq. ft.**
Basement (unfinished area)	493 sq. ft.
Garage	480 sq. ft.
Exterior Wall Framing:	2x6
Foundation Options:	**Plan #**
Daylight basement	H-877-4B
Standard basement	H-877-4
Crawlspace	H-877-4A

(All plans can be built with your choice of foundation and framing. A generic conversion diagram is available. See order form.)

BLUEPRINT PRICE CODE: B/C

UPPER FLOOR

REAR VIEW

STAIRWAY AREA IN CRAWLSPACE VERSION

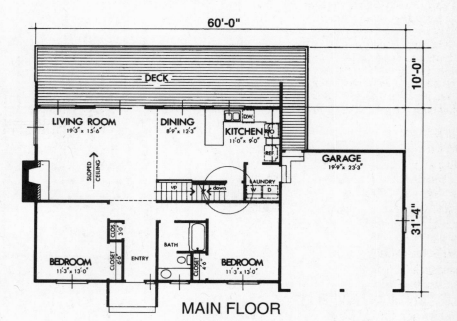

MAIN FLOOR

ORDER BLUEPRINTS ANYTIME!
CALL TOLL-FREE 1-800-820-1283

Plans H-877-4, -4A & -4B

PRICES AND DETAILS
ON PAGES 2-5

211

Small in Size, Big in Comfort

- Space-efficient and cost-effective, this stylish, feature-filled home is designed with comfort in mind.
- An angled entrance off the inviting covered porch opens to the 17-ft.-high foyer, which is brightened by a half-round clerestory window.
- The dramatic 17-ft. vaulted ceiling extends into the adjoining formal living areas. The living room features a stone fireplace, while the dining room is highlighted by an overhead plant shelf.
- A bay window brings great outdoor views into the eat-in kitchen, which serves the family room over a long snack bar.
- An atrium door in the family room offers access to a backyard deck. A half-bath, a pantry and a laundry room with garage access are within easy reach.
- Upstairs, the bay-windowed master suite is entered through elegant double doors and boasts a 12-ft. vaulted ceiling, a big walk-in closet and a private bath with twin sinks.
- Two additional bedrooms and a second full bath complete the upper floor.

Plan B-93004

Bedrooms: 3	Baths: 2½
Living Area:	
Upper floor	799 sq. ft.
Main floor	932 sq. ft.
Total Living Area:	**1,731 sq. ft.**
Standard basement	932 sq. ft.
Garage	420 sq. ft.
Exterior Wall Framing:	2x6

Foundation Options:

Standard basement

(All plans can be built with your choice of foundation and framing. A generic conversion diagram is available. See order form.)

BLUEPRINT PRICE CODE: **B**

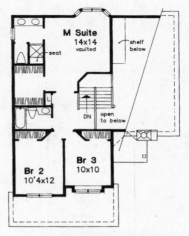

UPPER FLOOR

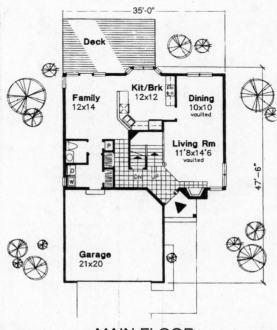

MAIN FLOOR

Plan B-93004

PRICES AND DETAILS ON PAGES 2-5

Deck and Spa!

- Designed for relaxation as well as for active indoor/outdoor living, this popular home offers a gigantic deck and an irresistible spa room.
- A covered porch welcomes guests into the entry hall, which flows past the central, open-railed stairway to the spectacular Great Room.
- Sliding glass doors on each side of the Great Room extend the living space to the huge V-shaped deck. The 22-ft. sloped ceiling and a woodstove add to the stunning effect.
- The master suite features a cozy window seat, a walk-in closet and private access to a full bath.
- The passive-solar spa room can be reached from the master suite as well as the backyard deck.
- The upper floor hosts two additional bedrooms, a full bath and a balcony hall that overlooks the Great Room.

Plans H-952-1A & -1B

Bedrooms: 3+	**Baths:** 2-3
Living Area:	
Upper floor	470 sq. ft.
Main floor	1,207 sq. ft.
Passive spa room	102 sq. ft.
Daylight basement	1,105 sq. ft.
Total Living Area:	**1,779/2,884 sq. ft.**
Garage	496 sq. ft.
Exterior Wall Framing:	2x6
Foundation Options:	**Plan #**
Daylight basement	H-952-1B
Crawlspace	H-952-1A
(All plans can be built with your choice of foundation and framing. A generic conversion diagram is available. See order form.)	
BLUEPRINT PRICE CODE:	**B/D**

REAR VIEW

UPPER FLOOR

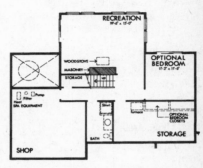

VIEW INTO PASSIVE SPA ROOM

MAIN FLOOR

DAYLIGHT BASEMENT

ORDER BLUEPRINTS ANYTIME!
CALL TOLL-FREE 1-800-820-1283

Plans H-952-1A & -1B

PRICES AND DETAILS
ON PAGES 2-5

209

Sensational Sun Catcher!

- A passive-solar sun room with two fully glazed walls and an all-glass roof offers comfortable, leisure living in this contemporary home.
- Inside, two huge gathering areas dominate the main floor. The family room is great for casual get-togethers; its nearness to the kitchen means appetizers are just a step or two away.

- With a big, bold fireplace, plus a view of the enormous back deck and access to the beautiful sun room, the living room makes the perfect spot for celebrating special occasions with family and friends.
- A full-sized bath is positioned between two pleasant bedrooms, the foremost of which offers a nice-sized window.
- The upper floor consists of the beautiful master suite, where you'll find a walk-in closet, a private bath and a handy storage area. A balcony provides a dramatic view of the living room.

Plans H-949-1, -1A & -1B	
Bedrooms: 3	**Baths:** 2
Living Area:	
Upper floor	428 sq. ft.
Main floor	1,373 sq. ft.
Passive sun room	165 sq. ft.
Total Living Area:	**1,966 sq. ft.**
Basement	1,373 sq. ft.
Garage	439 sq. ft.
Exterior Wall Framing:	**2x6**
Foundation Options:	**Plan #**
Daylight basement	H-949-1B
Standard basement	H-949-1
Crawlspace	H-949-1A

(All plans can be built with your choice of foundation and framing. A generic conversion diagram is available. See order form.)

BLUEPRINT PRICE CODE:	**B**

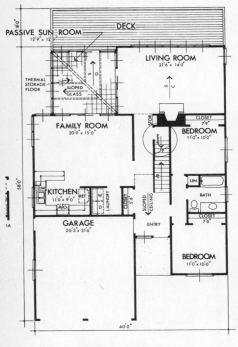

MAIN FLOOR

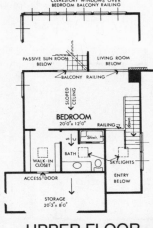

UPPER FLOOR

BASEMENT AREA IN CRAWLSPACE VERSION

FRONT VIEW

Spacious Economy

- This economical country cottage features wide, angled spaces and 9-ft., 4-in. ceilings in both the Great Room and the master bedroom for roomy appeal and year-round comfort.
- The Great Room boasts a cozy fireplace with a raised hearth and a built-in niche for a TV, making this room perfect for winter gatherings. On warm nights, a homey covered porch at the rear can be accessed through sliding glass doors.
- Amenities in the luxurious master bedroom include a large walk-in closet, a private whirlpool bath and a dual-sink vanity.
- The nicely appointed kitchen offers nearby laundry facilities and porch access. A serving bar allows for casual dining and relaxed conversation.
- The optional daylight basement includes a tuck-under, two-car garage.

Plan AX-94322

Bedrooms: 3	Baths: 2½
Living Area:	
Upper floor	545 sq. ft.
Main floor	1,134 sq. ft.
Total Living Area:	**1,679 sq. ft.**
Daylight basement	618 sq. ft.
Standard basement	1,134 sq. ft.
Tuck-under garage	516 sq. ft.
Exterior Wall Framing:	2x4

Foundation Options:
Daylight basement
Standard basement
Crawlspace
Slab
(All plans can be built with your choice of foundation and framing. A generic conversion diagram is available. See order form.)

BLUEPRINT PRICE CODE:	B

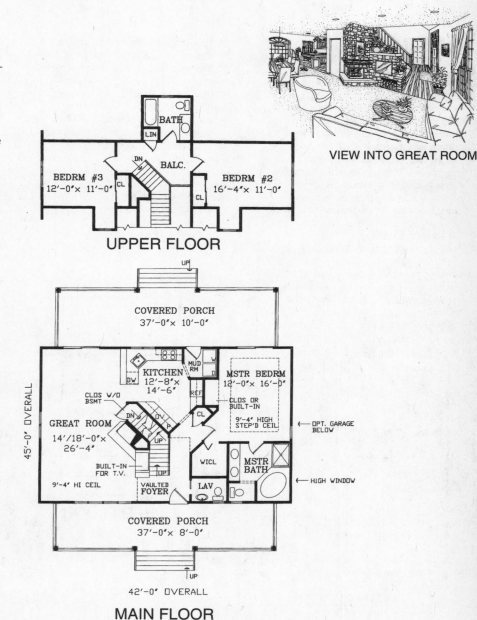

VIEW INTO GREAT ROOM

UPPER FLOOR

MAIN FLOOR

Vacation Home with Views

- The octagonal shape and window-filled walls of this home create a powerful interior packed with panoramic views.
- Straight back from the angled entry, the Great Room is brightened by expansive windows and sliding glass doors to a huge wraparound deck. An impressive spiral staircase at the center of the floor plan lends even more character.
- The walk-through kitchen offers a handy pantry. A nice storage closet and a coat closet are located between the entry and the two-car garage.
- The main-floor bedroom is conveniently located near a full bath.
- The upper-floor master suite is a sanctuary, featuring lots of glass, a walk-in closet, a private bath and access to concealed storage rooms.
- The optional daylight basement offers an extra bedroom, a full bath, a laundry area and a large recreation room.

Plans H-964-1A & -1B

Bedrooms: 2+	Baths: 2-3

Living Area:	
Upper floor	346 sq. ft.
Main floor	1,067 sq. ft.
Daylight basement	1,045 sq. ft.

Total Living Area:	1,413/2,458 sq. ft.
Garage	512 sq. ft.
Storage (upper floor)	134 sq. ft.

Exterior Wall Framing:	2x6

Foundation Options:	Plan #
Daylight basement	H-964-1B
Crawlspace	H-964-1A

(All plans can be built with your choice of foundation and framing. A generic conversion diagram is available. See order form.)

BLUEPRINT PRICE CODE:	A/C

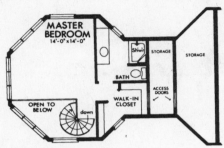

UPPER FLOOR

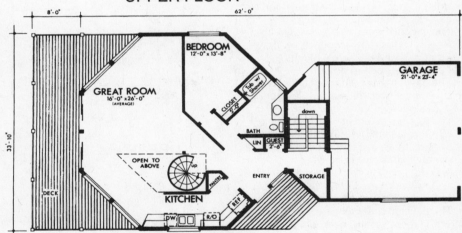

MAIN FLOOR

DAYLIGHT BASEMENT

Unique and Dramatic

- This home's unique interior and dramatic exterior make it perfect for a sloping, scenic lot.
- The expansive and impressive Great Room, warmed by a woodstove, flows into the island kitchen, which is completely open in design.
- The passive-solar sun room collects and stores heat from the sun, while offering a good view of the surroundings. Its ceiling rises to a height of 16 feet.
- Upstairs, a glamorous, skylighted master suite features an 11-ft. vaulted ceiling, a private bath and a huge walk-in closet.
- A skylighted hall bath serves the bright second bedroom. Both bedrooms open to the vaulted sun room below.
- The daylight basement adds a sunny sitting room, a third bedroom and a large recreation room.

Plans P-536-2A & -2D

Bedrooms: 2+	Baths: 2½-3½
Living Area:	
Upper floor	642 sq. ft.
Main floor	863 sq. ft.
Daylight basement	863 sq. ft.
Total Living Area:	**1,505/2,368 sq. ft.**
Garage	445 sq. ft.
Exterior Wall Framing:	2x6
Foundation Options:	**Plan #**
Daylight basement	P-536-2D
Crawlspace	P-536-2A

(All plans can be built with your choice of foundation and framing. A generic conversion diagram is available. See order form.)

BLUEPRINT PRICE CODE: B/C

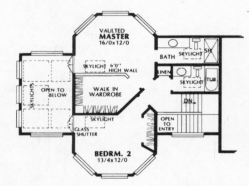

UPPER FLOOR

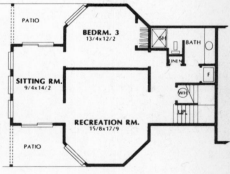

DAYLIGHT BASEMENT

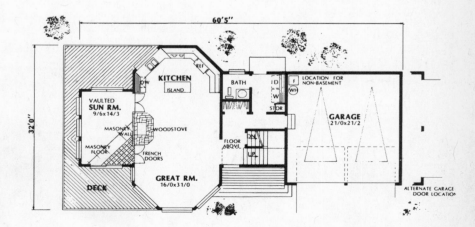

MAIN FLOOR

ORDER BLUEPRINTS ANYTIME!
CALL TOLL-FREE 1-800-820-1283

Plans P-536-2A & -2D

*PRICES AND DETAILS
ON PAGES 2-5*

205

REAR VIEW

Bright Ideas!

- Four clerestory windows, a boxed-out window and wing walls sheltering the entry porch give this home definition.
- Inside, an open room arrangement coupled with vaulted ceilings, abundant windows and a sensational sun room make this home a definite bright spot.
- The living room features a 22-ft.-high vaulted ceiling, a warm woodstove and a glass-filled wall that offers views into the sun room. A patio door in the sun room opens to a large backyard deck.
- The adjoining dining room flows into the kitchen, which offers a versatile snack bar. A handy laundry room is just steps away, near the garage.
- Upstairs, the intimate bedroom suite includes a 14-ft.-high vaulted ceiling, a view to the living room, a walk-in closet and a private bath.
- The optional daylight basement boasts a spacious recreation room with a second woodstove, plus a fourth bedroom and a third bath. A shaded patio occupies the area under the deck.

FRONT VIEW

Plans H-877-5A & -5B

Bedrooms: 3+	Baths: 2-3
Living Area:	
Upper floor	382 sq. ft.
Main floor	1,200 sq. ft.
Sun room	162 sq. ft.
Daylight basement	1,200 sq. ft.
Total Living Area:	**1,744/2,944 sq. ft.**
Garage	457 sq. ft.
Exterior Wall Framing:	2x6
Foundation Options:	**Plan #**
Daylight basement	H-877-5B
Crawlspace	H-877-5A

(All plans can be built with your choice of foundation and framing. A generic conversion diagram is available. See order form.)

BLUEPRINT PRICE CODE:	**B/D**

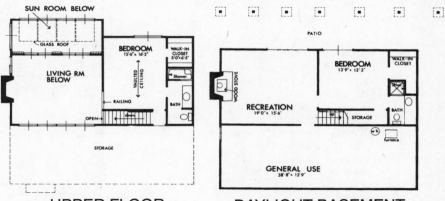

UPPER FLOOR   **DAYLIGHT BASEMENT**

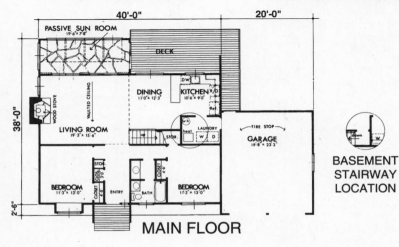

MAIN FLOOR

BASEMENT STAIRWAY LOCATION

ORDER BLUEPRINTS ANYTIME! CALL TOLL-FREE 1-800-820-1283

Plans H-877-5A & -5B

PRICES AND DETAILS ON PAGES 2-5

All Decked Out for Family Fun!

- Three decks help connect the interior of this clever home to the beautiful outdoors.
- The front deck includes a handy storage area—perfect for holding a stash of firewood or your collection of yard tools and fishing poles.
- You can almost smell the batter-fried walleye in the galley-style kitchen. Efficiency and smart design help make meal preparation easy.
- Lighted by the glow of a friendly fireplace, the huge living room has space enough for the biggest fish stories. It's a perfect end-of-the-day gathering spot for the whole family.
- On clear nights you can step out to the enormous back deck and hunt for constellations and shooting stars.
- The third deck gives the upper-floor master bedroom a romantic touch. A nice walk-in closet and a private bath add a luxurious feel.

Plan H-912-1A

Bedrooms: 3	Baths: 2
Living Area:	
Upper floor	379 sq. ft.
Main floor	894 sq. ft.
Total Living Area:	**1,273 sq. ft.**
Garage	245 sq. ft.
Exterior Wall Framing:	2x4

Foundation Options:

Crawlspace
(All plans can be built with your choice of foundation and framing. A generic conversion diagram is available. See order form.)

BLUEPRINT PRICE CODE: A

UPPER FLOOR

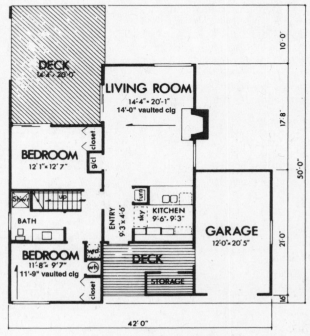

MAIN FLOOR

ORDER BLUEPRINTS ANYTIME!
CALL TOLL-FREE 1-800-820-1283

Plan H-912-1A

PRICES AND DETAILS
ON PAGES 2-5

203

Open Spaces

- This home offers several design options.
- For the plan with a crawlspace foundation and a bedroom/bath on the upper floor, order H-894-1A.
- For the plan with a crawlspace foundation and a dormitory on the upper floor, order H-894-2A.
- For the plan with a standard basement and a bedroom/bath on the upper floor, order H-894-1B.
- For the plan with a standard basement and a dormitory on the upper floor, order H-894-2B.
- For the plan with a daylight basement and a garage, plus a bedroom/bath on the upper floor, order H-894-1C.
- For the plan with a daylight basement and a garage, plus a dormitory on the upper floor, order H-894-2C.

Plans H-894-1A, -1B, -1C, -2A, -2B & -2C	
Bedrooms: 2+	**Baths:** 1-2
Living Area:	
Upper floor	336 sq. ft.
Main floor	1,056 sq. ft.
Total Living Area:	**1,392 sq. ft.**
Daylight basement	615 sq. ft.
Standard basement	1,056 sq. ft.
Tuck-under garage	441 sq. ft.
Exterior Wall Framing:	2x4
Foundation Options:	
Daylight basement	
Standard basement	
Crawlspace	

(All plans can be built with your choice of foundation and framing. A generic conversion diagram is available. See order form.)

BLUEPRINT PRICE CODE: **A**

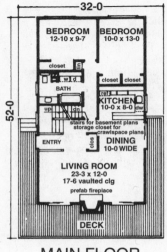

MAIN FLOOR

UPPER FLOOR

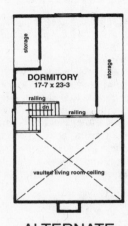

ALTERNATE UPPER FLOOR

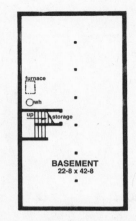

STANDARD BASEMENT

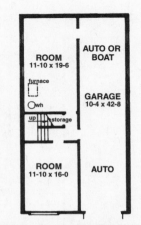

DAYLIGHT BASEMENT

Plans H-894-1A, -1B, -1C, -2A, -2B & -2C

Uniquely Stylish Retreat

- This vacation cabin includes both contemporary and rustic traits, creating a unique retreat for glorious getaways!
- Inside, the two-story living room, which features a charming corner fireplace and sliding glass doors to a sunny deck, serves as the heart of the home. It's the perfect place for family events.
- Meals and snacks are each handled smoothly in the well-planned kitchen.

A handy eating counter lets you spatula the morning's pancakes right from the grill to the plate.
- The two main-floor bedrooms are spacious and well lighted. The rear bedroom features access to the back deck. A full-sized bath is just down the hall from each.
- Upstairs, a lovely balcony overlooks the living room. It's a great spot for the kids to set up camp for a quiet day of play when the day's rainy. If needed, this spot can be used as a handy spare bedroom. A full bath and a closet add to the usefulness.

Plans H-915-1 & -1A	
Bedrooms: 2+	**Baths:** 2
Living Area:	
Upper floor	312 sq. ft.
Main floor	887 sq. ft.
Total Living Area:	**1,199 sq. ft.**
Standard basement	887 sq. ft.
Garage	297 sq. ft.
Exterior Wall Framing:	2x6
Foundation Options:	**Plan #**
Standard basement	H-915-1
Crawlspace	H-915-1A

(All plans can be built with your choice of foundation and framing. A generic conversion diagram is available. See order form.)

BLUEPRINT PRICE CODE:	**A**

MAIN FLOOR

- 44'-0"
- 38'-8"
- DECK
- LIVING ROOM 17'-0" x 12'-6" 14'-0" sloped clg
- PRE-FAB FIREPLACE
- BALCONY LINE
- BEDROOM 13'-0" x 13'-0"
- GARAGE 12'-2" x 21'-5"
- REF.
- KITCHEN 10'-4" x 8'-9"
- R/O
- W/D
- DW
- Tub w/ Shower
- CLOSET 4'-0"
- CLOSET 4'-0"
- LINEN
- ENTRY
- BATH 10'-4" x 5'-0"
- STORAGE
- DECK
- BEDROOM 13'-0" x 10'-4"

STAIRWAY AREA IN
- STOR

UPPER FLOOR

- OPEN TO LIVING ROOM
- SLOPED CEILING
- RAILING
- BALCONY/ BEDROOM 17'-0" x 11'-4" 10'-0" sloped clg
- SLOPED CEILING
- down
- CLOSET 3'-6"
- BATH 10'-0" x 5'-0"
- Sh'wr

Striking Angles

- This striking contemporary design is accented by dramatic angles, vertical siding and a private courtyard that extends from the side entrance to the covered front porch.
- The front entry flows between the formal areas, which are separated by a central open-railed staircase.
- To the left, the living room features a soothing fireplace and access to a big backyard deck. On the right, the dining room opens to the front courtyard.
- The efficient U-shaped kitchen boasts a walk-in pantry and a snack bar to the casual eating area. A convenient laundry closet and access to the side porch are nearby.
- Upstairs, the huge master bedroom opens to a quaint balcony overlooking the front courtyard. A walk-in closet supplements another closet in the dressing room, which leads to the private master bath.
- Two more large bedrooms share a spacious hall bath.

Plan E-1504

Bedrooms: 3	Baths: 2
Living Area:	
Upper floor	780 sq. ft.
Main floor	791 sq. ft.
Total Living Area:	**1,571 sq. ft.**
Garage	484 sq. ft.
Exterior Wall Framing:	2x6

Foundation Options:

Crawlspace

Slab

(All plans can be built with your choice of foundation and framing. A generic conversion diagram is available. See order form.)

BLUEPRINT PRICE CODE: **B**

UPPER FLOOR

MAIN FLOOR

ORDER BLUEPRINTS ANYTIME!
CALL TOLL-FREE 1-800-820-1283

Plan E-1504

PRICES AND DETAILS
ON PAGES 2-5

Advantageous Vantage Points

- The raised living and deck areas of this charming home take full advantage of the beautiful surrounding views!
- Enter on the basement level, where you'll find a pair of spacious bedrooms, each with a walk-in closet and private access to a full-size bath.
- At the heart of the main floor is the huge Grand Room—the perfect space for casual or formal entertaining. Guests can gather around the cozy fireplace or, if the weather's cooperative, they can step out to the extra-large main deck to enjoy the evening air.
- Sunny and cheerful, the morning room also walks out to the main deck.
- The incredible master suite has a long list of special features: two closets, a dressing area, an expansive bath with a spa tub and a separate shower, plus a private deck to bring you nearer to the outdoors whenever the mood hits.
- A fourth bedroom may also serve as a secluded study if so desired.

Plan EOF-44

Bedrooms: 3+	Baths: 2
Living Area:	
Main floor	1,256 sq. ft.
Daylight basement	541 sq. ft.
Total Living Area:	**1,797 sq. ft.**
Tuck-under garage	460 sq. ft.
Exterior Wall Framing:	2x4

Foundation Options:

Daylight basement

(All plans can be built with your choice of foundation and framing. A generic conversion diagram is available. See order form.)

BLUEPRINT PRICE CODE: **B**

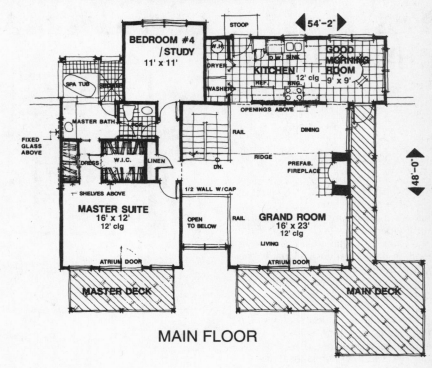

MAIN FLOOR

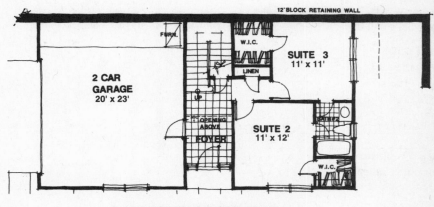

DAYLIGHT BASEMENT

ORDER BLUEPRINTS ANYTIME!
CALL TOLL-FREE 1-800-820-1283

Plan EOF-44

PRICES AND DETAILS
ON PAGES 2-5

199

Woodsy Forest Chalet

- There'll be plenty of sleeping room for family and guests with this five-bedroom forest chalet.
- Three separate decks bring the indoors out. Your grill can be stationed within easy reach, just outside the kitchen door. Two more balcony decks off upstairs bedrooms provide quiet retreats for early morning birdwatching or late night stargazing.

- The guest bedroom above the garage could double as a trophy room, card room, or private den.
- Abundant storage areas in the attic space under the eaves provide room for everything from winter clothes to fishing gear.
- Meanwhile, the wide 2-car garage frees up even more space for daily living. The one-car family keeps a boat high and dry in here!
- Bathrooms upstairs and down, plus a washer/dryer station central to the main floor keep housework and cleanup close at hand.

Plans H-804-2 & -2A	
Bedrooms: 5	**Baths:** 2
Living Area:	
Upper floor	767 sq. ft.
Main floor	952 sq. ft.
Total Living Area:	**1,719 sq. ft.**
Standard basement	952 sq. ft.
Garage	500 sq. ft.
Storage	sq. ft.
Exterior Wall Framing:	2x4
Foundation Options:	**Plan #**
Standard basement	H-804-2
Crawlspace	H-804-2A

(All plans can be built with your choice of foundation and framing. A generic conversion diagram is available. See order form.)

BLUEPRINT PRICE CODE:	B

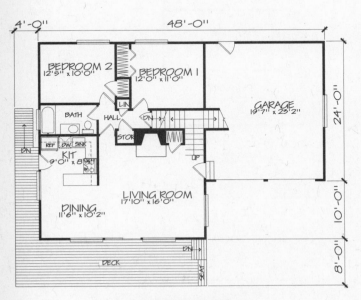

MAIN FLOOR

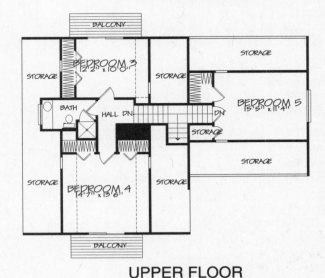

UPPER FLOOR

Plans H-804-2 & -2A

Scenic Site?

- A wraparound deck and multiple windows offering panoramic views make this the perfect vacation home for your lakeside, mountain or ocean lot.
- The large living room features floor-to-ceiling windows and is topped by an airy 20½-ft. vaulted ceiling. A rustic stone fireplace warms this space on chilly evenings.
- Sliding glass doors in the living room access the deck, which beckons you to step outside and soak up the view.
- A good-sized kitchen surrounds the family chef. A breakfast bar divides the kitchen from the living room.
- The main-floor bedroom has easy access to a full bath.
- Upstairs, a balcony overlooks the living room. Two secondary bedrooms with 12-ft. vaulted ceilings share a full bath.
- The furnace and water heater are located in the crawlspace or the basement, depending on which plan you choose.

Plans H-876-1 & -1A

Bedrooms: 3	Baths: 2
Living Area:	
Upper floor	592 sq. ft.
Main floor	960 sq. ft.
Total Living Area:	**1,552 sq. ft.**
Standard basement	960 sq. ft.
Garage	262 sq. ft.
Carport	232 sq. ft.
Exterior Wall Framing:	2x4
Foundation Options:	**Plan #**
Standard basement	H-876-1
Crawlspace	H-876-1A

(All plans can be built with your choice of foundation and framing. A generic conversion diagram is available. See order form.)

BLUEPRINT PRICE CODE: B

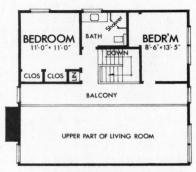

UPPER FLOOR

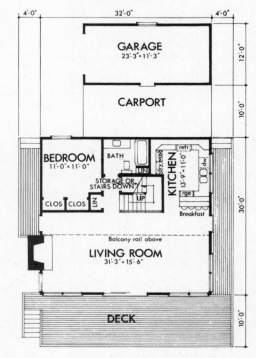

MAIN FLOOR

Romantic Retreat

- The romance and appeal of the Alpine chalet have remained constant over time. With more than 1,500 sq. ft. of living area, this chalet would make a great full-time home or vacation retreat.
- The L-shaped living room, dining room and kitchen flow together for casual living. This huge area is warmed by a freestanding fireplace and surrounded by an ornate deck, which is accessed through sliding glass doors.
- The main-level bedroom, with its twin closets and adjacent bath, could serve as a nice master suite.
- Upstairs, two large bedrooms share another full bath. One bedroom features a walk-in closet, while the other boasts its own private deck.
- The daylight basement offers laundry facilities, plenty of storage space and an extra-long garage.

Plan H-858-2

Bedrooms: 3	Baths: 2
Living Area:	
Upper floor	576 sq. ft.
Main floor	960 sq. ft.
Total Living Area:	**1,536 sq. ft.**
Daylight basement	530 sq. ft.
Tuck-under garage	430 sq. ft.
Exterior Wall Framing:	2x6

Foundation Options:

Daylight basement
(All plans can be built with your choice of foundation and framing. A generic conversion diagram is available. See order form.)

BLUEPRINT PRICE CODE: B

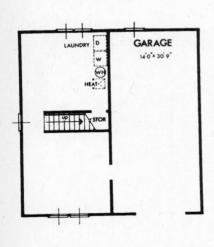

DAYLIGHT BASEMENT

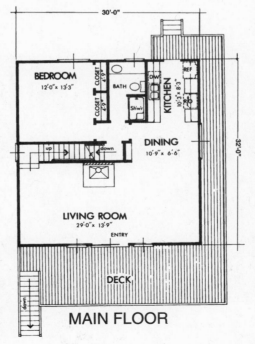

MAIN FLOOR

UPPER FLOOR

Plan H-858-2

PRICES AND DETAILS ON PAGES 2-5

PHOTO © 1990 EVERETT & SOULE

Unique Inside and Out

- This delightful design is as striking on the inside as it is on the outside.
- The focal point of the home is the huge Grand Room, which features a 23½-ft.-high vaulted ceiling, plant shelves and lots of glass, including a clerestory window. French doors flanking the fireplace lead to the covered porch and the two adjoining sun decks.
- The centrally located kitchen offers easy access from any room; a full bath, a laundry area and the garage entrance are nearby.
- The two main-floor master suites are another unique design element of the home. Each suite showcases a 13-ft. vaulted ceiling, a sunny window seat, a walk-in closet, a private bath and French doors that open to a sun deck.
- Upstairs, two guest suites under a 15-ft. vaulted peak overlook the Grand Room below.
- The multiple suites make this design a perfect shared vacation home.

Plan EOF-13

Bedrooms: 4	Baths: 3
Living Area:	
Upper floor	443 sq. ft.
Main floor	1,411 sq. ft.
Total Living Area:	**1,854 sq. ft.**
Garage	264 sq. ft.
Storage	50 sq. ft.
Exterior Wall Framing:	2x6

Foundation Options:

Crawlspace

(All plans can be built with your choice of foundation and framing. A generic conversion diagram is available. See order form.)

BLUEPRINT PRICE CODE: B

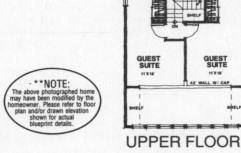

- **NOTE:
The above photographed home may have been modified by the homeowner. Please refer to floor plan and/or drawn elevation shown for actual blueprint details.

UPPER FLOOR

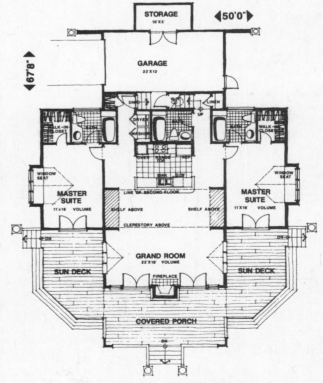

MAIN FLOOR

Dynamic Design

- This dynamic five-sided design is perfect for scenic sites. The front (or street) side of the home is shielded by a two-car garage, while the back of the home hosts a glass-filled living area surrounded by a spectacular deck.
- The unique shape of the home allows for an unusually open and spacious interior design.
- The living/dining room is further expanded by a 20-ft.-high vaulted ceiling. The centrally located fireplace provides a focal point while distributing heat efficiently.
- The space-saving galley-style kitchen is connected to the living/dining area by a snack bar.
- A large main-floor bedroom has two closets and easy access to a full bath.
- The upper floor is highlighted by a breathtaking balcony overlook. Also, two bedrooms share a nice-sized bath.
- The optional daylight basement includes a huge recreation room.

Plans H-855-1 & -1A

Bedrooms: 3	Baths: 2
Living Area:	
Upper floor	625 sq. ft.
Main floor	1,108 sq. ft.
Daylight basement	1,108 sq. ft.
Total Living Area:	**1,733/2,841 sq. ft.**
Garage	346 sq. ft.
Exterior Wall Framing:	2x6
Foundation Options:	**Plan #**
Daylight basement	H-855-1
Crawlspace	H-855-1A

(All plans can be built with your choice of foundation and framing. A generic conversion diagram is available. See order form.)

BLUEPRINT PRICE CODE:	**B/D**

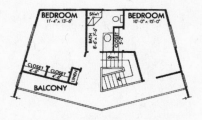

UPPER FLOOR

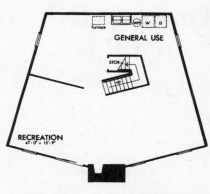

DAYLIGHT BASEMENT

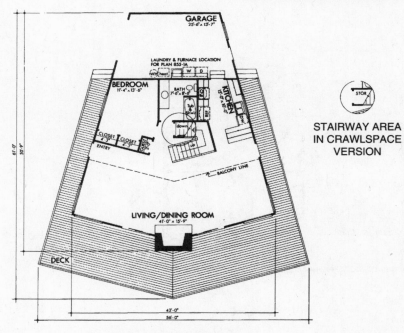

STAIRWAY AREA IN CRAWLSPACE VERSION

MAIN FLOOR

Unexpected Amenities

- Surprising interior amenities are found within the casual exterior of this good-looking design.
- A dramatic fireplace warms the comfortable formal areas. The living and dining rooms share a 20-ft. cathedral ceiling and high windows that flank the fireplace. Sliding glass doors access the outdoors.

- The efficient walk-through kitchen provides plenty of counter space, in addition to a windowed sink and a pass-through to the living areas.
- A large bedroom, a full bath and an oversized utility room complete the main floor. The utility room offers space for a washer and dryer, plus a sink and an extra freezer.
- Upstairs, the spacious and secluded master suite boasts a walk-in closet, a private bath and lots of storage space. A railed loft area overlooks the living and dining rooms.

Plan I-1249-A

Bedrooms: 2	**Baths:** 2

Living Area:

Upper floor	297 sq. ft.
Main floor	952 sq. ft.
Total Living Area:	**1,249 sq. ft.**
Standard basement	952 sq. ft.
Exterior Wall Framing:	**2x6**

Foundation Options:

Standard basement
Crawlspace
(All plans can be built with your choice of foundation and framing. A generic conversion diagram is available. See order form.)

BLUEPRINT PRICE CODE:	**A**

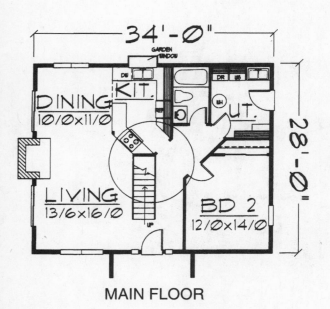

MAIN FLOOR

BASEMENT STAIRWAY LOCATION

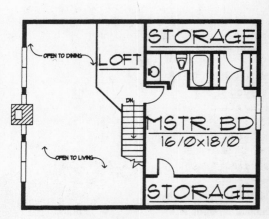

UPPER FLOOR

ORDER BLUEPRINTS ANYTIME!
CALL TOLL-FREE 1-800-820-1283

Plan I-1249-A

PRICES AND DETAILS
ON PAGES 2-5

193

Dominant and Deluxe Styling

- Vertical cedar siding, a dominant roofline and clerestory windows give this home an exciting facade.
- The interior spaces are just as inspiring, fully intended to take advantage of scenic views. The home's modest width also makes it ideal for narrow lots.
- The sunken living room is separated from the tiled foyer by an immense fireplace that rises to the peak of the cathedral ceiling. Skylights and sliding glass doors line the rear half of the room, which is surrounded by a deck.
- The adjacent dining room also has access to the deck. Extra eating space is provided by a roomy snack bar facing the efficient U-shaped kitchen.
- The oversized master suite has a large walk-in closet, a private bath and sliding glass doors to the deck.
- Upstairs, a balcony hall overlooks the living room and a portion of the foyer. The three upper-floor bedrooms boast private balconies and share a compartmentalized bath.
- The walk-out basement offers a recreation room and expansion space.

Plan AX-98597

Bedrooms: 4	**Baths:** 3

Living Area:

Upper floor	685 sq. ft.
Main floor	1,056 sq. ft.
Daylight basement (finished)	465 sq. ft.
Total Living Area:	**2,206 sq. ft.**
Daylight basement (unfinished)	585 sq. ft.
Garage	337 sq. ft.
Exterior Wall Framing:	2x4

Foundation Options:

Daylight basement
(All plans can be built with your choice of foundation and framing. A generic conversion diagram is available. See order form.)

BLUEPRINT PRICE CODE: **C**

UPPER FLOOR

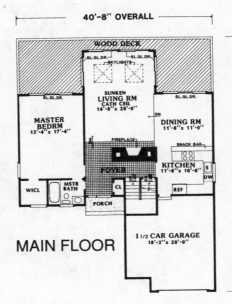

MAIN FLOOR

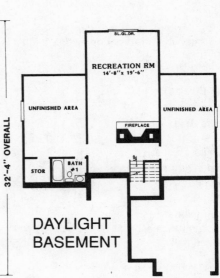

DAYLIGHT BASEMENT

Entertaining Inclinations

- This compact contemporary design is a perfect home for a sloping lot. It's also great for people who like to entertain.
- A railed, covered deck welcomes guests into the split-entry foyer. A short stairway leads to the main floor.
- The gorgeous sunken living room features a two-story window wall, a large fireplace and access to an interesting angular deck.
- Intimate dining is encouraged in the secluded corner dining room with a large picture window.
- The open kitchen boasts an island eating bar and a sunny breakfast nook with sliding glass doors.
- The sunken sleeping wing of the main floor offers access to the deck and a full bath.
- Upstairs, two open bedrooms may be partitioned for privacy or used as a loft study area. The balcony hall gives impressive views.

Plan LRD-2070

Bedrooms: 3	**Baths: 2**
Living Area:	
Upper floor	530 sq. ft.
Main floor	988 sq. ft.
Total Living Area:	**1,518 sq. ft.**
Standard basement	988 sq. ft.
Exterior Wall Framing:	2x6

Foundation Options:
Standard basement
Crawlspace
Slab
(All plans can be built with your choice of foundation and framing. A generic conversion diagram is available. See order form.)

BLUEPRINT PRICE CODE: B

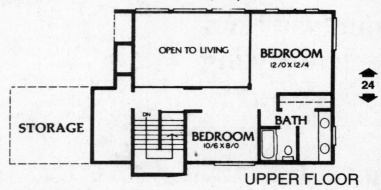

UPPER FLOOR

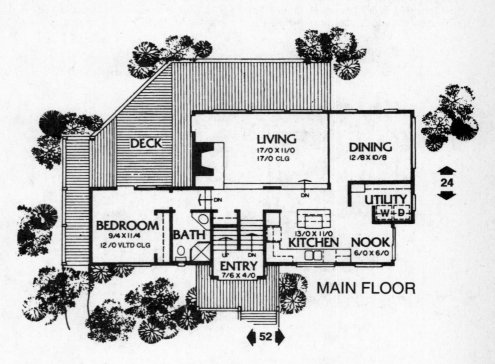

MAIN FLOOR

ORDER BLUEPRINTS ANYTIME!
CALL TOLL-FREE 1-800-820-1282

Plan LRD-2070

PRICES AND DETAILS
ON PAGES 8-1

121

Endearing Country Kitchen

- One of the most endearing features of this compact two-story design, the appealing country kitchen is spacious enough for large family gatherings yet intimate enough for romantic candlelight dinners.
- Steep rooflines, vertical siding and sharp transom windows accent the exterior of the home, giving it a strong contemporary look.

- Unfolding from the entry, the gracious family room is topped by a 17-ft. vaulted ceiling, and boasts a cozy fireplace. It opens to the formal dining room, creating a dramatic living space.
- Step outside to the patio through the kitchen to enjoy the warm weather.
- A handy utility closet and a half-bath are tucked near the entrance to the two-car garage.
- Upstairs, the master bedroom includes a private dressing area and access to the full bath. Two additional bedrooms, one with a neat built-in desk, complete the floor plan.

Plan B-7811	
Bedrooms: 3	Baths: 1½
Living Area:	
Upper floor	684 sq. ft.
Main floor	816 sq. ft.
Total Living Area:	**1,500 sq. ft.**
Standard basement	816 sq. ft.
Garage	399 sq. ft.
Exterior Wall Framing:	2x4

Foundation Options:

Standard basement
(All plans can be built with your choice of foundation and framing. A generic conversion diagram is available. See order form.)

BLUEPRINT PRICE CODE: B

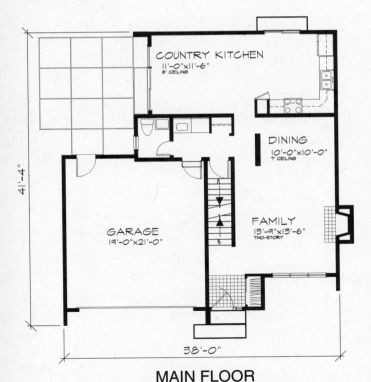

MAIN FLOOR

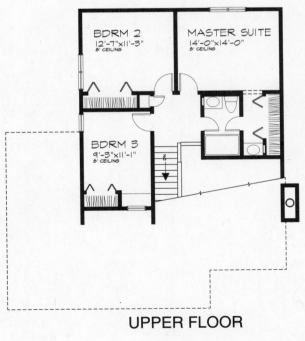

UPPER FLOOR

Plan B-7811

PRICES AND DETAILS ON PAGES 2-5

REAR VIEW

Wraparound Enticement

- A wraparound deck that gives fantastic panoramic views enhances the rear of this enticing home.
- The entry flows to the sunken living room, with its 16½-ft. ceiling. A central fireplace warms the room, and dramatic windows overlook the deck. Clerestory windows admit sunlight from above.
- Adjoining the living room, the dining room offers sliding glass doors to the deck. The kitchen's breakfast bar makes snacking or serving a breeze! Bright windows above the sink can serve as a pass-through to the deck.
- A full bath services a corner bedroom with windows facing the front yard.
- A cozy den to the right of the entry is topped by a 13-ft. vaulted ceiling. With a private deck, this room is an excellent choice for sleeping overnight guests or children returning to the nest.
- Upstairs, the master bedroom promises to spoil you with its private deck and roomy walk-in closet. A personal bath is a nice feature.

Plan LS-94142-H

Bedrooms: 2+	Baths: 2

Living Area:	
Upper floor	380 sq. ft.
Main floor	1,280 sq. ft.
Total Living Area:	**1,660 sq. ft.**
Daylight basement	1,173 sq. ft.
Exterior Wall Framing:	2x6

Foundation Options:

Daylight basement

(All plans can be built with your choice of foundation and framing. A generic conversion diagram is available. See order form.)

BLUEPRINT PRICE CODE:	**B**

MAIN FLOOR

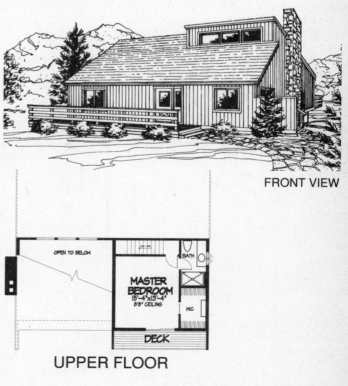

FRONT VIEW

UPPER FLOOR

ORDER BLUEPRINTS ANYTIME!
CALL TOLL-FREE 1-800-820-1283

Plan LS-94142-H

PRICES AND DETAILS
ON PAGES 2-5

189

Country Fun!

- Openness and affordability make this unique country home a good choice for a starter or empty-nester family.
- Whatever your needs, you're sure to enjoy the home's rustic flavor and the breezy porches extending along three of its four sides.
- Inside, the open-plan concept combines cooking, dining and relaxing, all under a dramatic centered balcony bridge and a 17-ft. vaulted ceiling!
- An eating bar and island cooktop attract the hungry and thirsty, while the exciting bayed woodstove area promises warmth and conversation.
- The main-floor master bedroom has a private bath with a sit-down dressing vanity; the toilet can be closed off with a pocket door. Escape to the back porch is easy through a French door.
- A skylighted bath serves the two upper-floor bedrooms. Nestled between them is an engaging loft for games or TV. Railings on both sides offer views of the living spaces below.

Plan LRD-7794

Bedrooms: 3	Baths: 3
Living Area:	
Upper floor	533 sq. ft.
Main floor	1,304 sq. ft.
Total Living Area:	**1,837 sq. ft.**
Standard basement	1,381 sq. ft.
Garage	576 sq. ft.
Exterior Wall Framing:	2x6

Foundation Options:

Standard basement

Crawlspace

(All plans can be built with your choice of foundation and framing. A generic conversion diagram is available. See order form.)

BLUEPRINT PRICE CODE: B

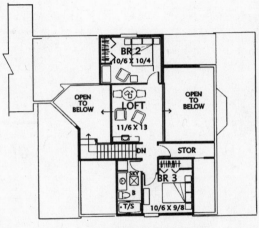

UPPER FLOOR

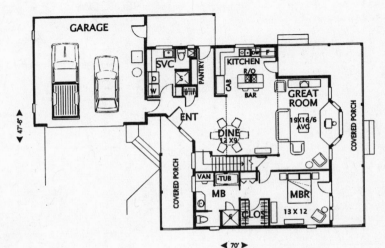

MAIN FLOOR

Plan LRD-7794

PRICES AND DETAILS
ON PAGES 2-5

Generous Living Areas

- Despite its compact floor plan, this contemporary, recreation-style home combines generous living areas both inside and out.
- A lovely covered entry porch protects visiting friends and family from rain, snow and other natural elements.
- Entertain guests in the charming living room while a glowing fire burns in the fireplace. Extend the invitation to include a meal served in the adjoining dining room. When weather permits, step out onto the deck to enjoy the sun's rays.
- Pocket doors open to reveal the pleasant family room. This room's openness to the well-designed kitchen means the family chef will be included in your conversations.
- One large main-floor bedroom and the two secondary bedrooms upstairs, complete the floor plan.

Plans H-3697-3 & -3A

Bedrooms: 3	Baths: 2
Living Area:	
Upper floor	528 sq. ft.
Main floor	1,344 sq. ft.
Total Living Area:	**1,872 sq. ft.**
Standard basement	1,344 sq. ft.
Garage	430 sq. ft.
Exterior Wall Framing:	**2x4**
Foundation Options:	**Plan #**
Standard basement	H-3697-3
Crawlspace	H-3697-3A

(All plans can be built with your choice of foundation and framing. A generic conversion diagram is available. See order form.)

BLUEPRINT PRICE CODE:	**B**

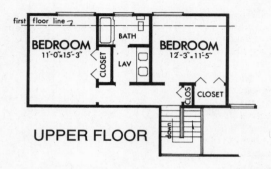

UPPER FLOOR

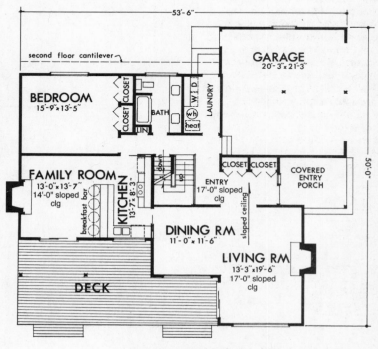

MAIN FLOOR

ORDER BLUEPRINTS ANYTIME!
CALL TOLL-FREE 1-800-820-1283

Plans H-3697-3 & -3A

PRICES AND DETAILS
ON PAGES 2-5

187

Pretty Starter Home

- Efficient and attractive, this pretty one-and-a-half story home is perfect as a retirement home or for a family just starting out.
- Guests will be drawn to the spacious living room, which is highlighted by a cute corner fireplace and access to a possible back patio.
- The well-equipped dining room features a handy wet bar and an interesting pass-through, each of which boasts glass shelves for elegant storage. A serving bar shared with the kitchen is a natural place to mull over the daily paper as you feast on morning muffins.
- With a secluded bath and a private door to the backyard, the master suite is ready to add some luxury to your life. The second main-floor bedroom suite has a walk-in closet and private access to a full bath.
- Upstairs, you'll find a unique gallery suitable for a variety of purposes, as well as lots of useful attic space.

Plan E-1223

Bedrooms: 2	Baths: 2
Living Area:	
Upper floor (gallery)	260 sq. ft.
Main floor	1,288 sq. ft.
Total Living Area:	**1,548 sq. ft.**
Garage and storage	560 sq. ft.
Exterior Wall Framing:	2x4

Foundation Options:
Crawlspace
Slab
(All plans can be built with your choice of foundation and framing. A generic conversion diagram is available. See order form.)

BLUEPRINT PRICE CODE: B

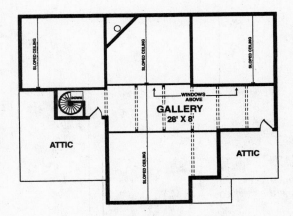

UPPER FLOOR

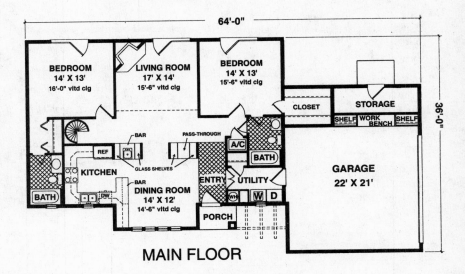

MAIN FLOOR

Casual Country

- Durable stone and decorative windows and dormers add unique style to this new-fashioned country home.
- The friendly wraparound porch is framed by rustic wood posts and accented by an attractive sidelighted front door. Inside, a high plant ledge adds decor to the two-story entry.
- French doors to the right of the entry offer peace and privacy to the study. For this reason, the room could also be used as a guest room.
- The dining room, opposite, is designed to comfortably accommodate those extra-large family gatherings.
- Casual meals can take place in the sunny breakfast nook or at the kitchen's handy breakfast bar.
- In the adjoining Great Room is a warm fireplace. A rear door expands this activity area to a backyard patio.
- Upstairs are three bedrooms and two baths. The spacious master bedroom offers a private bath with an oval garden tub and a dual-sink vanity.

Plan KD-1952

Bedrooms: 3+	Baths: 2½
Living Area:	
Upper floor	804 sq. ft.
Main floor	1,148 sq. ft.
Total Living Area:	**1,952 sq. ft.**
Garage and storage	547 sq. ft.
Exterior Wall Framing:	2x4

Foundation Options:

Slab

(All plans can be built with your choice of foundation and framing. A generic conversion diagram is available. See order form.)

BLUEPRINT PRICE CODE:	**B**

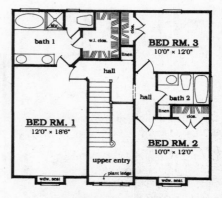

UPPER FLOOR

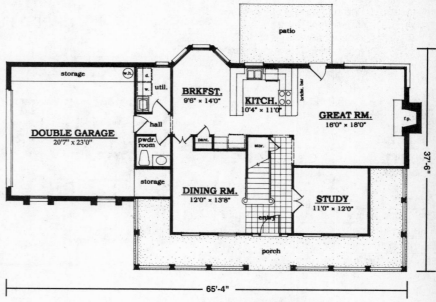

MAIN FLOOR

Living Pleasure

- Enjoy the quiet rustic feel of this pleasant design as it brings the outdoors in for your living pleasure.
- A cozy porch leads inside, where you'll enter the living room with its vaulted, two-story ceiling. Above it, a dramatic loft creates a romantic ambience.
- The living room also looks into the charming nook—get its fireplace blazing, relax and escape from it all as

you snuggle up with a loved one and some foamy hot chocolate on a blustery winter day.
- Enjoy meals in style in the formal dining room, where you can step out to the balcony to enjoy the fresh air.
- Spend the cool summer evenings stargazing from the rounded balcony, which gives you a great scenic overlook to the backyard as well.
- Vast closet space on the upper level helps to solve storage problems.

Plan GA-9603	
Bedrooms: 2+	**Baths:** 1
Living Area:	
Upper floor	655 sq. ft.
Main floor	1,110 sq. ft.
Total Living Area:	**1,765 sq. ft.**
Daylight basement	1,111 sq. ft.
Detached garage	333 sq. ft.
Exterior Wall Framing:	2x6

Foundation Options:

Daylight basement
(All plans can be built with your choice of foundation and framing. A generic conversion diagram is available. See order form.)

BLUEPRINT PRICE CODE: B

REAR VIEW

Room for Renters, In-Laws

- Beyond its rustic stone and cedar exterior, this charming cottage offers plenty of exciting, expandable space.
- The inviting foyer flows into the spectacular 12-ft., 9-in.-high vaulted Great Room, where a window-flanked stone fireplace is the center of attention. The adjoining den features sliding glass doors to a backyard deck.
- The bright, airy kitchen boasts a 12-ft. cathedral ceiling, a convenient eating bar and a sunny bayed dining room.
- Punctuated by skylights, the sleeping wing contains three bedrooms.
- The master bedroom has a private bath, a roomy walk-in closet and sliding glass doors to a quaint balcony. The two secondary bedrooms have independent access to a skylighted full bath.
- With its spacious Great Room, full-sized kitchen and dual bedrooms, the optional daylight basement is perfect for renters or in-laws.

Plan AHP-9425

Bedrooms: 3+	Baths: 2½-3½

Living Area:

Main floor	1,677 sq. ft.
Daylight basement	915 sq. ft.
Total Living Area:	**1,677/2,592 sq. ft.**
Tuck-under garage/utility room	762 sq. ft.

Exterior Wall Framing: 2x4 or 2x6

Foundation Options:
Daylight basement
Crawlspace
Slab
(All plans can be built with your choice of foundation and framing. A generic conversion diagram is available. See order form.)

BLUEPRINT PRICE CODE: B/D

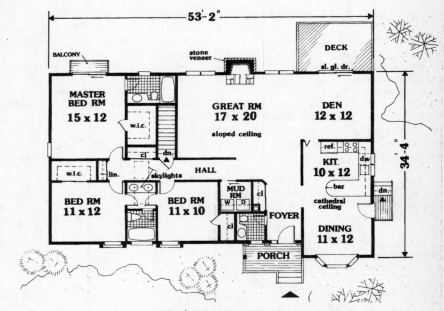

MAIN FLOOR

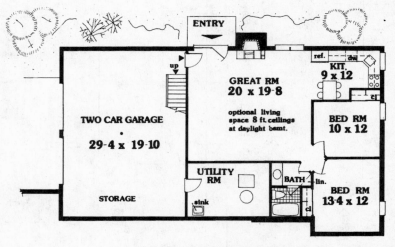

DAYLIGHT BASEMENT

Smart
Swing Suite

- A homey and appealing exterior is presented with this friendly two-story home. The shuttered entrance is topped with three decorative dormers.
- The dormers create a skylight effect and shed light upon the entry, the living room and the upper hallway. A boxed-out window and a 17-ft. vaulted ceiling further enhance the living room.
- The country kitchen is the perfect family haven for dining or just relaxing by the cozy fireplace. Sliding glass doors open to a backyard patio.
- For changing family needs, the swing suite is a nice extra. Designed to accommodate a returning or visiting child, an elderly parent or a home office, the swing suite is a smart addition to today's home.
- Upstairs, a full bath with a dual-sink vanity is nestled between two nice bedrooms.
- The master bedroom has private access to the bath and includes a walk-in closet and its own bright dormer.

Plan B-92037

Bedrooms: 2+	Baths: 2
Living Area:	
Upper floor	507 sq. ft.
Main floor	900 sq. ft.
Total Living Area:	**1,407 sq. ft.**
Standard basement	900 sq. ft.
Garage	380 sq. ft.
Exterior Wall Framing:	2x6
Foundation Options:	

Standard basement

(All plans can be built with your choice of foundation and framing. A generic conversion diagram is available. See order form.)

BLUEPRINT PRICE CODE:	**A**

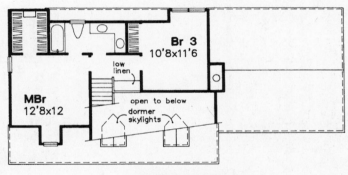

UPPER FLOOR

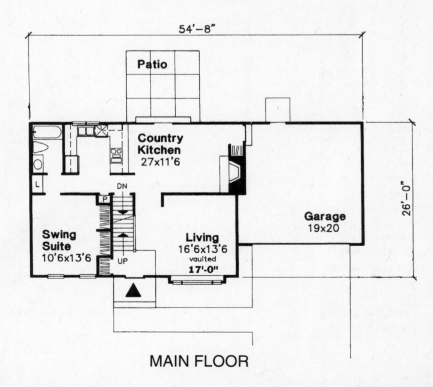

MAIN FLOOR

The Warmth of the Sun

- The benefit of the sun's warmth is maximized in this energy-efficient design. A sun space collects heat and distributes it throughout the house through sliding doors.
- Contemporary styling adds a beautiful image to any neighborhood.
- Just past the two-story entry, you'll find a huge Great Room with a sloped ceiling that rises to 17 feet. A cozy fireplace and access to the sun space add to its charm.
- Dazzling and invigorating, the spectacular sun space is a refreshing area that's perfect for relieving stress.
- The galley-style kitchen stands ready to serve any room in the house. On warm days you can step out a handy back deck and dine alfresco!
- Upstairs, you'll find a spacious master suite complete with a private dressing area. A loft can be used as a third bedroom if needed.

Plan B-605

Bedrooms: 2+	Baths: 1½
Living Area:	
Upper floor	653 sq. ft.
Main floor	731 sq. ft.
Sun space	179 sq. ft.
Total Living Area:	**1,563 sq. ft.**
Standard basement	731 sq. ft.
Garage	512 sq. ft.
Exterior Wall Framing:	2x6

Foundation Options:

Standard basement

(All plans can be built with your choice of foundation and framing. A generic conversion diagram is available. See order form.)

BLUEPRINT PRICE CODE:	**B**

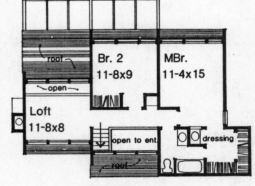

UPPER FLOOR

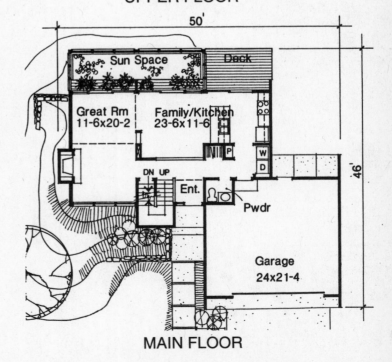

MAIN FLOOR

Delightful Traditional

- This delightful traditional design extends a warm invitation with its front and back covered porches.
- Off the front porch is a spacious central living space that combines the living room, dining room and kitchen.
- The living room boasts a dramatic fireplace that backs another fireplace in the adjoining master bedroom.
- The large kitchen features a cooktop island and lots of counter space. The kitchen is open to the dining area, which has French doors that provide access to the rear porch.
- Isolated from the secondary bedrooms, the master bedroom is a perfect private retreat. In addition to its romantic fireplace, the master suite has a huge private bath with dual dressing areas and a separate tub and shower.

Plan J-90015	
Bedrooms: 3	**Baths: 2½**
Living Area:	
Main floor	2,117 sq. ft.
Total Living Area:	**2,117 sq. ft.**
Standard basement	2,117 sq. ft.
Garage	528 sq. ft.
Exterior Wall Framing:	2x6

Foundation Options:

Standard basement

Crawlspace

Slab

(All plans can be built with your choice of foundation and framing. A generic conversion diagram is available. See order form.)

BLUEPRINT PRICE CODE: C

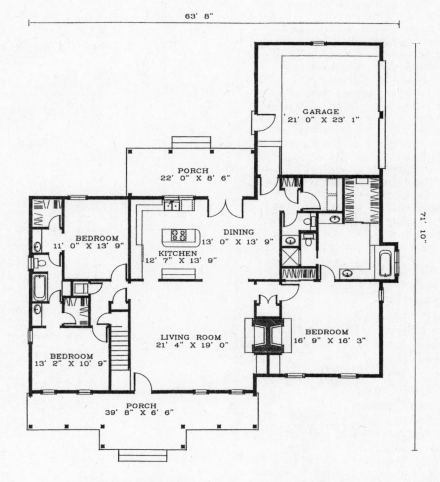

MAIN FLOOR

Mediterranean Masterpiece

- This home is truly a Mediterranean masterpiece, with its stucco exterior, arched entry and tile roof.
- An arched transom and sidelights embrace the front door, which opens to the welcoming foyer.
- Soaring 11-ft. ceilings enhance the living room, dining room, kitchen and foyer. Sliding glass doors in the dining room open to a nice backyard patio.
- Decorative plant ledges preside over the island kitchen, which includes a pantry.
- The fantastic family room features a fireplace, plus patio access.
- A handy laundry room and a half-bath are located near the garage entrance. The garage has extra storage space.
- The deluxe master suite boasts a spa tub, a separate shower, double sinks and a walk-in closet. Two additional bedrooms share a second full bath.

Plan U-92-113

Bedrooms: 3	**Baths:** 2½

Living Area:

Main floor (non-bsmt. version)	1,941 sq. ft.
Main floor (basement version)	1,983 sq. ft.
Total Living Area:	**1,941/1,983 sq. ft.**
Standard basement	1,961 sq. ft.
Garage	566 sq. ft.
Exterior Wall Framing:	**2x6**

Foundation Options:

Standard basement
Crawlspace
Slab

(All plans can be built with your choice of foundation and framing. A generic conversion diagram is available. See order form.)

BLUEPRINT PRICE CODE:	**B**

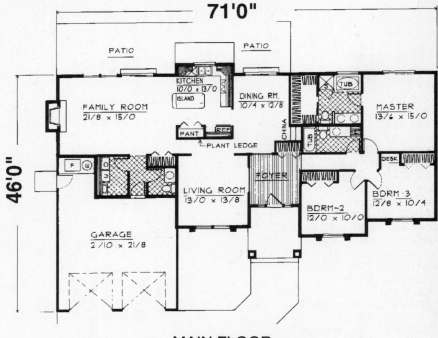

MAIN FLOOR

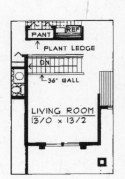

BASEMENT STAIRWAY LOCATION

ORDER BLUEPRINTS ANYTIME!
CALL TOLL-FREE 1-800-820-1283

Plan U-92-113

PRICES AND DETAILS
ON PAGES 2-5

179

Award Winner

- Filled with innovative features, this elegant one-story stucco home has won numerous national design awards.
- Accented by an overhead plant shelf, the marble-floored, 12-ft.-high foyer flows into the spacious Grand Room.
- Boasting a soaring 18-ft., 8-in. ceiling, the Grand Room offers an ale bar, a stunning two-way fireplace and glass doors to a backyard pool and spa area.
- The formal dining room, which also enjoys pool access, shares the Grand Room's high ceiling, fireplace and ale bar. A built-in buffet across the gallery overlooks a decorative fountain garden.
- The island kitchen's handy snack bar serves the sunny morning and gathering rooms, each with a 12-ft., 8-in. ceiling and a view of the covered veranda.
- The luxurious master suite features a 12-ft. ceiling, a sunken, glass-enclosed sitting area and private pool access. The master bath has a garden tub, a separate shower, a laundry closet and his-and-hers amenities. A media room and a pool bath complete the wing.
- Two more bedrooms boast 10-ft. ceilings and share a large dual-vanity bath with a 12-ft. ceiling.

Plan EOF-72

Bedrooms: 3	Baths: 3

Living Area:.

Main floor	3,600 sq. ft.
Total Living Area:	**3,600 sq. ft.**
Garage and golf cart storage	672 sq. ft.

Exterior Wall Framing: 8-in. concrete block

Foundation Options:

Slab

(All plans can be built with your choice of foundation and framing. A generic conversion diagram is available. See order form.)

BLUEPRINT PRICE CODE: **F**

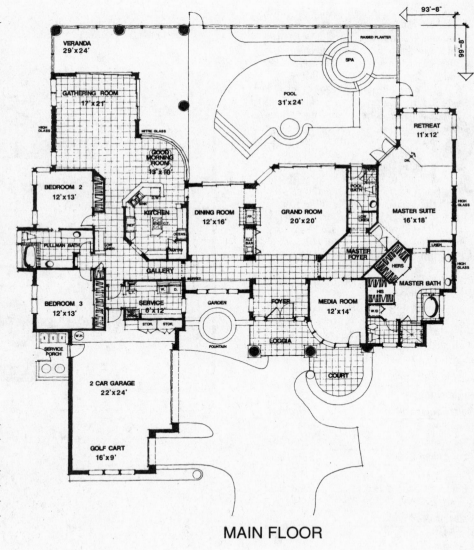

MAIN FLOOR

Worth the Wait!

- Retirement is definitely worth the wait in this exciting two-bedroom design.
- Circular wood louvers and a bold brick chimney delight the facade. The big three-car garage is oriented to the side and nicely disguised by windows.
- A high ceiling graces the entry and extends into the living room ahead. Windows alongside the fireplace offer a dramatic view of the backyard deck and spa you've always wanted.
- Another fireplace adds warmth and ambience to the double-doored den or home office to the right of the entry.
- The open kitchen is situated to serve both the breakfast area and the formal dining room. Also within easy reach are a walk-in pantry, a nice-sized laundry room and a door to the garage.
- The dining room's vaulted ceiling rises to meet a bright window wall. A glass door invites your guests outdoors for an eventful evening.
- When the bugs get bad, all can retreat to the roomy screened porch.
- Each bedroom has private access to a dual-vanity bath. The master bedroom also boasts a decorative plant shelf and deck access.

Plan B-94029

Bedrooms: 2+	Baths: 2
Living Area:	
Main floor	2,090 sq. ft.
Total Living Area:	**2,090 sq. ft.**
Screened porch	138 sq. ft.
Standard basement	2,090 sq. ft.
Garage	665 sq. ft.
Exterior Wall Framing:	2x6

Foundation Options:

Standard basement

(All plans can be built with your choice of foundation and framing. A generic conversion diagram is available. See order form.)

BLUEPRINT PRICE CODE: C

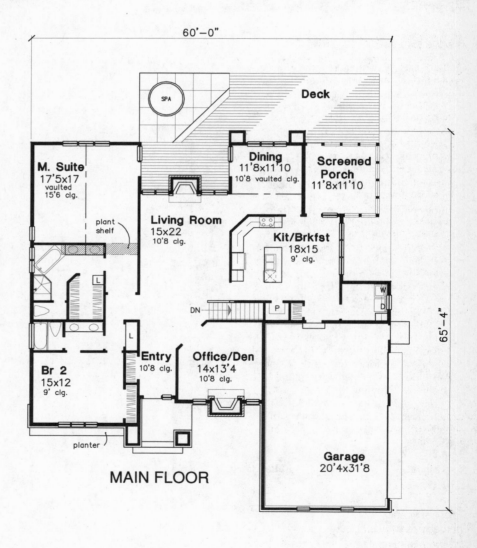

MAIN FLOOR

ORDER BLUEPRINTS ANYTIME!
CALL TOLL-FREE 1-800-820-1283

Plan B-94029

**PRICES AND DETAILS
ON PAGES 2-5**

177

Narrow-Lot Lake Home

- Under 24 ft. wide, this long, narrow home is perfect for lake lots or other sites with limited building space.
- Open and inviting, the combined living and dining rooms overlook both the screen porch and the L-shaped deck. The appealing fireplace can be enjoyed from both rooms.
- Centrally located, the well-designed kitchen has all the tools you'll need to prepare the catch of the day.
- Three good-sized bedrooms are secluded at the end of a long hallway. The largest bedroom sports a tidy private bath.
- On the lower floor, the spacious family room includes a fireplace and a pair of sliding glass doors that lead out to a large patio. The patio is protected by the deck above and a screen wall.
- Two more bedrooms, a utility room and a full bath complete the lower floor of this large recreation-style home.

Plan AX-97946

Bedrooms: 5	Baths: 3
Living Area:	
Main floor	1,204 sq. ft.
Lower floor	838 sq. ft.
Total Living Area:	**2,042 sq. ft.**
Screen porch	96 sq. ft.
Tuck-under garage	227 sq. ft.
Exterior Wall Framing:	**2x4**

Foundation Options:

Crawlspace

Slab

(All plans can be built with your choice of foundation and framing. A generic conversion diagram is available. See order form.)

BLUEPRINT PRICE CODE:	**C**

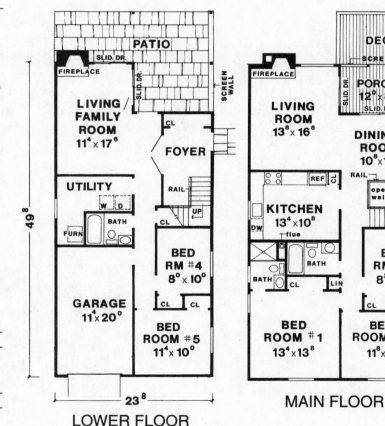

LOWER FLOOR

MAIN FLOOR

Sweet Memories

- With its sweet front porch and easygoing interior, this country-style home comfortably hosts the activities that turn into tomorrow's memories.
- Inside, the dining room off the foyer greets guests with a pretty picture of elegance. A corner cabinet keeps family china out of harm's way.
- At the rear of the home, the kitchen, the breakfast nook and the Great Room accommodate all sorts of events. A peninsula counter at the center of the

space puts hors d'oeuvres within arm's reach, while a recessed nook in the Great Room holds a big-screen TV.
- When the evening calls for a bit of romance, retreat to the master suite. Here, a corner fireplace creates a beautiful, comforting ambience. In the master bath, a garden tub will delight you for years to come.
- All of the rooms noted above include space-enhancing 10-ft. ceilings.
- Across the home, a central hall bath services the other two bedrooms, both of which are good-sized.

Plan J-9405

Bedrooms: 3	Baths: 2

Living Area:

Main floor (non-bsmt. version)	1,853 sq. ft.
Main floor (bsmt. version)	1,874 sq. ft.
Total Living Area:	**1,853/1,874 sq. ft.**
Standard basement	1,874 sq. ft.
Garage and storage	557/536 sq. ft.

Exterior Wall Framing:	2x4

Foundation Options:

Standard basement
Crawlspace
Slab
(All plans can be built with your choice of foundation and framing. A generic conversion diagram is available. See order form.)

BLUEPRINT PRICE CODE:	B

64-6

61-8

Bath

Owner's Bedroom
16-0x16-2

Porch
18-0x10-0

Storage
11-7x3-10

Laun.

Breakfast
11-6x10-6

Great Room
15-2x15-11

Bedroom
11-7x13-0

Garage
21-5x20-8

Kitchen
12-11x10-3

Dining
11-7x13-11

Foyer

Bath

Storage
15-5x3-0

Porch
20-10x8-4

Bedroom
11-7x12-6

MAIN FLOOR

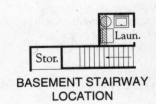

Laun.

Stor.

BASEMENT STAIRWAY LOCATION

Sumptuous Sunbelt Appeal

- A tile roof and a stucco facade marked by striking columns and an arched entry give this comfortable one-story a sumptuous Sunbelt appeal.
- French doors open to the foyer, where a columned half-wall defines the formal dining room.
- Double doors lead to a library, which could accommodate overnight guests.
- The foyer flows into the living room straight ahead, which is enhanced by sliding-glass-door access to a covered backyard lanai. A handsome fireplace with a built-in media center livens up the room even more.
- Greenhouse windows lend a dreamy brightness to the breakfast nook at the far end of the open kitchen.
- Nearby, two good-sized secondary bedrooms share a hall bath.
- The serene master bedroom boasts private lanai access through sliding glass doors in its bayed sitting area. A fireplace and a media center add to the cozy ambience.
- A luxurious garden tub graces the master bath, along with a separate shower and a private toilet.

Plan B-94014

Bedrooms: 3+	Baths: 2½
Living Area:	
Main floor	2,090 sq. ft.
Total Living Area:	**2,090 sq. ft.**
Garage	413 sq. ft.
Exterior Wall Framing:	8-in. concrete block

Foundation Options:

Slab
(All plans can be built with your choice of foundation and framing. A generic conversion diagram is available. See order form.)

BLUEPRINT PRICE CODE: **C**

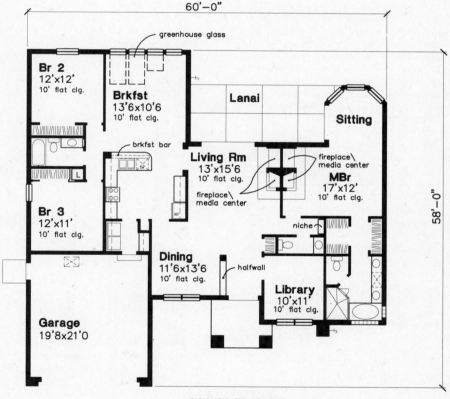

MAIN FLOOR

Plan B-94014

PRICES AND DETAILS
ON PAGES 2-5

New for Today

- This updated design has a charming Cape Cod look, with its round louvered vents, paned-glass windows and distinctive roof gables. Inside, however, this plan incorporates all of today's best new features in home design.
- Both the foyer and the living room boast ceilings that are 10 ft., 8 in. high. Beautiful transom windows are above the front door and above the windows flanking the living room fireplace.
- Elegant arched openings lead from the living room to the dining room, the kitchen and the bedroom hallway. The dining room offers a tall picture window and access to the deck and patio. A screen porch adds even more indoor/outdoor space.
- The gourmet kitchen includes an island counter and a sunny breakfast alcove.
- The master suite features a vaulted ceiling and private access to the deck. The luxurious master bath hosts a corner spa tub, a separate shower and a grooming table next to the sink.
- All ceilings are 9 ft. high unless otherwise indicated.

Plan B-91026

Bedrooms: 2+	Baths: 2
Living Area:	
Main floor	1,905 sq. ft.
Total Living Area:	**1,905 sq. ft.**
Standard basement	1,905 sq. ft.
Garage	406 sq. ft.
Exterior Wall Framing:	2x6

Foundation Options:

Standard basement
(All plans can be built with your choice of foundation and framing. A generic conversion diagram is available. See order form.)

BLUEPRINT PRICE CODE: B

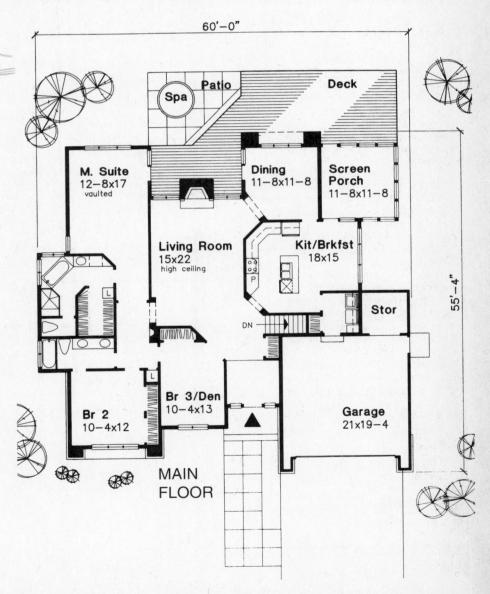

60'-0"

55'-4"

Spa Patio Deck

M. Suite 12–8x17 vaulted

Dining 11–8x11–8

Screen Porch 11–8x11–8

Living Room 15x22 high ceiling

Kit/Brkfst 18x15

DN

Stor

Br 2 10–4x12

Br 3/Den 10–4x13

Garage 21x19–4

MAIN FLOOR

ORDER BLUEPRINTS ANYTIME!
CALL TOLL-FREE 1-800-820-1283

Plan B-91026

PRICES AND DETAILS
ON PAGES 2-5

173

Southwestern Magic

- Casual, carefree spaces define the interior of this magical Southwestern-inspired design.
- Visually expanded by its openness to the other living areas, the sun-drenched living room features an oversized fireplace flanked by huge picture windows and access to the spacious covered patio.

- A peninsula snack bar distinguishes the casual eating nook from the efficient walk-through kitchen. Just steps away are laundry facilities, a full bath and a cozy den.
- The sleeping wing is secluded from the living area for privacy.
- Wake each morning in the master bedroom to the glowing rays of the sun. Highlights include a huge walk-in closet and a private bath with a dressing area.
- Two nice-sized secondary bedrooms share a full bath, completing the plan.

Plan H-1424-M1A

Bedrooms: 3+	**Baths:** 3

Living Area:

Main floor	2,461 sq. ft.
Total Living Area:	**2,461 sq. ft.**
Garage	455 sq. ft.

Exterior Wall Framing: 8-in. concrete block

Foundation Options:

Slab

(All plans can be built with your choice of foundation and framing. A generic conversion diagram is available. See order form.)

BLUEPRINT PRICE CODE: C

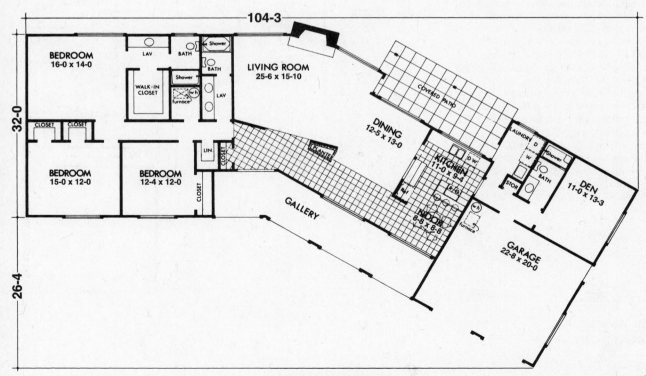

MAIN FLOOR

Plan H-1424-M1A

Country Invitation

- Dormer windows above a nostalgic covered porch highlight this country home's inviting facade.
- The 13-ft.-high sidelighted foyer opens into the formal living and dining rooms. The dining room is set off by a striking corner column and warmly lit by shuttered windows.
- A 13-ft. vaulted ceiling soars above the living room. Sliding glass doors lead to a covered backyard patio.
- The secluded master bedroom sprawls beneath a 12-ft., 9-in. vaulted ceiling. The master bath boasts a refreshing garden tub with a view of a courtyard through bright skywalls.
- A roomy secondary bedroom has easy access to a handy powder room.
- Skylights brighten the open kitchen, which is enhanced by a charming, bayed breakfast nook and a serving bar facing the family room.
- Patio access and a corner fireplace enhance the family room. From the 13-ft. vaulted ceiling, skylights drench the room with natural light.
- Two more bedrooms just off the family room share a full bath.

Plan HDS-99-236

Bedrooms: 4	Baths: 2½
Living Area:	
Main floor	2,330 sq. ft.
Total Living Area:	**2,330 sq. ft.**
Garage	477 sq. ft.
Exterior Wall Framing:	2x4

Foundation Options:

Slab

(All plans can be built with your choice of foundation and framing. A generic conversion diagram is available. See order form.)

BLUEPRINT PRICE CODE: C

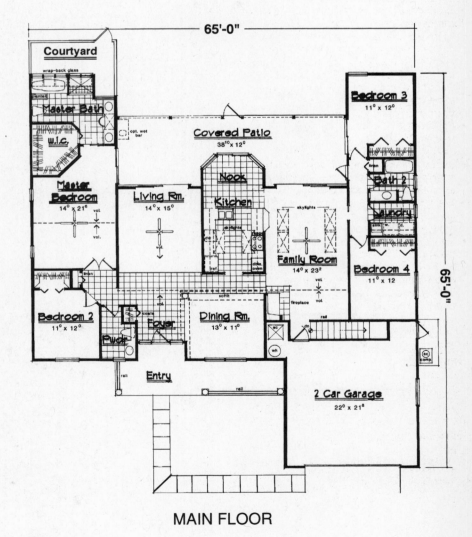

MAIN FLOOR

ORDER BLUEPRINTS ANYTIME!
CALL TOLL-FREE 1-800-820-1283

Plan HDS-99-236

PRICES AND DETAILS
ON PAGES 2-5

171

Exotic Mediterranean

- Exotic Mediterranean living is in store for the owners of this dramatic home.
- Its unique design is wrapped around a central courtyard and skylighted porch, allowing the living areas to bask in natural light while enjoying the views.
- Decorative columns, half-walls and plant ledges define the rooms, promoting openness and interaction.
- Adjoining the foyer are the formal spaces. The living room's 13-ft. cathedral ceiling is centered over a handsome fireplace with a Spanish tile hearth. The dining room is adorned by an octagonal stepped ceiling.
- The kitchen includes a handy snack bar and a pantry as it unfolds to the bright, angled breakfast nook.
- A long gallery leads to the home's three bedrooms. The master bedroom boasts an 11-ft. stepped ceiling and a French door to the porch. The roomy master bath showcases an exciting garden tub under a 16-ft., 4-in. gazebo ceiling!

Plan L-2360-MC

Bedrooms: 3	Baths: 2½
Living Area:	
Main floor	2,360 sq. ft.
Total Living Area:	**2,360 sq. ft.**
Garage	478 sq. ft.
Exterior Wall Framing:	2x4

Foundation Options:

Slab

(All plans can be built with your choice of foundation and framing. A generic conversion diagram is available. See order form.)

BLUEPRINT PRICE CODE:	C

REAR VIEW

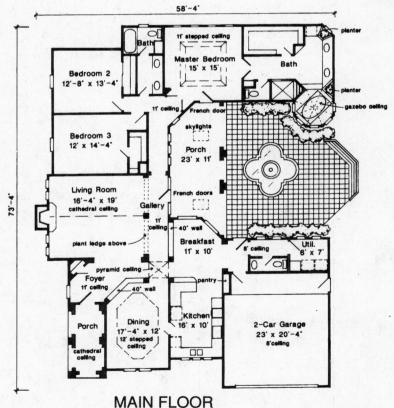

MAIN FLOOR

ORDER BLUEPRINTS ANYTIME!
CALL TOLL-FREE 1-800-820-1283

Plan L-2360-MC

PRICES AND DETAILS
ON PAGES 2-5

Splendid
Spanish Styling

- Spanish styling and a contemporary floor plan distinguish this moderately sized U-shaped ranch home.
- Three distinct wings envelop an exciting outdoor courtyard that could be used as a patio and pool area.
- A stunning glassed-in gallery connects the bedrooms to the living areas. The gallery opens to the courtyard in four places, providing easy access from any point in the home. It also floods the home with plenty of natural light.
- The extensive use of half-wall rails opens rooms up to one another and to the view through the gallery.
- The sunken living room is warmed by an inviting fireplace.
- The vaulted formal dining room looks out on the arcaded front porch.
- A cathedral ceiling crowns the master bedroom, which boasts a private bath, a walk-in closet and direct patio access.

REAR VIEW

Plan AX-97838

Bedrooms: 3	Baths: 2½

Living Area:

Main floor	1,665 sq. ft.
Total Living Area:	**1,665 sq. ft.**
Standard basement	1,650 sq. ft.
Garage	329 sq. ft.
Optional two-car garage	542 sq. ft.

Exterior Wall Framing: 2x4

Foundation Options:

Standard basement
Slab
(All plans can be built with your choice of foundation and framing. A generic conversion diagram is available. See order form.)

BLUEPRINT PRICE CODE: B

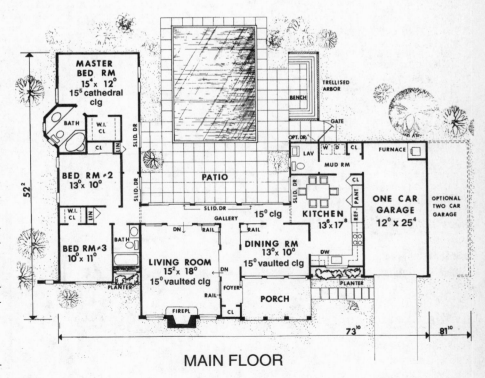

MAIN FLOOR

ORDER BLUEPRINTS ANYTIME!
CALL TOLL-FREE 1-800-820-1283

Plan AX-97838

PRICES AND DETAILS
ON PAGES 2-5
169

Spanish Styled So Right!

- Simply yet elegantly constructed, this Spanish-influenced design reflects that good feeling you've been searching for in a one-story home.
- Unfolding from the wide entry, the gracious living room promises to invigorate you. It features a fireplace with a raised hearth that extends the full width of the wall. Sliding glass doors open to the covered patio, which is framed in for added privacy.
- The casual living areas span the entire left side of the home, highlighted by a handy snack bar that divides the dining area and the U-shaped kitchen. Sliding glass doors in the family room offer access to the patio, with an adjoining storage compartment.
- Enjoy the pleasant features offered with the comfortable master bedroom—a spacious private bath, a separate dressing area and a large walk-in closet.
- Two additional bedrooms are generously sized, sharing

Plans H-1426-M1A & -M1B

Bedrooms: 3	Baths: 2
Living Area:	
Main floor	2,038 sq. ft.
Total Living Area:	**2,038 sq. ft.**
Garage and carport	441 sq. ft.
Storage	34 sq. ft.
Exterior Wall Framing:	2x6
Foundation Options:	**Plan #**
Slab with carport	H-1426-M1A
Slab with garage	H-1426-M1B

(All plans can be built with your choice of foundation and framing. A generic conversion diagram is available. See order form.)

BLUEPRINT PRICE CODE: C

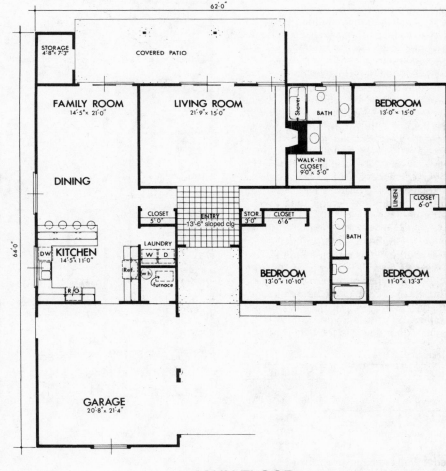

MAIN FLOOR

Plans H-1426-M1A & -M1B

PRICES AND DETAILS
ON P. 5S 3.5

Look No Further

- If you're looking for a move-up ranch with plenty of deilightful features, look no further.
- A covered, railed porch opens to an entry that leads you into the 13-ft.-high vaulted living room. A fireplace warms this generous space, and a French door leads out to a big backyard deck.
- The adjoining formal dining room features greenhouse windows that bathe the room in light and offer a full view of the deck. A handy pass-through extends from the U-shaped kitchen.
- A nearby Keeping Room is topped by an 11-ft., 8-in. vaulted ceiling and has its own deck access. Curl up beside the fireplace in an overstuffed chair, and let yourself nod off on a rainy autumn Saturday.
- Awaken each day to a hearty breakfast served in the 11-ft., 8-in. vaulted breakfast nook. Its proximity to the Keeping Room's fireplace is an amenity you'll appreciate on winter mornings.
- The sleeping wing of the home includes the master suite with its 12½-ft. vaulted ceiling and private luxury bath. A French door opens to the deck.

Plan B-86118

Bedrooms: 3	Baths: 2½
Living Area:	
Main floor	2,004 sq. ft.
Total Living Area:	**2,004 sq. ft.**
Standard basement	2,004 sq. ft.
Garage	609 sq. ft.
Exterior Wall Framing:	2x4

Foundation Options:

Standard basement

(All plans can be built with your choice of foundation and framing. A generic conversion diagram is available. See order form.)

BLUEPRINT PRICE CODE: C

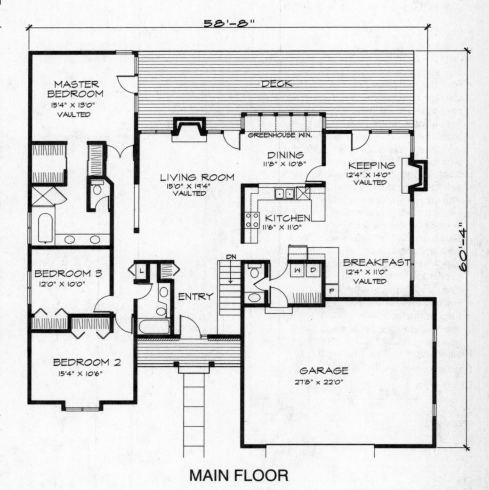

MAIN FLOOR

Classic Beauty

- Stately columns, bright windows and a symmetrical design give this charming home an aura of lasting beauty.
- Highlighted by a trio of fantail transom windows, the gallery-style foyer flows past decorative Roman columns into the living room.
- Boasting a 12-ft. vaulted ceiling, the living room features a handsome fireplace flanked by glass.
- Pantry shelves separate the living room from the dining room and the kitchen, which offers a unique curved counter. A laundry/utility area and access to a two-car garage and a covered backyard porch are nearby.
- The sleeping wing has its own porch access. The wonderful master bedroom is enhanced by a lovely bow window that views into a sunny courtyard. The master bath showcases an oval garden tub, a separate shower, a dual-sink vanity and a roomy walk-in closet.
- Two additional bedrooms share a second full bath.
- Unless otherwise specified, 9-ft. ceilings are found throughout the home.

Plan J-9402

Bedrooms: 3	Baths: 2
Living Area:	
Main floor (without basement)	1,800 sq. ft.
Main floor (with basement)	1,908 sq. ft.
Total Living Area:	**1,800/1,908 sq. ft.**
Standard basement	1,800 sq. ft.
Garage	497 sq. ft.
Exterior Wall Framing:	2x4

Foundation Options:

Standard basement

Crawlspace

Slab

(All plans can be built with your choice of foundation and framing. A generic conversion diagram is available. See order form.)

BLUEPRINT PRICE CODE: B

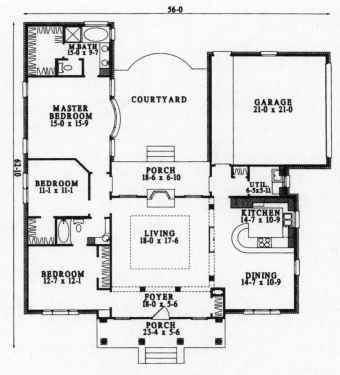

MAIN FLOOR

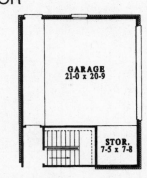

BASEMENT STAIRWAY LOCATION

Plan J-9402

PRICES AND DETAILS
ON PAGES 2-5

Sprawling Contemporary

- Room to roam is what this sprawling contemporary ranch offers, plus plenty of little surprises.
- The rustic wood exterior is enhanced by corner trapezoid windows that add dramatic curb appeal and interior enjoyment.
- In from the double-door entry, the vaulted foyer affords a panoramic view of the entire living area.

- Sparkling transom windows are accentuated by a sloped ceiling in the sunken living room.
- The formal dining room overlooks the living room and the dramatic conversation pit nestled around the heartwarming fireplace.
- Also overlooking the conversation pit, the family room features a built-in wet bar and sliding glass doors to a covered rear porch.
- The sleeping wing includes a large master bedroom with a sloped ceiling, sliding glass doors out to the patio and a stunning private bath.

Plan AX-703-B	
Bedrooms: 3	**Baths:** 2
Living Area:	
Main floor	2,128 sq. ft.
Total Living Area:	**2,128 sq. ft.**
Standard basement	2,128 sq. ft.
Garage and storage	565 sq. ft.
Exterior Wall Framing:	2x4
Foundation Options:	
Standard basement	
Slab	

(All plans can be built with your choice of foundation and framing. A generic conversion diagram is available. See order form.)

BLUEPRINT PRICE CODE:	C

MAIN FLOOR

STORAGE

COVERED PORCH

UTILITY

TWO CAR GARAGE
21⁰ x 23⁴

PATIO

FAMILY ROOM
13⁰ x 24²
13⁰ vaulted clg

KITCHEN
13⁴ x 13⁶

PANTRY

SERVICE ENTRY

SLID. DR.

DRESSING   BATH   BAR

MASTER BED ROOM
12⁶ x 18⁸
11⁰ vaulted clg

WALK-IN CLOSET

BATH

STOR

location of bsm't stair

SEAT
CONVERSATION PIT
8⁶ clg
FIREPLACE

DINING ROOM
13⁰ x 11²

REF

RAIL

BED ROOM #3
12⁶ x 11⁸

BED ROOM #2
10² x 11⁸

FOYER
12⁰ sloped clg   RAIL

SUNKEN LIVING ROOM
13⁶ sloped clg
15⁰ x 20⁰

PORCH

58-8

84-8

Plan AX-703-B

REAR VIEW

Soaring Center

- This home's dramatic central living and dining rooms share a vaulted ceiling that soars to an astounding 20 feet! Clerestory windows flood the rooms with refreshing natural light.
- A charming front porch leads to the sidelighted entry, which offers two wide openings to the formal living and dining rooms. An elegant see-through fireplace and adjoining cabinets create a cozy ambience for both rooms.
- Two separate French doors open to a covered porch. An adjoining patio offers a barbecue grill and an outdoor spa.
- The isolated master suite is enhanced by a 14-ft. ceiling and private backyard access. The stunning bath includes a lovely corner garden tub.
- Easily accessed from the dining room, the island kitchen boasts a neat snack bar and a spacious morning room that is perfect for cheery breakfasts. The rooms share a 10-ft. ceiling.
- In the opposite wing are three more bedrooms with 9-ft. ceilings, two of which offer private baths. One bedroom may be used as a quiet study.

Plan DD-2704-1

Bedrooms: 3+	Baths: 4
Living Area:	
Main floor	2,704 sq. ft.
Total Living Area:	**2,704 sq. ft.**
Standard basement	2,704 sq. ft.
Garage and shop	591 sq. ft.
Exterior Wall Framing:	2x4

Foundation Options:

Standard basement

Crawlspace

Slab

(All plans can be built with your choice of foundation and framing. A generic conversion diagram is available. See order form.)

BLUEPRINT PRICE CODE:	D

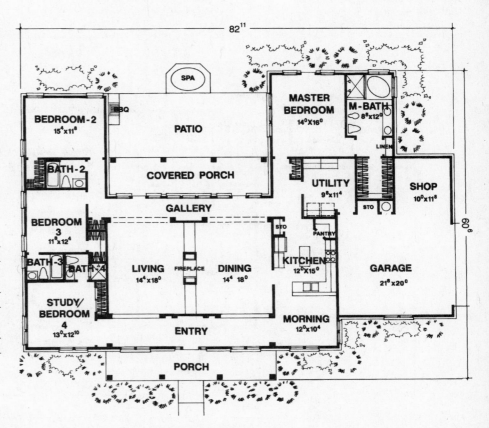

MAIN FLOOR

ORDER BLUEPRINTS ANYTIME! **CALL TOLL-FREE 1-800-820-1283**   Plan DD-2704-1   **PRICES AND DETAILS ON PAGES 2-5**

Center of Attention

- The covered front porch of this cozy three-bedroom ranch gives the home its country flavor.
- The focal point of the interior is an impressive stone fireplace that separates the Great Room from the formal dining room. The Great Room is further enhanced by a dramatic cathedral ceiling.

- The dining room offers sliding glass doors to a backyard patio.
- Attached to the dining room is a space-efficient kitchen that easily serves the bay-windowed breakfast nook. Garage access and a laundry/utility room are close by.
- The spacious master bedroom includes a unique compartmentalized bath with a walk-in closet, a dressing area and a separate tub.
- Serviced by another full bath at the opposite end of the home are two good-sized secondary bedrooms.

Plan C-8710

Bedrooms: 3	**Baths:** 2
Living Area:	
Main floor	1,670 sq. ft.
Total Living Area:	**1,670 sq. ft.**
Garage	427 sq. ft.
Storage	63 sq. ft.
Exterior Wall Framing:	2x4

Foundation Options:
Crawlspace
Slab
(All plans can be built with your choice of foundation and framing. A generic conversion diagram is available. See order form.)

BLUEPRINT PRICE CODE: **B**

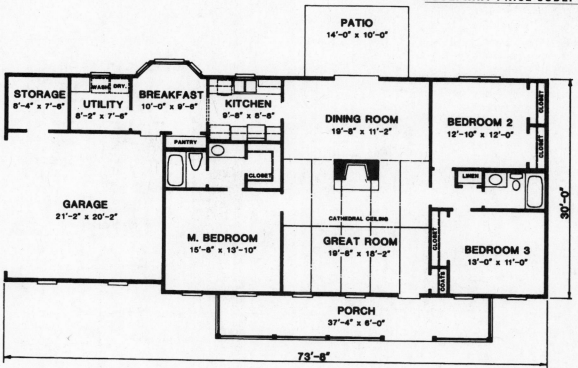

MAIN FLOOR

ORDER BLUEPRINTS ANYTIME!
CALL TOLL-FREE 1-800-820-1283

Plan C-8710

PRICES AND DETAILS
ON PAGES 2-5

163

Affordable Luxury

- This fantastic, open design is well planned and luxurious. Designed for indoor/outdoor enjoyment, the activity areas are oriented for maximum views of the backyard living spaces.
- Handsome double doors off the covered entry open to an airy 12-ft.-high foyer. The spacious central family room ahead features a dramatic fireplace, an adjoining media center and a 10-ft. ceiling. Sliding glass doors open to the spectacular covered patio.

- The formal dining room, kitchen and breakfast nook unfold from the family room. The kitchen is neatly positioned to serve each of the living areas and boasts a pantry and a large snack bar.
- The secondary sleeping wing houses two bedrooms and a full bath, and is conveniently accessible from the patio.
- The super master suite at the opposite end of the home also opens to the patio and is complete with a huge walk-in closet and a luxurious private bath with a dual-sink vanity and a whirlpool tub. A courtesy door allows direct access to the bath from the adjacent den/study, which may include a wet bar.

Plan HDS-99-144	
Bedrooms: 3+	**Baths:** 2
Living Area:	
Main floor	1,869 sq. ft.
Total Living Area:	**1,869 sq. ft.**
Garage	400 sq. ft.
Exterior Wall Framing:	2x4
Foundation Options:	

Slab
(All plans can be built with your choice of foundation and framing. A generic conversion diagram is available. See order form.)

BLUEPRINT PRICE CODE: B

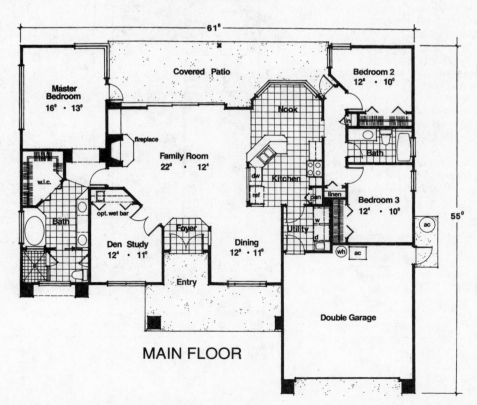

MAIN FLOOR

ORDER BLUEPRINTS ANYTIME!
CALL TOLL-FREE 1-800-820-1283

Plan HDS-99-144

PRICES AND DETAILS
ON PAGES 3-5

162

Modest Charm

- Wide paned windows and a covered front porch lend beguiling charm to this cheerful one-story home.
- The open and efficient—yet modest—floor plan is perfect for young or starting families.
- Flanking the entry are the formal dining room, with an angled front window, and the vaulted living room.
- Directly opposite the living room is the vaulted family room. Defined by decorative columns and featuring sliding glass doors to the rear deck, this room allows a view straight from the front of the home to the back.
- The family room is open to the generous kitchen. This work space is brightened by a window above the sink, and includes a handy pantry.
- Secluded at the rear corner of the home, the master suite offers plenty of closet space and a private dual-sink bath.
- Convenient laundry facilities are tucked away nearby.
- Across the home, two secondary bedrooms share another full bath. Each room enjoys a nice view to the outside.

Plan B-90005

Bedrooms: 3	Baths: 2
Living Area:	
Main floor	1,636 sq. ft.
Total Living Area:	**1,636 sq. ft.**
Standard basement	1,636 sq. ft.
Garage	374 sq. ft.
Exterior Wall Framing:	2x4

Foundation Options:

Standard basement
(All plans can be built with your choice of foundation and framing. A generic conversion diagram is available. See order form.)

BLUEPRINT PRICE CODE: **B**

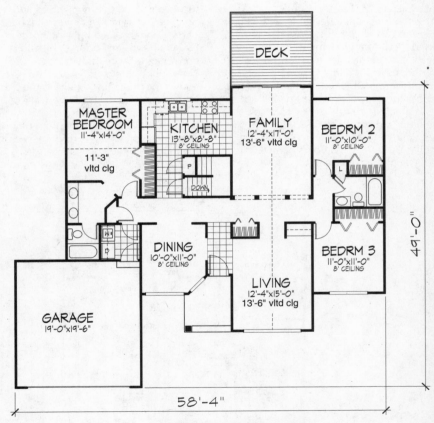

MAIN FLOOR

High-Energy Living!

- Weather-defying concrete block laid in a running bond pattern helps this clever one-story home reduce its energy use.
- A passive sun room works as a solar heat collector and storage chamber. Its glass walls and roof enclose an aesthetically fascinating room that's both practical and beautiful.
- A lovely clerestory window delivers extra sunlight to the living room. Here,

you'll find lots of space for entertaining, plus access to the sun room.
- A second large gathering area is the family room, where a woodstove creates a warm and friendly glow.
- The U-shaped kitchen stands poised to serve a variety of areas. The nearby dining room works well for either casual or formal meals.
- Across the home, the spacious master suite boasts a walk-in closet and a private bath.
- Two additional bedrooms each feature a pretty window seat and close proximity to a full-size bath.

Plan H-3720-M1

Bedrooms: 3	Baths: 2½
Living Area:	
Main floor	2,060 sq. ft.
Sun room	159 sq. ft.
Total Living Area:	**2,219 sq. ft.**
Standard basement	2,060 sq. ft.
Garage	550 sq. ft.
Exterior Wall Framing:	2x6

Foundation Options:

Standard basement
(All plans can be built with your choice of foundation and framing. A generic conversion diagram is available. See order form.)

BLUEPRINT PRICE CODE:	C

MAIN FLOOR

Exciting Angles and Amenities

- The interior of this elegant stucco design oozes in luxury, with an exciting assortment of angles and glass.
- Beyond the 14-ft.-high foyer and gallery is a huge parlour with an angled stand-behind ale bar and an adjoining patio accessed through two sets of glass doors.
- The diamond-shaped kitchen offers a sit-down island, a spacious walk-in pantry and a pass-through window to a summer kitchen.
- Opposite the kitchen is an octagonal morning room surrounded in glass and a spacious, angled gathering room with a fireplace and a TV niche.
- The luxurious master suite features a glassed lounge area and a spectacular two-sided fireplace, and is separated from the three secondary bedroom suites. The stunning master bath boasts a central linen island and an assortment of amenities designed for two.
- The library could serve as a fifth bedroom or guest room; the bath across the hall could serve as a pool bath.
- An alternate brick elevation is included

Plan EOF-59

Bedrooms: 4+	Baths: 4
Living Area:	
Main floor	4,021 sq. ft.
Total Living Area:	**4,021 sq. ft.**
Garage	737 sq. ft.
Exterior Wall Framing:	2x6

Foundation Options:
Slab
(All plans can be built with your choice of foundation and framing. A generic conversion diagram is available. See order form.)

BLUEPRINT PRICE CODE: **G**

MAIN FLOOR

Plan EOF-59

REAR VIEW

Decks, Sun for Outdoor Fun!

- A huge deck that extends the entire length of the back of the home, and the extensive use of windows and skylights bring to life the fun of the outdoors.
- From the entry, you can step right into the enormous living room/dining room area. Gather friends and family around the blazing fireplace and lead the group in holiday sing-alongs.

- Summer events belong on the awesome deck. Fire up the grill, turn up the music and dance the night away!
- The family room's 15-ft. sloped ceiling features four solar-collecting roof panels, which, combined with a specially designed 4-in.-thick concrete floor, forms a passive sun room system.
- Skylights and deck access are highlights in the master suite. Two additional bedrooms are found on the main floor.
- Two bedrooms in the daylight basement provide space for growing families or sleepover guests.

Plans H-2108-1A & -1B	
Bedrooms: 3+	**Baths:** 2-3
Living Area:	
Main floor	1,753 sq. ft.
Daylight basement	1,753 sq. ft.
Total Living Area:	**1,753/3,506 sq. ft.**
Garage and storage	624 sq. ft.
Exterior Wall Framing:	2x6
Foundation Options:	**Plan #**
Daylight basement	H-2108-1B
Crawlspace	H-2108-1A
(All plans can be built with your choice of foundation and framing. A generic conversion diagram is available. See order form.)	
BLUEPRINT PRICE CODE:	**B/F**

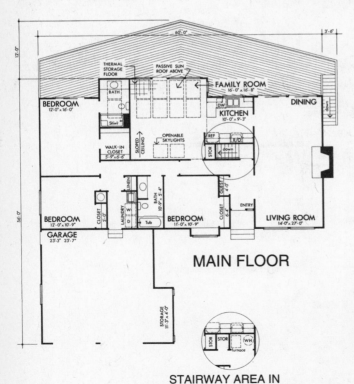

MAIN FLOOR

STAIRWAY AREA IN CRAWLSPACE VERSION

DAYLIGHT BASEMENT

FRONT VIEW

Plans H-2108-1A & -1B
PRICES AND DETAILS ON PAGES 2-5

Indoor/Outdoor Delights

- A curved porch in the front and a garden sun room in the back make this home an indoor/outdoor delight.
- Inside, a roomy kitchen is open to a five-sided, glassed-in dining room that views out to the porch.
- The living room features a fireplace nestled into a radiant glass wall that adjoins the gloriously sunny garden room—the perfect spot for morning tea!

- Wrapped in windows, the garden room accesses the backyard as well as a large storage area in the unobtrusive, side-entry garage.
- The master suite is no less luxurious, featuring a sumptuous master bath with a garden spa tub, a corner shower and a walk-in closet.
- Each of the two remaining bedrooms has a boxed-out window and a walk-in closet. A full bath with a corner shower and a dual-sink vanity is close by.
- A stairway leads to a bonus room and attic, which provide more potential living space.

Plan DD-1852

Bedrooms: 3	Baths: 2
Living Area:	
Main floor	1,680 sq. ft.
Garden room	240 sq. ft.
Total Living Area:	**1,920 sq. ft.**
Bonus room	316 sq. ft.
Attic	309 sq. ft.
Standard basement	1,680 sq. ft.
Garage and storage	570 sq. ft.
Exterior Wall Framing:	2x4

Foundation Options:

Standard basement
Crawlspace
Slab

(All plans can be built with your choice of foundation and framing. A generic conversion diagram is available. See order form.)

BLUEPRINT PRICE CODE:	B

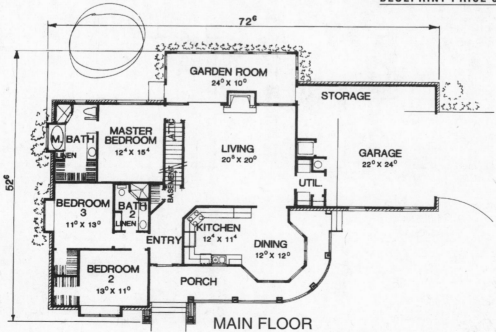

MAIN FLOOR

ORDER BLUEPRINTS ANYTIME!
CALL TOLL-FREE 1-800-820-1283

Plan DD-1852

PRICES AND DETAILS
ON PAGES 2-5

157

Updated Creole

- This Louisiana-style raised cottage features a tin roof, shuttered windows and three pairs of French doors, all of which add to the comfort and nostalgic appeal of this Creole classic.
- The French doors enter from the cool and relaxing front porch to the formal living areas and a front bedroom.
- The central living room, which features a 12-ft. ceiling, merges with the dining room and the kitchen's eating area. A fireplace warms the whole space while more French doors access a porch.
- The efficient kitchen offers a 12-ft. flat ceiling, an angled snack bar and a bayed nook with a 12-ft. sloped ceiling.
- A secluded master suite showcases a private bath, fit for the most demanding tastes. Across the home, the secondary bedrooms include abundant closet space and share a full bath.
- This full-featured, energy-efficient design also includes a large utility room and extra storage space in the garage.

Plan E-1823

Bedrooms: 3	Baths: 2
Living Area:	
Main floor	1,800 sq. ft.
Total Living Area:	**1,800 sq. ft.**
Garage	550 sq. ft.
Exterior Wall Framing:	2x6

Foundation Options:

Crawlspace

Slab

(All plans can be built with your choice of foundation and framing. A generic conversion diagram is available. See order form.)

BLUEPRINT PRICE CODE: B

MAIN FLOOR

Plan E-1823

Luxurious
Inside and Out

- The beautiful exterior of this grand one-story home is a true indicator of the luxury within.
- Pillars accentuate the entrance of the home as well as the entrance to the exciting Grand Room. A gorgeous covered porch, featuring a summer kitchen, waits just beyond.
- The sunken Gathering Room boasts high, arched openings, a corner fireplace and a pretty window seat.
- Perfect for formal meals, the private dining room is sure to provide an extraordinary eating experience. Nearby, the island kitchen also serves the sunny morning room.
- The spectacular master suite has a sunken entertainment retreat, a two-way fireplace and access to the outside. The master bath offers a sinfully elegant tub and a sunken shower. A huge walk-in closet fits any wardrobe.
- Quiet and peaceful, the corner library easily converts to a bedroom, if needed.
- A guest suite also features a courtyard, a walk-in closet and its own bath.

Plan EOF-1

Bedrooms: 4+	Baths: 4
Living Area:	
Main floor	3,903 sq. ft.
Total Living Area:	**3,903 sq. ft.**
Garage	748 sq. ft.
Exterior Wall Framing:	2x4

Foundation Options:

Slab

(All plans can be built with your choice of foundation and framing. A generic conversion diagram is available. See order form.)

BLUEPRINT PRICE CODE:	**F**

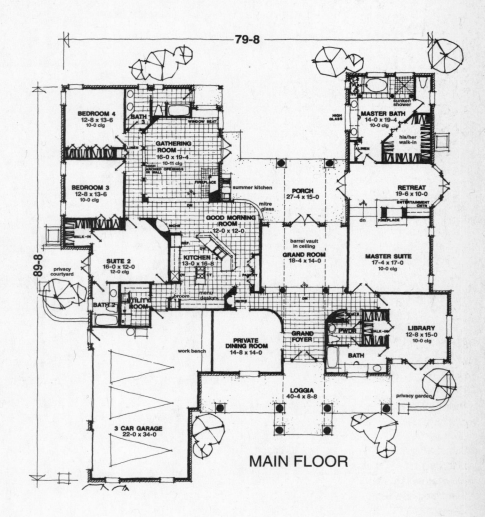

MAIN FLOOR

Versatile
Sun Room

- This cozy country-style home offers an inviting front porch and an interior just as welcoming.
- The spacious living room features a warming fireplace and windows that overlook the porch.
- The living room opens to a dining area, where French doors access a covered porch and a sunny patio.
- The island kitchen has a sink view, plenty of counter space, and a handy pass-through to the adjoining sun room. The bright sun room is large enough to serve as a formal dining room, a family room or a hobby room.
- The private master suite is secluded to the rear. A garden spa tub, dual walk-in closets and separate dressing areas are nice features found in the master bath.

Plan J-90014

Bedrooms: 3	Baths: 2½
Living Area:	
Main floor	2,190 sq. ft.
Total Living Area:	**2,190 sq. ft.**
Standard basement	2,190 sq. ft.
Garage	465 sq. ft.
Storage	34 sq. ft.
Exterior Wall Framing:	2x6

Foundation Options:

Standard basement

Crawlspace

Slab

(All plans can be built with your choice of foundation and framing. A generic conversion diagram is available. See order form.)

BLUEPRINT PRICE CODE:	C

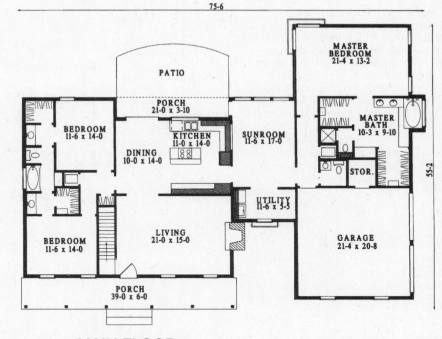

MAIN FLOOR

Plan J-90014

PRICES AND DETAILS
ON PAGES 2-5

REAR VIEW

Sunny Disposition!

- A wide assortment of windows and glass give the interior of this striking one-story a bright, sunny disposition!
- Entertaining is easy with two huge areas to do it in: the huge living room and the even larger family room. The living room boasts a big, handsome fireplace to add cheer to any occasion.
- A woodstove provides the same warm glow in the family room. A glass roof above the room creates an unforgettable connection to the outside world.
- Serving both areas is the efficient corner kitchen, where a nice-sized pantry will hold all the canned goods you need.
- Across the home, the master suite features a walk-in closet and a private bath. Two additional bedrooms are near a full bath.

Plans H-3722-1 & -1A

Bedrooms: 3	Baths: 2½
Living Area:	
Main floor	2,023 sq. ft.
Total Living Area:	**2,023 sq. ft.**
Standard basement	2,023 sq. ft.
Garage	466 sq. ft.
Exterior Wall Framing:	2x6
Foundation Options:	**Plan #**
Standard basement	H-3722-1
Crawlspace	H-3722-1A

(All plans can be built with your choice of foundation and framing. A generic conversion diagram is available. See order form.)

BLUEPRINT PRICE CODE: C

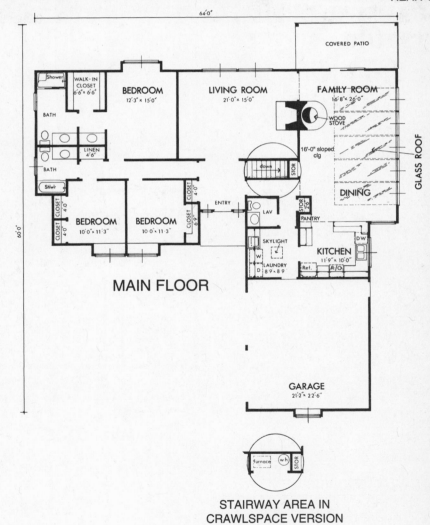

MAIN FLOOR

STAIRWAY AREA IN CRAWLSPACE VERSION

ORDER BLUEPRINTS ANYTIME!
CALL TOLL-FREE 1-800-820-1283

Plans H-3722-1 & -1A

**PRICES AND DETAILS
ON PAGES 2-5**

153

This Is It!

- This comfortable design is just the plan you're looking for. The affordable design includes all the features—both inside and out—today's family needs.
- The first days of spring will feel even better when you settle into a rocker on the porch and watch the kids play a game of Kick the Can in the front yard.
- Inside, the dining room awaits formal dinners. Built-in china cabinets replace the stairway to the basement in the crawlspace and slab versions.
- In the kitchen, a snack bar is the perfect place to feed the kids a snack. The sunshine that pours into the morning room will rouse the spirits of even the sleepiest family member.
- Friends and family will show up at your home to celebrate the Fourth of July on your fun-packed deck.
- In the busy living room, plenty of room is available to dance to your favorite music or gather the clan together to watch the newest release on video.
- When you need a break, retreat to the master suite, where you can savor the peace and quiet in the sitting area.

Plan DD-1716

Bedrooms: 3	Baths: 2
Living Area:	
Main floor	1,738 sq. ft.
Total Living Area:	**1,738 sq. ft.**
Standard basement	1,466 sq. ft.
Garage	425 sq. ft.
Exterior Wall Framing:	2x4

Foundation Options:

Standard basement

Crawlspace

Slab

(All plans can be built with your choice of foundation and framing. A generic conversion diagram is available. See order form.)

BLUEPRINT PRICE CODE: B

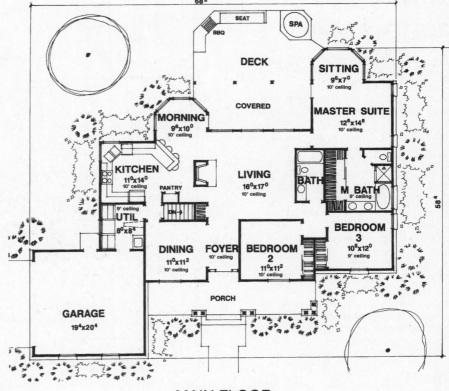

MAIN FLOOR

Intriguing Combination

- This intriguing home is finished with a combination of wood siding and brick, giving it a warm, rustic look.
- Geared for formal entertaining as well as family living, the home offers distinct activity zones. A built-in china hutch and a fireplace add style and function to the formal spaces at the front of the home. Both the living and dining rooms are set off by decorative columns.
- The large-scale family room features a 13-ft. ceiling, a fireplace and a built-in entertainment center. The skylighted sun room and the breakfast area include sloped ceilings and French doors opening to the patio. Typical ceiling heights elsewhere are 9 feet.
- The master suite has a 14-ft. sloped ceiling, private access to the patio and its own fireplace. The adjoining bath offers abundant storage space and a garden tub with glass-block walls.
- Three additional bedrooms and two baths are on the other side of the home.

Plan E-3102

Bedrooms: 4	Baths: 3
Living Area:	
Main floor	3,158 sq. ft.
Total Living Area:	**3,158 sq. ft.**
Garage	559 sq. ft.
Storage	64 sq. ft.
Exterior Wall Framing:	2x6

Foundation Options:

Crawlspace

Slab

(All plans can be built with your choice of foundation and framing. A generic conversion diagram is available. See order form.)

BLUEPRINT PRICE CODE: E

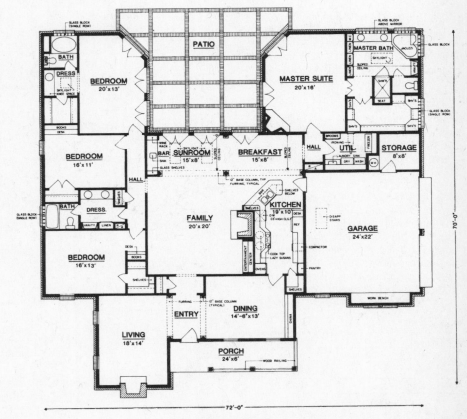

MAIN FLOOR

ORDER BLUEPRINTS ANYTIME!
CALL TOLL-FREE 1-800-820-1283

Plan E-3102

PRICES AND DETAILS
ON PAGES 2-5

151

Photo by Jane Kirkpatrick

Center of Attention

- At the center of this dramatic contemporary design is the octagonal solarium, a great spot to soak up sunlight year-round.
- Rustic stonework around the entry, vertical siding and sparkling windows highlight the home's exterior.
- Inside, the living areas surround the solarium, allowing for smooth flow of traffic while creating distinct spaces.

- Warmed by a woodstove, the spacious family room also has access to the backyard via a sliding glass door.
- A built-in buffet in the casual eating nook makes serving large holiday meals a snap. The U-shaped kitchen is conveniently located nearby.
- The delightful master bedroom will pamper your every need. A cavernous walk-in closet, access to the backyard and a skylighted private bath with a soothing oval tub are among its special amenities.
- Two good-sized secondary bedrooms and a full bath round out the floor plan.

Plans H-3719-1 & -1A	
Bedrooms: 3	**Baths:** 2½
Living Area:	
Main floor	2,842 sq. ft.
Sun room	324 sq. ft.
Total Living Area:	**3,166 sq. ft.**
Partial basement	1,558 sq. ft.
Garage	850 sq. ft.
Storage	132 sq. ft.
Exterior Wall Framing:	2x6
Foundation Options:	**Plan #**
Partial basement	H-3719-1
Crawlspace	H-3719-1A

(All plans can be built with your choice of foundation and framing. A generic conversion diagram is available. See order form.)

BLUEPRINT PRICE CODE:	E

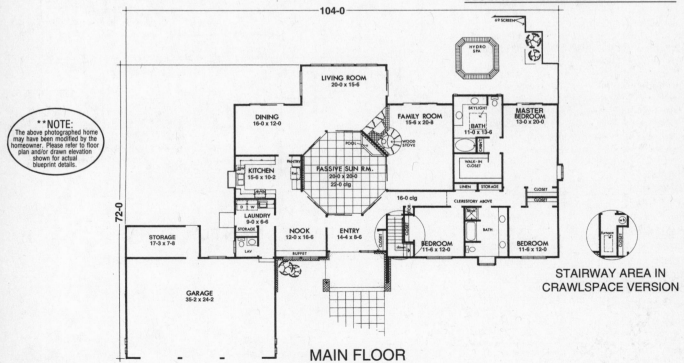

NOTE:
The above photographed home may have been modified by the homeowner. Please refer to floor plan and/or drawn elevation shown for actual blueprint details.

MAIN FLOOR

STAIRWAY AREA IN CRAWLSPACE VERSION

Plans H-3719-1 & -1A

*PRICES AND DETAILS
ON PAGES 2-5*

Photo by Mark Englund/HomeStyles

Family Zone

- This home's welcoming exterior and well-zoned floor plan make it an ideal family abode.
- Inside, the columned entry is flanked by the formal dining room on the left and the living room on the right.
- Straight ahead, the spacious family room, breakfast nook and kitchen form a sunny trio that opens to a backyard deck. A wet bar is centrally located. The family room flaunts a fireplace and built-in bookshelves; both the U-shaped kitchen and the family room are topped by vaulted ceilings.
- Three secondary bedrooms to the right include ample closet space and share a compartmentalized bath.
- Luxuriously isolated from the other bedrooms, the master suite features a majestic bath with a dual-sink vanity and a separate tub and shower.

Plan B-87145

Bedrooms: 4	Baths: 2
Living Area:	
Main floor	2,472 sq. ft.
Total Living Area:	**2,472 sq. ft.**
Standard basement	2,470 sq. ft.
Garage	455 sq. ft.
Exterior Wall Framing:	2x4

Foundation Options:
Standard basement
(All plans can be built with your choice of foundation and framing.
A generic conversion diagram is available. See order form.)

BLUEPRINT PRICE CODE: C

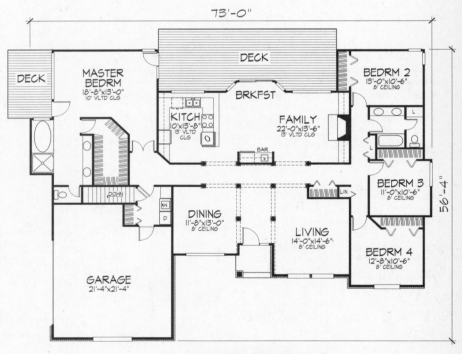

MAIN FLOOR

**NOTE:
The above photographed home may have been modified by the homeowner. Please refer to floor plan and/or drawn elevation shown for actual blueprint details.

ORDER BLUEPRINTS ANYTIME!
CALL TOLL-FREE 1-800-820-1283

Plan B-87145

PRICES AND DETAILS
ON PAGES 2-5

149

Open Invitation

- Classic shutters, distinctive columns and a covered country porch invite you to explore this fine family home.
- Inside, oversized windows allow sunlight to flood the dining area. A handy snack bar fronts the kitchen and serves the adjoining Great Room, providing the perfect space for Super Bowl hors d'oeuvres.
- The Great Room, with its soaring 12½-ft. vaulted ceiling and generous floor space, allows for an abundance of furniture and ample space to mingle. Built-in shelves flank the cozy fireplace.
- A sprawling rear patio embraces the back of the home, and brick steps lead to the backyard. Whether you're barbecuing with friends or worshipping the sun, this haven is sure to please.
- The owner's bedroom enjoys a walk-in closet and a gracious master bath. At the opposite corner of the home, two additional bedrooms with ample closet space share a full bath. The front bedroom features a 10-ft. ceiling.

Plan J-9426

Bedrooms: 3+	Baths: 2

Living Area:

Main floor	1,689 sq. ft.
Total Living Area:	**1,689 sq. ft.**
Standard basement	1,689 sq. ft.
Garage and storage	467 sq. ft.
Exterior Wall Framing:	2x4

Foundation Options:

Standard basement
Crawlspace
Slab
(All plans can be built with your choice of foundation and framing. A generic conversion diagram is available. See order form.)

BLUEPRINT PRICE CODE: B

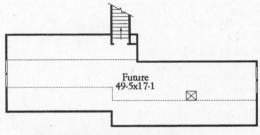

UPPER FLOOR

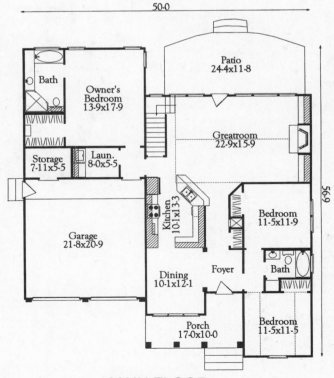

MAIN FLOOR

Plan J-9426

PRICES AND DETAILS
ON PAGES 2-5

Tall and Proud

- This stately home's proud exterior gives way to a luxurious and impressive interior.
- The step-down parlour is the home's centerpiece, and boasts a 13-ft.-high ceiling and a full-wall fireplace and entertainment center.
- The master suite features a step-down sitting room and a corner fireplace. The opulent master bath has a linen island, a morning kitchen and a bidet.
- The library offers private access to the main hall bath.
- Graceful arches and a high, coffered ceiling adorn the formal dining room.
- The spacious kitchen includes a cooktop island, a walk-in pantry, a menu desk, a vegetable sink and a bright good morning room.
- Each of the three secondary suites has a large closet and direct access to a bath.
- The huge Gathering Room boasts wraparound glass and another fireplace and entertainment wall.

Plan EOF-58

Bedrooms: 4+	Baths: 4
Living Area:	
Main floor	4,021 sq. ft.
Total Living Area:	**4,021 sq. ft.**
Garage	879 sq. ft.
Exterior Wall Framing:	2x4

Foundation Options:
Slab
(All plans can be built with your choice of foundation and framing. A generic conversion diagram is available. See order form.)

BLUEPRINT PRICE CODE: G

MAIN FLOOR

ORDER BLUEPRINTS ANYTIME!
CALL TOLL-FREE 1-800-820-1283

Plan EOF-58

PRICES AND DETAILS
ON PAGES 2-5
147

REAR VIEW

Scenic Surround

- Designed for a sloping, scenic lot, this home features a wraparound deck that takes in the view from any direction.
- An entry bridge leads you across to the front hall, which steps down into a sunken living room warmed by a rustic stone fireplace. The adjoining formal dining room opens to the living room, making the most of the fireplace and the view to the rear deck and beyond.
- The kitchen and adjacent dining nook also overlook the rear deck. The two rooms share a handy serving counter.
- The master suite boasts its own bath and private deck access. Two secondary bedrooms share a full hall bath.
- The daylight basement versions of this home includes a recreation room with a fireplace, as well as a third full bath and plenty of space for storage and extra bedrooms if you need them.

Plans H-2083, -A & -B

Bedrooms: 3+	Baths: 2-3
Living Area:	
Upper floor	1,660 sq. ft.
Daylight basement	1,660 sq. ft.
Total Living Area:	**1,660/3,320 sq. ft.**
Garage	540 sq. ft.
Exterior Wall Framing:	2x4
Foundation Options:	**Plan #**
Daylight basement (concrete)	H-2083
Daylight basement (wood)	H-2083-B
Crawlspace	H-2083-A

(All plans can be built with your choice of foundation and framing. A generic conversion diagram is available. See order form.)

BLUEPRINT PRICE CODE:	**B/E**

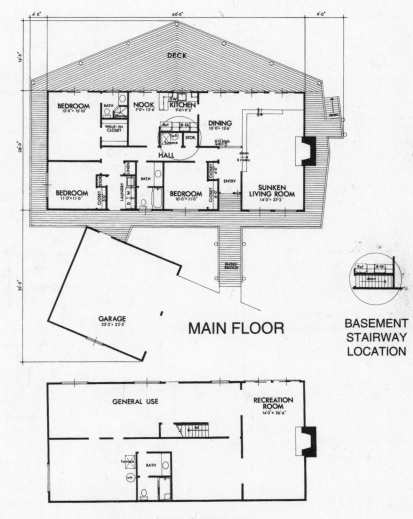

MAIN FLOOR

BASEMENT STAIRWAY LOCATION

DAYLIGHT BASEMENT

Plans H-2083, -A & -B

PRICES AND DETAILS ON PAGES 2-5

Rustic, Relaxed Living

- The screened porch of this rustic home offers a cool place to dine on warm summer days. The covered front porch provides an inviting welcome and a place for pure relaxation.
- With its warm fireplace and surrounding windows, the home's spacious living room is ideal for unwinding indoors. The living room unfolds to a nice-sized dining area that overlooks a backyard patio and opens to the screened porch.
- The U-shaped kitchen is centrally located and features a nice windowed sink. A handy pantry and a laundry room adjoin to the right.
- Three large bedrooms make up the home's sleeping wing. The master bedroom boasts a roomy private bath with a step-up spa tub, a separate shower and two walk-in closets.
- The secondary bedrooms share a compartmentalized hall bath.

Plan C-8650	
Bedrooms: 3	**Baths: 2**
Living Area:	
Main floor	1,773 sq. ft.
Total Living Area:	**1,773 sq. ft.**
Daylight basement	1,773 sq. ft.
Garage	441 sq. ft.
Exterior Wall Framing:	2x4
Foundation Options:	

Daylight basement
Crawlspace
Slab
(All plans can be built with your choice of foundation and framing. A generic conversion diagram is available. See order form.)

BLUEPRINT PRICE CODE:	**B**

MAIN FLOOR

ORDER BLUEPRINTS ANYTIME!
CALL TOLL-FREE 1-800-820-1283

Plan C-8650

PRICES AND DETAILS
ON PAGES 2-5

145

Well-Appointed Walk-Out Design

- The hipped roof and covered entry give this well-appointed home a look of distinction.
- Inside, the foyer leads directly into the expansive Great Room, which boasts a 13-ft. vaulted ceiling, an inviting fireplace, a built-in entertainment center and a dramatic window wall that overlooks an exciting full-width deck with a hot tub!
- A half-wall separates the Great Room from the nook, which is open to the U-shaped kitchen. The impressive kitchen includes a snack bar, a walk-in pantry and a greenhouse window.
- The isolated master suite offers a vaulted ceiling that slopes up to 9 feet. A French door opens to the deck and hot tub, while a pocket door accesses the sumptuous master bath with a spa tub under a glass-block wall.
- Two more bedrooms in the walk-out basement share another full bath. The optional expansion areas provide an additional 730 sq. ft. of space.

Plan S-41792

Bedrooms: 3	Baths: 3
Living Area:	
Main floor	1,450 sq. ft.
Partial daylight basement	590 sq. ft.
Total Living Area:	**2,040 sq. ft.**
Garage	429 sq. ft.
Unfinished expansion areas	730 sq. ft.
Exterior Wall Framing:	2x6

Foundation Options:

Partial daylight basement
(All plans can be built with your choice of foundation and framing. A generic conversion diagram is available. See order form.)

BLUEPRINT PRICE CODE: C

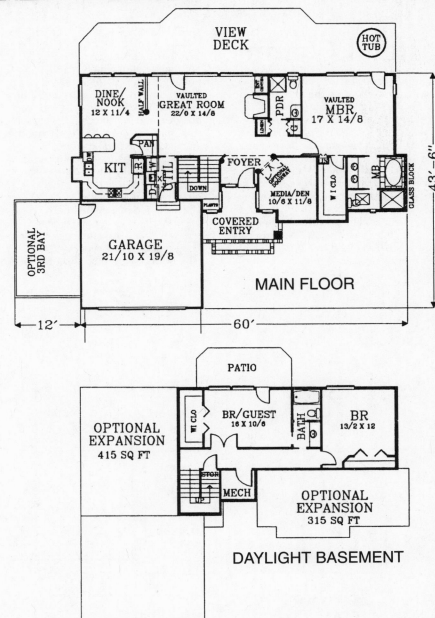

MAIN FLOOR

DAYLIGHT BASEMENT

Plan S-41792

PRICES AND DETAILS
ON PAGES 2-5

Tasteful Charm

- Columned covered porches lend warmth and charm to the front and rear of this tasteful traditional home.
- Sidelight and transom glass brightens the entry foyer, which shares a 10-ft. ceiling with the elegant dining room.
- The dining room provides a quiet spot for formal meals, while a Palladian window arrangement adds light and flair.
- The spacious living room offers a warm fireplace and an adjacent TV cabinet. The dramatic ceiling vaults to a height of 11 ft., 8 inches. French doors give way to the skylighted rear porch, which is finished with lovely brick pavers.

Two brick steps descend to the adjoining patio, which is also beautifully paved with brick.
- The gourmet kitchen offers a built-in oven/microwave cabinet, a separate cooktop and an island snack bar with a sink. Its 10-ft. ceiling extends into the sunny breakfast nook.
- The oversized laundry room includes a handy half-bath, a wall-to-wall storage cabinet, a hanging rod, a large sink and nearby porch access.
- The secluded master bedroom boasts a 12-ft. vaulted ceiling and a large walk-in closet. In the private master bath, a glass-block divider separates the whirlpool tub from the shower stall.

Plan J-9414

Bedrooms: 3	Baths: 2½
Living Area:	
Main floor	1,974 sq. ft.
Total Living Area:	**1,974 sq. ft.**
Standard basement	1,974 sq. ft.
Garage and storage	518 sq. ft.
Exterior Wall Framing:	2x4

Foundation Options:
Standard basement
Crawlspace
Slab
(All plans can be built with your choice of foundation and framing. A generic conversion diagram is available. See order form.)

BLUEPRINT PRICE CODE: **B**

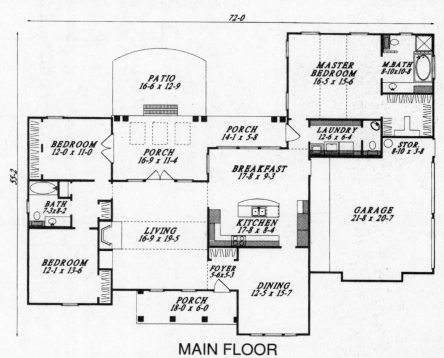

BASEMENT STAIRWAY LOCATION

MAIN FLOOR

ORDER BLUEPRINTS ANYTIME!
CALL TOLL-FREE 1-800-820-1283

Plan J-9414

PRICES AND DETAILS
ON PAGES 2-5

143

Mediterranean Spice Is Nice!

- An exotic stucco facade, an inviting courtyard, gorgeous windows and a stunning backyard lanai flavor this marvelous Mediterranean-style home.
- Past the courtyard, the covered entry leads through French doors to a grand Great Room, which features a soaring 13-ft. ceiling. Three sets of French doors open onto the lanai.
- Lazy summer breezes will sweep through the four stately columns gracing the lanai, which can be reached from the breakfast nook and the master bedroom, as well as the Great Room.
- The well-appointed kitchen is enhanced by a convenient built-in desk, a center island and a 10-ft. ceiling.
- Cheery windows brighten the adjoining breakfast nook.
- On the other side of the home, the sumptuous master suite boasts two overhead plant shelves, two entrances to the lanai and two large walk-in closets. The full bath features a platform tub and a dual-sink vanity.
- Around the corner, a full bath is shared by two bedrooms; one of these may be used as a den, if desired.

Plan B-92002

Bedrooms: 2+	Baths: 2
Living Area:	
Main floor	1,859 sq. ft.
Total Living Area:	**1,859 sq. ft.**
Garage	390 sq. ft.
Exterior Wall Framing:	2x6
Foundation Options:	

Slab
(All plans can be built with your choice of foundation and framing. A generic conversion diagram is available. See order form.)

BLUEPRINT PRICE CODE: **B**

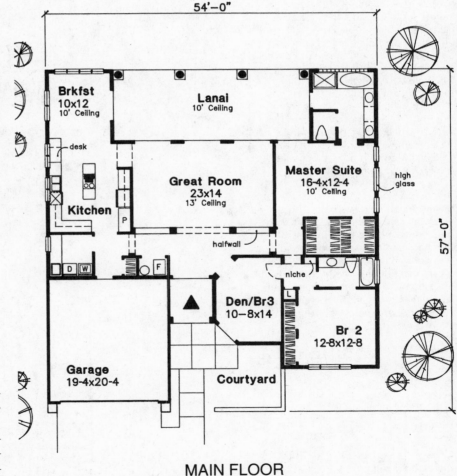

MAIN FLOOR

Plan B-92002

PRICES AND DETAILS ON PAGES 2-5

Country Corner

- Victorian-style trim and an ornate veranda give this home an adorable country look; the side-entry garage makes it adaptable to a corner lot.
- A fireplace anchors the gorgeous living room. Gather around the hearth on cold winter nights with steaming mugs of hot chocolate and soak in the warmth.
- The 13½-ft. cathedral ceiling that crowns the kitchen and dining room adds volume. Step out to the covered porch to smell the scents of spring.
- The sleeping wing includes a roomy master suite, which boasts a private bath with a walk-in closet and time-saving amenities like a dual-sink vanity. French doors open to the porch.
- Down the hall, two secondary bedrooms feature loads of closet space. One bedroom has a built-in desk; the other has a sunny bay window and a 10-ft. volume ceiling.
- An optional loft or game room with a half-bath and a wet bar is accessed via a circular stairway in the foyer.
- Unless otherwise noted, all rooms feature airy 9-ft. ceilings.

Plan L-647-VA

Bedrooms: 3+	Baths: 2-2½
Living Area:	
Main floor	1,604 sq. ft.
Optional loft/bath	367 sq. ft.
Total Living Area:	**1,971 sq. ft.**
Optional storage	55 sq. ft.
Garage	511 sq. ft.
Exterior Wall Framing:	2x4

Foundation Options:

Slab

(All plans can be built with your choice of foundation and framing.
A generic conversion diagram is available. See order form.)

BLUEPRINT PRICE CODE: B

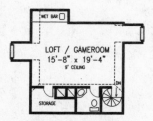

OPTIONAL LOFT

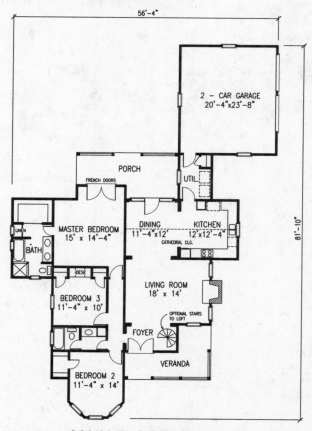

MAIN FLOOR

ORDER BLUEPRINTS ANYTIME!
CALL TOLL-FREE 1-800-820-1283

Plan L-647-VA

PRICES AND DETAILS
ON PAGES 2-5

141

Attractive Energy Savings

- With energy savings estimated at 50 to 60 percent, this earth-sheltered design will appeal to any smart-shopping consumer. It's intended to face within 10 degrees of the south to maximize its solar benefits.
- Skylights and an open courtyard allow natural light to stream into each room and brighten up the day.
- The entry opens to an air-lock vestibule and into the home through a set of double doors.

- At the heart of the home is the spacious and open living room. Its large size is perfect for big celebrations, while its cozy fireplace comes in handy on intimate evenings of just you two.
- A skylight lets the sunshine pour into the lovely corner kitchen.
- At the opposite corner of the home is the master bedroom, which boasts a walk-in closet and a private bath. Sliding glass doors lead out to its own personal deck.
- A second bedroom is just a step away, down a skylighted hallway. A full bath, a convenient study and a den are a little farther down the hall. The den serves nicely as a third bedroom.

Plan B-7943

Bedrooms: 2+	Baths: 2½
Living Area:	
Main floor	1,678 sq. ft.
Total Living Area:	**1,678 sq. ft.**
Garage	440 sq. ft.
Exterior Wall Framing:	2x4 and concrete
Foundation Options:	

Slab
(All plans can be built with your choice of foundation and framing. A generic conversion diagram is available. See order form.)

BLUEPRINT PRICE CODE: **B**

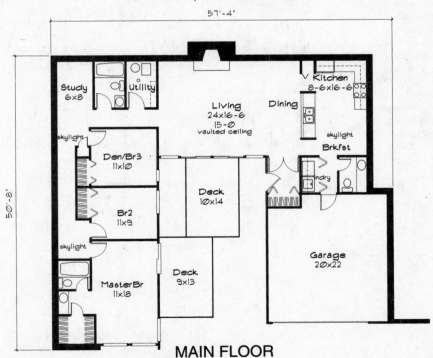

MAIN FLOOR

Plan B-7943

Sweet Home

- The sweet facade of this charming home looks as if it were plucked straight out of a European hamlet. The stone exterior, decorated dormers and cute porch combine to present a charming invitation to guests.

- Inside, the floor plan takes advantage of the compact square footage. A tiled foyer leads into a unique curved gallery that wraps around the central Great Room. On the left, a half-wall allows a view into the dining room.

- A wall of windows adds brightness and cheer to the Great Room, where a shuttered pass-through to the kitchen lets the chef visit with guests. French doors open to a railed deck that is the perfect site for drinks with friends.

- Between the kitchen and the breakfast nook, a serving counter provides a spot to set snacks. The kitchen's island cooktop makes meal preparation easier.

- The Great Room, the breakfast nook and the kitchen boast 12-ft. ceilings. All other rooms feature 9-ft. ceilings.

- The master suite's sunny bay serves as a cozy sitting area to retreat to each day.

Plan DW-1892

Bedrooms: 3	Baths: 2

Living Area:

Main floor	1,892 sq. ft.
Total Living Area:	**1,892 sq. ft.**
Standard basement	1,892 sq. ft.
Exterior Wall Framing:	2x4

Foundation Options:

Standard basement
Crawlspace
Slab

(All plans can be built with your choice of foundation and framing. A generic conversion diagram is available. See order form.)

BLUEPRINT PRICE CODE: B

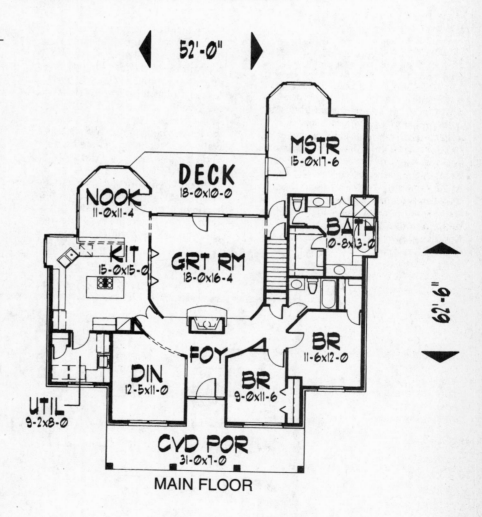

52'-0"

62'-6"

NOOK
11-0x11-4

DECK
18-0x10-0

MSTR
15-0x17-6

KIT
15-0x15-0

GRT RM
18-0x16-4

BATH
10-8x13-0

DIN
12-5x11-0

FOY

BR
9-0x11-6

BR
11-6x12-0

UTIL
9-2x8-0

CVD POR
31-0x7-0

MAIN FLOOR

Plan DW-1892

Unbelievable Amenities

- This sprawling estate has amenities that won't quit!
- Beautiful views of the surrounding gardens are possible from virtually any inside area. The backyard features a gazebo overlooking an inviting pool and spa. The blueprints show the gazebo, the patio and the garden walls.
- At the center of the floor plan is an expansive Gathering Room with an ale bar, a cozy fireplace and French doors to a spacious lanai.
- The island kitchen is conveniently located between the morning room, with greenhouse glass, and the dining room, with a stepped ceiling.
- The above-mentioned rooms and the welcoming gallery are all enhanced by 14-ft. ceilings.
- A two-way fireplace warms both the living room, with its 13-ft. vaulted ceiling, and the library, with its 12-ft. vaulted ceiling.
- A third fireplace adds ambience to the stunning master suite, which features a sunken retreat. A 15½-ft. vaulted ceiling presides over the opulent private bath.

Plan EOF-69

Bedrooms: 4	Baths: 3½
Living Area:	
Main floor	3,836 sq. ft.
Total Living Area:	**3,836 sq. ft.**
Garage	952 sq. ft.
Exterior Wall Framing:	2x6

Foundation Options:

Slab

(All plans can be built with your choice of foundation and framing. A generic conversion diagram is available. See order form.)

BLUEPRINT PRICE CODE: F

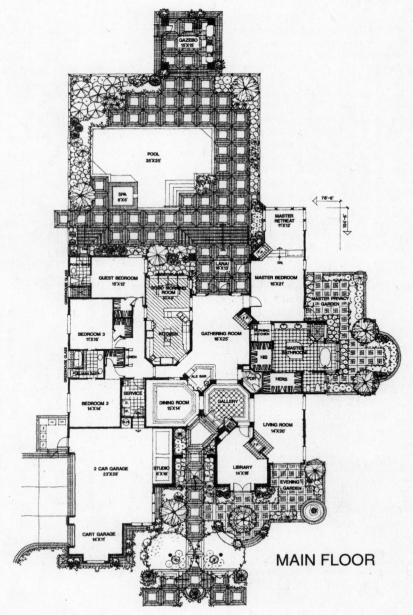

MAIN FLOOR

ORDER BLUEPRINTS ANYTIME!
CALL TOLL-FREE 1-800-820-1283

PRICES AND DETAILS
ON PAGES 2-5

Lively Styling

- A lively mixture of European and country styling makes this one-story a wonderfully eclectic retreat.
- The angled entry opens to the naturally lit living room, which features a warm fireplace flanked by cabinets and a media center.
- The dining room offers sliding French doors to a wraparound backyard deck.
- The kitchen is paired with a bayed breakfast nook, which flaunts French-door access to the deck.
- High glass lights the master bedroom, while private sliding French doors lead to the deck. All of the above-mentioned rooms are enhanced by 12-ft. ceilings.
- More daylight drenches the master bath, which hosts a garden tub and a separate shower under a 9-ft. ceiling.
- Another good-sized bedroom boasts a built-in desk and a nearby bath. Both rooms have 9-ft. ceilings.
- A swing suite to the left of the entry sports a window seat and an airy 10-ft. ceiling. This room could serve as a den, an office or a guest room, swinging from function to function as family needs change.

Plan B-94008

Bedrooms: 2+	Baths: 2
Living Area:	
Main floor	1,795 sq. ft.
Total Living Area:	**1,795 sq. ft.**
Basement	1,795 sq. ft.
Garage	454 sq. ft.
Exterior Wall Framing:	2x6

Foundation Options:

Daylight basement

Standard basement

(All plans can be built with your choice of foundation and framing. A generic conversion diagram is available. See order form.)

BLUEPRINT PRICE CODE:	**B**

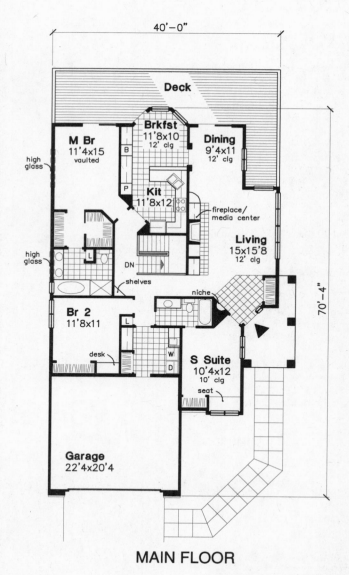

MAIN FLOOR

ORDER BLUEPRINTS ANYTIME!
CALL TOLL-FREE 1-800-820-1283

Plan B-94008

PRICES AND DETAILS
ON PAGES 2-5

137

Graceful Wings

- Past the inviting entrance to this graceful contemporary home, the skylighted foyer awaits guests with a dramatic 14½-ft. vaulted ceiling.
- Off the foyer, the dining room is embraced by a wall of windows and a 9-ft. tray ceiling. The spacious country kitchen has a bright skylight and sliding glass doors to a huge wraparound deck.
- The spectacular Great Room's vaulted ceiling soars to 19 ft., 8 in., greeting a row of large clerestory windows. Flanked by sliding doors, the exciting corner fireplace warms the entire area.
- The main-floor sleeping wing contains three bedrooms. The master bedroom boasts a 9-ft. tray ceiling, a private bath and two closets.
- The optional walk-out basement includes a fabulous sunken family room with a second fireplace and sliding glass doors to a spacious patio.
- The family room is flanked by a hobby room and a versatile den or study.
- Two additional bedrooms share a hall bath. The corner bedroom is large enough to accommodate an in-law or a "boomerang" child.

Plan AX-97837

Bedrooms: 3+	Baths: 2½-3½
Living Area:	
Main floor	1,816 sq. ft.
Daylight basement (finished)	1,435 sq. ft.
Total Living Area:	**1,816/3,251 sq. ft.**
Utility and storage	381 sq. ft.
Garage	400 sq. ft.
Exterior Wall Framing:	2x4
Foundation Options:	
Daylight basement	
Crawlspace	
Slab	

(All plans can be built with your choice of foundation and framing. A generic conversion diagram is available. See order form.)

BLUEPRINT PRICE CODE:	B/E

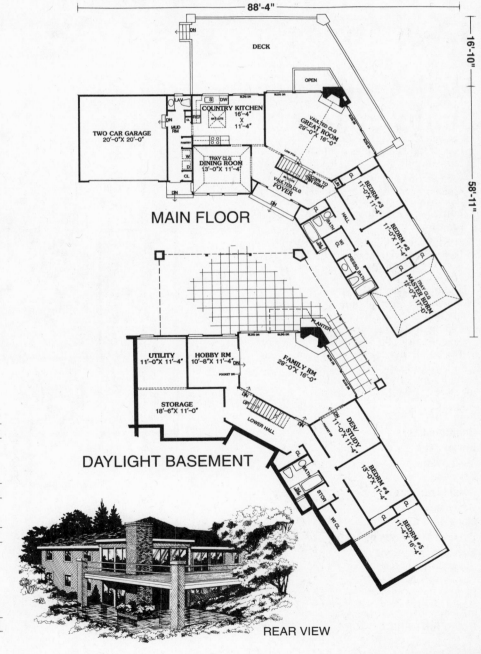

MAIN FLOOR

DAYLIGHT BASEMENT

REAR VIEW

High Ceilings, Sunny Spaces

- Lots of glass, a sunny solarium and a large terrace make this elegant one-story perfect for indoor/outdoor living.
- The solarium at the rear of the home has glass walls and a sunroof. Sliding doors in the family room open to this refreshing space.
- The bayed dining nook overlooks the rear terrace, which is also accessible from the solarium.
- The kitchen is open to the family room and has a snack bar joining it to the dinette. The formal dining room and the living room, which features a cathedral ceiling and a fireplace, are also easily reached from the kitchen.
- The hall bath is close to the living areas as well as to the two front-facing bedrooms. The master bedroom suite offers its own luxurious bath.

Plan AHP-9125

Bedrooms: 3	Baths: 2
Living Area:	
Main floor	1,703 sq. ft.
Solarium	96 sq. ft.
Total Living Area	**1,799 sq. ft.**
Basement	1,766 sq. ft.
Garage	462 sq. ft.
Exterior Wall Framing	2x4 or 2x6

Foundation options:

Standard basement

Crawlspace

Slab

(All plans can be built with your choice of foundation and framing. A generic conversion diagram is available. See order form.)

BLUEPRINT PRICE CODE	B

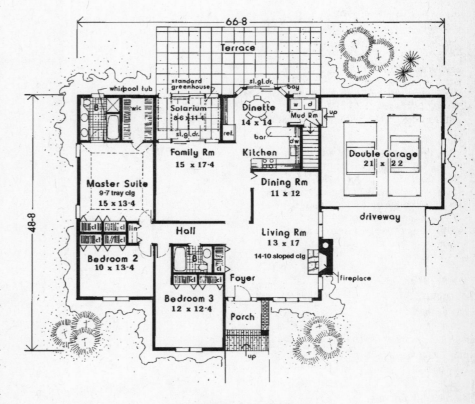

MAIN FLOOR

ORDER BLUEPRINTS ANYTIME!
CALL TOLL-FREE 1-800-820-1283

Plan AHP-9125

PRICES AND DETAILS
ON PAGES 2-5

135

Gabled Delight

- Family and friends will delight in this home's gracious facade, complete with a covered front porch, picturesque shutters and decorative gables.
- The entry sweeps guests straight ahead into the central living room, where two sets of French doors open to a rear covered porch. A built-in wet bar, enclosed behind bifold doors, accommodates festive occasions, while the fireplace is perfect for quiet nights.
- A short hallway off the living room leads to the boxed-out breakfast nook

and the U-shaped kitchen. An island cooktop, lots of counter space and two windows highlight the work area.
- The formal dining room lies conveniently nearby and overlooks the front porch.
- Across the home, the sleeping quarters are housed in a wing of their own. The master bedroom enjoys private access to the rear porch, as well as a lush bath with dual sinks, a garden tub, a separate shower, a private toilet and two walk-in closets.
- The three secondary bedrooms share a neat hall bath.

Plan J-8518-1	
Bedrooms: 4	**Baths: 2½**
Living Area:	
Main floor	2,587 sq. ft.
Total Living Area:	**2,587 sq. ft.**
Garage and storage	564 sq. ft.
Exterior Wall Framing:	2x4

Foundation Options:

Crawlspace
(All plans can be built with your choice of foundation and framing. A generic conversion diagram is available. See order form.)

BLUEPRINT PRICE CODE: D

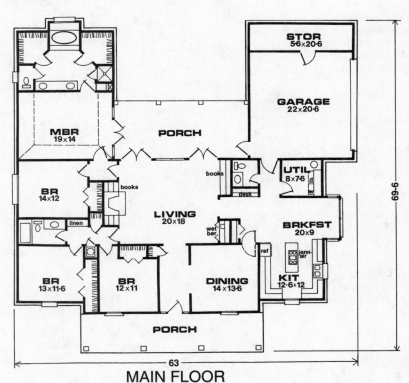

MAIN FLOOR

Plan J-8518-1
PRICES AND DETAILS
ON PAGES 2-5

Tropical Villa

- This stunning tropical villa features an open floor plan, a striking stucco facade, a clay-tile roof and numerous windows.
- The shaded entryway, crowned by a clerestory window, opens into the expansive living room and the equally spacious dining room, both brightened by lavish full-length windows and enhanced by 12-ft. vaulted ceilings.
- The gourmet kitchen features generous counter space, a handy pantry and an angled snack bar. The adjoining breakfast nook provides scenic views of a backyard pool and patio.
- A family area, set off from the nook by a two-way fireplace, offers a wet bar and outdoor views through tall windows.
- The incredible master suite shows off a 12-ft. vaulted ceiling, a walk-in closet, a two-way fireplace and patio access. The luxurious master bath offers a whirlpool tub, a separate shower, a dual-sink vanity and a private toilet.
- Two additional bedrooms feature ample closet space and share a full bath of their own. The third bedroom could serve as a den or guest room.
- Ceilings in all rooms are at least 9 ft. high for added spaciousness.

Plan B-89003

Bedrooms: 2+	Baths: 2½
Living Area:	
Main floor	2,235 sq. ft.
Total Living Area:	**2,235 sq. ft.**
Two-car garage	564 sq. ft.
Three-car garage	756 sq. ft.
Exterior Wall Framing:	2x4

Foundation Options:
Slab
(All plans can be built with your choice of foundation and framing. A generic conversion diagram is available. See order form.)

BLUEPRINT PRICE CODE:	C

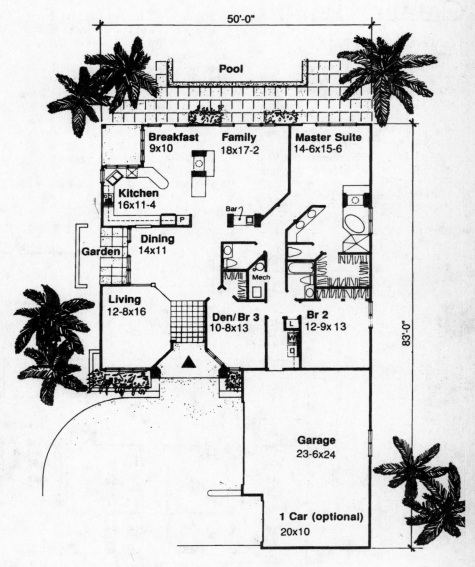

MAIN FLOOR

Creative Home for Sloped Lot

- This creative country-style home is warm and inviting. Its walkout lower level can accommodate a sloping lot.
- Expansive front and rear porches are ideal for entertaining. Access to the rear porch is possible from the Great Room, the dining room and the master bedroom. A second bedroom opens to the front porch.
- All three bedrooms have private baths! The master bath also offers dual walk-in closets and a luxurious garden tub.
- The huge gourmet kitchen offers a built-in desk, a pantry closet and a handy work island. All main-floor rooms and porches are enhanced by 10-ft. ceilings.
- Adjacent to the garage on the basement level is room for a future playroom or home office. The basement level is expanded by 9-ft., 4-in. ceiling heights. Other expansion is possible in the attic/loft area.

Plan HDS-99-160

Bedrooms: 3	Baths: 3
Living Area:	
Main floor	2,500 sq. ft.
Total Living Area:	**2,500 sq. ft.**
Partial daylight basement	492 sq. ft.
Tuck-under garage	811 sq. ft.
Exterior Wall Framing:	2x4

Foundation Options:

Partial daylight basement
(All plans can be built with your choice of foundation and framing. A generic conversion diagram is available. See order form.)

BLUEPRINT PRICE CODE: D

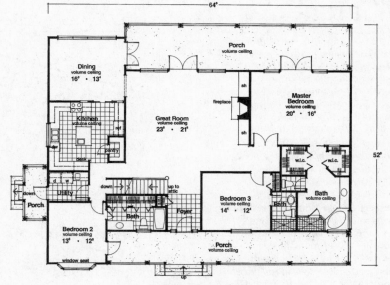

MAIN FLOOR

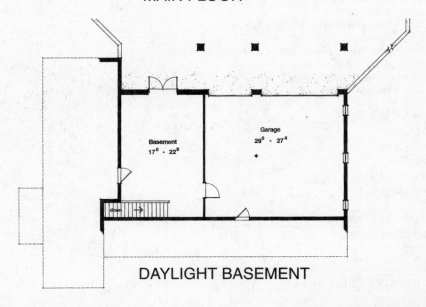

DAYLIGHT BASEMENT

Plan HDS-99-160

PRICES AND DETAILS
ON PAGES 2-5

Sun Catcher

- The most striking feature of this unique contemporary design is a two-story, glass-faced masonry wall built to collect and store passive solar heat.
- The home's 21-ft. vaulted entry has a view to the floor above and is topped by a sun roof. To the left, two bedrooms, one of which features a window seat, share a full bath. To the right you'll find plenty of storage space and a double garage.
- Upstairs, a balcony hallway overlooks the entry below. The hall opens into a 16-ft. vaulted Great Room warmed by a woodstove set up on a raised stone hearth. A long window seat looks out on the front of the home. Clerestory windows let in sunlight from overhead.
- The walk-through kitchen opens into the dining area as well as the Great Room. A range oven topped by a grill is a gourmet touch.
- Sliding doors in the dining room access a backyard patio.
- The master suite is secluded from the traffic of the common living areas. It boasts a private bath, a walk-in closet and a cozy window seat.

Plan H-2112-1B

Bedrooms: 3	Baths: 2½
Living Area:	
Main floor	1,166 sq. ft.
Daylight basement	693 sq. ft.
Total Living Area:	**1,859 sq. ft.**
Garage	434 sq. ft.
Exterior Wall Framing:	2x6

Foundation Options:
Daylight basement
(All plans can be built with your choice of foundation and framing. A generic conversion diagram is available. See order form.)

BLUEPRINT PRICE CODE: B

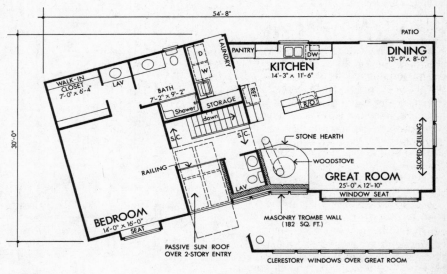

MAIN FLOOR

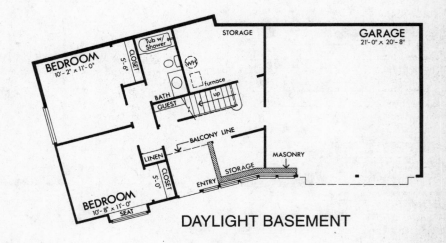

DAYLIGHT BASEMENT

Designed for Relaxed Living

- A simple exterior with a covered front porch and decorative shutters gives a relaxed look to this country home.
- The covered porch entrance opens directly into the spacious living room, which boasts a handsome fireplace. Glass doors in the adjoining dining room open to a screened back porch with outdoor access.
- The roomy kitchen includes an island counter and a windowed sink. A bright bay-windowed breakfast area, a pantry and a laundry closet are nearby.
- The secluded master bedroom is enhanced by a private, compartmentalized bath and a walk-in closet.
- Two additional bedrooms are serviced by a second full bath.
- The two-car garage is entered from the side and includes a sizable storage room for lawn and garden equipment.

Plan C-7549

Bedrooms: 3	Baths: 2
Living Area:	
Main floor	1,627 sq. ft.
Total Living Area:	**1,627 sq. ft.**
Screened porch	140 sq. ft.
Daylight basement	1,627 sq. ft.
Garage	407 sq. ft.
Storage	63 sq. ft.
Exterior Wall Framing:	2x4

Foundation Options:

Daylight basement
Crawlspace
Slab

(All plans can be built with your choice of foundation and framing. A generic conversion diagram is available. See order form.)

BLUEPRINT PRICE CODE:	B

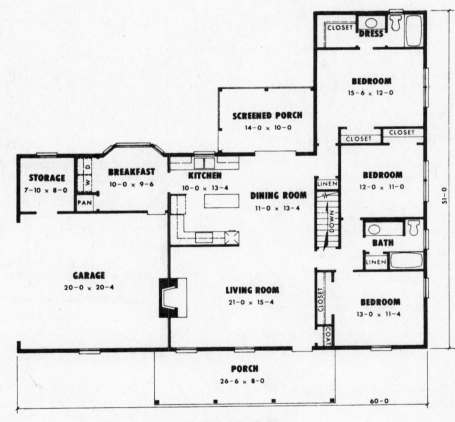

MAIN FLOOR

Plan C-7549

PRICES AND DETAILS
ON PAGES 2-5

REAR VIEW

Earth's Embrace

- This earth-sheltered home combines the livability of a conventional house with the good sense of energy-efficient features. All rooms benefit from proper solar orientation, and, though three exterior walls of the home are covered with earth, skylights make the interior light and airy.
- The Great Room is a highlight of the plan, with a corner fireplace, corner window walls and sliding glass doors to the south-facing patio.
- The walk-through kitchen includes a skylighted breakfast area and a handy wet bar facing the Great Room.
- Clustered away from the living areas, the master bedroom enjoys a private, compartmentalized bath, while two secondary rooms share a hall bath.
- The elevation of the garage above the living areas can be varied from a full flight of stairs to no stairs at all.
- Blueprints for this home include framing plans for two kinds of roof structures—a concrete roof that will support up to two feet of earth, and a wood-truss roof for use without earth.
- Note: Earth-sheltered houses should not be considered in high-water-table areas.

Plan B-502

Bedrooms: 2+	Baths: 2
Living Area:	
Main floor	1,712 sq. ft.
Total Living Area:	**1,712 sq. ft.**
Garage	440 sq. ft.
Exterior Wall Framing:	2x6
Foundation Options:	

Slab
(All plans can be built with your choice of foundation and framing. A generic conversion diagram is available. See order form.)

BLUEPRINT PRICE CODE:	**B**

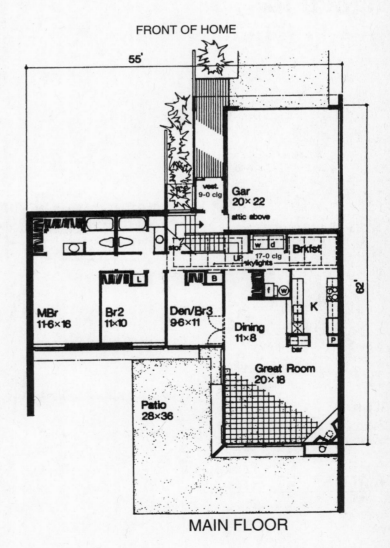

FRONT OF HOME

MAIN FLOOR

Tropical Design

- A hipped roof with twin gables and a dramatic tropical porch are among the exterior features of this attractive home.
- Double glass doors open to a tiled foyer with a long view into the Great Room and the covered patio beyond.
- The formal dining room to the left boasts a trio of tall windows that overlook the front porch.
- The expansive central Great Room offers a charming view of the covered back patio through sliding glass doors.
- An angled snack bar with a sink is featured in the kitchen, which is also equipped with a walk-in pantry and a bayed breakfast area with patio access.
- The master suite also enjoys generous views of the outdoors, including an angled window wall and sliding glass doors that offer private access to the patio. The master bath features a large walk-in closet, a dual-sink corner vanity and a separate tub and shower.
- The secondary bedrooms are entered from a separate hallway; each bedroom has a sunny window seat.
- All volume ceilings are 10-ft. high. A 12-ft. ceiling presides over the foyer.

Plan HDS-99-174

Bedrooms: 3	Baths: 2
Living Area:	
Main floor	1,627 sq. ft.
Total Living Area:	**1,627 sq. ft.**
Garage	413 sq. ft.
Exterior Wall Framing:	2x4

Foundation Options:

Slab

(All plans can be built with your choice of foundation and framing. A generic conversion diagram is available. See order form.)

BLUEPRINT PRICE CODE:	B

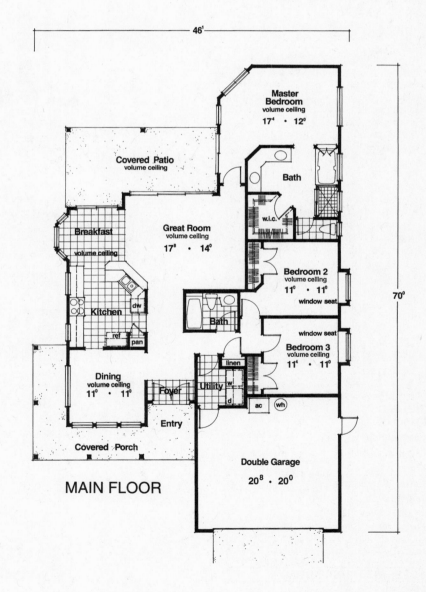

MAIN FLOOR

128

ORDER BLUEPRINTS ANYTIME!
CALL TOLL-FREE 1-800-820-1283

Plan HDS-99-174

PRICES AND DETAILS
ON PAGES 2-5

Captivating Cottage

- Regal metal-roofed bays give a European flair to this captivating cottage design.
- Elegant French doors usher guests in from the covered porch to a dramatic columned gallery.
- On the left, the island kitchen boasts a 12-ft. vaulted ceiling and outdoor access via sliding glass doors.
- A 19-ft. vaulted ceiling presides over the bayed dining room and the expansive central Great Room. Features here include a focal-point fireplace, built-in shelves and sliding glass doors to a second covered porch.
- An angled door leads to the secluded master bedroom, with its 12-ft. vaulted ceiling. Sliding doors provide private access to the backyard. Two closets and a whirlpool bath complete the suite.
- High 10-ft. ceilings enhance the two secondary bedrooms, which share a hall bath. A laundry closet is nearby.
- The side-entry garage is beautifully concealed behind a lovely bay window.

Plan AX-94313

Bedrooms: 3	Baths: 2
Living Area:	
Main floor	1,685 sq. ft.
Total Living Area:	**1,685 sq. ft.**
Standard basement	1,685 sq. ft.
Garage	434 sq. ft.
Exterior Wall Framing:	2x4

Foundation Options:

Standard basement

Crawlspace

Slab

(All plans can be built with your choice of foundation and framing. A generic conversion diagram is available. See order form.)

BLUEPRINT PRICE CODE:	**B**

VIEW INTO GREAT ROOM

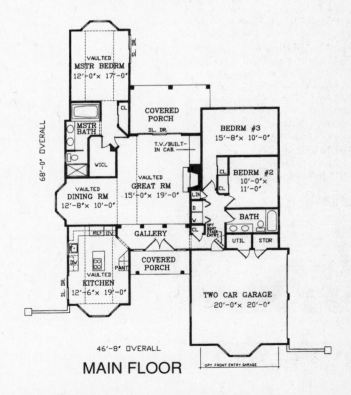

MAIN FLOOR

ORDER BLUEPRINTS ANYTIME!
CALL TOLL-FREE 1-800-820-1283

Plan AX-94313

PRICES AND DETAILS
ON PAGES 2-5

127

Charming Guest Cottage

- A charming guest cottage makes this home a unique find.
- Incorporated with the detached garage, the cottage's cozy covered porch opens to a comfortable living area, which shares an efficient serving counter with the galley-style kitchen.
- A full bath and a bedroom with a large walk-in closet complete the cottage.
- The foyer of the main home unfolds to a spacious living room, which boasts a dramatic 16-ft. cathedral ceiling and a cozy fireplace.
- The sun-drenched dining room features French-door access to a covered porch.
- The efficient kitchen includes a neat serving counter and a handy laundry area behind pocket doors.
- Elegant double doors open to the master bedroom, which features a 16-ft. cathedral ceiling and attractive plant ledges above the two walk-in closets. The master bath flaunts a garden tub and a separate shower.
- French doors open to a cozy study, which could serve as a second bedroom.

Plan L-270-SA

Bedrooms: 2+	Baths: 3
Living Area:	
Main floor	1,268 sq. ft.
Guest cottage	468 sq. ft.
Total Living Area:	**1,736 sq. ft.**
Garage and storage	573 sq. ft.
Exterior Wall Framing:	2x4

Foundation Options:

Slab

(All plans can be built with your choice of foundation and framing. A generic conversion diagram is available. See order form.)

BLUEPRINT PRICE CODE: B

REAR VIEW

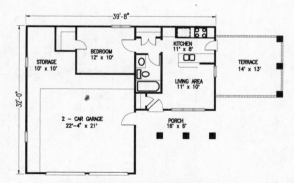

GUEST COTTAGE

MAIN FLOOR

Plan L-270-SA

PRICES AND DETAILS
ON PAGES 2-5

Wonderful One-Story

- Brick columns, arches with keystones, and transom windows set the tone for the luxurious, light-filled spaces found within this wonderful one-story home.
- The L-shaped living and dining rooms offer sweeping views of the front yard and the lanai. The lanai would make a great poolside entertainment area, with its built-in barbecue grill, serving counter and sink.
- The U-shaped kitchen is open to the glassed-in morning room and the family room with fireplace. The kitchen features an island counter and an eating bar/pass-through to the family room.
- The isolated master bedroom has French doors that lead to the lanai and a bath with all the amenities.
- Another full bath offers easy access from the lanai as well as from the three bedrooms. These bedrooms, the bath and the utility room have standard 8-ft. ceilings. All remaining rooms are enhanced by 10-ft. ceilings.

Plan DD-2139

Bedrooms: 4	Baths: 2
Living Area	
Main floor	2,139 sq. ft.
Total Living Area:	**2,139 sq. ft.**
Standard basement	2,139 sq. ft.
Garage	587 sq. ft.
Exterior Wall Framing:	2x4

Foundation Options:

Standard basement
Crawlspace
Slab
(All plans can be built with your choice of foundation and framing. A generic conversion diagram is available. See order form.)

BLUEPRINT PRICE CODE:	C

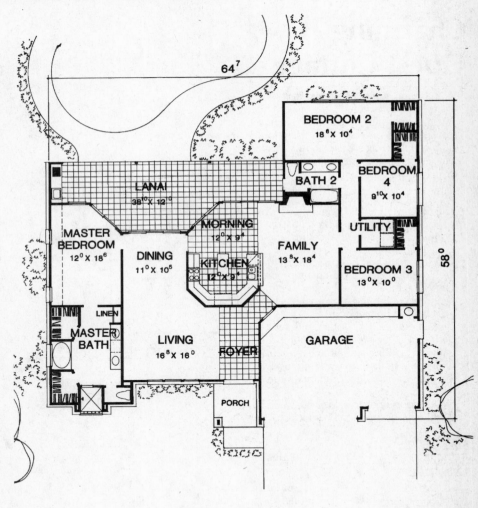

MAIN FLOOR

Private Courtyard

- Designed with privacy in mind, this European-style home is oriented around a sunny porch and courtyard.
- Three French doors topped by fantail transoms highlight the home's facade.
- Inside, the spacious living room is enhanced by a dramatic corner fireplace and a high 14-ft. ceiling. All other rooms feature 9-ft. ceilings.
- The adjoining central entry area links the living room and the dining room to the courtyard and its covered porch.
- Double doors open into the kitchen, where an angled eating bar and a cool wet bar serve a bayed breakfast area. A French door opens to the courtyard.
- The master suite also has courtyard access and includes a private bath. A separate dressing area offers a makeup table, a second sink and a walk-in closet with built-in shelves.
- Double doors off the living room open to the other sleeping wing, where two additional bedrooms feature walk-in closets and share a second full bath.

Plan E-1911

Bedrooms: 3	Baths: 2
Living Area:	
Main floor	1,961 sq. ft.
Total Living Area:	**1,961 sq. ft.**
Garage	484 sq. ft.
Storage	60 sq. ft.
Exterior Wall Framing:	2x6

Foundation Options:

Slab

(All plans can be built with your choice of foundation and framing. A generic conversion diagram is available. See order form.)

BLUEPRINT PRICE CODE: B

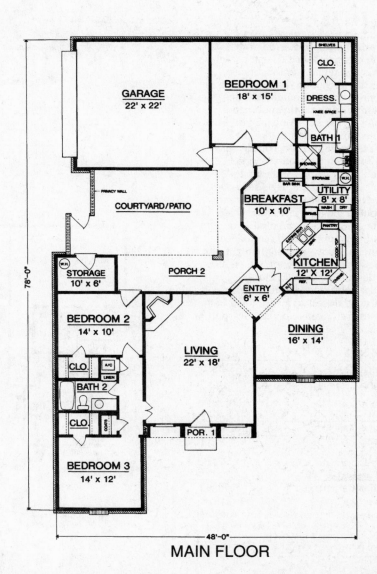

MAIN FLOOR

124

ORDER BLUEPRINTS ANYTIME!
CALL TOLL-FREE 1-800-820-1283

Plan E-1911

PRICES AND DETAILS
ON PAGES 2-5

Series of Surprises

- Deceptively simple outside, this Southwestern-inspired design contains a series of delightful surprises inside.
- Especially large for a home of this size, the living room is a natural gathering place for visiting family and friends throughout the day. A rustic woodstove enhances the warmth of the space.
- Meal preparation will no doubt be a family affair in the well-equipped kitchen. Its close proximity to the dining room means dinner will be served piping hot every time.
- Step out to the sun nook through a sliding glass door in the dining room to enjoy the warmth of the summer sun.
- A skylighted private bath highlights the spacious master bedroom, which also includes a large walk-in closet.
- Another good-sized bedroom has dual closets and access to a skylighted bath.
- This design is available with a carport or a garage.

Plans H-1433-1A & -1B

Bedrooms: 2	Baths: 2
Living Area:	
Main floor	1,558 sq. ft.
Sun nook	140 sq. ft.
Total Living Area:	**1,698 sq. ft.**
Carport	462 sq. ft.
Storage	92 sq. ft.
Exterior Wall Framing:	2x6
Foundation Options:	**Plan #**
Slab (carport)	H-1433-1A
Slab (garage)	H-1433-1B

(All plans can be built with your choice of foundation and framing. A generic conversion diagram is available. See order form.)

BLUEPRINT PRICE CODE:	B

REAR VIEW

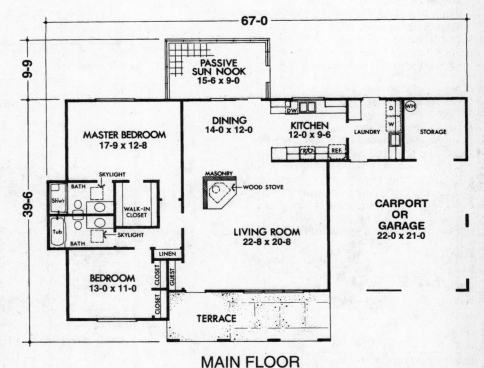

MAIN FLOOR

ORDER BLUEPRINTS ANYTIME!
CALL TOLL-FREE 1-800-820-1283

Plans H-1433-1A & -1B

PRICES AND DETAILS
ON PAGES 2-5

123

Look Out Below!

- This home, which includes a daylight basement with tons of living space in addition to the main floor, is perfect for that beautiful—but difficult—sloping lot. The design is also carefully planned to take advantage of scenic vistas.
- The entry leads into the heart of the home, where many hours will be spent in years to come. On the right, guests will enjoy chatting in front of the Great Room's corner woodstove.
- The breakfast nook merges with the open kitchen, creating a casual setting for any meals. In the kitchen, an island

cooktop with a snack bar allows a parent to prepare dinner while the kids have an after-school snack.
- Nearby, the amenity-packed master suite goes far beyond the average bedroom. Here, an enormous walk-in closet provides storage space for even the largest shoe collection.
- Sliding glass doors open to a huge deck with lots of room for lawn chairs, the grill and plenty of friends.
- Downstairs, a substantial recreation room is a great place for an entertainment center and a pool table. The kids can host friends here for sleepovers and birthday parties.
- A central bath with a dual-sink vanity services two more bedrooms. A handy laundry room is nearby.

Plan LRD-5295

Bedrooms: 3	Baths: 2½
Living Area:	
Main floor	1,229 sq. ft.
Daylight basement	1,033 sq. ft.
Total Living Area:	**2,262 sq. ft.**
Unfinished storage room	96 sq. ft.
Garage and shop	541 sq. ft.
Exterior Wall Framing:	2x6

Foundation Options:
Daylight basement
(All plans can be built with your choice of foundation and framing. A generic conversion diagram is available. See order form.)

BLUEPRINT PRICE CODE: C

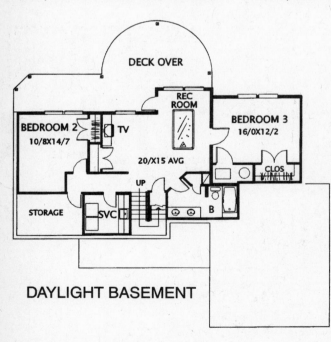

DAYLIGHT BASEMENT

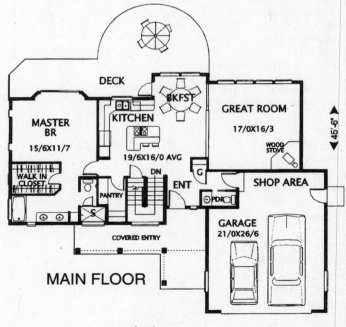

MAIN FLOOR

◄ 58' ►

Plan LRD-5295

PRICES AND DETAILS
ON PAGES 2-5

Tranquil Living

- A railed porch promotes tranquil living in this traditional family home.
- Sunny transom windows top the entry, which opens directly into the living room. A fireplace and built-in shelves make the living room an inviting spot for get-togethers.
- The open dining area can be adapted to suit both casual and formal occasions, and the well-planned kitchen features an island cooktop with a snack bar. Beautiful French doors extend an invitation to retreat to the quiet backyard porch on summer evenings.
- Convenient access to the garage eases the strain of unloading groceries.
- A romantic fireplace adds an intimate and peaceful glow to the master bedroom. The master bath features dual vanities and a luxurious raised tub under a picture window.
- Across the home are two more bedrooms with walk-in closets, private vanities and a shared bath.
- An enormous, versatile area upstairs is available to meet your evolving needs.

Plan J-9505

Bedrooms: 3+	Baths: 2½
Living Area:	
Main floor	2,117 sq. ft.
Total Living Area:	**2,117 sq. ft.**
Future upper floor	1,385 sq. ft.
Standard basement	2,117 sq. ft.
Garage	528 sq. ft.
Exterior Wall Framing:	2x6

Foundation Options:

Standard basement

Crawlspace

Slab

(All plans can be built with your choice of foundation and framing. A generic conversion diagram is available. See order form.)

BLUEPRINT PRICE CODE: C

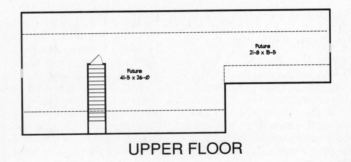

UPPER FLOOR

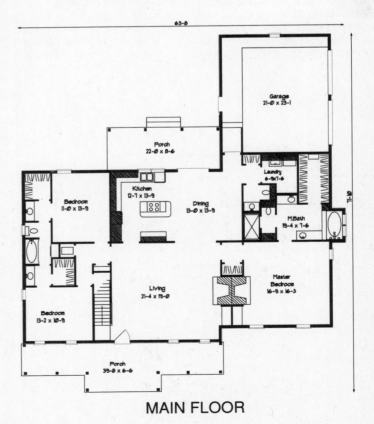

MAIN FLOOR

ORDER BLUEPRINTS ANYTIME!
CALL TOLL-FREE 1-800-820-1283

Plan J-9505

PRICES AND DETAILS
ON PAGES 2-5

121

REAR VIEW

Courtyard Classic

- An intriguing courtyard entrance introduces this classic U-shaped home.
- Inside, the entry flows easily to all parts of the home, which is zoned for privacy and natural flow of traffic.
- The open living spaces are grouped together under a 11½-ft. vaulted ceiling.
- A crackling fireplace lights the expansive living room, which also offers sliding glass doors to the backyard deck that spans the home's entire width.

- Meals in the boxed-out dining room sparkle with sunlight in the afternoon, and take on starlit ambience at night.
- The U-shaped kitchen lies at the heart of the living areas. It shares a cozy breakfast bar with the family room.
- In the sleeping wing, the master suite boasts built-in shelves, two closets, a full bath and sliding glass doors to the deck. Two secondary bedrooms share a hall bath. Laundry facilities are tucked away nearby.
- The daylight basement includes another bedroom and a full bath, a game room, a party room equipped with a fireplace, and a general-use area.

Plans H-3683-1 & -1A	
Bedrooms: 3+	**Baths:** 2-3
Living Area:	
Main floor	1,560 sq. ft.
Daylight basement	1,560 sq. ft.
Total Living Area:	**1,560/3,120 sq. ft.**
Garage	429 sq. ft.
Storage	74 sq. ft.
Exterior Wall Framing:	2x4
Foundation Options:	**Plan #**
Daylight basement	H-3683-1
Crawlspace	H-3683-1A
(All plans can be built with your choice of foundation and framing. A generic conversion diagram is available. See order form.)	
BLUEPRINT PRICE CODE:	**B/E**

BASEMENT STAIRWAY LOCATION

FAMILY RM
HALL
LAUNDRY
w   d
CLOSET
BEDROOM

DAYLIGHT BASEMENT

BEDROOM
11'-3" × 14'-0"
CLOS
CLOS
STOR
GAME ROOM
21'-0" × 25'-0"
PARTY ROOM
22'-10" × 13'-3"
BATH
Shower
STOR
STOR
heat
GENERAL USE
22'-8" × 11'-3"

MAIN FLOOR

58'-0"
DECK
6'-0"
BEDROOM
11'-6" × 14'-4"
CLOS
shelves
CLOS
FAMILY RM
12'-0" × 18'-3"
vaulted ceiling
breakfast bar
KITCHEN
8'-6" × 9'-0"
dw
rng
ref
DINING
11'-3" × 10'-0"
LIVING RM
13'-8" × 23'-3"
vaulted ceiling
CLOS
CLOS
STORAGE
48'-6"
BATH
Shower
STOR
heat
LAUNDRY
w   d
ENTRY
BATH
LIN
CLOSET
CLOSET
BEDROOM
11'-5" × 10'-0"
BEDROOM
11'-5" × 13'-5"
ENTRANCE COURT
GARAGE
19'-4" × 22'-2"

Plans H-3683-1 & -1A
PRICES AND DETAILS
ON PAGES 2-5

Split-Level with Personality

- The blueprints for this multi-level home include two exteriors with distinct personalities: the contemporary version pictured here and a traditional version with lap siding and natural stone.
- A trellis-covered porch gives way to a skylighted entry that opens into the living room. Here, a boxed-out window and a fireplace are nice touches.
- Up a short stairway, the kitchen and dining area are separated by a work island fronted by a curved serving bar. Sliding glass doors in the dining area, which overlooks the living room, open to a backyard deck.
- Down the hall, the master bedroom features a dressing area with a vanity, plus a walk-in closet and private access to a full bath.
- The basement contains a family room with its own beckoning fireplace, which stands next to built-in shelves. A bonus area is easily divisible into two bedrooms.
- This design's spacious common areas and modest square footage make it a smart choice for a vacation home.

Plan B-4-4	
Bedrooms: 2+	**Baths: 2**
Living Area:	
Main floor	1,012 sq. ft.
Partial basement	332 sq. ft.
Bonus room	268 sq. ft.
Total Living Area:	**1,612 sq. ft.**
Garage	419 sq. ft.
Exterior Wall Framing:	2x4
Foundation Options:	

Partial basement
(All plans can be built with your choice of foundation and framing. A generic conversion diagram is available. See order form.)

| **BLUEPRINT PRICE CODE:** | **B** |

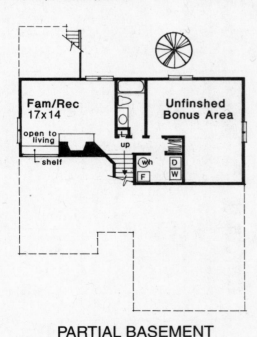

PARTIAL BASEMENT

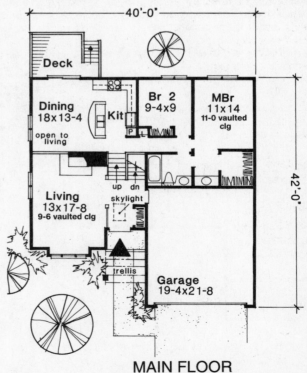

MAIN FLOOR

Cozy Bungalow

- This pleasing L-shaped design packs a lot of living space into its floor plan.
- The large family room at the center of the home extends to two outdoor living spaces: a screened porch and a big patio or deck. For colder days, the warm fireplace will come in handy.
- Formal occasions will be well received in the spacious living/dining room at the front of the home. Each area offers a nice view of the front porch.
- The airy kitchen includes a pantry, a windowed sink and lots of counter space. Attached is a cozy breakfast bay and, beyond that, a laundry room.
- Secluded to the rear of the sleeping wing, the master suite boasts a private symmetrical bath with a garden tub, a separate shower and his-and-hers vanities and walk-in closets.
- Two secondary bedrooms and another full bath complete the sleeping wing.

Plan C-8620

Bedrooms: 3	Baths: 2
Living Area:	
Main floor	1,950 sq. ft.
Total Living Area:	**1,950 sq. ft.**
Daylight basement	1,950 sq. ft.
Garage	420 sq. ft.
Exterior Wall Framing:	2x4

Foundation Options:

Daylight basement
Crawlspace
Slab

(All plans can be built with your choice of foundation and framing. A generic conversion diagram is available. See order form.)

BLUEPRINT PRICE CODE: B

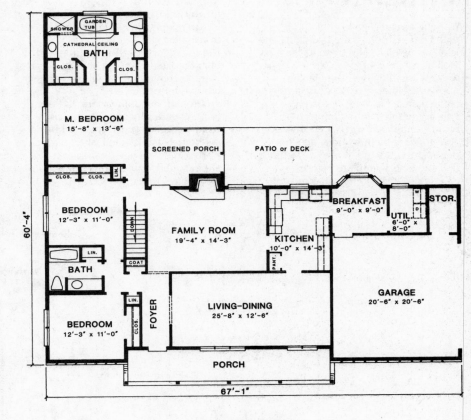

MAIN FLOOR

Plan C-8620

PRICES AND DETAILS
ON PAGES 2-5

Formal Yet Fun

- Upright and elegant in front and filled with French doors at the back, this one-level home has an air of composure as well as excitement.
- A gazebo ceiling over the breakfast nook brings height and stature to the kitchen area.
- This home's accommodating game room, centralized wet bar, skylighted rear porch and courtyard space that's perfect for a hot tub, make it a terrific place to entertain in any season.

- A secluded fourth bedroom with a nearby full bath is just the thing for the independent teenager or the private overnight guest.
- The living room's 14-ft. ceilings and high fireplace chimney give the room volume and imbue the whole home with a soaring grace.
- A porch off the utility room, a tiled front foyer, a spacious kitchen and large closets throughout contribute to the home's frank practicality.
- Plans for a detached, two-car garage are included with the blueprints.

Plan L-2516-C	
Bedrooms: 4	**Baths:** 3
Living Area:	
Main floor	2,516 sq. ft.
Total Living Area:	**2,516 sq. ft.**
Exterior Wall Framing:	2x4
Foundation Options:	

Slab
(All plans can be built with your choice of foundation and framing. A generic conversion diagram is available. See order form.)

BLUEPRINT PRICE CODE:	**D**

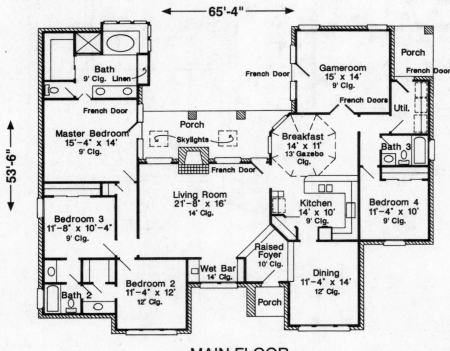

MAIN FLOOR

ORDER BLUEPRINTS ANYTIME!
CALL TOLL-FREE 1-800-820-1283

Plan L-2516-C

PRICES AND DETAILS
ON PAGES 2-5

117

Open Plan

- This openly comfortable home defines function and style, with a sharp window wall to brighten the central living areas.
- In from the front deck, the living/family room boasts a fireplace, a cathedral ceiling and soaring views.
- The galley-style kitchen offers a bright sink, with a laundry closet and carport access nearby.
- The secluded and spacious master bedroom features private deck access, a walk-in closet and a private bath.

Plan C-8160

Bedrooms: 3	Baths: 2
Living Area:	
Main floor	1,669 sq. ft.
Total Living Area:	**1,669 sq. ft.**
Daylight basement	1,660 sq. ft.
Carport	413 sq. ft.
Storage	85 sq. ft.
Exterior Wall Framing:	2x4

Foundation Options:
Daylight basement
Crawlspace
Slab
(All plans can be built with your choice of foundation and framing. A generic conversion diagram is available. See order form.)

BLUEPRINT PRICE CODE: B

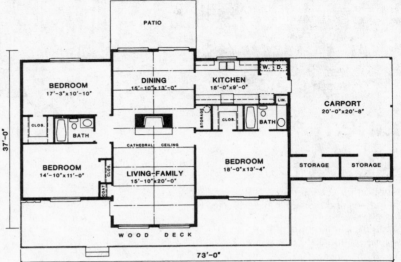

MAIN FLOOR

Plan C-8160

Rustic Welcome

- This appealing home boasts a rustic exterior offering guests a friendly welcome. Inside, the Great Room boasts a massive fireplace and an 11-ft., 8-in. cathedral ceiling.
- Off the dining room, the galley-style kitchen flows into the breakfast room.
- The master suite features a walk-in closet and a compartmentalized bath.
- On the opposite side of the home, two additional bedrooms share a second full bath.

Plan C-8460

Bedrooms: 3	Baths: 2
Living Area:	
Main floor	1,670 sq. ft.
Total Living Area:	**1,670 sq. ft.**
Daylight basement	1,600 sq. ft.
Garage	427 sq. ft.
Storage	63 sq. ft.
Exterior Wall Framing:	2x4

Foundation Options:
Daylight basement, crawlspace, slab
(All plans can be built with your choice of foundation and framing. A generic conversion diagram is available. See order form.)

BLUEPRINT PRICE CODE: B

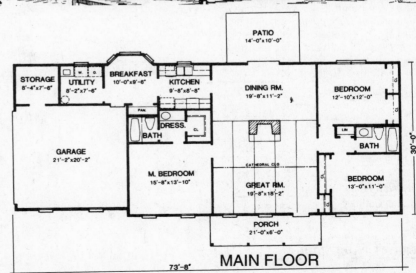

MAIN FLOOR

Plan C-8460

Prominent Portico

- A prominent portico accented by dramatic windows and a Spanish tile roof draws attention to this home. Grand double doors open into a foyer with an airy 14-ft. ceiling.
- Straight ahead, an elegant curved gallery frames the living room, which opens to a skylighted patio. Arched openings along one wall add high style.
- The quiet den and the formal dining room feature striking 12-ft. ceilings.
- The island kitchen boasts a big pantry and a neat pass-through to the patio, which offers a summer kitchen with a bar sink. A powder room is nearby.
- A 14-ft. vaulted ceiling, plus a fireplace set into a media wall make the family room a fun indoor gathering place.
- Two secondary bedrooms share a split bath with a dual-sink vanity.
- Across the home, a three-way fireplace and an entertainment center separate the master bedroom from its bayed sitting room. An exercise area, a wet bar and a posh bath are other pleasures!
- Unless otherwise mentioned, every room features a 10-ft. ceiling.

Plan HDS-99-242

Bedrooms: 3+	Baths: 3½
Living Area:	
Main floor	3,556 sq. ft.
Total Living Area:	**3,556 sq. ft.**
Garage	809 sq. ft.
Exterior Wall Framing:	8-in. concrete block

Foundation Options:

Slab

(All plans can be built with your choice of foundation and framing. A generic conversion diagram is available. See order form.)

BLUEPRINT PRICE CODE:	F

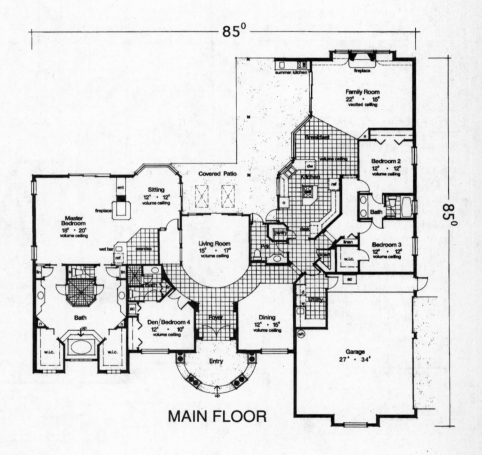

MAIN FLOOR

Roomy, Open Floor Plan

- An interesting mixture of exterior finish materials, including diagonal and vertical cedar siding, wood shingles and brick veneer, adds definition to this appealing one-story home.
- The interior packs a lot of punch as well, featuring an open floor plan accented by several skylights.
- Just off the foyer, the living and dining rooms flow together beneath a stunning 16-ft.-high cathedral ceiling. Skylights and expansive picture windows brighten the area, which is warmed by

an optional three-way fireplace that is shared with the family room.
- The skylighted family room also has a 16-ft. cathedral ceiling, as well as a wall of glass overlooking the backyard. Another option is a built-in entertainment center or shelving unit .
- The sunny kitchen features a 16-ft. ceiling topped with a skylight. A convenient island separates the kitchen from the breakfast room, which boasts a 15-ft. ceiling. The nearby laundry room includes extra closet space.
- The impressive master suite showcases a large sleeping area, two closets and a skylighted bath with a cathedral ceiling.
- The two remaining bedrooms share a second full bath.

Plan AX-98603	
Bedrooms: 3	**Baths:** 2
Living Area:	
Main floor	1,615 sq. ft.
Total Living Area:	**1,615 sq. ft.**
Standard basement	1,615 sq. ft.
Garage	400 sq. ft.
Exterior Wall Framing:	2x4
Foundation Options:	
Standard basement	
Crawlspace	
Slab	

(All plans can be built with your choice of foundation and framing. A generic conversion diagram is available. See order form.)

BLUEPRINT PRICE CODE:	B

MAIN FLOOR

72'-4"
32'-4"

W.D. **BKFST. AREA**
CL.
DN
DN
GAR.

BASEMENT STAIRWAY LOCATION

CL. **W. D.** **LAUNDRY RM.**
UTIL.

BKFST. AREA 8⁴x11⁴

DW **S.** **KITCHEN** 9x13⁴
KIT. ISLAND **SKYLITE**
REF.

SL.GL.DR.
FAMILY RM. CATH'DL. CLG. 15x13⁴
SKYLITE
OPT. BUILT -IN

CATH'DL. CLG.
MSTR. BTH. **SKYLITE**
BTH. #2 **W.I.CL.**

MSTR.BDRM. 15x13⁴
CL. **CL.**

TWO CAR GARAGE 20x20⁰

CATH'DL. CLG. **SKYLITE**
DINING RM. 10⁰x12⁴
LIVING RM. 12x13⁴
RAIL
OPT.FIREPLACE

FOY
LIN
CL.
CL.

BDRM.#3 10x10⁰
BDRM.#2 11x11⁰

Rustic Beauty

- If you're looking for a rustic design with an innovative floor plan, this beautiful home is for you!
- Cedar siding and eye-catching stone combine for an engaging, low-maintenance facade.
- The large, tiled entry is brightened by sidelights and high, angled windows that rise to meet the 15½-ft. ceiling.
- Straight ahead, the sunken Great Room offers a 16½-ft. ceiling and wonderful views of the backyard. A low, see-through fireplace allows the window area to be uninterrupted. A French door accesses a wraparound covered porch.
- The galley-style kitchen offers a 16½-ft. ceiling and a convenient serving bar for snacks and hors d'oeuvres.

- The windowed breakfast nook is a comfortable spot for pleasant dining. A 15½-ft. ceiling adds openness.
- A lengthy utility room makes laundry a breeze. The nearby two-car garage has an attic storage area.
- Off the main entry, two good-sized bedrooms with 11½-ft. ceilings are serviced by a roomy full bath and a powder room.
- Across the home, the raised master bedroom boasts a 9½-ft. ceiling and sliding glass doors to a private deck. A nice dressing area features a walk-in closet and a makeup table. A French door opens to a large patio that is enclosed by a stone wall.
- The private master bath is brightened by a skylight and shows off a corner tub, a separate shower and two sinks.

Plan SAN-4004

Bedrooms: 3	Baths: 2½
Living Area:	
Main floor	1,900 sq. ft.
Total Living Area:	**1,900 sq. ft.**
Garage	576 sq. ft.
Storage (above garage)	341 sq. ft.
Exterior Wall Framing:	2x6

Foundation Options:
Slab
(All plans can be built with your choice of foundation and framing. A generic conversion diagram is available. See order form.)

BLUEPRINT PRICE CODE: B

VIEW INTO GREAT ROOM

MAIN FLOOR

DECK

MASTER BEDROOM
15' x 12'

COVERED PORCH

GREAT ROOM
20' x 20'

NOOK
9' x 9'

UTILITY
19'0" x 6'6"

KITCHEN
8'6" x 14'0"

GARAGE
24' x 24'

BEDROOM
12' x 12'

BEDROOM
10' x 14'

56'-0"

95'-0"

ORDER BLUEPRINTS ANYTIME!
CALL TOLL-FREE 1-800-820-1283

Plan SAN-4004

PRICES AND DETAILS
ON PAGES 2-5

113

Rustic Comfort

- Rustic charm highlights the exterior of this design, while the interior is filled with all the latest comforts.
- The wide, covered porch opens to a roomy entry, where two 7-ft.-high openings with decorative railings view into the dining room.
- Straight ahead lies the sunken living room, which features a 16-ft.-high vaulted ceiling with exposed beams. The fireplace is faced with floor-to-ceiling fieldstone, adding to the rustic look. A rear door opens to a large patio with luscious plant areas.

- The large and functional U-shaped kitchen features a china niche with glass shelves. Other bonuses include the adjacent sewing/hobby room, the oversized utility room and the storage area and built-in workbench in the side-entry garage.
- The secluded master suite hosts a sunken sleeping area with built-in bookshelves. One step up is a cozy sitting area that is defined by brick columns and a railed room divider. Double doors open to the deluxe bath, which offers a niche with glass shelves.
- Across the home, two more bedrooms share a second full bath.

Plan E-1607	
Bedrooms: 3	**Baths:** 2
Living Area:	
Main floor	1,600 sq. ft.
Total Living Area:	**1,600 sq. ft.**
Standard basement	1,600 sq. ft.
Garage	484 sq. ft.
Storage	132 sq. ft.
Exterior Wall Framing:	2x6

Foundation Options:
Standard basement
Crawlspace
Slab
(All plans can be built with your choice of foundation and framing. A generic conversion diagram is available. See order form.)

BLUEPRINT PRICE CODE:	**B**

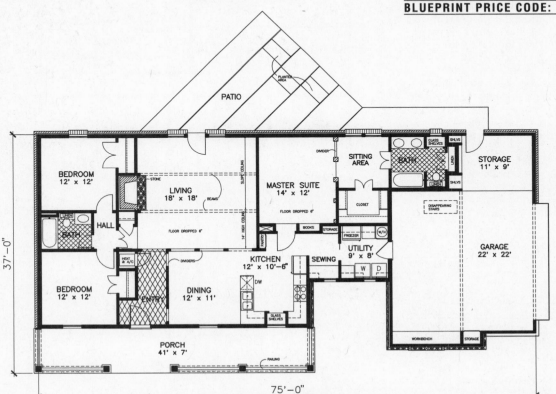

MAIN FLOOR

Low-Profile Getaway

- This Spanish-style one-level bungalow keeps a low profile and lets you disappear into your own world of privacy and comfort.
- The kitchen and family room are extended by the backyard patio. It is covered and has a parapet wall, adding a new dimension to your privacy.
- The sunken family room invites quiet conversation around a warm fireplace.
- The elongated living room is accented by a raised-hearth fireplace with a stucco finish and arched opening.
- Bedroom closets are roomy and plentiful. The deep U-shaped kitchen means efficiency and cleanliness. Even the laundry is convenient to the entry and dining areas, just off the kitchen.
- The flat garage roof extends over the front entry to create a kind of pergola that can be hung full of welcoming flowers. The whole house is the perfect canvas for a gardener's creative touch.
- Decorate it in warm Southwestern motifs, and turn this lovely home into your dream vacation place!

Plan H-1400-M1B

Bedrooms: 3	Baths: 2½
Living Area:	
Main floor	1,836 sq. ft.
Total Living Area:	**1,836 sq. ft.**
Garage	480 sq. ft.
Exterior Wall Framing:	2x6

Foundation Options:

Slab
(All plans can be built with your choice of foundation and framing. A generic conversion diagram is available. See order form.)

BLUEPRINT PRICE CODE: B

MAIN FLOOR

ORDER BLUEPRINTS ANYTIME!
CALL TOLL-FREE 1-800-820-1283

Plan H-1400-M1B

PRICES AND DETAILS
ON PAGES 2-5

111

Sweetly Appealing

- The efficient floor plan and moderate square footage of this interesting one-story is sure to appeal to a wide variety of home owners.
- A walk-up front porch, lap siding and Palladian windows convey its traditional charm to passersby.
- Inside, the sizable Grand Room is at the heart of the home. It features a mood-setting fireplace, a handy ale bar and access to a back deck via a pair of pretty French doors.
- Gourmet cooks and weekend chefs will find a happy home in the island kitchen. Situated nicely between the casual morning room and the formal dining room, it's destined to be the source of many great meals.
- Romantic and roomy, the master suite offers two closets, a secluded bath with a garden tub and its own pair of French doors to the back deck.
- At the front of the home is a library that easily converts to a bedroom, and a second suite with its own private bath.

Plan EOF-25

Bedrooms: 2+	Baths: 2½
Living Area:	
Main floor	1,758 sq. ft.
Total Living Area:	**1,758 sq. ft.**
Garage	400 sq. ft.
Exterior Wall Framing:	2x6

Foundation Options:

Slab
(All plans can be built with your choice of foundation and framing. A generic conversion diagram is available. See order form.)

BLUEPRINT PRICE CODE: B

MAIN FLOOR

Plan EOF-25

PRICES AND DETAILS
ON PAGES 2-5

Youthful Exuberance!

- With its free-flowing interior and breezy outdoor spaces, this historic home exudes a youthful exuberance.
- The sprawling central living room offers a refreshing wet bar and plenty of room for movement, yet is equally suited for quiet moments. The corner fireplace splashes the walls and windows with dancing light. Select a book from either of the bookshelves, curl up on the couch and escape!

- A clever bayed area in the master bedroom would make a nice exercise nook. A nearby French door opens to the skylighted sun porch, while twin walk-in closets lead the way to an almost sinfully sumptuous private bath.
- Your children or guests will enjoy their spacious bedrooms, large closets and private bath access.
- The family cook can work magic in the well-appointed kitchen, where a peninsula cooktop greatly simplifies meal preparation. Plentiful cupboards line the oversized eating area.
- A vast, unfinished attic provides limitless options for future expansion.

Plan E-2107

Bedrooms: 3+	Baths: 2½
Living Area:	
Main floor	2,123 sq. ft.
Total Living Area:	**2,123 sq. ft.**
Unfinished attic/future space	556 sq. ft.
Standard basement	2,123 sq. ft.
Garage	483 sq. ft.
Storage	76 sq. ft.
Exterior Wall Framing:	2x6

Foundation Options:

Standard basement
Crawlspace
Slab
(All plans can be built with your choice of foundation and framing. A generic conversion diagram is available. See order form.)

BLUEPRINT PRICE CODE: C

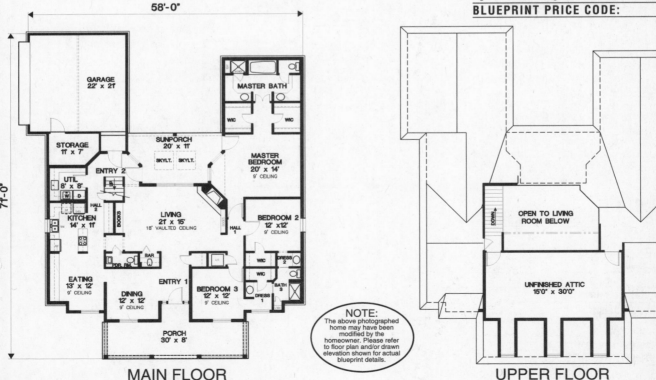

NOTE:
The above photographed home may have been modified by the homeowner. Please refer to floor plan and/or drawn elevation shown for actual blueprint details.

MAIN FLOOR

UPPER FLOOR

ORDER BLUEPRINTS ANYTIME!
CALL TOLL-FREE 1-800-820-1283

Plan E-2107

PRICES AND DETAILS
ON PAGES 2-5

109

A Real Original

- This home's round window, elegant entry and transom windows create an eye-catching, original look.
- Inside, high ceilings and tremendous views let the eyes wander. The foyer provides an exciting look at the expansive deck and the inviting spa through the living room's tall windows. The windows frame a handsome fireplace, while a 10-ft. ceiling adds volume and interest.
- To the right of the foyer is a cozy den or home office with its own fireplace, 10-ft. ceiling and dramatic windows.
- The spacious kitchen/breakfast area features an oversized snack bar island and opens to a large screen porch. Within easy reach are the laundry room and the entrance to the garage.
- The bright formal dining room overlooks the deck and boasts a ceiling that vaults up to 10 feet.
- The secluded master suite looks out to the deck as well, with access through a patio door. The private bath features a dynamite corner spa tub, a separate shower and a large walk-in closet.
- A second bedroom and bath complete the main floor.

Plan B-90065

Bedrooms: 2+	Baths: 2
Living Area:	
Main floor	1,889 sq. ft.
Total Living Area:	**1,889 sq. ft.**
Standard basement	1,889 sq. ft.
Garage	406 sq. ft.
Exterior Wall Framing:	2x6

Foundation Options:

Standard basement

(All plans can be built with your choice of foundation and framing. A generic conversion diagram is available. See order form.)

BLUEPRINT PRICE CODE: B

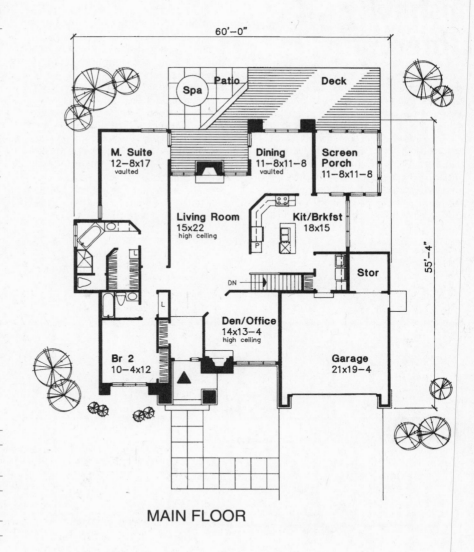

MAIN FLOOR

Distinctly Different

- This traditional, ranch-style home offers three distinct living areas—a formal area for entertaining, a casual one to enjoy everyday life in and a sleeping wing when you want privacy.
- An inviting porch greets visitors and ushers them into a welcoming foyer. On the right, the living room extends to the formal dining room, providing a large yet intimate place to entertain.
- A versatile family room at the rear of the home serves as the focal point of casual

gatherings. This good-sized room is a comfortable spot to watch a movie, enjoy a book or catch up on family matters. You will spend plenty of easy, bug-free, summer afternoons on the screened porch nearby.
- The efficient kitchen includes lots of counter space to prepare meals, and a roomy pantry that maximizes storage space. The sunny breakfast bay is great for casual meals and morning pastries.
- Across the home, the spacious master bedroom is a peaceful retreat. A neat dressing area with a dual-sink vanity and a large walk-in closet leads to the master bath, where a raised tub ends the day with a splash!

Plan C-8625

Bedrooms: 3	Baths: 2½
Living Area:	
Main floor	2,306 sq. ft.
Total Living Area:	**2,306 sq. ft.**
Screened porch	276 sq. ft.
Daylight basement	2,306 sq. ft.
Garage and storage	583 sq. ft.
Exterior Wall Framing:	2x4

Foundation Options:
Daylight basement
Crawlspace
Slab
(All plans can be built with your choice of foundation and framing. A generic conversion diagram is available. See order form.)

BLUEPRINT PRICE CODE: C

MAIN FLOOR

SCR. PORCH 23'-0" x 12'-0"

BATH

CLOSET

M. BEDROOM 17'-0" x 13'-6"

STEP

LINEN

DRESSING

CLOSET

FAMILY ROOM 22'-6" x 13'-6"

DOWN

KITCHEN 10'-0" x 13'-6"

BREAKFAST 10'-0" x 13'-0"

BATH

UTILITY

CLOSET

LINEN

BATH

PANTRY

BEDROOM 14'-0" x 12'-0"

COATS

BEDROOM 12'-0" x 12'-0"

CLOSET

FOYER

LIVING ROOM 16'-0" x 15'-0"

DINING ROOM 10'-0" x 12'-6"

GARAGE 22'-0" x 20'-0"

32'-8"

PORCH

STORAGE

93'-10"

ORDER BLUEPRINTS ANYTIME!
CALL TOLL-FREE 1-800-820-1283

Plan C-8625

PRICES AND DETAILS
ON PAGES 2-5

107

Bring Everyone Together

- You won't want to leave this home's most endearing feature—the sunken conversation pit. It is central to what it means to "get away from it all." Relax in the built-in sofa that borders the huge fireplace, and rediscover casual living at its most unique!
- The wide front deck is just as inviting. Partly covered, partly exposed, it provides the best of both sun and shade.
- Windows in the elevated roof dome high above the living room provide warm natural light all day long.
- The master bedroom enjoys a huge walk-in closet and its own private bath.
- Kitchen and utility rooms make use of the home's geometric shape. Each nook area is handled with maximum efficiency in mind.
- The open concept among the home's living, dining, conversation and deck areas makes this the perfect place for large- or small-scale entertaining.

Plan H-2

Bedrooms: 3	Baths: 2
Living Area:	
Main floor	1,664 sq. ft.
Total Living Area:	**1,664 sq. ft.**
Exterior Wall Framing:	2x4

Foundation Options:

Crawlspace

(All plans can be built with your choice of foundation and framing. A generic conversion diagram is available. See order form.)

BLUEPRINT PRICE CODE:	**B**

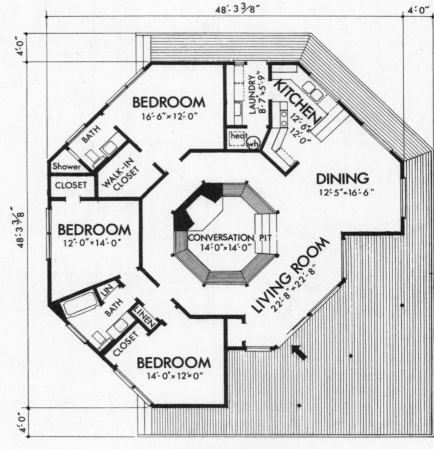

MAIN FLOOR

Plan H-2

Innovative Living

- This plan is decidedly contemporary in its exterior design; its interior layout, dropping six feet below the entry level, is both innovative and functional.
- The sidelighted, 18½-ft.-high entry issues a strong statement about the surprises that await inside.
- Brightened by a striking set of clerestory windows, the expansive family room is perfect as both a space for formal gatherings and informal football parties. A 15½-ft. sloped ceiling, a charming fireplace and a sliding glass door out to a covered patio highlight the space.
- Open to the living area, the U-shaped kitchen provides numerous amenities to indulge the family chef, including a tidy pantry closet and ample cupboard and counter space.
- A 15-ft. sloped ceiling tops the humongous master bedroom, which features a wall of windows, backyard access and a private bath.
- The secondary bedroom lies across the home, and accesses another full bath.

FRONT VIEW

Plan H-938-1A

Bedrooms: 2	Baths: 2
Living Area:	
Main floor	1,789 sq. ft.
Total Living Area:	**1,789 sq. ft.**
Garage	529 sq. ft.
Exterior Wall Framing:	2x6

Foundation Options:

Crawlspace
(All plans can be built with your choice of foundation and framing. A generic conversion diagram is available. See order form.)

BLUEPRINT PRICE CODE: B

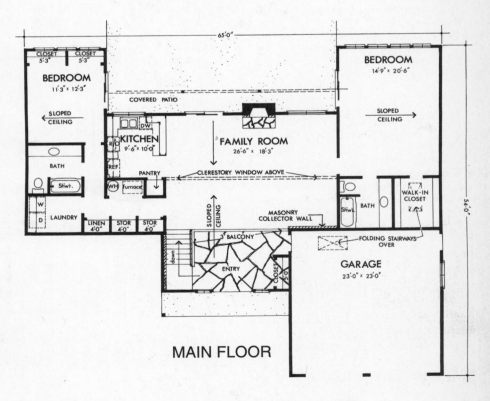

MAIN FLOOR

ORDER BLUEPRINTS ANYTIME!
CALL TOLL-FREE 1-800-820-1283

Plan H-938-1A

PRICES AND DETAILS
ON PAGES 2-5

105

Angled Solar Design

- This passive-solar design with a six-sided core is angled to capture as much sunlight as possible.
- Finished in natural vertical cedar planks and stone veneer, this contemporary three-bedroom requires a minimum of maintenance.
- Double doors at the entry open into the spacious living and dining areas.

- The formal area features a 14-ft. domed ceiling with skylights, a freestanding fireplace and three sets of sliding glass doors. The central sliding doors lead to a glass-enclosed sun room.
- The bright eat-in kitchen merges with the den, where sliding glass doors lead to one of three backyard terraces.
- The master bedroom, in the quiet sleeping wing, boasts ample closets, a private terrace and a luxurious bath, complete with a whirlpool tub.
- The two secondary bedrooms share a convenient hall bath.

Plan K-534-L

Bedrooms: 3	Baths: 2
Living Area:	
Main floor	1,647 sq. ft.
Total Living Area:	**1,647 sq. ft.**
Standard basement	1,505 sq. ft.
Garage	400 sq. ft.
Exterior Wall Framing:	2x4 or 2x6

Foundation Options:

Standard basement
Slab
(All plans can be built with your choice of foundation and framing. A generic conversion diagram is available. See order form.)

BLUEPRINT PRICE CODE: B

VIEW INTO LIVING ROOM AND DINING ROOM

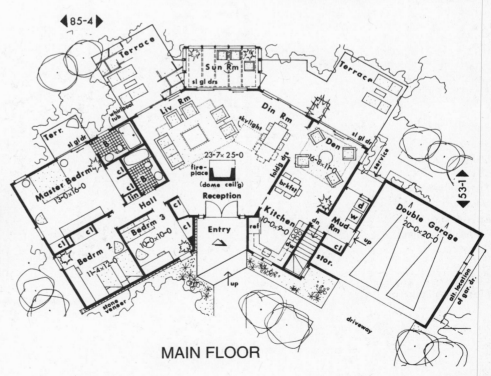

MAIN FLOOR

ORDER BLUEPRINTS ANYTIME!
CALL TOLL-FREE 1-800-820-1283

Plan K-534-L

PRICES AND DETAILS
ON PAGES 2-5

Modern Charmer

- This attractive plan combines country-style charm with a modern floor plan.
- The central foyer ushers guests past a study and on into the huge living room, which is highlighted by an 11-ft. ceiling, a corner fireplace and access to a big, covered backyard porch.
- An angled snack bar joins the living room to the bayed nook and the efficient kitchen. The formal dining room is easily reached from the kitchen and the foyer. A utility room and a half-bath are just off the garage entrance.
- The master suite, isolated for privacy, boasts a magnificent bath with a garden tub, a separate shower, double vanities and two walk-in closets.
- Two more bedrooms are located on the opposite side of the home and are separated by a hall bath.
- Ceilings in all rooms are at least 9 ft. high for added spaciousness.

Plan VL-2069

Bedrooms: 3	Baths: 2½
Living Area:	
Main floor	2,069 sq. ft.
Total Living Area:	**2,069 sq. ft.**
Garage	460 sq. ft.
Exterior Wall Framing:	2×4

Foundation Options:

Crawlspace
Slab
(All plans can be built with your choice of foundation and framing. A generic conversion diagram is available. See order form.)

BLUEPRINT PRICE CODE: C

REAR VIEW

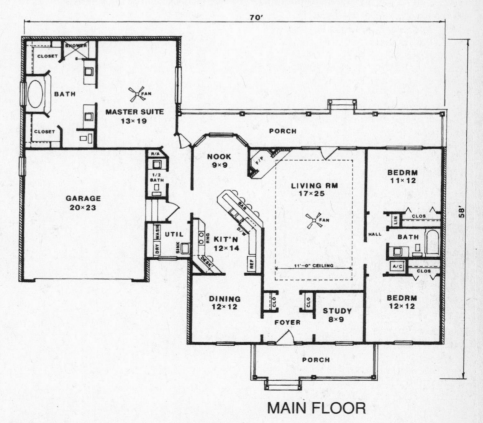

MAIN FLOOR

ORDER BLUEPRINTS ANYTIME!
CALL TOLL-FREE 1-800-820-1283

Plan VL-2069

PRICES AND DETAILS
ON PAGES 2-5

103

Character Plus Warmth

- The warmth and character provided by the cozy sun room enhances the flavor and appeal of this contemporary one-story design.
- In from the double-door entry, the combined living and dining room unfolds in splendor. Topped by a 14-ft. vaulted ceiling and accessing the sun room, this space will be the setting of many special times to come.
- Relax at the end of a long day in the spacious family room. A wonderful woodstove, as well as a cup of hot cocoa served from the nearby kitchen, help erase your winter chill.
- Many nights of sweet dreams lie ahead in the pleasant master bedroom. It boasts a large walk-in closet and a charming private bath.
- Two identically sized bedrooms, each with a boxed-out window, share another full bath

Plans H-3720-1 & -1A

Bedrooms: 3	Baths: 2½
Living Area:	
Main floor	2,034 sq. ft.
Sun room	159 sq. ft.
Total Living Area:	**2,193 sq. ft.**
Standard basement	2,034 sq. ft.
Garage	551 sq. ft.
Exterior Wall Framing:	2x6
Foundation Options:	**Plan #**
Standard basement	H-3720-1
Crawlspace	H-3720-1A

(All plans can be built with your choice of foundation and framing. A generic conversion diagram is available. See order form.)

BLUEPRINT PRICE CODE:	**C**

REAR VIEW

MAIN FLOOR

STAIRWAY AREA IN CRAWLSPACE VERSION

PLAN H-2107-1B

Solarium for a Sloping Lot

- Experience the cheer of solarium living and the environmentally responsible economics of passive-solar heat in this exclusive, moderately sized home.
- Depending upon the slope of your lot, this design can be adapted to fit.
- Use the two-story solarium as an exercise room, a conservatory for exotic plants, or a craft space.
- Living, dining, and entry areas meet and merge in a way that makes the home's living space seem even larger. Vaulted ceilings span the entire complex of rooms, giving them volume.
- Finish the basement according to your needs. Develop another bedroom there, or customize for hobbies.
- The master bedroom has a 7-ft. closet.
- Balconies abound, and the slanted front entry gable only adds to the intrigue of this home's dramatic lines.

Plans H-2107-1 & -1B

Bedrooms: 3	Baths: 2
Living Area:	
Main floor	1,505 sq. ft.
Basement	779 sq. ft.
Total Living Area:	**2,284 sq. ft.**
Tuck-under garage/storage	600 sq. ft.
Exterior Wall Framing:	2x6
Foundation Options:	**Plan #**
Daylight basement	H-2107-1B
Standard basement	H-2107-1

(All plans can be built with your choice of foundation and framing. A generic conversion diagram is available. See order form.)

BLUEPRINT PRICE CODE:	**C**

PLAN H-2107-1

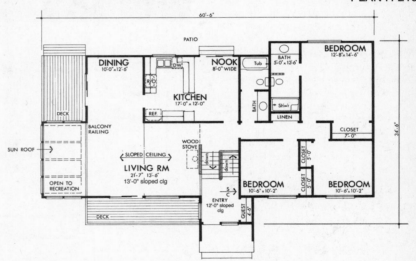

MAIN FLOOR

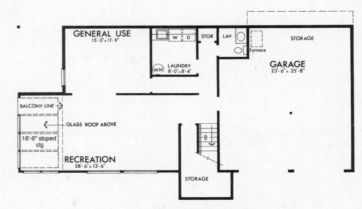

BASEMENT

Plans H-2107-1 & -1B

PRICES AND DETAILS
ON PAGES 2-5

Classic Country-Style

- At the center of this rustic country-style home is an enormous living room with a flat beamed ceiling and a massive stone fireplace. A sunny patio and a covered rear porch are just steps away.
- The adjoining eating area and kitchen provide plenty of room for casual dining and meal preparation. The eating area is visually enhanced by a 14-ft. sloped ceiling with false beams. The kitchen includes a snack bar, a pantry closet and a built-in spice cabinet.
- The formal dining room gets plenty of pizzazz from a stone-faced wall and an arched planter facing the living room.
- The secluded master suite has it all, including a private bath, a separate dressing area and a large walk-in closet with built-in shelves.
- The two remaining bedrooms have big closets and easy access to a full bath.

Plan E-1808	
Bedrooms: 3	**Baths:** 2
Living Area:	
Main floor	1,800 sq. ft.
Total Living Area:	**1,800 sq. ft.**
Garage	605 sq. ft.
Exterior Wall Framing:	2x4

Foundation Options:
Crawlspace
Slab
(All plans can be built with your choice of foundation and framing. A generic conversion diagram is available. See order form.)

BLUEPRINT PRICE CODE:	B

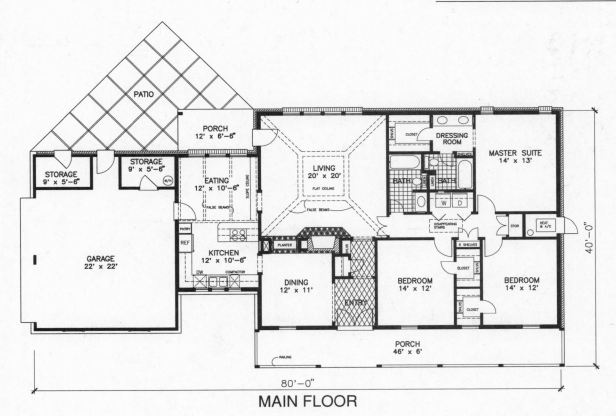

MAIN FLOOR

Plan E-1808

PRICES AND DETAILS ON PAGES 2-5

All Good Things

- This stone-sturdy home pleases the eye with a rustic, country facade and a multitude of interior luxuries.
- Designed with your loved ones in mind, the family room, island kitchen and bayed breakfast nook flow into each other for a feeling of togetherness. From the nook, a huge backyard deck is quickly accessible.

- For formal gatherings, the living and dining rooms serve effortlessly.
- The master suite epitomizes comfort, with its private deck and adjoining office space. Opulence is apparent in the master bath, which features a spa tub and two walk-in closets.
- A stunning guest suite delivers a private deck and a kitchen area. With its full bath, it's the perfect spot for relatives who are enjoying their golden years.

Plan DD-3152

Bedrooms: 3+	**Baths:** 3½
Living Area:	
Main floor	3,152 sq. ft.
Total Living Area:	**3,152 sq. ft.**
Standard basement	3,152 sq. ft.
Garage	610 sq. ft.
Exterior Wall Framing:	2x4
Foundation Options:	
Standard basement	
Crawlspace	
Slab	

(All plans can be built with your choice of foundation and framing. A generic conversion diagram is available. See order form.)

BLUEPRINT PRICE CODE: E

MAIN FLOOR

116² · 67¹¹

DECK · BRKFST. 13⁶ X 9⁶ 9⁰ CLG · DECK · KITCHEN UNIT · DECK

M. BATH 9⁰ CLG · WIC · SPA · WIC

MASTER SUITE 12⁴ X 18⁶ 11⁰ CLG · OFFICE/ MEDIA/ BR.4 13⁰ X 12⁰ 9⁰ CLG · LIVING 16⁰ X 19⁶ 11⁰ CLG · ISLAND KITCHEN 12⁰ X 13⁶ 9⁰ CLG · PANTRY · FAMILY 14² X 19⁰ 9⁰ CLG · SITTING 8⁰ X 11⁴ 9⁰ CLG · GUEST SUITE 13⁰ X 14⁸ 9⁰ CLG

NICHE · WIC · NICHE · LINEN · WIC · BATH

BEDRM 2 11⁸ X 12¹⁰ 9⁰ CLG · BATH 2 · LINEN · STUDY/ BEDRM 3 12⁸ X 13² 11⁰ CLG · ENTRY 11⁰ CLG · DINING 12⁰ X 15² 11⁰ CLG · UTIL. · STAIRS DOWN · STORAGE · PWDR.

PORCH · SERVICE PORCH · COATS

3-CAR GARAGE 23⁰ X 26⁰

Surrounded by Ease and Light

- For your great escapes, why not escape conventionality altogether, and discover an entirely new kind of living? This octagonal design highlights an easy-living floor plan with clerestory windows in its layered roof.
- Kitchen, dining, and living areas address one another for flow and simplicity.

- Each bedroom enjoys access to a bath and a different view to the outdoors.
- The kitchen lies near a laundry room, plus pantry space, for utility efficiency.
- The living room's circular configuration is instantly cozy. A wide deck overlook gives it focus in the daytime; a huge fireplace gives it ambience at night.
- Order this plan with a basement, and double the size of your living area; customize the space as a relaxing recreation room, using a second fireplace as your anchor.

Plans H-821-1 & -1A	
Bedrooms: 3	**Baths:** 2½
Living Area:	
Main floor	1,699 sq. ft.
Total Living Area:	**1,699 sq. ft.**
Daylight basement	1,699 sq. ft.
Exterior Wall Framing:	2x4
Foundation Options:	**Plan #**
Daylight basement	H-821-1
Crawlspace	H-821-1A

(All plans can be built with your choice of foundation and framing. A generic conversion diagram is available. See order form.)

BLUEPRINT PRICE CODE: B

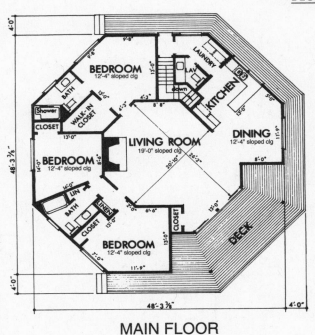

MAIN FLOOR

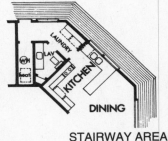

STAIRWAY AREA IN CRAWLSPACE VERSION

Plans H-821-1 & -1A

PRICES AND DETAILS ON PAGES 2-5

Aura of Calm

- With its simple floor plan and inviting facade, this home exudes an aura of calm and contentment.
- The quiet front porch allows plenty of room for a rocker or swing, and recalls nostalgic days of simpler living.
- Double doors introduce a long foyer that leads straight to the central living room. Here, a trio of skylights paints the room with natural light. A fireplace is paired with built-in shelves for books and favorite board games. Sliding glass

doors open to a wood deck just waiting to host a backyard barbecue!
- The kitchen boasts many modern touches, including a lazy Susan pantry and a unique circular island. Double doors swing inward to reveal a sweet porch, where you may instruct the dairy man to leave your weekly order.
- You'll find the master bedroom to be a desirable getaway. A cathedral ceiling tops the sleeping space, as well as the bath. Here, two walk-in closets await, in addition to a stunning whirlpool tub and an eye-opening shower.

Plan J-9304	
Bedrooms: 3+	**Baths:** 2
Living Area:	
Main floor	1,878 sq. ft.
Total Living Area:	**1,878 sq. ft.**
Upper floor (future area)	500 sq. ft.
Standard basement	1,878 sq. ft.
Garage and storage	595 sq. ft.
Exterior Wall Framing:	2x4

Foundation Options:

Standard basement
Crawlspace
Slab
(All plans can be built with your choice of foundation and framing. A generic conversion diagram is available. See order form.)

BLUEPRINT PRICE CODE:	**B**

MAIN FLOOR

58-0

Garage
22-6~22-3

Wood Deck
18-0~18-0

Porch

Laun.

Stor.

Brkfst.
9-5~8-6

Master
Bedroom
13-5~16-4
11-9 clg.

Bedroom
12-2~11-0

Living
16-10~17-1
9-0 clg.

Bath

Kitchen

12-8~14-3

M.Bath

Bedroom
12-2~10-7

Foyer
9-0 clg.

Dining
12-1~13-7
9-0 clg.

Porch

13-5~15-9

11-9 clg.

Porch
22-0~6-5

70-8

UPPER FLOOR

Future
16-8~7-6

Future
17-6~21-7

Shady Porches, Sunny Patio

- Designed with stylish country looks, this attractive one-story also has shady porches and a sunny patio for relaxed indoor/outdoor living.
- The inviting foyer flows into the spacious living room, which is warmed by a handsome fireplace.
- The adjoining dining room has a door to a screened-in porch, which opens to the

backyard and serves as a breezeway to the nearby garage
- The U-shaped kitchen has a pantry closet and plenty of counter space. Around the corner, a space-efficient laundry/utility room exits to a big backyard patio.
- The master bedroom is brightened by windows on two sides and includes a wardrobe closet. The compartmentalized master bath offers a separate dressing area and a walk-in closet.
- Another full bath serves two additional good-sized bedrooms.

Plan C-7557	
Bedrooms: 3	**Baths:** 2
Living Area:	
Main floor	1,688 sq. ft.
Total Living Area:	**1,688 sq. ft.**
Daylight basement	1,688 sq. ft.
Garage	400 sq. ft.
Exterior Wall Framing:	2x4
Foundation Options:	
Daylight basement	
Crawlspace	
Slab	

(All plans can be built with your choice of foundation and framing. A generic conversion diagram is available. See order form.)

BLUEPRINT PRICE CODE: **B**

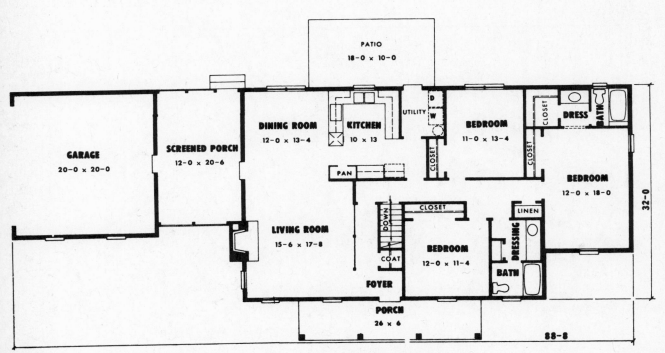

MAIN FLOOR

Plan C-7557

**PRICES AND DETAILS
ON PAGES 2-5**

Sun-Splashed One-Story

- This unique angled design offers spectacular backyard views, a delightful sun room and two enticing terraces.
- The reception hall opens to the huge combination living and dining area, which is enhanced by a 13½-ft.-high ceiling. A stone fireplace and walls of glass add to the expansive look and the inviting atmosphere.

- The adjoining family room, kitchen and nook are just as appealing. The family room features a built-in entertainment center and sliding glass doors that access the energy-saving sun room. The comfortable kitchen has a handy snack counter facing the sunny dinette.
- The sleeping wing offers three bedrooms and two baths. The master suite boasts a 13½-ft. sloped ceiling, a private terrace, a large walk-in closet and a personal bath with a whirlpool tub. The two remaining bedrooms are just steps away from another full bath.

Plan AHP-9330

Bedrooms: 3	Baths: 2
Living Area:	
Main floor	1,626 sq. ft.
Sun room	146 sq. ft.
Total Living Area:	**1,772 sq. ft.**
Standard basement	1,542 sq. ft.
Garage	427 sq. ft.
Exterior Wall Framing:	2x4 or 2x6

Foundation Options:
Standard basement
Crawlspace
Slab
(All plans can be built with your choice of foundation and framing. A generic conversion diagram is available. See order form.)

BLUEPRINT PRICE CODE:	B

MAIN FLOOR

Creative Luxury

- A stunning facade and a creative floor plan combine to produce a truly luxurious home.
- The 17-ft., 10-in.-high foyer is flanked by a den with a nearby full bath, and the sunken formal dining room. Both rooms offer 13-ft. ceilings.
- Straight ahead, the sunken living room is topped by a 13-ft. ceiling and offers access to a covered patio through sliding glass doors. A summer kitchen services the patio on warm evenings.
- Patio access through sliding glass doors enhances the master bedroom.
- Twin walk-in closets with plant shelves above line the path to the sunken master bath. Here, amenities include a raised tub and a glass-block shower.
- Connected to the living room by a wet bar, the open kitchen is bordered by a quaint breakfast nook. From the nook, French and sliding doors open to the summer kitchen and patio.
- A beautiful fireplace warms the family room, while window-lined walls let in cheery sunlight.
- Two large secondary bedrooms flaunt exotic plant shelves and private access to a split bath.
- Unless otherwise noted, all rooms have 11-ft. ceilings.

Plan HDS-99-237

Bedrooms: 3+	Baths: 3
Living Area:	
Main floor	2,636 sq. ft.
Total Living Area:	**2,636 sq. ft.**
Garage	536 sq. ft.
Exterior Wall Framing:	8-in. concrete block

Foundation Options:

Slab
(All plans can be built with your choice of foundation and framing. A generic conversion diagram is available. See order form.)

BLUEPRINT PRICE CODE: D

MAIN FLOOR

Rustic Ranch Appeal

- Multiple gables, wood siding and shingles, and trapezoid windows with heavy beam details give this ranch a rustic yet contemporary appeal.
- The dramatic foyer is bathed in sun from the transom windows, and overlooks the vaulted living room, with its fireplace and open stairwell.
- The island kitchen opens to the breakfast room and beyond to the rear deck, where a greenhouse may be positioned.
- The kitchen is designed to handle more than one cook! A step-in pantry is close by.
- The sleeping wing incorporates three bedrooms and two full baths. The master suite features sliding glass doors to a private balcony.
- The daylight basement may be finished to provide a recreation room, plus two additional bedrooms and storage galore!

Plan AX-98053

Bedrooms: 5	Baths: 3
Living Area:	
Main floor	1,724 sq. ft.
Daylight basement (finished)	766 sq. ft.
Total Living Area:	**2,490 sq. ft.**
Daylight basement (unfinished)	881 sq. ft.
Garage	455 sq. ft.
Exterior Wall Framing:	2x4

Foundation Options:

Daylight basement

(All plans can be built with your choice of foundation and framing. A generic conversion diagram is available. See order form.)

BLUEPRINT PRICE CODE:	C

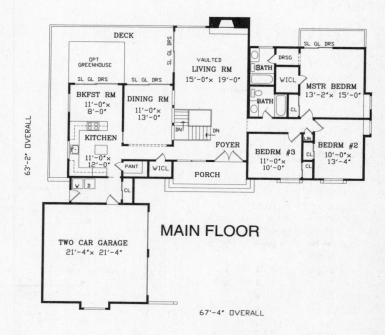

MAIN FLOOR

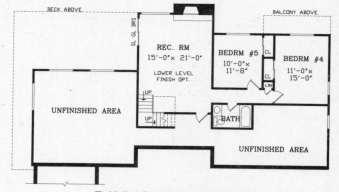

DAYLIGHT BASEMENT

Escape to the Outdoors

- Merge yourself with the outdoors in this gorgeous design! A huge wraparound deck lets you enjoy the sunshine any time of day.
- Just past the entry, you'll find an enormous living room/dining room area that's ideal for entertaining large crowds. When it's just you two, snuggle up by the cozy fireplace.
- Another spacious gathering spot is the family room. Sliding glass doors lead from both areas to the incredible deck.
- Between the family room and the dining room is the well-equipped kitchen.
- The master suite boasts a walk-in closet and a private bath.
- Below, the daylight basement offers a nice-sized recreation room, a full bath and room for future expansion.
- The daylight basement has two foundation versions: wood-framed (H-2083-1B) or concrete (H-2083-1).

BASEMENT STAIRWAY LOCATION

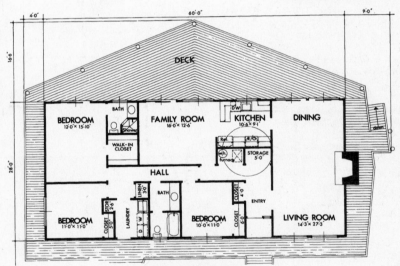

REAR VIEW

Plans H-2083-1, -1A & -1B	
Bedrooms: 3	**Baths:** 2-3
Living Area:	
Main floor	1,660 sq. ft.
Daylight basement	1,660 sq. ft.
Total Living Area:	**1,660/3,320 sq. ft.**
Garage	541 sq. ft.
Exterior Wall Framing:	2x4
Foundation Options:	**Plan #**
Daylight basement (concrete)	H-2083-1
Daylight basement (wood)	H-2083-1B
Crawlspace	H-2083-1A
(All plans can be built with your choice of foundation and framing. A generic conversion diagram is available. See order form.)	
BLUEPRINT PRICE CODE:	B/E

MAIN FLOOR

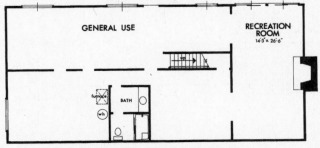

DAYLIGHT BASEMENT

Plans H-2083-1, -1A & -1B

PRICES AND DETAILS ON PAGES 2-5

Breezy Beauty

- A nostalgic covered front porch, a backyard deck and a sprawling screened porch combine to make this beautiful one-story home a breezy delight.
- The front entry opens into the Great Room, which is crowned by a soaring 12-ft.-high cathedral ceiling. A handsome fireplace is flanked by built-in bookshelves and cabinets.
- The large, bayed dining room offers a 9-ft. tray ceiling and deck access through French doors.

- The adjoining kitchen boasts plenty of counter space and a handy built-in recipe desk.
- From the kitchen, a side door leads to the screened porch. A wood floor and deck access highlight this cheery room.
- A quiet hall leads past a convenient utility room to the sleeping quarters.
- The secluded master bedroom is enhanced by a spacious walk-in closet. The private master bath includes a lovely garden tub, a separate shower and dual vanities.
- Two more bedrooms with walk-in closets share a hall bath.

Plan C-8905

Bedrooms: 3	Baths: 2
Living Area:	
Main floor	1,811 sq. ft.
Total Living Area:	**1,811 sq. ft.**
Screened porch	240 sq. ft.
Daylight basement	1,811 sq. ft.
Garage	484 sq. ft.
Exterior Wall Framing:	2x4

Foundation Options:

Daylight basement
Crawlspace
(All plans can be built with your choice of foundation and framing. A generic conversion diagram is available. See order form.)

BLUEPRINT PRICE CODE: **B**

MAIN FLOOR

DECK 28-0 x 12-0

BATH — GARDEN TUB — SHOWER

BEDROOM 2 11-0 x 13-6

WALK-IN CLOSET

DINING 12-0 x 13-6 TRAY CEILING

DW · SINK · S UNIT · REFG · OVEN

KITCHEN 10-0 x 13-6 · DESK · PANTRY

SCR. PORCH 12-0 x 20-0

GARAGE 22-0 x 22-0

DRY · WASH

UTILITY

MASTER BEDROOM 12-0 x 18-0

HALL

BATH · LINEN

DESK · COATS · DOWN

CATHEDRAL CEILING W/ FALSE BEAMS

BOOKS

BEDROOM 3 12-0 x 11-4

WALK-IN CLOSET

GREAT ROOM 19-0 x 17-6

HEARTH · BOOKS

PORCH 25-0 x 6-0

50-0

38-4

89-6

Open Invitation

- The wide front porch of this friendly country farmhouse presents an open invitation to all who visit.
- Highlighted by a round-topped transom, the home's entrance opens directly into the spacious living room, which features a warm fireplace flanked by windows.
- The adjoining dining area is enhanced by a lovely bay window and is easily serviced by the updated kitchen's angled snack bar.
- A bright sun room off the kitchen provides a great space for informal meals or relaxation. Access to a covered backyard porch is nearby.
- The good-sized master bedroom is secluded from the other sleeping areas. The lavish master bath includes a garden tub, a separate shower, a dual-sink vanity and a walk-in closet.
- Two more bedrooms share a second full bath. A laundry/utility room is nearby.
- An additional 1,007 sq. ft. of living space can be made available by finishing the upper floor.
- All ceilings are 9 ft. high for added spaciousness.

Plan J-91078

Bedrooms: 3	**Baths: 2**

Living Area:

Main floor	1,846 sq. ft.
Total Living Area:	**1,846 sq. ft.**
Future upper floor	1,007 sq. ft.
Standard basement	1,846 sq. ft.
Garage	484 sq. ft.

Exterior Wall Framing:	2x6

Foundation Options:

Standard basement
Crawlspace
Slab
(All plans can be built with your choice of foundation and framing. A generic conversion diagram is available. See order form.)

BLUEPRINT PRICE CODE:	**B**

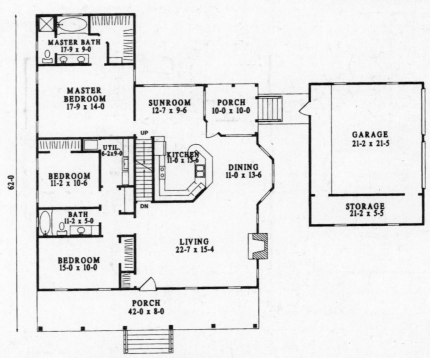

MAIN FLOOR

Plan J-91078

Outdoor Surprises!

- A private entry courtyard topped by an intricate trellis draws attention to this beautiful brick home.
- The drama continues inside, where you'll find high ceilings, sprawling openness and breathtaking views of the many outdoor living spaces.
- The central hearth room is a great spot to welcome your guests and keep them entertained with its dazzling fireplace and media center combination.
- Appetizers and refreshments can be served at the long snack bar extending from the triangular kitchen.
- Plenty of space for formal mingling is offered in the spacious living and dining room expanse beyond. The screened porch, adjoining patio and panoramic views will inspire hours of conversation.
- Ideal for the empty nester, this home includes two private bedroom suites. The master suite boasts his-and-hers closets, vanities and toilets.
- The studio at the front of the home could also serve as an extra bedroom or home office.

Plan EOF-86-B

Bedrooms: 2+	Baths: 2½
Living Area:	
Main floor	1,830 sq. ft.
Total Living Area:	**1,830 sq. ft.**
Screened porch	134 sq. ft.
Garage	433 sq. ft.
Exterior Wall Framing:	2x4

Foundation Options:

Slab
(All plans can be built with your choice of foundation and framing. A generic conversion diagram is available. See order form.)

BLUEPRINT PRICE CODE: B

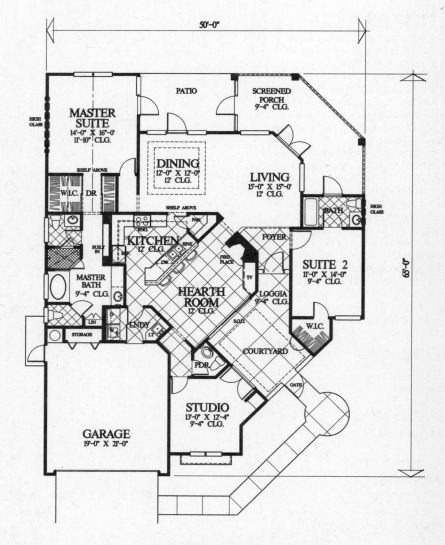

MAIN FLOOR

Affordable
Charm

- An inviting columned porch introduces this affordable home.
- Inside, soaring ceilings and attention to detail highlight the efficient floor plan.
- The foyer leads to an eat-in kitchen, which includes a handy built-in pantry. A great 10-ft. ceiling enhances this sunny space.
- A convenient serving counter connects the kitchen to the open dining room. A beautiful bay window is topped by a half-round transom.
- The adjacent living room features an energy-efficient fireplace and French-door access to an inviting rear deck.
- A dramatic 14-ft. vaulted ceiling soars above the living and dining rooms.
- The spacious master bedroom boasts a striking 11-ft. vaulted ceiling, a large walk-in closet and private access to the hall bath.
- Two additional bedrooms and a linen closet round out the floor plan.

Plan B-93015

Bedrooms: 3	Baths: 1
Living Area:	
Main floor	1,227 sq. ft.
Total Living Area:	**1,227 sq. ft.**
Standard basement	1,217 sq. ft.
Garage	385 sq. ft.
Exterior Wall Framing:	2x6

Foundation Options:

Standard basement

(All plans can be built with your choice of foundation and framing. A generic conversion diagram is available. See order form.)

BLUEPRINT PRICE CODE: A

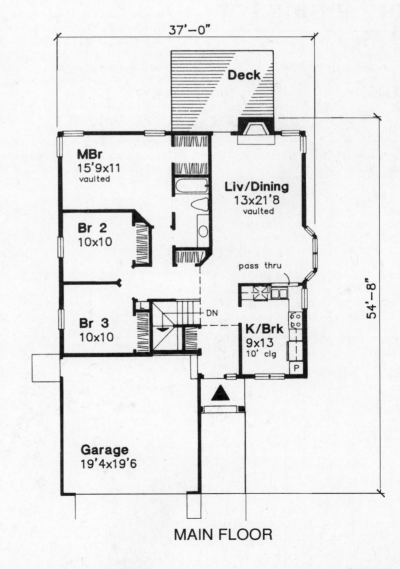

MAIN FLOOR

Plan B-93015

PRICES AND DETAILS
ON PAGES 2-5

Comfy Home for Sloping Lot

- This contemporary plan was especially designed to deliver comfort and stability to almost any sloping lot.
- The entry gains spacial variety from the double doors and the open balustrade on the staircase that leads up to the living spaces on the main floor.
- Here, a generous-sized living room is separated from the entry by a massive fireplace. Wraparound windows offer a view to the front of the home.

- The dining room is tucked into a corner of the main floor, thus maintaining its own identity. It is open on one end to the living room for extra seating when the holidays an require extended table. Sliding glass doors open to a rear deck.
- Down one level, the master suite has a sunny window seat and a private bath. Two secondary bedrooms share a full hall bath.
- In the daylight basement, a recreation room contains a fireplace and functions as a playroom for your kids or as extra entertainment space when friends visit.
- A double garage is included in both foundation versions of this plan.

Plans H-2045-4 & -4A

Bedrooms: 3+	**Baths: 2½-3½**

Living Area:	
Main floor	1,516 sq. ft.
Daylight basement	1,034 sq. ft.
Total Living Area:	**1,516/2,550 sq. ft.**
Tuck-under garage	429 sq. ft.
Exterior Wall Framing:	**2x6**
Foundation Options:	**Plan #**
Daylight basement	H-2045-4
Crawlspace	H-2045-4A

(All plans can be built with your choice of foundation and framing. A generic conversion diagram is available. See order form.)

BLUEPRINT PRICE CODE:	**B/D**

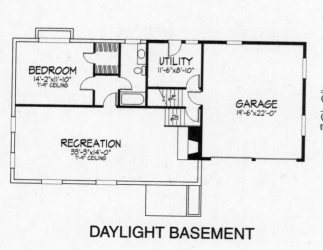

DAYLIGHT BASEMENT

MAIN FLOOR

Emphasis on Accessibility

- Designed with special or changing family needs in mind, this charming, affordably sized cottage home is fully handicapped-accessible.
- The inviting covered entrance opens into the bright and airy living room. Enhanced by a 12-ft. vaulted ceiling, the living room also boasts dramatic corner windows and a warm fireplace.
- The adjoining kitchen shares the living room's vaulted ceiling and features a cleverly designed serving counter with knee space below. Sliding glass doors open to a backyard patio or deck. This outside area could be adapted for wheelchair use by adding a ramp.
- The master bedroom includes an oversized walk-in closet and a bright sitting area with a 10½-ft. raised ceiling. The master bath has a handicapped-accessible shower.
- The two secondary bedrooms share a second full bath. A neat laundry closet is convenient to each of the bedrooms.

Plan B-92017

Bedrooms: 3	Baths: 2

Living Area:	
Main floor	1,180 sq. ft.
Total Living Area:	**1,180 sq. ft.**
Exterior Wall Framing:	2x6

Foundation Options:

Slab

(All plans can be built with your choice of foundation and framing. A generic conversion diagram is available. See order form.)

BLUEPRINT PRICE CODE: **A**

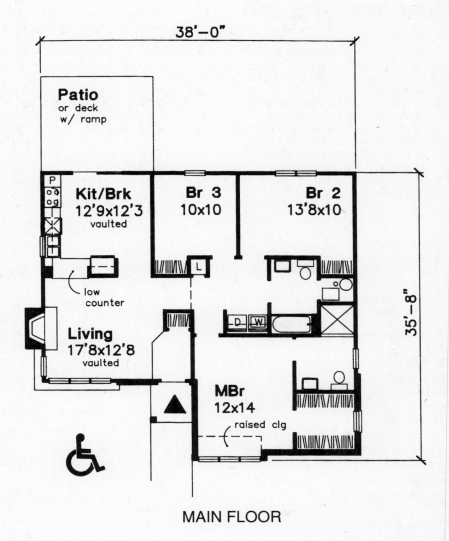

MAIN FLOOR

Plan B-92017

PRICES AND DETAILS
ON PAGES 2-5

Sunny Breakfast Porch

- The charm of yesteryear's front porch is brought into contemporary focus with this design's unique sun porch/breakfast room. What a glorious spot to greet each new day!

- This stylish home offers other dramatic spaces, including a large vaulted living and dining room combination. From the entryway, you can view the massive corner fireplace, the rear deck through sliding glass doors and the railed stairway to the basement.

- The master bedroom is also vaulted and boasts its own deck access. Double walk-in closets and a private bath with a plant shelf and a garden tub are other extras you'll come to appreciate.

- A nearby secondary bedroom would make a great nursery or child's room for young families. Singles and empty nesters might turn this space into a cozy den for casual relaxing.

- Sunny weather begs you to step out to the rear deck and fire up the barbecue.

Plan B-86136

Bedrooms: 1+	Baths: 2
Living Area:	
Main floor	1,421 sq. ft.
Total Living Area:	**1,421 sq. ft.**
Standard basement	1,421 sq. ft.
Garage	400 sq. ft.
Exterior Wall Framing:	2x4

Foundation Options:

Standard basement

(All plans can be built with your choice of foundation and framing. A generic conversion diagram is available. See order form.)

BLUEPRINT PRICE CODE: A

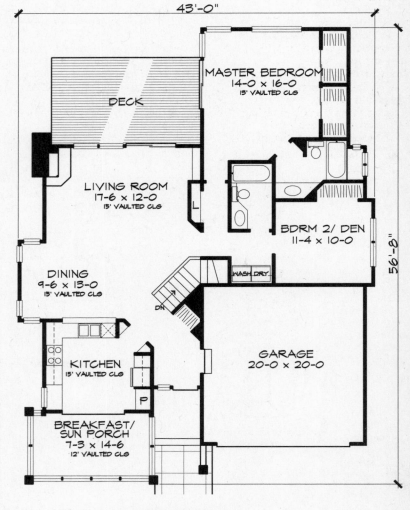

MAIN FLOOR

43'-0"

56'-8"

DECK

MASTER BEDROOM
14-0 x 16-0
15' VAULTED CLG

LIVING ROOM
17-6 x 12-0
15' VAULTED CLG

BDRM 2/ DEN
11-4 x 10-0

DINING
9-6 x 13-0
15' VAULTED CLG

WASH DRY

DN

KITCHEN
15' VAULTED CLG

GARAGE
20-0 x 20-0

P

BREAKFAST/
SUN PORCH
7-3 x 14-6
12' VAULTED CLG

No Place Like Home

- An arched transom window, a louvered vent over the garage and a smart side deck demonstrate why there is no place like this one-story home.
- The living areas flank the foyer to the right, while the bedrooms lie down a straight hallway ahead.
- Flowing together for an open feeling, the living room and dining room overlook the deck; sliding glass doors in the dining room provide access. Built-in bookshelves and a fireplace lend warm character, and a 3-ft. wall separates this area from the hallway.
- The kitchen is blessed with a windowed sink, plenty of counter space and a pantry for extra storage.
- An eating bar serves well for casual meals and after-school snacks.
- To the back of the home, the master suite features a private bath and a large walk-in closet.
- Two secondary bedrooms share a hall bath nearby. Each room provides ample closet space.

Plans U-87-102A & -102B	
Bedrooms: 3	**Baths:** 2
Living Area:	
Main floor (crawlspace version)	1,326 sq. ft.
Main floor (basement version)	1,374 sq. ft.
Total Living Area:	**1,326/1,374 sq. ft.**
Standard basement	1,348 sq. ft.
Garage	492 sq. ft.
Exterior Wall Framing:	2x4 or 2x6
Foundation Options:	**Plan #**
Standard basement	U-87-102B
Crawlspace	U-87-102A

(All plans can be built with your choice of foundation and framing. A generic conversion diagram is available. See order form.)

BLUEPRINT PRICE CODE: **A**

BASEMENT STAIRWAY LOCATION

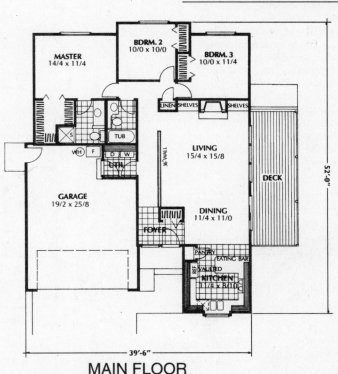

MAIN FLOOR

Plans U-87-102A & -102B

PRICES AND DETAILS
ON PAGES 2-5

Open Forum

- This home's combined living and dining area provides a restful place for both stimulating conversation and elegant dining with friends and family.
- A corner fireplace casts a flickering glow near the exit to the backyard deck, where there's plenty of room to relax on brisk fall nights. You can almost hear the geese as they wing southward!
- If you're a budding entrepreneur, you'll appreciate the quiet den. There's enough room for your computer, fax machine and filing cabinets. A closet lets you use the room to sleep overnight guests or welcome a newborn addition to the family in style.
- In the master bedroom, a cozy window seat may prove to be a favorite spot to soak up the early morning sun with a cup of gourmet brew. A private bath makes this room the perfect hideaway.
- Summer evenings take on an extra special feel when they're enjoyed on the front porch. Feel free to kick back and thumb through the latest issue of your favorite magazine while the neighbors quietly stroll by.

Plan B-86126

Bedrooms: 2+	Baths: 2
Living Area:	
Main floor	1,270 sq. ft.
Total Living Area:	**1,270 sq. ft.**
Standard basement	1,270 sq. ft.
Garage	385 sq. ft.
Exterior Wall Framing:	2x4

Foundation Options:

Standard basement

(All plans can be built with your choice of foundation and framing. A generic conversion diagram is available. See order form.)

BLUEPRINT PRICE CODE: A

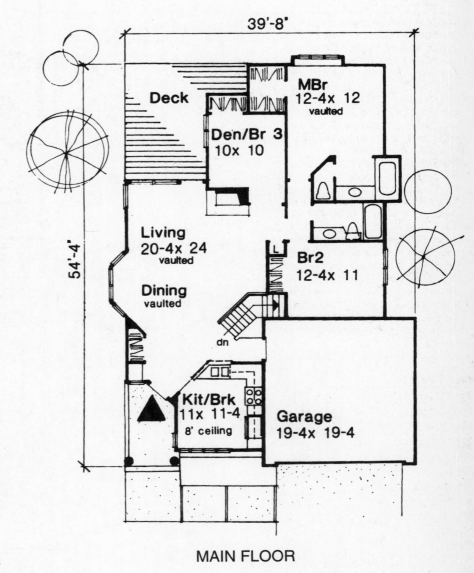

MAIN FLOOR

Eclectic Fun

- Staggered garage doors and a nostalgic front porch give this home's facade an eclectic flavor. Inside, a fun floor plan keeps boredom at bay.
- Central to the free-flowing interior are the Great Room and the adjoining dining room, where cozy fireside gatherings and exquisite meals are practically guaranteed! A boxed-out window arrangement gives great views of a patio in the side yard.
- The kitchen's raised eating bar serves double duty as a pass-through when the food is piping hot and ready to eat! Bright windows above the sink bathe the room in natural light.
- Spoil yourself with a cup of Darjeeling tea in the master bedroom's sitting area, which overlooks a cute courtyard. The refreshing shower and the twin vanities in the skylighted master bath ease preparation for special evening events.
- Is sewing your favorite hobby? Pursue it avidly at the sewing table in the large utility room, while enjoying the colorful courtyard.
- All rooms are enhanced by 9-ft. ceilings.

Plan S-82694

Bedrooms: 3	Baths: 2
Living Area:	
Main floor	1,441 sq. ft.
Total Living Area:	**1,441 sq. ft.**
Standard basement	1,381 sq. ft.
Garage	458 sq. ft.
Exterior Wall Framing:	2x6

Foundation Options:

Standard basement
Crawlspace
Slab

(All plans can be built with your choice of foundation and framing. A generic conversion diagram is available. See order form.)

BLUEPRINT PRICE CODE:	**A**

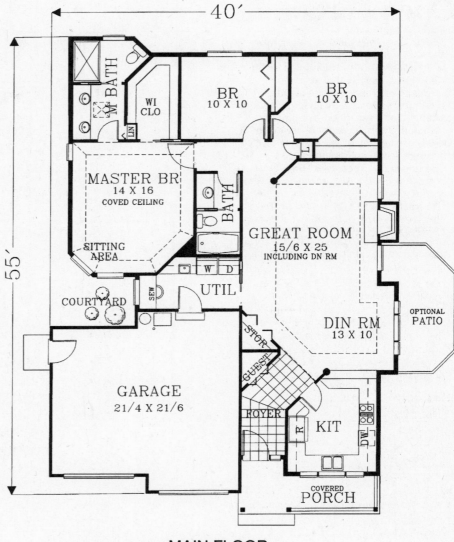

MAIN FLOOR

Plan S-82694

PRICES AND DETAILS
ON PAGES 2-5

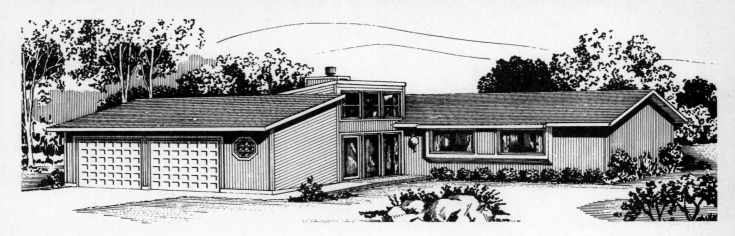

Cost-Conscious

- This modest, three-bedroom plan offers many amenities and is designed as a primary residence or a vacation home.
- A sunny, vaulted entry soars to a height of 15 ft., 9 in. and is brightened by large clerestory windows that also add architectural interest to the facade.
- The entry leads into the generous living room, which is warmed by a fireplace. The living room and dining area flow together to give you the space you need for large-scale entertaining.
- Down the hall, the master suite boasts a large closet and a private bath that's a must for today's busy families.
- The two secondary bedrooms each include a cozy window seat. What a wonderful spot for reading a bedtime story to young children. Older kids and teenagers will love having a quiet place that's all their own.
- The secondary bedrooms have easy access to a skylighted hall bath. Sun splashes across the nearby utility room through another skylight, adding a touch of cheer to laundry chores.
- The garage has a windowed storage area you might use as a workshop.

Plan H-1436-1A

Bedrooms: 3	Baths: 2
Living Area:	
Main floor	1,086 sq. ft.
Total Living Area:	**1,086 sq. ft.**
Garage and storage	543 sq. ft.
Exterior Wall Framing:	2x6

Foundation Options:

Crawlspace
(All plans can be built with your choice of foundation and framing. A generic conversion diagram is available. See order form.)

BLUEPRINT PRICE CODE:	A

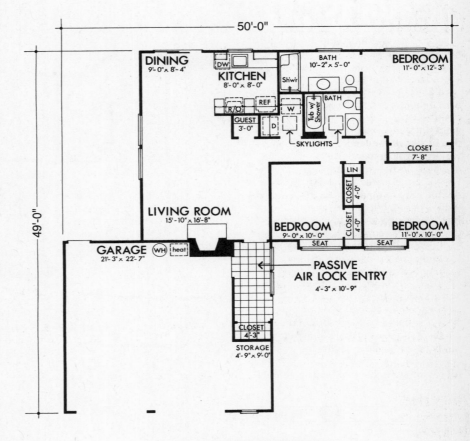

MAIN FLOOR

Feeling Fresh?

- You will after breathing the clean, invigorating air from this home's roomy patio and airy screen porch!
- If you'd rather stay inside, you can pass the time in the Great Room, which is crowned by an 11½-ft. ceiling and features a handsome fireplace. Line up some snacks on the pass-through to the kitchen and eat up!
- Perhaps mornings are your time to shine; if so, you'll love the breakfast room, which boasts bright windows and smooth access to the kitchen.
- Who doesn't love a place of their own? The smallest of the bedrooms could easily become just that—a sewing room, a private library or simply a special refuge for peace and quiet.
- The master suite finishes this home's enchanting spell. It includes a spacious walk-in closet and a bath with a zesty shower that has room for two. A 12-ft. vaulted ceiling nicely expands the sleeping chamber.
- Unless otherwise noted, all rooms boast 9-ft. ceilings.

Plan B-91023

Bedrooms: 2+	Baths: 2
Living Area:	
Main floor	1,530 sq. ft.
Total Living Area:	**1,530 sq. ft.**
Screen porch	178 sq. ft.
Standard basement	1,530 sq. ft.
Garage	387 sq. ft.
Exterior Wall Framing:	2x6

Foundation Options:

Standard basement

(All plans can be built with your choice of foundation and framing. A generic conversion diagram is available. See order form.)

BLUEPRINT PRICE CODE:	B

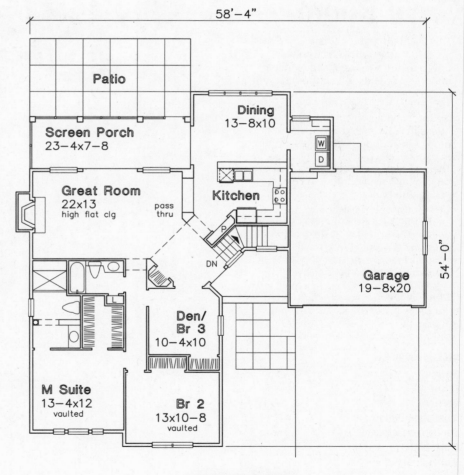

MAIN FLOOR

Patio Embraces Great Room

- This vacation home's Great Room lives up to its name, with a handsome fireplace and six sets of sliding glass doors that open to a wraparound patio or deck.
- The efficient U-shaped kitchen includes a pantry and a convenient snack bar. Meals may be served in the dining area of the Great Room, complete with built-in cabinet space.
- The secluded master bedroom boasts a private bath with outdoor access. A central full bath services the two secondary bedrooms.
- Two storage rooms adjoin the carport, which is stationed near the kitchen for effortless unloading of groceries.
- In the basement version, the stairs are located behind the fireplace.

Plan AX-98376

Bedrooms: 3	Baths: 2
Living Area:	
Main floor	1,386 sq. ft.
Total Living Area:	**1,386 sq. ft.**
Standard basement	1,386 sq. ft.
Carport and storage	376 sq. ft.
Exterior Wall Framing:	2x4

Foundation Options:

Standard basement

Crawlspace

Slab

(All plans can be built with your choice of foundation and framing. A generic conversion diagram is available. See order form.)

BLUEPRINT PRICE CODE:	A

VIEW INTO GREAT ROOM

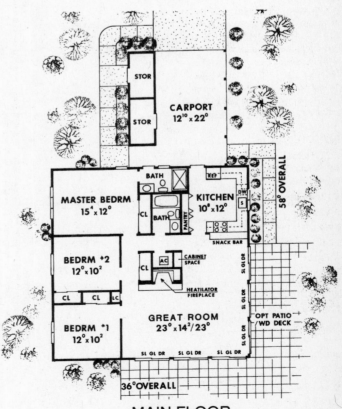

MAIN FLOOR

ELEVATION A

ELEVATION B

Relaxed Ranch

- A cozy covered porch adds an old-fashioned warmth to this comfortable ranch-style home.
- Inside, vaulted ceilings enhance the spacious living and dining rooms. A dramatic fireplace warms the entire area. Sliding glass doors in the dining room open to a private backyard patio.
- The efficiently designed kitchen is easily accessed from the dining area and features a U-shaped counter and a window above the sink.
- The master suite is located away from the main activity areas and features a walk-in closet and a private bath.
- Two nice-sized secondary bedrooms share a hall bath.
- Plans for the home are available with a gabled roof (Elevation A) or a hip roof (Elevation B). Please specify your preference when ordering.

Plan U-91-103

Bedrooms: 3	Baths: 2
Living Area:	
Main floor	1,256 sq. ft.
Total Living Area:	**1,256 sq. ft.**
Garage	419 sq. ft.
Exterior Wall Framing:	2x6

Foundation Options:

Crawlspace

Slab

(All plans can be built with your choice of foundation and framing. A generic conversion diagram is available. See order form.)

BLUEPRINT PRICE CODE: A

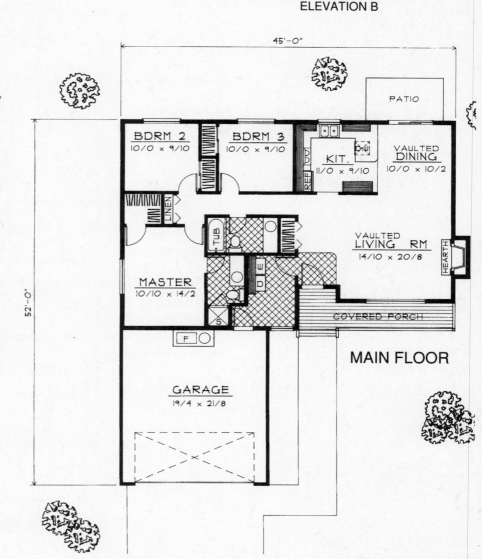

MAIN FLOOR

Cost-Saving Contemporary

- The simple yet distinctive lines of this compact design allow you to build an affordable home that isn't short on style.
- Visitors will be sheltered from the wind and rain by the recessed, covered entry.
- Natural light streams into the 15-ft.-high vaulted entry through a striking clerestory window.
- Refined comfort is the order of the day in the distinctive living room. Warmed by a majestic fireplace, distinguished by a spindle-topped half-wall and open to the sun-splashed dining room, this space easily hosts both formal and casual occasions.
- The efficient galley-style kitchen has everything you'll need to prepare healthy meals for your family. Its close proximity to the laundry room allows you to complete multiple tasks at the same time.
- Two good-sized bedrooms, one with a pair of wardrobe closets, share a full bath, rounding out the floor plan.

Plan H-1434-1A

Bedrooms: 2	Baths: 1
Living Area:	
Main floor	1,027 sq. ft.
Total Living Area:	**1,027 sq. ft.**
Garage	457 sq. ft.
Exterior Wall Framing:	2x6

Foundation Options:

Crawlspace

Slab

(All plans can be built with your choice of foundation and framing. A generic conversion diagram is available. See order form.)

BLUEPRINT PRICE CODE: A

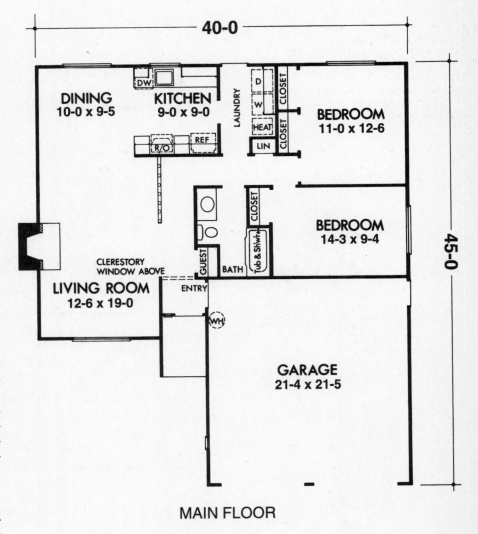

MAIN FLOOR

Open Areas Expand Ranch

- A spacious living and dining room combination, along with high ceilings in the family room, kitchen and master suite, gives this plan an open, airy feel.
- The living and dining area shares a brick hearth and an impressive 10-ft. tray ceiling.
- The kitchen shares an eating bar and a 14-ft.-high vaulted ceiling with the adjoining family room. A built-in

indoor barbecue grill is another extra found in the kitchen. A half-bath and a nice-sized laundry room with outdoor access are nearby.
- The family room features sliding glass doors to a covered rear porch.
- The master suite is enhanced by an elegant 9-ft.-high tray ceiling, a wardrobe closet, a private bath and sliding glass doors to the rear porch.
- The corner bedroom includes a walk-in closet and is brightened by windows on two sides.
- An additional bedroom and another full bath complete the bedroom wing.

Plan AX-97731	
Bedrooms: 3	**Baths:** 2½
Living Area:	
Main floor	1,547 sq. ft.
Total Living Area:	**1,547 sq. ft.**
Standard basement	1,427 sq. ft.
Garage	400 sq. ft.
Exterior Wall Framing:	2x4

Foundation Options:

Standard basement
Slab
(All plans can be built with your choice of foundation and framing. A generic conversion diagram is available. See order form.)

BLUEPRINT PRICE CODE:	B

MAIN FLOOR

Mediterranean Delight

- Perfect for sunny climes, this delightful stucco home offers luxurious living spaces within a narrow-lot design.
- A clerestory window above the front door spotlights the plant shelves that frame the Great Room.
- The spectacular Great Room features a 12-ft. vaulted ceiling, a striking fireplace and access to a secluded patio.
- Efficiently designed, the cozy kitchen includes a sunny breakfast room, an angled serving bar and close proximity to the two-car garage.
- Isolated at the rear of the home, the master suite offers a 9½-ft. vaulted ceiling, a large walk-in closet and a lavish bath with a soothing garden tub.
- The den adjacent to the master suite could also serve as a guest or additional bedroom.
- The front-facing bedroom boasts a charming boxed-out window and easy access to a full bath.

Plan B-90502

Bedrooms: 2+	Baths: 2
Living Area:	
Main floor	1,200 sq. ft.
Total Living Area:	**1,200 sq. ft.**
Garage	387 sq. ft.
Exterior Wall Framing:	2x4

Foundation Options:

Slab

(All plans can be built with your choice of foundation and framing. A generic conversion diagram is available. See order form.)

BLUEPRINT PRICE CODE:	**A**

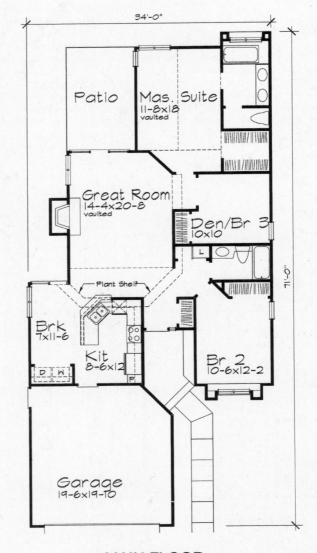

MAIN FLOOR

Nice and Narrow

- Fun and functional covered porches in the front and rear of this unique design let you enjoy outdoor views and maintain some privacy, even in a narrow, 42-ft.-wide plan.
- The house is built around a central and spacious living room with an angled fireplace, an airy dining room and a kitchen with open counter and wet bar.

- A side entry opens to the living room near the master suite, while a second living room entry opens onto a back porch.
- The secluded master suite has a private bath with an angled tub, a walk-in closet and separate vanities.
- Two additional bedrooms are well separated from the master suite for privacy and share a second bath.
- A utility room is conveniently located off the kitchen.
- Ample storage space is available at the back of the garage.

Plan E-1511	
Bedrooms: 3	**Baths:** 2
Living Area:	
Main floor	1,599 sq. ft.
Total Living Area:	**1,599 sq. ft.**
Garage	484 sq. ft.
Storage	96 sq. ft.
Exterior Wall Framing:	2x6
Foundation Options:	
Crawlspace	
Slab	

(All plans can be built with your choice of foundation and framing. A generic conversion diagram is available. See order form.)

BLUEPRINT PRICE CODE:	B

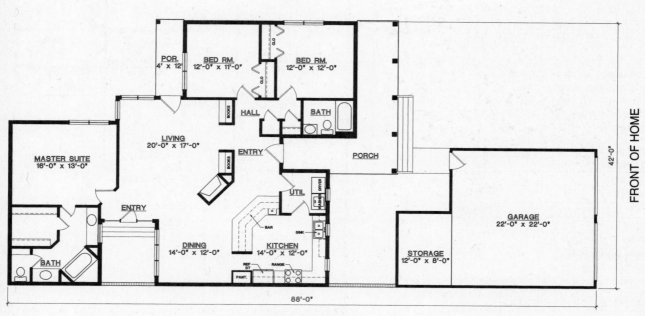

MAIN FLOOR

Plan E-1511

PRICES AND DETAILS
ON PAGES 2-5

Cuddle Up
by the Fire!

- This compact cottage's huge Great Room features a cozy fireplace that's perfect for romantic nights cuddled up with your significant other.
- The strong, rustic exterior is highlighted by a stone and siding facade and is accented by a charming wood fence.
- From the entry, you can step right into the incredible Great Room. You can fit all the relatives here during holiday festivities! While the fireplace helps heat up chilly nights, access to a spacious back deck lets you step outside to bask in the warmth of the summer days.
- Waffles and strawberries make a succulent morning meal in the sunny breakfast room.
- Surprisingly large is the master suite, which boasts a walk-in closet and a dynamic private bath with a luxurious corner tub.
- Two more bedrooms are found on the opposite side of the home. Each is just a step from a nice full-sized bath.

Plan C-8610

Bedrooms: 3	Baths: 2
Living Area:	
Main floor	1,575 sq. ft.
Total Living Area:	**1,575 sq. ft.**
Garage and storage	454 sq. ft.
Exterior Wall Framing:	2x4

Foundation Options:

Crawlspace

Slab

(All plans can be built with your choice of foundation and framing. A generic conversion diagram is available. See order form.)

BLUEPRINT PRICE CODE:	**B**

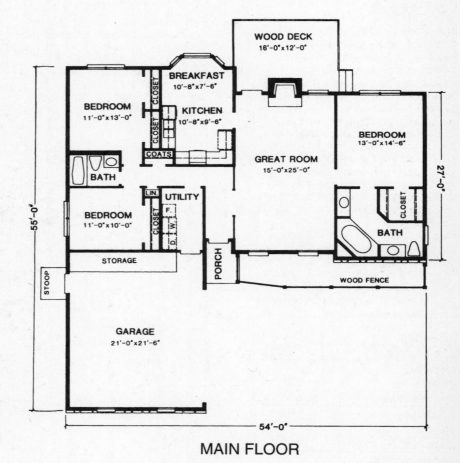

MAIN FLOOR

Looking Good!

- Good looks and versatility add to the appeal of this economical home.
- The simple exterior is spruced up with a brick entry and a fashionable pot shelf.
- Inside, a large and bright expanse combines dining, entertaining and pure relaxation. The allure of a fireplace is maximized with the addition of a built-in media center, a decorative display niche and a handy wood box; the 13-ft. vaulted ceiling adds a spatial element.
- A half-wall or railing may be used to set off the kitchen and breakfast area, which are neatly located near the laundry closet and the two-car garage.
- Sliding glass doors open to a large deck that is nestled between the kitchen and the living room.
- Window seats lend warmth to the secondary bedrooms, one of which may be used as a den or study.
- The master bedroom's 10½-ft. vaulted ceiling ends at its dressing area and private bath. The separate vanity allows good use of your time.

Plan B-95003

Bedrooms: 2+	Baths: 2
Living Area:	
Main floor	1,280 sq. ft.
Total Living Area:	**1,280 sq. ft.**
Standard basement	1,280 sq. ft.
Garage	400 sq. ft.
Exterior Wall Framing:	2x6

Foundation Options:

Standard basement

(All plans can be built with your choice of foundation and framing. A generic conversion diagram is available. See order form.)

BLUEPRINT PRICE CODE:	**A**

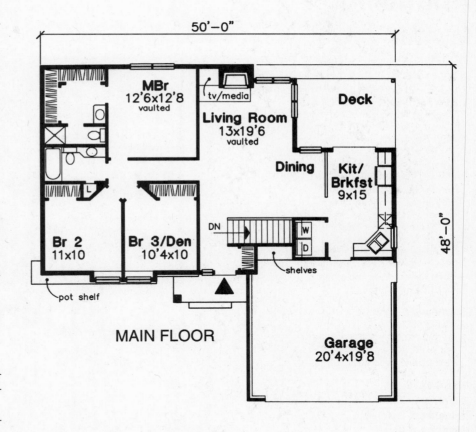

MAIN FLOOR

Abundant Living

- This contemporary ranch-style home offers three generously sized bedrooms and abundant living space in just over 1,500 square feet.
- A massive corner fireplace anchors the living room, where a pair of windows looks out to the world.
- Opposite the living room, a quiet dining room awaits quiet intimacy or festive fetes. It is removed amply from the kitchen to minimize noise.
- The family room stretches to include the kitchen. Sliding glass doors join the family room to the backyard.
- Two secondary bedrooms line the passage to the master bedroom. Here, a private bath, bright windows and ample closet space combine to bring peace to your life.

Plan AX-8595-A

Bedrooms: 3	Baths: 2
Living Area:	
Main floor	1,520 sq. ft.
Total Living Area:	**1,520 sq. ft.**
Standard basement	1,520 sq. ft.
Garage	452 sq. ft.
Exterior Wall Framing:	2x4

Foundation Options:
Standard basement
Slab
(All plans can be built with your choice of foundation and framing. A generic conversion diagram is available. See order form.)

BLUEPRINT PRICE CODE: **B**

MSTR BEDRM
15'-8" × 12'-0"

BEDRM #2
10'-0" × 11'-0"

BATH

BATH

KIT
9'-6" × 12'-0"

FAMILY RM
16'-0" × 12'-0"

54'-0" OVERALL

BEDRM #3
10'-0" × 11'-0"

FOY

DINING RM
10'-0" × 11'-0"

TWO CAR GARAGE
21'-6" × 21'-0"

LIVING RM
17'-0" × 13'-0"

PORCH

54'-8" OVERALL

MAIN FLOOR

At One with the Sun

- An open floor plan and large windows on every side of this design allow you to take full advantage of the sun.
- The 12-ft. vaulted, pass-through kitchen opens to a cheerful 12-ft. vaulted sun porch that's the perfect spot to start your day. A serving counter makes the kitchen available to the adjoining formal dining area.
- The dining and living rooms flow together nicely, and are enhanced by 12-ft. vaulted ceilings and views of the large rear deck. A corner fireplace radiates warmth to the living area.
- The master bedroom has twin walk-in closets and a private bath. A 13-ft. vaulted ceiling adds a spacious feel; sliding glass doors open to the deck.
- Another full bath services a nearby secondary bedroom that may be used as a cozy den or home office.
- The full basement offers more potential living space. A guest suite, a family room or a hobby and craft area would nicely round out the floor plan.

Plan B-91012

Bedrooms: 1+	Baths: 2
Living Area:	
Main floor	1,421 sq. ft.
Total Living Area:	**1,421 sq. ft.**
Standard basement	1,421 sq. ft.
Garage	400 sq. ft.
Exterior Wall Framing:	2x4

Foundation Options:

Standard basement

(All plans can be built with your choice of foundation and framing. A generic conversion diagram is available. See order form.)

BLUEPRINT PRICE CODE: A

REAR VIEW

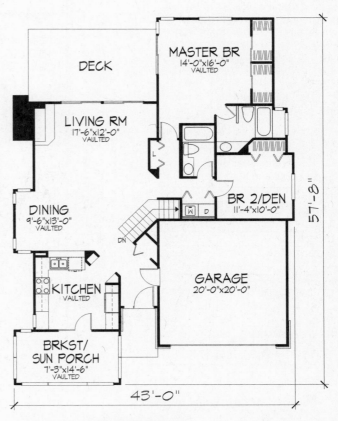

MAIN FLOOR

Plan B-91012

PRICES AND DETAILS
ON PAGES 2-5

Extra! Extra!

- With its extra perks and modest, easy-to-maintain square footage, this home is one that you and your family will want to read all about!
- At the front of the home, a graceful arch and handsome columns frame the entry, showcasing the beautiful double doors and the transom above.
- Inside, the vaulted foyer ushers guests directly into the living areas. No matter what the occasion, this comfortable trio, which includes the living room, the dining room and the kitchen, guarantees worry-free gatherings.
- An angled serving bar off the kitchen holds snacks and beverages when you entertain. During family feasts in the dining room, this is a great spot to keep reserves of the main dish. On a summer night, nothing could be better than a simple meal on the patio.
- As each day comes to a close, you'll savor moments of quiet time in the peaceful master suite. Here, a large walk-in closet and a good-sized bath easily accommodate two busy people.

Plan J-9424

Bedrooms: 3	Baths: 2
Living Area:	
Main floor	1,499 sq. ft.
Total Living Area:	**1,499 sq. ft.**
Standard basement	1,499 sq. ft.
Garage	447 sq. ft.
Storage	65 sq. ft.
Exterior Wall Framing:	2x4

Foundation Options:

Standard basement

Crawlspace

Slab

(All plans can be built with your choice of foundation and framing. A generic conversion diagram is available. See order form.)

BLUEPRINT PRICE CODE: A

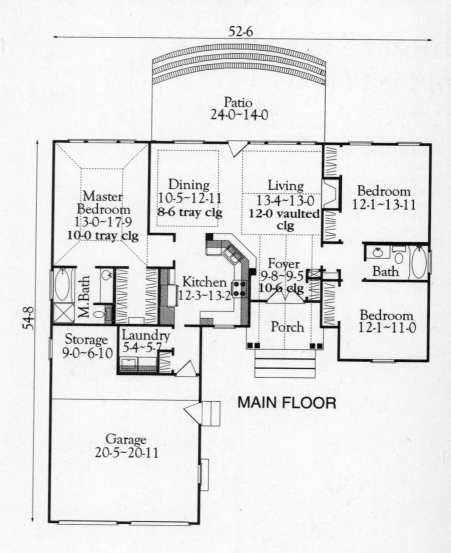

MAIN FLOOR

52-6

54-8

Patio
24-0~14-0

Master Bedroom
13-0~17-9
10-0 tray clg

Dining
10-5~12-11
8-6 tray clg

Living
13-4~13-0
12-0 vaulted clg

Bedroom
12-1~13-11

M. Bath

Kitchen
12-3~13-2

Foyer
9-8~9-5
10-6 clg

Bath

Storage
9-0~6-10

Laundry
5-4~5-7

Porch

Bedroom
12-1~11-0

Garage
20-5~20-11

Great Retirement or First Home

- A host of quality features, such as high ceilings and a huge Great Room, adds to the livability of this terrific two-bedroom home.
- Articulating the exterior is a boxed-out window whose graceful arch is echoed by the detailing of the front porch.
- A roomy foyer accented by columns and a 10-ft.-high ceiling introduces the interior, which is dominated by a

fantastic Great Room. Here, the central fireplace is framed by sliding glass doors that open to a covered lanai with a 10-ft. vaulted ceiling.

- An arched opening leads from the Great Room to the kitchen/breakfast area, where the ceiling vaults up to a 10-ft. height. An arched pass-through just beyond the corner sink keeps the kitchen open to the Great Room.
- Each of the bedrooms has private access to a full bath. The master suite includes a 10-ft. vaulted ceiling, two walk-in closets and a bath with a dual-sink vanity and a sit-down shower.

Plan B-92020	
Bedrooms: 2	**Baths:** 2
Living Area:	
Main floor	1,275 sq. ft.
Total Living Area:	**1,275 sq. ft.**
Garage	263 sq. ft.
Exterior Wall Framing:	2x4

Foundation Options:

Slab
(All plans can be built with your choice of foundation and framing. A generic conversion diagram is available. See order form.)

BLUEPRINT PRICE CODE: A

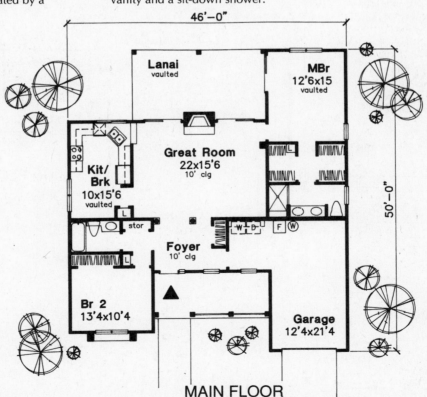

MAIN FLOOR

Bright, Roomy Interior

- Vertical wood siding, stone accents and breathtaking triple clerestory windows give this one-story a fabulous facade.
- The covered porch opens to a roomy foyer, which flows into a spacious family room. This bright activity area is highlighted by a fireplace and a 17-ft. vaulted ceiling with exposed beams. Sliding glass doors open to a backyard patio with a wrought-iron railing.
- The adjoining dining room also overlooks the patio, creating a sunny, enjoyable atmosphere.
- The galley-style kitchen boasts a sunny breakfast area for informal dining.
- The secluded master suite has two walk-in closets and a private bath.
- Two additional bedrooms, also with walk-in closets, share another full bath.

Plan C-8356

Bedrooms: 3	Baths: 2
Living Area:	
Main floor	1,457 sq. ft.
Total Living Area:	**1,457 sq. ft.**
Daylight basement	1,457 sq. ft.
Garage	434 sq. ft.
Exterior Wall Framing:	2x4

Foundation Options:

Daylight basement
Crawlspace
(All plans can be built with your choice of foundation and framing. A generic conversion diagram is available. See order form.)

BLUEPRINT PRICE CODE:	**A**

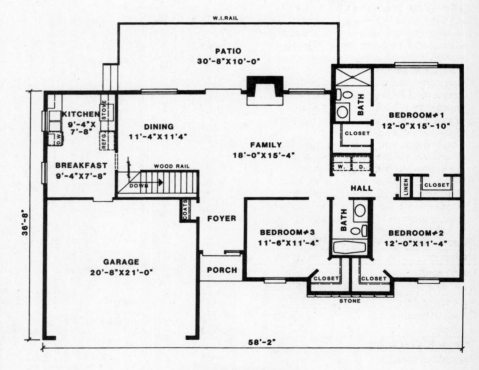

MAIN FLOOR

B-90040

B-90042

B-90047

Triple-Take

- This well-planned 1,390-sq.-ft. ranch offers three different exterior looks to give home buyers a choice and chance to find the right one for them. Each elevation is sold separately. Please specify your elevation of choice when you place your order.
- The entry opens to an airy Great Room and formal dining area, which are topped by a 13-ft. vaulted ceiling. In the corner of the Great Room, a fireplace cheerfully crackles.
- The kitchen, with handy garage access, overlooks the breakfast room and rear patio beyond sliding glass doors.
- The three bedrooms are highlighted by a double-doored master suite with a soaring 10-ft. vaulted ceiling, a window seat, a walk-in closet and a private bath.

Plans B-90040, B-90042 & B-90047

Bedrooms: 3	**Baths:** 2

Living Area:	
Main floor	1,390 sq. ft.
Total Living Area:	**1,390 sq. ft.**
Standard basement	1,382 sq. ft.
Garage	387 sq. ft.
Exterior Wall Framing:	2x6

Foundation Options:

Standard basement

(All plans can be built with your choice of foundation and framing. A generic conversion diagram is available. See order form.)

BLUEPRINT PRICE CODE:	**A**

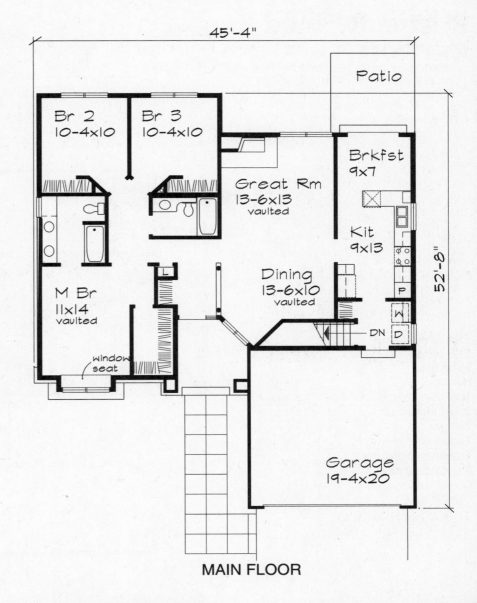

MAIN FLOOR

Plans B-90040, B-90042 & B-90047

PRICES AND DETAILS
ON PAGES 2-5

Rustic, Refined

- This home offers opportunities for enjoying the outdoors, with its lavish use of glass and wood deck or optional greenhouse.
- The rustic exterior sports vertical cedar siding contrasted with stone veneer. The home's tuck-under garage and rear-view orientation make it perfect for scenic, sloped lots.
- Built-in shelves, a bay window and a fireplace grace the large living room.
- The two dining areas and the kitchen all face a rear deck. If you wish, convert the deck into a greenhouse and add 168 sq. ft. of space.
- The daylight basement is a self-sufficient unit, making it a perfect suite for guests, elderly parents or your boomerang child. In addition to a bedroom and bath, it includes a family room with a fireplace, a kitchenette and sliding glass doors to the backyard.

Plan AX-98483

Bedrooms: 3+	**Baths:** 2-3

Living Area:	
Main floor	1,528 sq. ft.
Daylight basement (finished)	504 sq. ft.
Total Living Area:	**1,528/2,032 sq. ft.**
Daylight basement (unfinished)	243 sq. ft.
Tuck-under garage	619 sq. ft.
Exterior Wall Framing:	2x4

Foundation Options:

Daylight basement
Crawlspace

(All plans can be built with your choice of foundation and framing.
A generic conversion diagram is available. See order form.)

BLUEPRINT PRICE CODE: **B/C**

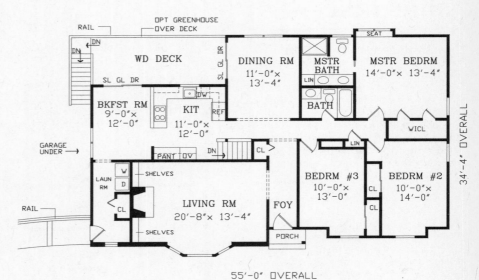

MAIN FLOOR

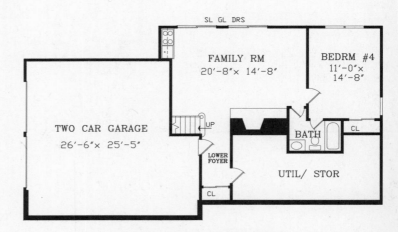

DAYLIGHT BASEMENT

Porch Pleasures

- The highlight of this rambling one-story is the wraparound porch that stretches along the front of the home. Friends and family will spend countless hours here enjoying gentle summer breezes, easy conversation and tall, icy colas.
- Inside, the good-sized living room serves as the focal point of the home. This space is equally suited to help the kids with their homework and to entertain friends and colleagues in an elegant setting.

- The dining room and the kitchen adjoin seamlessly, forming an open area where you will savor many meals. This design allows dinner guests and family to visit with the resident cook without getting underfoot.
- A soaring 10-ft. ceiling tops all of these rooms, as well as the two secondary bedrooms nearby.
- In the master bedroom, a 9-ft. sloped ceiling adds a splash of style. The incredible master bath includes two walk-in closets and a dressing area, so you won't disturb a sleeping spouse.

Plan DD-1452

Bedrooms: 3	Baths: 2
Living Area:	
Main floor	1,452 sq. ft.
Total Living Area:	**1,452 sq. ft.**
Garage and storage	496 sq. ft.
Exterior Wall Framing:	2x4

Foundation Options:

Crawlspace
Slab
(All plans can be built with your choice of foundation and framing. A generic conversion diagram is available. See order form.)

BLUEPRINT PRICE CODE:	**A**

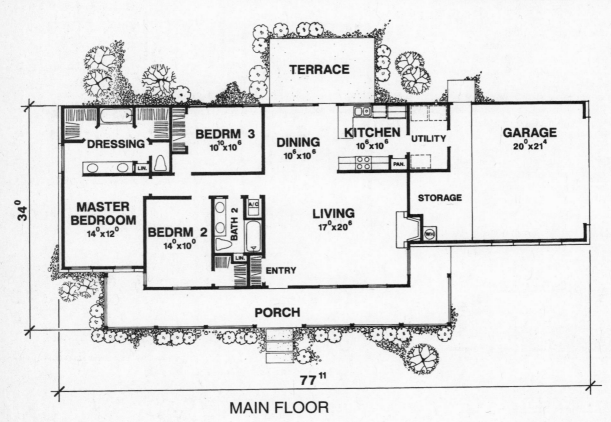

MAIN FLOOR

Plan DD-1452
PRICES AND DETAILS
ON PAGES 2-5

Pretty Little Garden Home

- This garden home is designed to fit on a narrow lot, making it the perfect plan for cost-conscious builders or those looking for a cozy weekend retreat.
- An angled front entryway adds interior interest. It leads into the kitchen, which features a built-in pantry closet and elegant corner glass shelves. Another set of glass shelves graces the entry.
- A handy serving bar extends from the kitchen into the dining area, which flows into the living room. A raised ceiling in the living room elegantly defines this area. A French door opens to a covered rear porch.
- The master suite boasts a private bath and a walk-in closet. A quiet sitting area provides you with a place to reflect at day's end or curl up with a good book.
- A secondary bedroom has its own walk-in closet and easy access to a full bath.
- In the garage, disappearing stairs lead up to storage space for seasonal lawn equipment; there's also a handy storage alcove at the back of the garage.

Plan E-1108

Bedrooms: 2	Baths: 2
Living Area:	
Main floor	1,150 sq. ft.
Total Living Area:	**1,150 sq. ft.**
Garage and storage	471 sq. ft.
Exterior Wall Framing:	2x4

Foundation Options:

Crawlspace
Slab

(All plans can be built with your choice of foundation and framing. A generic conversion diagram is available. See order form.)

BLUEPRINT PRICE CODE: **A**

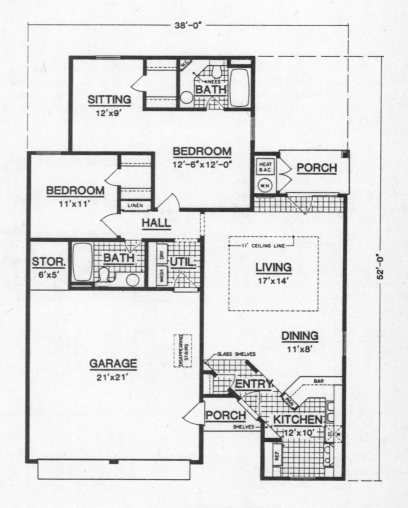

MAIN FLOOR

High-Profile Contemporary

- This design does away with wasted space, putting the emphasis on quality rather than on size.
- The angled floor plan minimizes hall space and creates smooth traffic flow while adding architectural appeal. The roof framing is square, however, to allow for economical construction.
- The spectacular living and dining rooms share a 16-ft. cathedral ceiling and a fireplace. Both rooms have lots of glass overlooking an angled rear terrace.
- The dining room includes a glass-filled alcove and sliding patio doors topped by transom windows. Tall windows frame the living room fireplace and trace the slope of the ceiling.
- A pass-through joins the dining room to the combination kitchen and family room, which features a snack bar and a clerestory window.
- The sleeping wing provides a super master suite, which boasts a skylighted dressing area and a luxurious bath. The optional den, or third bedroom, shares a second full bath with another bedroom that offers a 14-ft. sloped ceiling.

Plan K-688-D

Bedrooms: 2+	**Baths:** 2½

Living Area:	
Main floor	1,340 sq. ft.
Total Living Area:	**1,340 sq. ft.**
Standard basement	1,235 sq. ft.
Garage	484 sq. ft.
Exterior Wall Framing:	2x4 or 2x6

Foundation Options:

Standard basement
Slab
(All plans can be built with your choice of foundation and framing. A generic conversion diagram is available. See order form.)

BLUEPRINT PRICE CODE:	A

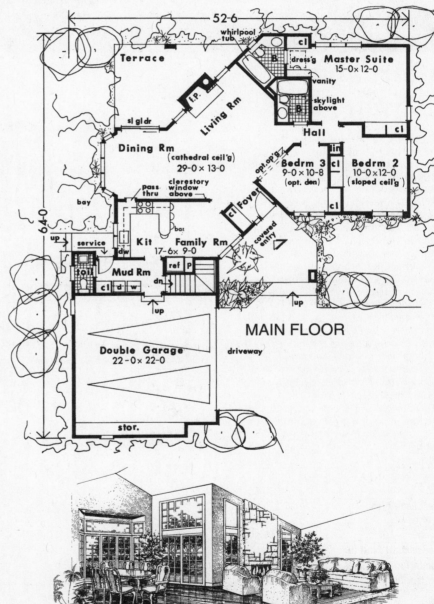

MAIN FLOOR

Terrace
whirlpool tub
cl
B
dress'g Master Suite 15-0 x 12-0
vanity
skylight above
f.p.
Living Rm
B
sl gl dr
Hall
cl
Dining Rm (cathedral ceil'g) 29-0 x 13-0
opt op'g
Bedrm 3 9-0 x 10-8 (opt. den)
cl
Bedrm 2 10-0 x 12-0 (sloped ceil'g)
clerestory window above
bay
pass thru
cl Foyer
cl
covered entry
service
Kit
Family Rm 17-6 x 9-0
dw
bar
Mud Rm
ref P
cl d w
dn
up
up
Double Garage 22-0 x 22-0
driveway
stor.
52-6
64-0
up

VIEW INTO DINING ROOM AND LIVING ROOM

Plan K-688-D
PRICES AND DETAILS ON PAGES 2-5

Affordable Comfort

- Compact, simple and easy to build, this rustic ranch design offers plenty of comfortable living space for the small family or the empty nester.
- A covered porch leads into a spacious living room with an airy beamed ceiling and a large fireplace. A French door beside the fireplace leads out to a patio where you'll love gathering with friends for summer barbecues.
- The efficient kitchen features a snack bar that extends to the dining room, where railed half-walls offer a view of the living room.
- The master suite boasts a private bath and a walk-in closet.
- Two more bedrooms share a hall bath.
- The garage includes a separate, sealed-off storage area, as well as a built-in work bench for those who enjoy at-home projects.
- This design's rustic interior and exterior styling make it a great vacation home.

Plan E-1207

Bedrooms: 3	Baths: 2
Living Area:	
Main floor	1,230 sq. ft.
Total Living Area:	**1,230 sq. ft.**
Garage	512 sq. ft.
Storage	56 sq. ft.
Exterior Wall Framing:	2x6

Foundation Options:

Crawlspace

Slab

(All plans can be built with your choice of foundation and framing. A generic conversion diagram is available. See order form.)

BLUEPRINT PRICE CODE:	**A**

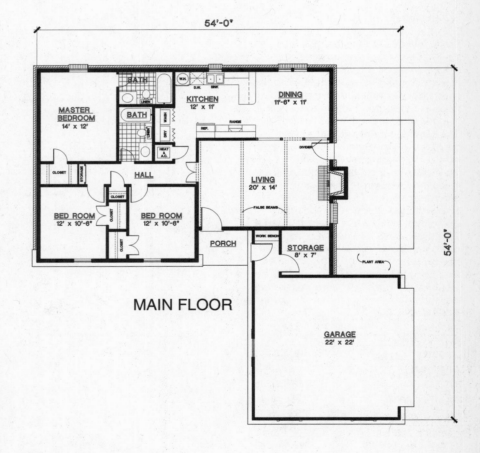

MAIN FLOOR

Southwestern Flavor

- The influence of the ancient designs of the Southwest and Central America is evident in this stucco home.
- Wrought-iron gates open to an L-shaped courtyard, where a tile or brick walk leads to a front porch covered with a clay-tile roof.
- Inside, a short hallway leads to the generous living room, which is warmed by a corner fireplace with a fan-shaped hearth. The living room is spacious enough to accommodate a formal dining set.
- The U-shaped kitchen opens directly into an informal dining nook.
- The master suite boasts its own bath and private access to the patio. The second bedroom has easy access to a full bath.
- An enclosed garage or open carport is available by specifying your preference.

Plans H-1399-1A & -1B

Bedrooms: 2	Baths: 2
Living Area:	
Main floor	1,300 sq. ft.
Total Living Area:	**1,300 sq. ft.**
Garage	390 sq. ft.
Carport	412 sq. ft.
Exterior Wall Framing:	2x6
Foundation Options:	**Plan #**
Slab (with garage)	H-1399-1B
Slab (with carport)	H-1399-1A

(All plans can be built with your choice of foundation and framing. A generic conversion diagram is available. See order form.)

BLUEPRINT PRICE CODE:	**A**

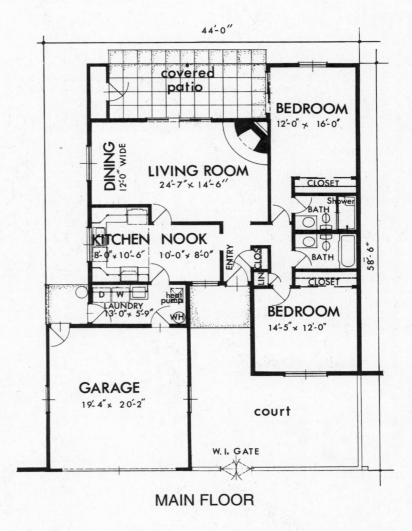

MAIN FLOOR

A Circle of Simplicity

- This one-bedroom circular retreat is the perfect open and airy vacation home. The simplicity of the floor plan and the lofty nature of the vaulted ceilings create a feeling of complete freedom.
- The glass-sheathed Great Room offers panoramic views through its wall of windows. The room functions as both a living room and the home's dining area.

A round fireplace casts a warm glow in all directions and double doors lead out to the deck.
- The arrow-shaped kitchen provides plenty of counter and storage space.
- Windows in the bedroom afford you the scenic view your lot enjoys, without compromising your privacy.
- The nearby bath and adjoining hallway are illuminated by skylights.
- The large deck is the perfect spot for nature-watching or embracing a sunset.
- A double garage and roomy laundry facilities ease the vacation experience.

Plan H-961-1A

Bedrooms: 1	Baths: 1
Living Area:	
Main floor	1,018 sq. ft.
Total Living Area:	**1,018 sq. ft.**
Garage	452 sq. ft.
Exterior Wall Framing:	2x4

Foundation Options:

Crawlspace
(All plans can be built with your choice of foundation and framing. A generic conversion diagram is available. See order form.)

BLUEPRINT PRICE CODE: A

MAIN FLOOR

GARAGE
21'-3" x 21'-3"

ALTERNATE GARAGE DOOR LOCATION

64'-0"

42'-0"

7'-6"

LAUNDRY
D W

W/O

KITCHEN
13'-0" x 13'-0"
13'-0" sloped clg

heat
WH STOR

GUEST
4'-0"

ENTRY

REF DW

Tub w/ Shower

BATH

BEDROOM
13'-10" x 16'-2"
14'-0" sloped clg

S.C.

SKYLIGHTS

STORAGE LIN CLOSET 5'-0" CLOSET 5'-0" STOR

GREAT ROOM
33'-0" x 14'-2"
14'-10" sloped clg

SLOPED CEILING

PRE-FAB FIREPLACE

DECK

Living Is Easy!

- Filled with popular features but affordably sized, this charming country home is a great choice for a new family.
- Past the inviting covered front porch and beyond a decorative open railing, the spacious living room is brightened by a lovely bay window with a built-in seat. A handsome fireplace adds warmth to the area.

- The efficient U-shaped kitchen offers a stylish eating bar and a windowed sink.
- The adjoining dining room is large enough for any occasion, and offers handy sliding glass doors to a sunny backyard patio.
- In the sleeping wing of the home, the good-sized master bedroom features two closets and a private bath.
- The two secondary bedrooms share a nice full bath, which includes a handy laundry closet.

Plan AX-98602

Bedrooms: 3	Baths: 2
Living Area:	
Main floor	1,253 sq. ft.
Total Living Area:	**1,253 sq. ft.**
Basement	1,253 sq. ft.
Garage	368 sq. ft.
Exterior Wall Framing:	2x4

Foundation Options:
Daylight basement
Standard basement
Crawlspace
Slab
(All plans can be built with your choice of foundation and framing. A generic conversion diagram is available. See order form.)

BLUEPRINT PRICE CODE: A

MAIN FLOOR

Attention: Smart Shoppers

- Get the most out of your lot and your pocketbook by building this beautiful three-bedroom home.
- A friendly front porch and a brick-accented facade assure you of the nice, warm interior that awaits.
- Upon entering, the airy vaulted ceilings will immediately catch your eye. Next you'll be drawn to the exciting two-way fireplace and a pleasant backyard view through sliding glass doors.
- Opposite the living room, the family room's fireplace wall includes a shuttered TV niche. Plenty of windows brighten the family room, dining room and kitchen, which flow together to create a sun-drenched spaciousness.
- With a central island workstation and a corner pantry, the kitchen promises efficient traffic flow and use of space.
- The bedroom wing is also smartly arranged, with the laundry closet conveniently placed in the middle. The master suite is secluded for peace and privacy behind its full bath and oversized walk-in closet.

Plan BRF-1372

Bedrooms: 3	**Baths:** 2

Living Area:	
Main floor	1,372 sq. ft.
Total Living Area:	**1,372 sq. ft.**
Garage	420 sq. ft.
Exterior Wall Framing:	2x4

Foundation Options:

Slab

(All plans can be built with your choice of foundation and framing. A generic conversion diagram is available. See order form.)

BLUEPRINT PRICE CODE:	**A**

NOTE:
The above photographed home may have been modified by the homeowner. Please refer to floor plan and/or drawn elevation shown for actual blueprint details.

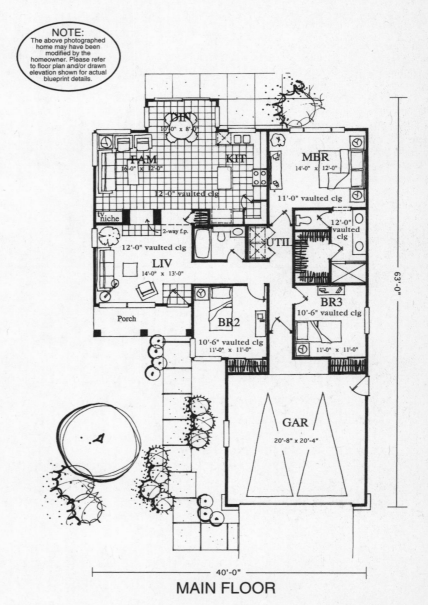

MAIN FLOOR

Options Galore

- This home is adaptable to nearly any lot. It's available in three different foundation versions to fit a sloped or a flat site.
- The ranch design is timeless. As you enter, common living spaces are to the left and the sleeping wing is to the right.
- The generous living room is warmed by a fireplace flanked by built-in shelves. A triple window arrangement lets in lots of sun and provides a stunning view of

your scenic lot. Sliding glass doors access a side patio or deck.
- The kitchen is within easy serving distance of the dining room, which is positioned to handle the overflow crowd during large-scale entertaining.
- On the other side of the home, the master suite features dual closets, a sunny window seat and a private bath. Two more bedrooms share a full bath.
- The basement versions include a rec room and space for two bedrooms, a full bath and laundry facilities.

Plans H-2088-2, -2A & -2B		
Bedrooms: 3+		**Baths:** 2-3
Living Area:		
Main floor (crawlspace vesion)		1,349 sq. ft.
Maln floor (basement version)		1,328 sq. ft.
Basement		1,213 sq. ft.
Total Living Area:		**1,349/2,541 sq. ft.**
Garage (crawlspace version)		474 sq. ft.
Garage (basement versions)		509 sq. ft.
Exterior Wall Framing:		**2x4**
Foundation Options:		**Plan #**
Daylight basement		H-2088-2
Standard basement		H-2088-2B
Crawlspace		H-2088-2A

(All plans can be built with your choice of foundation and framing. A generic conversion diagram is available. See order form.)

BLUEPRINT PRICE CODE:	**A/D**

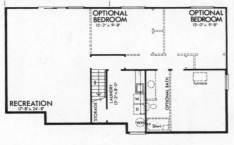

BASEMENT

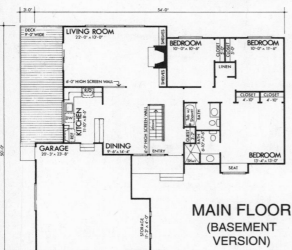

MAIN FLOOR
(BASEMENT VERSION)

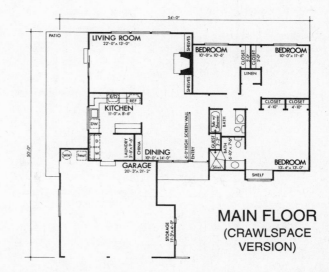

MAIN FLOOR
(CRAWLSPACE VERSION)

Plans H-2088-2, -2A & -2B

PRICES AND DETAILS
ON PAGES 2-5

Tudor Cottage

- Charming Tudor features dress up the facade of this three-bedroom cottage design, which functions as a first home or a romantic weekend retreat.
- The natural stone that highlights the exterior is repeated in the fireplace in the living room. What a wonderful spot to unwind after a day of skiing! A half-wall topped by cedar dividers separates the living room from the dining area.
- The galley kitchen boasts a pantry closet and opens directly into the dining area, for ease in serving meals. Easy traffic flow between the living room and the dining area allows guests to mingle comfortably when you entertain.
- The master suite includes a walk-in closet and a private bath, amenities you may not have expected in a home of this size.
- Across the hall, two more bedrooms share another full bath.
- Storage space in and above the garage gives you plenty of room to keep yard equipment and the barbecue grill. If this is a second home, use these areas to store seasonal recreation equipment, and save time packing up the car.

Plan E-1110

Bedrooms: 3	Baths: 2
Living Area:	
Main floor	1,149 sq. ft.
Total Living Area:	**1,149 sq. ft.**
Garage and storage	288 sq. ft.
Exterior Wall Framing:	2x6

Foundation Options:
Crawlspace
Slab
(All plans can be built with your choice of foundation and framing. A generic conversion diagram is available. See order form.)

BLUEPRINT PRICE CODE: A

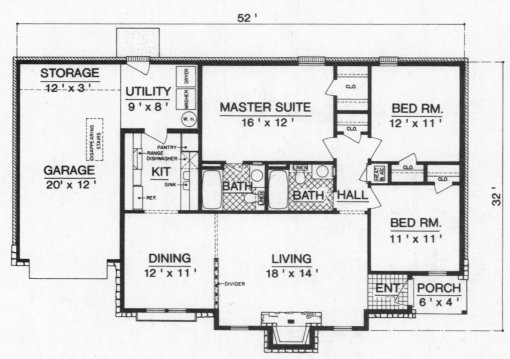

MAIN FLOOR

Style and Economy

- Interesting style and smart economics make this charming one-story design an attractive choice for any prospective home owner.
- A central hallway provides a private traffic pattern, beginning at the front entry, which is partially screened from the living room and dining alcove.
- The huge living room is the perfect place to gather family and friends during festive holiday activities. It features a dramatic vaulted ceiling and a cozy fireplace to set a sparkling mood. Clerestory windows above brighten the entire area.
- Conveniently close to the laundry room, the L-shaped kitchen lets you handle two tasks at once. A windowed sink gives you a view of the outdoors when cleaning up after meals.
- Two big bedrooms offer plenty of closet space and are just steps from a full-sized bath. A nearby linen closet is sure to come in handy.

Plan H-1385-1A

Bedrooms: 2	Baths: 1
Living Area:	
Main floor	1,076 sq. ft.
Total Living Area:	**1,076 sq. ft.**
Garage	296 sq. ft.
Exterior Wall Framing:	2x4
Foundation Options:	

Crawlspace
(All plans can be built with your choice of foundation and framing. A generic conversion diagram is available. See order form.)

BLUEPRINT PRICE CODE:	A

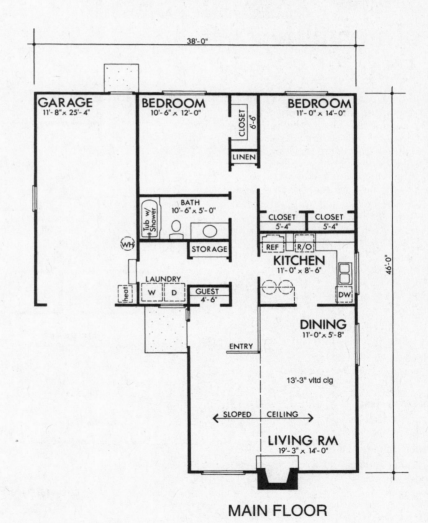

MAIN FLOOR

Plan H-1385-1A

PRICES AND DETAILS
ON PAGES 2-5

Comfortable L-Shaped Ranch

- From the covered entry to the beautiful and spacious family gathering areas, this comfortable ranch-style home puts many extras into a compact space.
- Straight off the central foyer, an inviting fireplace and a bright bay window highlight the living and dining area, while sliding glass doors open to a wide backyard terrace.
- The combination kitchen/family room features a large eating bar. The nearby mudroom offers a service entrance, laundry facilities, access to the garage and room for a half-bath.
- In the isolated sleeping wing, the master bedroom boasts a private bath and plenty of closet space. Two additional bedrooms share another full bath.

Plan K-276-R

Bedrooms: 3	Baths: 2+
Living Area:	
Main floor	1,245 sq. ft.
Total Living Area:	**1,245 sq. ft.**
Standard basement	1,245 sq. ft.
Garage	499 sq. ft.
Exterior Wall Framing:	2x4 or 2x6

Foundation Options:

Standard basement
Crawlspace
Slab
(All plans can be built with your choice of foundation and framing. A generic conversion diagram is available. See order form.)

BLUEPRINT PRICE CODE: A

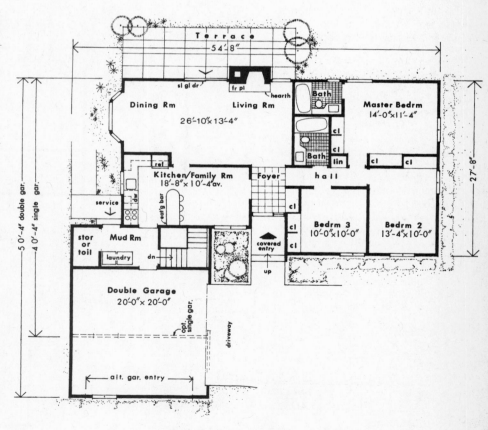

MAIN FLOOR

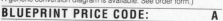

Shelter from the Storm

- This home's covered entry, brick exterior and built-in planter make it a cozy shelter from the storms of life.
- Inside, the convenient entry hall neatly divides the living spaces from the sleeping quarters. It also accesses the two-car garage.
- The walk-through kitchen lies adjacent to the dining room, and boasts a bright window over the sink.

- An 11½-ft. vaulted ceiling lends an open, airy feeling to the living room and dining room area, while plenty of natural light adds gentle brilliance.
- The dining room gazes over the front yard, while the living room enjoys two more windows and sliding glass doors to an expansive deck. A crackling fireplace glows on rainy days and chilly evenings.
- The larger of the two bedrooms features a private bath and two closets. The other bedroom also includes two closets, and has exclusive use of the hall bath nearby.

Plan H-866-M2A

Bedrooms: 2	Baths: 2
Living Area:	
Main floor	1,199 sq. ft.
Total Living Area:	**1,199 sq. ft.**
Garage	521 sq. ft.
Exterior Wall Framing:	2x4

Foundation Options:

Crawlspace
(All plans can be built with your choice of foundation and framing. A generic conversion diagram is available. See order form.)

BLUEPRINT PRICE CODE: A

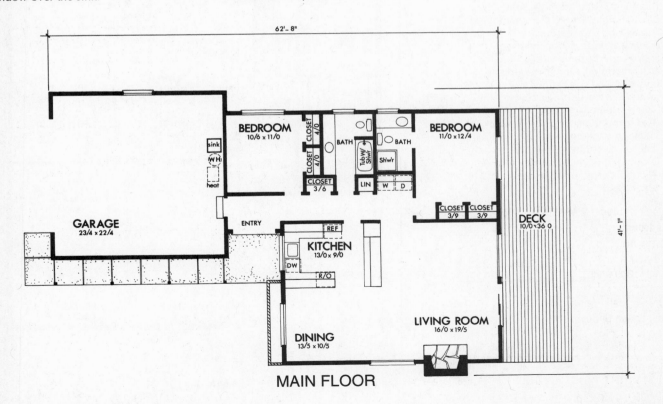

MAIN FLOOR

ORDER BLUEPRINTS ANYTIME!
CALL TOLL-FREE 1-800-820-1283

Plan H-866-M2A

PRICES AND DETAILS
ON PAGES 2-5

Gardener's Hacienda

- Whether clad with stucco or masonry block, this Spanish-style home is strictly casual from one end to the other.
- The front entry is surrounded by stone walls and a wrought-iron gate. A raised-bed planter there provides a built-in seat at one end.
- The carport offers easy access and freedom from clutter.
- The covered patio in the rear of the home is visited by sliding glass doors from the master bedroom and living room, and comes equipped with storage for a golf cart or other items.
- Take your morning coffee from the kitchen directly into the garden room, and grab the newspaper from the front entry courtyard through yet another sliding door. Then sit and enjoy the fire.
- The living room fireplace is set at an angle to encourage casual socializing.
- The master suite has a walk-through closet and its own private bath.
- A cupola crowns the home's varied rooflines.

Plans H-1404-1A & -M1A

Bedrooms: 2	Baths: 2
Living Area:	
Main floor	1,510 sq. ft.
Total Living Area:	**1,510 sq. ft.**
Carport	400 sq. ft.
Exterior Wall Framing:	2x6
Foundation Options:	**Plan #**
Slab (stucco)	H-1404-1A
Slab (concrete)	H-1404-M1A

(All plans can be built with your choice of foundation and framing. A generic conversion diagram is available. See order form.)

BLUEPRINT PRICE CODE: B

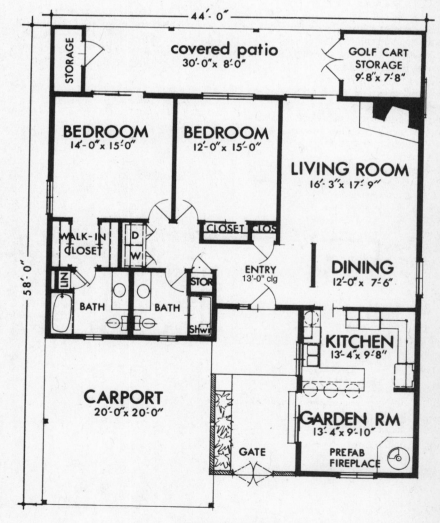

MAIN FLOOR

**WOOD EXTERIOR
REAR VIEW**

Photo by: Karl Bischoff

Panoramic Views

- This home lets you take maximum advantage of a particularly scenic or woodsy lot. Its octagonal design directs the focus of decking and window views outward in all directions.
- A fireplace warms the spacious living and dining area, where two sets of sliding glass doors offer deck access.
- The well-planned kitchen is adjacent to the laundry room, to minimize the time spent on chores.
- Bedrooms gain added character from the home's unusual angles. The master bedroom is secluded and boasts a private bath with a spacious shower.
- The basement option gives you a fourth bedroom with a nearby bath—perfect for an aging parent or a boomerang child! A cozy downstairs den lets you work or study in privacy.
- Plans can be ordered for either a wood or a stucco exterior.

**STUCCO EXTERIOR
REAR VIEW**

NOTE:
The above photographed home may have been modified by the homeowner. Please refer to floor plan and/or drawn elevation shown for actual blueprint details.

Plans H-942-1, -1A, -2 & -2A	
Bedrooms: 3+	**Baths:** 2-3
Living Area:	
Main floor	1,564 sq. ft.
Daylight basement	1,170 sq. ft.
Total Living Area:	**1,564/2,734 sq. ft.**
Tuck-under garage	394 sq. ft.
Exterior Wall Framing:	2x6
Foundation Options:	**Plan #**
Daylight basement (wood)	H-942-1
Daylight basement (stucco)	H-942-2
Crawlspace (wood)	H-942-1A
Crawlspace (stucco)	H-942-2A

(All plans can be built with your choice of foundation and framing. A generic conversion diagram is available. See order form.)

BLUEPRINT PRICE CODE:	**B/D**

DAYLIGHT BASEMENT

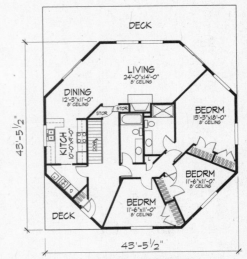

MAIN FLOOR

Plans H-942-1, -1A, -2 & -2A

*PRICES AND DETAILS
ON PAGES 2-5*

Peak of Perfection

- This home, with expansive outdoor spaces and a relaxed interior, culminates at a central peak in the roof.
- Inside, all rooms are topped by a unique vaulted ceiling; it slopes from the center of the home, where its 15½-ft. height is supported by a king post, down to each of the four sides, where it measures 7½ ft. at the lowest point.
- The living room is dominated by a striking fireplace and breathtaking views

to the outdoors. Sliding glass doors lead to a wraparound deck bordered on two sides by a built-in seat.
- The kitchen shares a serving counter with both the living room and the bright dining room. Easy access to the front deck simplifies impromptu summer meals outside.
- The sleeping quarters are grouped together for privacy. The primary bedroom features sliding glass doors to the rear deck, and a private, compartmentalized bath. The secondary bedrooms share a hall bath nearby.
- Blueprints for this home include plans for a detached, two-car garage.

Plan H-913-1A

Bedrooms: 3	Baths: 2
Living Area:	
Main floor	1,504 sq. ft.
Total Living Area:	**1,504 sq. ft.**
Detached garage	528 sq. ft.
Exterior Wall Framing:	2x4

Foundation Options:

Crawlspace
(All plans can be built with your choice of foundation and framing. A generic conversion diagram is available. See order form.)

BLUEPRINT PRICE CODE:	B

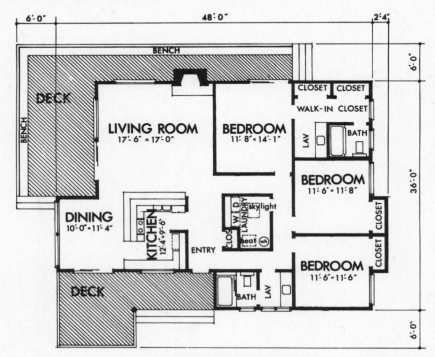

MAIN FLOOR

Just Beachy!

- This home offers outdoor living spaces, sunny windows, and open rooms. In other words, it's the ideal beach retreat.
- The open carport underneath the home includes a good-sized storage room to hold beach umbrellas, shovels and pails and other vacation paraphernalia.
- Upstairs, the living room provides plenty of room for rambunctious games of charades or Pictionary. Under its 11½-ft. vaulted ceiling, a corner fireplace will warm those chilled bones.
- French doors open to a rear deck that is the perfect spot to savor a cup of coffee and watch the waves roll in. This breezy space is also great for displaying a colorful wind-sock collection.
- The breakfast nook also has French doors to the deck, plus a snack counter where you can grab a quick bite. The dining room awaits those nights when you want a more formal setting.
- Across the home, the master suite's deck access gives you an escape. A dressing area leads to the bath.
- A secondary bedroom at the front of the home boasts a private deck.
- Unless otherwise noted, every room includes a soaring 10-ft. vaulted ceiling.

Plan HDS-99-251

Bedrooms: 2	Baths: 2
Living Area:	
Main floor	1,549 sq. ft.
Total Living Area:	**1,549 sq. ft.**
Tuck-under carport	1,429 sq. ft.
Enclosed storage under home	106 sq. ft.
Exterior Wall Framing:	2x4

Foundation Options:

Pier
(All plans can be built with your choice of foundation and framing. A generic conversion diagram is available. See order form.)

BLUEPRINT PRICE CODE: B

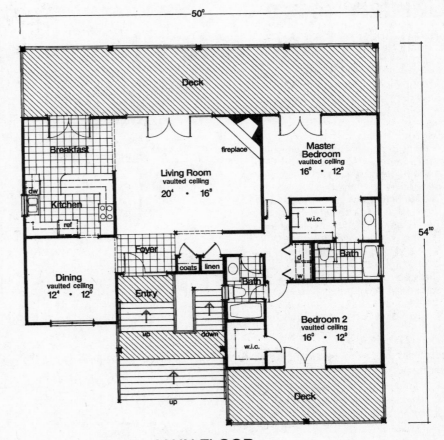

MAIN FLOOR

Garden Room Warms Home

- From the sklighted air-lock entry hall, it's possible to proceed in privacy to any part of this contemporary home.
- A soaring living room with a 16-ft. vaulted ceiling, lofty clerestory windows and a massive fireplace extends to the peaceful passive-solar garden room.
- A sunny dining area overlooking a back deck opens from the living room.
- The kitchen easily serves the dining room as well as a cozy family room.
- Two standard-sized bedrooms share a common bath, while the master bedroom at the rear of the house boasts its own full bathroom.
- The basement plan (H-2111-1B) features a huge recreation room with a fireplace, an extra bedroom with a bath, storage space and a handy workshop.

Plans H-2111-1A & -1B

Bedrooms: 3+	Baths: 2-3
Living Area:	
Main floor (crawlspace version)	1,448 sq. ft.
Main floor (basement version)	1,497 sq. ft.
Passive garden room	92 sq. ft.
Daylight basement	1,387 sq. ft.
Total Living Area:	**1,540/2,976 sq. ft.**
Garage	395 sq. ft.
Exterior Wall Framing:	2x6
Foundation Options:	**Plan #**
Daylight basement	H-2111-1B
Crawlspace	H-2111-1A

(All plans can be built with your choice of foundation and framing. A generic conversion diagram is available. See order form.)

BLUEPRINT PRICE CODE:	**B/D**

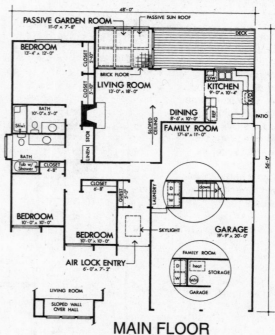

MAIN FLOOR

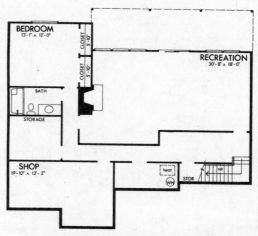

DAYLIGHT BASEMENT

Out of the Ordinary

- With its 13-ft., 8-in. vaulted ceiling, this home's spacious Great Room takes it convincingly out of the ordinary!
- The Great Room includes an impressive fireplace and easy access—both physically and visually—to a large backyard deck.
- The kitchen/breakfast area includes a delightfully sunny bay window and a 13-ft., 8-in. vaulted ceiling.

- The master suite features a 12-ft. vaulted ceiling, and has a split bath and a large walk-in closet. This is the spot for relaxation! Try cozying up to the trio of windows and finishing off that favorite novel, or simply catch an afternoon nap.
- The den may be used as an attractive and convenient home office, or as a third bedroom for your growing family. But why stop there? You may turn it into a playroom or even an exciting media room for the weekends.
- Basement stairs are convenient to both the front entry and the garage door.

Plan B-88056	
Bedrooms: 2+	**Baths:** 2
Living Area:	
Main floor	1,338 sq. ft.
Total Living Area:	**1,338 sq. ft.**
Standard basement	1,338 sq. ft.
Garage	380 sq. ft.
Exterior Wall Framing:	2x4
Foundation Options:	

Standard basement
(All plans can be built with your choice of foundation and framing. A generic conversion diagram is available. See order form.)

BLUEPRINT PRICE CODE:	**A**

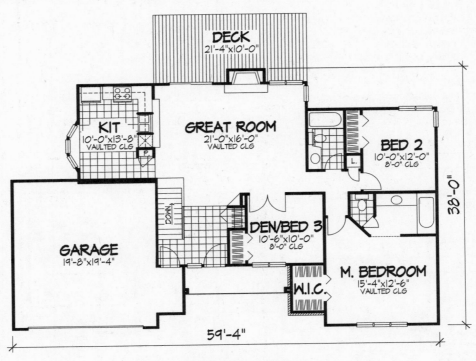

MAIN FLOOR

It's All Yours

- This efficient, affordable design masterfully blends a modest square footage with open spaces, high ceilings and numerous amenities.
- Outside, the covered entry shelters visitors from the elements as it ushers them into the warm interior.
- Straight ahead, the spacious living room shares a soaring 13-ft. ceiling with the dining room.
- At the heart of the living room, a warm fireplace sets a casual, comfortable

mood. An overhead plant shelf defines the dining room as it lends a stylish touch to formal meals.
- A set of double doors swings open to a backyard deck, where you will drink in the splendor of many magnificent spring and summer afternoons.
- In the nearby kitchen, plenty of room is available to set up a more casual eating area for day-to-day meals.
- Across the home, the master bedroom showcases a 12½-ft. ceiling. Its luxurious bath offers a relaxing whirlpool tub.

Plan B-95005	
Bedrooms: 2+	**Baths:** 2
Living Area:	
Main floor	1,577 sq. ft.
Total Living Area:	**1,577 sq. ft.**
Standard basement	1,577 sq. ft.
Garage	420 sq. ft.
Exterior Wall Framing:	2x6
Foundation Options:	
Standard basement	

(All plans can be built with your choice of foundation and framing. A generic conversion diagram is available. See order form.)

BLUEPRINT PRICE CODE:	**B**

MAIN FLOOR

A Real Charmer

- This charming design is exceptionally livable. Maximum use of space allows for four bedrooms within its modest square footage.
- The living room and dining area flow together to create a large, open expanse suitable for entertaining on any scale. A formal holiday dinner with all the trimmings is as at home here as your raucous Super Bowl bash.
- The U-shaped kitchen surrounds the family chef, making dinner a joy to cook and serve. There's plenty of cabinet space, and a big pantry closet holds all your food essentials, plus some hidden goodies!
- The master suite boasts features you'd only expect to find in a larger home. The walk-in closet is tucked into a corner off the roomy private bath.
- Three secondary bedrooms share another bath. A door closes off the sleeping wing from the rest of the home.
- A wide backyard patio is a great place for stargazing on summer nights.
- Outdoor storage holds yard equipment.

Plan E-1211

Bedrooms: 4	Baths: 2
Living Area:	
Main floor	1,235 sq. ft.
Total Living Area:	**1,235 sq. ft.**
Carport	274 sq. ft.
Storage	51 sq. ft.
Exterior Wall Framing:	2x6

Foundation Options:

Crawlspace

Slab

(All plans can be built with your choice of foundation and framing. A generic conversion diagram is available. See order form.)

BLUEPRINT PRICE CODE: A

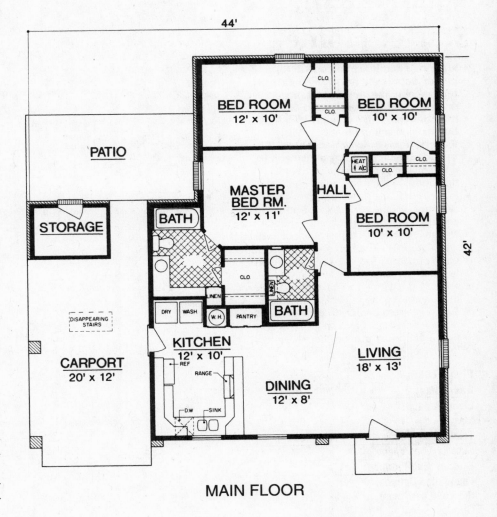

MAIN FLOOR

Plan E-1211

PRICES AND DETAILS ON PAGES 2-5

Smart, Sharp Starter Home

- Ideal for a family starting out, or for a pair of empty nesters looking for a cozy retirement home, this sharp, compact one-story will steal your heart away!
- Its design makes it extremely affordable, but you'll also find plenty of stylish features, some of which offer hints of a Victorian style, including a cute porch with spindlework detailing and half-timbering on the front-facing gable.
- Inside, the living room is surprisingly spacious. It's the perfect spot for hosting get-togethers with friends and family.
- The galley-style kitchen is efficient and well equipped. The laundry room's close proximity lets you keep an eye on two tasks at once.
- Nearby, the dining room features access to a pleasant patio in back.
- Two nice-sized bedrooms provide a place for the both of you as well as your new addition; or use the spare bedroom for visiting relatives.

Plan J-8632

Bedrooms: 2	Baths: 1
Living Area:	
Main floor	889 sq. ft.
Total Living Area:	**889 sq. ft.**
Standard basement	889 sq. ft.
Exterior Wall Framing:	2x4

Foundation Options:

Standard basement
Crawlspace
Slab
(All plans can be built with your choice of foundation and framing. A generic conversion diagram is available. See order form.)

BLUEPRINT PRICE CODE: AA

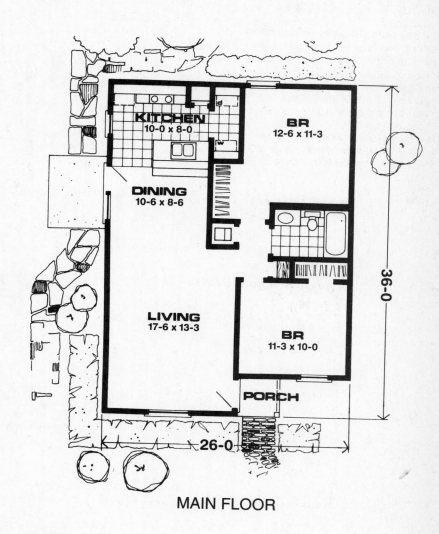

MAIN FLOOR

Away at Last!

- Just one sight of this clever home will remind you that you've escaped the cares of everyday life. A huge, angled wraparound deck hints at the time you'll spend relaxing outdoors.
- A comfortable floor plan makes maximum use of the home's modest square footage.
- The entry opens, on one side, to the massive living room. Here, sliding glass doors lead to the deck, and large

windows with transoms create a wall of windows. The natural beauty of the outside view renders interior decorating unnecessary.
- A lovely fireplace warms this space and imbues chilly afternoons—and quiet evenings—with romantic charm.
- The U-shaped kitchen shares a breakfast bar with the living room. It also features a window over the sink.
- Two bedrooms, one with dual closets, share a full bath. A nice-sized hall closet provides extra storage space.

Plan H-786

Bedrooms: 2	Baths: 1
Living Area:	
Main floor	880 sq. ft.
Total Living Area:	**880 sq. ft.**
Exterior Wall Framing:	2x4

Foundation Options:

Crawlspace
(All plans can be built with your choice of foundation and framing. A generic conversion diagram is available. See order form.)

BLUEPRINT PRICE CODE: AA

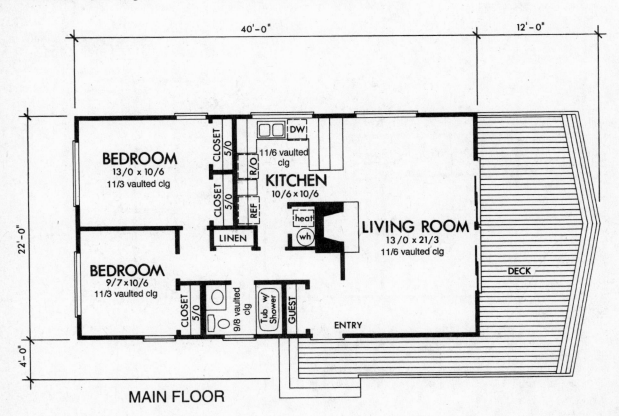

MAIN FLOOR

Plan H-786

Two-Bedroom Country Cottage

- This two-bedroom country-style cottage includes some surprising amenities for a home of modest size. It's a cozy primary home or a vacation retreat.
- The long, covered front porch is just the spot for sitting with guests and enjoying a glass of iced tea before moving inside for dinner.
- Past the porch, you enter a generous family room that's warmed by an inviting fireplace.

- The family room flows into a dining area with bright windows.
- The kitchen features a doorway that leads directly into the garage for ease in unloading groceries on shopping day. A big pantry is located in the adjoining laundry room.
- A screened porch allows you to stay dry while you enjoy the sound of the spring rain.
- The master bedroom boasts direct access to the screened porch, as well as a walk-in closet and a private bath.
- A secondary bedroom includes plenty of closet space and its own access to a shared hall bath.

Plan C-7520

Bedrooms: 2	Baths: 2
Living Area:	
Main floor	1,420 sq. ft.
Total Living Area:	**1,420 sq. ft.**
Screened porch	174 sq. ft.
Daylight basement	1,350 sq. ft.
Garage	444 sq. ft.
Storage	42 sq. ft.
Exterior Wall Framing:	2x4

Foundation Options:
Daylight basement
Crawlspace
Slab
(All plans can be built with your choice of foundation and framing. A generic conversion diagram is available. See order form.)

BLUEPRINT PRICE CODE:	A

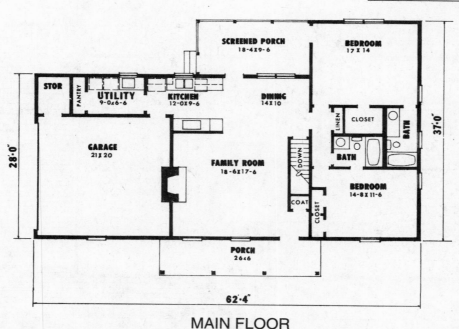

MAIN FLOOR

Classic Economy

- This quaint home uses simple and clean exterior lines for economical construction and a classic look.
- Above the living and dining rooms, a 12-ft. vaulted ceiling soars. The fireplace blazes warmly and points the way to a deck that addresses the backyard with relaxed grace.
- In the kitchen, you'll find a place for everything and everything in its place. The island presents itself unobtrusively, yet provides plenty of room for late-night pizza parties or quick breakfasts.
- Two secondary bedrooms lead to the master suite, which offers a walk-in closet and a 12½-ft. vaulted ceiling in the sleeping chamber. A private bath completes this cozy retreat.
- The home's two-car garage nestles up to the utility room and guest closet.

Plan B-88085

Bedrooms: 3	Baths: 2
Living Area:	
Main floor	1,561 sq. ft.
Total Living Area:	**1,561 sq. ft.**
Standard basement	1,561 sq. ft.
Garage	455 sq. ft.
Exterior Wall Framing:	2x4

Foundation Options:

Standard basement

(All plans can be built with your choice of foundation and framing. A generic conversion diagram is available. See order form.)

BLUEPRINT PRICE CODE:	**B**

Floor Plan

- BDRM 2 — 11'-8"x11'-4" — 8'-0" CLG.
- BDRM 3 — 10'-6"x10'-4" — 8'-0" CLG.
- DECK — 19'-0"x10'-8"
- M. BDRM — 14'-0"x12'-0" — VAULTED CLG.
- LIVING — 24'-0"x14'-8" — VAULTED CLG.
- DINING
- W.I.C.
- W. D.
- BRKFST — 9'-4"x11'-8" — 8'-0" CLG.
- KIT
- DOWN
- P. DESK
- IS.
- PLANT SHELF
- GARAGE — 21'-4"x21'-4"
- 58'-8"
- 50'-0"

MAIN FLOOR

Stylish Tradition

- Classic styling is captured in this home's traditional exterior, which is accented with a half-round transom window and an inviting porch.
- Inside, the open foyer shares an 11-ft., 4-in. ceiling with the spacious living room. A fireplace adds a comforting glow to all gatherings, while French doors lead to an expansive rear terrace.
- The formal dining room is neatly tucked away for quiet conversation over a memorable meal.
- The walk-through kitchen is located between the dining room and the casual dinette. Sliding French doors open to the side yard and a second terrace. Morning coffee will taste great in the fresh air!
- The perfect location of the laundry area provides a service entrance from the garage or the outdoors.
- The secluded master bedroom includes a walk-in closet and direct terrace access through sliding French doors. A whirlpool tub anchors the private master bath, where a separate shower gives you another bathing option.
- Two additional bedrooms share an oversized hall bath. The larger bedroom boasts a 10-ft., 4-in. ceiling.

Plan AHP-9622	
Bedrooms: 3	**Baths:** 2
Living Area:	
Main floor	1,470 sq. ft.
Total Living Area:	**1,470 sq. ft.**
Standard basement	1,502 sq. ft.
Garage	420 sq. ft.
Exterior Wall Framing:	2x4 or 2x6

Foundation Options:
Standard basement
Crawlspace
Slab
(All plans can be built with your choice of foundation and framing. A generic conversion diagram is available. See order form.)

BLUEPRINT PRICE CODE:	A

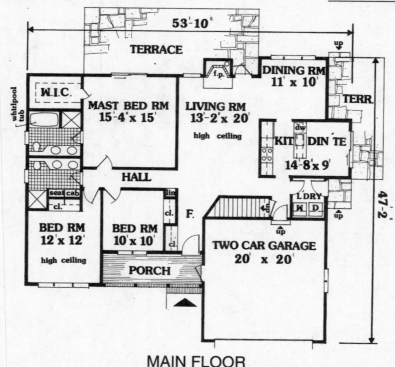

MAIN FLOOR

Two Courtyards

- This home is entered through a lovely gated courtyard. The master suite has access to a second courtyard at the back of the design.
- Inside, a formal dining room with a window seat adjoins a living room warmed by a fireplace. The two spaces are separated by a divider with a wet bar and built-in bookshelves that open to the living room. Adjustable glass shelves hang from the ceiling above. Use the divider top as a buffet server.
- The kitchen flows into a casual dining area that includes bright windows and plenty of storage space.
- A doorway in the living room accesses a three-season screened porch that opens to a side patio.
- The master suite boasts several handy amenities, including a walk-in closet, a personal bath with a dual-sink vanity and access to the rear courtyard, which is surrounded by a 6-ft. privacy fence.
- Two secondary bedrooms flank a full hall bath that is accessible to the home's common living areas.

Plan E-1508

Bedrooms: 3	Baths: 2
Living Area:	
Main floor	1,565 sq. ft.
Total Living Area:	**1,565 sq. ft.**
Screened porch	128 sq. ft.
Garage and storage	486 sq. ft.
Exterior Wall Framing:	2x6

Foundation Options:

Crawlspace

Slab

(All plans can be built with your choice of foundation and framing. A generic conversion diagram is available. See order form.)

BLUEPRINT PRICE CODE: B

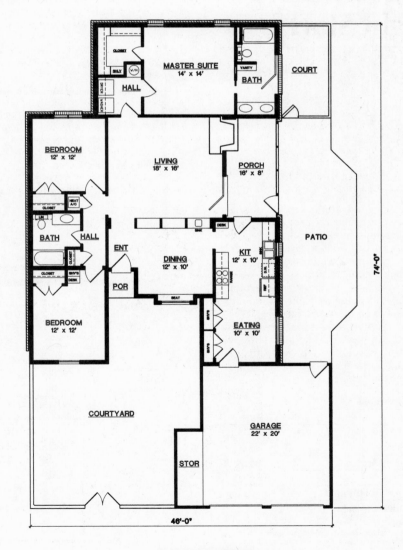

MAIN FLOOR

Plan E-1508

PRICES AND DETAILS ON PAGES 2-5

Off to the Right Start

- This modest-sized home provides a cozy nest for a young family just starting out. The simple design also makes it ideal for single adults or a family on the lookout for a peaceful vacation getaway.
- Inside, a corner fireplace in the spacious living room offers a cozy centerpiece to gather around. Sink into your favorite overstuffed chair and kick back with a good book and a refreshing beverage. On more festive evenings, the fireplace will warm the crowd during a boisterous round of charades.
- During the summer months, family and guests will gravitate to a wide side deck for tasty barbecued dinners and animated conversation.
- A private bath in each of the bedrooms makes this home well suited for putting up guests on the weekend.
- Every room features a space-enhancing 11-ft., 10-in. ceiling. Adjustable shelves along many of the walls offer ample storage space for books, games and other sundries.

Plan SAN-5008

Bedrooms: 2	Baths: 2
Living Area:	
Main floor	784 sq. ft.
Total Living Area:	**784 sq. ft.**
Garage	576 sq. ft.
Exterior Wall Framing:	2x4

Foundation Options:

Crawlspace
(All plans can be built with your choice of foundation and framing. A generic conversion diagram is available. See order form.)

BLUEPRINT PRICE CODE: **A**

MAIN FLOOR

Adorable and Affordable

- This affordably sized one-story cottage is filled with surprising features and brimming with country charm.
- Past the covered front porch, the inviting entry flows directly into the combination living/dining room. An airy 10-ft. vaulted ceiling and two bay windows add a feeling of spaciousness to the area, while a two-sided fireplace extends its warmth to the adjoining family room and kitchen.
- The kitchen includes a pantry and an island cooktop/snack bar and merges with the family room for an open yet intimate atmosphere. Sliding glass doors open to the side yard.
- The sleeping wing is oriented to the back of the home. The master suite features a roomy walk-in closet and a private bath with a garden spa tub, a separate shower and a dual-sink vanity.
- Two additional bedrooms share the main bath.

Plan S-11094

Bedrooms: 3	Baths: 2
Living Area:	
Main floor	1,370 sq. ft.
Total Living Area:	**1,370 sq. ft.**
Standard basement	1,310 sq. ft.
Garage	460 sq. ft.
Exterior Wall Framing:	**2x6**

Foundation Options:

Standard basement

Crawlspace

Slab

(All plans can be built with your choice of foundation and framing. A generic conversion diagram is available. See order form.)

BLUEPRINT PRICE CODE: A

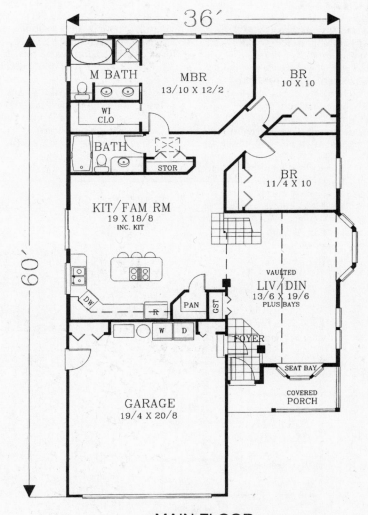

MAIN FLOOR

Warm Welcome

- Warm, wood siding and unique window treatments welcome family and friends to this appealing home!
- Step from the foyer to the open activity areas. Here, a corner fireplace and a lovely bow window imbue the living room with simple charm.
- Nearby, the dining room's wall of French doors overlooks a sprawling rear deck. The scent of summer blooms will distinguish summer parties that extend to the outdoors.
- The neat kitchen reserves a corner for casual eating and boasts another French door to the rear deck. The large laundry room nearby includes an outside service entrance.
- For a measure of privacy, this efficient design clusters the sleeping quarters in their own wing.
- The master bath contributes a walk-in closet, a whirlpool tub and dual sinks to your comfort. A vaulted, 10-ft. ceiling tops the bedroom.
- Two other bedrooms share a hall bath.

Plan HFL-1910-JO	
Bedrooms: 3	**Baths:** 2
Living Area:	
Main floor	1,387 sq. ft.
Total Living Area:	**1,387 sq. ft.**
Standard basement	1,387 sq. ft.
Garage and storage	493 sq. ft.
Exterior Wall Framing:	2x6

Foundation Options:

Standard basement
Slab
(All plans can be built with your choice of foundation and framing. A generic conversion diagram is available. See order form.)

BLUEPRINT PRICE CODE:	**A**

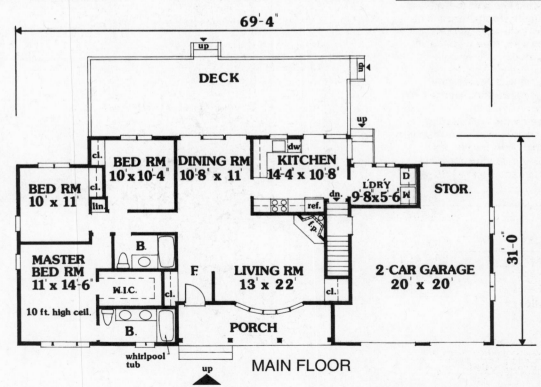

MAIN FLOOR

Compact One-Story

- A lovely porch, fishscale shingles and durable brick dress up this compact one-story home.
- The porch offers access into the home and into the adjoining two-car garage.
- The main entry separates the master bedroom and the main living areas from the secondary bedroom wing.
- With its 15-ft. sloped ceiling and soaring brick fireplace, the living room dramatically introduces the home. The handy pass-through from the kitchen makes serving or entertaining a breeze.
- Flowing from the living room is the bright dining area, which may be extended to a covered back porch.
- Recessed fluorescent lighting illuminates the kitchen, which is conveniently located at the center of the floor plan.
- The removed master bedroom has its own porch access, in addition to a large walk-in closet and a private bath.
- The secondary bedrooms also have walk-in closets and share another bath.

Plan E-1425

Bedrooms: 3	Baths: 2
Living Area:	
Main floor	1,407 sq. ft.
Total Living Area:	**1,407 sq. ft.**
Garage and storage	544 sq. ft.
Exterior Wall Framing:	2x6

Foundation Options:

Crawlspace

Slab

(All plans can be built with your choice of foundation and framing. A generic conversion diagram is available. See order form.)

BLUEPRINT PRICE CODE: A

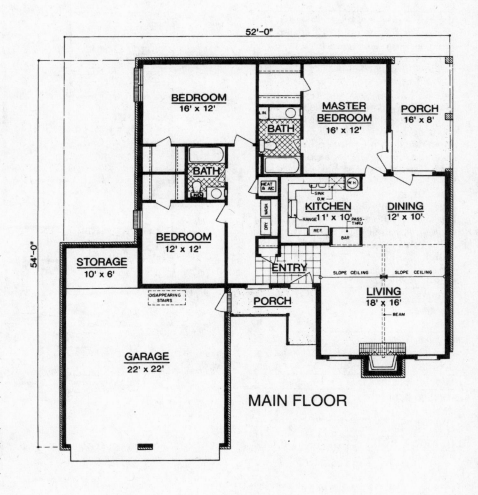

52'-0"

54'-0"

BEDROOM 16' x 12'

MASTER BEDROOM 16' x 12'

PORCH 16' x 8'

BATH

BATH

KITCHEN 11' x 10'

DINING 12' x 10'

BEDROOM 12' x 12'

STORAGE 10' x 6'

ENTRY

SLOPE CEILING   SLOPE CEILING

DISAPPEARING STAIRS

PORCH

LIVING 18' x 16'

BEAM

GARAGE 22' x 22'

MAIN FLOOR

Plan E-1425

PRICES AND DETAILS ON PAGES 2-5

Simply Stylish

- Affordable does not mean styleless. This plan illustrates the point with exterior character from a covered front porch with stately columns and an interior full of pleasant surprises.
- Once inside, there is an exciting view into the vaulted-ceilinged living room with its two-sided corner fireplace and adjacent double-doored den. The den can accommodate hobby functions, a home office with quaint corner window seat, a reading or TV room, or a third bedroom.
- The U-shaped kitchen opens to a spacious eating area with rear deck access through a French door.
- The master suite offers a vaulted ceiling with a plant shelf focal point. There is also a private bathroom and a spacious walk-in closet.

Plan B-88062

Bedrooms: 3	Baths: 2
Living Area:	
Main floor	1,408 sq. ft.
Total Living Area:	**1,408 sq. ft.**
Standard basement	1,408 sq. ft.
Garage	441 sq. ft.
Exterior Wall Framing:	2x4

Foundation Options:

Standard basement
(All plans can be built with your choice of foundation and framing. A generic conversion diagram is available. See order form.)

BLUEPRINT PRICE CODE:	**A**

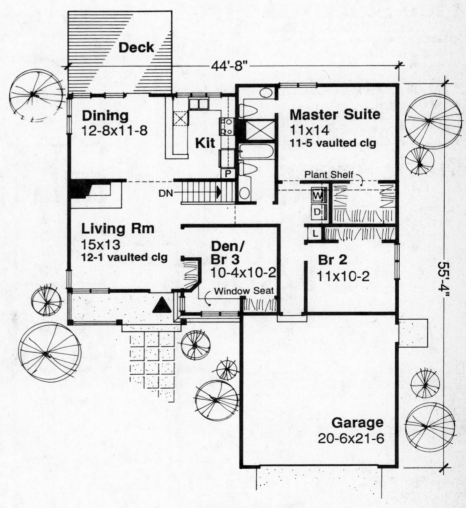

MAIN FLOOR

European Flair

- Arched window arrangements, striking stone and metal roofing above the garage give this home a European flair.
- The living room features a 10-ft. vaulted ceiling and a warm fireplace.
- The adjacent dining room includes a pass-through to the kitchen.
- An inviting bayed breakfast nook is a great spot for a leisurely cup of coffee.
- In the 10-ft. vaulted master suite are two walk-in closets and a private bath.
- Double doors introduce a quiet den or extra bedroom with bathroom access.

Plan B-94024

Bedrooms: 2+	Baths: 2
Living Area:	
Main floor	1,431 sq. ft.
Total Living Area:	**1,431 sq. ft.**
Standard basement	1,431 sq. ft.
Garage	380 sq. ft.
Exterior Wall Framing:	2x6

Foundation Options:

Standard basement

(All plans can be built with your choice of foundation and framing. A generic conversion diagram is available. See order form.)

BLUEPRINT PRICE CODE: A

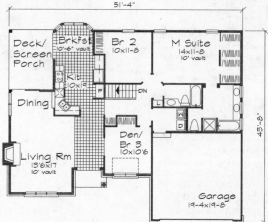

Plan B-94024

MAIN FLOOR

Rustic Appeal

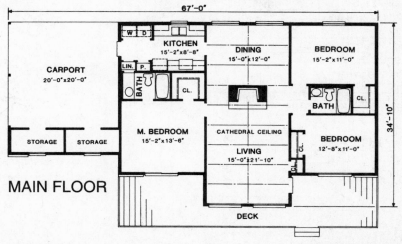

- Rustic stone and wood, plus high windows, give this home appeal.
- A massive central stone fireplace is the focal point of the majestic living room, which is accented by a 15-ft. cathedral ceiling with exposed beams. Behind the fireplace, the cathedral ceiling continues into the dining room.
- The kitchen features a sunny sink and easy service to the dining room.
- The master suite boasts a private master bath and sliding glass doors to the deck.

Plan C-7360

Bedrooms: 3	Baths: 2
Living Area:	
Main floor	1,454 sq. ft.
Total Living Area:	**1,454 sq. ft.**
Daylight basement	1,454 sq. ft.
Carport	400 sq. ft.
Storage	120 sq. ft.
Exterior Wall Framing:	2x4

Foundation Options:

Daylight basement

Crawlspace

Slab

(All plans can be built with your choice of foundation and framing. A generic conversion diagram is available. See order form.)

BLUEPRINT PRICE CODE: A

MAIN FLOOR

Plan C-7360

PRICES AND DETAILS **ON PAGES 2-5**

Affordable Excitement

- This affordable home adds excitement with pretty exterior touches and, on the interior, vaulted ceilings, pleasant views and a extra-large master bedroom!
- Fishscale shingling and an attractive railed fence give the outside of the home a charming appeal.
- Inside, the spacious living room is the perfect place to gather with family and friends. Its charming corner fireplace gives a warm, friendly glow to your special occasions, while a brilliant wraparound window bathes the whole room in glorious light.
- The L-shaped kitchen offers an efficient, open layout that's ideal for quick, carefree meal preparation. A bay window in the nearby dining area makes a cheery spot for a quick morning meal.
- When the weather's nice, step out to the back deck and enjoy the morning air.
- Surpisingly big, the master bedroom boasts a walk-in closet, a private dressing area and access to the full bath.

Plan B-116-8506

Bedrooms: 2	Baths: 1
Living Area:	
Main floor	1,123 sq. ft.
Total Living Area:	**1,123 sq. ft.**
Standard basement	1,123 sq. ft.
Garage	380 sq. ft.
Exterior Wall Framing:	2x4

Foundation Options:

Standard basement
(All plans can be built with your choice of foundation and framing. A generic conversion diagram is available. See order form.)

BLUEPRINT PRICE CODE:	**A**

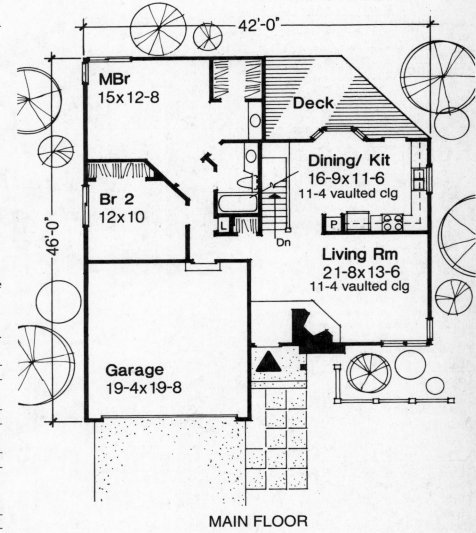

MAIN FLOOR

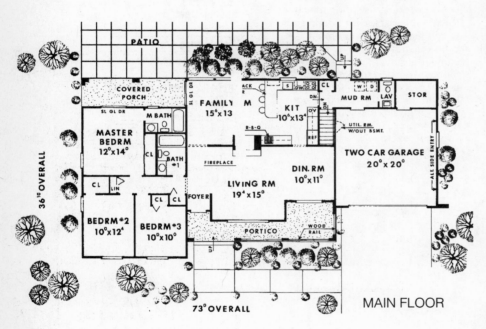

MAIN FLOOR

PATIO

COVERED PORCH

SL GL DR

MASTER BEDRM 12⁰x14⁰

M BATH

CL

BATH #1

CL LIN

BEDRM #2 10⁰x12⁴

CL CL

BEDRM #3 10⁰x10⁰

FOYER

FAMILY M 15⁶x13

KIT 10⁶x13⁴

FIREPLACE

R-B-Q

LIVING RM 19⁴x15⁰

DIN. RM 10⁰x11⁰

PORTICO

WOOD RAIL

UP

MUD RM

LAV

STOR

UTIL. RM. W/OUT BSMT.

REF

TWO CAR GARAGE 20⁰x20⁰

ALL SIDE ENTRY

36¹⁰ OVERALL

73⁰ OVERALL

Southwestern Seasoning

- Arched openings to a portico and a tile roof offer a Southwestern flavor to this stucco ranch.
- Formal living areas overlook the portico at the front of the home. A two-way fireplace is shared between the front rooms and the informal areas to the rear.
- The rear-oriented fireplace includes a barbecue. A snack bar separates the kitchen from the adjoining family room. Sliders open to a covered porch and a patio beyond.
- Laundry facilities and a half-bath are located near the garage entrance.
- A master bedroom with private porch access, two secondary bedrooms and two full baths complete the floor plan.

Plan AX-98273

Bedrooms: 3	Baths: 2 ½
Space:	
Main floor	1,548 sq. ft.
Total Living Area	**1,548 sq. ft.**
Basement	1,472 sq. ft.
Garage	400 sq. ft.
Exterior Wall Framing	2x4

Foundation options:

Standard Basement

Slab

(All plans can be built with your choice of foundation and framing. A generic conversion diagram is available. See order form.)

BLUEPRINT PRICE CODE   B

INTERIOR ELEVATION

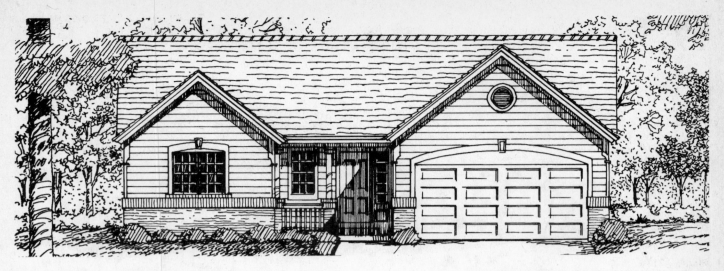

Starting Out

- For a young family starting out, or empty nesters savoring some newfound freedom, this well-planned ranch-style home fits the bill just perfectly.
- The recessed, covered entry affords a bit of privacy, while also shielding visitors from the rain and wind.
- Inside, the combined family and dining rooms provide a comfortable place to enjoy some time together. Plenty of room is available to spread out and work on crafts or projects, while a fireplace adds a warm glow.

- Sliding glass doors open to a secluded porch, an ideal site to set up a pair of wicker rockers. As spring rolls into town, settle back with a soda and watch the new season unfold.
- When friends come over to watch the game, the serving bar between the family room and the kitchen holds reserves of chips and pretzels. A built-in desk in the breakfast nook is great for grabbing phone calls.
- In the master suite, curl up on the cozy window seat to read a favorite novel or the latest issue of *People*. The private bath boasts a dual-sink vanity.

Plan BRF-1324

Bedrooms: 2+	**Baths: 2**

Living Area:

Main floor	1,324 sq. ft.
Total Living Area:	**1,324 sq. ft.**
Standard basement	1,324 sq. ft.
Garage	453 sq. ft.

Exterior Wall Framing: 2x4

Foundation Options:

Standard basement
Crawlspace
Slab

(All plans can be built with your choice of foundation and framing. A generic conversion diagram is available. See order form.)

BLUEPRINT PRICE CODE: A

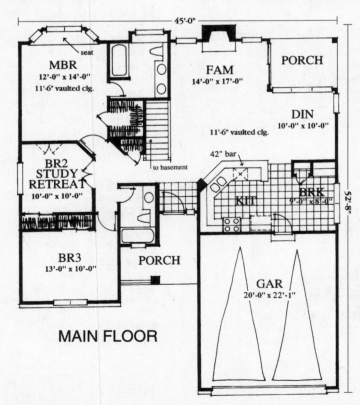

MAIN FLOOR

STAIRWAY AREA IN CRAWLSPACE AND SLAB VERSIONS

The Easy Life

- This affordable one-story home makes easy living, along with today's most up-to-date amenities, readily available.
- The covered entry to the side of the home opens directly into the home's common living areas. An 11-ft., 8-in. vaulted ceiling crowns the open living and dining area, while sunlight pours in through a cheery boxed-out window and a fireplace adds a homey glow.
- The kitchen includes a bar to the living areas, plus room for casual meals.
- At day's end, you'll love to retreat to the inviting master suite, highlighted by an 11-ft. vaulted ceiling and a private bath.

Plan B-87116

Bedrooms: 2+	Baths: 2
Living Area:	
Main floor	1,270 sq. ft.
Total Living Area:	**1,270 sq. ft.**
Standard basement	1,270 sq. ft.
Garage	374 sq. ft.
Exterior Wall Framing:	2x4

Foundation Options:

Standard basement

(All plans can be built with your choice of foundation and framing. A generic conversion diagram is available. See order form.)

BLUEPRINT PRICE CODE:	A

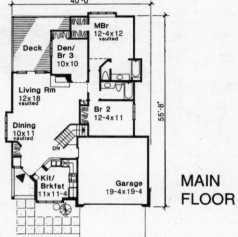

MAIN FLOOR

Plan B-87116

Rustic Ranch

- A rustic exterior and a relaxed interior define this warm ranch-style home.
- The living room flows into the bayed dining room, which opens to a patio. Both rooms are enhanced by 14-ft. vaulted ceilings and a central fireplace.
- The functional kitchen includes a snack bar to the dining room, a pantry and plenty of cabinet space.
- The master bedroom boasts a mirrored dressing area, a private bath and abundant closet space.
- The third bedroom includes a cozy window seat.

Plan NW-521

Bedrooms: 3	Baths: 2
Living Area:	
Main floor	1,187 sq. ft.
Total Living Area:	**1,187 sq. ft.**
Garage	448 sq. ft.
Exterior Wall Framing:	2x6

Foundation Options:

Crawlspace

(All plans can be built with your choice of foundation and framing. A generic conversion diagram is available. See order form.)

BLUEPRINT PRICE CODE:	A

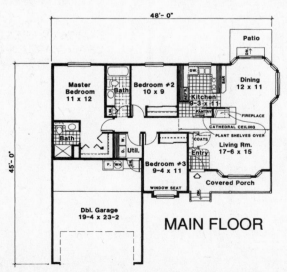

MAIN FLOOR

The Pursuit of Leisure

- With a serene exterior and an easy floor plan, this one-story home allows plenty of space in which to pursue your favorite leisurely pastimes. Further, its well-designed floor plan comfortably accommodates everyday living.
- To the left of the entry, the massive living room hosts a lovely fireplace and a breakfast bar shared with the U-shaped kitchen. This work space is brightened by a windowed sink.
- The feeling of spaciousness in these areas is magnified by a vaulted, exposed-beam ceiling.
- Sliding glass doors in the living room lead to a large wraparound deck. Ideal for festive summer barbecues and languid sunset-watching, you're sure to spend much of your time here.
- On the other side of the home, two bedrooms dwell at the end of a short hallway. They share a roomy bath.
- A hall storage closet is a nice bonus; take advantage of this extra space.
- Laundry facilities are tucked away in the corner of the two-car garage.

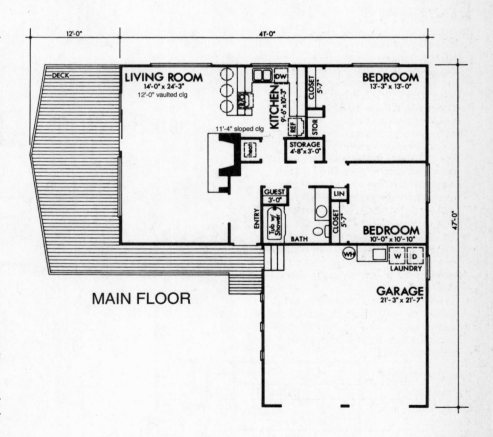

MAIN FLOOR

Plan H-786-3

Bedrooms: 2	Baths: 1
Living Area:	
Main floor	1,025 sq. ft.
Total Living Area:	**1,025 sq. ft.**
Garage	459 sq. ft.
Exterior Wall Framing:	2x4

Foundation Options:

Crawlspace

(All plans can be built with your choice of foundation and framing. A generic conversion diagram is available. See order form.)

BLUEPRINT PRICE CODE:	**A**

First-Home Features

- The first-time home buyer will be delighted with the features included in this 1,040-sq.-ft. ranch design.
- The entry opens into the good-sized living room, which is brightened by corner windows. A handy serving counter that extends from the kitchen makes serving snacks or drinks an easy option when entertaining.
- The L-shaped kitchen provides enough room for a dining area. Sliding glass doors usher in the sun while providing access to the large deck in the backyard. The deck is the perfect spot for a warm-weather barbecue!
- The master bedroom offers two closets, one of which is a walk-in, as well as a personal dressing area with its own vanity and a private entrance to the main bath.
- A secondary bedroom makes a great nursery or guest room. Singles or empty nesters might prefer to use this space for a home office, a casual den or an exercise room.

Plan UDG-90015

Bedrooms: 2	Baths: 1
Living Area:	
Main floor	1,040 sq. ft.
Total Living Area:	**1,040 sq. ft.**
Standard basement	1,040 sq. ft.
Garage	400 sq. ft.
Exterior Wall Framing:	2x4

Foundation Options:

Standard basement

(All plans can be built with your choice of foundation and framing. A generic conversion diagram is available. See order form.)

BLUEPRINT PRICE CODE:	**A**

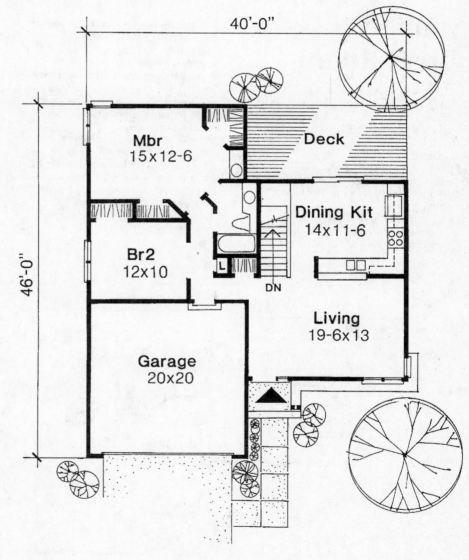

MAIN FLOOR

Plan UDG-90015

PRICES AND DETAILS
ON PAGES 2-5

Vaulted Great Room

- The covered entry of this rustic ranch welcomes you in to a dramatic Great Room with a cozy fireplace. An open, airy feel flows throughout the house with lofty 9-ft. ceilings and minimum hallway space.
- The Great Room's 13½-ft. vaulted ceiling peaks over the adjoining dining area which boasts a lovely built-in china hutch.
- Adjacent to the dining area is a spacious customized kitchen featuring a boxed-out garden window. The angled

counter ends with a cooktop and snack bar. In the basement version, the refrigerator and cooktop create a separate island.

- A pocket door opens to the laundry room, which includes a sink and plenty of counter space. With access from the two-car garage, this area also serves as a mudroom.
- The master bedroom is nestled into one corner with private access to the patio. This luxury suite includes a skylighted private bath featuring a designer shower, a dual-sink vanity, a garden tub and a generous linen closet.
- The remaining two bedrooms are serviced by the full bath across the hall.

Plan LRD-100193

Bedrooms: 3	Baths: 2
Living Area:	
Main floor	1,190 sq. ft.
Total Living Area:	**1,190 sq. ft.**
Standard basement	1,190 sq. ft.
Garage	495 sq. ft.
Exterior Wall Framing:	2x6

Foundation Options:

Standard basement
Crawlspace
(All plans can be built with your choice of foundation and framing. A generic conversion diagram is available. See order form.)

BLUEPRINT PRICE CODE:	A

MAIN FLOOR

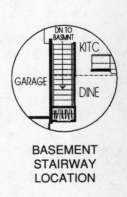

BASEMENT STAIRWAY LOCATION

Quiet Class

- This lovely home's unassuming facade quickly reveals a classy interior.
- A skylight-punctuated cathedral ceiling expands the space shared by the living and dining rooms.
- The spiffy country kitchen has room for your breakfast table and more! Sliding glass doors open to a backyard patio.
- The fantastic master bedroom flaunts backyard views and a private skylighted bath.
- This home is available with an optional first-floor plan that includes a two-car garage.

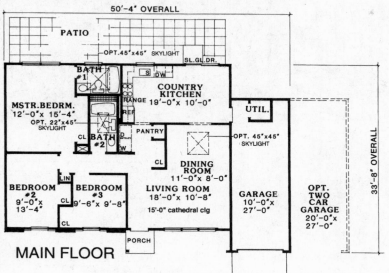

MAIN FLOOR

Plan AX-98818

Plan AX-98818

Bedrooms: 3	Baths: 2
Living Area:	
Main floor	1,190 sq. ft.
Total Living Area:	**1,190 sq. ft.**
Standard basement	1,296 sq. ft.
Garage and utility room	270 sq. ft.
Optional two-car garage	540 sq. ft.
Exterior Wall Framing:	2x4

Foundation Options:
Standard basement, Crawlspace, Slab
(All plans can be built with your choice of foundation and framing. A generic conversion diagram is available. See order form.)

BLUEPRINT PRICE CODE: **A**

Smart and Compact

- Compact and affordable, this home is a smart choice for new homeowners, second-home buyers or retirees.
- The covered front porch, decorative post and bright windows give the home its warm appeal.
- The living area centers around an impressive Great Room with a 12-ft. vaulted ceiling, a fireplace and a built-in bookcase. The kitchen/dining room combination faces an expandable area.
- The roomy master suite includes a cozy window seat, a large walk-in closet and a private bath.

MAIN FLOOR

Plan B-8317

Bedrooms: 2+	Baths: 2
Living Area:	
Main floor	1,016 sq. ft.
Total Living Area:	**1,016 sq. ft.**
Exterior Wall Framing:	2x4

Foundation Options:
Slab
(All plans can be built with your choice of foundation and framing. A generic conversion diagram is available. See order form.)

BLUEPRINT PRICE CODE: **A**

Plan B-8317

PRICES AND DETAILS
ON PAGES 2-5

Sunny and Cost-Efficient

- This home's big bright windows and economical square footage allow you to keep costs down without sacrificing aesthetics.
- The entry is brightened by clerestory windows, while the 14-ft. vaulted living room features floor-to-ceiling windows and is the perfect spot for hosting afternoon tea.
- The 9-ft. dining room has sliding glass doors opening to a backyard deck.

Invite the neighbors over for barbecue ribs on a warm summer day. The neat U-shaped kitchen includes a space-saving laundry closet and a pantry.
- The 11-ft.-high vaulted master bedroom offers a wonderful view of the backyard. The private master bath makes mornings run a little smoother.
- Two secondary bedrooms and another full bath round out the main floor.
- The full basement can be finished to provide more living space. Wouldn't a home office or a playroom be nice?
- This home's many windows and modest size make it a great choice for a vacation home.

Plan B-90066	
Bedrooms: 3	**Baths:** 2
Living Area:	
Main floor	1,135 sq. ft.
Total Living Area:	**1,135 sq. ft.**
Standard basement	1,135 sq. ft.
Garage	288 sq. ft.
Exterior Wall Framing:	2x4

Foundation Options:

Standard basement
(All plans can be built with your choice of foundation and framing. A generic conversion diagram is available. See order form.)

BLUEPRINT PRICE CODE:	A

MAIN FLOOR

54'-0"

31'-8"

Deck

Master Br 12-4x11-4 vaulted

Dining 9x11-4

Kit 9-6x10

Pan D W

DN

Br 2 10-4x10

Br 3 10x11-4

Living 19x12 vaulted

Garage 12-4x22

Rustic Recreational

- Touches of natural stone on the facade and chimney of this recreational design give it a relaxed, rustic look.
- The plan is fronted by a large deck. There's another deck in the backyard.
- The living/family room is crowned by a 15-ft., 4-in. cathedral ceiling that adds an air of spaciousness. Transom windows that reach to the peak of the roof enhance the effect. A fireplace is the room's natural focal point.

- Built-in cabinets serve as a room divider between the living room and the dining room.
- The galley-style kitchen opens to the dining room at one end and a utility room with a storage closet at the other.
- The master suite is separated from the secondary sleeping quarters for maximum privacy. The suite includes its own bath, a walk-in closet and sliding glass doors that open to the front deck.
- Two more bedrooms boast lots of closet space and share a full bath.
- The double carport includes two roomy storage areas.

Plan C-1454	
Bedrooms: 3	**Baths:** 2
Living Area:	
Main floor	1,454 sq. ft.
Total Living Area:	**1,454 sq. ft.**
Carport	400 sq. ft.
Storage	100 sq. ft.
Exterior Wall Framing:	2x4

Foundation Options:
Crawlspace
Slab
(All plans can be built with your choice of foundation and framing. A generic conversion diagram is available. See order form.)

BLUEPRINT PRICE CODE: A

Wood Deck

Utility

Kitchen 9'4" x 8'6"

Dining Room 14'10" x 11'2"

Bedroom 12'8" x 10'10"

Carport 20' x 20'

Bath

Bath

Master Bedroom 15'2" x 13'4"

Living/Family Room 14'10" x 15'

Bedroom 12'8" x 10'10"

Storage

Storage

34'10"

Wood Deck

Sun Shade

Wood Deck

67'

MAIN FLOOR

Affordable Country Living

- This affordable country cottage, with its Great Room, wraparound porch and master suite, is enhanced by many features found only in larger, more expensive homes.
- Located past the entrance, the Great Room is warmed by a fireplace and features a 10-ft.-high vaulted ceiling.

- Measuring close to 8 ft. at its widest points, the wraparound porch has more than enough room for rocking chairs or porch swings.
- The sunny kitchen, which has a large pantry and a convenient eating bar, shares a 10-ft.-high vaulted ceiling with the adjoining dining room.
- The master suite boasts a roomy walk-in closet and a private bath.
- A large hall bath and a compact laundry closet are convenient to the two remaining bedrooms.

Plan BOD-13-9A	
Bedrooms: 3	Baths: 2
Living Area:.	
Main floor	1,302 sq. ft.
Total Living Area:	**1,302 sq. ft.**
Garage	484 sq. ft.
Exterior Wall Framing:	2x4

Foundation Options:

Crawlspace
Slab
(All plans can be built with your choice of foundation and framing. A generic conversion diagram is available. See order form.)

BLUEPRINT PRICE CODE: **A**

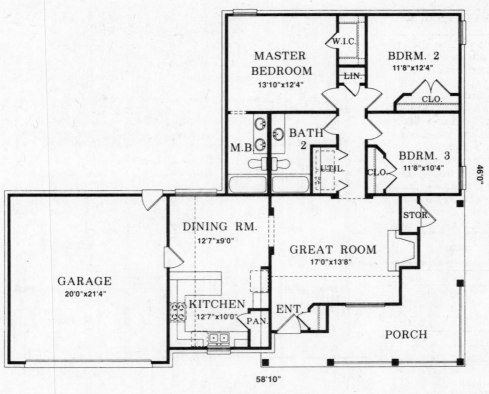

MAIN FLOOR

Rustic Ranch

- This ranch-style home offers a warm facade featuring a railed front porch and stone accents.
- Inside, the inviting living room includes an eye-catching fireplace, patio access and a sloped, beamed ceiling.
- The dining room adjoins the efficient U-shaped kitchen, which includes a pantry and a broom closet.
- The master suite offers a large walk-in closet and a roomy master bath.
- At the other end of the home, two secondary bedrooms with abundant closet space share another full bath.

Plan E-1410

Bedrooms: 3	Baths: 2
Living Area:	
Main floor	1,418 sq. ft.
Total Living Area:	**1,418 sq. ft.**
Garage	484 sq. ft.
Storage	38 sq. ft.
Exterior Wall Framing:	2x4

Foundation Options:

Crawlspace
Slab
(All plans can be built with your choice of foundation and framing. A generic conversion diagram is available. See order form.)

BLUEPRINT PRICE CODE:	**A**

MAIN FLOOR

Plan E-1410

Ritzy Rambler

- This inviting one-story home is full of fancy touches not usually associated with such an economical floor plan!
- A quaint, covered porch adorns the entry, which leads first to two secondary bedrooms and the well-placed laundry facilities between them.
- At the back of the home, the family room faces a warm fireplace.
- With a versatile center island, the adjoining kitchen and breakfast nook promise easy food preparation. Sliding glass doors lead to a backyard patio.
- Occupying a secluded corner, the master bedroom boasts a roomy walk-in closet and a private bath.

Plan NW-531

Bedrooms: 3	Baths: 2
Living Area:	
Main floor	1,214 sq. ft.
Total Living Area:	**1,214 sq. ft.**
Garage	380 sq. ft.
Exterior Wall Framing:	2x6

Foundation Options:

Crawlspace
(All plans can be built with your choice of foundation and framing. A generic conversion diagram is available. See order form.)

BLUEPRINT PRICE CODE:	**A**

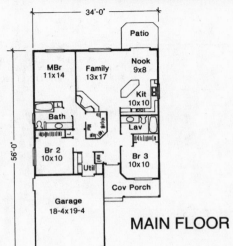

MAIN FLOOR

Plan NW-531

**PRICES AND DETAILS
ON PAGES 2-5**

Relax in a Sun Room Porch

- Classic styling is captured in this home's elegant exterior, accented with half-round windows.
- The graceful foyer has a sloped ceiling and flows into a huge entertaining space. The living and dining rooms share a fireplace and a view of the adjoining patio through exciting rear glass walls.
- A large casual living space is created with a sunny eating area and large kitchen. The addition of a sun room porch provides extra space for relaxing or entertaining.
- At the opposite end of the home, the master suite is the perfect quiet retreat. The bedroom features a tray ceiling and a private patio. A large walk-in closet and a personal bath are also included.
- Two secondary bedrooms and another full bath complete the floor plan.

Plan AHP-9370

Bedrooms: 3	Baths: 2
Living Area:	
Main floor	1,248 sq. ft.
Sunroom porch	125 sq. ft.
Total Living Area:	**1,373 sq. ft.**
Standard basement	1,248 sq. ft.
Garage and storage	507 sq. ft.
Exterior Wall Framing:	2x4 or 2x6

Foundation Options:

Standard basement

Crawlspace

Slab

(All plans can be built with your choice of foundation and framing. A generic conversion diagram is available. See order form.)

BLUEPRINT PRICE CODE: A

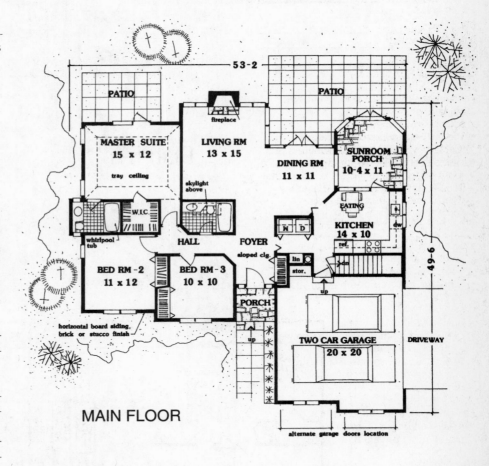

MAIN FLOOR

Roomy One-Story

- A wonderfully open floor plan is the keynote of this charming one-story country-style home.
- The inviting living room features a fireplace with built-in bookshelves or a media center. The adjoining dining room offers a large picture window that floods the eating area and the galley-style kitchen with natural light.

- The kitchen has easy access to the utility room and the garage.
- The sleeping wing includes three good-sized bedrooms and generous closet space. The master suite has a private bath, while the two secondary bedrooms share a full bath.
- Another special feature is the extra storage space located in the garage.
- This design is available with wood siding (shown) or with a brick exterior. Please specify your choice when ordering. Also specify 2x4 or 2x6 exterior wall framing.

Plan J-8274

Bedrooms: 3	**Baths:** 2

Living Area:

Main floor	1,441 sq. ft.
Total Living Area:	**1,441 sq. ft.**
Standard basement	1,441 sq. ft.
Garage	447 sq. ft.
Exterior Wall Framing:	2x4 or 2x6

Foundation Options:

Standard basement
Crawlspace
Slab
(All plans can be built with your choice of foundation and framing. A generic conversion diagram is available. See order form.)

BLUEPRINT PRICE CODE:	**A**

67'0"

34'0"

MASTER BEDROOM 13'2" X 15'3"

LIVING 15'2" X 19'0"

DINING 9'4" X 10'0"

STOR. 7'0" X 5'4"

STORAGE 13'0" X 5'0"

KITCHEN 9'0" X 11'8"

GARAGE 20'4" X 22'0"

BEDROOM 13'4" X 11'8"

BEDROOM 12'2" X 13'9"

UTILITY 9'0" X 5'5"

PORCH 16'6" X 5'0"

MAIN FLOOR

Plan J-8274

PRICES AND DETAILS
ON PAGES 2-5

Twice as Nice

- This plan functions nicely as a primary residence or a vacation home, making it doubly worthy of a second look.
- Clerestory windows and a big backyard deck accent the deceptively simple exterior of the design.
- Inside, the entry hallway leads to the generously sized living room, where a fireplace casts a warm glow. A row of clerestory windows combines with the 14½-ft vaulted ceiling to create a spacious feel.
- The walk-through kitchen opens directly to the dining area.
- Two main-floor bedrooms share a full bath. The master bedroom features his-and-hers closets.
- A fun backyard deck is just the place to relax and soak up the sun or enjoy a scenic view. It hosts coffee and dessert or a barbecue shindig with equal ease.
- The daylight basement plan boasts an extra bedroom and bath, lots of storage space and a tuck-under two-car garage.
- The crawlspace version include plans for a detached, two-car garage.

Plans H-2105-1 & -1A

Bedrooms: 2+	Baths: 1-2
Living Area:	
Main floor	1,008 sq. ft.
Daylight basement	528 sq. ft.
Total Living Area:	**1,008/1,536 sq. ft.**
Tuck-under garage	428 sq. ft.
Exterior Wall Framing:	2x4
Foundation Options:	**Plan #**
Daylight basement	H-2105-1
Crawlspace	H-2105-1A

(All plans can be built with your choice of foundation and framing. A generic conversion diagram is available. See order form.)

BLUEPRINT PRICE CODE:	**A/B**

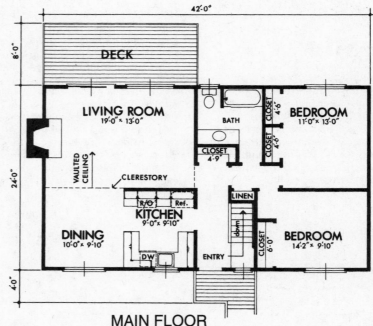

MAIN FLOOR

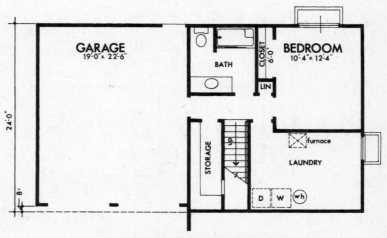

DAYLIGHT BASEMENT

Easy to Build

- This compact vacation or retirement home is economical and easy to build. As versatile as it is affordable, this home is suitable for a scenic, sloping or narrow lot.
- The main entrance is located on the side of the home, near the carport, which includes two storage areas.
- An impressive 12-ft., 4-in. sloped ceiling presides over the open living and dining rooms. A corner fireplace warms the entire area, while sliding glass doors provide access to a fabulous railed, wraparound deck.

- The efficient kitchen includes an 11-ft. sloped ceiling, a convenient laundry closet and deck access.
- Down the hall, the two front bedrooms feature high, triangular windows on the street side. The master bedroom boasts a 12-ft., 4-in. ceiling, two wardrobe closets and a private bath with an oversized, sit-down shower.
- The two secondary bedrooms are expanded by 11½-ft. ceilings and share the hall bath. Both baths have 11-ft. sloped ceilings.
- The optional daylight basement offers space for a recreation room that opens to the backyard.

Plans H-18 & -18-A	
Bedrooms: 3	**Baths:** 2
Living Area:	
Main floor (crawlspace version)	1,056 sq. ft.
Main floor (basement version)	1,104 sq. ft.
Total Living Area:	**1,056/1,104 sq. ft.**
Daylight basement	1,104 sq. ft.
Carport and storage	320 sq. ft.
Exterior Wall Framing:	2x4
Foundation Options:	**Plan #**
Daylight basement	H-18
Crawlspace	H-18-A

(All plans can be built with your choice of foundation and framing. A generic conversion diagram is available. See order form.)

| **BLUEPRINT PRICE CODE:** | **A** |

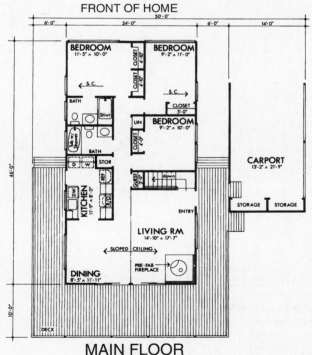

MAIN FLOOR
(CRAWLSPACE VERSION)

MAIN FLOOR
(BASEMENT VERSION)

Photo by Mark Englund/HomeStyles

Everything You'll Need

- This perfect—and affordable—home offers everything your family will need to keep you comfortable for many years to come. A charming porch out front provides a pleasant setting where you can savor a refreshing beverage.
- Inside, the tiled entry includes a handy coat closet for guests and a lovely arch with two elegant columns to introduce the dining room. A beautiful bay window and a French door make this room a stylish spot for formal meals.
- The nearby kitchen features a fun snack bar with room for three. The kids will love to gather here for peanut butter and jelly sandwiches. The sunny eating nook is great for casual family meals.
- In the Great Room, an entertainment center holds your stereo equipment, VCR and TV, with extra space to display family photos. A 10-ft., 8-in. vaulted ceiling soars above, while a fireplace adds ambience to the room.
- The master suite, which also boasts a 10-ft., 8-in. ceiling, provides a quiet refuge for the heads of the household. Highlights of the master bath include a spa tub and a dual-sink vanity.

Plan S-3295

Bedrooms: 3	Baths: 2
Living Area:	
Main floor	1,597 sq. ft.
Total Living Area:	**1,597 sq. ft.**
Garage	380 sq. ft.
Exterior Wall Framing:	2x6

Foundation Options:

Crawlspace
(All plans can be built with your choice of foundation and framing. A generic conversion diagram is available. See order form.)

BLUEPRINT PRICE CODE: B

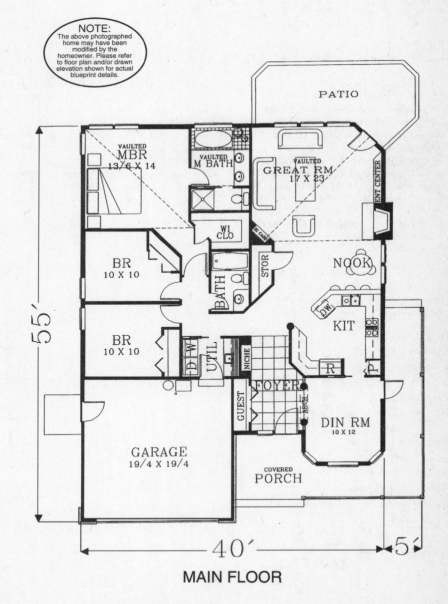

NOTE:
The above photographed home may have been modified by the homeowner. Please refer to floor plan and/or drawn elevation shown for actual blueprint details.

MAIN FLOOR

Build It Yourself

- Everything you need for a leisure or retirement retreat is neatly packaged in this affordable, easy-to-build design.
- The basic rectangular shape features a unique wraparound deck, entirely covered by a projecting roofline.
- A central fireplace and a vaulted ceiling that rises to 10 ft. visually enhance the cozy living and dining rooms.
- The efficient kitchen offers convenient service to the adjoining dining room. In the crawlspace version, the kitchen also includes a snack bar.
- Two main-floor bedrooms share a large full bath.
- The daylight-basement option is suitable for building on a sloping lot and consists of an extra bedroom, a general-purpose area and a garage.

Plans H-833-7 & -7A

Bedrooms: 2+	Baths: 1
Living Area:	
Main floor	952 sq. ft.
Daylight basement	676 sq. ft.
Total Living Area:	**952/1,628 sq. ft.**
Tuck-under garage	276 sq. ft.
Exterior Wall Framing:	2x6
Foundation Options:	**Plan #**
Daylight basement	H-833-7
Crawlspace	H-833-7A

(All plans can be built with your choice of foundation and framing. A generic conversion diagram is available. See order form.)

BLUEPRINT PRICE CODE:	**AA/B**

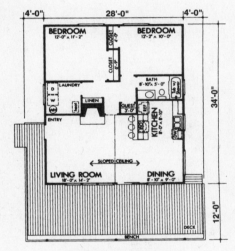

MAIN FLOOR
Crawlspace version

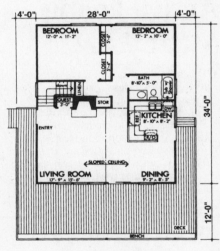

MAIN FLOOR
Basement version

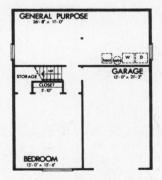

DAYLIGHT BASEMENT

Plans H-833-7 & -7A

**PRICES AND DETAILS
ON PAGES 2-5**

Active Living Made Easy

- This home is perfect for active living. Its rectangular design allows the use of truss roof framing, which makes construction easy and economical.
- The galley-style kitchen and the sunny dining area are kept open to the living room, forming one huge activity space. Two sets of sliding glass doors expand the living area to the large deck.

- The secluded master bedroom offers a private bath, while the remaining bedrooms share a hall bath.
- The two baths, the laundry facilities and the kitchen are clustered to allow common plumbing walls.
- Plan H-921-1A has a standard crawlspace foundation and an optional solar-heating system. Plan H-921-2A has a Plen-Wood system, which utilizes the sealed crawlspace as a chamber for distributing heated or cooled air. Both versions of the design call for energy-efficient 2x6 exterior walls.

Plans H-921-1A & -2A	
Bedrooms: 3	**Baths:** 2
Living Area:	
Main floor	1,164 sq. ft.
Total Living Area:	**1,164 sq. ft.**
Exterior Wall Framing:	2x6
Foundation Options:	**Plan #**
Crawlspace	H-921-1A
Plen-Wood crawlspace	H-921-2A

(All plans can be built with your choice of foundation and framing. A generic conversion diagram is available. See order form.)

| **BLUEPRINT PRICE CODE:** | **A** |

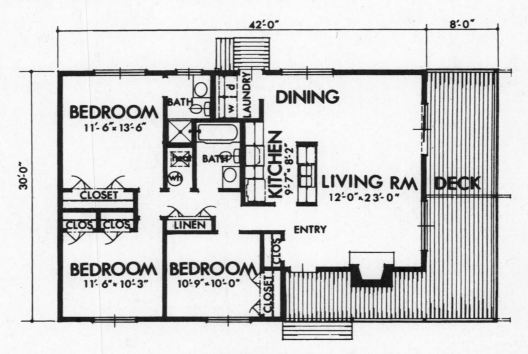

MAIN FLOOR

Adorable and Affordable

- This charming one-story home has much to offer, despite its modest size and economical bent.
- The lovely full-width porch has old-fashioned detailing, such as the round columns, decorative railings and ornamental molding.
- An open floor plan maximizes the home's square footage. The front door opens to the living room, where a railing creates a hallway effect while using very little space.
- Straight ahead, the dining room adjoins the island kitchen, while offering a compact laundry closet and sliding glass doors to a large rear patio.
- Focusing on quality, the home also offers features such as a 10-ft. tray ceiling in the living room and a 9-ft. stepped ceiling in the dining room.
- The three bedrooms are well proportioned. The master bedroom includes a private bathroom, while the two smaller bedrooms share another full bath. Note that the fixtures are arranged to reduce plumbing runs.

Plan AX-91316

Bedrooms: 3	Baths: 2
Living Area:	
Main floor	1,097 sq. ft.
Total Living Area:	**1,097 sq. ft.**
Basement	1,097 sq. ft.
Garage	461 sq. ft.
Exterior Wall Framing:	2x4

Foundation Options:

Daylight basement

Standard basement

Slab

(All plans can be built with your choice of foundation and framing. A generic conversion diagram is available. See order form.)

BLUEPRINT PRICE CODE:	A

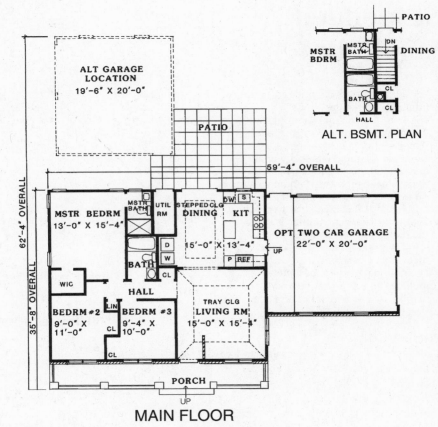

MAIN FLOOR

ALT. BSMT. PLAN

VIEW INTO LIVING ROOM AND DINING ROOM

Plan AX-91316

PRICES AND DETAILS
ON PAGES 2-5

Suspended Sun Room

- This narrow-lot design is a perfect combination of economical structure and luxurious features.
- The living and dining rooms flow together to create a great space for parties or family gatherings. A 16-ft. sloped ceiling and clerestory windows add drama and brightness. A fabulous deck expands the entertaining area.
- An exciting sun room provides the advantages of passive-solar heating.
- The sunny, efficient kitchen is open to the dining room.
- A full bath serves the two isolated main-floor bedrooms.
- The optional daylight basement includes an additional bedroom and bath as well as a tuck-under garage and storage space.

Plans H-951-1A & -1B

Bedrooms: 2+	Baths: 1-2
Living Area:	
Main floor	1,075 sq. ft.
Sun room	100 sq. ft.
Daylight basement	662 sq. ft.
Total Living Area:	**1,175/1,837 sq. ft.**
Tuck-under garage	311 sq. ft.
Exterior Wall Framing:	2x6
Foundation Options:	**Plan #**
Daylight basement	H-951-1B
Crawlspace	H-951-1A

(All plans can be built with your choice of foundation and framing. A generic conversion diagram is available. See order form.)

BLUEPRINT PRICE CODE:	**A/B**

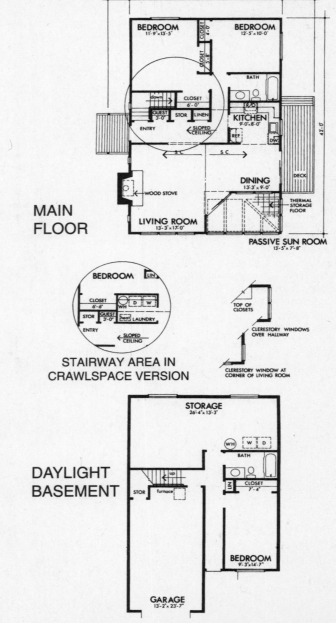

MAIN FLOOR

STAIRWAY AREA IN CRAWLSPACE VERSION

CLERESTORY WINDOWS OVER HALLWAY

CLERESTORY WINDOW AT CORNER OF LIVING ROOM

DAYLIGHT BASEMENT

Super Compact Contemporary

- Sensible for singles, a young couple or empty-nesters, this one-bedroom plan carefully organizes 775 sq. ft. of floor space into a comfortable, contemporary home that fits on nearly every lot.
- The entry hall, which leads into the living and dining areas, contains a guest closet and storage space.
- The living room is warmed by a fireplace and features a ceiling that vaults to 13 ft. high. Sliding glass doors access a sheltered deck.
- Clerestory windows funnel natural light into the kitchen. The dining room is brightened by a wall of windows that stretches to the ceiling, which vaults to a height of nearly 16 feet.
- The bathroom has its own clerestory window that shines into the vaulted area from almost 14 ft. above.
- The large bedroom features double wardrobe closets and a ceiling that slopes to almost 16 ft. high. Sunlight pours into the room through huge windows.
- The laundry area is handy to both the bedroom and the bath.

Plan H-917-1A

Bedrooms: 1	Baths: 1
Living Area:	
Main floor	775 sq. ft.
Total Living Area:	**775 sq. ft.**
Garage	245 sq. ft.
Exterior Wall Framing:	2x4

Foundation Options:

Crawlspace

(All plans can be built with your choice of foundation and framing. A generic conversion diagram is available. See order form.)

BLUEPRINT PRICE CODE:	**AA**

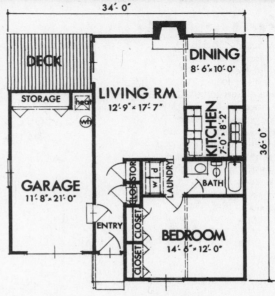

MAIN FLOOR

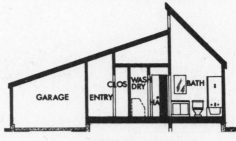

INTERIOR SECTION

REAR SECTION

Plan H-917-1A
PRICES AND DETAILS
ON PAGES 2-5

Sweet Petite

- This home's modest—and affordable— square footage belies the open spaces and numerous amenities found inside. The charming stone exterior and a beautiful arched window arrangement lend a sweet air to the entire design.
- Inside, the entry flows directly into the living room. Whether you prefer kicking back with a pile of movies, poring over a stack of magazines or visiting with friends and family, this room serves as the perfect home base for any activity.
- Between the living room, the dining room and the kitchen, a serving counter holds snacks when you entertain and provides a casual spot to grab a bagel when you're on the run.
- At the end of the day, the master bedroom is a refreshing sight. The highlights of the private bath include a dual-sink vanity and a huge tub.
- A versatile bedroom nearby can be adapted to meet your personal needs. How about a nursery, a guest room or a home office? Take your pick.
- The living room, the dining room and the kitchen share a 10-ft. sloped ceiling. The master bedroom boasts a 9-ft. sloped ceiling, and the second bedroom also includes a 10-ft. sloped ceiling.

Plan DD-1234

Bedrooms: 1+	Baths: 2
Living Area:	
Main floor	1,234 sq. ft.
Total Living Area:	**1,234 sq. ft.**
Garage and storage	494 sq. ft.
Exterior Wall Framing:	2x4

Foundation Options:

Slab

(All plans can be built with your choice of foundation and framing. A generic conversion diagram is available. See order form.)

BLUEPRINT PRICE CODE:	**A**

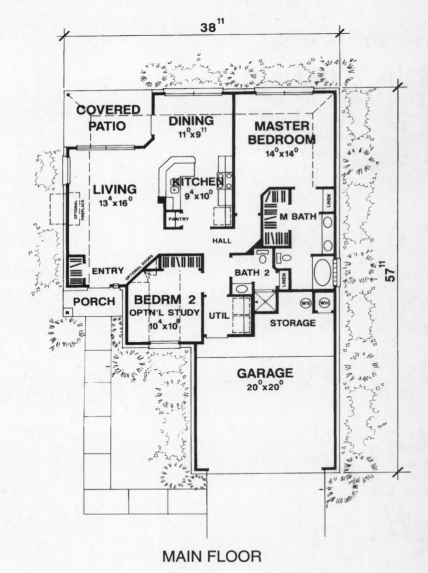

MAIN FLOOR

Narrow Plan, Wide Views

- Here's a plan that lends itself to a narrow building lot, yet offers maximum viewing at its farther end, where it addresses the outdoors with plenty of windows and a spacious deck that spans the width of the home.
- It's those little touches, like the front entry planter, the living room fireplace and the snack bar in the kitchen that give this home character.
- With the daylight basement option, enjoy three bedrooms, each with its own private full bath, plus add a second fireplace, recreation room, and useful shop or hobby space in the general-use area.
- Without the daylight basement option, the master bedroom is expanded to replace the stairwell.
- An 11-ft. 8-in. vaulted ceiling rises over the dining and living areas.

Plans H-866-2B & -2C	
Bedrooms: 2+	**Baths:** 2-3
Living Area:	
Main floor	1,338 sq. ft.
Daylight basement	1,170 sq. ft.
Total Living Area:	**1,338/2,508 sq. ft.**
Garage	528 sq. ft.
Exterior Wall Framing:	2x6
Foundation Options:	**Plan #**
Daylight basement	H-866-2B
Crawlspace	H-866-2C

(All plans can be built with your choice of foundation and framing. A generic conversion diagram is available. See order form.)

BLUEPRINT PRICE CODE:	A/D

DAYLIGHT BASEMENT

MAIN FLOOR

Plans H-866-2B & -2C

PRICES AND DETAILS
ON PAGES 2-5

Photo by Mark Englund/HomeStyles

Life-Sized Doll Cottage

- Pretty as a picture, this adorable many-gabled cottage brings a touch of old New England to your retreat, and dresses up a forest glade with propriety and style.
- Compact and efficient, the plan is comfortably open. The kitchen shares a snack bar with the bay-windowed dining area. The living room is made even more spacious by the addition of a 9-ft. ceiling, lots of glass and access to a large deck.
- The living room fireplace has a built-in storage space for firewood.
- You'll love the kitchen's box shape for vacation ease and efficiency.
- The master bedroom has two closets and its own bath. The second bedroom also enjoys its own bath.

Plan B-91007

Bedrooms: 2	Baths: 2
Living Area:	
Main floor	1,199 sq. ft.
Total Living Area:	**1,199 sq. ft.**
Exterior Wall Framing:	2x6

Foundation Options:
Slab
(All plans can be built with your choice of foundation and framing. A generic conversion diagram is available. See order form.)

BLUEPRINT PRICE CODE: A

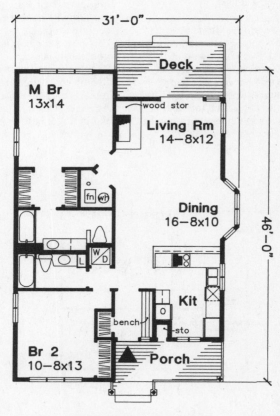

MAIN FLOOR

Rough-and-Ready

- This simple, efficient vacation house is equally suitable as a carefree hunting lodge, boat port, snowmobile station, or fishing house.
- Hunkered against the weather, yet open to the sun and views, the roofline reaches out over the deep deck and is accented by exposed beams that can be trimmed for a decorative flavor.

- The dining, living, and kitchen areas form a circle around an efficient or beautiful woodstove of your choosing, so that its heat can be felt everywhere.
- Plenty of closets and an ample garage encourage the storage of sports paraphernalia and outdoor equipment.
- A sofa-sleeper in the living room helps you accommodate relatives or guests during longer retreats.
- The U-shaped kitchen makes quick meals a breeze.
- A washer and dryer can be conveniently placed in the garage.

Plan H-786-1

Bedrooms: 1	Baths: 1
Living Area:	
Main floor	761 sq. ft.
Total Living Area:	**761 sq. ft.**
Garage	418 sq. ft.
Exterior Wall Framing:	2x4

Foundation Options:

Crawlspace
(All plans can be built with your choice of foundation and framing. A generic conversion diagram is available. See order form.)

BLUEPRINT PRICE CODE:	**AA**

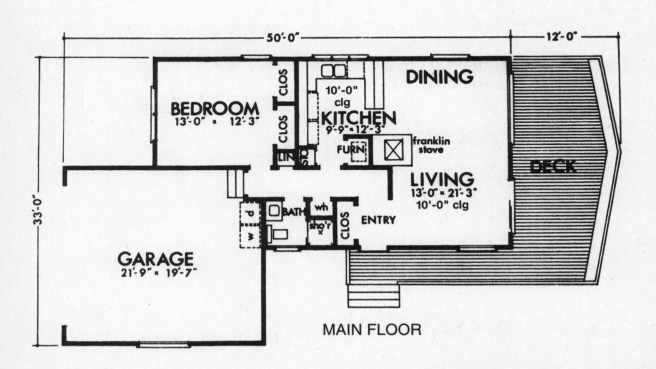

MAIN FLOOR

Plan H-786-1

PRICES AND DETAILS
ON PAGES 2-5

Blueprint Order Form

Complete this order form in just three easy steps. Then mail in your order or, for faster service, call toll-free.

1. Blueprints & Accessories

BLUEPRINT CHART

Price Code	1 Set	4 Sets	7 Sets	Reproducible Set*
AAA	$245	$295	$330	$430
AA	$285	$335	$370	$470
A	$365	$415	$450	$550
B	$405	$455	$490	$590
C	$445	$495	$530	$630
D	$485	$535	$570	$670
E	$525	$575	$610	$710
F	$565	$615	$650	$750
G	$605	$655	$690	$790
H	$645	$695	$730	$830
I	$685	$735	$770	$870

A reproducible set is produced on erasable paper for the purpose of modification. It is only available for plans with prefixes A, AG, AGH, AH, AHP, APS, AX, B, BOD, BRF, C, CC, CDG, CPS, DCL, DD, DW, E, EOF, FB, G, GA, GL, GSA, H, HDS, HFL, HOM, IDG, J, JWA, K, KD, KLF, L, LRD, LS, M, NBV, NW, OH, PH, PI, RD, S, SDG, SG, SUL, SUN, THD, TS, U, UD, UDA, UDG, V, WH. Prices subject to change

Mirror-Reverse Sets: $50 surcharge. From the total number of sets you ordered above, choose the number you want to be reversed. *Note: All writing on mirror-reverse plans is backwards. Order at least one regular-reading set.*

Itemized Materials List: One set $50; each additional set $15. Details the quantity, type, and size of materials needed to build your home.

Description of Materials: Sold in a set of two for $50 (for use in obtaining FHA or VA financing).

Typical How-To Diagrams: One set $20; two sets $30; three sets $40; four sets $45. General guides on plumbing, wiring, and solar heating, plus information on how to convert from one foundation or exterior framing to another. *Note: These diagrams are not specific to any one plan.*

2. Sales Tax & Shipping

Determine your subtotal and add appropriate local state sales tax, plus shipping and handling (see chart below).

SHIPPING & HANDLING

	1–3 Sets	4–6 Sets	7 or More Sets	Reproducible Set
U.S. Regular (5–6 business days)	$17.50	$20.00	$22.50	$17.50
U.S. Express (2–3 business days)	$29.50	$32.50	$35.00	$29.50
Canada Regular (2–3 weeks)	$20.00	$22.50	$25.00	$20.00
Canada Express (5–6 business days)	$35.00	$40.00	$45.00	$35.00
Overseas/Airmail (7–10 businessdays)	$57.50	$67.50	$77.50	$57.50

3. Customer Information

Choose the method of payment you prefer. Include check, money order, or credit card information, complete name and address portion, and mail, fax, or call using the information at the right.

SS22

COMPLETE THIS FORM

Plan Number _____ **Price Code** _____

Foundation _____
(Review your plan carefully for foundation options—basement, pole, pier, crawlspace, or slab. Many plans offer several options; others offer only one.)

Number of Sets: $_____
- [ ] **One Set** (See chart at left)
- [ ] **Four Sets**
- [ ] **Seven Sets**
- [ ] **One Reproducible Set**

Additional Sets _____ $_____
($40 each)

Mirror-Reverse Sets _____ $_____
($50 surcharge)

Itemized Materials List $_____
Only available for plans with prefixes AH, AHP, APS*, AX*, B*, BOD*, C, CAR, CC, CDG*, CPS, DD*, DW, E, G, GSA, H, HFL, HOM, I*, IDG, J, K, L, LMB*, LRD, NW*, P, PH, R, S, SG*, SUN, THD, U, UDA, UDG, VL, WH, YS.
*Not available on all plans. Please call before ordering.

Description of Materials $_____
Only for plans with prefixes AHP, C, DW, H, J, K, P, PH, SUL, VL, YS.

Typical How-To Diagrams $_____
- [ ] Plumbing
- [ ] Wiring
- [ ] Solar Heating
- [ ] Foundation & Framing Conversion

SUBTOTAL $_____

SALES TAX Minnesota residents add 6.5% $_____

SHIPPING & HANDLING $_____

GRAND TOTAL $_____

- [ ] Check/money order enclosed (in U.S. funds) payable to HomeStyles
- [ ] VISA   [ ] MasterCard   [ ] AmEx   [ ] Discover

Credit Card # _____ **Exp. Date** _____

Signature _____

Name _____

Address _____

City _____ **State** ____ **Country** _____

Zip _____ **Daytime Phone** (____) _____
- [ ] Please check if you are a contractor.

Mail form to: Sunset/HomeStyles
P.O. Box 75488
St. Paul, MN 55175-0488

Or fax to: (612) 602-5002

FOR FASTER SERVICE
CALL 1-800-820-1283

SS22

Before You Order

Once you've chosen the one or two house plans that work best for you, you're ready to order blueprints. Before filling in the form on the facing page, note the information that follows.

How Many Blueprints Will You Need?

A single set of blueprints will allow you to study a home design in detail. You'll need more for obtaining bids and permits, as well as some to use as reference at the building site. If you'll be modifying your home plan, order a reproducible set (see page 2).

Figure you'll need at least one set each for yourself, your builder, the building department, and your lender. In addition, some subcontractors—foundation, plumber, electrician, and HVAC—may also need at least partial sets. If they do, ask them to return the sets when they're finished. The chart below can help you calculate how many sets you're likely to need.

Blueprint Checklist

____ Owner's set(s)

____ Builder usually requires at least three sets: one for legal documentation, one for inspections, and a minimum of one set for subcontractors.

____ Building department requires at least one set. Check with your local department before ordering.

____ Lending institution usually needs one set for a conventional mortgage, three sets for FHA or VA loans.

____ TOTAL SETS NEEDED

Blueprint Prices

The cost of having an architect design a new custom home typically runs from 5 to 15 percent of the building cost, or from $5,000 to $15,000 for a $100,000 home. A single set of blueprints for the plans in this book ranges from $245 to $685, depending on the house's size. Working with these drawings, you can save enough on design fees to add a deck, a swimming pool or a luxurious kitchen.

Pricing is based on "total finished living space." Garages, porches, decks and unfinished basements are not included.

Building Costs

Building costs vary widely, depending on a number of factors, includ-

Price Code (Size)	1 Set	4 Sets	7 Sets	Reproducible Set
AAA (under 500 sq. ft.)	$245	$295	$330	$430
AA (500- 999 sq. ft.)	$285	$335	$370	$470
A (1,000- 1,499 sq. ft.)	$365	$415	$450	$550
B (1,500- 1,999 sq. ft.)	$405	$455	$490	$590
C (2,000- 2,499 sq. ft.)	$445	$495	$530	$630
D (2,500- 2,999 sq. ft.)	$485	$535	$570	$670
E (3,000- 3,499 sq. ft.)	$525	$575	$610	$710
F (3,500- 3,999 sq. ft.)	$565	$615	$650	$750
G (4,000- 4,499 sq. ft.)	$605	$655	$690	$790
H (4,500- 4,999 sq. ft.)	$645	$695	$730	$830
I (5,000 & above)	$685	$735	$770	$870

ing local material and labor costs and the finishing materials you select.

Foundation Options & Exterior Construction

Depending on your site and climate, your home will be built with a slab, pier, pole, crawlspace or basement foundation. Exterior walls will be framed with either 2 by 4s or 2 by 6s, determined by structural and insulation standards in your area. Most contractors can easily adapt a home to meet the foundation and/or wall requirements for your area. Or ask for a conversion how-to diagram (see page 2).

Service & Blueprint Delivery

Service representatives are available to answer questions and assist you in placing your order. Every effort is made to process and ship orders within 48 hours.

Returns & Exchanges

Each set of blueprints is specially printed and shipped to you in response to your specific order; consequently, requests for refunds

cannot be honored. However, if the prints you order cannot be used, you may exchange them for another plan from any Sunset home plan book. For an exchange, you must return all sets of plans within 30 days. A nonrefundable service charge will be assessed for all exchanges; for more information, call the toll-free number on the facing page. Note: Reproducible sets cannot be exchanged.

Compliance with Local Codes & Regulations

Because of climatic, geographic and political variations, building codes and regulations vary from one area to another. These plans are authorized for your use expressly conditioned on your obligation and agreement to comply strictly with all local building codes, ordinances, regulations and requirements, including permits and inspections at time of construction.

Architectural & Engineering Seals

With increased concern about energy costs and safety, many cities and states now require that an architect or engineer review and "seal" a blueprint prior to construction. To find out whether this is a requirement in your area, contact your local building department.

License Agreement, Copy Restrictions & Copyright

When you purchase your blueprints, you are granted the right to use those documents to construct a single unit. All the plans in this publication are protected under the Federal Copyright Act, Title XVII of the United States Code and Chapter 37 of the Code of Federal Regulations. Each designer retains title and ownership of the original documents. The blueprints licensed to you cannot be used by or resold to any other person, copied or reproduced by any means. The copying restrictions do not apply to reproducible blueprints. When you buy a reproducible set, you may modify and reproduce it for your own use.

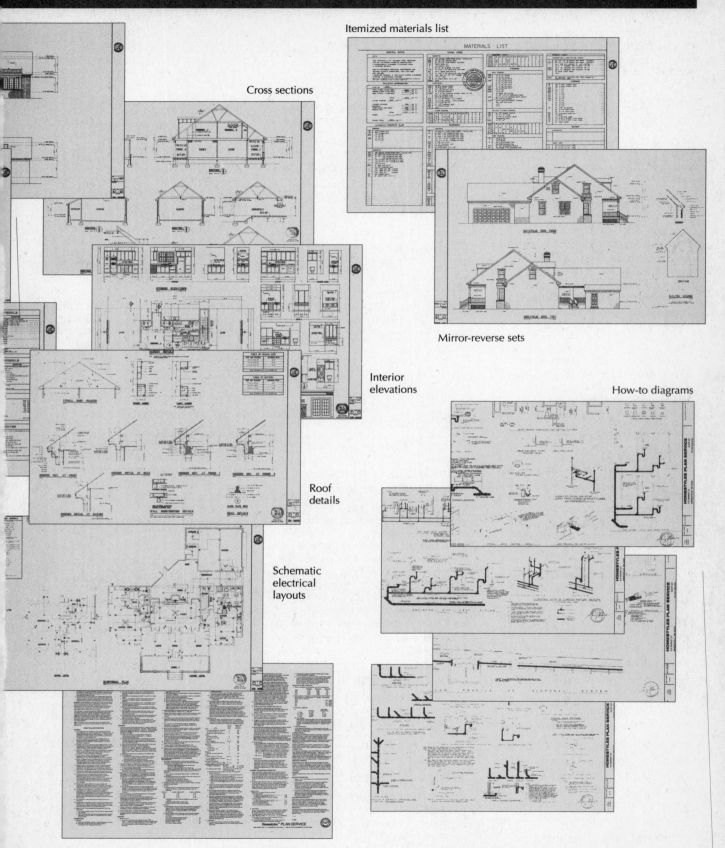

Itemized materials list

MATERIALS LIST

Cross sections

Mirror-reverse sets

Interior
elevations

How-to diagrams

Roof
details

Schematic
electrical
layouts

General specifications